The Best of

Elementary
Science Activities

The Best of

WonderScience

Elementary
Science Activities

AMERICAN
INSTITUTE
OF PHYSICS

Delmar Publishers®

I(T)P® An International Thomson Publishing Company

Albany • Bonn • Boston • Cincinnati • Detroit • London • Madrid
Melbourne • Mexico City • New York • Pacific Grove • Paris • San Francisco
Singapore • Tokyo • Toronto • Washington

Cover Design: Brucie Rosch
Cover Illustration: Loel Barr

Delmar Staff
Publisher: William Brottmiller
Senior Editor: Jay Whitney
Production Coordinator: James Zayicek
Art and Design Coordinator: Carol Keohane
Senior Editorial Assistant: Glenna Stanfield

COPYRIGHT © 1997
By Delmar Publishers
a division of International Thomson Publishing Inc.

The ITP logo is a trademark under license.

Printed in the United States of America

For more information, contact:

Delmar Publishers
3 Columbia Circle, Box 15015
Albany, New York 12212-5015

International Thomson Editores
Campos Eliseos 385, Piso 7
Col Polanco
11560 Mexico D F Mexico

International Thomson Publishing Europe
Berkshire House 168-173
High Holborn
London, WC1V 7AA
England

International Thomson Publishing GmbH
Konigswinterer Strasse 418
53227 Bonn
Germany

Thomas Nelson Australia
102 Dodds Street
South Melbourne, 3205
Victoria, Australia

International Thomson Publishing Asia
221 Henderson Road
#05-10 Henderson Building
Singapore 0315

Nelson Canada
1120 Birchmount Road
Scarborough, Ontario
Canada, M1K 5G4

International Thomson Publishing-Japan
Hirakawacho Kyowa Building, 3F
2-2-1 Hirakawacho
Chiyoda-ku, Tokyo 102
Japan

1 2 3 4 5 6 7 8 9 10 XXX 02 01 00 99 98 97

Library of Congress Cataloging-in-Publication Data
Kessler, James H.
        The best of WonderScience: elementary science activities / James H. Kessler, Andrea Bennett.
            p. cm.
        Includes index.
        ISBN 0-8273-8094-1
        1. Science—Study and teaching (Elementary)—United States.
    2. Science—Study and teaching—United States—Activity programs.
    I. Bennett, Andrea T. II. Title.
    LB1585.3.K47 1996
    372.3'5—dc20   96-19106
                                                                        CIP

DESCRIPTIVE TABLE OF CONTENTS

TABLE OF CONTENTS

PREFACE

Introduction

Publication of *WonderScience* magazine began ten years ago as a result of a conference on science education hosted by the world's largest scientific organization, the American Chemical Society (ACS). Scientists and science educators from around the country agreed that *learning* science can only be accomplished by *doing* science. Hence, *WonderScience* was created to offer hands-on science learning experiences for elementary school children.

Over the years, *WonderScience* has explored many science concepts using a hands-on, guided inquiry approach in which students work through activities while being challenged with questions along the way. These questions are intended to encourage students to interpret their observations, to analyze and draw conclusions, and to suggest possible alternative approaches and explanations for their observations. To make the hands-on experiences accessible to all, careful attention is paid to developing activities that make use of easily obtained, inexpensive materials. *WonderScience*'s interdisciplinary approach integrates science with math by emphasizing measuring skills, calculation, and mathematical reasoning skills along with the use of charts, graphs, maps, and other applications. *WonderScience* activities also explore the relationships between science concepts and history and technology.

National Science Education Standards

Today's teachers are responsible for preparing their students to confront the heavily scientific, highly technical world of the 21st century. To help teachers accomplish this difficult task, the new National Science Education Standards will serve as a guideline. The Standards describe what all students, regardless of background or circumstances, should be able to do in science as a result of their science education, K-12. The Standards promote a citizenry capable of making informed personal and social decisions, holding meaningful and productive jobs, and experiencing, understanding, and enjoying the natural world around them.

Achieving science literacy will require a long-term commitment to change, as well as support from all levels of our educational system. This book is designed to help teachers implement science education reform at ground zero.

The National Science Education Standards provide guidelines for six integral components of science education. These include science teaching, professional development, assessment, science content, education programs, and education systems. This book of *WonderScience* activities is designed to help teachers implement the science content standards. The content standards outline what students should know, understand, and be able to do in natural science. To make the *WonderScience* book as effective a resource as possible for teachers, it is recommended that educators integrate its use with the implementation of the other related National Science Education Standards, in particular, teaching and assessment.

The Best of WonderScience and the Content Standards

The National Science Education Content Standards are divided into eight categories. They are:

Unifying Concepts and Processes   Earth and Space Science

Science as Inquiry   Science and Technology

Physical Science   Science in Personal and Social Perspectives

Life Science   History and Nature of Science

The first category, Unifying Concepts and Processes, is a broad, overarching standard that applies to science learning from K-12. The hands-on, guided inquiry approach of *WonderScience*, with its emphasis on the process skills of experimentation, observation, measurement, and reasoning from evidence, addresses this standard. Since the underlying philosophy and approach of *WonderScience* supports this standard, a discussion of the standard will be addressed here rather than repeated at the beginning of each unit.

Unifying Concepts and Processes

Unifying Concepts and Processes, includes principles and abilities that students should be developing over the entire course of their education. This category includes concepts and process skills that cross all disciplines and all grade levels, and therefore is presented for grades K through 12. This standard includes conceptual and procedural elements designed to promote critical thinking skills and an understanding of the basic principles that explain the natural and designed world. The fundamental unifying concepts are:

- Systems, order, and organization
- Evidence models, and explanation
- Constancy, change, and measurement
- Evolution and equilibrium
- Form and function

Systems, Order, and Organization

Analyzing science topics in terms of systems helps students keep track of concepts, objects, organisms, and events referred to in other content standards. Students develop an understanding of regularities in systems and by extension, the broader world around them. Many *WonderScience* units are based on the understanding of systems, order, and organization at the level of the solar system, Earth systems, human body systems, and atomic and molecular systems.

Evidence, Models, and Explanation

Observations provide evidence on which to base scientific explanations. Using evidence to understand interactions allows students to hypothesize about other changes in their world, both natural and designed. Since the processes of science can best be understood by doing science, *WonderScience* activities are focused on students doing a variety of hands-on science activities. Through this experimentation, students develop skills of observation, modeling, data collection, and reasoning based on empirical evidence.

Constancy, Change, and Measurement

The natural and designed world is one of both constancy and change. Some properties of objects and processes, such as the density of a substance, the freezing point of water, and the acceleration of gravity, remain constant. Other properties, such as the speed and direction of a moving object, the air temperature over a 24-hour period, and the growth and development of an organism are properties that change. *WonderScience* activities are designed for students to observe these characteristics of constancy and change, and to quantify them with measurement when possible. Emphasis is placed on accuracy and precision, and on using the appropriate measurement tools and units.

Evolution and Equilibrium

Evolution involves a series of changes that results in the present form and function of objects, organisms, and natural and designed systems. Several *WonderScience* units include elements of the evolution of designed systems including the units on magnification, inventions, and measuring.

Equilibrium, the physical state in which forces and changes occur in opposite and off-setting directions, can be described in terms of steady state, balance, and homeostasis. The concept of equilibrium is dealt with directly in the sections Motions and Forces, Transfer of Energy, Physical Changes, and Water, and indirectly in other sections.

Form and Function

The form or shape of an object or system is often related to its use or function. *WonderScience* activities repeatedly focus on the complementary nature of form and function, and thereby help students explain function by referring to form and explain form by referring to function. The interrelationship of form and function exists on many different levels of organization, from the molecular level to the complex multicellular level. For example, several *WonderScience* units explore the direct relationship of a molecule's structure and shape to its function. This form/function relationship is also explored in living things such as plants, humans, and other animals.

Science As Inquiry

The second category of the Content Standards, Science as Inquiry, is divided into abilities students need to do scientific inquiry and understandings they should have about scientific inquiry. *WonderScience* promotes scientific inquiry abilities through its guided inquiry-based approach. These abilities include: (1) identifying questions that can be answered through scientific investigations, (2) designing and conducting scientific investigations, (3) using appropriate tools and techniques to gather, analyze, an interpret data, (4) developing descriptions, explanations, predictions, and models using evidence, (5) thinking critically and logically to make relationships between evidence and explanations, (6) recognizing and analyzing alternative explanations and predictions, (7) communicating scientific procedures and explanations, and (8) using mathematics in all aspects of scientific inquiry.

These skills allow students to develop very important understandings about scientific inquiry. Through *WonderScience* experimentation, students discover that different types of questions lead to different types of scientific investigations. Investigations may involve experimenting, creating models, collecting specimens, or making observations. Students learn that scientific explanations are based on reproducible evidence and use scientific principles, and that it is the role of a scientist to evaluate these explanations, challenge faulty reasoning, and suggest alternative explanations. It is through this process, students come to realize, that science advances.

The Remaining Six Content Standards

Physical Science	Science and Technology
Life Science	Science in Personal and Social Perspectives
Earth and Space Science	History and Nature of Science

The remaining six categories of the content standards are Physical Science, Life Science, Earth and Space Science, Science and Technology, Science in Personal and Social Perspectives, and History and Nature of Science.

To see how a particular standard is supported by one or more *WonderScience* units, refer to the National Science Education Standards listing that follows. If a teacher approaches the book by unit rather than by standard, the same information can be obtained by checking the National Science Education Standards box at the bottom of the "Teacher Page" at the front of each unit. The standards addressed by that unit will be indicated and can be used to search the NSE listing in the front of the book for more information.

Although most *WonderScience* activities were written prior to the release of the standards, the activities can be used very effectively to support the understandings envisioned by the standards. An example is the unit on calcium. The activities involving calcium can be used to support the science as inquiry standard of abilities necessary to do scientific inquiry, the physical science standard of properties and changes of properties in matter, the life science standard of structure and function in living systems, and the science in personal and social perspective standard of personal health. As teachers plan their science lessons, reference to the National Science Education Standards list and to the "Teacher Page" at the beginning of each unit will help identify how each unit supports the standards teachers are working toward. We hope that teachers will find a ready source of hands-on science activities related to the Standards a valuable resource in helping to achieve the goals of effective elementary science education.

Abilities necessary to do scientific inquiry

Section 1, Science Process Skills

Estimating: Use appropriate tools and techniques, including mathematics to answer a question.

Measuring: Develop ability to make accurate measurements.

Designing Structures: Design and conduct a scientific investigation to solve a problem.

Inventing: Design, construct, and evaluate a new product.

Section 2, Science and Recreation

Science of the Playground: Use critical thinking to establish relationships between evidence and explanations regarding motions of playground equipment.

Physics of Baseball: Examine various aspects of the game of baseball through investigations involving modeling.

Chemistry of Art: Investigate various materials used in art by modeling their use and making observations.

Toys in Space: Develop descriptions, explanations, predictions, and models of the behavior of various toys in orbit based on observation and evidence.

Section 3, Science and Technologies

Soaps and Detergents: Use appropriate tools and techniques, including mathematics, to answer questions regarding the chemical nature of soaps and detergents.

Bubbles: Develop observation skills by comparing bubbles produced by different bubble blowers.

Adhesives: Conduct scientific investigations which involve making accurate measurements and controlling variables to test the effectiveness of various adhesives.

Lubricants: Investigate the properties of lubricants using critical thinking skills to formulate explanations and predictions.

Fibers and Fabrics: Use appropriate tools and techniques to compare the properties of natural and synthetic fibers.

Section 4, Water

Properties of Water: Develop descriptions, predictions, and models to explain various physical properties of water.

Surface Tension: Use critical thinking skills to explain relationships between observed phenomena and the surface tension of water.

Capillarity: Conduct investigations to observe and develop explanations of how capillarity and absorption are related.

Evaporation and Condensation: Use observation skills to develop descriptions, predictions, and models, using evidence to understand and explain water's properties of evaporation and condensation.

Section 5, Food Science

Food Nutrients: Use observations to generate explanations and make predictions about how various food nutrients function.

Calcium: Conduct investigations to answer various questions about the chemical properties of calcium.

Food Additives: Use appropriate tools and techniques to investigate different types of food additives.

Soda Pop Science: Conduct investigations into the chemical nature of soda, which involve observation and control of variables.

Section 6, Materials Science

Plastics: Observe different properties of plastics to formulate explanations and predictions pertaining to its use in society.

Rubber: Conduct investigations to observe the properties of rubber.

Metals: Investigate properties of metals by making predictions and observations.

Insulation: Compare the insulating characteristics of various materials and use critical thinking skills to establish cause and effect relationships.

Recycling: Develop descriptions, explanations, and predictions by conducting investigations that model recycling techniques.

Section 7, Physical Changes

Chemical Particles: Make observations and develop explanations about the behavior of various particles in solution.

Density: Make and test predictions, develop explanations about why objects sink or float, and use mathematics to calculate density.

Mixtures: Observe and develop explanations about how substances combine to form mixtures and ways to separate them.

More Mixtures: Conduct investigations to observe and compare the ability of various substances to mix.

Diffusion: Apply critical thinking to explain the movement of molecules through different mediums.

Crystals: Conduct investigations to observe crystal formation.

Section 8, Chemical Changes

Chemicals and Chemical Reactions: Observe various chemical reactions to develop explanations about the nature of chemicals.

More Chemical Reactions: Observe changes that occur as a result of chemical reactions and use critical thinking skills to modify them.

Acids and Bases: Investigate through observation the chemical properties and reactions of acids and bases.

Plant Chemistry: Explore the properties of some chemicals found in plants.

Carbon Dioxide: Observe chemical and physical properties of carbon dioxide and develop explanations and predictions about its chemical behavior.

Section 9, Earth and Space Science

Rocks: Collect and test various rock samples for characteristic identifying properties.

Earthquakes: Conduct scientific investigations to observe the effects of earthquakes on different structures and materials.

Weather: Construct and use appropriate tools and techniques to gather, analyze and interpret weather data.

Solar Energy: Construct and use tools to observe the conversion of solar energy to heat energy.

Solar System: Use observations to develop descriptions and explanations about the solar system.

Section 10, Energy

Energy: Think critically and logically to identify different types of observed energy converting events.

Static Electricity: Observe various phenomena to develop explanations about static electricity.

Electric Circuits: Use appropriate tools and techniques to gain and analyze information about the operation of an electric circuit.

Heat: Conduct investigations to observe and explain the effects of temperature on the behavior of a gas.

Magnets: Construct and use appropriate tools and techniques to detect, analyze and explain magnetism.

Section 11, Motions and Forces

Forces: Conduct investigations to observe the effects and explain the forces of friction and gravity.

Air Pressure: Use critical thinking skills to explain observed air pressure phenomena.

Aerodynamics: Construct and operate various flying vehicles to develop explanations and predictions regarding the effects of air resistance.

Hovering: Construct and observe the motion of a hovercraft to develop an understanding of the forces involved in hovering.

Balance: Develop descriptions, explanations and predictions by observing effects of gravity on balance.

Wheels: Make use of tools and techniques, including mathematics to develop explanations regarding the motion of a wheel.

Section 12, Sound

Sound and Hearing: Conduct investigations to observe and explain how the ears detect sound.

Physics of Music: Create different instruments to observe how various factors influence sound production.

Echoes: Investigate ways to produce and detect reflected sound to develop explanations regarding echoes.

Section 13, Light

Vision: Conduct investigations to observe and explain how the eyes detect images.

Colors: Describe and explain what color is and how it is detected through observation and modeling.

Colors in Light: Observe refracted light from different sources to describe and explain the visible light spectrum.

Optical Illusions: Investigate, observe and formulate explanations of how the brain perceives certain images detected by the eyes.

Magnifiers: Construct and use appropriate tools to investigate, observe, and explain the magnifying power of different materials.

Reflection: Observe and explain the ways in which light reflects off the surfaces of different materials.

Understandings about scientific inquiry

Section 1, Science Process Skills

Investigating the Unseen: Develop an understanding that different types of questions require different types of investigations.

Section 6, Materials Science

Polymers: Develop understanding that scientific investigations may lead to new ideas and phenomena for study.

Section 9, Earth and Space Science

Stars and Constellations: Develop understanding that some scientific investigations involve observing and describing objects, as well as making models.

Section 8, Chemical Changes

Chemicals and Chemical Reactions: Investigate the properties of some common chemicals and their behavior.
More Chemical Reactions: Experiment with more chemical reactions.
Acids and Bases: Explore the chemical reactions of acids and bases.
Plant Chemistry: Use chemical reactions to learn more about the chemicals present in plants.
Carbon Dioxide: Discover the chemical properties of carbon dioxide.

Section 9, Earth and Space Science

Rocks: Investigate the properties of rocks that make them useful for so many purposes.

Section 10, Energy

Static Electricity: Discover which materials tend to be more easily charged with static electricity.
Electric Circuits: Experiment with materials which are good conductors and others which are good insulators.
Heat: Observe the effects of heat on the behavior of a gas.
Magnets: Investigate the magnetic behavior of some substances.

Section 12, Sound

Echoes: Experiment with different materials to test their ability to reflect sound.

Section 13, Light

Color: Create color mixtures and investigate ways to separate colors in a mixture.
Colors In Light: Experiment with different materials that diffract light.
Magnifiers: Observe the magnifying powers of different materials.

Motions and forces

Section 1, Science Process Skills

Designing Structures: Examine the influence of various forces on building structures.
Inventing: Construct and launch a jet propulsion vehicle.

Section 2, Science and Recreation

Science of the Playground: Investigate the motion of various pieces of playground equipment.
Physics of Baseball: Explore the motions and forces associated with the game of baseball.
Toys in Space: Learn about the factors that influence the motion of objects orbiting the Earth.

Section 9, Earth and Space Science

Earthquakes: Model the motions of the Earth's crust during a simulated earthquake.
Weather: Measure relative wind speeds and model the motion of a tornado.
Solar System: Observe indirectly the motions of the Earth and the moon.
Stars and Constellations: Investigate the motion of the Earth by observing the stars.

Section 11, Motions and Forces

Forces: Explore the effect of forces such as friction on the motion of an object.
Aerodynamics: investigate how the shape of an object influences the force of air resistance on the object's motion.
Balance: Observe how an object's weight affects its center of gravity and consequently its balance.
Wheels: Discover the variables that affect the motion of a wheel.

Transfer of energy

Section 1, Science Process Skills

Inventing: Explore inventions that involve an energy transfer from one form to another.

Section 2, Science and Recreation

Science of the Playground: Energy is associated with the mechanical motion of playground equipment.

Section 5, Food Science

Food Nutrients: Learn about the role of food in providing the body with energy.

Section 6, Materials Science

Rubber: Use the energy stored in a twisted rubber band to propel a small vehicle.
Metals: Investigate how mechanical, sound, heat, and electrical energy are transferred through metals.
Insulation: Experiment with materials which impede the transfer of heat from warmer objects to cooler objects.

Section 7, Physical Changes

Crystals: Learn about a special type of crystal that converts light energy into electrical energy.

Section 8, Chemical Changes

More Chemical Reactions: Investigate energy transfers associated with chemical reactions.

Section 9, Earth and Space Science

Earthquakes: Discover how stored energy is released during an earthquake.
Solar Energy: Investigate the conversion of solar energy into heat and electrical energy.

Section 10, Energy

Energy: Investigate different forms of energy and means of energy transfer.
Static Electricity: Learn about the causes and behavior of this special form of energy.
Electric Circuits: Experiment with the transfer of electrical energy to light energy.

Section 12, Sound

Sound and Hearing: Investigate energy transferred by vibrations in the form of sound.
Physics of Music: Experiment with sound production.
Echoes: Discover how to produce and detect echoes.

Section 13, Light

Colors: Observe colors produced when light is refracted.
Colors in Light: Investigate the color spectrum of refracted light.

Populations and ecosystems

Section 6, Materials Science

Recycling: Learn how decomposers naturally recycle resources in an ecosystem.

Section 9, Earth and Space Science

Earthquakes: Examine the dramatic effects that earthquakes can have on an ecosystem.
Solar Energy: Investigate ways in which the sun's energy is utilized in an ecosystem.

Section 10, Energy

Energy: Discover how solar energy is changed into chemical energy in an ecosystem.

Diversity and adaptations of organisms

Section 1, Science Process Skills

Designing Structures: Learn about animal homes and other structures built by animals.

Section 3, Science and Technologies

Adhesives: Learn about organisms that produce their own adhesives for a variety of purposes.
Fibers and Fabrics: Investigate relationship between certain animal fibers and their function.

Section 4, Water

Surface Tension: Discover an insect with a unique adaptation.

Section 6, Materials Science

Rubber: Investigate a product that results from a unique adaptation.
Insulation: Explore various adaptations that serve as insulators for animals.

Section 9, Earth and Space Science

Rocks: Discover how adaptations of extinct organisms are studied by modeling cast and mold fossils.

EARTH AND SPACE SCIENCE

CONTENT STANDARD D:

As a result of their activities in grades 5-8, all students should develop an understanding of

✔ Structure of the earth system

✔ Earth's history

✔ Earth in the solar system

Structure of the earth system

Section 1, Science Process Skills

Investigating the Unseen: Discover how probes are used to study the Earth's structure.

Section 3, Science and Technologies

Soaps and Detergents: Investigate water's behavior as a solvent.

Section 4, Water

Properties of Water: Experiment and observe the dissolving power of water.
Evaporation and Condensation: Explore the mechanisms of evaporation and condensation and their effects on the atmosphere.

Section 6, Materials Science

Recycling: Learn about natural recycling that occurs in soil.

Section 7, Physical Changes

Chemical Particles: Explore water's role as a solvent.
Mixtures: Investigate the properties of water that make it the "universal solvent."
Diffusion: Further explore the dissolving properties of water.

Section 8, Chemical Changes

Plant Chemistry: Learn how plants have played a role in the structure of the Earth system.
Carbon Dioxide: Explore the behavior of this important atmospheric gas.

Section 9, Earth and Space Science

Rocks: Investigate different rocks that make up the Earth's crust.
Earthquakes: Explore the causes, effects, and methods of studying earthquakes.
Weather: Construct tools to measure atmospheric phenomena.

Earth's history

Section 9, Earth and Space Science

Rocks: Discover how fossils are created.

Earth in the solar system

Section 1, Science Process Skills

Investigating the Unseen: Learn about the use of probes to study the solar system.

Section 2, Science and Recreation

Toys in Space: Investigate the force of gravity through the behavior of toys taken into space.

Section 9, Earth and Space Science

Solar Energy: Explore the sun's role as the major source of energy for phenomena on the Earth's surface.
Solar System: Learn about the components of our solar system.
Stars and Constellations: Detect the Earth's motion by observing the stars.

Section 11, Motions and Forces

Forces: Investigate the influence of the force of gravity on the way objects move.

SCIENCE AND TECHNOLOGY

CONTENT STANDARD E:
As a result of their activities in grades 5-8, all students should develop

✔ Abilities of technological design
✔ Understandings about science and technology

Abilities of technological design

Section 1, Science Process Skills

Estimating: Propose methods for estimating a variety of unknown quantities.
Designing Structures: Design, implement, and evaluate the quality of paper bridges.
Inventing: Design and create a simple time piece.

Section 2, Science and Recreation

Physics of Baseball: Create a new sport using various pieces of sporting equipment.

Section 5, Food Science

Food Additives: Design a thickness test for liquids.

Section 6, Materials Science

Recycling: Design and test ways to separate materials for recycling.

Section 8, Chemical Changes

More Chemical Reactions: Design an experiment to modify temperature change in a chemical reaction.

Section 11, Motions and Forces

Hovering: Design, modify and test different hovercraft vehicles.

Understandings about science and technology

Section 1, Science Process Skills

Investigating the Unseen: Develop understanding that technology is essential to science because it provides instruments and techniques that enable observation of objects and phenomena that would be otherwise unobservable.

Section 3, Science and Technologies

Soaps and Detergents: Develop understanding that technological solutions to problems, such as phosphate-containing detergents, have intended benefits and may have unintended consequences.

Section 6, Materials Science

Recycling: Discover that technological solutions, such as the wide variety and availability of different product materials, often carry risks. Attempts to reduce the risks these materials hold for our environment has resulted in new recycling technology.

Section 5, Food Science

Food Additives: Develop understanding that scientists propose solutions relating to human needs, such as determining nutritional requirements.

Section 13, Light

Magnifiers: Develop understanding that technology is essential to science because it provides instruments and techniques that enable observation of objects and phenomena that would be otherwise unobservable.

SCIENCE IN PERSONAL AND SOCIAL PERSPECTIVES

CONTENT STANDARD F:

As a result of activities in grades 5-8, all students should develop an understanding of

✔ Personal health

✔ Populations, resources, and environments

✔ Natural hazards

✔ Risks and benefits

✔ Science and technology in society

Personal health

Section 5, Food Science

Food Nutrients: Learn about nutritional requirements necessary for growth and development.
Calcium: Discover the ways in which the body uses calcium.

Populations, resources, and environments

Section 6, Materials Science

Recycling: Discover how recycling conserves a variety of finite natural resources.

Natural hazards

Section 6, Materials Science

Recycling: Discover how recycling reduces hazards caused by large scale waste disposal.

Section 9, Earth and Space Science

Earthquakes: Investigate the risks and potential damage associated with earthquakes.
Weather: Learn about the potential hazard to ecosystems caused by some weather phenomena.

Section 10, Energy

Static Electricity: Investigate lightning, a powerful and often destructive force of static electricity.

Science and technology in society

Section 1, Science Process Skills

Designing Structures: Discover materials and methods used in modern architecture.

Section 2, Science and Recreation

Chemistry of Art: Learn about a technological product (and art form) that has had a tremendous effect on society.

Section 3, Science and Technologies

Soaps and Detergents: Learn how and why scientists developed phosphate-free detergents.
Lubricants: Discover the important role of lubricants in keeping a variety of modern devices operating properly.
Fibers and Fabrics: Explore the variety of fabrics developed for different uses.

Section 5, Food Science

Food Additives: Investigate different food additives developed in response to society's need for flavorful, fresh food.

Section 6, Materials Science

Polymers: Learn how the development of synthetic rubber helped meet the demand for rubber during war time.
Plastics: Explore the tremendous variety of ways plastic has affected modern life.
Rubber: Learn about some high-tech uses of rubber.
Recycling: Explore the environmental cost of having such a large quantity of products available.

Section 7, Physical Changes

Mixtures: Investigate techniques for separating and identifying substances in a mixture.
More Mixtures: Learn about the development of special mixtures used to make color film for photography.

Section 8, Chemical Changes

Carbon Dioxide: Learn how the need for containers for carbonated beverages led to the development of a new type of plastic bottle.

Section 9, Earth and Space Science

Solar Energy: Explore different ways to harness the sun's energy.
Solar System: Learn how probes are used to provide information about our solar system.

Section 10, Energy

Electric Circuits: Investigate how electric circuits operate in countless devices.

Section 11, Motions and Forces

Aerodynamics: Discover how an understanding of aerodynamics led to the development and improvement of airplanes.
Wheels: Explore the tremendous impact of wheels on society.

Section 13, Light

Magnifiers: Discover the technological advances of different instruments used to magnify.

HISTORY AND NATURE OF SCIENCE

CONTENT STANDARD G:

As a result of activities in grades 5-8, all students should develop an understanding of

✔ Science as a human endeavor

✔ Nature of science

✔ History of science

Science as a human endeavor

Section 6, Materials Science

Plastics: Learn about the work of a female plastics chemist.
Polymers: Discover a scientist that invents new polymers.
Rubber: Learn about Charles Goodyear's contribution to the rubber industry.

Section 7, Physical Changes

More Mixtures: Discover the work of a female chemist who develops new kinds of photographic film.

Section 11, Motions and Forces

Aerodynamics: Explore the accomplishments of two women in the field of aerodynamics.

Nature of science

Section 2, Science and Recreation

Toys in Space: Investigate ways astronauts conduct experiments to learn more about microgravity.

Section 11, Motions and Forces

Air Pressure: Learn about a German Scientist's historic experiment with air pressure.

History of science

Section 1, Science Process Skills

Measuring: Learn how different ancient civilizations developed their own measurement systems.
Designing Structures: Discover the ways in which people in different parts of the world use different materials to build homes and other structures.
Inventing: Learn about the contributions of several inventors.

Section 3, Science and Technologies

Soaps and Detergents: Discover the origins of soap production, over 2000 years old.

Section 5, Food Science

Food Additives: Learn how people have used food additives to preserve and enhance the flavor of foods for thousands of years.

Section 7, Physical Changes

Chemical Particles: Explore the challenge of one chemical engineer to develop a chemical to prevent helium balloons from leaking.

Section 10, Energy

Heat: Learn about the first hot air balloons.

Section 11, Motions and Forces

Wheels: Explore the history of the wheel.

Reviewers of
The Best of WonderScience

Kenneth G. Blom
Director of Science
Niskayuna Central School District
Niskayuna, New York

W. H. Breazeale
Francis Marion University
Florence, South Carolina

Linda Estes
Lindenwood College
St. Charles, Missouri

Karen K. Lind
University of Louisville
Louisville, Kentucky

David J. Martin Ph.D.
Kennesaw State College
Marietta, Georgia

JoAnn Kosko Simmons
Elementary Teacher
Selkirk, New York

This unit introduces students to some of the ideas and techniques involved in estimating. Estimating is a quick and useful tool when objects are too numerous to count, too long to measure, or too heavy to weigh. The disadvantage of estimating is that sometimes a small inaccuracy in the beginning of an estimate can lead to a very large inaccuracy at the end. This unit encourages students to think carefully about what they are trying to estimate and to consider all the factors that might influence that estimate.

Estimate–Investigate!

In *Estimate–Investigate!*, students are given four steps necessary to make their estimates. This estimating process could be done as a class or in groups. Ask students to think about why their estimates vary. What variables need to be considered in making this estimate as close to reality as possible? It should be made clear to students that this is not the only way to make this estimate. See if your students can suggest other ways.

Quicker than the Count

In *Quicker than the Count*, students practice estimating a large number of objects by placing them onto a grid of a known number of small squares. Grids are used by scientists counting cells in laboratories as well as by officials whose job it is to estimate the number of people in a large crowd. See if students can suggest other ways a grid might be used to count large numbers of objects such as stars in the sky, bees on a hive, or plants in a corn field.

How Many Books? Just Take a Look!

In *How Many Books? Just Take a Look!*, students see that estimating the total number of books in a bookcase gets more and more accurate as students get more information about the number of books on each shelf. Students will see that when making an estimate, the more detailed and complete the information, the better the estimate can be.

The Long and Short of It

In *The Long and Short of It*, students discover that estimating can become more accurate with practice. Students estimate the length of a shoe lace while it is laced and tied and then check their estimate by measuring the actual length of the lace. They then estimate the length of another tied lace and should find that their estimate is closer the second time.

Time Flies—When You're Having Fun!

In *Time Flies—When You're Having Fun!*, students test their ability to estimate time. Time is difficult to estimate because our perception of time is closely associated to what we are doing. Ask students which hour seems longer: an hour spent doing homework or an hour spent playing their favorite game.

Picture-Perfect (almost) Estimates

In *Picture-Perfect (almost) Estimates*, students use a reference to make some estimates. In the photograph of the neighborhood, the length of the street can be estimated by using a car as a reference. An important factor to consider is the difference in size between objects in the foreground and background of the picture. To make up for this difference, a reference object in one part of the picture should be used to measure distances only in that area. An estimate of the number of birds in the middle photograph may be made using the grid method form *Quicker than the Count*. However, students should be aware that unlike the activity with lentils, we cannot tell from the photograph if some birds are hidden behind other birds.

RELEVANT NATIONAL SCIENCE EDUCATION STANDARDS

The activities in this unit can be used to support the teaching of the following standards:

✔ **Science as Inquiry**
   Abilities necessary to do scientific inquiry

✔ **Science and Technology**
   Abilities of technological design

Estimate-Investigate!

Estimating is very important. You do it all the time. But don't try to estimate how often, because you usually do it without even thinking about it! You estimate about how long it will take you to get ready for school and then wake up according to that estimate. (Sometimes that one's a little off.) You might estimate the cost of things you want to buy at the store to see if you have enough money to buy them.

Sometimes you may have to make more difficult estimates, and you may not know how to make them. The following activity gives you a step-by-step way to do these difficult estimates and to become an excellent estimator!

Here's an example of a tricky estimate and a way to go about making it easier:

What is the total amount of water that students drink from water fountains in your whole school in a single day?

Step 1

Think about how much water an average student drinks at an average visit to the water fountain. How many cups do you think it is? Less than 1/2, between 1/2 and 1, or more than 1?

Write down your number.

Step 2

The next question is how many times per day does the average student visit the water fountain? Some may go more often than others and some may not go at all, but you want the average amount. *Write down your number.*

Step 3

You now have an estimate of the amount of water a student drinks at each visit to the fountain from Step 1. You also have an estimate of the number of times a student goes to the fountain in a day from Step 2. If you multiply these together, you get an estimate of the amount an average student drinks from the fountain in a day.

Write down your answer.

Step 4

Once you have an estimate of the amount an average student drinks from the fountain in a day from Step 3, multiply that number by the number of students in your school. *Write down your answer.*

This is an estimate of the amount of water students drink from water fountains in your whole school in a single day! And that's what you were looking for!

How much money is spent at lunch time in one day at your school?

Now try to estimate these!

What is the total number of times that a student writes his or her name in a week?

What is the distance a student walks in school during an average school day?

How many times do you think students say "Hi" during a school day?

ILLUSTRATIONS, BOB BOURDEAUX

Quicker than the COUNT

People who work in laboratories sometimes need to estimate the number of tiny organisms or cells in a sample of liquid. By placing a drop of the liquid on a tiny grid of squares under a microscope and counting the cells in a few squares, the total number of cells in the sample can be estimated. This is much quicker than counting all the cells in the sample. To get an idea of how it works, try the activity below with a partner.

1 Cut the index card into four equal strips. Tape the pieces together to make a square barrier as shown. Place the barrier around the grid of squares below.

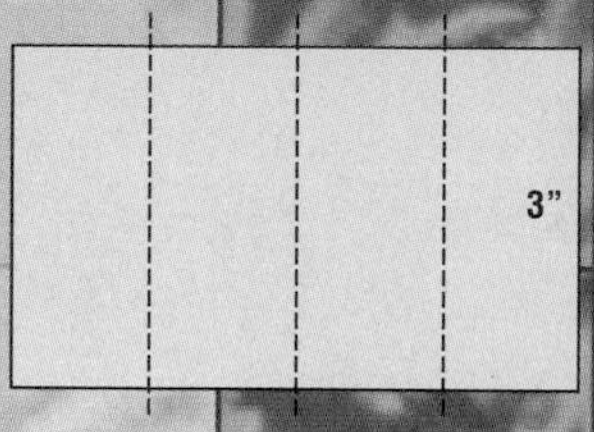

3"

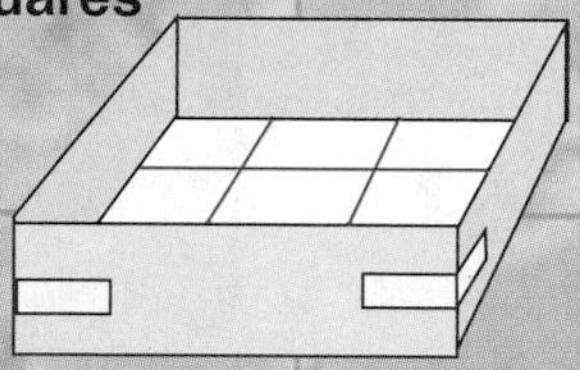

YOU WILL NEED:

3 × 5 index card (1 for each group)

dried lentils (2 teaspoons for each grou

teaspoon

blunt-tipped scissors

tape

2 Place 2 level teaspoons of lentils onto the center of the grid. Hold the barrier in place, and shake your grid back and forth to spread the lentils evenly among the squares.

3 Count the lentils in 1 square. Your partner should count them in another square. Add the numbers together and write down the sum. Divide the sum by 2 to get the average number of lentils in each of the two squares.

4 Since there are 9 squares, multiply the average number you got by 9 to get the total number of lentils in two level teaspoons.

You and your partner should count all the lentils on the grid to see how close your estimate was!

...one thousand two hundred and thre one thousand two hun and four...one thousan hundred and five. There's got to be better way!

4

How many books? Just take a look!

YOU WILL NEED:

bookcase with at least 3 shelves filled with books

Sometimes store owners actually count every single product on the shelves of their store. This is called doing an **inventory**. Doing an inventory takes a lot of time. Sometimes the store has to be closed while the inventory is being done. Therefore, instead of doing an inventory every time, someone in the store usually just looks at the shelves and makes a quick estimate of what needs to be ordered. Let's see how good you are at estimating what's on the shelf!

1 Look at each shelf on the bookcase. Do not count the individual books. Make an estimate of the total number of books in the bookcase. Your partner should also make an estimate. Write your estimates down and keep them secret.

2 You and your partner should now count the books on a single shelf. Based on the number you counted, you and your partner can change your estimates if you want. Write down your new estimate but don't show it to anyone.

3 Now, count the books on the second shelf. You can each change your estimates again if you want. Write down your new estimates.

4 Count the books on the remaining shelves. Write down the total.

How close was your first estimate to the actual number? How close was your partner's?

How much closer were your second and third estimates compared with your first?

1 Pick a nice thick book with a lot of pages. You and your partner should look to see how many pages are in the whole book.

2 Your partner should call out a page number and you should estimate where this page is and open up the book to see how close you came.

3 Try it several more times to see how much you improve.

The long and short of it

We estimate **distance** or **length** all the time. For a quick game of baseball or soccer, you estimate the distance between the bases or the length of the field. When you get your hair cut, you may ask them to take off *about* an inch or inch and a half. When you give someone directions somewhere, you might tell them to go *about* 2 miles and make a right. In the activity below, try estimating distances in some different ways.

1 It's not easy to estimate the length of a shoelace when it is laced and tied. Look at one of your shoes or your partner's shoe if your shoes don't have laces. Estimate the length of the shoelace and write it down.

2 Take out one of the laces and measure it. Write down the actual length. Don't let anyone else see the actual length. You may have been pretty far off but that's OK. You will get a chance to improve.

3 Now look at someone else's shoe with the lace still in it. Think about your own shoe and shoelace and estimate the length of this other shoelace. Write down your estimate. Ask for the actual length and record it.

Was this estimate closer than the one you did for your own shoe?

4 Now that you know the length of your shoelace, estimate how many shoelaces long the room is. Write down your estimate. Now measure the length of the room with your shoelace.

How close was your estimate?

5 Now that you know the length of the room in shoelaces, you should be able to make a good estimate of the width in shoelaces. Write down your estimate and then make your measurement.

Were you closer this time?

Don't lace that shoe yet! You'll need it in Time Flies—When You're Having Fun!

6

Time flies—
when you're having fun!

We estimate time all the time! You say "I'll be there in *about* 5 minutes" or "To go that far will probably take you *about* three hours." Speaking of time, you probably shouldn't spend too much more time with a laceless shoe, so try the activity below and see how time flies when you're having fun!

YOU WILL NEED:

clock or watch with a second hand

shoelace and unlaced shoe

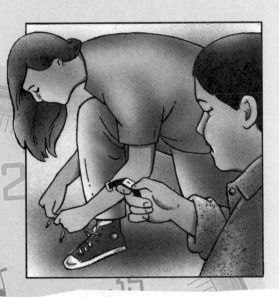

1 Estimate the shortest amount of time you think it will take you to lace and tie your shoe. Write down your estimate and then GO! Have your partner time you. Write down the actual amount of time it took.

2 Now that your partner has seen how long it took you to lace and tie your shoe, he or she should make an estimate and then start lacing!

Whose estimate was closer? Why do you think so?

You've probably said, "I'll be done with this in about one minute" or "That will take me just a minute." Well let's see how well you and your partner can estimate just how long one minutes really is!

YOU WILL NEED:

clock or watch with a second hand

1 Sit so that you can see a clock or watch and your partner cannot. Tell your partner that you will say "Go" and begin asking interview questions.
Your partner must answer the questions and then say "Stop" when one minute has gone by.

Interview Questions:
What is your full name?
Can you spell that please?
What are the names of your brothers and sisters?
What is your home address?
How long have you lived there?
Do you have any pets?
What are they?
What are their names?
What was the best thing you did during your last vacation?

2 After your partner says "Stop," check the time and write it down. **How did your partner do?** Now switch seats, and you try to tell when one minute has gone by.

Picture-
Perfect
(almost)
Estimates

Can you estimate the length of this curved street using clues you find in the picture?

Can you estimate the number of birds in this picture? Does Quicker Than the Count give you any ideas?

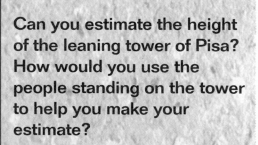

Can you estimate the height of the leaning tower of Pisa? How would you use the people standing on the tower to help you make your estimate?

To learn more about the tower and what makes it lean, look up "Pisa" in an encyclopedia.

This unit concentrates on the concept of measuring. The purpose of the unit is not to focus on a particular measuring system but to get students thinking about different techniques for measuring and why measuring is important. There are many quantities that can be measured (temperature, speed, weight, voltage, pressure, loudness, etc.), a variety of tools that can be used to measure them, and a choice of units in which a measurement can be expressed. This unit focuses on the measurement of length, one of the most fundamental quantities that we measure.

How Do You Measure Up?

How Do You Measure Up? describes how ancient people first began to measure the lengths of objects in a systematic way. Students learn how common units of length, such as the inch and foot, were first established, and will discover some of the problems with the early definitions of these units. Before starting the activity, have students make a copy of the chart pictured.

Measurement Matters

Measurement Matters lists some good measurement techniques. Stress the importance of these, and try to continually reinforce them as your students conduct the activities in this and other units.

Going Around in Circles

Going Around in Circles compares two different methods of measuring the length of a curved line. This activity is designed to challenge the notion that only straight lines can be easily measured.

Measurement: The Long and Short of It

In *Measurement: The Long and Short of It*, students use measurement tools to measure things that are extremely large and extremely small. In the first activity, a sextant and graph paper are used to make a scale drawing to find the height of a flagpole or other tall object. In the second activity, the thickness of a single page in a book can be calculated by measuring the thickness of a large number of pages with an ordinary ruler and then dividing by the number of pages. In both activities, students use an indirect method of measurement.

Picture Yourself a Ruler

Picture Yourself a Ruler challenges students to estimate the length of objects that appear in pictures by comparing their size to other objects in the pictures whose lengths are known. This is similar to an activity in the Estimating Unit. Special help is given for estimating the height of the Washington Monument in the first picture. In the beach picture, students should use the person nearest the water for best results. We estimated the young boy's height to be about 4 1/2 feet. Using him as a measuring device, the beach, along the water's edge, was about 84 feet long.

RELEVANT NATIONAL SCIENCE EDUCATION STANDARDS

The activities in this unit can be used to support the teaching of the following standards:

✔ Science as Inquiry
   Abilities necessary to do scientific inquiry

✔ History and Nature of Science
   History of science

How Do You

People who lived in ancient civilizations needed a way to measure and compare the sizes of different things. Several of these civilizations invented ways of measuring using parts of the body! The **cubit**, for example, was equal to the distance from the end of the elbow to the tip of the middle finger. There was a big problem with this way of measuring, which you can discover in the following activity.

1 Ancient Romans often used their thumb to measure the length of objects. The width of a man's thumb was called an **uncia** (un-see-a). The English word **inch** comes from this word. Place your thumb on a yardstick or measuring tape and measure its width. Is it exactly one inch wide? Record the width of your thumb in inches on the chart. Also measure and record the width of your adult partner's thumb.

2 Use your thumb to measure the length of this page. What is its length in your thumb widths, or uncia? Ask your partner to measure the page in his or her thumb widths. Do you think your adult partner will use more, fewer, or the same number of uncia as you did?

3 Twelve uncia equaled a **foot**, which was about the same length as a real man's foot. How many of your thumb widths equal the length of your foot? Ask your adult partner to measure his or her foot in the same way. Measure the actual length, in inches, of your foot and your partner's foot. Record these measurements on your chart.

4 Three feet equaled a **yard**. A yard was defined as the distance from the end of a man's nose to the tip of the middle finger of his outstretched arm. Get your adult partner to help you measure this distance on your body. Write the distance on your chart. Is this distance exactly three times the length of your foot? Measure and record this distance for your adult partner.

Measure Up?

5 The *cubit* was the length of a man's arm from his elbow to the tip of his middle finger. Today, the cubit is defined as 18 inches long. Get your adult partner to help you measure the distance from your elbow to the end of your middle finger, and record it on your chart. Is it longer or shorter than a modern 18-inch cubit? Measure and record the distance from your adult partner's elbow to the middle finger. How close is it to a modern cubit?

6 Look at your completed chart. Two cubits are supposed to equal exactly one yard. Do two of your cubits equal a yard? What about your adult partner's?

7 Pretend that you need to find out the length of the room you are in, but you don't have a ruler, yardstick, or other measuring instrument. Which of the body parts listed on the chart would you use, and why?

8 Actually use this part of your body to measure the length of the room. Then ask your adult partner to use his or her same body part to measure the room's length. Does your partner's measurement agree with yours?

What is the main problem with measuring units based on body parts? Is there any advantage?

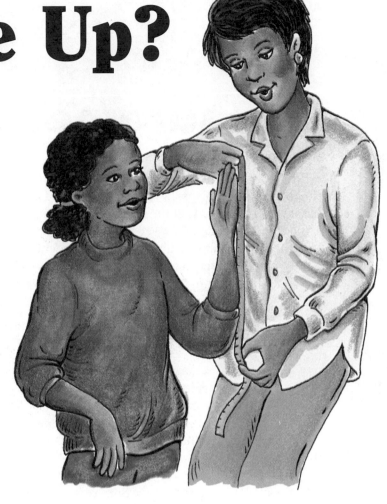

Body Part	Unit	Length		
		Actual	**Yours**	**Partner's**
	Uncia	1 inch		
	Foot	12 inches		
	Cubit	18 inches		
	Yard	36 inches		

---

* All activities in *WonderScience* have been reviewed for safety by Dr. Jack Breazeale, Francis Marion University, Florence, SC, and Dr. Jay Young, Chemical Health and Safety Consultant, Silver Spring, MD.

Measurement Matters!

The first measurement systems were invented thousands of years ago. Many ancient civilizations, including the Babylonians, Egyptians, Greeks, and Romans, developed their own measurement systems based upon parts of the body. Body parts made convenient measuring tools because everybody had them and they were always available whenever something needed to be measured. The problem was that body parts on different people were different sizes. When measuring a certain object or distance, a person with a huge foot would get a measure different from that of a person with a very short foot. There was a need for a more consistent way to measure things.

As civilization progressed, and countries began to trade with one another and merge together, there became a need for a single system of measurement that could be used by all countries. In the late 17th century, some people saw a need for a simple system of measurement that would be used by all countries of the world. This began the development of the modern **metric** system, which today is officially called the **International System of Units**, or SI. The United States is one of only about five countries that does not require the use of the metric system in daily life.

One of the most basic things to measure is **length**, or **distance**. Length describes how long an object or part of an object is. *Height*, *thickness*, and *width* are other words for length. Distance describes how far it is from one point to another. In SI, the basic unit of length or distance is the meter.

There are several important rules to remember whenever you are using a measuring instrument to find out the length of an object:

- Never measure from the end of the measuring instrument. There is often no line at the very end. This can make your measurement inexact.
- If possible, place the object to be measured directly on the measuring instrument, or place the instrument directly on the object.
- When reading a measuring instrument, always line your eye up directly with the point you are measuring.
- For greatest accuracy, repeat your measurement at least three times and average your results.

In this unit, you will investigate several different ways to measure length and distance. You will learn how to find the length of something that is really, really small and something that is very, very tall. You will also learn how you can measure the distance along a curved or crooked path. Finally, you will be challenged to estimate the length of different objects.

GOING ROUND IN CIRCLES

You will need

1 stiff small paper plate
ruler with hole near the end
brass paper fastener
ball point pen
cloth measuring tape
chalk
concrete or paved sidewalk
string

Can you measure a length or distance if it is all squiggly and wavy? Sure! If a bicycle or a car has an ***odometer***, it measures the distance the bike or car travels, whether you are traveling up or down a hill, around curves, or turning a corner. In this activity, you will make a WonderWheeler that you can use to measure the distance traveled along a crooked path.

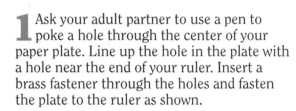

1 Ask your adult partner to use a pen to poke a hole through the center of your paper plate. Line up the hole in the plate with a hole near the end of your ruler. Insert a brass fastener through the holes and fasten the plate to the ruler as shown.

2 Use the end of the ruler that sticks out as a handle to push the paper plate across a table or other flat surface. If the plate wobbles, tighten the fastener or use a stiffer plate.

3 Make a mark near the edge of the plate as shown in the illustration. Use the measuring tape to measure the ***circumference*** of the plate (circumference is the distance around the outside edge of a circle). Write the circumference on the plate. Your WonderWheeler is now ready to use!

4 Have your adult partner use chalk to draw a curvy line along the sidewalk or asphalt surface. Position your Wonder Wheeler so that the bold mark touches one end of the curvy chalk line. Push the WonderWheeler along the line. Keep your eye on the bold mark and count how many turns the WonderWheeler makes including any fraction of a turn.

5 To find the distance traveled along the curvy line, multiply the number of turns you counted by the circumference, then add any fraction of a turn. How long is the line?

6 Another way to measure a curvy line is to lay a string directly on the line from one end to the other. Try it with the line your adult partner drew. To find out how long the curvy line is, just measure the string! Were the results of your string and WonderWheeler measurements similar? Which method do you think is better for measuring what sorts of things. Why do you think so?

MEASUREMENT: THE LONG

S ome objects are too long or too tall to measure easily with a ruler or tape measure. A different kind of measuring instrument or method must be used. In this activity, you will make a measuring instrument called a **sextant** that you can use to measure the height of really tall things such as a flagpole, a giant tree, or a skyscraper.

You will need

protractor	metal washer
straw	meter stick or metric
tape	tape measure
string (12–15 cm)	plain square graph paper*

1 Tie one end of the string to the center hole along the flat edge of the protractor. Tie the other end of the string to the washer. Tape the straw across the middle of the protractor as shown. When the protractor is held so that the straw is level with the ground, the string should hang freely along the zero mark on the protractor.

Protractor
Tape
Soda Straw
String, 10 cm
Washer

2 You are now ready to use your sextant to measure the height of a tall object. Find a flagpole (or other tall object). Use the meter stick or tape measure to measure and mark a spot ten meters away from the bottom of the flagpole.

3 Squat down at this spot so that when you hold your sextant at a height of 1 meter above the ground, you can tilt the sextant to sight the top of the flagpole through the straw. Ask your adult partner to write down the number on the protractor across which the string now hangs. This number shows the angle at which you have sighted the top of the flagpole.

4 To figure out the height of the flagpole, you will need to make a scale drawing on the graph paper. The length of each square on the graph paper will represent 1 meter. Draw a horizontal line 10 squares long across the center of the graph paper. This line represents the 10-meter distance you stood away from the flagpole.

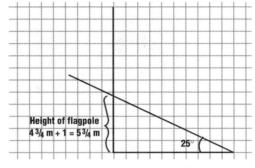

Height of flagpole
4 3/4 m + 1 = 5 3/4 m
25°

* Graph paper is on the inside back cover of your *WonderScience*.

5 At the left end of the horizontal line, draw a long vertical line representing the flagpole. From the right end of the horizontal line, have your adult partner help you use the protractor to draw a line at the same angle at which you sighted the top of the flagpole. The point at which this line crosses the flagpole line marks the top of the flagpole.

6 To find the height of the flagpole in meters, first count how many graph squares tall your drawing of the flagpole is. Then add 1 to this number to take care of the fact that you sighted the flagpole from 1 meter above the ground. What is the height of your flagpole?

S ee whether you can use your sextant to find the height of other tall objects!

1 m
10 m
25°

AND SHORT OF IT!

You will need

thick book
   (at least 300 pages)
metric ruler

Some things, such as the thickness of a sheet of paper, are too small to measure directly with an ordinary ruler or measuring tape. But if you're clever, you may be able to find a way to get a very close approximation of these small measurements. In the activity below, you will figure out the thickness of a single sheet of paper by first measuring the thickness of a larger number of sheets, and then dividing that thickness by the number of sheets to find the thickness of a single sheet. To be most accurate, you will need to do this at least three times and average your results.

1 On a separate sheet of paper, make a chart like the one below.

2 Count out and measure the thickness of exactly 100 pages near the front of the book. Be sure the pages are evenly lined up before measuring. Record the thickness on your chart next to Trial 1. Divide this measurement by 100 to calculate the thickness of a single page. Record this value on your chart.

3 Count out and measure the thickness of exactly 100 pages near the middle of the book. Record this thickness next to Trial 2 in your chart. Divide by 100 to calculate the thickness of a single page, and record.

4 Count out and measure the thickness of exactly 100 pages near the end of the book. Record this thickness next to Trial 3 in your chart. Divide by 100 to calculate the thickness of a single page, and record.

5 Add the three values in the right-hand column of your chart together. Divide the sum you get by 3 to figure out the average thickness of a sheet of paper.

6 How could you find out the thickness of a penny in a similar way? Could you find the thickness of a tissue in a box of tissues in the same way? What would you need to do to the stack of tissues before you measured them?

	100 pages	1 page
Trial 1		
Trial 2		
Trial 3		
TOTAL		
Average		

Picture Yourself a Ruler!

If you want to get an idea of how big or small something is, you can **estimate** its size if you know the approximate size of something else nearby. You can even do this for objects in a picture! See whether you can estimate the height of the Washington Monument and the length of the beach in the pictures below.

1 In the picture at left, the Washington Monument is surrounded by flagpoles and people. If you assume that most of the people are about 5 1/2 feet tall, how would you go about estimating the height of a flagpole? (You may want to use a ruler to help you.) Once you have estimated the flagpole height, you can use the same method to estimate the height of the monument! Turn this page upside down to compare your estimate with the actual height of the monument.

2 Can you estimate the length of the beach by the water's edge in the picture below? If you used a person in the picture, which person would you use and why? Turn the page upside down for our estimate of the length of the beach.

Try using your own height in a picture to estimate the height or distance of something in the picture!

ANSWERS: Height of the Washington Monument—555 ft. Length of the beach in picture—84 ft.

This unit introduces students to some of the principles involved in designing structures. Students investigate the factors effecting bridge, beam, and dome strength as well as considerations involved when designing homes and sky scrapers.

A WonderScience Construction Challenge

In *A WonderScience Construction Challenge*, students are challenged to design and construct a bridge from one-half sheet of paper. Although suggestions for different designs are given, see what students can devise *before* trying the suggested designs. Students should discover how important it is for a bridge to have a component either above or below the road surface to increase the amount of weight the bridge can support.

There's No Place Like Home!

There's No Place Like Home! features the different materials used around the world to construct different types of homes. Two of the most important considerations in home building are emphasized: (1) what materials are available and (2) how to use the materials to design and construct a home that will work well in the particular environment.

Reach For the Sky

In *Reach for the Sky*, students discover that as buildings get taller, the base needs to be more massive. In fact, sky scrapers usually have such a deep foundation that the Earth itself becomes its massive base. In this activity, students observe that a tower made of paper cups is much more stable when the bottom cup is weighted with pennies.

Beam Me Up

Beam Me Up illustrates the importance of the orientation of certain building materials, such as beams, in the construction of a building. When oriented in a particular direction, a building component is very flexible, but when placed in another direction, the component is very rigid and strong.

The Mighty Dome

The activities in *The Mighty Dome* demonstrate that fragile material such as egg shell and papier-mache can support a surprising amount of weight if the material is shaped like a dome. A dome shape distributes the forces of the weight on it and can withstand a great amount of weight.

An Unusual Home . . . A Geodesic Dome

In *An Unusual Home . . . A Geodesic Dome*, students work together to build an interesting structure. Because the structure is made of straws it is light enough to be hung from a string and displayed in the classroom. You might also want to introduce students to the history of the geodesic dome and its creator, Buckminster Fuller.

Animal Architects

Animal Architects shows the relation among the physical sciences, natural sciences, and technology in the context of designing structures. Challenge students to think of structures built by humans that might be based on the work of these animal architects.

RELEVANT NATIONAL SCIENCE EDUCATION STANDARDS

The activities in this unit can be used to support the teaching of the following standards:

✔ Science as Inquiry
   Abilities necessary to do scientific inquiry

✔ Physical Science
   Properties and changes of properties in matter
   Motions and forces

✔ Life Science
   Diversity and adaptation

✔ Science and Technology
   Abilities of technological design

✔ History and Nature of Science
   History of science

WonderScience Construction Challenge *

If you wanted to build a structure such as a bridge, a house, or even a baseball stadium, there are always two important questions you first need to answer:

1) What kind of building materials am I able to get?
and
2) How can I *design* the structure so that it will work using those materials?

Try to find the best way to use a material to build a strong structure in the *WonderScience Construction Challenge* below!

You will need

sheets of typing paper, cut in half
   lengthwise
two stacks of books of equal height
   (about 10 cm)
blunt-end scissors
metric ruler
pennies

THE CHALLENGE!

Your *WonderScience* Construction Challenge is to build the strongest bridge you can, using only 1/2 sheet of paper!

THE RULES:

1. The bridge can be made only from 1/2 sheet of plain white paper. You can use less paper, but not more.

2. You may not use glue, tape, or any other materials.

3. You may bend, fold, or cut the paper any way you like.

4. The two stacks of books must be at least 10 cm high and placed at least 12 cm apart.

THE TEST:

After you have made your bridge, test the strength by gently stacking pennies, one at a time, in the middle of the bridge.

See how many pennies your bridge can support without caving in. Our record is 54 pennies! Can you beat it?

* All activities in *WonderScience* have been reviewed for safety by Dr. Jack Breazeale, Francis Marion College, Florence, SC; Dr. Jay Young, Chemical Health and Safety Consultant, Silver Spring, MD; and Dr. Patricia Redden, Saint Peter's College, Jersey City, NJ.

Here are some design ideas to get you started. Try these and come up with a design of your own!

THE FLAT BRIDGE

Lay your piece of paper between the books. Test the bridge by placing pennies, one at a time, on the middle of the bridge. Is this bridge very strong? Cut the piece of paper lengthwise to make two long strips. Lay one strip on top of the other. Is this bridge stronger than the first one?

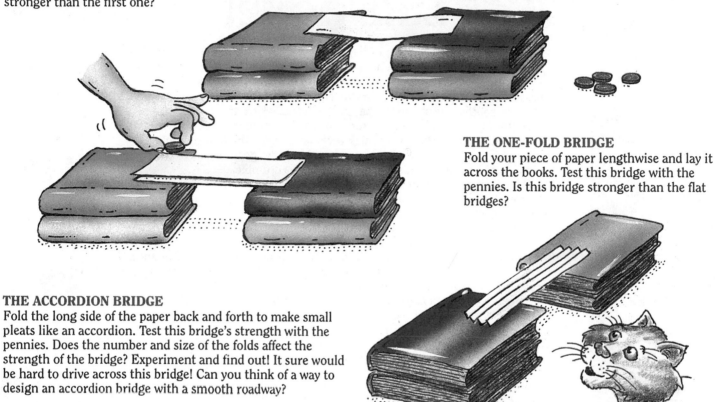

THE ONE-FOLD BRIDGE

Fold your piece of paper lengthwise and lay it across the books. Test this bridge with the pennies. Is this bridge stronger than the flat bridges?

THE ACCORDION BRIDGE

Fold the long side of the paper back and forth to make small pleats like an accordion. Test this bridge's strength with the pennies. Does the number and size of the folds affect the strength of the bridge? Experiment and find out! It sure would be hard to drive across this bridge! Can you think of a way to design an accordion bridge with a smooth roadway?

THE ARCHED BRIDGE

Cut the paper in half lengthwise. Place one strip between the two stacks of books to make an arch. (You may need to cut the strip so that the arch is the same height as the books.) Place the second strip across the books and the arch and test with the pennies. Does the arch make the bridge stronger?

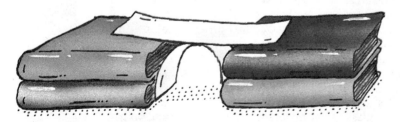

THE WALLED BRIDGE

Fold each long side of the paper up so that your bridge has walls on both long sides. Test the bridge with the pennies. Does the size of the walls make a difference in the strength of the bridge? Experiment to find out. Can you design a bridge with both walls and an arch?

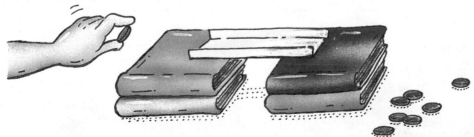

THERE'S NO PLACE LIKE HOME!

People in different parts of the world have different materials that they can use to build their homes and other structures. When building a home, they have to think of how to use these materials to build a house that will work well for *where* and *how* they live.

In the southwestern part of the United States, where there is a lot of clay and little wood, people build houses from *adobe*, a mixture of clay, straw, and water. Adobe houses have very thick walls which keep the houses cool in the hot dry desert weather. Adobe houses would not be good in places where it rains a lot because too much water makes adobe crumble.

The weather in certain tropical islands in the Pacific ocean is hot, but wet. People who live there make their houses from materials that are easy to find such as palm leaves, woven grasses, and bamboo. Sometimes they build the houses on stilts to keep them off the wet ground and to let breezes move under the house, helping to keep it cool.

Most Eskimos in Alaska and Canada built their houses out of sod or snow. These dome-shaped houses are called *igloos*. The *dome* shape of the igloo made it very strong and able to withstand powerful winter storms.

Some American Indians used to build dome-shaped houses made of poles, leaves, and tree bark. These houses were called *wigwams*. Indian tribes that moved a lot often built cone-shaped *tepees* out of buffalo skins or bark. Tepees could be easily built and taken apart quickly. Some Indians lived in more permanent structures called lodges made from logs and sod.

When early American settlers came to New England, they found the ground covered with large stones. They used these stones to build stone houses and fences that you still see in New England today.

The northwest part of the United States and Canada have plenty of forests, so most of the houses in these areas are made of wood. In China, where there are few forests, there are hardly any wooden houses. The Chinese people use tile, concrete, and stone to build beautiful *pagodas* and other buildings. In parts of Africa, where tall grasses grow, people weave the stems of dried grass together to make *thatch* huts. In Tibet, some people even make their houses out of *wool!* They shear the wool from ox-like animals called *yaks*. The wool walls keep the houses warm through the cold winter months.

Most houses in the United States today are built of wood, brick, stone, concrete, aluminum, or even glass. What materials were used to build your house or apartment?

All of the houses pictured on this page have been described above. How many can you identify?

Illustration by Martha Vaughan

REACH FOR THE SKY!

Building houses is one thing, but building *skyscrapers* is another! In this activity, try to build the tallest paper cup skyscraper you can, that can stand up to a terrible windstorm!

1 Use a very thin layer of glue on the rim and bottom of each cup to build a *skyscraper* that is 4 cups tall.

2 Let the glue dry for about 10 minutes. Stand about 1 meter in front of your skyscraper and wave your *WonderScience* magazine up and down to make a windstorm.

3 If your skyscraper is still standing, glue some more cups onto it to make it even taller! Test your tower again with the windstorm. How tall a skyscraper can you build that will not fall over in the windstorm?

4 Fill the bottom of your skyscraper with 40-50 pennies. Does this help the skyscraper stand up through the windstorm? See how high you can build your skyscraper with this heavy base.

You will need
7-oz plastic or paper cups
white liquid glue
40-50 pennies

BEAM ME UP!

One of the first steps in building a house or other building is to construct a frame. The frame supports the building just like your skeleton supports your body. Most houses have a wooden frame. Skyscrapers and tall office buildings usually have a steel frame. The parts of the frame that go across the building are called **beams**. Beams help hold up the upper levels and roof of the building. Try the following activity to find out how beams should be used to support the most weight without bending or breaking.

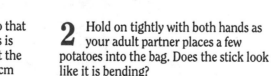

You will need
meter stick or yard stick
bag with handles
potatoes

1 Hold one end of the meter stick so that the flat end side with the numbers is facing up. Ask your adult partner to put the handles of the plastic bag about 10–15 cm from the other end of the stick.

2 Hold on tightly with both hands as your adult partner places a few potatoes into the bag. Does the stick look like it is bending?

3 This time, turn the stick so that the side with the numbers faces sideways. Have your adult partner put the same potatoes into the bag and see if the stick bends. Add some more potatoes to see if the stick will bend. Why do you think the stick bends when positioned in one direction but not when positioned in the other?

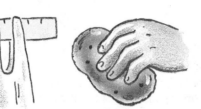

If beams are shaped like your stick, how should the beams in the frame of a skyscaper be turned to support the most weight without bending or breaking?

THE MIGHTY DOME!

A *dome* is a structure that looks like an upside-down bowl. Some famous buildings with domes are the Astrodome, the Taj Mahal in India, and the United States Capitol building. Something about the shape of a dome makes it very strong as you will see in the next activities!

1 Place the paper towel on the table. Arrange your egg shell domes on the paper towel in a square. Place the cardboard square on top of the domes so that the edge of the cardboard sticks out about 3 cm past each dome.

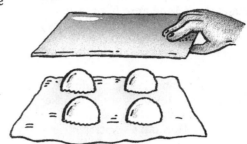

You will need

4 egg shell halves
square piece of stiff cardboard
    (20 cm x 20 cm)
magazines or thin books
paper towel

2 Start placing magazines or thin books one by one on the cardboard. How many do you think you can stack before the domes will break? Keep *stacking* until you hear the domes *cracking*! Were the domes stronger than you thought they would be? How do you think the dome shape makes fragile material like egg shell so strong?

- -

1 Completely cover your work area with newspapers. Ask your adult partner to cut four holes in the bottom of a cardboard box. Blow up and tie the balloons and place them in the holes as shown.

You will need

1 1/2 cups flour
1 cup water
large bowl
spoon
4 small round balloons (about 12 cm
    across when inflated)
cardboard box
blunt-end scissors
cookie sheet
4 paper towels
newspapers
10-pound bag of potatoes

2 Mix the flour and water in a bowl and stir until it is a smooth paste. Cut or tear each paper towel into four strips lengthwise.

3 Put both sides of a paper towel strip in the paste and pull the strip between your fingers to make sure that the strip is completely coated on both sides.

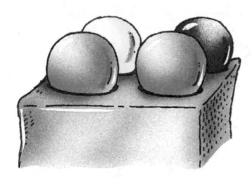

4 Lay the strip across the balloon so that the center of the strip is over the top of the balloon. Cross four strips over each balloon so that the strips completely cover the top and sides of each balloon.

5 Use your hands to mold the pasted paper towels into nice smooth dome shapes. Find a sunny spot to put the box and let your domes dry thoroughly for *at least three days!*

6 When your domes are completely dry, use a pencil or pen to carefully pop the balloons. Discard the balloons, and trim the bottom edge of the domes so that they sit evenly on a flat surface.

Let's see how strong these domes are!

Place the domes on a piece of newspaper. Place a tray or cookie sheet upside down on the domes. Put a telephone book on the tray. If your domes didn't crack, add another telephone book. If your domes are still okay, add a 10-pound bag of potatoes.

If your domes haven't cracked at all, take everything off of them, except for the tray or cookie sheet. Take your shoes off and ask your adult partner to help you gently step up onto middle of the the tray to stand on your *WonderScience* super-strong domes!

BRIDGE; TUNNEL; ARCHES; IGLOOS; THATCH; TEPEES   Answers

22

AN UNUSUAL **HOME** . . . A GEODESIC **DOME!**

You will need
60 flexible plastic straws
tape

A *geodesic dome* is a special kind of dome that can be easily put together and quickly taken apart. Geodesic domes, like the one in the lower right-hand corner of this page, were designed by a famous American architect named Buckminster Fuller. Geodesic domes are lightweight but very strong. You can build your own geodesic dome!

When connecting straws to make your geodesic dome, always insert the long end of one straw into the short end of the other, pushing all the way up to the flexible joint.

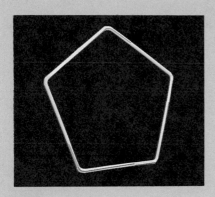

1 Connect five straws together to make a pentagon. A pentagon is a shape that has five sides that are all the same length. (The flexible joints of the straws make the corners of the pentagon).

2 Use the rest of the straws to make 11 more pentagons. Make sure all the pentagons are the same size.

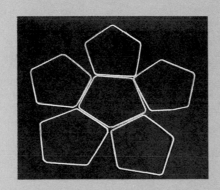

3 Place one pentagon on the table and tape five pentagons around it as shown.

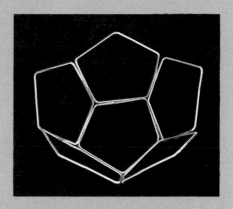

4 Lift the surrounding pentagons, so that their neighboring sides touch. Tape the sides of the pentagons which are touching each other together. You have now built half of your geodesic dome.

5 Repeat steps 3 and 4 with the rest of your pentagons to build the other half of your geodesic dome.

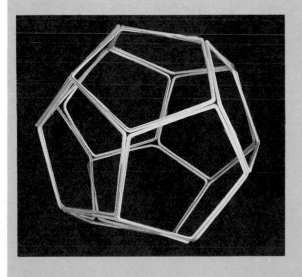

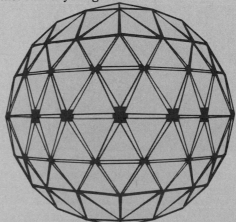

6 Tape the two halves together to complete your geodesic dome!

Most geodesic domes are made from shapes with six sides called hexagons. Can you figure out how to use straws to build a geodesic dome of hexagons?

ANIMAL ARCHITECTS

Many animals build homes and other structures similar to the ones built by humans. Some animals even make their own building materials! The silkworm, for example, makes the strong and stretchy silk threads it uses to spin a cocoon. Here are some of our favorite animal architects. Can you think of others?

BEAVERS make their homes by building dams across rivers and streams. Beaver dams are made from logs, sticks, rocks, and mud. Some dams are as long as three football fields! Most of the dam is below the waters' surface but the top is always above water. The beavers live in hollowed-out rooms inside the dam which they enter through hidden underwater tunnels.

Can you find the seven beaver tails hidden in the drawing?

Illustration by Tina Mion

SPIDERS build strong, sticky webs to catch their food. The strands which come straight out from the middle of the web are strong, but *not* sticky. The strands which go around the web are strong and *very* sticky!

Put the letters of the same color together and unscramble them to find the answers to the clues below.

a. It crosses a river or a road.
b. Underground or underwater passageway.
c. Curved structures under some bridges.
d. Homes of snow and ice.
e. Woven grass for building.
f. Cone-shaped American Indian homes.

ANTS build homes by digging a maze of underground tunnels and rooms. The tunnels underneath an ant hill may go as deep as 40 feet and have more than a million ants living in them!

See how many paths you can find from the opening at the top of the tunnel to the queen's chamber at the bottom. You must enter every chamber, but may never retrace or cross your path! We found 10 different paths, but we know there are more!

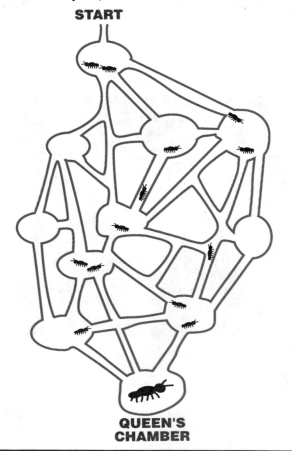

START

QUEEN'S CHAMBER

Answers can be found on the bottom of page 6.

24

Inventing

This unit offers students an opportunity to create some simple devices and then to modify them to work better or differently. Inventions included deal with the major technological areas of time-keeping, transportation, communication, and electricity.

It's Time to Invent

In *It's Time to Invent*, students make two different types of 10-second timers. Through trial and error and a series of small adjustments, students should be able to make timers that count exactly 10 seconds every time. Students are challenged to invent a timer using a string and a weight. It is fairly easy to come up with a pendulum-type timer. The key to this timer is finding the exact length of string that would result in a given number of swings in a given amount of time every time.

Invent-a-Jet

Invent-a-Jet offers a fun way to learn about jet propulsion. If your engine tubes are getting crushed by the rubber bands, use a longer strip of paper to increase the thickness of the tube walls when the paper is rolled up. If you have room, you could set up two or more launch strings to race your jet propulsion vehicles.

Let's Hear it for Inventions

In *Let's Hear it for Inventions*, students make the well-known and time-honored cup and string communication system. Although this may be a familiar activity, students are often amazed when they actually try it. The activity includes some new twists, such as using two cups at each end as separate mouth and ear pieces and hooking one cup to the speaker of a portable tape player and listening to a cup at the other end as an earphone.

Another Bright Idea

In *Another Bright Idea*, students should first look closely at the inside of the flashlight and the bulb to try to figure out how the flashlight works. As students work together to make their own electrical device, encourage them to note how the design of the device is similar to that of the flashlight. Try adding extra batteries, and see what happens.

Your Imagination Creation

Your Imagination Creation is a Rube Goldberg-type inventing activity. It can be an excellent mental exercise for students to determine the necessary orientation and relationship between the different components of the invention so that it could actually work.

RELEVANT NATIONAL SCIENCE EDUCATION STANDARDS

The activities in this unit can be used to support the teaching of the following standards:

✔ Science as Inquiry
   Abilities necessary to do scientific inquiry

✔ Physical Science
   Motions and forces
   Transfer of energy

✔ Science and Technology
   Abilities of technological design

✔ History and Nature of Science
   History of science

IT'S TIME TO INVENT!

Some very old and important inventions are devices for measuring time. It is hard to figure out when these devices were first invented, but it was well over 1000 years ago. The most important thing about a time-keeping device is that it do the same thing in the same amount of time over and over again. In the activities below, you can make two different types of 10-second timers and then invent a timing device of your own!

You will need

water
2 paper cups
pencil
tape
straw
blunt end scissors
watch with second hand

1 Use your scissors to cut a piece of straw about 6 cm long. Ask your adult partner to use a pencil to poke a hole near the top of your paper cup so that the straw can fit snugly into the hole. Adjust your straw so that it is half in and half out of the cup.

2 Cut another cup so that it fits under the straw to catch the water that will come out. Fill your large cup with water to the very top. You will have to put your finger over the straw so that the water doesn't come out.

3 When your adult partner says "GO," take your finger off the straw as your partner calls out the seconds while looking at a watch. Remember how many seconds it took for the water to stop coming out of the straw.

4 If it took more or less than 10 seconds, you will have to figure out how much to move the straw up or down on your cup. Pour out the rest of the water and remove the straw. Dry off any water on the outside of the cup and tape over your first hole.

5 Ask your adult partner to use a pencil to carefully poke a new hole. Put your straw in and fill the cup to the same height as before. Repeat step 3 to see if you are closer to 10 seconds. Continue to adjust the height of your straw until you make an exact 10-second timer!

You can also make a 10-second sugar timer!

You will need

clear plastic cup	tape
paper or plastic cup	watch with second hand
paper	sugar
pencil	metric ruler
blunt end scissors	tablespoon

1 On a piece of paper, draw a circle about 12 cm in diameter and cut it out. (It doesn't have to be a perfect circle.) Use your scissors to cut a slit from anywhere on the outside of the circle to the center.

2 Slide the cut ends of the paper against each other to form a cone. Adjust the size of your cone so that the top is a little bigger than the top of your plastic cup. Tape the cone to hold it together. Use your scissors to snip the tip off the cone so there is a small hole at the bottom. Place the cone in your cup as shown.

3 Place 1 heaping tablespoon of sugar in another cup. When your adult partner says "GO," pour all of the sugar into your cone as your adult partner calls out the seconds while looking at a watch. Remember how many seconds it took for all the sugar to go through the cone.

See if you can figure out what changes to make in your sugar clock so that it is an exact 10-second timer!

Invent your own clock!

If you had a string and a weight, could you make a 10-second timer? How would you do it? How would you make it work the same way every time?

Could a dripping faucet and a cup be made into a type of clock? Could you mark off the minutes and even the hours with a faucet clock? If you could recycle the water, it would be a better clock. How could you do it? Would you use the faucet or something else?

* All activities in *WonderScience* have been reviewed for safety by Dr. Jack Breazeale, Francis Marion University, Florence, SC; Dr. Jay Young, Chemical Health and Safety Consultant, Silver Spring, MD; and Dr. Patricia Redden, Saint Peter's College, Jersey City, NJ.

Invention: What's New?

Throughout history, people have invented products that have changed the world! Cars and planes, telegraphs and telephones, radios and televisions, computers and satellites, electric lights, and X-ray machines are a few examples of some very important inventions.

Inventing takes imagination, creativity, and the desire to make something useful and different! Inventing isn't easy. It usually takes many tries and many changes before the invention is exactly right.

An invention is different from a discovery. A *discovery* is the first understanding of something about the natural world, such as gravity. Gravity was always there, it just took people a long time to understand it. But when a person uses this understanding of gravity to make a new product, such as an elevator, that is an *invention*.

Inventors sometimes use ordinary materials that are easy to find. They also use knowledge that has been discovered by other people over the years. In fact, most inventions are improvements to products that already exist. What makes inventors special is that they look at ideas, products, and the needs of people in new ways to make other new and useful products.

An invention doesn't always have to be a product. It can also be a new way of making a product. The *assembly line* was a new way to manufacture cars. In a car assembly line, the car moves slowly ahead as each new part is added to it. The assembly line was an important invention. It was soon used in the production of many other products.

Many of the inventions we use today seemed impossible only a few years ago. People have invented robots that can write, play music, do surgery, explore the surface of other planets, and help build cars and other machines. Inventors have also created new ways of looking into the body using magnetism and sound waves. They have also invented lasers that can be used in communication systems and to cure people of certain diseases. There are now telephones that allow you to see the person you are talking to. There are also solar-powered televisions and atomic clocks that are off by only one-tenth of a second every 100,000 years!

None of these modern inventions would have been possible without the many inventions before them. The first inventions were probably hand-made blades and axes produced by prehistoric people thousands of years ago. Later, people wove fabric to replace animal hides and invented the first plows for farming. These people produced the bow and arrow, the dugout boat, and the sail for transportation on water. They also began using the wheel for making pottery and for the first carts.

One of the greatest inventions ever was a way of removing iron from iron ore (the rock in which iron is found). Once things could be made out of iron, a tremendous number of inventions were possible.

The following is a list of inventions that many people believe to be some of the most important in history. Look at each invention and think about why it was so important. Explain to your adult partner how you think each invention helped people in a very important way.

windmill for grinding grain	steam engine	X-ray	radio	plastics
irrigation	locomotive	telegraph	airplane	computer
mechanical clock	electricity production	telephone	satellite	television
paper making	light bulb			
printing press	automobile			
telescope	factory-made fertilizer			
microscope	vaccine			

Have fun doing the activities in the rest of your *WonderScience*, and most of all, be inventive!

INVENT-A-JET

Over the years, there have been many inventions in the area of *transportation*. Boats, cars, trains, and planes have all caused big changes in our society. One of the major inventions in transportation was the jet engine. In the activity below, we'll give you a few hints to start you off, then you can design your own jet propulsion vehicle!

1 Cut your piece of paper lengthwise into three equal strips. Roll the first strip into a tube so that the hole is about 1/2 cm in diameter. Use two or three pieces of tape to hold the tube closed. Use your other two strips to make tubes that are 1 cm and 2 cms in diameter.

2 Blow your balloons up a few times to stretch them out. Ask your adult partner to help you attach a balloon to each tube. Put about half the tube into the opening of the balloon. Wrap a rubber band over the balloon and tube. Be sure not to crush the tube. The widest tube may fit snugly inside the balloon without using a rubber band. These are your three jet engines.

3 Tie one end of your string to a door knob or something else that will not move when the string is pulled tight. This is your launch string. Thread the other end of the string through a straw and tie the string to something firm across the room. Make sure the string is tight and level. The straw is your launch vehicle.

4 Blow up the balloon on your narrowest tube engine by blowing through the tube. Pinch the balloon so that no air comes out. Be sure not to crush the tube.

5 Ask your adult partner to help you tape the engine to the launch vehicle as shown. Launch your vehicle by allowing air to rush out of the engine. How fast and far did it go? How do you think the other engines will do? Try them and see!

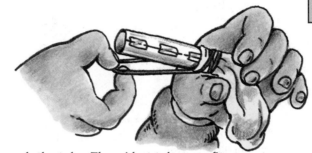

Straw
(Launch vehicle)

Tube
(Jet engine)

Can you invent another kind of vehicle, engine, or launch string that will work better?
Would more than one engine on a launch vehicle help?
What problems could this cause? How about a flexible straw? See whether you or your adult partner can invent a launch vehicle that goes the fastest and furthest!

Let's HEAR it for Inventions!

Inventions in **communication** have also been very important. The radio, television, telegraph, telephone, computer, and satellite are all inventions that have helped people communicate over long distances. Try the activity below and then see if you can invent a better way to communicate over long distances without having to scream!

You will need

4 paper cups (7 oz)
kite string (at least 10 meters)
pencil or ball point pen
blunt end scissors

1 Use your pencil to poke a small hole in the center of two paper cups. Put the end of the string through the bottom of one of the cups. Tie a knot so that the string won't come out of the bottom of the cup. Do the same thing with the other cup at the other end of the string.

2 Have your adult partner hold the other cup a distance away so that the string is tight. Ask your partner to speak into the cup while you listen. Have your partner speak more and more quietly and see if you can still hear.

3 Pluck the string and see how it sounds. Scrape your fingernails along the string. If you had a tape player, could you invent a way to record these strange sound effects? Try it! Could you invent a way to listen to music being played in another room? Try it and see!

4 If you had more cups and string, could you get someone else in on the conversation? How about inventing a way to talk and hear without switching the cups back and forth between your mouth and ear? This would be more like the ear and mouth parts of a modern telephone receiver.

Try using different string or cups to see which works best.

See what else you can invent using your cup and string communication system!

Another Bright Idea

Throughout the years, *electricity* has been used in many different types of inventions. From light bulbs to hearing aids, electricity has been used by inventors to produce many useful products to solve many different problems. In the following activity, you can make your own electrical device. See if you can invent new uses or make changes to the device so that it has different uses!

You will need

flashlight (with 2 size D batteries)
aluminum foil
paper
tape
glass or plastic bottle
blunt end scissors

1 Take out the batteries and bulb from a flashlight. Tape the two batteries together with the plus and minus ends touching as shown. Lay the stacked batteries on a piece of paper and roll them up in the paper to form a paper tube around the batteries. Tape the tube closed. Trim off the extra paper so that the paper tube is the same length as the batteries.

2 Cut a rectangle of paper that is about 10 cm long and 5 cm wide. Tear off a strip of aluminum foil that is about 10 cm wide and about 30 cm long. Wrap the aluminum foil around the width of the paper until the whole strip of alminium foil is used up and both sides of the paper are covered with several layers of aluminum foil.

3 Place the paper and aluminum foil on the open end of an empty bottle. Use a sharpened pencil to poke a hole all the way through the aluminum foil and paper. The hole should be the same diameter as the pencil.

4 Push the glass part of the flashlight bulb through the hole until the metal part of the bulb is firmly pressed against the aluminum foil. Tape the paper and aluminum foil to the sides of the paper tube so that the bottom tip of the bulb sits on the little bump on the top of the battery.

5 Tear off a strip of aluminum foil about 5 cm wide and about 20 cm long. Keep folding it in half lengthwise until you have a long thick wire. Tape one end of the wire firmly to the end of the bottom battery.

6 Test your electrical device by touching the free end of your wire to the aluminum around the bulb. The bulb should light! If it does not, check to make sure that the aluminum foil is touching the metal part of the bulb, that the bottom of the bulb is touching the top of the battery, and that the wire is firmly attached to the end of the bottom battery.

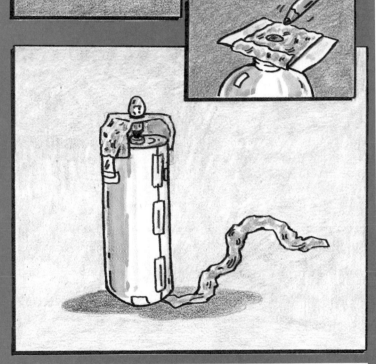

What could you invent with this device?

Could it be used to check what objects conduct electricity? Put a key, a metal spoon, or a pair of scissors between your wire and the aluminum foil around the bulb. If the bulb lights, the object conducts electricity!

How about a door-opening detector? If you had enough aluminum foil, could you invent a way to make the light go on when someone opens the door to your room?

Think of other inventions and try them out!

YOUR IMAGINATION
CREATION!

As you learned already, inventing takes a lot of imagination and creativity. Inventors need to put things together in ways that were never thought of and done before. In the activity below, you can put things together in some very unusual ways to make your own *WonderScience* wacky inventions!

Look at the three strange inventions below. One is *a door closer*, another is a *light turner offer*, and the other is an *egg cracker*. Pick two or three parts from each of these inventions and put them together to create your own invention! See if you can invent a door knocker, a plant waterer, or a pancake flipper. Try to come up with your own parts to make your own crazy invention!

After working out your ideas on paper, discuss your invention with your adult partner. If you decide to actually try your invention, be sure to work with an adult.

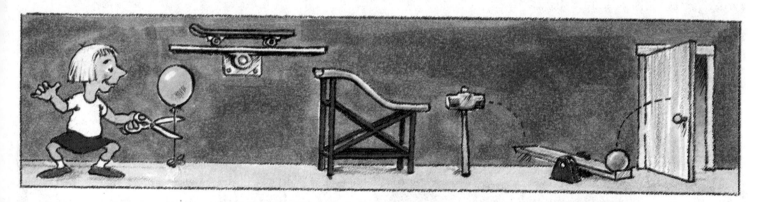

Robert Bourdeaux

This unit introduces students to several methods scientists use to seek information about objects and phenomena that, for a variety of reasons, cannot be observed directly.

It's in the Bag!

Because of the unusual nature of this unit, several activities require that you prepare in advance "mystery" objects for students to describe or identify. In *It's in the Bag!* you will need to put five different food samples in brown paper bags for your students to try to name using senses other than sight. Select foods that have distinctive odors, textures, or tastes such as the ones suggested.

Accelerators: They're Smashing!

A focus of the issue is how scientists have learned about the inside of the atom. Today, scientists know that atoms are not only made up of protons, neutrons, and electrons but also a host of other particles including *gluons* and *quarks*. They have discovered and are continually learning about these particles through the use of particle accelerators (or atom smashers). In *Accelerators: They're Smashing!* a slanted paper tube is used as a model of a particle accelerator and an inverted pie pan serves as an atom to be explored. By observing what happens when a marble is accelerated down the tube and crashes into a "mystery" object hidden beneath the pie pan, students can begin to understand how scientists use particle accelerators to infer information about the inside of the atom. You might want to put a thick cord around the entire activity to prevent the marbles from rolling away. Bring up the idea that the marble is a "probe" being used to explore the model atom.

Probing Possibilities!

Probing Possibilities! shows students that the amount that can be learned about an object is related to the size of the probe used.

The Inside Story!

In *The Inside Story!* students try to identify the hidden object inside a balloon. The marble, coin, and bouillon cube have some similar characteristics and must be distinguished. The paper clip and the pen cap may also present a challenge.

RELEVANT NATIONAL SCIENCE EDUCATION STANDARDS

The activities in this unit can be used to support the teaching of the following standards:

✔ Science as Inquiry
  Understandings about scientific inquiry

✔ Physical Science
  Properties and changes of properties in matter

✔ Life Science
  Regulation and behavior

✔ Earth and Space Science
  Structure of the earth system
  Earth in the solar system

✔ Science and Technology
  Understandings about science and technology

It's in the Bag!

Scientists often need to get information about objects or places that they can't see. A scientist may want to know what it is like at the center of the earth, or at the bottom of the ocean, or inside an ancient mummy case. How can scientists learn about things when they can't even see them? Sometimes they can get a lot of information by using their other senses! Find out how well you can identify "mystery foods" by using your senses of hearing, touch, smell, and taste.

Be sure to wash your hands before starting this activity.

1 Have your adult partner pick at least five of the mystery foods above. Ask your partner to place each food in a separate paper bag. Number each bag starting with the number 1.

2 Your job is to figure out what is in each bag without using your sense of sight. You must use your four other senses in the following order: hearing, touching, smelling, and tasting.

3 On a separate sheet of paper, make a large chart like the one on page 3. You will use this chart to write down your observations about what you sensed for each bag.

4 **HEARING:** Shake or move each bag and listen for clues about the mystery food inside. (Example: When you shake or move the bag, you might sense that the food is small and hard). Write these observations in the chart under ***Hearing*** for that bag. See how much you can find out just by hearing the mystery food!

You will need

5 new, unused paper bags	cereal
pencil	slice of bread
5 small food samples such as:	grape
potato chip	piece of orange
chocolate chip cookie	piece of banana
chocolate chips	piece of carrot
raisins	piece of apple
	piece of celery
	peppermint stick

5 **TOUCHING:** Turn your head away and close your eyes while putting your hand into the bag. ***Do not look in the bag.*** Touch the mystery food. See if you can sense its shape and size. Is it a regular shape such as a sphere, disk, or cube, or is it irregular with lots of dents and angles? What else can you find out about the mystery food with your sense of touch? Is it smooth or rough, hard or soft, moist or dry? Remember to record your observations in the chart.

 6 **SMELLING:** Open the bag slightly but don't look in. Close your eyes and smell what is in the bag. Write down what you think the mystery food smells like. Does it smell minty or spicy? Does it smell like chocolate or banana? Can you describe the smell?

7 At this point, look at your chart and see if you can take a guess at what the mystery food is. Write down what you think it is under the word "Guess" in the chart.

 8 **TASTING:** Close your eyes and ask your adult partner to put a small piece of the mystery food on your tongue. Move it around in your mouth and chew it. Can you tell what it is? Was the guess you made after smelling it correct?

9 Try the same activity with different mystery foods and let your adult partner be the mystery food senser! It's not as easy as it smells!

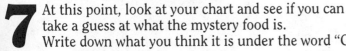

BAG	Hearing	Touching	Smelling	Guess	Tasting
1					
2					
3					
4					
5					

---

* All activities in *WonderScience* have been reviewed for safety by Dr. Jack Breazeale, Francis Marion University, Florence, SC; Dr. Jay Young, Chemical Health and Safety Consultant, Silver Spring, MD; and Dr. Patricia Redden, Saint Peter's College, Jersey City, NJ.

How do scientists learn about places and things that they can't even see? How do scientists know that the center of the earth is made of very hot iron and nickel if no one has ever seen it? How can scientists learn about the size of a star or what it is made of when the star is so far away that it can't be seen even through the most powerful telescope? How did scientists find out that atoms are made of tiny particles when the particles are too small to be seen even through an electron microscope?

There are many ways to learn about objects that we can't see. *It's In the Bag!* required your senses of hearing, touch, smell, and taste to find out about objects you couldn't see. Good scientists often use all of their senses to investigate the unknown. But sometimes just using their senses is not enough. They have to find other ways to investigate things they can't see, like the center of the Earth, distant stars, and the tiny particles that make up atoms. For example, scientists have figured out how to study the mountains and valleys of the ocean floor by using sound waves!

Sometimes scientists use a *probe* to investigate places and things they can't reach or see directly. One kind of probe you probably already know about is a space probe. A space probe is a spacecraft that is sent somewhere in the solar system or beyond to gather and send back information. It is gone for a very long time so there are no astronauts inside. The spacecraft Voyager II was a space probe sent in 1977 to photograph and learn about the planets Jupiter, Saturn, Uranus, and Neptune. It took Voyager II almost 15 years to fly past all four planets. The pictures and other information about the planets were much better than scientists ever could have had without using the probe.

There are many different kinds of probes used by scientists. X-rays are probes used to look inside the human body. Radio signals are used to find out about distant stars. Sound waves can be used to help find oil deep below the Earth's surface and to study a baby inside a pregnant woman. You may have seen a cook use a toothpick as a probe to tell if the inside of a cake is done cooking! In the activity *The Inside Story!*, a probe needs to be smaller than the object it is studying.

Scientists have come up with probes that are even small enough to study the inside of atoms! You probably know that atoms are made up of *protons*, *neutrons*, and *electrons*. The protons and neutrons form the *nucleus* at the center of the atom. Protons and neutrons are larger and heavier than electrons. The electrons move at very high speed around the outside of the nucleus. Scientists want to learn what protons and neutrons are made of. They have built huge instruments called *particle accelerators* or *atom smashers* to try to figure this out. In *Accelerators*, you can learn about one type of particle accelerator called the Continuous Electron Beam Accelerator Facility (CEBAF). Find out how it works and even build your own model particle accelerator!

Have fun as you learn more about special methods and instruments scientists use to explore the places and things we can't see!

PROBING POSSIBILITIES!

You will need

blindfold
roll of paper towels
pencil or pen
"mystery object" (iron, coffee pot, T.V., radio, or other familiar object of similar size and weight)

You know that scientists can use probes to learn about the objects around them. A doctor might use an X-ray as a probe to look inside the human body. A geologist might use a long metal tube as a probe to learn more about the rock deep inside the Earth. For a probe to be useful, it must be smaller than the object being studied and about the same size as the details you are trying to learn about. Discover this for yourself in the activity below!

1 Have your adult partner find a "mystery object" for you to try to identify.

2 Stand directly in front of a table and cover your eyes with a blindfold. Keep the blindfold on until the end of the activity.

3 Ask your adult partner to place the mystery object in the center of the table directly in front of you. You are not allowed to touch the object directly with your hands!

4 Have your partner place the roll of paper towels in your hands. Use the roll of paper towels as a probe to gently touch and explore the mystery object. Try to describe and identify the object.

5 Now have your adult partner give you a pencil (or pen) to use as a probe instead of the paper towels. Does this smaller probe make it easier or more difficult to describe and identify the mystery object?

ACCELERATORS:

You read already that scientists have been able to build giant devices called particle accelerators for learning about the inside of atoms. By firing high-speed electrons or other tiny particles at the atom, scientists can find out what the inside of the atom is like. By seeing how the electron acts when it hits the atom, scientists can learn about the location, size, and shape of particles inside the atom.

In the following activity, you can make a model of an accelerator and of an atom. A pie pan is your atom and a hidden object under the pan is the inside of the atom. An inclined tube will be your accelerator and marbles will be the particles you fire at your atom. Your challenge is to figure out the location, size, and shape of the hidden object. **GOOD LUCK!**

You will need

geometrically shaped objects such as:

wooden blocks (rectangle, circle, triangle)

can of tuna fish

baby food jar

bath soap (unopened bar)

marbles

aluminum pie pan

tape

sheet of paper

thick book

large tabletop or uncarpeted floor

1 Roll your paper into a tube so that the diameter of the tube is a little wider than the diameter of a marble. Tape the paper so the tube can't unroll. Test it to make sure a marble can roll freely through the tube.

2 Have your adult partner select an object without telling you what it is. Your partner should tape the object to the inside of a pie pan. Your partner should turn the pan upside down so that you can't see the object underneath. The object should be thick enough to allow a marble to roll freely under the pan.

3 Prop up one end of the tube on a book. Aim the tube so that a marble will go through the tube and under the pie pan. Let a marble roll through the tube. Does it strike the hidden object? If so, notice which direction it bounces off.

4 Move the tube a small distance in either direction and fire another marble. If you move the tube enough times, and fire enough marbles, you should be able to figure out the location of the hidden object. Do you think you can also figure out its size and shape?

THEY'RE SMASHING!

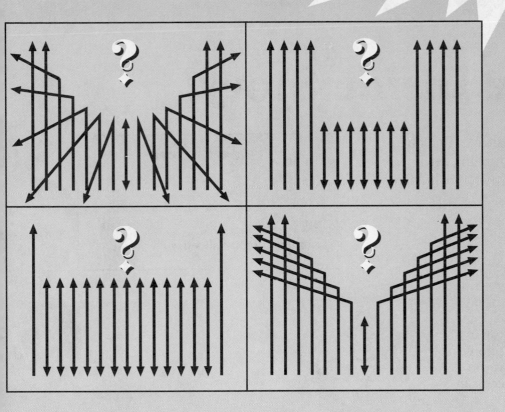

By looking at how the marbles bounce off you should be able to get information about the size and shape of the hidden object. Look at the diagram at left. What can you tell about the size and shape of each object?

5 On a piece of paper, draw what you think the size and shape of your hidden object is. Roll a few more marbles down the ramp from different places. Do you still think your guess about the object is right? If not, do some more firings to get some extra information.

6 Repeat the activity with a different object taped under the pie pan. Do you get better at figuring out the location, size, and shape of the hidden object?

Quark Quest

Scientists at the Continuous Electron Beam Accelerator Facility (CEBAF) near Williamsburg, Virginia, are very interested in learning more about the protons and neutrons in the nucleus of an atom. They have built a giant particle accelerator that is one mile around to find out what protons and neutrons are made of and how they are held together. Here's how the accelerator works. A beam of electrons travels through the accelerator building up speed. When the electrons reach the end of the accelerator, they will be traveling at almost the speed of light! The electrons will then crash into the atoms of a sample of matter placed at the end of the accelerator. Most of the electrons will miss the protons and neutrons in the atoms of the sample. But some electrons will strike the protons and neutrons in the nucleus and will bounce off and knock out one or more pieces of the nucleus. By analyzing the electrons that bounce off and the loose pieces of the nucleus that fly out, scientists can learn a lot about the inner workings of atoms. Scientists doing experiments like this have already found out that protons and neutrons are made up of even smaller particles called **quarks**. Are quarks made of even smaller particles? To find out, scientists will have to do even more experiments using even bigger accelerators like the 54-mile Superconducting Super Collider (SSC) being built in Texas!

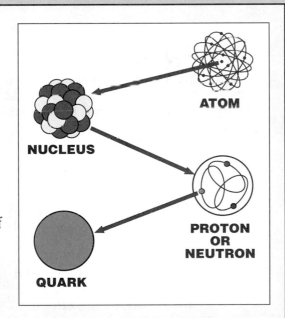

ATOM

NUCLEUS

PROTON OR NEUTRON

QUARK

The Inside Story!

Just like scientists can find out what's inside an atom, see if you can identify what is hidden inside a balloon.

1 Ask your adult partner to separately place a penny, a marble, a bouillon cube, a paper clip, and a pen cap in each of five differently colored balloons. Make sure that you do not know which object is in which balloon.

2 Your partner should blow up each balloon until it is fairly large and then tie it. Your partner should tell you the objects being used but not which object is in which balloon.

3 See if you can figure out which object is in which balloon by touching and moving the balloon. You can pick it up and shake it, twirl it, spin it, or bounce it. *Be sure not to burst the balloon.*

WONDERSCIENCE

Unit 6
Science of the Playground

This unit introduces students to some of the physical principles involved in common playground equipment. It is not necessary to visit a playground to conduct all of the activities in this unit. Several activities include alternate instructions using common items to model playground equipment.

WonderScience Playground Challenge

In *WonderScience Playground Challenge*, a playground slide is used to understand some of the factors effecting the motion of an object down a slide. There are a large number of variables that may affect how fast an object will be going when it reaches the bottom of the slide and, consequently, how far from the end of the slide it will land. The activity enables students to explore some of these variables.

Spin Out!

Spin Out! involves using a record player or turntable to simulate a playground merry-go-round. It provides a safe way of discovering how factors such as a person's weight, where they are standing on the merry-go-round, and the speed at which the merry-go-round is turning affect the likelihood of a person's flying off. The activity begins with a series of questions, and then has students reconsider the questions after performing the activity. Choice B is the correct answer to all of the questions.

A Swinging Good Time!

In *A Swinging Good Time!* students investigate what factors affect how long it takes for a playground swing to go back and forth. Expected results for the activity are printed upside-down at the bottom of the page. These results are valid if the swinging motion is not too large. If the angle or distance through which the swing moves is fairly large, the Swing Time *will* be affected. As an extension to the activity, you might challenge students to discover how large the swinging motion has to be before there is a noticeable change in the Swing Time.

Oh Say Can You Seesaw!

In *Oh Say Can You Seesaw!* students investigate the balancing process on a seesaw. If students use more than one penny on either end of the seesaw, be sure the pennies are stacked, rather than spread out. Students should discover that if there are twice as many pennies in one stack, it needs to be only half as far away from the center of the seesaw as the other stack. (See Balance Unit)

A New Twist!

A New Twist! requires a swing with long ropes that can be twisted to allow your child or student to spin around. Chain swings should *not* be used because the links will not unwind consistently. Students should rotate faster when their legs are tucked in.

RELEVANT NATIONAL SCIENCE EDUCATION STANDARDS

The activities in this unit can be used to support the teaching of the following standards:

✔ Science as Inquiry
  Abilities necessary to do scientific inquiry

✔ Physical Science
  Motions and forces
  Transfer of energy

WonderScience
Playground Challenge

If you let something go down a slide, how far away from the bottom of the slide does it land? Some things go a lot farther than others before hitting the ground. Your *WonderScience* Playground Challenge is to find something that goes the farthest distance after leaving the end of the slide!

Be sure to have your adult partner with you when doing the *WonderScience* playground challenge.

Rules of the Challenge:

1 All objects must be released from the same point near the top of the slide. Mark this point with a piece of tape.

2 Objects cannot be pushed or helped down the slide in any way.

3 Distance should be measured from a point directly below the end of the slide to the nearest point where the object hits the ground.

> **Be sure to stand**
> **to the side of the slide until the object has**
> **hit the ground and stopped moving**

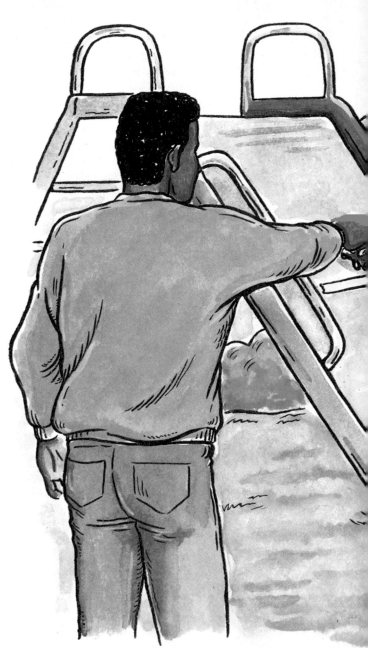

Getting Started...Some things to think about and try:

Should the object slide or roll?
Try some objects that slide and some that roll, and see if it seems to make a difference in how far they go.

Should the object be big or small?
Do bigger or smaller objects seem to go farther?

What should the shape of the object be?
Try objects that are rectangular, round, or irregularly shaped. Does shape seem to make a difference? Does it seem to matter how much of the object is in contact with the slide?

ADULT SAFETY TIP:
*If you use an empty can,
use a screwdriver or the back of a metal
spoon to carefully press any sharp edges
down against the inside of the can.
Cover the rim of the can with two layers
of adhesive tape for safe handling.*

Should the object go straight down the slide or bounce off the sides?

Roll a ball down the center of the slide and then at an angle so that it bounces off one of the sides. Which method makes the ball go farthest?

Do heavier or lighter objects go farther?

Try a small empty box such as a shoe box. Now almost fill the box with some stones or dirt and tape the top closed. Which goes farther?

Does it matter what the outside of the object is made of?

Cover the bottom of your box with wax paper, aluminum foil, or cloth to see if these different materials affect the distance the box travels.

Should the object be hollow or solid?

Compare how far hollow and solid objects of about the same shape and size go. You might try an empty can and an identical unopened can. Let them both roll down the slide. Which can goes the farthest? Find out what happens if you turn them on the end and let them slide down. Was sliding or rolling better? For which can?

Look at the results of all of your tests. Describe to your adult partner the kind of object you think should go the farthest. Can you think of a real object with all these qualities?

---

* All activities in *WonderScience* have been reviewed for safety by Dr. Jack Breazeale, Francis Marion University, Florence, SC; Dr. Jay Young, Chemical Health and Safety Consultant, Silver Spring, MD; and Dr. Patricia Redden, Saint Peter's College, Jersey City, NJ.

Playing with Physics!

If someone asks you to describe a physics lab, you probably think of a place where there is lots of electronic equipment, or a darkened room where scientists experiment with lasers, or a room filled with computers that track satellites and other spacecraft. You probably DO NOT think of an ordinary playground where scientists can push one another on swings, slide down slides, and use the seesaw. But you can learn a lot of physics at a playground.

One thing that physicists do is study moving objects. From the tiniest particles even smaller than an atom, to the most giant of galaxies, physicists try to describe how and why things move. What better place to study moving things than at the playground? You can see things swing back and forth, spin around, and move up and down.

A playground slide is something you can use to study the motion of sliding and rolling objects. Objects placed at the top of the slide build up speed as they move down the slide. The object that is going the fastest when it reaches the end should go the farthest before hitting the ground.

To win the *WonderScience* Playground Challenge, you need to choose the object that will have the greatest speed at the bottom of the slide. An object that bumps into the side of the slide on the way down will lose some of its speed, so it probably won't win. If an object rolls, some of its energy is used to make it turn around and around instead of just going forward, so maybe it won't win either. If the surface of the object is sticky or rough, there may be a lot of friction and the object won't go as fast. The shape of the object and whether it is hollow or solid also affects how fast it will go. Think about all of these things when choosing the best object for the Challenge.

A swing is like a giant **pendulum** that moves back and forth. In "A Swinging Good Time" you will find out what makes a swing move back and forth more quickly or more slowly. In "Here's a New Twist" you will twist the ropes of the swing together and then explore ways to change how fast it unwinds.

A playground merry-go-round is like a turning record on a record player. You won't be using a real merry-go-round for this *WonderScience* activity, but you can use a record player as a model of a merry-go-round. Your experiment can show you how motion in a circle affects objects at different positions on the record player.

The seesaw works best when the two sides are balanced. How can you make it work if the persons sitting on each side don't weigh the same? Make your own miniature seesaw and find out in "Oh Say Can You Seesaw."

Spin out!

In the activity below, you will use a record player as a model of a popular piece of playground equipment— a merry-go-round. Pennies will represent the people. Before you start, think and talk about the questions below with your adult partner, try to answer the questions, and then do the activity to see if you were right!

You will need

record player with at least
  two speeds
old record album that is OK to scratch or
  cardboard disk with a hole in the middle
pennies
tape

Imagine that you are standing on a merry-go-round that is going faster and faster:

Where are you more likely to fly off?
A) Standing near the center
B) Standing near the outside
C) It doesn't matter where you stand

When are you more likely to fly off?
A) When the merry-go-round is going slowly
B) When the merry-go-round is going quickly
C) The speed of the merry-go-round doesn't make a difference

What is the weight of a person who is more likely to fly off?
A) A person who weighs a whole lot
B) A person who doesn't weigh much at all
C) Weight doesn't make a difference

Where do you stand if you want to move faster?
A) Near the center
B) Near the outside edge
C) It doesn't matter; everyone goes the same speed

1 Place the album or cardboard on the record player. Set the record player on its slowest speed, but do not turn it on yet. Place one penny on the album near the center. Turn on the record player. Does the penny fly off?

2 Turn the record player off, and allow it to stop spinning. Place another penny about halfway between the center and the outside edge of the album. Turn on the record player. Does this new penny fly off? Try a penny near the outside edge of the album.

3 Repeat steps 1 and 2 with the record player set at the next highest speed. How do your results compare with what happened at the lowest speed? If you have an even higher speed, try that next. How do your results compare with what happened at the other two speeds?

4 Reset the record player to its slowest speed. Repeat steps 1 and 2, using a stack of 2 pennies taped together. Is the result different from that of a single penny? Try a stack of 4 pennies.

5 Experiment to find the highest stack of pennies you can get to stay on the spinning record player. Where on the record player did you place the stack? At what speed was the record player spinning?

Look at the four questions at the beginning of the activity. Based on the experiment you just finished, would you like to change any of your answers?

A Swinging Good Time!

About how long do you think it takes for a swing to go back and forth once when you are sitting in it? Does it always take the same amount of time? Find out in the activity below. If you can't get to a playground to try this activity, you can still do it at home or school. Instead of a swing, use a pendulum made by hanging a metal washer from a string. The washer represents you sitting in the swing.

You will need

a playground swing
watch or clock with second hand
metal washers
string

1 Sit in the swing. Have your adult partner time how long it takes for you to swing back and forth 30 times. (Or time how long it takes your pendulum to swing 30 times.) Divide the time by 30 to see how long it takes to swing back and forth once. This is your Swing Time.

2 Do you think your Swing Time depends on how big your back and forth motion is? Have your adult partner time you as you swing high back and forth 30 times. Then do 30 very small back and forth swings, and see how long it takes. Repeat your measurements at least twice. How does the swinging distance affect the time?

3 What do you think would happen to your Swing Time if you weighed a lot more? To find out, ask your adult partner to sit in the swing. (If you are using a pendulum, add a few more washers.) Time your adult partner's 30 swings. Did the extra weight seem to make a difference?

4 All swings are not the same. If you can find a swing that is longer or shorter than the one you used, repeat steps 1 and 2 with the new swing.

5 With your adult partner, make a pendulum with your washer and string. Make your string longer or shorter and repeat steps 1 and 2. Does the length of the string affect your Swing Time? Do your results match the results at the bottom of this page?

YOUR SWING TIME IS NOT AFFECTED BY EITHER YOUR WEIGHT OR BY THE DISTANCE THROUGH WHICH YOU SWING. THE ONLY THING THAT CHANGES THE SWING TIME IS THE LENGTH OF THE SWING.

Oh Say Can You Seesaw!

You will need

seesaw or ruler

tape

pencil

2 books of the same thickness
  (about 4 cm)

pennies

When sitting on a seesaw, you have probably noticed that a person who doesn't weigh much can balance a heavy person if the people are positioned at different places along the seesaw. In the following activity, you can use a real seesaw or a ruler as the seesaw and pennies as the people.

1 You and your adult partner should sit on opposite ends of the seesaw. If you both lift your feet off the ground, which one of you tilts down to the ground? If your adult partner is heavier, where should he or she sit on the seesaw so that it would be balanced? Try it and find out.

2 If you sat halfway between your end and the center of the seesaw, where would your adult partner have to sit so that the two of you will be balanced?

3 If you can't get to a seesaw, you and your adult partner can make a model of one! Take a flat ruler and tape a pencil across the back of the center of the ruler. Place the pencil and ruler between two books as shown. It may not balance right away, but you can use pennies to make it balance.

4 Place a penny at each end of the ruler. Adjust the pennies back and forth until the ruler is balanced. Now stack another penny on one of the pennies. How do you have to move the pennies to get the ruler to balance?

5 Now stack another penny so that you have three pennies stacked on one side and one on the other. See if you can make them balance. How many pennies can you stack and still be able to balance them with one penny at the other end?

6 With the large stack of pennies still on one side, add another penny to the end with one. What are the two ways you could make the ruler balance? Try other combinations and see if you can begin to predict where the different stacks of pennies will need to be to balance the ruler.

A New Twist!

Some swings that are hung from long ropes can be twisted so that as they unwind, they spin around and around. When used in this way, a swing can help you learn about spinning objects. You may have seen ballerinas or figure skaters pull their arms in very close to their bodies when they want to spin really fast. You can see how this works in the activity below. You can also find out how changing the mass, size, or shape of an object changes the way it spins.

You will need

rope swing (do not use a chain swing)

clock or watch with second hand

paper

pencil

1 On a separate piece of paper, make a chart like the one below. Sit in the swing and ask your adult partner to turn you around 8–10 turns. Count the number of complete turns the swing is twisted, and record this number in your chart.

2 Stretch your legs straight out in front of you. Ask your adult partner to time how many seconds it takes for the swing to completely unwind. Record the unwinding time next to Trial 1 in your chart.

3 Repeat steps 1 and 2, and record the unwinding time next to Trial 2. Take the two unwinding times and add them together. Now divide this number by 2 to get the average unwinding time. Record this number in your chart.

4 Do you think the swing will unwind faster or slower if you tuck your legs under the swing? Try it and see! Use the same number of turns as before. Record the number of turns and the unwinding time in the chart for "Legs Tucked." Repeat this step and average your results.

5 What do you think will happen if you start with your legs outstretched and then tuck them in as the swing is unwinding? How about if you start with your legs tucked and then stretch them out? Try it and find out.

6 Experiment with different numbers of turns and combinations of tucked and outstretched legs. Predict each time how long your unwinding time will be.

		Turns	Unwinding Time	Average
Legs Outstretched	Trial 1			
	Trial 2			
Legs Tucked	Trial 1			
	Trial 2			

		Turns	Predicted Time	Actual Time
Legs Outstretched and Tucked	Trial 1			
	Trial 2			

This unit introduces students to some of the science involved in playing baseball. The activities require no special baseball equipment and are equally appealing to girls and boys.

A New Spin on Throwing a Curve!

In *A New Spin on Throwing a Curve!* students examine the behavior of Ping-Pong and Styrofoam balls thrown from paper tubes. The purpose is to discover, first of all, that a spinning ball always curves. The trick to throwing a curve ball is to make the ball spin a lot. Students should discover that the direction in which the ball spins is the same as the direction in which it curves.

The behavior of a baseball has a lot to do with aerodynamics—the way air flows around the ball. Changing the surface of the ball, such as making it rougher, changes the aerodynamics and, consequently, the behavior of the ball as it travels through the air. Students can confirm this in the first activity by finding that a rougher ball spins faster when thrown from the tube and curves more. Similarly, the stitches on a baseball cause it to curve more. If baseballs were seamless and smooth, they would curve less and be much easier to hit. On the other hand there would be a lot fewer home runs, because it would be much harder for hitters to put the extra backspin on a ball needed to give it the lift and distance to clear the outfield fence.

Batter Up! and Catch That Fly!

In *Batter Up!* students investigate "reaction time" as it relates to a baseball batter. A batter's reaction time helps determine the amount of time available to make the decision to swing, which is very important in hitting a quickly moving object such as a pitched baseball. *Catch That Fly!* also relates to reaction time, but in the context of fielding. Students should notice that reaction time can be improved through practice.

Go the Distance

In *Go the Distance* students test the importance of a balanced stance in baseball. Standing with legs spread apart significantly increases reach distance. Standing this way lowers a player's center of gravity and broadens the base of support, both of which make a player more stable and less likely to topple over when reaching out to throw, hit, or catch a ball.

A Sports Spectacular!

A Sports Spectacular! encourages students to appreciate how the equipment, playing field, and rules of a sports game must be uniquely suited to one another. Students are challenged to use their creativity to invent some unique sports of their own.

RELEVANT NATIONAL SCIENCE EDUCATION STANDARDS

The activities in this unit can be used to support the teaching of the following standards:

✔ Science as Inquiry
   Abilities necessary to do scientific inquiry
✔ Physical Science
   Motions and forces
✔ Life Science
   Regulation and behavior
✔ Science and Technology
   Abilities of technological design

A New Spin on

The key to throwing a good curve ball is throwing the ball fast enough and putting a lot of sideways spin on the ball. In the activity below, see if you can find out how to make a spinning ball curve in different directions!

Note: Do this activity outdoors when it is not windy.

You will need

toilet paper tube

medium sandpaper

2 Ping-Pong balls and a rough styrofoam ball

water-soluble marker

1 Color one-half of the Ping-Pong ball with your marker. Place the ball in the tube. With the tube in your right hand, move the tube quickly across your body so that the ball flies out of the tube with sideways spin. Which way does the ball curve?

2 Fling the ball out of the tube again, just as before, but this time notice the direction in which the ball is spinning. If you're not sure, try flinging the ball from the tube again, and get your adult partner to help you watch the ball to see its direction of spin.

3 What do you think will happen if you fling the ball with your left hand? If you are not left-handed, you may have trouble putting a lot of spin on the ball. You can ask your adult partner to fling it out of the tube. In what direction did the ball curve this time? In what direction did it spin?

4 Use the tube and ball to try some "overhead" and "underhand" throws. Let your partner also try throwing the ball from the tube. Notice each time the direction in which the ball spins and the direction in which it curves. When a ball is thrown the same way, does it always spin in the same direction and curve the same way?

5 Based on your observations, can you predict the direction in which a ball will curve based upon the direction in which it spins? Test your prediction by seeing if it holds true when you fling the ball from the tube in different ways.

Throwing a Curve!

The greater the amount of spin on the ball, the more the ball curves. One way to make your ball spin more is to make either the surface of the ball or the surface of the inside of the tube rougher. This increases the amount of friction between the ball and the tube, causing the ball to spin rather than slide out of the tube.

6 Ask your adult partner to hold a piece of sandpaper flat on your work surface. Scrape one of the Ping-Pong balls back and forth on the sandpaper to make it very rough over the entire surface.

7 Now use the rough and smooth Ping-Pong balls to do the same throws you did before. Does one curve more than the other?

8 Try using a rough styrofoam ball the same size as the Ping-Pong ball. Does the styrofoam ball behave differently when thrown from the tube? What is it about the styrofoam ball that might explain this difference?

9 You can also ask your adult partner to help you make a tube out of sandpaper so that the rough side of the paper is on the inside of the tube. Try flinging the Ping-Pong balls and styrofoam ball from this tube. Do the balls behave differently than when thrown from the smooth tube?

* All activities in *WonderScience* have been reviewed for safety by Dr. Jack Breazeale, Francis Marion University, Florence, SC and Dr. Jay Young, Chemical Health and Safety Consultant, Silver Spring, MD.

Let's Play Ball!

Baseball is one of America's favorite pastimes. It's also a great example of physics in action. An important area of physics is the study of **motion**, or trying to understand what makes certain objects move the way they do. When you try to figure out how to hit or throw a baseball so it will move a certain way, you are really doing physics!

Baseball pitchers use principles of physics to throw the wackiest curveballs and the fastest fastballs. In *Throwing a Curve!*, you should have found that a spinning ball, depending on its rate and direction of spin, can soar upward, curve to one side, or fall more quickly than usual. The Ping-Pong balls that you used were either smooth or rough all over. A baseball, on the other hand, has raised stitches that make its surface uneven and cause it to spin through the air in some unusual ways. By gripping the seams in a certain way, the pitcher can make the ball spin in a particular way, causing the ball to move the way the pitcher wants it to.

Batters can use physics to hit the ball so it will travel the farthest and possibly result in a home run. By swinging under the ball and hitting it about 2 cm below center, the batter can give the ball a fairly large backspin. Backspin causes the ball to stay up instead of falling as fast as it ordinarily would. You may have discovered this in *Throwing a Curve*. Because the ball rises, it travels farther. But too much backspin pushes the ball backwards and can result in a pop-up fly. In order to put backspin on a ball, there must be enough friction between the bat and the ball. The amount of friction depends on the roughness of the surfaces of the ball and bat. Years ago, hitters would carve grooves in their bats or add pine tar to make the bat rougher where it contacts the ball. Today, this is a violation of baseball rules.

To be a really great batter today, you have to have a strong arm, a keen eye, and a very fast reaction time. In *Batter Up*, measure your reaction time and see if you have the potential to be the next Hank Aaron or Babe Ruth!

Fielders use physics to catch fly balls, to scoop up grounders, and to accurately throw the ball to teammates. In *Catch That Fly!*, you can see if you can react fast enough to catch a ball immediately after you see it!

The way that baseball players stand when they are waiting to hit, catch, or throw the ball can also be explained with physics. Standing with your feet wide apart gives your body a wide support base. Bending at your waist or knees also puts more of your body nearer to the ground, or as physicists would say, lowers your "center of gravity." Discover for yourself why stance is so important to baseball-playing success!

Baseball and other sports depend a lot on the characteristics of the ball and other equipment being used. Think about these characteristics as you do the last activity in which you can create your own sport!

Batter Up!

The average 90-mile-per-hour fastball leaves the pitcher's hand and travels to home plate in just .41 seconds. It takes a good high school batter about .28 seconds to bring the bat around and make contact with the ball. This means that in order to hit the ball, the batter must see the ball coming and decide whether or not to swing after just .13 seconds of the ball's flight!

In this activity, you will see if you are able to make such a decision in .13 seconds by measuring your *reaction time*. Your reaction time is the time it takes for you to recognize and respond to a signal. If your reaction time is only one or two thousandths of a second more than .13 seconds, it can mean that your bat won't make contact with the ball at all.

You will need

stiff paper (file folder or index card stock)

sheet of tracing paper or plain white paper

blunt-tip scissors

1 Use the tracing paper to transfer the picture of the bat, with its number scale, onto a piece of stiff paper. Cut the bat out.

2 The scale on the bat shows the number of seconds it takes for the bat to fall through a certain distance. By catching the dropped bat in the right way, you can use the scale to measure your reaction time.

3 Ask your adult partner to hold the bat at the top. Then place your thumb and forefinger on either side of the bottom edge of the bat. When your partner drops the bat, catch it as quickly as you can. Read your reaction time on the card. Is your reaction time short enough for you to react to a 90-mile-per-hour fastball? What about your adult partner's reaction time?

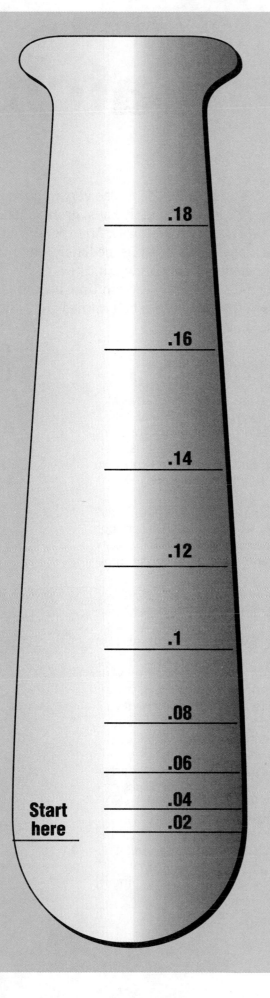

.18

.16

.14

.12

.1

.08

.06

.04

Start here .02

Catch That Fly!

Reaction time is also very important for catching fly balls, ground balls, and thrown balls. An experienced fielder reacts almost immediately when the ball is hit or thrown. In the activity below, see if your reaction time improves as you try to catch a ball immediately after it comes into view.

1 Stand with your arms at your sides and with the palms of your hands touching your legs. Your adult partner should stand behind you with a tennis ball in one hand.

2 Your partner should hold the tennis ball far enough over your head so that you cannot see it. Without telling you when it is being dropped, your partner should drop the ball in front of you.

3 When the ball passes into your view, try to react quickly enough to bring your hands up and catch it. It is not easy at first, but after a few tries you will probably begin to improve.

4 If you get really good at catching, your adult partner can make things a little more challenging by dropping the ball a bit to the right or left or by giving it a gentle downward throw instead of simply dropping it.

"Go the Distance"

You will need

cloth measuring tape (or meter stick or yardstick)

tape

pencil

sheet of paper

The next time you go to a baseball game or see one on television, look at the way the baseball players stand. Batters, fielders, and base runners always seem to crouch down with their feet spread apart and their knees bent. See if you can figure out why in the activity below!

1 Make a chart on your sheet of paper that looks like the one on this page. Ask your adult partner to help you find a wall where you can tape a little "X" about waist-high on the wall.

2 Also use tape to mark an "X" on the ground about 20 cm (8 inches) directly in front of the "X" on the wall. Stand facing the wall with your feet together directly on the spot marked "X". Reach as far as you can with your right arm, touching the farthest point possible on the wall without falling over. Have your adult partner measure how far you were able to reach.

3 On your chart, record your **reach distance** under the "0" for **distance between feet**. How do you think your reach distance might change if you stand with your feet separated?

4 Stand with your feet apart so that each foot is a distance of 10 cm (4 inches) from the X. Try reaching as far as you can this time. Write down your reach distance under the 20 cm for distance between feet.

5 Measure and record your reach distances when your feet are separated by distances of 40 cm (about 16 inches) and 80 cm (about 32 inches).

6 Based upon your experiment, think of reasons why a baseball fielder might stand with legs wide apart. Can you think of why a batter waiting to hit the ball might also stand with legs apart?

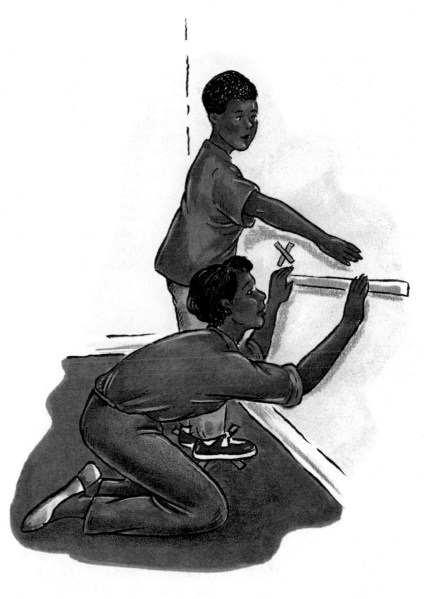

distance between feet	0	20 cm	40 cm	80 cm
reach distance				

A Sports Spectacular!

The way a sport is played depends a lot on the characteristics of the ball and the other equipment that is used. The size, shape, weight, and material of the baseball, bat, and mitt have a large effect on the way baseball is played. The distance between pitcher's mound and home plate and between the bases, and the way the rest of the baseball diamond is designed, are also very important to the game. When a sport such as baseball is invented, the ball, other equipment, design of the of field, number of players, rules, and the object of the game all have an effect on each other and are all worked out together. If a baseball were like a beach ball and the bat were like a Ping-Pong paddle, the field, object of the game, and rules would be very different!

Answer these questions before doing the "Create your own sport" activity below:

1 Name all the sports you can that use balls that are filled with air. Pick one of these sports and explain how the air-filled ball behaves in a way that is important to that sport. Now imagine what it would be like if the ball were solid. How might the object or rules of the game need to change?

2 Which games use balls that are heavy for their size? Pick one of these games and explain how the heaviness of the ball affects the way the game is played. How would the rules of the game have to change if the ball were a lot lighter?

Create your own sport!

Write down each of the items in columns A, B, C, and D on separate pieces of paper. Place the papers from each column upside down in separate piles. Mix the papers up within each pile. Choose one paper from each pile. Invent a sport that uses all the items you picked. You need to state the object of the game, how many players on a team, the rules of play, how points are scored, etc. **GOOD LUCK!**

A	B	C	D
tennis ball	baseball bat	basketball hoop	baseball diamond
bowling ball	tennis racket	volleyball net	tennis court
Ping-Pong ball	croquet mallet	soccer goal	football field
football	golf club	bowling pins	golf course
golf ball	pool cue	football goalpost	bowling alley
basketball	Ping-Pong paddle	golf hole	basketball court

This unit introduces students to several of the different ways that chemistry is involved in art. The main objective is for students to discover that chemistry is a central component of the materials and processes in art.

The Dilution Solution!

In *The Dilution Solution!* students make a series of dilutions with watercolor paints. Using watercolors makes the concept of dilution easier to understand because the decrease in color intensity with more dilution is easy to see. The activity also allows students to experiment with mixing different dilutions of color to achieve predicted results.

Become An Art Master...with the Power of Plaster!

In Become An Art Master...with the Power of Plaster! students are introduced to the characteristics of plaster and to its use in the art of sculpture. The impression in the plaster is the mirror image of the toy used to make the impression. When clay is pressed into the impression and removed, the image is reversed again, matching the original toy.

Picture This!

In the short article about photography, students learn about the fascinating chemistry that goes into making a photograph as well while considering the idea of a photograph as a work of art.

Vegetable Dyes—They're Hard To "Beet"!

In *Vegetable Dyes—They're Hard To "Beet"!* students should understand that in order for a dye to work, the dye molecules must interact and bind to the molecules of the material being dyed. You might want to point out that certain chemicals are added to commercial dyes to enhance this interaction.

WonderScience Mystery Art!

In *WonderScience Mystery Art!* students use wax in their art work. The chemicals that make up wax repel water so the watercolors will color the paper but not the wax.

Pick the Right Paint For Your Palette!

Pick the Right Paint For Your Palette! demonstrates that different types of paint are needed to paint different kinds of surfaces. Students readily see that paints made with water and paints made with oil can have very different qualities and uses.

RELEVANT NATIONAL SCIENCE EDUCATION STANDARDS

The activities in this unit can be used to support the teaching of the following standards:

✔ Science as Inquiry
   Abilities necessary to do scientific inquiry

✔ Physical Science
   Properties and changes of properties in matter

✔ Science in Personal and Social Perspectives
   Science and technology in society

THE DILUTION SOLUTION!*

An important skill that artists need when working with watercolor paints is to know how to *dilute* the paints. Diluting something means to make it less strong by adding something else to it; for example, adding water to concentrated orange or grape juice. People working with paint or other chemicals need to know how to dilute the chemical to the exact strength they need for a particular job. When artists dilute watercolors, they add more and more water to the paint. As the paint becomes more dilute, it becomes lighter and lighter in color. In this activity, you will learn to dilute paints similar to the way a chemist dilutes other chemicals. You will see that you can control how light or dark the paint gets and what colors are created when paints are mixed together!

1 Put on an old shirt or smock that's okay to get stained. Take the *red, blue*, and *yellow* watercolor bricks out of the tray. Break each one in half. Put each 1/2 brick into a separate plastic bag.

2 Ask your adult partner to use the back of a metal tablespoon to crush the paint into a powder inside the bag.

You will need

set of dry watercolors
medium watercolor brush
2 sheets of white art paper (or construction paper)
water
teaspoon
metal tablespoon
3 zip-closing plastic bags
18 small (3.5 oz) clear plastic cups
masking tape
crayon
old shirt or smock

3 Line up three plastic cups and place three tablespoons of warm water into each one. Carefully pour your crushed blue paint into the first cup and stir until all the paint is dissolved.

4 Take one teaspoon of water from the first cup and place it in the second cup and stir. Next, take one teaspoon from the second cup and place it in the third cup and stir.

You have just made a *dilution* of paint that goes from the least dilute (the darkest one) to the most dilute (the lightest one) with one medium dilution in between. Use your masking tape and crayon to put a dilution number on each cup. Label the darkest paint **1**, the middle paint **2**, and the lightest paint **3**.

* All activities in *WonderScience* have been reviewed for safety by Dr. Jack Breazeale, Francis Marion College, Florence, SC; Dr. Jay Young, Chemical Health and Safety Consultant, Silver Spring, MD; and Dr. Patricia Redden, Saint Peter's College, Jersey City, NJ.

5 Repeat steps 2, 3, and 4 using the red and yellow paint bricks. Label these cups **1**, **2**, and **3** from dark to light as you did with the blue paint.

6 Look at the two *dilution color triangles* below. In the triangle on the left, **Yellow 1** means the darkest yellow, **Red 2** is the medium red, and **Blue 3** is the lightest blue.

7 To start the first color triangle, mix 1 teaspoon of **Yellow 1** with one teaspoon of **Red 2** in a clean plastic cup. What color did you get? Write the color in the circle between the two arrows. Next, mix 1 teaspoon of **Red 2** with one teaspoon of **Blue 3**. Write in the color you got. Finish the color triangle by mixing 1 teaspoon of **Blue 3** with one teaspoon of **Yellow 1**. Did you get the color you expected? Write the color you got in the circle.

8 On a clean white sheet of paper make three of your own Dilution Color Triangles like the one below on the left. Use different dilutions of your different colored paints. Instead of writing in the color you get, use your paint brush to paint in your color-mixing results!

9 In the triangle on the right, the final colors are given. Your job is to experiment to find which paints mixed together will give you these results. Write in the color and dilution number you used in the boxes.

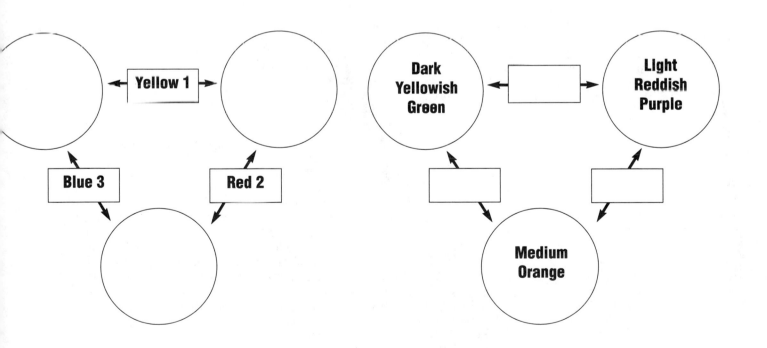

GET SMART... WITH THE CHEMISTRY OF ART!

Did you know that you are *always* using chemicals when you create any work of art? The paper you draw or paint on is made from wood which is made of chemicals. The wood is processed with other chemicals to make different types of paper that work well with different types of *paints*, *crayons*, *markers*, *pencils*, or *chalk*. These things that you put on the paper are also made of chemicals!

The main part of most *paints* is usually either water or some type of oil, which are both very useful chemicals. To give the paint color, chemicals called *pigments* are added to the paint. Pigments are very special chemicals because different pigments appear different colors when light hits them. Pigments can look black, white, or almost any color depending on which ones are used, the type of light that hits them, and how the pigments are mixed together. Many of these chemical pigments are found in vegetables, fruit, flowers, and other natural things as you will see in the activity on dyes. Many other useful pigments are made in the laboratory using other chemicals.

Crayons are made mostly of wax, which is made form the chemicals in *petroleum.* You can learn more about petroleum and wax in the activity on Mystery Art. The liquid in *markers* is often made from a type of chemical called a *solvent*. Different solvents are used with different chemical dyes or pigments that give the markers their colors. Chemicals are also important in *pencils.* The part of the pencil we call "lead" is actually made mostly of clay and a chemical called *graphite*. The more clay added to the graphite, the harder the lead in the pencil. The main chemical in *chalk* is called *calcium carbonate*. Calcium carbonate is found in nature in a mineral called *limestone,* which is made mostly from the shells of tiny organisms!

The art of *sculpture* also uses a lot of chemistry. Sculptures can be made of wood, metal, plaster, clay, marble, plastic, glass, or almost any other material! But no matter what material the artist uses, it will always act in its own certain way because of the chemicals that make up the material. When the artist tries to carve, bend, chip, smooth, or shape material to make a sculpture, the chemicals that make up the material will control how it can be shaped.

Making and dyeing thread and cloth to create works of art on fabric, also uses a lot of chemistry. In a process called *batik*, which began in Indonesia, dye and wax are used with cloth to make beautiful designs on fabric. Metal can even be used in cloth to make a work of art. Some of the threads in old *tapestries* were actually made from real gold or silver metal! Because of the way the *atoms* in gold or silver are connected together, both these metals can be made into many shapes and can be pulled into long thin threads, which can be woven into fabrics. We won't be making gold or silver threads, but you can experiment with *dyeing* different types of fabric with natural dyes in the activity on dyes. You could even take three different colored cloths from this activity and braid them into a cloth bracelet!

All artwork, including newer forms of art such a photography, color printing, and computer art, uses chemistry in many different ways. So the next time you are at a museum or art show or are just looking at a picture, remember that an artist using chemicals made it all possible!

Illustration by Lori Seskin-Newman

BECOME AN ART MASTER...
—WITH THE POWER OF PLASTER!

Chemistry is very important when making a sculpture. In this activity, you will use a substance called *plaster of paris* which is made of chemicals that harden when water is added. Artists often use plaster to make a *mold* for a statue. They use the mold to shape *solid* material on the inside or outside of the mold or to pour *liquid* material into it, which will later harden. The chemicals that make up the mold and the solid or liquid material used to make the sculpture all work together to make the sculpture that the artist is trying to create.

You will need

newspaper
2 disposable pie tins
1/2 cup dry plaster of paris
spoon
water
modeling clay
small hard plastic toy
 figure

1 Completely cover your work area with newspapers. In a pie tin, mix 1/2 cup of dry plaster of paris with 1/4 cup of water. Mix thoroughly with a spoon until smooth. Carefully mix in a little more plaster of paris to thicken the mixture.

2 After the plaster has set for a few minutes, touch it gently with your finger to test its hardness. When it feels like soft modeling clay, scrape it out of the tin and work it between your hands into a ball.

3 Put the ball of plaster back into the pan and press it down with the palm of your hand so it is like a thick pancake.

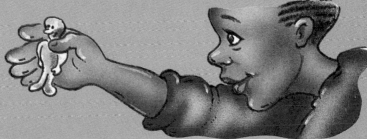

4 Take a small hard plastic toy figure like a dinosaur or other animal and press it deep down into the plaster. Leave it in for a few seconds and then carefully take it out. Your figure should have made a detailed *impression* in the plaster. That impression is now your mold.

5 After the plaster hardens, take a piece of soft modeling clay and roll it into a ball between your hands. Press the clay down firmly inside the mold. Make sure that the clay fills up every part of the impression in your mold.

6 Carefully remove the clay from the mold to see your *WonderScience* clay sculpture.

PICTURE THIS!

Photography is another area of art that uses a lot of chemistry. When you take a picture, light comes into the camera and hits the film. The film is usually made of a certain type of plastic, covered with a mixture of chemicals called the *emulsion*. Most film emulsions are made of tiny crystals of a certain type of *salt* that contains *silver*. These crystals are mixed into a special kind of gelatin which coats the plastic to make the film. When you take a picture of some object, light from the object hits the emulsion, and a *chemical reaction* happens to the crystals!

At this point, you cannot yet see an *image* of the object on your film. To make the image, even more chemistry is used in a process called *developing*. In developing, different chemicals react with the crystals on the film that you used to take your picture. The crystals that were hit with different amounts of light or different colors of light react in different ways to these chemicals. These different reactions cause the image of the object to appear on the film. But we're not done yet because this image is only the *negative*, it's still not the finished picture!

In the image on a negative, the dark parts of the object look light and the light parts of the object look dark. To straighten all this out, you have to make a *print* from the negative which uses even more chemistry! To make a print, light is sent through the negative and onto special photographic paper which contains its own chemicals. This paper is then treated with some other—you guessed it—chemicals, and your picture is finally ready!

Illustration by Lori Seskin-Newman

VEGETABLE DYES—THEY'RE HARD TO "BEET"!

Another area in the **chemistry of art** is the dyeing of fabrics. The chemicals in dyes that give them their color are called **pigments**. These chemicals and the chemicals in the fabric have to work together so that the dye **molecules** will connect to the cloth molecules, to color the cloth. If the dye and the cloth molecules work well together, the dye will not come out (run) even when the cloth is washed!

You will need

newspaper
paper towels
white unlined paper
white 100% cotton cloth
    (from an old rag)
white cotton/synthetic cloth
    (from an old rag)
raw carrot
raw beet
raw red cabbage
grater
three small plates
blunt-end scissors
3 zip-closing plastic bags
6 plastic cups
warm water
laundry detergent

1 Put on old clothes or a smock that is okay to get stained. Cover your work area with newspaper. Ask your adult partner to grate about 1/8 cup of carrot, beet, and red cabbage onto separate plates.

2 Place each of the three vegetables into its own plastic bag. Add about 1/4 cup of warm water to each bag and close tightly.

3 You and your adult partner should now press the vegetable and water inside the bag with your hand for two or three minutes, until a lot of the pigment from the vegetables has colored the water.

4 Open one corner of each bag and pour the colored water into three separate cups.

5 Use your scissors to cut the 100% cotton cloth, the paper, and the cotton/synthetic cloth into three strips each, about 3 cm wide and about 15 cm long.

6 Place one strip of each material into each vegetable dye. Let the materials stay in the dye overnight. The next day, take them all out and place them on paper towels to dry.

7 Which dye seemed to work best with which material?

8 Let's see how well the dye molecules will stay on the material when it is washed. Fill three separate cups halfway with warm water. Put the three dyed materials in each of the three cups. Ask your adult partner to help you move them up and down for one or two minutes.

9 Did any of the pigments run? Which pigment stuck best to its material? Which one got washed away the most easily? Have your adult partner put some laundry detergent in the cups. Move the materials up and down. Which dyes were able to stay on which materials when washed in soapy water?

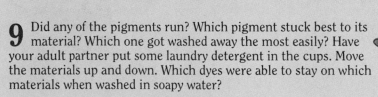

WonderScience
Mystery Art!

It may be hard to believe, but the wax in a beautiful white candle is made from *petroleum*, the thick dark oil pumped from beneath the Earth in oil wells. A process called *distillation* is used to separate the different chemicals in the oil. Some of the chemicals separated in this process are used to make candle wax. Wax is used in many different ways in art. It is used to make crayons, it can be carved and set in plaster to make a mold, or it can be used on cloth with dye in a special art form called *batik*. In the following activity, you will use wax to make your own *WonderScience* Mystery Art!

1 On a sheet of paper, use your candle to draw a picture of a tree, person, house, animal, car, or anything you want. Press down hard enough so you are sure the wax gets on the paper, but not hard enough to break the candle. It will be very difficult to see what you are drawing since you are using white wax on white paper, but do the best you can.

2 Now cover your wax drawing with watercolors. Use a dilute (watery) paint so you are sure to cover the entire area of your drawing.

3 Do the watercolors bind to the wax and the paper in the same way? Which one does the watercolor bind to the best? Do you think this has anything to do with the chemicals in the watercolors, the wax, and the paper?

4 Look at the picture below. Put a clean sheet of paper over the drawing and trace the picture as best you can using your candle. Paint over your tracing with different watercolors to see the picture you drew.

Could wax and watercolors be used to send secret messages in invisible writing? Try it and see!

PICK THE RIGHT PAINT FOR YOUR PALETTE!

Many times an artist needs to decide what type of paint is best for the material or surface he or she will be painting. Paints made with *water* work well on certain surfaces but not on others. Artists may even want to experiment with making their own paints to find the best one for the surface they are trying to paint. Try the activity below to see what we mean.

1 Break the chalk in half and put one half in a plastic bag. Close the bag and ask your adult partner to use the back of a spoon to crush the chalk into a powder inside the bag.

2 Pour the powdered chalk into one of your cups. Repeat Step 1 with the other half-piece of chalk and pour that powder into the other cup.

You will need

1 piece of colored chalk
1 zip closing plastic bag
water
mineral oil
sheet of waxed paper (about 15 cm x 15 cm)
two small clear plastic cups
two small paintbrushes
metal tablespoon

3 In one cup, add a little water and stir until most of the chalk looks like it has colored the water. In the other cup, add a little mineral oil and stir until most of the chalk has colored the oil. How does the paint in the two cups compare? Which one is darker? Which one is thicker? Are there any other differences?

4 Take a piece of waxed paper and use a paintbrush to paint your name using the water and chalk paint. Now use a different paintbrush to paint your name using the oil and chalk paint. Which one works better? How is the chemistry in this activity similar to the chemistry in the activity *Mystery Art*?

People really do need different paints for different jobs. Paints mixed in water are called *water-based* paints, and paints mixed in oil are called *oil-based* paints. Each one is good for its own job because the chemicals in oil and water can stick well to certain surfaces but not to others!

You may notice that your oil-based paint doesn't dry! That's okay, because special chemicals are added to store-bought oil-based paints to make them dry!

This unit introduces students to thinking about the way ordinary objects, such as toys, would behave in orbit in what scientists call "microgravity." Students make toys, see how they work, predict how they would behave in microgravity, and then compare their answers to the way some toys actually did act in orbit. The space shuttle Endeavor's flight in early 1993 included a cargo of 30 different toys for the astronauts to play with and study. Each toy relied in some way on gravity to make it work on Earth. The toys should behave very differently in orbit.

Space Hoppers

In *Space Hoppers*, students make paper "grasshoppers" of different sizes. When students tap the nose of a grasshopper down onto the table, it flips into the air. Gravity causes the grasshopper to come back down again. If used in orbit, these grasshoppers would not come back down.

Cosmic Catch!

In *Cosmic Catch!* students construct a ball-and-cup toy. On Earth, gravity is used to get the ball to drop back into the cup. Aboard the shuttle, the astronauts would have to find some other way to get the ball to go into the cup!

Out-of-This-World Boomerang!

In *Out-of-This-World Boomerang!* students make a miniature boomerang that should work pretty well on Earth. Be sure to use cardstock, which has about the same weight and texture as a manila file folder. The flight of the spinning boomerang is affected not only by gravity, but also by air resistance. On the shuttle, the boomerang might go in a circle but it wouldn't fall to the shuttle floor.

Space Waves?

In *Space Waves?* students make and observe a popular ocean-in-a-bottle toy. On Earth, gravity causes the water and oil in the bottle to separate into two distinct layers because the water is more dense than the oil. The question is whether the weightless environment of the shuttle would result in the same effect. On the shuttle, the oil and water still would not mix but one would not necessarily be layered above or below the other.

Information and resources related to a previous (1985) "Toys in Space" shuttle program, including a videotape of the astronauts actually using the toys on the shuttle, is available from your Local NASA Regional Service Center. Ask about the 1993 "Toys in Space" launch also.

RELEVANT NATIONAL SCIENCE EDUCATION STANDARDS

The activities in this unit can be used to support the teaching of the following standards:

✔ Science as Inquiry
   Abilities necessary to do scientific inquiry

✔ Physical Science
   Motions and forces

✔ Earth and Space Science
   Earth in the solar system

SPACE

Astronauts on an upcoming space shuttle mission will be testing toy grasshoppers like these to find out how they flip while in orbit. Make some grasshoppers yourself and see how well they flip on Earth. Then imagine trying to make them flip in space!

1 Cut out three paper squares. Use the bottom corner of this page as a pattern for your squares. One should have sides 10 centimeters long. The others should have sides of 7.5 cm and 5 cm.

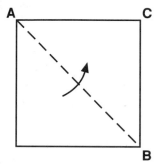

2 Make the largest grasshopper first. Take the square with 10 cm sides and fold it diagonally to make a triangle as shown.

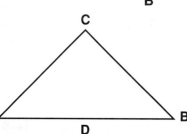

3 Fold up the corners labeled A and B until they touch C. The shape is now a diamond or square.

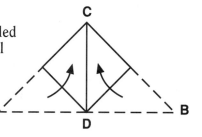

4 Fold inward along the center crease of the diamond from step 3. The shape is now a triangle again.

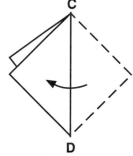

5 Fold up the two tips at the angle shown in the diagram to give the grasshopper its legs. Corner C is the grasshopper's nose. Be sure to make the creases very sharp.

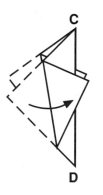

6 Place your grasshopper on a flat table. Make sure its nose is higher than its tail as shown. Using your index finger, strike downward on its nose to make it flip. Strike the very tip of its nose to get the best flip.

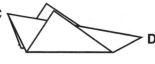

10 cm

7.5 cm

5 cm

HOPPERS

7 Do you think that smaller grasshoppers will hop farther than your big grasshopper? Make your prediction. Then make smaller grasshoppers from the squares that are 7.5 and 5 cm on a side.

Be sure that all three grasshoppers are made from the same kind of paper.

8 Make a chart like the one below. Flip each grasshopper three times. Measure and record in centimeters how far each hops and estimate how high each jumps. Decide which grasshopper is the best flipper.

		Big Hopper	Middle Hopper	Small Hopper
First jump	Length			
	Height			
Second jump	Length			
	Height			
Third jump	Length			
	Height			

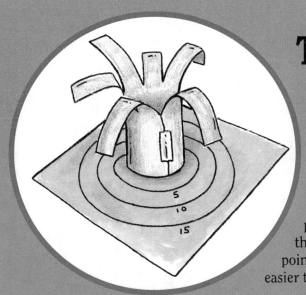

The Grasshopper Game

With green construction paper, make a plant with long leaves for your grasshopper to land in. See how far you can move away from your plant and still land your grasshopper in it. You can make lots of grasshoppers of different sizes and colors. Each player gets points for every grasshopper that flips into the plant. The farther away the grasshopper is, the more points scored. Draw circles around the plant to make it easier to measure the distances.

The Astronaut Challenge:

Will the astronauts be as successful with the grasshoppers as you are? What problems will they have in making the grasshoppers flip? Where should they place the plant target?

★ All activities in *WonderScience* have been reviewed for safety by Dr. Jack Breazeale, Francis Marion University, Florence, SC; Dr. Jay Young, Chemical Health and Safety Consultant, Silver Spring, MD; and Dr. Patricia Redden, Saint Peter's College, Jersey City, NJ.

That Freefall Feeling

On television, we see astronauts and other objects floating about inside the Space Shuttle. Things float around so freely that the astronauts have to strap themselves in place and use Velcro to attach their equipment to walls. As you can imagine, they have to be really careful when they eat to keep their food under control.

Why do things float around inside the shuttle while it is orbiting the Earth? Many people think it is because the shuttle is so far from the pull of Earth's gravity, but this is *not* the reason. The same gravity force that keeps you in your chair here on the Earth's surface also keeps the shuttle in orbit. Without Earth's gravity, the orbiting shuttle would fly off into interplanetary space!

So if Earth's gravity is pulling down on the shuttle, just as it is pulling down on you, how does the shuttle stay in orbit? Compare the shuttle to a fast-pitched baseball. When you throw a baseball horizontally, it drops lower and lower and finally hits the ground. The faster you throw the ball, the farther it goes before it hits the ground. What do you think would happen if you could throw the baseball hard enough for it to travel at the same speed as the Space Shuttle? The shuttle travels at the incredible speed of about 18,000 miles per hour (29,000 kilometers per hour). It travels so fast and far that the Earth curves away from it as it falls. So the shuttle just falls around and around the Earth without ever reaching the ground, until it slows down to come in for a landing.

How do the astronauts feel as they fall around the Earth? Imagine jumping off a high diving board. If you sat on a bathroom scale as you fell toward the water, what would the scale read? "Zero," of course. Since you and the scale are falling at the same rate, you do not push down on the scale and it reads "zero." You are *weightless*! Sky divers and riders falling down high roller coaster hills have this same weightless feeling.

The same thing happens to the shuttle astronauts when they are in orbit. The shuttle, the astronauts, and all of their equipment are falling at the same rate around the Earth. So the astronauts and their food, tools and toys all seem to float in the cabin. If an astronaut were to sit on a bathroom scale while in orbit, it would read "zero" just as it did for you jumping off the diving board.

The word physicists use to describe the astronauts' condition is freefall because that is exactly what the astronauts are doing. *Microgravity* is also used since it is the official NASA term for this *freefall* experience.

Play with each toy in this *WonderScience* issue. Think about how you would use the toy if it floated around you and never fell toward your feet. Is it a better toy for Earth or space?

Special thanks to Dr. Carolyn Sumners, Project Director, "Toys in Space," Houston Museum of Natural Sciences.

The Astronauts' Toy Box

I n one of the earlier shuttle missions, astronauts carried certain toys into space to find out how they would work in microgravity. The toys included a wind-up car, a Slinky, a spinning top, a back-flipping mouse, paper airplanes, and the toys described below. Read about these three toys, then decide how you think each performed aboard the shuttle. After you make your predictions, turn the page upside down to find out what really happened!

Magnetic Marbles

Magnetic marbles are small hollow plastic balls. Each has a little bar magnet inside. On Earth, they can join together to make chains or circles. Do you think they will attach to each other in space the way they did on Earth?

Aboard the Space Shuttle, two magnetic marbles not only will attract each other, but will rotate around the point where they attach! When Astronaut Jeffrey Hoffman joined some marbles into a chain, and then added a new marble, the whole chain wriggled back and forth! When he added enough marbles to the chain, the two ends floated close enough together that their magnetic attraction closed the chain into a circle!

Ball and Jacks

When you play jacks, you must bounce the ball, pick up some jacks, and catch the ball. Does the ball bounce differently in space? How will the jacks behave?

Playing jacks in space is a very different game! First of all, a dropped ball doesn't fall! Astronaut Rhea Seddon found that instead she had to throw the ball toward a wall and wait for it to bounce off and return to her. She also found that when she opened her hand to release the jacks, just the tiny force from opening her fingers caused the jacks to start drifting apart. She learned to be very careful releasing the jacks so they wouldn't float out of reach!

Yo-Yo

Usually a yo-yo moves down its string, and a jerk from your hand brings it back up again. Do you think a yo-yo will work in space? Why or why not?

Believe it or not, a yo-yo works beautifully in space! It moves easily down the string, and when it reaches the end bounces backward along the string. Astronaut Dave Griggs found that difficult tricks like "Shooting the Moon" are easier to perform in space. But tricks like "Walking the Dog" where the yo-yo has to "sleep" at the bottom of the string don't work. This is because in microgravity, there is nothing to keep the yo-yo down, so it rebounds right back up the string!

69

COSMIC CATCH!

The Ball & Cup is a traditional toy found in many cultures around the world. Soon it will be found in space! Astronauts aboard the shuttle are going to try to use the ball and cup in orbit. Make your own ball and cup for use on Earth, and then predict what the astronauts will have to do in space to get the ball to land in the cup!

You will need

blunt-tip scissors
masking tape
ruler
Ping-Pong ball

plastic tablespoon
small paper cup
piece of string (about 60 cm long)

1 Place the Ping-Pong ball inside the cup. The cup should be just slightly larger than the Ping-Pong ball. If the cup is taller than the ball, trim it down until the ball just fits in the cup. The smaller the cup, the more challenging your toy will be.

2 Tape the bottom of the cup to the bowl of the spoon as shown. Tape one end of the string to the Ping-Pong ball and tie the other to the handle of the spoon at a point near the cup. Wrap the string around the spoon handle until the ball and cup are about 30 centimeters apart.

3 Hold the handle with one hand and let the ball hang down. With a swinging motion, make the ball swing up and into the cup. It must stay in the cup and not bounce out.

4 If you can't get the ball into the cup, make the string shorter by wrapping more of it around the handle. If it gets too easy, make the string longer.

The Astronaut Challenge:

Once you can catch the ball, think about how you are using the toy. Can the astronauts use it the same way in space? What would happen if they did? How should they get the ball into the cup? Is this toy easier or harder to use in space? Hint: Think about how the toys worked in space.

Out-of-This-World Boomerang!

When you send a boomerang spinning through the air, it is supposed to come back to you. Most boomerangs need a space about as big as a football field to turn around. The astronauts have only the shuttle's middeck which is about 4 meters wide. For the astronauts, a special small 4-blade boomerang has been designed. Follow these instructions to make a boomerang like the one the astronauts use.

You will need

card stock (from a manila file folder)
blunt-tip scissors
pencil

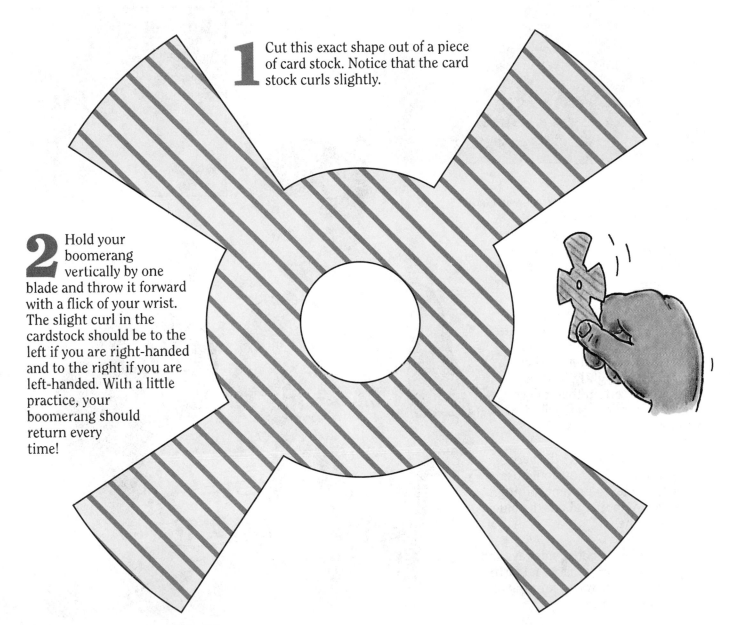

1 Cut this exact shape out of a piece of card stock. Notice that the card stock curls slightly.

2 Hold your boomerang vertically by one blade and throw it forward with a flick of your wrist. The slight curl in the cardstock should be to the left if you are right-handed and to the right if you are left-handed. With a little practice, your boomerang should return every time!

The Astronaut Challenge:

Does gravity make this boomerang turn around? Is the boomerang falling as it returns? Watch to see how the boomerang's spin changes during flight. Is this a change in direction, angle, or rate of spin? Is this change caused by the air or by gravity? Do you think that the astronauts will be successful in throwing this boomerang?

SPACE WAVES?

Have you ever seen an "Ocean-in-a-Bottle" that you can buy at a toy or novelty store? In this activity, you can make your own "Ocean-in-a-Bottle." Discover how this toy works, and then imagine what might happen if you could take it into orbit!

You will need

newspaper

clear plastic 1 liter soda bottle

clear mineral oil or light-colored vegetable oil

water

blue food coloring

funnel (optional)

1 Cover your work surface with a double layer of newspaper. Rinse out the bottle and take off any labels. Be certain to rinse away any soap you might have used in soaking and cleaning the bottle.

2 Fill the bottle half-full with water. Add blue food coloring drop by drop until your ocean is a color you like. Then put the lid on tightly. Tilt the bottle to be certain that it does not leak. If it does, you will need another bottle.

3 Fill the bottle to the very top with oil. You could use a funnel to prevent spilling. What do you notice about the blue water and the oil?

4 Hold your bottle sideways and slowly rock it back and forth. Notice the waves forming on your miniature ocean.

The Astronaut Challenge:

How do you think this toy would work in orbit? Would the liquids separate at all? Think about what causes them to make two layers in the bottle. Tilt your bottle and think about the effect gravity has on the two different liquids in the bottle.

WONDER SCIENCE

This unit introduces students to some of the science behind soaps and detergents. The emphasis in this unit is for students to recognize variables in an experiment and to understand why they need to be controlled.

If Cleaning is Urgent Use Soap or Detergent

In *If Cleaning is Urgent Use Soap or Detergent*, soap and detergent are compared for cleaning ability. Every attempt is made at controlling variables in this activity, and you may want to explore the concept of controlling variables with your students. There are several questions you could ask, such as why it is important to mix the same amount of each soap or detergent in the same amount of water? Why is the same amount of each mixture used on the lipstick? Why is the cotton swab not used to rub the lipstick? Why is the lipstick smoothed before testing it with the mixtures? Challenge students to think of other cleaning tests for soap and detergent while focusing on the importance of controlling variables.

Which Mixture is the Best Mixer?

Which Mixture is the Best Mixer? demonstrates the ability of soap and detergent to make oil and water mix. Under the conditions in this activity, the oil and water separate again after two or three minutes but they do mix much better with the soap or detergent than without it.

Totally Sudsational...Dude!

In *Totally Sudsational...Dude!*, students can have fun testing soap and detergent for suds-making ability. The activity also provides an opportunity for developing the math skills of measurement, calculating volume, and data recording.

To Bubble or Not to Bubble, That is the Question

To Bubble or Not to Bubble, That is the Question introduces the concept that dissolving certain substances in water can affect the way water behaves with soap and detergent. Water containing dissolved calcium or magnesium salts is often called "hard" water. Table salt is used as the dissolved substance because it is safe, readily available, and has a similar effect on soap's sudsing ability.

A Total Washout?

A Total Washout? offers students a chance to do some indirect reasoning to draw conclusions from their observations. Students determine how effective fresh water and salt water are at rinsing out shampoo from a cotton ball. One way to figure this out is to see how much shampoo is left in the cotton ball after rinsing. Students should discover that the salt water left more shampoo in the cotton ball and was therefore the less effective rinser.

RELEVANT NATIONAL SCIENCE EDUCATION STANDARDS

The activities in this unit can be used to support the teaching of the following standards:

✔ **Science as Inquiry**
   Abilities necessary to do scientific inquiry

✔ **Physical Science:**
   Properties and changes of properties in matter

✔ **Earth and Space Science**
   Structure of the earth system

✔ **Science and Technology**
   Understandings about science and technology

✔ **Science in Personal and Social Perspectives**
   Science and technology in society

✔ **History and Nature of Science**
   History of science

If cleaning is urgent

What do soap, dish detergent, shampoo, and laundry detergent, all have in common? Everyone knows they are all used for cleaning! In the following activity, you can test these grime busters on different surfaces to see which ones clean best!

Soap and detergent can sting your eyes. Be careful doing these experiments.

You will need

sheet of white unlined paper	food grater	measuring spoons
lipstick	cotton swabs	water
pencil	soap	plastic or paper cups
masking tape	dish detergent	white cloth rag
blunt-end scissors	laundry detergent	wax paper
ruler	shampoo	
	measuring cups	

1 Cut your piece of paper in half lengthwise and use your ruler to divide it into 5 spaces as shown. Label the spaces "water," " soap," "dish detergent," shampoo," and "laundry detergent." Lay a piece of wax paper over the chart and fold the wax paper around the chart and tape it on the back.

2 Use your masking tape and pencil to label your cups "water," "soap," "dish detergent," "shampoo," and "laundry detergent." Place ½ cup of water into each cup. Ask your adult partner to help you use a grater to grate two tablespoons of soap onto a dish. Place all of your grated soap into the "soap" cup and stir with a cotton swab until the soap flakes dissolve.

3 Add 2 tablespoons each of dish detergent, shampoo, and laundry detergent to their labeled cups and stir with separate cotton swabs until they are well mixed. Place each cup in front of its space on the chart.

4 Use a lipstick to make a streak on the wax paper across your chart. Use your finger to smooth out the lipstick so that it looks like the same thickness across all 5 spaces.

Caution: Graters have sharp edges. Be careful.

use Soap or Detergent

5 Use a separate cotton swab to put one drop of each liquid on the lipstick in each space. Do not touch the lipstick with your swab. Wait 3–5 minutes and rinse off the drops in a thin stream of water from the faucet. Which liquid cleaned the lipstick the best? Which cleaned it the worst?

6 On your other half piece of paper, make the same chart you made before, but this time, don't cover it with wax paper. Make another streak of lipstick and smooth it out. Does the lipstick go on differently than before?

7 Add one drop of each liquid to the lipstick, wait 3–5 minutes, and rinse. Did the liquids clean the paper differently than the wax paper? Hold your chart up to the light to see your results better.

8 Put a streak of lipstick on a piece of white rag. Smooth it out, add the drops of liquid, wait, and rinse. Did the liquids clean the lipstick from the cloth as well as from the paper or wax paper?

9 Put a little lipstick on each of the five fingertips of one hand. Rub your thumb and fingertips together to even out the lipstick. Dip one finger at a time into each liquid.

> **You can conserve and recycle by saving your cups of soap and detergent for the activities.**

10 Ask your adult partner to rub each of your fingertips with a separate cotton swab for 3 seconds and rinse. Which liquid cleaned the lipstick off your finger the best? Was this the same as for the cloth, paper, and wax paper?

---

* All activities in *WonderScience* have been reviewed for safety by Dr. Jack Breazeale, Francis Marion University, Florence, SC; Dr. Jay Young, Chemical Health and Safety Consultant, Silver Spring, MD; and Dr. Patricia Redden, Saint Peter's College, Jersey City, NJ.

Get the Real Dirt on Soap and Detergent

Every time you wash your clothes, wash the dishes, wash your hands, or take a shower or bath, you are using chemicals to help you clean. The chemicals you are using are the ones in soaps and detergents!

People have been making soap for about 2,000 years! The old way of making soap was to first put ashes from burnt wood into a big barrel with a small hole at the bottom. Water was then poured into the barrel and allowed to drip slowly through the ashes and out the bottom into a container. Next, animal fat was melted in a big kettle over a fire and the liquid from the wood ashes was stirred in. A *chemical reaction* soon took place between the liquid and the fat. This caused a layer of white soap to form at the top of the mixture. Today, soap is usually made with plant oils instead of animal fat and often contains perfumes, coloring, moisturizers, and certain other chemicals.

Detergent is not nearly as old as soap. It has been made in factories for only about 70 years. Detergent is made from the chemicals in *petroleum* instead of the ones in animal fat that were in the first soap. Detergent and soap work in a similar way to help people clean.

But before soap and detergent can help you clean, you need to get dirty the right way! If dirt or dust simply gets on a surface, it can usually be cleaned off with a dry cloth or water alone. But if oil or grease gets mixed in with the dirt, then you need soap or detergent to help clean it away. This is because water cannot hook on to oil or grease. Water just slides along the oil or grease but can't "grab" on to it to wash it away. This is why people say "oil and water don't mix." Water molecules and oil molecules need something to help them attach to each other. That's the job of soap and detergent! The soap and detergent molecules are special because they have one end that attaches well to water and another end that attaches well to oil. The soap or detergent molecule "hooks" the dirty oil and water together. Then extra water washes the "hooked" water and dirty oil away.

But where does all this oil come from? Your skin gives off oil all the time! When dirt mixes with this oil, water alone won't work to wash it away. You need to use some kind of soap or detergent. When oil from your scalp mixes with dirt on your hair, you use shampoo to get the job done. Dirt also gets on your clothes and mixes with oil from your skin. We use laundry detergent to wash this oily dirt away. Oil and grease from food make it very difficult to clean dishes with just water. That's why dish detergent is used to help wash dishes clean.

Have fun doing the activities in this month's *WonderScience* while learning about the amazing qualities of soap and detergent!

Which MIXTURE is the best MIXER?

You learned that soap and detergent work by helping water and oil to mix. You can try the following activity to see which soap or detergent makes oil and water mix the best!

You will need

5 zip-closing plastic bags	soap
vegetable oil	dish detergent
measuring cups	laundry detergent
measuring spoons	shampoo
water	grater
newspapers	

1 Cover your work surface with a double layer of newspaper. You can use your soap and detergent mixtures from the first activity or make new mixtures using the instructions in the first activity.

2 Use your masking tape and pencil to label 5 plastic bags "water," "soap," "dish detergent," "shampoo," and "laundry detergent." Ask your adult partner to help you pour ½ cup of water into each bag. Now add 3 tablespoons of oil to each bag. Close the bags and make sure they are sealed tightly.

3 Look at your bag marked "water." Do the oil and water mix? Shake the bag hard up and down three or four times. Hold the bag still. Do the oil and water stay mixed or do they separate again?

4 Now add 2 tablespoons of each soap or detergent mixture to each of the four labeled bags. You and your adult partner should hold one bag in each hand and shake them hard 3 or 4 times.

5 Which soap or detergent seemed to make the oil and water mix the best? How did the other ones work? Which soap or detergent would you use to clean an oily mess? Why?

77

Totally
Sudsational...Dude!

An important quality of soaps and detergents is how much suds they make and how long the suds last. Suds help spread out the soap and detergent molecules so more of them can work on the greasy dirt. Let's see which of your solutions is the sudsiest!

You will need

5 small cups	5 straws
bar soap	measuring spoons
dish detergent	water
laundry detergent	metric ruler
shampoo	newspapers

1 Cover your work surface with a double layer of newspaper. Use your soap and detergent mixtures from the first activity or make new mixtures by following the instructions in the first activity.

2 Place 2 tablespoons of each mixture into its own labeled cup. Tilt the cup away from you and use a straw to blow gently into the liquid to produce bubbles. **Be sure to blow into the liquid—Do not suck the liquid in.** Let the bubbles pour out of the cup and pile up on the newspaper. Keep blowing until all the liquid in the cup is used up.

3 Use a ruler to measure the length of the pile. Also measure how wide and high the pile of bubbles is. Multiply the length by the width by the height to find the *volume* of your pile.

4 Use separate straws to blow bubbles from the rest of your cups and record your results. Which mixture makes the biggest volume of bubbles?

Mixture	Length of pile	Width of pile	Height of pile	Volume of pile L × W × H
Soap				
Dish detergent				
Shampoo				
Laundry detergent				

See if you can tell the difference between your cleaning solutions by blowing one bubble of each.

1 Put a teaspoon of each soap or detergent mixture into its labeled cup. Dip one end of a straw into one of your liquids. Take the straw out and gently blow into the other end to make a bubble. Look at the size of the bubble. What else do you notice about it?

2 Make a bubble from each of your liquids using a separate straw. Observe each bubble very closely. Do the bubbles from each liquid look the same? In what ways are they different? Can you tell which liquid was used to make a bubble just by looking at the bubble? Ask your adult partner to help you try it!

"To bubble or not to bubble, that is the question"

Sometimes, certain chemicals can get dissolved in water that can change the way water and soap or detergent work together. Let's see if dissolving table salt in water changes the amount of suds your soap can make!

1 Hold a bar of soap in your hands. Ask your adult partner to slowly pour a cup of warm water over the soap as you move the soap in your hands to make suds.

2 Look at the amount of suds you made and then rinse off your hands. Add two tablespoons of salt to a cup of warm water and stir until most or all of the salt dissolves.

3 Hold the soap again as you did before. Ask your adult partner to slowly pour the salt water over the soap as you move your hands to make suds. What did you notice?

Try blowing a bubble like you did on the bottom of page 6, but this time, add ½ teaspoon of salt to your soap or detergent mixture. Good Luck!

THE FATE OF PHOSPHATE

For a long time, most laundry detergents had chemicals in them called phosphates. Phosphates were used in detergent to help clean clothes but they are also a very good fertilizer for plants! When people washed clothes, the phosphates would go down the drain with the water, and some of them ended up in lakes. The phosphates made small green plants called *algae* grow much faster than normal. The algae began using up so much oxygen in the water that the fish began to die. Bacteria on the dead fish used up even more oxygen. Pretty soon, there was not enough oxygen for the algae and it died too. Scientists traced the problem to the phosphates in the detergent. They started experimenting with chemicals that worked as well as phosphates for cleaning but did not cause algae to grow. They soon found different chemicals to replace the phosphates, and today most laundry detergents have no harmful phosphates.

A TOTAL WASHOUT?

You saw that soap makes better suds in fresh water than in salt water. Now let's see if fresh water or salt water is better for rinsing suds away!

You will need

shampoo
water
5 plastic or paper cups (8 oz)
2 cotton balls

measuring spoons
salt
2 straws
masking tape
pencil

1 Label one cup "shampoo," another cup "salt water," and your other three cups, "fresh water." Fill all of your cups about half-full of water. To the "shampoo" cup, add 3 tablespoons of shampoo and stir. To the "salt" cup, add 3 tablespoons of salt and stir. Add nothing to the three "fresh water" cups.

2 Set your five cups up as shown. Dunk both cotton balls at the same time all the way into the shampoo cup until they are both completely soaked. Squeeze them out over the cup until almost no more liquid will come out of them.

3 Dunk one cotton ball into fresh water and one into salt water to try to rinse out the shampoo. Move the cotton balls up and down and continue to move and squeeze them under water to try to get the shampoo out.

4 Squeeze out the cotton balls over their cups until no more water will come out. Which cotton ball do you think has the most shampoo left in it? Can you tell by feeling the cotton balls? How about by smelling them? Put the cotton balls down and rinse off and dry your hands. Make sure you know which cotton ball was in salt water and which was in fresh water.

5 Dunk each cotton ball into a separate cup of fresh water. Move and squeeze them under water to get any shampoo out that is still there. Take both cotton balls out of the water and squeeze them over their cups.

6 Which cotton ball seems to have put more shampoo into the water? To make sure, use a separate straw to blow air into each cup to see which one makes the most bubbles. By looking at the amount of bubbles now, can you tell whether rinsing the cotton ball in salt water or fresh water in step 3 got out more of the shampoo?

WONDER SCIENCE

This unit introduces students to some of the scientific properties of soap bubbles. The key to the success of many of the activities is the quality of the bubble solution. Below are some tips for making and working with a bubble solution.

Bubble solution works best if it is made a couple of days ahead of time. After making the solution, be sure to test it before students try it. You should be able to blow a bubble at least 10 cm (about 4 inches) in diameter. Dip a finger in the bubble solution and poke the bubble you have just blown. If it doesn't burst, your bubble solution is good. If it bursts, you might want to add a little more detergent. Always store the bubble solution in a closed container to keep it from drying out.

One thing that causes a soap bubble to burst is the *evaporation* of water from the bubble. Sugar and some other substances can help prevent the water from evaporating. As an extension, have students test to find out how much added sugar makes the best bubble solution. Students can compare either the size or the duration of the bubbles produced from different bubble solution recipes.

Bubble Blowers

Bubble Blowers suggests several common household items that can be used to produce free floating bubbles. Students should examine how the size and shape of a bubble compares to the size and shape of the opening through which it was blown. Many young people expect that a larger opening will produce a larger bubble. They are also likely to predict that a square opening will produce a square or rectangular bubble.

It's a Frame-Up!

It's a Frame-Up! enables students to examine how soap films form on toothpick frames of regular geometric shapes. You might want to extend this activity by making frames of other shapes.

Don't Burst My Bubble!

In *Don't Burst My Bubble!* students explore how long soap bubbles of different sizes last. Larger bubbles should burst sooner due to more rapid evaporation.

A Bagful of Bubbles! and Hoop it Up!

A Bagful of Bubbles! and *Hoop it Up!* explore several interesting characteristics of soap bubbles and films which are interesting to observe.

Bubbles Aloft!

Bubbles Aloft! challenges students to see who can keep a bubble in the air the longest without touching it. One way is to blow the bubble over a layer of denser gas on which the bubble will float rather than sink. This is why a bubble should stay aloft inside the aquarium with baking soda and vinegar. The baking soda and vinegar chemically react to produce carbon dioxide. Because a soap bubble is lighter than carbon dioxide, it will float on the layer of carbon dioxide in the aquarium.

RELEVANT NATIONAL SCIENCE EDUCATION STANDARDS

The activities in this unit can be used to support the teaching of the following standards:

✔ Science as Inquiry
   Abilities necessary to do scientific inquiry

✔ Physical Science
   Properties and changes of properties in matter

BUBBLE BLOWERS

Soap bubbles are really fun, especially when you use unusual objects as bubble blowers. In the activity below, you can use objects of different shapes and sizes to make bubbles from a special bubble solution!

Bubble Solution Recipe

First, you need to make up some bubble solution. Mix 4 parts of water to 1 part of liquid detergent. For example, measure out 2 cups of water and add 1/2 cup of detergent. Add the detergent to the water, and stir gently. Add about 1 teaspoon of sugar to the solution to make longer lasting bubbles. Put your bubble solution in a shallow baking pan or tray.

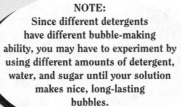

NOTE:
Since different detergents have different bubble-making ability, you may have to experiment by using different amounts of detergent, water, and sugar until your solution makes nice, long-lasting bubbles.

STRAWS—
Dip one end of the straw into the bubble solution. Remove the straw and slowly blow into the other end to make a bubble. How big a bubble can you blow? Try using fat and skinny straws, and straws of different lengths. What kind of straw makes the best bubble blower?

PIPE CLEANERS—
You can use pipe cleaners to make bubble blowers in different shapes. Bend pipe cleaners into circles, triangles, or squares, making sure to leave the end of the pipe cleaner to use as a handle. Does changing the shape of the pipe cleaner change the shape of the bubble?

Do not suck soap solution up through the straw.

STRAWBERRY BASKETS—

Dip a strawberry basket into the bubble solution, and then whirl it through the air. How many bubbles does it make? What shape and size are the bubbles?

STRAWS AND STRING—

One way to make a giant bubble is to run a piece of heavy string through two straws and tie it into a loop. The string should be about 6 times the length of one of the straws. Dip the loop into a large pan of bubble solution to cover it with soap film. Holding a straw in each hand, run with it through the air, twisting the straws in opposite directions to release the bubble. This takes practice! Once you get good at it, you can try using a longer string to make even bigger bubbles.

COAT HANGER—

If you have a large enough pan of bubble solution, you can use a coat hanger to make a really big bubble. Use the hook of the hanger as a handle, and dip the frame of the hanger into the bubble solution to cover it with soap film. Hold the hanger away from your body, and move it slowly through the air. As you finish moving the hanger through the air, twist it a little bit to release the soap bubble. What is the biggest soap bubble you can make? How does the size of the soap bubble change if you move the hanger faster through the air? What happens if you move the hanger farther before releasing the bubble?

The end of the coat hanger could be sharp— be careful.

---

* All activities in *WonderScience* have been reviewed for safety by Dr. Jack Breazeale, Francis Marion University, Florence, SC and Dr. Jay Young, Chemical Health and Safety Consultant, Silver Spring, MD.

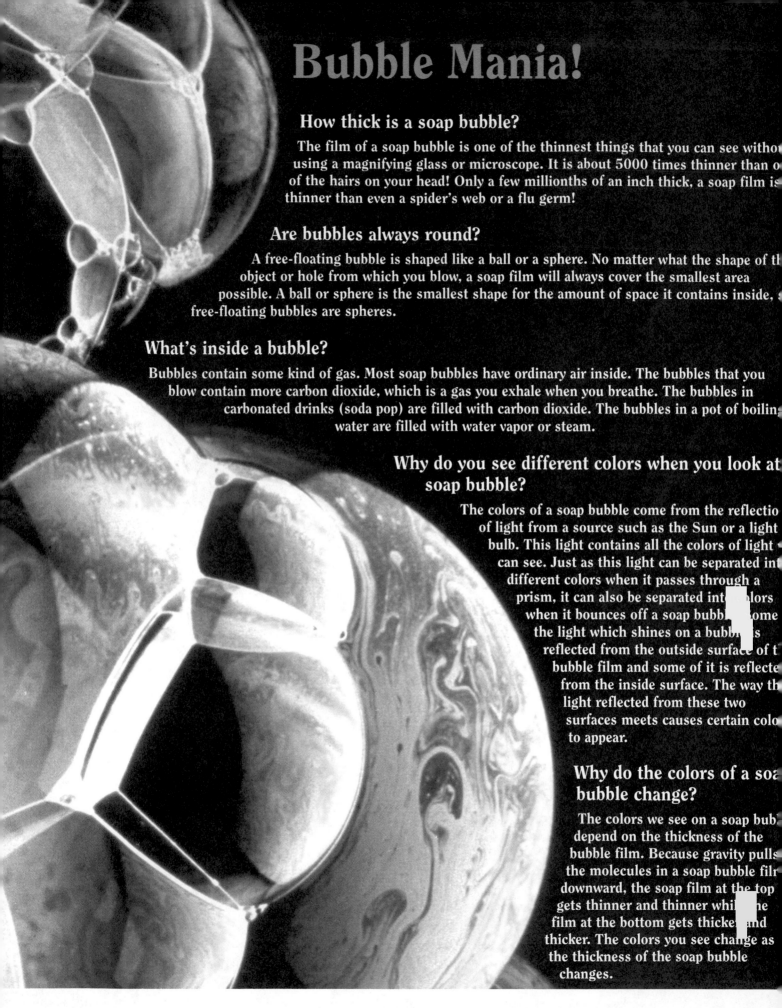

Bubble Mania!

How thick is a soap bubble?

The film of a soap bubble is one of the thinnest things that you can see witho[ut] using a magnifying glass or microscope. It is about 5000 times thinner than o[ne] of the hairs on your head! Only a few millionths of an inch thick, a soap film is thinner than even a spider's web or a flu germ!

Are bubbles always round?

A free-floating bubble is shaped like a ball or a sphere. No matter what the shape of th[e] object or hole from which you blow, a soap film will always cover the smallest area possible. A ball or sphere is the smallest shape for the amount of space it contains inside, [so] free-floating bubbles are spheres.

What's inside a bubble?

Bubbles contain some kind of gas. Most soap bubbles have ordinary air inside. The bubbles that you blow contain more carbon dioxide, which is a gas you exhale when you breathe. The bubbles in carbonated drinks (soda pop) are filled with carbon dioxide. The bubbles in a pot of boilin[g] water are filled with water vapor or steam.

Why do you see different colors when you look at [a] soap bubble?

The colors of a soap bubble come from the reflectio[n] of light from a source such as the Sun or a light bulb. This light contains all the colors of light [we] can see. Just as this light can be separated int[o] different colors when it passes through a prism, it can also be separated int[o c]olors when it bounces off a soap bubbl[e. S]ome [of] the light which shines on a bubb[le i]s reflected from the outside surfa[ce of t]he bubble film and some of it is reflecte[d] from the inside surface. The way th[e] light reflected from these two surfaces meets causes certain colo[rs] to appear.

Why do the colors of a soa[p] bubble change?

The colors we see on a soap bub[ble] depend on the thickness of the bubble film. Because gravity pulls the molecules in a soap bubble fil[m] downward, the soap film at the top gets thinner and thinner whil[e t]he film at the bottom gets thicke[r a]nd thicker. The colors you see change as the thickness of the soap bubble changes.

IT'S A FRAME-UP!

You will need

toothpicks
modeling clay or plasticine
deep bowl, at least 10 cm tall
 and 20 cm across
bubble solution (see *Bubble
 Blowers* activity for recipe)
straw

You should have noticed that the soap bubbles you blow are round, or ***spherical***. You can use frames to make soap films form different shapes and patterns. In the activity below, you will make frames that are shaped like a ***triangular prism*** and a ***cube***. Beware! The patterns of the soap films on these frames might be different from what you expect!

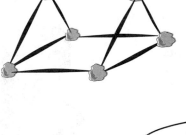

1 Mold the modeling clay into 14 small balls (each about 1 cm in diameter).

2 Use toothpicks and clay balls to make a frame like the one shown here. This shape has three sides and is called a triangular prism. Completely submerge the frame in the soap solution. Carefully remove it, touching only the clay balls.

3 Look at the soap film on the prism frame. You should see three flat soap films meeting each other at equal angles down the center of the frame.

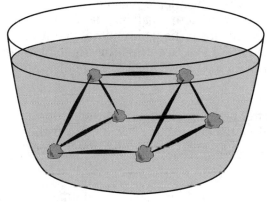

4 Now make a frame in the shape of a cube like the one shown here. A cube has four sides. How do you think the soap film will form on this frame?

5 Dip the cube frame in the solution and carefully remove it. Study the soap film on the frame. Are you surprised at the pattern of the soap film? If you study the pattern, you should see that there are never more than three soap films meeting along an edge or four edges meeting at a point!

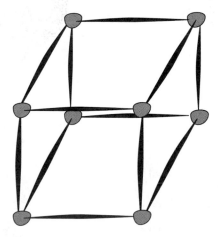

6 Dip the end of the straw into the bubble solution to wet it. **Very carefully**, touch the wet straw where the soap films meet in the center of the cube frame.
Gently blow, and you should see the soap film form a tiny cube in the center of the frame. If you continue to blow gently, this cube will grow larger. Study this new pattern. Are there still three films meeting at an edge?

Don't Burst My Bubble!

What kinds of bubbles last the longest? Try to find out in the activity below!

1 Ask your adult partner to use the sharpened pencil to poke a small hole in the center of the bottom of one of the small paper cups. You will use this cup as the bubble blower in the rest of this activity.

2 Place some bubble solution in a shallow pan or bowl. Dip the mouth of your bubble blower cup into the solution. When you lift it out, you should see a soap film across the mouth of the cup.

3 Gently blow through the hole in the bottom of the cup. The film should begin to form a bubble. When the bubble is about 3 cm tall, stop blowing. This is your small bubble. Place the cup with its bubble on the table and watch until the bubble bursts. Practice using the cup to blow small, medium (about 5 cm), and large (about 7 cm) bubbles.

4 After blowing a bubble with your cup, carefully place the cup inside a box to protect the bubble from air drafts. This should help the bubble last longer.

5 Use the cup to blow small, medium, and large bubbles, timing how long each lasts. Start timing when you place the cup and bubble on the table inside the box. Stop timing when the bubble bursts. Record your times on a chart like the one below. Repeat three times for bubbles of each size.

6 Add the three times you have recorded under **Small bubbles** together and record. Divide this number by three to find the *average* time that a small bubble lasts. Write your answer down. Fill in the chart the same way under **Medium bubbles** and **Large bubbles**.

7 What did you find out in your experiment? Is there any difference in how long small, medium, and large bubbles last?

	Small bubbles	Medium bubbles	Large bubbles
Trial 1	_____ sec	_____ sec	_____ sec
Trial 2	_____ sec	_____ sec	_____ sec
Trial 3	_____ sec	_____ sec	_____ sec
Total time	_____ sec	_____ sec	_____ sec
Average time	_____ sec	_____ sec	_____ sec

A Bagful of Bubbles!

You will need

zip-lock bag (quart size works best)

plastic straw

bubble solution (see *Bubble Blowers* activity)

What do a turtle shell, a bee's honeycomb, and a bag full of bubbles have in common? Fill a bag with bubbles and find out!

Place 1 tablespoon of bubble solution in the plastic bag. Close the bag almost completely, leaving just enough space to slip the straw into the bag. Blow through the straw to fill the bag with bubbles. Study the bubbles that form. Are the sides of the bubbles curved or flat? How do their sizes and shapes compare? Do most of them have the same number of sides?

Many of the bubbles inside your bag should be **hexagons** (six-sided shapes). Lots of examples of hexagons can be found in nature. Spiderwebs, some insects' eyes, and certain plant stems are based on a hexagon shape.

Double Bubbles

Bubbles like wet things. A straw dipped in bubble solution can poke through a bubble without popping it because the molecules of bubble solution on the straw will join together with the molecules of the soap film. You can use this idea to blow one bubble inside another!

You will need

pie pan (or other flat-bottomed container)

straw

bubble solution

Mix 1/4 cup water, 1/4 cup detergent, and 1 teaspoon sugar in the pie pan. Use the straw to blow a bubble in the middle of the pie pan. Remove the straw. Can you blow a second bubble inside the first? Dip the end of the straw in some bubble solution and carefully push it through the bubble until it touches the bubble solution in the pan. Slowly blow another bubble inside the first. Your inside bubble will be smaller, but see how big you can make it before it joins the outer bubble!

HOOP IT UP!

Can you imagine what it would be like to be inside a giant soap bubble? With a little effort and some help from your adult partner and a friend, you can find out!

Tie the four strings to the hula hoop so they are fairly evenly spaced around the hoop. Pour about 1 inch of bubble solution in the wading pool, and lay the hoop in the middle of the pool. Stand bare-footed (or in shoes covered with plastic bags) in the center of the hoop. Ask your adult partner and a friend to stand on either side of the pool and hold two of the strings on the hula hoop. Have them slowly raise the hoop straight up until it is higher than your head. You should be enclosed in a cylinder of soap film!

(You may need to do this several times before you are successful. The entire hula hoop and string should be wet with soapy solution. If the soap film keeps breaking, try adding more detergent to the solution.)

You will need

child's wading pool or large washtub
hula hoop
8–10 cups of bubble solution
4 pieces of string, about 45 cm long

BUBBLES ALOFT!

You will need

aquarium (or other large waterproof container)
1/2 box of baking soda
1/2 bottle of vinegar
bubble solution
bubble blower (use one from a commercial bottle of bubble solution or make one from a pipe cleaner)

Have a contest with your adult partner to see who can keep a soap bubble aloft the longest without touching it.
Then try the activity below.

Have your bubble solution and bubble blower ready. Sprinkle the baking soda evenly over the bottom of the aquarium. Pour the vinegar over the baking soda. Blow some bubbles so that they float downward toward the top of the aquarium. What happens? Can you explain why?

This unit introduces students to the properties of an important group of substances called *lubricants*. Students will learn that lubricants can be solids, liquids, or gases and that the main job of lubricants is to reduce friction.

Let's Lube-A-Cube!

In *Let's Lube-A-Cube!* students get a good idea of how well certain lubricants can reduce the friction between two surfaces. The activity also shows that water is not as good a lubricant as students might think it is.

Thick or Thin—Who Will Win?

Thick or Thin—Who Will Win? deals with an important quality of lubricants called *viscosity*. The viscosity of a lubricant is a measure of its thickness and its resistance to flow. A lubricant's viscosity is an important factor in deciding whether it should be used for a particular purpose. If the lubricant is too viscous, it could clog or slow down moving parts; if it's not viscous enough, it could break down too easily, causing machine parts to heat up and wear out.

Synovial Fluid—Your Body's Super Lubricant!

Synovial Fluid—Your Body's Super Lubricant! relates the topic of lubricants to Life Science and specifically to your students' own bodies.

Test Your Aim With a Graphite Game!

In the activity, *Test Your Aim With a Graphite Game!* graphite from an ordinary pencil is used in a game to show that even certain solids can be good lubricants.

From Here to There on a Cushion of Air!

From Here to There on a Cushion of Air! shows how a gas, in this case air, can be used as a lubricant. If you cannot get the plate to glide on a cushion of air, try a lighter plate, a more forceful balloon, or a combination of both.

Lip and Leafy Lubricants

Lip and Leafy Lubricants demonstrates how certain lubricants, in this case petroleum jelly, can be used to prevent loss of moisture. Leaves, like human lips, have tiny openings from which moisture evaporates. The right lubricant can prevent a leaf as well as your lips from drying and cracking.

RELEVANT NATIONAL SCIENCE EDUCATION STANDARDS

The activities in this unit can be used to support the teaching of the following standards:

✔ Science as Inquiry
   Abilities necessary to do scientific inquiry
✔ Physical Science
   Properties and changes of properties in matter
✔ Life Science
   Structure and function in living systems
✔ Science in Personal and Social Perspectives
   Science and technology in society

LET'S *LUBE-A-CUBE!**

You will need

unflavored gelatin (5 envelopes)
square baking pan (8 in × 8 in × 2 in)
liquid dish detergent
vegetable oil
2 bowls
watch with a second hand
butter knife
8-oz cup
mixing bowl

NOTE: Although gelatin is edible, do not eat the gelatin cubes after they have been handled or after a lubricant has been applied to them.

1 Cover your work surface with a double or triple layer of newspaper or paper towels. In a mixing bowl, dissolve 5 envelopes of unflavored gelatin in 2 1/2 cups of hot tap water to make quadruple-strength gelatin.

2 Apply a very thin coating of vegetable oil to the inside of the pan so that the gelatin will not stick when removed. Pour the gelatin mixture into the baking pan and place the pan in the refrigerator until the gelatin is firm (about 3-4 hours).

3 When the gelatin is firm, ask your adult partner to use the butter knife to cut the gelatin into cubes about 1 in x 1 in x 1 in (about 64 cubes).

4 Place about 15 gelatin cubes into a bowl. Place an empty bowl about 15 cm (approx. 6 in) away from the cube bowl.

5 When your adult partner says *"GO,"* start picking up the gelatin cubes, **ONE AT A TIME,** using **only** your thumb and index finger. Each time you pick up a cube, place it in the other bowl and then go get another! See how many cubes you can transfer in 15 seconds. Record the number transferred in the chart.

---

* All activities in *WonderScience* have been reviewed for safety by Dr. Jack Breazeale, Francis Marion College, Florence, SC; Dr. Jay Young, Chemical Health and Safety Consultant, Silver Spring, MD; and Dr. Patricia Redden, Saint Peter's College, Jersey City, NJ.

6 Put all the gelatin cubes back into one bowl. Pour 1/4 cup of *dish detergent* over the cubes. Have your adult partner gently mix the detergent and the cubes to make sure that the cubes are well-coated. You can add more detergent if necessary.

7 When your adult partner says *"GO,"* use the same method as before to transfer as many cubes as possible in 15 seconds. Record your results.

8 Discard the cubes and detergent and wash and dry both bowls. Put about 15 new cubes into one of the bowls. Pour 1/4 cup of *water* over the cubes. Again, your adult partner should make sure the cubes are thoroughly coated. See how many cubes you can transfer in 15 seconds and record your results.

9 Discard the cubes and water and dry both bowls. Place about 15 new cubes into one of the bowls. This time, pour 1/4 cup of *vegetable oil* over the cubes. Make sure the cubes are well-coated. See how many cubes you can transfer this time in 15 seconds and record your results.

10 With which liquid were you able to transfer the *most* cubes? Was this the best lubricant or the worst? With which liquid were you able to transfer the *fewest* cubes? Was this the best or worst lubricant?

NUMBER OF CUBES TRANSFERRED			
CUBES WITH NO LUBRICANT	CUBES WITH DISH DETERGENT	CUBES WITH WATER	CUBES WITH OIL

SLIP SLIDING AWAY!

A squeaky hinge, a wheel rubbing against its axle, and even your own hands rubbing together all have something in common: *friction*. Whenever two surfaces touch or slide or roll against each other, friction is produced. Friction causes the things that are rubbing together to heat up and to wear down. Cars, trucks, boats, trains, airplanes, and industrial machines all have many mechanical parts that rub against each other all the time. These parts would heat up, wear down, and completely stop working if it weren't for *lubricants*.

The job of any lubricant is to lessen the amount of friction between two surfaces that move against each other. A quick experiment will show you how lubricants do this. Rub your hands together very quickly so that the friction you produce will heat the palms of your hands. Now squirt a little liquid dish detergent on your hands and rub them together again. Your hands did not get as warm this time because the detergent acted as a lubricant. The detergent filled up and covered many of the tiny bumps, cracks, and ridges on your hands. Because the chemicals in detergent slide easily over each other, coating your hands with detergent made your hands slide over each other more easily and with less friction. Because the lubricating detergent reduced the amount of friction, less heat was produced.

Different types of chemicals are used to make different types of lubricants. Because of their different chemicals, some lubricants work better in cold rather than hot temperatures or in dry rather than wet weather. The chemicals in a lubricant might also make it better for lubricating tiny, lightweight parts such as the gears in a wristwatch rather than bigger, heavier parts such as the axles of a train engine. There are even some lubricants that are not used to lubricate mechanical parts at all. Some lubricants, such as certain oils, are used to make moisturizers, cold cream, and soap.

Most lubricants are *liquids*. Oil from plants, animals, and the oil pumped from under the ground can all be made into liquid lubricants. There are also some *solids* that can be used as lubricants. The talc found in baby powder, the graphite used in pencils, and certain types of wax are all solids that can be added to lubricants or used as lubricants themselves. There are also lubricants that are something like a liquid *and* something like a solid, such as thick grease or petroleum jelly. Even *gases* can be used as lubricants. A thin "cushion" of air blown between two surfaces can reduce friction very well and act as an excellent lubricant.

Your *WonderScience* activities investigate all four types of lubricants in interesting and exciting ways! *HAVE FUN!*

Illustration by Lori Seskin-Newman

THICK OR THIN—WHO WILL WIN?

You will need

three tall narrow jars with lids, such as
  olive jars or baby food juice jars
vegetable oil
transparent shampoo
transparent dish detergent

> ONE IMPORTANT FEATURE OF A LIQUID LUBRICANT IS ITS THICKNESS AND ITS ABILITY TO FLOW. THIS QUALITY IS CALLED THE LUBRICANT'S VISCOSITY. TRY THESE TWO ACTIVITIES TO SEE WHICH LUBRICANT IS MORE OR LESS VISCOUS THAN THE OTHERS.

1 Fill each jar about 4/5 full of one of the following: vegetable oil, shampoo, and dish detergent. Put the lids on tightly.

2 You and your adult partner should shake the jars hard and fast to create tiny bubbles in the liquids (you can shake two jars while your adult partner shakes one).

3 Shake the jars for the same amount of time and then place them in a row on a table. Look at the smallest bubbles in each jar. Find the jar where these bubbles are moving the fastest. Is this liquid the most viscous or the least viscous?

4 Now find the jar where the tiny bubbles are moving the slowest. Is this liquid the most or the least viscous? What about the jar where the bubbles are between the slowest and the fastest? How does the viscosity of this liquid compare to the other two?

You will need

3 tall narrow jars
vegetable oil
transparent shampoo
transparent dish detergent
3 chocolate chips
watch with a second hand

1 Fill each jar with one of the following: vegetable oil, shampoo, and dish detergent. Do not put on the lids.

2 Gently place a chocolate chip in one of the liquids. Time how long it takes to reach the bottom. Record the number of seconds in the chart.

3 Do the same thing with the other two jars. For the jar with the shortest time for the chip to reach the bottom, is the liquid in that jar more viscous or less viscous than the other liquids?

SECONDS TO REACH BOTTOM		
OIL	SHAMPOO	DISH DETERGENT

FROM HERE TO THERE ON *A CUSHION OF AIR!*

Illustrations by Tina Mion

1 Ask your adult partner to use the pencil to make a hole in the center of the plate.

You will need
lightweight disposable plastic
    dinner plate
plastic straw
balloon
rubber band
pencil
blunt-end scissors
very smooth table or counter top

2 Cut a 5 cm (2 in) piece of straw. Put about 1/2 of the straw into the opening of the balloon and attach the balloon to the straw with a rubber band. (Do not put the rubber band on so tightly that it crushes the straw).

3 Turn the plate upside down on a smooth table or counter top. To inflate the balloon, blow into the straw sticking out of the balloon. Pinch the balloon just above the straw to keep the air from escaping.

4 Without letting the air escape, push the straw through the back of the plate. Now let the air out of the balloon. Gently push your plate and see how easily it moves with air as a lubricant!

TEST YOUR AIM WITH A GRAPHITE GAME!

You will need

old smock or apron
1 cardboard box
7 8-oz clear plastic cups
glue
3 ping-pong balls
1 dark crayon
masking tape
1 piece of paper
#2 pencil
emery board or sand paper

NOTE: With powdered graphite on your fingers, do not touch walls, clothes, or furniture!

1 Put a 5-cm (approx. 2 in) piece of masking tape on each cup. Using your crayon, mark 2 cups "25," 2 cups "50," 2 cups "75," and 1 cup "100".

2 Glue the bottoms of the 7 marked cups to the bottom of the inside of the box as shown. Place the box on the floor about 1 meter (approx. 3 feet) from where you will be shooting.

3 Place an emery board on a piece of paper and rub the point of the pencil on the emery board. Tap the emery board on the paper so that the graphite dust falls onto the paper. Rub the pencil again until you have collected a little pile of powdered graphite.

4 Put your index finger in the graphite and rub your finger and thumb together for about 1 minute to thoroughly coat them with the graphite powder. Notice how your thumb and finger get slippery as the graphite acts as a lubricant.

5 Put a ping-pong ball between your thumb and index finger as shown. Aim the ball at the cups and squeeze your index finger and thumb together. If your fingers are well-lubricated, the ball should shoot out toward the cups.

6 If the ping-pong ball lands in a cup, you get the number of points on the cup. Play against your adult partner and see who scores the most points in three shots. **REMEMBER: ALL** players must use the powdered graphite lubricant! The graphite will wash off your fingers easily with soap and warm water.

LIP AND LEAFY LUBRICANTS

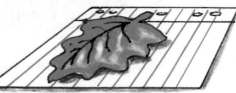
ALTHOUGH LUBRICANTS ARE USUALLY USED TO REDUCE FRICTION IN MACHINES, SOME ARE USED TO PREVENT THINGS FROM DRYING OUT. PETROLEUM JELLY CAN REDUCE FRICTION, BUT CAN ALSO BE USED TO KEEP YOUR LIPS FROM DRYING AND CHAPPING. LET'S SEE HOW IT WORKS!

You will need

two fresh green leaves from a tree (do not use thick leaves or leaves with shiny coatings)
petroleum jelly
2 sheets of paper

1 Coat the front and back of one of the leaves with a very thin layer of petroleum jelly. Do not do anything to the other leaf.

2 Place each leaf on a separate piece of paper. Put both leaves in the same room on a shelf or table top. Check your leaves each day for a week to see which one seems to be drying out first.

3 What do you think causes one of the leaves dry out? What do you think petroleum jelly does to keep the other leaf from drying out? Do you think petroleum jelly keeps your lips moist the same way it keeps the leaf moist?

Illustration by Lori Seskin-Newman

SYNOVIAL FLUID— YOUR BODY'S SUPER LUBRICANT!

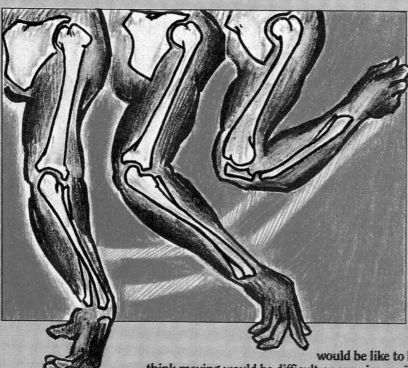

Illustration by Tina Mion

Lubricants are even important inside your own body! Wherever two or more bones come together so that you can bend, you have what is called a *joint*. Your elbow, knee, and hip are examples of large joints that help you move. What keeps the bones in a joint sliding against each other so smoothly rather than scraping against each other and wearing down? *Synovial fluid*, a very special lubricant made by your body, does the job! This fluid is clear, viscous, and one of the very best lubricants known. Where in your body is this great lubricant made? Right where the bones in your joints come together there is a very thin layer called the *synovial membrane*. This *membrane* makes just enough synovial fluid to keep your joints well-lubricated and bending easily. Sometimes, because of an accident or disease, the body makes too much *synovial fluid*. This extra fluid can cause the joints to swell, making it difficult for a person to bend and move. This is what happens to a person who has *arthritis*. The person's *synovial membrane* swells and makes bending a joint uncomfortable or even very painful. Too much synovial fluid is bad, but think what it would be like to have too little synovial fluid or none at all! Do you think moving would be difficult or even impossible? Could you run, walk, sit down, turn your head, or even use a pencil without synovial fluid lubricating your joints? We are lucky that our bodies produce one of the most wondrous lubricants in the world!

The activities in this unit introduce students to the topic of adhesives. Students will have an opportunity to learn how adhesives work on the microscopic and molecular level, and to test the strength of different types of tape and glue, make their own glue and paste, produce artwork with adhesives, and learn about adhesives found in nature.

Make Your Own Sticky-O-Meter!!

In *Make Your Own Sticky-O-Meter!!* students create a device for measuring and comparing the bonding strength of different glues made from food. This activity encourages students to design equipment, record data, and interpret information from a chart.

Today's Tape—Tremendous and Terrific, But Tacky

In *Today's Tape—Tremendous and Terrific, But Tacky* a simple method is used to measure the adhesive quality of different tapes on various surfaces. Again, equipment building and data recording and interpreting are emphasized.

On Target With Adhesives!

Simple adhesives are used in *On Target With Adhesives!* to make a target game for some friendly competition between students.

Make a Hit With Piñatas

Make a Hit With Piñatas encourages students to use adhesives in a creative way while learning about the customs of another country.

Tricky Sticky Riddles

Tricky Sticky Riddles uses a form of poetry to show that, in addition to manufactured adhesives, many plants and animals also make and use adhesives.

RELEVANT NATIONAL SCIENCE EDUCATION STANDARDS

The activities in this unit can be used to support the teaching of the following standards:

✔ Science as Inquiry

  Abilities necessary to do scientific inquiry

✔ Physical Science

  Properties and changes of properties in matter

✔ Life Science

  Diversity and adaptations of organisms

You will need

1 large plastic or pressed foam cup (32 oz)
5 foam cups (8 oz)
ruler
string
honey
pancake syrup
peanut butter
jam or jelly
spoon
tape
pennies
aluminum foil
plastic wrap
4 small paper plates
pencil

1 Cover your work surface with a double layer of paper towels or newspaper. Turn your 32-oz cup upside down on the table. Balance the ruler on the cup.

2 Make a handle for one of the other cups out of string by taping the two ends of a piece of string to opposite sides of the cup near the rim. **NOTE:** The handle should be long enough so that the bottom of the cup touches the table when the handle is placed over one end of the balanced ruler.

3 Make a shorter string handle for another cup. Tape the two ends of a piece of string to this cup so that it will be about 3 inches (approx. 8 cm) off the table when the handle is placed over the other end of the balanced ruler.

4 Hang the cups from opposite ends of the ruler and tape each cup handle to the ruler to hold the handles in place. Put a small paper plate under the cup with the long handle.

5 Using a spoon, smear a layer of honey on the bottom of the long-handled cup and push the cup down onto the plate. Lay a pencil on top of the cup and underneath the center of the ruler.

* All activities in *WonderScience* have been reviewed for safety by Dr. Jack Breazeale, Dr. Jay Young, and Dr. Patricia Redden.

OWN STICKY-O-METER!!*

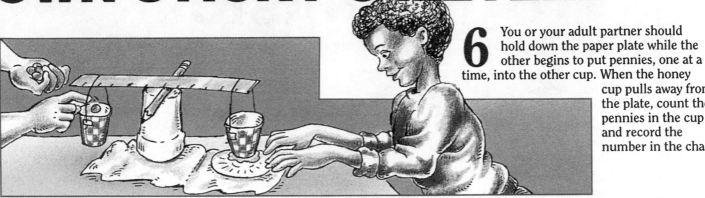

6 You or your adult partner should hold down the paper plate while the other begins to put pennies, one at a time, into the other cup. When the honey cup pulls away from the plate, count the pennies in the cup and record the number in the chart.

7 Now cover the plate with aluminum foil. Put the same amount of honey on the bottom of the cup as you used the first time. Stick the cup to the aluminum foil and start adding pennies to the other cup. When the honey cup becomes "unglued," record the number of pennies in the chart. If the number of pennies is different than before, is the bond between the cup and aluminum foil stronger or weaker than the bond between the cup and the paper plate?

8 Now cover the plate with plastic wrap. Put the same amount of honey on the cup and stick the cup to the plastic. Add pennies again until the cup becomes "unglued." Record the number of pennies in the chart. When using honey as the adhesive, to which material does the cup form the strongest bond: *paper, aluminum,* or *plastic?*

9 Repeat your experiments using jelly, peanut butter, and pancake syrup as you did with the honey to see which one forms the strongest bond between the cup and the paper. **NOTE:** You will need a different cup and a new paper plate for each different "food glue."

10 You and your adult partner can try mixing some of your food glues together to see who can come up with the stickiest glue! You can tell who wins by using your Sticky-O-Meter!

	NUMBER OF PENNIES			
	HONEY	JELLY	PEANUT BUTTER	PANCAKE SYRUP
PAPER PLATE				
ALUMINUM FOIL				
PLASTIC WRAP				

99

STICKING TO THE BASICS

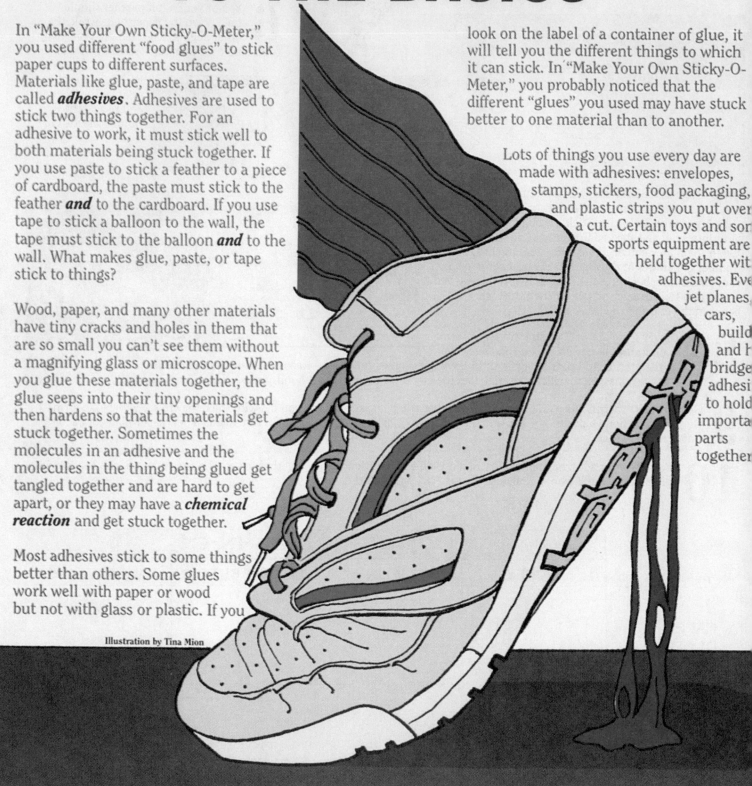

In "Make Your Own Sticky-O-Meter," you used different "food glues" to stick paper cups to different surfaces. Materials like glue, paste, and tape are called **adhesives**. Adhesives are used to stick two things together. For an adhesive to work, it must stick well to both materials being stuck together. If you use paste to stick a feather to a piece of cardboard, the paste must stick to the feather **and** to the cardboard. If you use tape to stick a balloon to the wall, the tape must stick to the balloon **and** to the wall. What makes glue, paste, or tape stick to things?

Wood, paper, and many other materials have tiny cracks and holes in them that are so small you can't see them without a magnifying glass or microscope. When you glue these materials together, the glue seeps into their tiny openings and then hardens so that the materials get stuck together. Sometimes the molecules in an adhesive and the molecules in the thing being glued get tangled together and are hard to get apart, or they may have a **chemical reaction** and get stuck together.

Most adhesives stick to some things better than others. Some glues work well with paper or wood but not with glass or plastic. If you

Illustration by Tina Mion

look on the label of a container of glue, it will tell you the different things to which it can stick. In "Make Your Own Sticky-O-Meter," you probably noticed that the different "glues" you used may have stuck better to one material than to another.

Lots of things you use every day are made with adhesives: envelopes, stamps, stickers, food packaging, and plastic strips you put over a cut. Certain toys and some sports equipment are held together with adhesives. Even jet planes, cars, build and h bridge adhesi to hold importa parts together

TODAY'S TAPE—TREMENDOUS AND TERRIFIC, BUT *TACKY*

1 Place two chairs back to back. Support a ruler on the backs of the chairs so that the numbers on the ruler are facing the floor.

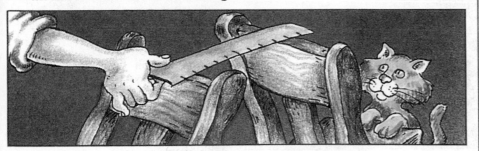

2 Cut a six-inch piece of each type of tape. If any piece of tape is not the correct width, trim it so that it is 1/2 inch (approx. 1.3 cm) wide.

3 Tape about 2 inches (approx. 5 cm) of one of the tapes to the open end of a plastic bag so that the bag hangs open when you hold the top of the tape. Tape exactly 1 inch (approx. 2.5 cm) of the other end of the tape to the surface of the ruler facing the floor.

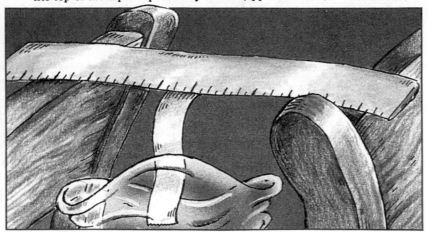

4 Start putting pennies, one at a time, in the plastic bag. Keep putting pennies in the bag until the tape pulls off from the bottom of the ruler. Count the pennies in the bag and record the number in the chart.

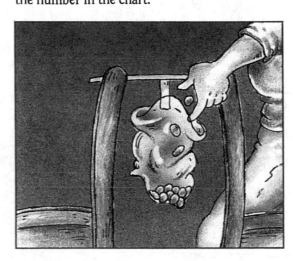

5 Repeat steps 3 and 4 with the different tapes and see which tape sticks longest to the ruler. Make sure you place the pennies into the bag at the same rate for each experiment.

6 Wrap the ruler with a piece of newspaper and repeat steps 3–5 to see which tape sticks best to newspaper. **NOTE:** Use your other ruler to be sure to stick exactly 1 inch (approx. 2.5 cm) of tape to the newspaper as you did with the bare ruler. Why do you want to stick the same length of tape to the ruler each time?

7 Wrap the ruler with aluminum foil. Repeat steps 3–5 to see how well each tape sticks to aluminum foil. Record your results.

NUMBER OF PENNIES		
PLASTIC RULER	NEWSPAPER	ALUMINUM FOIL
FIRST-AID TAPE		
CELLOPHANE TAPE		
MASKING TAPE		

ADHESIVES

Make a **HAPPY NEW YEAR!!** *WONDERSCIENCE* **ADHESIVE POSTER** using adhesives in as many different ways as you can!
Be a creative *WonderScience* Artist!

1 Make three bowls of flour-and-water paste: In each of the three bowls, add 1/4 cup of water to 1/2 cup of flour and mix until smooth. Add different food coloring to each of the three bowls and mix.

2 Have your adult partner crack open an egg and separate the white into a bowl and discard the yolk. The egg white is your clear glue.

3 Use your colored paste, ribbon, cloth, yarn, aluminum foil, colored toothpicks (color them with crayons), different-colored tapes, egg white glue, and glitter!

ON TARGET WITH ADHESIVES!

1 Use some different-sized cups, jars, jar lids, coins, and other circular objects to draw about 15 circles of different sizes on your cardboard. There should be at least 1 inch (approx. 2.5 cm) of space between a circle and any of the circles around it.

2 Using numbers from 10 to 100, write the point value for each circle inside that circle. The smallest circles should be worth the most and the biggest circles should be worth the least.

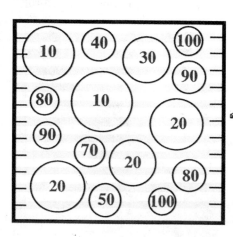

3 Make 12 small marks, 1 inch apart (approx. 2.5 cm) down both sides of your cardboard. Attach each piece of tape, with the sticky side up, across the board at each mark.

4 *WONDERSCIENCE* ADHESIVE TARGET INSTRUCTIONS:

A. Object of game:
   1. Score a total of as many points as you can in three drops.

B. How to play:
   1. Place the target on the floor with the tape side up.
   2. Stand over the target with the ping-pong ball touching your nose.
   3. Drop the ball onto the target. Each player gets three drops in a row.

C. Scoring:
   1. If the ball sticks to the tape and covers any part of a circle, the player gets the points in that circle.
   2. If the ball sticks to the tape and covers a part of more than one circle, the player gets the higher score from the two circles.
   3. If the ball sticks to the tape but does not cover any part of any circle, the player gets zero.
   4. If the ball hits and bounces completely off the target, the player gets zero.
   GOOD LUCK!

Illustration by Lori Seskin-Newman

MAKE A HIT WITH PIÑATAS

¿Qué es una PIÑATA?   (What is a PIÑATA?)

Piñatas are from Mexico, the country just south of the United States. The older-style piñatas were made from decorated clay jars and filled with candy, fruit, and gifts. During the Christmas celebration in Mexico, the piñatas were hung overhead and children wearing blindfolds would try to break them open with a stick to get the prizes inside. Today, piñatas are usually made from *papier mâché* (strips of paper dipped in paste and allowed to dry and harden) but are still filled with candy and prizes and decorated in beautiful colors.

You will need
1/2 cup flour
1 cup water
bowl
newspaper
spoon
balloons (inflated)
crepe paper

1 Pour the flour and water into a bowl and mix with a spoon until the paste is smooth.

2 Tear the newspaper into strips about 2 inches wide (approx. 5 cm) and between 6 inches (approx. 15 cm) and one foot (approx. 30.5 cm) long.

3 Dip the newspaper strips all the way into the paste and then pull the strips between your fingers to wipe off the extra paste.

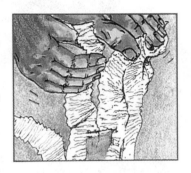

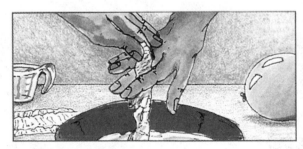

4 Lay the pasted newspaper strips on the balloon. You can attach different kinds of balloons together to make piñatas with different shapes. Keep adding your papier mâché strips until the balloons are almost completely covered.

5 Leave a small part of the balloon uncovered so you can pop the balloon when the papier mâché is dry to create a hollow piñata that you can fill with candy and prizes.

Illustrations by Lori Seskin-Newman

6 Let your piñata dry (about 2 or 3 days). Use colorful crepe paper with tape or glue to decorate your *WonderScience* piñata!

7 Your adult partner can hang your piñata as a decoration or let you break it open for the prizes inside!

TRICKY STICKY RIDDLES

Many adhesives we use every day are made in factories, but there are also many adhesives that occur in nature and have their own important uses for plants and animals.

Read the riddles and pick the picture that best answers the riddle.

After solving these riddles about natural adhesives, write your own riddle about *the sticky tongue a chameleon shoots out of its mouth to catch insects.*

1 I stick to boats and ships and rocks
And underneath the rusty docks.

2 Down your drainpipe I can glide
Along my sticky,
slimy slide.

3 With every sticky thread
I weave
There's one more guest
who cannot leave.

4 Dirt and mud and sticky stuff
For my nest, that's enough.

5 When the wind makes me fall to the ground
near your toes
Pry me apart to stick on your nose.

6 I stick to the rocks at the oceanside
I bend but don't wash away with the tide.

7 Inside my stem, beneath the fluff
Is filled with latex, that sticky stuff.

8 To make sticky honey
takes hours and hours
Of collecting nectar
from my favorite flowers.

9 Look at me closely and you will see
The sticky sap that comes out of me.

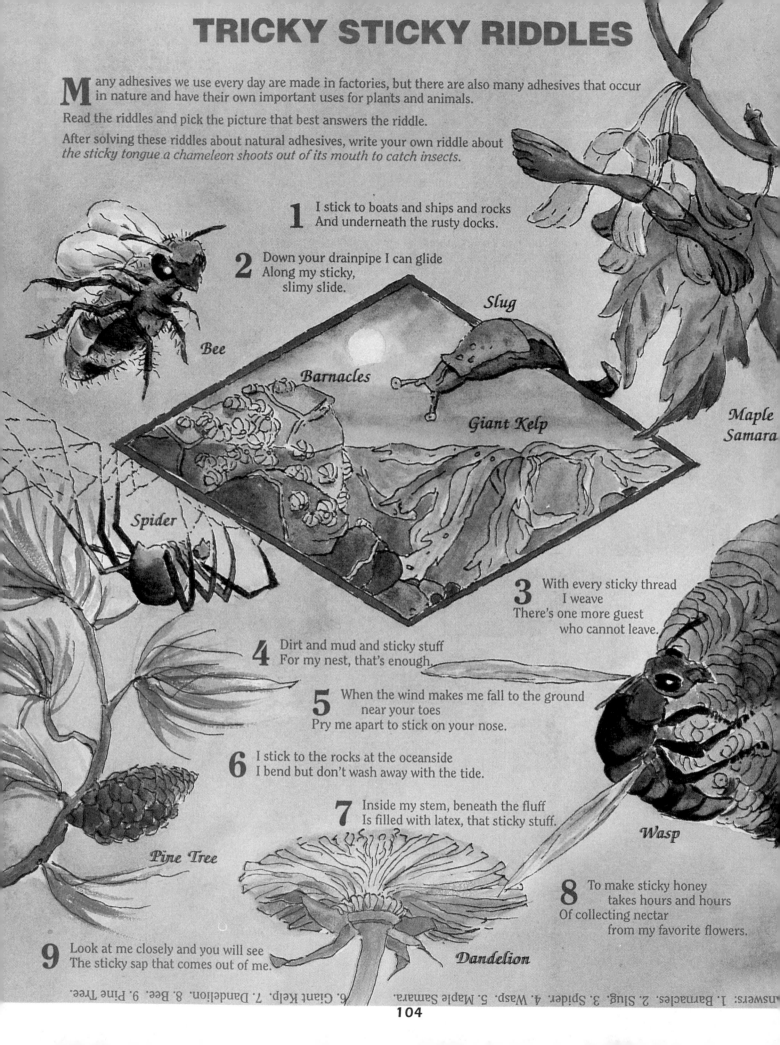

Bee
Slug
Barnacles
Giant Kelp
Maple Samara
Spider
Pine Tree
Dandelion
Wasp

Answers: 1. Barnacles. 2. Slug. 3. Spider. 4. Wasp. 5. Maple Samara. 6. Giant Kelp. 7. Dandelion. 8. Bee. 9. Pine Tree.

This unit introduces students to some of the properties of fibers and fabrics. The activities take very common materials that students do not normally view in a scientific context and show that there are scientific ways of experimenting with these materials to learn more about them.

Fibers to Thread—a New Twist!

In *Fibers to Thread—a New Twist!* students observe that the seemingly flimsy fibers of a cotton ball, when twisted, can make a thread that is so strong they will be unable to break it.

What a Mesh!

In *What a Mesh!* students can create a fabric weave projection system with a flashlight, a stocking, and a magnifying glass. The distances between the flashlight, magnifying glass, and wall will need to be adjusted to get a clear focused view of the fabric weave.

Wear and Tear

In *Wear and Tear* students will investigate how the tightness of the fabric weave effects the durability of the fabric. You might also want to ask students if it is possible to tell from this activity why stockings run the way they do when they get snagged.

Drip Busters!

Drip Busters! shows that different fibers have different abilities to absorb liquid. The activity also enables students to measure in metric units, to record measurements, and to analyze their results.

From Diapers...to Denim!

From Diapers...to Denim! is a good review of the major qualities of fabrics and fibers in the context of their many uses in clothing designed for a variety of activities.

RELEVANT NATIONAL SCIENCE EDUCATION STANDARDS

The activities in this unit can be used to support the teaching of the following standards:

✔ Science as Inquiry
   Abilities necessary to do scientific inquiry

✔ Physical Science
   Properties and changes of properties in matter

✔ Life Science
   Diversity and adaptations of organisms

✔ Science in Personal and Social Perspectives
   Science and technology in society

Fibers to Thread—
a New Twist!

1 Stretch out a cotton ball or take a piece of cotton from a roll so that you have a piece between 20 and 30 cm long and about 2 to 3 cm wide. Do the same thing with a synthetic puff or fluff ball.

2 Pull off a piece of lamb's wool which is also 20 to 30 cm long and 2 to 3 cm wide. You should now have three strips of fibers. Write **"Cotton," "Wool,"** and **"Synthetic"** on separate pieces of tape and attach each piece to one end of its fiber strip. Put all the strips on a black piece of paper.

3 Make a **"Fiber Facts"** chart like the one below. Carefully remove three individual fibers from each fiber strip. Measure the length of each fiber in millimeters and write down the *average* length in the chart under **"average length."** (To get the average, add the three lengths together and divide the sum you get by three.)

4 Look very closely at the fibers. Which fibers look the thickest? Which fibers look the skinniest? Use a scale from 1 to 3 with 1 being the skinniest and 3 being the thickest and fill in the chart under **"Thickness."**

You will need

cotton balls or box of rolled cotton sheet
lamb's wool (from foot care area of drug or grocery store)
cosmetic "puff" or "fluff" balls (synthetic fiber ball or blend of synthetic and cotton fibers)

black construction paper	metric ruler
sheet of white paper	plastic bucket
masking tape	broom or mop handle
ball point pen	

Fiber Facts

Type of fiber	Average Length	Thickness (1,2, or 3)	Bends (1,2, or 3)	Strength (1,2, or 3)
Cotton				
Wool				
Synthetic				

5 Take another close look at your fibers. Which fibers have the most wrinkles and bends in them? Use a scale from 1 to 3 with 1 being the fewest bends and 3 being the most bends and fill in the chart under **"Bends."**

6 Gently pull each fiber until it breaks. Which fiber seems the strongest? Use a scale from 1 to 3 with 1 being the weakest and 3 being the strongest and fill in the chart under **"Strength."**

Look at the information in your Fiber Facts chart and predict which fiber will make the strongest thread. Let's test them and find out!

7 Ask your adult partner to hold one end of your cotton strip. Twist the cotton strip 5 times to make a thick thread. With your adult partner, gently pull the thread in opposite directions to see how strong it is, but don't let it break. Now twist it 5 more times and test its strength. Did the added twisting make it stronger?

8 Repeat step 7 with your two other fiber strips and see which fiber makes the strongest thread. Was your prediction correct?

9 Go outside and tie one end of one of your threads to the handle of a plastic bucket and tie the other end to a broom handle as shown. See how many books or unopened food cans you can put in the bucket before the thread breaks. Test each type of thread in this way to see which fiber makes the strongest thread. Is this a good test to compare the strength of the different threads? How could you improve it?

★ All activities in *WonderScience* have been reviewed for safety by Dr. Jack Breazeale, Francis Marion College, Florence, SC; Dr. Jay Young, Chemical Health and Safety Consultant, Silver Spring, MD; and Dr. Patricia Redden, Saint Peter's College, Jersey City, NJ.

Fabulous Fibers Form Fantastic Fabrics!

We use fibers and fabrics every day in so many different ways that sometimes we forget or don't think about how important they are.

Fiber made from glass is called fiberglass and can be used for filters, insulation in the walls of houses, or mixed with other chemicals to make the bodies of boats or cars. Other fibers are used to make the filling in bed comforters and thick winter coats. Fibers are also used to make cotton balls and the padding for adhesive bandages and diapers. But the most common use of fibers is to make *thread*. Thread is made by twisting fibers so that they connect to each other to make a long string. You saw how this worked in the activity *Fibers to Thread*. The thread is then intertwined in a method called *weaving* to make *fabric*.

The most common use of fabric is to make clothes, but fabric is used for many other things such as cloth suitcases, parachutes, sails for sailboats, flags, and trampolines. The qualities of a certain type of fabric that make it right for a certain use depend on which fibers were used to make it, how the fibers were twisted to make the threads, and the type of weave that was used to make the fabric.

Most fibers come from two major sources: living plants and animals, and factories. Cotton fibers, for example, come from the cotton plant. Wool fibers are sheared from sheep and silk fibers are made by silkworms. Fibers made in factories are called "synthetic" fibers. These include materials such as nylon, rayon, and polyester. Believe it or not, many of these synthetic fibers are made from *petroleum*. All these fibers have different characteristics because of the different *atoms* and *molecules* that make up the fibers and the ways these atoms and molecules are connected to each other.

Using these different fibers, people have been able to create threads and fabrics with different qualities. Certain fabrics are very strong and take a long time to tear or wear out. This ability of a fabric to last a long time is called *durability*. Another quality of fabrics is stretchiness or *elasticity*. Because of the fibers used and the way the threads are woven together, certain fabrics are more elastic than others. Some fabrics can pick up and hold moisture better than others. This quality is called *absorbency*. Some fabrics are good to wear in the winter because they keep your body's warmth from escaping. This is the *insulating* quality of a fabric. Some of the other major characteristics of fabrics are softness, ability to be dyed, washability, and easy airflow through the fabric or breathability. All these characteristics depend on which fibers make up the thread, how the thread is made, and how the thread is woven to make the fabric.

Other important qualities can be given to fabrics by adding certain chemicals to them. Some fabrics can be changed so that they will NOT absorb water. These fabrics are called *water resistant.* Water and many other liquids made with water can be wiped off of the fabric before sinking in. Other fabrics can be treated with chemicals so that it is harder for the fabric to catch on fire. These fabrics are called *flame resistant.*

What a Mesh!

One very important characteristic of a fabric is how the threads are woven over and under each other to make the fabric. The tightness or looseness of the weave and the type of weave can have a big effect on how the final fabric looks, whether it can stretch, how well it absorbs, how strong it is, and how it can be used. Try this experiment to learn about the tightness and style of weave of different fabrics.

1 Darken a room and place a nylon stocking over a flashlight. Pull the stocking tightly over the front of the flashlight and shine the light in the direction of a white piece of paper or a white wall.

2 Notice the amount of light that passes through the fabric and hits the wall. The more light that passes through the fabric, the looser the weave. Move the flashlight closer and further from the wall and tilt it at different angles until you can see the type of weave used to make the stocking.

3 Move a magnifying glass forward and back between the flashlight and the wall until the weave is in focus. You may also have to move the flashlight further or closer to the magnifier to get the weave into focus. What can you tell about the style and tightness of the weave?

4 Now test your two other pieces of fabric in the same way to compare the style and tightness of the weave of each fabric. Which fabric allowed the most light to pass through? Which allowed the least? Which fabric do you think had the tightest weave, which had the loosest? Try a piece of lace or another fabric with an interesting weave to see how it looks with your WonderScience fabric projector system!

The type of weave you saw in the nylon stocking gives it certain qualities. One of these important qualities is the stretchiness of the stocking. Another word for stretchiness is *elasticity*. The stocking weave is special because it gives the stocking elasticity in different directions. You can investigate the elasticity of a stocking by doing a simple experiment!

First measure the *length* of an *unstretched* stocking in centimeters. Now, ask your adult partner to help you stretch the stocking lengthwise as far as it can go! Now measure it in centimeters again. If you divide the *unstretched* length into the *stretched* length, you will see how many times its normal length the stocking can stretch. Now try the same experiment with the *width* of the stocking. Is the stocking more elastic lengthwise or widthwise or about the same? Can you explain this from the type of weave you saw with the flashlight?

Wear and Tear
The "H●le" Truth

ave you ever noticed how the fabric on the elbows of shirts and the knees of pants seems to wear out the fastest? The fabrics that we wear to work and play have to be strong enough not to tear or wear away too quickly. This quality is called **durability.** In the following activity, you will test the durability of three different types of fabric with a ball acting as your elbow or knee!

You will need

3 different pieces of fabric (nylon stocking, light-weight cotton, denim)

1 baseball or heavy rubber ball

extra coarse sandpaper

sheet of paper

pencil

1 Wrap one of your pieces of fabric tightly around the ball and hold the fabric together with your hand. On your own piece of paper, make a **"Fabric Wear and Tear"** chart like the one at the bottom of the page.

2 Ask your adult partner to hold the sandpaper down on a flat surface while you drag the ball across it. Don't press down on the ball, just let the weight of the ball drag across the sandpaper.

3 Look at the fabric where it scraped along the sandpaper. Was there any wear after just one scrape? Continue to scrape the fabric and to count each scrape until you notice some wear on the fabric.

4 The first time you notice some wear on the fabric, record the number of scrapes in your chart under **"First Wear"** for that fabric.

5 Continue scraping the fabric and counting each scrape until you break through the fabric, making a tear or a hole. Record the number of scrapes in your chart under **"Breakthrough"** for that fabric.

6 Which fabric needed the most scrapes to show the first signs of wear? Which needed the least? Which fabric lasted the longest between the first signs of wear and the breakthrough point?

Which fabric qualities do you think were most important for the durability of your fabrics?

A) Type of fiber in the thread
B) Strength of the thread
C) Type or tightness of weave

Fabric Wear & Tear

Type of fabric	Number of scrapes	
	First Wear	Breakthrough
Nylon		
Cotton		
Denim		

110

Drip Busters!

You will need

cotton balls or box of rolled cotton sheet

lamb's wool (from foot care section of drug or grocery store)

cosmetic "puff" or "fluff" balls (synthetic fiber or synthetic and cotton blend)

bowl

3 small (3–5 oz) plastic or glass cups

metric ruler

masking tape

ball point pen

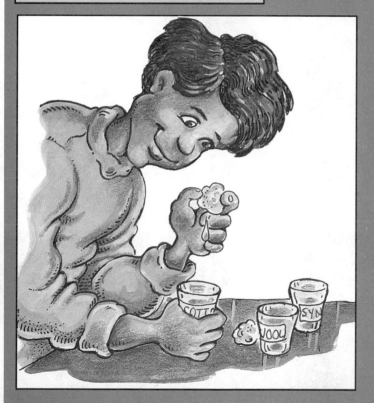

Type of fabric	Height of water
Cotton	
Wool	
Synthetic	

Another very important quality of fibers and fabric is how well they can pick up and hold liquids. This quality is called **_absorbency_**. Cloth towels are made of fibers that are very absorbent. If you look closely at a towel, you will see that it is not a flat piece of fabric. It has little loops of thread sticking out from the surface so that a towel has more absorbing fibers than if it were just a flat piece of fabric. In the following activity, you can test different types of fibers for absorbency to see which fibers should be used to make towels.

1 Use the same amount of cotton, synthetic, and wool fibers to make a ball out of each fiber about the size shown. Use your pen and masking tape to label three cups **"cotton," "wool,"** and **"synthetic."**

2 Pour about 1 cup of water into a bowl. Dunk your ball of cotton one time into and out of the water as quickly as you can. Be sure the ball goes completely under water but only for a split second. Immediately place the ball in the cup labeled cotton. Do the same thing with the ball of wool and the ball of synthetic fiber and place each in its separate cup.

3 Squeeze as much water as you can from each fiber ball and make sure that all the water from each ball goes into its proper cup. Put your fiber ball next to its cup.

4 Line up your cups and use a ruler to measure the height of the water in each cup. Make an **"absorbency"** chart like the one below and fill in the height of the water in each cup. Which fiber ball was the most absorbent? Which was the least absorbent?

5 Look at your wet balls of fiber. Do you notice any differences between them? Does one feel harder or more compact than the others? Is there a difference in how easily you can pull them apart? Do you think this has anything to do with how absorbent they are?

6 Can you think of any reasons why this absorbency test might **_not_** be the most accurate experiment to test water absorbency? See if you can come up with another water absorbency test you think would be better and try it out! Good luck!

From Diapers . . . to Denim!

Different activities require people to wear special clothing made from certain types of fabric. Look at each person on this page and decide which fabric qualities are important to that person. Write down the fabric qualities next to the person and explain to your adult partner why those qualities are important to the person wearing the fabric.

Durability	Elasticity	Absorbency	Insulation	Softness
Washability	Breathability	Flame retardance	Water resistance	Dyeability

Fill in the fabric qualities you think are important to each person.

Firefighter _____

Cyclist _____

Arctic explorer _____

Football player _____

Horseback rider _____

Skier _____

Baby _____

Unit 15
Properties of Water

This unit introduces students to some of the properties of water. Many of the observable behaviors of water can be explained by referring to the structure and composition of water molecules themselves. Water molecules are composed of two atoms of hydrogen and one atom of oxygen. Because of the different characteristics of the oxygen and hydrogen atoms, the electrons in a water molecule spend more time near the oxygen atom than the hydrogen atoms. Since electrons are negatively charged, the area around the oxygen atom is slightly negative and the area around the hydrogen atoms is slightly positive. Molecules that have this type of charge separation are called *polar* molecules. It is this polar property of water molecules that gives water many of its unusual characteristics. The polar nature of a water molecule can be illustrated like this:

Because of this polar aspect of water, water molecules have a mutual attraction between their positive and negative ends. This attraction can be illustrated like this:

This attraction accounts for water's tendency to cling to itself or its *cohesiveness*. Water molecules also adhere to other substances (*adhesiveness*) that are composed of polar molecules or atoms and molecules that are charged.

Water Drops Unite! and Racedrop Raceway!

The activities in *Water Drops Unite!* and *Racedrop Raceway!* depend on this cohesion and adhesion of water.

Solving Dissolving

In *Solving Dissolving,* dissolving can also be explained, in part, by the polar water molecules' attraction to the polar or charged particles of the substance being dissolved. Heating water makes the water molecules move more quickly, resulting in more water molecules attaching to the substance and agitating it more vigorously. This dissolves the substance more quickly.

Ice of a Different Color

In *Ice of a Different Color,* the nature of the water molecule can also explain the structure and strength of pure ice versus ice with impurities. Because of the shape of water molecules and their polarity, they arrange themselves into a regular pattern when water freezes to form ice. Salt and sugar both dissolve in water and interfere with this regular arrangement of water molecules.

Water: From H to O

The polarity of water molecules also accounts for the phenomena in *Water: From H to O.* Surface tension, capillarity, and static electricity's effects on water can all be explained by understanding the polar nature of water.

Wondering about Water

Wondering about Water gives students a chance to do some creative thinking and writing about water.

RELEVANT NATIONAL SCIENCE EDUCATION STANDARDS

The activities in this unit can be used to support the teaching of the following standards:

✔ **Science as Inquiry**
  Abilities necessary to do scientific inquiry
✔ **Physical Science**
  Properties and changes of properties in matter
✔ **Life Science**
  Structure and function in living systems
✔ **Earth and Space Science**
  Structure of the Earth system

Water Drops *UNITE!*

One very important quality of water is its attraction to different surfaces. The attraction and attaching of a substance to **itself** is called *cohesion*. The attraction and attaching of a substance to **something else** is called *adhesion*. In the following activities, notice the way water attaches to itself and how it attaches or doesn't attach to other surfaces.

You will need

2 pieces of cardboard (about 24 cm x 40 cm)	tape
2 sheets of white, unlined paper	water
wax paper	watch with second hand
pencil	eye dropper
metric ruler	plastic straw

1 Use a pencil or pen to draw or trace the dark circles on the water drop game board onto one of your sheets of paper. Tape the paper to one of your pieces of cardboard at the corners. Make sure the paper lies very flat.

2 Place a piece of wax paper over the game board and tape it down at the corners. Be sure there are no bumps or wrinkles in the wax paper. You should be able to see the game board clearly through the wax paper.

3 Use your dropper or straw to put drops of water in each of the outer circles. Each drop should be made up of two or three drops of water.

4 Ask your adult partner to time you as you tilt and move the game board to make the drops of water connect to each other into one big drop of water.

5 When you have one big drop of water, tilt the board to move your drop to the center circle. Stop the clock and check your time.

Did the drops of water connect to each other easily? How well did the water stick to the wax paper? Did the size of a drop affect how fast the drop moved?

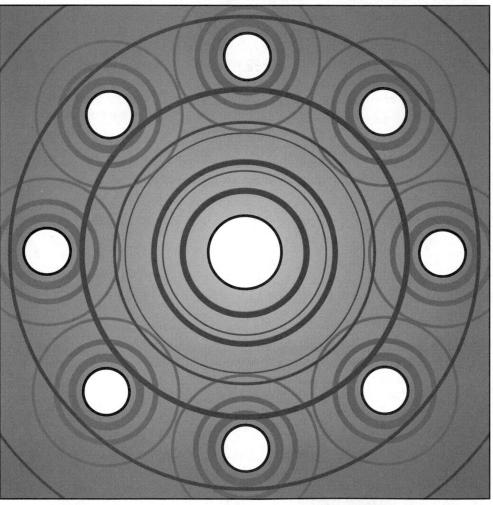

T ry another game! Instead of tilting and moving your game board to bring the water drops together, use a plastic straw to drag them together. They should stick better to the straw than to the wax paper, so you should be able to pull them along the wax paper until you have one big water drop in the middle! See how quickly you can do it!

RACEDROP RACEWAY!

1 Repeat steps 1 and 2 with the water race track below. Place one or two drops of water together to make one drop in the starting area. This is your *race drop!*

Challenge your partner to beat your time!

2 Ask your adult partner to time you as you tilt and move the board to make your race drop go as fast as it can around the track. Be careful not to let your race drop touch the sides of the track. Every time it touches a side, two seconds should be added to your total time.

FINISH

3 Experiment with different size race drops to see which size gives you the best combination of speed and control!

START

IMPORTANT: *In the activities on these pages, do not allow your drops to sit in one place on the wax paper for too long because they may begin to soak in a little. If this happens, simply remove the old wax paper and tape down a new piece.*

All activities in *WonderScience* have been reviewed for safety by Dr. Jack Breazeale, Francis Marion University, Florence, SC; Dr. Jay Young, Chemical Health and Safety Consultant, Silver Spring, MD; and Dr. Patricia Redden, Saint Peter's College, Jersey City, NJ.

WATER, WATER, EVERYWHERE...

It's just about everywhere! It covers almost 3/4 of the Earth's surface! It makes up about 2/3 of your body's weight! Every living thing needs it to survive! It's amazing! It's incredible! It's the one and only, your friend and mine, that multi-talented substance we know and love! Let's hear it for that wild and wonderful wizard of wetness— **WATER!**

To help understand what makes water so special, we have to think small, very small. You may already know that everything in the world is made up of *atoms*. When two or more atoms join together, they make a *molecule*. A molecule of water is made up of three atoms: one *Oxygen* atom and two *Hydrogen* atoms. That's why scientists call water H_2O. When water molecules get near each other, they *attract*. This is what gives water some of its very interesting qualities.

The first two activities showed that one of these special characteristics of water is the way it connects to itself and holds together. This is called *cohesion*. You also saw that water clings to other things. This is called *adhesion*. Cohesion and adhesion are caused by the attraction of water molecules to each other and to other things.

The cohesion and adhesion of water molecules also help them move up the very thin tubes in the roots and stems of plants. This movement of a liquid up tiny tubes or spaces is called *capillary action*. Water molecules are attracted to the sides of the tube and to each other as they move up the tubes. This water brings the plants the nutrients they need to live. The cohesion of water molecules also helps form raindrops. In a cloud, water molecules join together until the drops get big enough to fall as rain.

Water molecules can also form a kind of "skin" on the surface of water. The water molecules at the surface are attracted to each other and are also pulled down by the molecules beneath them. These attractions pull the water molecules at the surface very close together. This results in what scientists call *surface tension*. Surface tension helps a drop of water hold its shape. It also lets some insects walk around on the surface of the water.

Water molecules can also *dissolve* many different things. The water molecules are attracted to the atoms and molecules of the substance being dissolved. The water molecules attach to these atoms or molecules. The water molecules pull and bump into them so much that the substance begins to fall apart. This action of water molecules lets you dissolve sugar, salt, or other substances in water. We can then use the liquid with the dissolved substance in it for different jobs.

Water molecules also act in a special way when water freezes. When most liquids freeze, their molecules get closer together and the substance shrinks or *contracts*. But when water freezes, water molecules get farther apart and the water *expands*. After water has expanded to form ice, it is able to float on liquid water. This is very helpful in nature. When lakes freeze, the ice forms on the surface and the water underneath stays liquid. This helps living things in the water survive during the winter.

Have fun with these activities on water. As you do the activities, think about how water molecules make this dazzling and dynamic liquid do the dynamic things it does!

SOLVING DISSOLVING

A very important quality of water is its ability to *dissolve* many substances. Different things affect how well water dissolves a certain amount of a substance: the amount of water used, the temperature of the water, and how fast the water is moving. In the following activity, you can investigate these three aspects of dissolving!

You will need

sugar cubes   water
sugar   plastic spoons
measuring spoons   3 clear plastic cups

1 Place 1/4 cup of cold tap water and 1/4 cup of hot tap water into two separate cups.

2 Place a sugar cube in the center of each cup and observe the cubes very closely. Which cube dissolved the fastest? Why do you think this happened?

3 You also know that stirring water helps make a substance dissolve faster. Rinse out your cups and place ¼ cup of warm water into each of three cups.

4 Place 1 teaspoon of sugar into each cup. Ask your adult partner to stir one cup slowly while you stir one cup very quickly. Leave the other cup alone. Which sugar dissolved the fastest? Why do you think this happened?

5 Do you think you can dissolve 3 teaspoons of sugar in less time than your partner can dissolve 1? Should your water be warmer or colder than your partner's? Should you stir quickly or slowly? Do you think using extra water would help? Try it and see!

Stalagmites and stalactites

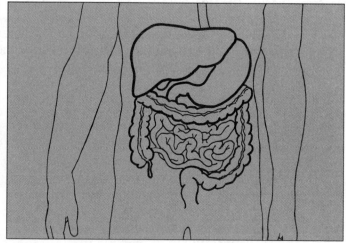

PHOTO COURTESY LURAY CAVERNS, VIRGINIA

Digestive system

Explain to your partner or teacher how dissolving is important in each of these pictures.

ICE
OF A DIFFERENT COLOR

You learned that water molecules come together in a very special way when water freezes. In the activity below, see if water freezes the same way when salt or sugar are dissolved in it.

You will need

water	three 12-oz plastic or paper cups
ice cube tray	masking tape
food coloring (three different colors)	pencil
	newspaper
freezer	coarse sandpaper
sugar	empty coffee can
salt	sand, gravel, or dirt

1 Cover your work surface with a layer of newspaper. Label your cups "tap," "salt," "sugar." Put 1 cup of cold tap water in each cup.

2 Add 1 level teaspoon of salt to the salt cup and stir until as much salt dissolves as possible. Add 1 level teaspoon of sugar to the sugar cup and stir until as much sugar dissolves as possible.

3 Put 1 drop of a different color food coloring in each cup. Write the color on the cup's label. Take each cup and carefully pour enough liquid to make 3 or 4 cubes of each color in the ice cube tray. Put the tray in the freezer before going to bed.

4 The next day, take out one cube of each color and put the rest back in the freezer. Look at the three cubes very closely. Do you see a difference among them? Describe the differences. Feel each ice cube. Describe the way they feel.

5 Rub each cube on your piece of sandpaper. Is there a difference in the sound they make? Does any cube seem easier to sand down than another?

6 Fill an empty coffee can with sand, gravel, or dirt. Put the lid on and tape it all around so the lid is very secure. Place one of each type of ice cube from the freezer on a hard surface outside.

7 Drop the can on each cube from 5 cm above the ground. Remove the can and observe what happened to each cube. Did you expect these results? Why? Do the same experiment again with a new set of cubes to check your results.

Which cube do you think will melt first? Do an experiment to find out!

*Caution: The **empty** coffee can may have sharp edges. Be careful when filling it. The **filled** coffee can is heavy. Do not drop it on your fingers or toes.*

Water: From H to O

The structure of water molecules makes water act in some interesting ways. The three activities below show some of these wonders of water!

How many drops of water do you think you can stack on a penny?

Place a clean dry penny on your work surface. Use a straw or eye dropper to place drops of water on the penny one by one. Count the drops as you put them on. Watch from the side as the water builds up. The surface tension will finally break, causing the water to spill. Dry your penny off and see if you can pile on more drops the next time!

Surface Tension

To test water's capillary action is a piece of cake. As you read already, water has the ability to climb up thin tubes and tiny holes. This is called capillary action. Even when certain things are dissolved in water, the water can still move up tiny tubes and spaces. This lets you make a capillarity dessert!

Ask your adult partner to help you make a 3-oz package of strawberry or cherry gelatin. Cut a cube of angel food cake and a cube of pound cake about 5 cm on each side. Have your adult partner pour about ¼ cup of gelatin into each of two clear plastic cups. While the gelatin is still liquid, gently put the angel food cake cube in one cup and the pound cake cube in the other. Ask your adult partner to help you so that you add the cubes at the same time.

Watch as the gelatin moves up into the cake. In which cake does it move up the fastest? Why do you think this is so? Put your cups in the refrigerator and add some whipped cream when they are gelled. Then eat your delicious capillarity dessert!

Capillarity

Obviously, water is an amazing liquid, but this one will really surprise you! See what happens when you bring a charged balloon near a thin stream of water!

Blow up a balloon. Turn the water on in your sink very slightly so that it makes a very thin stream. Rub the balloon on your hair to give the balloon an electric charge. Bring the charged side of the balloon near the water. What happens? Why do you think this happened?

Electricity

Wondering about Water

What if Wally and Wilma Waterman Were in a World Where Water Was Wacky?

In What Ways Would Wally and Wilma's World

of Weird Water be Warped?

Think about how strange the World Would be if Water Were different.

Look at the ideas below and Write a short story

about Wally and Wilma Waterman Wandering

in a Way-out World of Whimsical Water.

Be creative and have fun! You could even illustrate your story!

1. **What if water adhered strongly to many substances?**

   How well would your windshield wipers work?
   How easily could you dry off after a bath or shower?
   What would it be like to walk outside after a rain?

2. **What if water were not very cohesive?**

   Could you pour a glass of water?
   How big would puddles get?
   Could most plants survive?

3. **What if water did not dissolve things?**

   Could you make a cake?
   Could you wash with soap?
   Would ocean water be salty?

4. **What if ice were to sink in water?**

   Could aquatic animals and plants live through a cold winter?
   Would there be any liquid water to drink in a long cold winter?
   How long would you have to wait to go skating outside?

5. **What if water did not have surface tension?**

   Would there be icicles?
   What would rain be like?
   Could we drip drops from an eye dropper?

The activities in this unit introduce students to a property of liquids called *surface tension*. The unit deals only with the surface tension of water since it is an excellent example of surface tension and is safe and convenient to observe. The surface tension of water refers to the layer of water molecules on the water's surface which acts as a strong but flexible "film" or "skin."

In any amount of water, each water molecule is attracted in many different directions by the molecules around it. But the molecules on the water's surface have so few water molecules in the air above them that they are only minimally attracted in an upward direction. Since the water molecules on the surface are pulled mainly down and in by the water molecules below them, they form a tighter, more uniform surface tension layer on top of the water.

Surfin' Surface Tension

Throughout this unit, the term "float" was avoided to describe the position of an object on the water's surface due to surface tension. An object floats in a liquid if it is less dense than the liquid. But an object can rest on the surface of a liquid, as a result of surface tension, even if it is more dense than the liquid. The paper clips on the skier in *Surfin' Surface Tension* are more dense than water. They do not float, but rest on the water's surface tension layer.

Surfin' Surface Tension and How to Give Pepper Some Pep!

In *Surfin' Surface Tension* and *How to Give Pepper Some Pep!*, detergent was used to disrupt or "break" the water's surface tension. When placed in water the detergent molecules interfere with the orderly arrangement of water molecules and "breaks" the water's surface tension layer.

Putting Your Two Cents In

In *Putting Your Two Cents In,* students have a chance for some friendly competition and cooperation in an educational activity about surface tension. The number of pennies that can be added before the water overflows is surprising.

Water Walking—They Take It In Stride and Great Strides In Poetry—Water Strider Limericks

In *Water Walking—They Take It In Stride,* students can relate the concept of surface tension to an insect which they may have observed in nature. The limericks in *Great Strides In Poetry—Water Strider Limericks* give students a chance to use literature in a creative way to learn about surface tension.

RELEVANT NATIONAL SCIENCE EDUCATION STANDARDS

The activities in this unit can be used to support the teaching of the following standards:

✔ Science as Inquiry
  Abilities necessary to do scientific inquiry

✔ Physical Science
  Properties and changes of properties in matter

✔ Life Science
  Diversity and adaptations of organisms

SURFIN' SURFACE TENSION*

1 Open your envelope so it can be used like a regular piece of paper. Trace two water-skiers on your envelope and cut them both out. Bend their feet as shown.

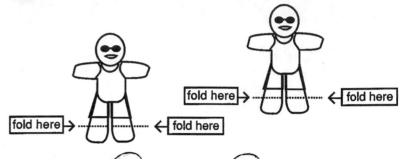

2 Roll four small pieces of tape with the sticky side out. Stick a piece of rolled tape to the middle of each paper clip, and then stick one foot of each skier to each piece of tape. Now your skiers should be firmly attached to their clips.

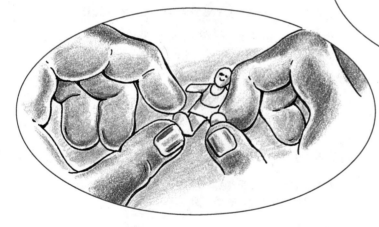

3 Put your skiers aside and fill a cup with water. Take a paper clip and hold it by one end and place it in the water. Does it sink or stay on the surface? Take a second paper clip, hold it by one long edge, and place it in the water. What happens to this one?

4 Now take the third paper clip and place its flat surface very carefully on the water. Try this until you can make the paper clip stay on top of the water. (Dry the paper clip between tries.)

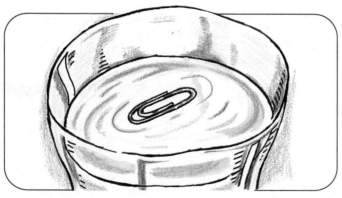

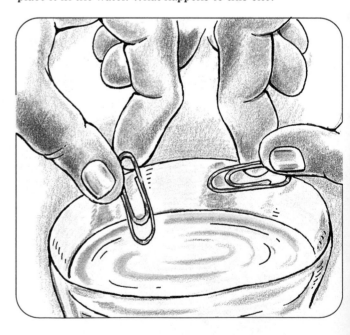

* All activities in *WonderScience* have been reviewed for safety by Dr. Jack Breazeale, Dr. Jay Young, and Dr. Patricia Redden.

5 Fill the baking pan half-full of water. Hold one of your skiers by the head, and very carefully lower it until the clips are resting flat on the water. Put your finger in the water behind your skier and gently push it along the surface of the water. Observe what the water looks like around the edges of the skier's clips. Are the clips breaking through the water's surface? What do you think is keeping them up?

6 Race your skiers! Put both skiers in the water at one end of the pan. Blow air *very gently* behind them and see which one reaches the other side first! (Don't blow too hard or you'll *wipe out!!!*) If one skier does sink, try to put it right back onto the water's surface. Does it still stay up? Why or why not?

7 If you now have two wet skiers, you may need to make a new one out of dry paper and paper clips. Place a new skier on the surface of the water in the baking pan. Dip a dry cotton swab into the water at the edge of the pan farthest away from the skier. What happens to the skier?

8 Now, dip a cotton swab with dish detergent on it into the baking pan at the farthest place from the skier. *Now* what happens? Which swab causes the skier to sink? How could you explain what happens?

Before you try making and racing any more skiers, be sure that you thoroughly rinse out and dry the baking pan. If there is *any* detergent left in the pan, the skiers will not be able to stay on the surface.

More fun! Make your skier into a surfer by attaching it sideways to only *one* paper clip. How does your surfer work compared to your skier?

Water's Secret "Skin"

You know that some things you have in your house float and other things sink. Some plastic toys and certain kinds of soap and wood all float when placed in water. But many things sink in water, such as silverware, nails, and gravel.

In the "Surfin' Surface Tension" activity, you saw that paper clips are very special because they usually sink; but when placed on the water in a certain way, they *don't!* There are only a few very special objects like paper clips with just the right size, shape, and weight to stay on the surface of the water when we expect them to sink. Try some other objects such as a dime or a hair pin and see if they're special too!

Since paper clips normally sink, what could be keeping them on the surface of the water? The paper clips don't sink because they are resting on a strong layer of water molecules. The water molecules at the surface form a "skin", because they are being attracted to each other and to the water molecules under them. This strong attraction of water molecules at the surface is known as *surface tension,* and that's what is holding the paper clips up! If you look closely at your paper clips on water, you can see the clips pushing down on the layer of water but not breaking through.

Do you remember what happened to your skiers in "Surfin' Surface Tension" when you added detergent to the water? Adding soap to water makes the attraction of the water molecules at the surface much less than it was. We say that "the surface tension was broken" by the detergent, which allowed the skiers to sink. You'll get another chance to see how detergent affects surface tension in "Dish Detergent Dynamos."

In "Water Walking—They Take It In Stride", you will learn how an insect uses the water's surface tension to push its way along the top of a creek or a pond. In "Putting Your Two Cents In", you'll see that water filled *over* the top of a cup won't spill because water's surface tension holds it in!

Discover the power of water's strong outer layer!

HOW TO GIVE PEPPER SOME *PEP!*

You will need
8-oz cup or small bowl
black pepper
baby powder
liquid dish detergent

Safe Science Tip:
Both baby powder and pepper can irritate eyes, nose, and throat. Shake both the pepper and the baby powder away from your face.

1 Fill the cup with water and cover the surface of the water with a thin layer of pepper.

2 Place a drop of detergent in the middle of the pepper. Describe what happens. Does any pepper sink or does it just move? What do you think is making the pepper move? Put a second drop of detergent in the water. Does the pepper do the same thing again? Why or why not?

3 Wash out the cup very well, but this time put baby powder on the water instead of pepper. Add a drop of detergent as in step 2. What happens this time? Is it different from the pepper? Why do you think it acts this way?

PUTTING YOUR TWO CENTS IN

You will need
8-oz plastic cup
pencil and paper for recording
200 pennies
paper towels

HOW MANY PENNIES CAN YOU PUT IN A CUP FILLED WITH WATER BEFORE IT OVERFLOWS? LET'S HAVE A CONTEST!

1 There are two jobs in this game. One player carefully puts the pennies in the cup one by one. The other player keeps count on a piece of paper of how many pennies go into the cup before the water overflows.

2 Put a triple layer of paper towels on your work surface. Fill a cup all the way to the top with water. Place the cup on the work surface between you and your adult partner.

3 Predict how many pennies can be put in the cup before it overflows. Record your prediction and your adult partner's prediction on your paper.

4 Start placing pennies in the cup. Make sure you count them correctly so that you can tell whose prediction is closest.

What's keeping the water from overflowing? How many pennies went into the cup before the water overflowed?

Now try a new game!

1 Fill the cup with water again.

2 Take turns with your adult partner putting pennies in the cup.

3 Whoever puts the penny in that makes the water overflow is the loser.

WATER WALKING— THEY TAKE IT IN *STRIDE*

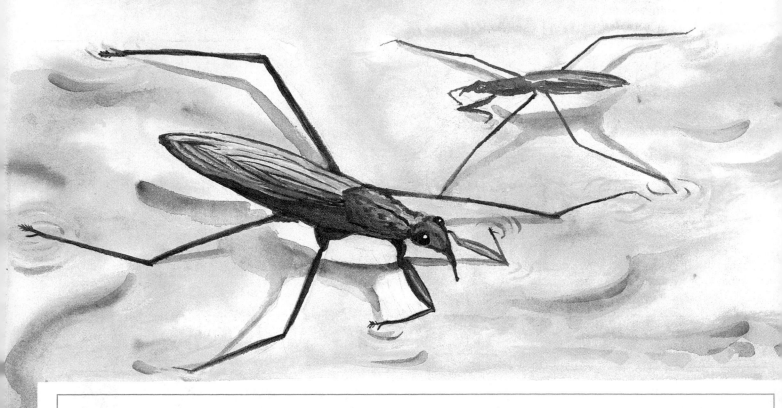

In "Surfin' Surface Tension", your water-skiers were able to stand on the top of the water without sinking. They were made of tape, paper, and paper clips, which normally sink when wet. If your skiers were real people, could they stand on the surface of the water? Believe it or not, some insects can!

Have you ever been to a stream or a pond and noticed a large insect gliding on top of the water? If it had six long, thin legs, you probably saw a *water strider.* Water striders move around on the water's surface. How do they do it?

The water strider has special hairs on the ends of its feet that act like snowshoes or your skier's paper clips. These special hairs don't break through the water's surface. Did you notice that the paper clips dented the water but didn't go through? The water strider's feet do the same thing—they dent the water's surface but they don't break through. The front and back legs (with the special hairs) keep the water strider on top of the water while its middle legs paddle it around the pond.

by Jennifer Snyder

DISH DETERGENT DYNAMOS!!!

You will need

cinnamon
8-oz clear plastic cup
liquid dish detergent
white typing paper

1 Fill the cup as full as possible without letting the water overflow.

2 Sprinkle a thin layer of cinnamon on the surface of the water.

3 Place a drop of dish detergent on the cinnamon. Watch the pattern that forms when the detergent "breaks" the water's surface tension.

4 Gently place the piece of typing paper flat on the water's surface and pick up the design made of cinnamon.

5 Lay the paper flat with the cinnamon side up and allow your cinnamon design to dry.

6 Wash out the cup very thoroughly and try this activity again, but this time drop the dish detergent in a different spot on the layer of cinnamon. You should get a different design this time and every time you try it!

YOU CAN EVEN RACE A BOAT BECAUSE OF THE SURFACE TENSION OF WATER!

1 Using your index card, cut out a little boat like the one in the drawing. Make sure you put a notch in the back of the boat.

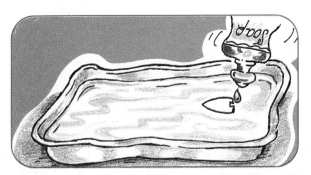

2 Place the boat gently on the water and place a drop of dish detergent in the notch. Your boat should go, go, *GO!!*

You will need

1 index card
blunt-tip scissors
baking pan
liquid dish detergent

3 Try making boats of different shapes and try racing boats with your adult partner. Remember to wash the pan *very* well after *each* time you use the detergent or your boat won't go.

GREAT *STRIDES* IN POETRY—
WATER STRIDER LIMERICKS

A limerick is a poem that has only five lines. The last words in the *first, second,* and *fifth* lines all rhyme. Also, the last words in the *third* and *fourth* lines rhyme with each other but not with the other three. Most limericks tell a little story and are usually funny. Here are some limericks about *water striders* for you to read with your adult partner. When you see how they work, take the lines of the scrambled limericks and try to put them in order. Then, you and your adult partner can write some water strider limericks of your own!

We all know a strider named Link
On water, he would not sink
He'd zoom on the surface
With speed as his purpose.
You'd miss him if you would blink.

The bodies of striders are thin—
Not much fatter than needle or pin.
On water they're speedy
All others are needy
When racing, it's striders who win!

The first line of each limerick is given. See if you can put the other four lines in order by writing them in the spaces provided.

When hiking you often see striders—

On ponds they do paddle

No noise and no rattle

You shouldn't mistake them for spiders.

On the surface where water is tighter.

❖

Striders have feet that are hairy.

On purpose they're made

For water and not for the prairie.

But don't be afraid—

Up close, to some, they look scary.

❖

The water's surface is tight.

This mixture, you see,

The strider's body is light.

Makes skimming for striders all right!

(And I'm sure you'll agree)

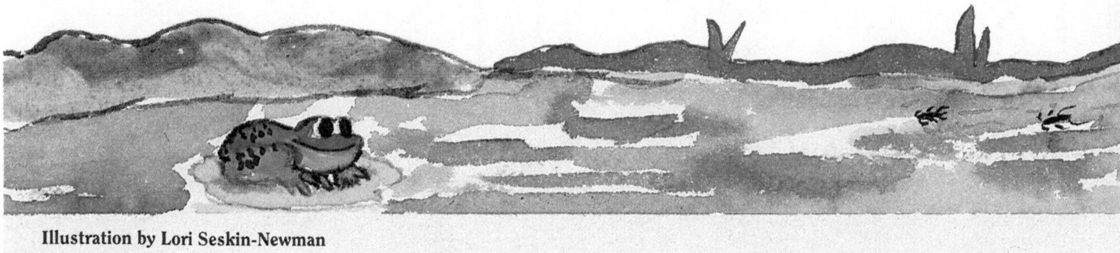

When hiking you often see striders—

_____

_____

_____

_____

❖

Striders have feet that are hairy.

_____

_____

_____

_____

❖

The water's surface is tight.

_____

_____

_____

_____

Illustration by Lori Seskin-Newman

The activities in this unit deal with the movement of water up narrow tubes or between the tiny fibers that make up paper and cloth. This upward traveling of water is known as capillary action or *capillarity*. After conducting the activities, students should understand some of the causes of capillarity and see that it is involved in many aspects of daily life including drying off with cloth towels, absorbing liquids with paper towels, mops, and sponges, and the health and growth of plants.

The hair-like fibers in cloth and paper are so close together that water molecules can move up them. This upward movement is due to the fact that water molecules in contact with these solid surfaces are more attracted to those surfaces than to each other. This same attraction occurs when water is offered the opportunity to travel up most narrow-gauge tubes.

Soak Those Sharks! and Celery Climb

In *Soak Those Sharks!,* students can compare the relative capillary action of different types of absorbent materials. *Celery Climb* lets students chart the movement of color water up the tiny tubes which run the length of celery stalks.

The Return of the Sharks

Two of the activities in this unit emphasize the graphing of data as well as the need to control variables. *The Return of the Sharks* uses information from *Soak Those Sharks!* to create a bar graph. In *Celery Climb!*, students create a line graph from the data generated in the celery activity. Both graphs are then used as the basis for questions on the relative rates of capillarity of the materials used in the activities. In both investigations, the need to recognize and to control variables should be stressed.

Soggy Socks!

Soggy Socks! enables students to compare the capillary action of two materials used to filter water from soil.

A Day at Capillarity Park

A Day at Capillarity Park reinforces the recognition of capillary action in nature and in other everyday situations.

RELEVANT NATIONAL SCIENCE EDUCATION STANDARDS

The activities in this unit can be used to support the teaching of the following standards:

✔ Science as Inquiry
   Abilities necessary to do scientific inquiry

✔ Physical Science
   Properties and changes of properties in matter

✔ Life Science
   Structure and function in living systems

notch

You will need

- paper towels
- brown paper bag
- old white, cotton sweat sock
- sheet of typing paper
- blue food color
- 33 × 23 × 5 cm baking pan (13 × 9 × 2 in.)
- blunt-tipped scissors
- pencil
- hanger
- string
- metric ruler
- tape
- spoon

1 Trace the shark shape onto the piece of typing paper and cut it out. (Have your adult partner supervise all cutting.) Measure the shark from notch to tail and record the length: _____ cm.

2 Use the typing paper shark shape to cut sharks from the sock, the paper bag, and a paper towel. You should now have four sharks.

5 Tie a string to the hook of the hanger and suspend the hanger from a cupboard handle (or some other convenient hook over the counter or table) so that just the noses of the sharks are in the ocean up to the notch. Record the time that the sharks took their dive _____.

6 Leave the sharks' noses in the ocean until one of the sharks is completely soaked. Remove the sharks and record the time here: _____. Lay the sharks on a paper-towel-covered surface and let them dry.

9 Try making sharks out of other materials to see how absorbent they are. (Be sure to check with your adult partner before cutting out any new sharks!) Experiment with different kinds of cloth, blotting paper, cotton batting, and foam sheeting. Think of the uses of each of the materials. Are they mainly for soaking up liquids, or do they have other uses?

SHARKS!

LET'S SEE HOW WELL DIFFERENT MATERIALS SOAK UP WATER! WHICH MATERIAL DO YOU EXPECT TO WORK BEST?

3 Tape the sharks' tails to the bottom of the hanger so that the sharks' tails are evenly spaced across. The sharks' notches should be even with each other.

4 Fill the baking pan half full of water and add four drops of blue food coloring. Stir to make a blue "ocean" in the pan. Put the ocean on a table or counter that has been covered with paper towels.

7 Measure the distance from each shark's notch to the blue line left by the ocean and record those distances in the chart. Also, figure out the amount of time it took for the most absorbent shark to become soaked and record it here: _____ min. (You'll need this number for the next activity.)

8 Look at the distances you recorded for each shark in the chart. Which shark was the first one soaked? If you spilled a glass of milk on the table, which material would get the milk up most quickly? Which materials would you NOT want to use to clean up the spill?

SHARK CHART				
	Sweat sock	Paper towel	Paper bag	Typing paper
Distance ocean traveled (in cm)				

131

WHAT'S UP WITH CAPILLARITY

Did you ever wonder how water can travel up a paper towel when just a corner of the towel is dipped in the water? Get a paper towel and take a close look at it. (Use a magnifying glass, if you have one.) Do you see how uneven and rough the paper appears? This is because it is made of hundreds of tiny threads (called fibers) woven together. These fibers are so small and close together that water molecules can travel between them up the towel.

This "water traveling" (or CAPILLARITY) happens because the molecules of water closest to the paper fibers hold more to the fibers than to each other. This causes the water to move up between the fibers. You can see this "climbing" action of water by doing a simple activity. You will need a glass of water and a wooden spoon. Dip the rounded handle of the wooden spoon into the water. Bend down so that the surface of the water is on your eye level. Do you notice that the water appears to be "climbing" up the sides of the spoon's handle? This is because the water molecules close to the handle hold more to the wood of the handle than to the other water molecules around them.

Water not only travels by capillarity between fibers and up the sides of wooden spoon handles; water can also move up narrow tubes in the same way. You will be able to see this movement when you do the activity called "The Celery Climb." One of the things you should look for when you have all your data from the activity is how fast the water climbs the celery. Does this change as time goes by? In what way?

The tiny tubes that run the length of celery stalks are very similar to the small tubes that can be found in most other green plants. The job of these tubes is to carry water from the plant's roots to its leaves. The plant then uses this water to make its own food. You can see how this process works in a plant other than celery by buying a white carnation, cutting two centimeters off the bottom of its stem, and placing the flower stem-side down in a glass of colored water. Watch what happens to the white petals of the carnation after it has been in the colored water for several hours. Look at the cut part of the flower stem with a magnifying glass. Can you see the ends of the tubes that carried the colored water to the petals? Here's a challenge for you: How could you use capillary action to make a carnation with petals of two different colors?

You were able to compare capillarity in several different types of materials when you did the activity called "Soak Those Sharks!" Later in this issue, you can see how capillary action can separate a mixture of soil and water by doing the "Soggy Socks" experiment.

Don't forget to make a visit to Capillarity Park to see how many examples of capillary action you can find.

ILLUSTRATION BY TINA MION

THE RETURN OF THE SHARKS!!

You will need

your measurements from "Soak Those Sharks!"
pencil
metric ruler

You will be taking the information from your "Shark Chart" to make a bar graph. You will then use your bar graph as you think about some of the materials that you tested.

Here is a sample of how to set up your bar graph.

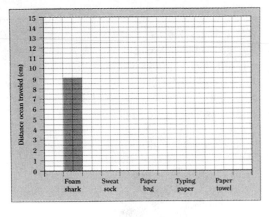

This bar graph shows that when a sample foam shark was placed in the ocean for the same amount of time as your sharks, it had a blue water line that ended up 9 cm from the notch. The actual shark looked like the one pictured at left when it was taken out of the ocean.

Take the distances that the ocean traveled on your four sharks and make a bar graph of the information on the grid below.
Use two blocks for each bar, and allow a space of two empty blocks between each bar.

Which shark has the tallest bar? Was this shark able to soak up the most or the least blue water during the time the sharks were in the ocean? What can you say about the size of the bars compared to how quickly the ocean traveled up each shark?

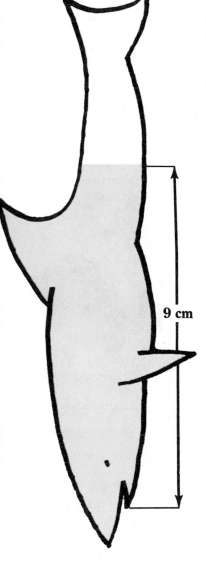

9 cm

How does the sample foam shark compare to your sharks? Does foam soak up water more or less quickly than typing paper? More or less quickly than a sweat sock?

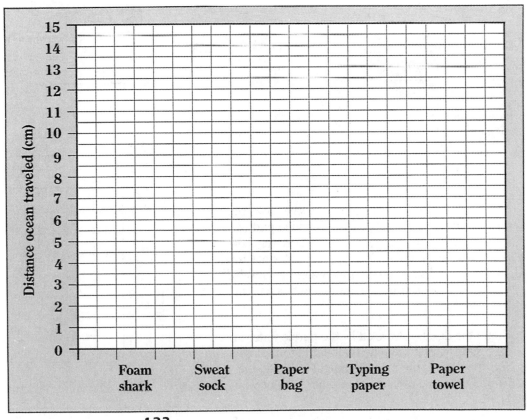

CELERY CLIMB

You will need
- 4 same-size stalks of fresh celery with leaves (use the pale-green inside stalks)
- kitchen knife • crayon or pencil • metric ruler
- 4 clear 8-oz plastic cups half-full of purple water (Use 10 drops of red food color and 10 drops of blue food color for each half cup of water)
- paper towels • swivel-type vegetable peeler

1 Lay the 4 pieces of celery in a row on the table or counter so that the place where the stalks and the leaves meet matches up. Have your adult partner cut the ends of the celery so that the stalks are all 10 cm in length.

2 Put the 4 stalks in the cups of purple water (1 stalk/cup) and record the time that you put them in: _____

3 Label 4 paper towels in the following way: "2 hours," "4 hours," "6 hours," and "8 hours."

4 Every 2 hours from the time that you put the celery into the cups, remove one of the stalks and put it onto the correct towel. For example, the stalk that you remove after 2 hours in the purple water will be placed on the "2 hours" towel. The next stalk that you remove 2 hours later will be placed on the "4 hours" towel, and so on.

SAFETY TIP
Be sure to have your adult partner do all the cutting and peeling in this activity!

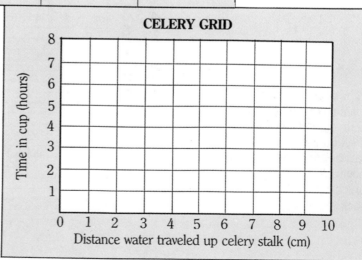

CELERY CHART					
	0 Hours	2 Hours	4 Hours	6 Hours	8 Hours
Distance purple water traveled (in cm)					

5 After each stalk is removed from the water, ask your adult partner to carefully peel the rounded part of the celery stalk with the vegetable peeler. This will allow you to see how far up the stalk the purple water has traveled. Measure the distance the purple water has traveled up the stalk and record this amount (in centimeters) in the chart above.

6 Graph the distance traveled by the purple water in each stalk against the time on the grid to the right. Connect the dots. Is the result a straight line? Did the water travel the same distance each time? Why or why not?

CELERY GRID

Time in cup (hours) vs. Distance water traveled up celery stalk (cm)

SOGGY SOCKS!

LET'S SEE HOW CAPILLARY ACTION CAN FILTER CLEAR WATER FROM MUDDY WATER! BE SURE TO HAVE YOUR ADULT PARTNER SUPERVISE ALL CUTTING FOR THIS ACTIVITY.

1 Fill 2 of the jars ⅓ full of soil.

2 Add water to the soil until the jars are ⅔ full. Stir the mixture well in both jars.

3 Cut off the band at the top of the sock, then cut a strip from the sock that is 3 cm wide and 30 cm long. This strip is your "sock filter." Cut another 3 × 30 cm strip from your paper towel to make your "paper filter."

4 Set up your 4 jars and filters as follows: Put the empty jars side by side on the counter or table. Stack the books next to the empty jars to make a 13 cm high "platform." Set the mud-filled jars on the platform on the edge closest to the empty jars. Stir the muddy water again. Place one end of your filters to the same depth in each muddy water jar, the other ends in the empty jars. Record the time that you start filtering: _____

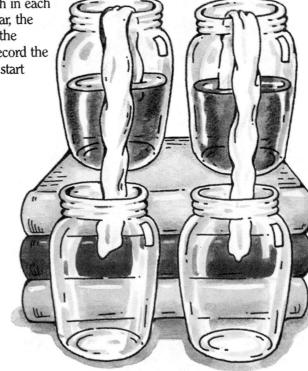

5 Observe the filters during the next few hours and record your observations below.

Sock Filter:

Paper Filter:

Compare the water in the 2 jars that started out empty. After 3 hours, which jar contains more water? What explanation do you have for this?

Is the water just as clear in both jars, or is there a difference? If there is a difference, what could have caused it?

Try making capillarity filters out of other kinds of materials, such as felt, old terry-cloth towels, or blotting paper. Observe the filters in action to discover what it is about the different materials that makes them work as filters.

A Day at Capillarity Park

OBJECTIVE: Find and circle all examples of capillarity that you can find, then explain why you chose those examples.

136

This unit introduces students to the processes of *evaporation* and *condensation*. Students discover that evaporation is the process which changes a liquid to a gas and that different liquids may evaporate at different rates. Students will also explore the process of condensation which changes a gas to a liquid. Students should see that evaporation and condensation are opposite or reverse processes.

"Water, Water Everywhere, But Not a Drop to Drink"

In *"Water, Water Everywhere, But Not a Drop to Drink"*, evaporation and condensation are both at work. At the end of this activity, the water in the cup does not taste salty because only water molecules evaporated from the salty water, leaving the salt behind. These water molecules condensed on the plastic wrap and fell into the cup as pure water. This process of purifying liquids is known as *distillation*. Note: It is possible for mold to grow in water if left for a long period of time (several days), so have a student taste a drop from the cup in the first few hours after putting the water outside.

Lose Some Weight—Evaporate!

Lose Some Weight—Evaporate! shows that alcohol evaporates more quickly than water. Since the attraction between one alcohol molecule and another is not as strong as the attraction between one water molecule and another, alcohol molecules break away from each other more easily and evaporate more quickly.

Dew Drop Inn

In *Dew Drop Inn* students can observe evaporation and condensation on a small scale and relate these observations to effects of evaporation and condensation they have seen on a larger scale at home, in the car, or at school.

Frosty the Snow Can

Frosty the Snow Can demonstrates that under the right conditions, frost can form directly from water vapor in the air.

Earth Day

Earth Day shows the connection between evaporation and condensation and the environment and encourages students to become environmentally aware. After reading the article, you could encourage students to think of ways they can help clean and protect the environment.

Evaporation—A Paint Sensation!

Evaporation—A Paint Sensation! uses different paints to reinforce the idea that different liquids may have different rates of evaporation and therefore different times required to dry.

RELEVANT NATIONAL SCIENCE EDUCATION STANDARDS

The activities in this unit can be used to support the teaching of the following standards:

✔ **Science as Inquiry**
   Abilities necessary to do scientific inquiry

✔ **Physical Science**
   Properties and changes of properties in matter

✔ **Earth and Space Science**
   Structure of the Earth system

"WATER, WATER EVERYWHERE, BUT NOT

Imagine you are shipwrecked on a desert island in the middle of the ocean. You have food and some supplies from your ship but not a single drop of drinking water. You have to figure out some way to make the salt water from the ocean safe to drink! What can you do? (You'd better think *quickly*)!

You will need

large bowl
heavy glass cup (shorter than the bowl is deep)
teaspoon
clear plastic food wrap
clear cellophane tape
penny
blue food coloring
newspaper or paper towels
salt

1 Put tap water in a bowl to a depth of about 5 cm (approx 2 in.) Add ten drops of blue food coloring and 2 or 3 teaspoons of salt. Mix well until the salt is dissolved. This is your ocean. (**Note:** Ocean water is not actually blue, but appears blue due to the reflection of light.)

2 Stand the heavy glass cup in the center of the bowl so it is surrounded by the blue saltwater.

3 Put a *loose* covering of plastic food wrap over the top of the bowl. Tape the plastic wrap to the sides of the bowl so that no air can get in or out. *Make sure the plastic wrap is not pulled tightly across the top of the bowl.*

* All activities in *WonderScience* have been reviewed for safety by Dr. Jack Breazeale, Francis Marion College, Florence, SC; Dr. Jay Young, Chemical Health and Safety Consultant, Silver Spring, MD; and and Dr. Patricia Redden, Saint Peter's College, Jersey City, NJ.

138

A DROP TO DRINK" *

4 Tape a penny to the outside of the plastic wrap directly over the center of the glass. Make sure that the weight of the penny makes the plastic wrap slant way down toward the center of the glass.

5 Put the bowl on a flat surface outside, where it will get a lot of sunshine.

Note: When moving the bowl, be sure that none of the blue saltwater splashes into the glass. Check the bowl every hour for four hours. Do not leave the bowl outside for more than four hours, because mold may eventually grow in the water.

6 Do you see any droplets of water forming on the bottom of the plastic wrap? How do you think this water got there?

7 Leave the bowl in the sunny spot until it has been exposed for four hours. At the end of four hours, take off the plastic wrap and lift the glass out of the salty blue water.

8 What color is the water in the glass? What do you think happened to the blue food coloring? Make sure your hands are clean, and put your finger in the glass to get a drop or two of water on the tip of your finger. Taste the water. Is it still salty? **CONGRATULATIONS!** You have found a way to make drinking water from ocean water: **YOU'RE SAVED!**

EVAPORATION AND CONDENSATION— THE DYNAMIC DUO!

Illustration by Tina Mion

Have you ever looked into a glass of water and wondered what water really is? You can't tell simply by looking, but the water in the glass, which is a *liquid*, is actually made of billions of tiny particles called *molecules*. The molecules which make up water are very close to one another and are always jiggling around and bumping into each other. A container of water is sort of like a shoe box full of ping-pong balls being shaken back and forth very quickly. The ping-pong balls, like the molecules of a *liquid*, touch and hit each other all the time but can still move around from place to place.

Not every molecule of a *liquid* stays so close to its neighbor molecules. Some molecules are able to escape from the *liquid* and become a *gas!* One way to help molecules break away from a *liquid,* to become a *gas*, is to heat the *liquid*. Letting water stand in a sunny spot, in a warm room, or even in your hand will heat the water and make its molecules move faster. Some molecules near the surface will gain enough speed to break away from the other molecules and to go up into the air as a *gas*. This process is called *evaporation*.

When the molecules of a *liquid evaporate*, to become a *gas*, they spread out and move around much faster than when they were part of the *liquid*. In fact, if the ping-pong balls in the shoe box are like the molecules of a *liquid*, then the molecules of a *gas* are like the same number of ping-pong balls spread out and flying in all directions in a large room!

We know that *evaporation* happens when the molecules of a *liquid* become a *gas*, but the opposite can also happen: the molecules of a *gas* can form a *liquid!* One way a *gas* can become a *liquid* is if the *gas* is cooled. Cooling a *gas* slows down its molecules. If the molecules slow down enough and get close enough together, like the ping-pong balls in the shoe box, they will form a *liquid*. This change from a *gas* to a *liquid* is called *condensation*.

CONDENSATION is the opposite of *EVAPORATION*.

In "Water Water Everywhere, But Not a Drop to Drink," you use both *EVAPORATION and CONDENSATION* to purify water. Energy from the sun makes the water molecules in the bowl move faster. Some of these water molecules have enough speed to break away from the others and to go up into the air inside the bowl as a *gas*. This is *evaporation*. When these fast-moving water molecules in the air bump into each other and into the bottom of the plastic wrap, some of them begin to slow down. As they slow down, some get so close together that they begin to form tiny drops of water again. This is *condensation*. This process is similar to what happens when *clouds* and *rain* form. Energy from the sun causes water molecules from oceans, lakes, rivers and streams to *evaporate*. Up in the atmosphere, where temperatures are cooler, the water molecules slow down, get closer together and *condense* into tiny drops of *liquid* water forming *clouds*. As more water molecules condense, the drops of water get bigger and bigger until they fall to the earth as *rain*.

Sometimes, when enough water molecules are in the air and the temperature near the ground is cool enough, the water molecules *condense* to form *dew*. If the temperature drops below the freezing point (0° C or 32° F), the water in the air can change directly to ice, forming *frost*.

LOSE SOME WEIGHT—EVAPORATE!

You will need

2 large plastic cups (32 oz)
2 disposable paper or plastic cups (8 oz)
1 straight pin
1 plastic drinking straw
1 paper towel
rubbing alcohol
water
metric ruler
blunt-end scissors
tablespoon
safety goggles, one per person

1 Put on your safety goggles. Measure the length of the straw and ask your adult partner to push the pin through the exact center of the straw.

2 Stand the two large cups near each other on the table and rest the pin on the rims of the two cups to make a balance. If the straw is not well-balanced, ask your adult partner to push the pin through the straw again in a slightly different spot.

3 Pour about 2 tablespoons of water into one of the smaller cups. Ask your adult partner to pour about 2 tablespoons of rubbing alcohol in the other smaller cup. **Be sure to replace the cap on the alcohol bottle.**

4 Cut 2 strips of paper towel measuring 2.5 cm (approx. 1 in) wide and 15 cm (approx. 6 in) long.

5 Have your adult partner dip one strip in the cup of alcohol while you dip the other strip in the cup of water. Make sure both strips get completely wet.

6 Take your strip out of the water and have your adult partner take the strip out of the alcohol. Touch the strips to the inside of the cups so that some of the excess liquid drips off.

7 Hang your water strip on one end of the straw while your adult partner hangs the alcohol strip on the other end. Move the strips on the straw until the straw is balanced again.

8 Watch the straw as the water and the alcohol evaporate. Which side seems to be losing weight the fastest? What is causing one side to lose weight faster than the other? Does water or alcohol evaporate faster? How can you tell?

DEW DR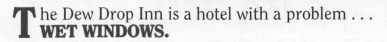P INN

The Dew Drop Inn is a hotel with a problem . . . **WET WINDOWS.**

In the **winter** it is colder outside the hotel than inside, and water forms on the **inside** of the windows.

In the **summer** it is colder inside the hotel than outside, and water forms on the **outside** of the windows. Can you explain why? The following experiment may help you figure it out.

Illustration by Neal Clodfelter

You will need
clear glass jar with lid
ice
water

1 Ask your adult partner to put hot tap water in the jar until it is half full. Put the lid on the jar and place it on a table.

2 Watch the sides of the jar. Is water forming on the **inside** of the jar or on the **outside?** From what you learned about **evaporation** and **condensation** on page 4, can you explain why? Is this jar like the Dew Drop Inn windows in the summer or winter?

3 Pour the water out of the jar and dry the inside and outside of the jar. Now fill the jar half way with cold tap water and add a few ice cubes to make the water really cold. Put the lid on the jar and place the jar on a table. If you do not see any water drops forming, try the experiment in the bathroom or kitchen, where the air may have more water molecules in it.

4 This time are the water drops forming on the **inside** or **outside** of the jar? Why? Is this jar like the Dew Drop Inn windows in the summer or winter?

FROSTY THE SNOW CAN

❄ ❄

You will need

clean, empty metal food can
(label removed)
crushed ice or small ice cubes
salt
teaspoon
dish towel
adhesive tape

In "Dew Drop Inn," you saw that water molecules as a gas in the air will change into liquid water on the outside of a container if the container is cold enough. You have learned that this process of changing from a gas to a liquid is called **condensation.** Let's see what happens if the container is *REALLY COLD!*

CAUTION: The open end of a metal can may have sharp and jagged edges. If you see any jagged edges, have your adult partner use the back of a spoon to press them down against the inside of the can. Whether you see sharp edges or not, cover the rim with a double layer of adhesive tape.

1 Dry the outside of the can with the dish towel.

2 Place three heaping teaspoons of salt in the can. Fill the can about half way with crushed ice. Add three more teaspoons of salt. Fill the can almost to the top with ice and add another three teaspoons of salt. (Adding salt to the ice keeps the temperature of the melting ice lower than normal, making the surroundings much colder than ice alone.)

3 Hold the can near the top and mix the ice-salt mixture with a spoon. Keep stirring until you see a thin layer of frost form on the side of the can.

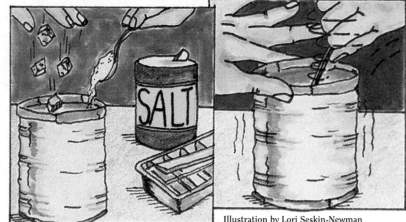

Illustration by Lori Seskin-Newman

4 Did you notice any water form on the outside of the can? Do you think the water molecules in the air could have changed directly to ice? This is the same process that causes *frost* to form on cold mornings.

EARTH DAY

Life on earth would be impossible without water. Plants, animals, and other forms of life need a constant supply of water to survive. Evaporation and condensation form the clouds and rain which provide the water for these living things. But in some places, pollution in the air makes rain not as healthy for plants and animals as it should be. On Earth Day, people make a special effort to solve this problem and some of our Earth's other pollution and environmental troubles.

The first Earth Day was on April 22, 1970. Earth Day was started by people who were very worried about our environment. They believed that cars, people, and certain industries were polluting our land, air, and water so much that the environment was becoming unhealthy for plants, people, other animals, and all living things.

Today, people are still very concerned about the environment. You can help save and protect the environment by asking your teacher or librarian about Earth Day activities in your school or community.

GET INVOLVED—
YOU CAN MAKE A DIFFERENCE!

Here are some ways you can help protect the environment:

- Help in cleaning up litter around streams, lakes, and fields

- Plant trees in your community (trees help control the amount of carbon dioxide and oxygen in the air and help keep soil from washing away).

- Recycle paper, glass, aluminum, plastic, and other recyclable material.

- Buy things that are made from recycled material.

- Buy products with a minimal amount of packaging.

- Save water by not watering your lawn too much and by not leaving the water running while you brush your teeth or wash the dishes.

- Teach your friends, family, and neighbors about Earth Day and the importance of helping the environment.

EVAPORATION— A PAINT SENSATION!

We use the process of evaporation every time we use paint. Paint is made by adding colored powder to water, oil, or certain other liquids. In ancient times, people mixed ground flowers, leaves, and clay with water to make different colored paints. In colonial America, the colonists added things like coffee grounds and egg yolks to water to make paint.

When paint is exposed to air, the liquid in the paint evaporates, leaving a solid finish. Some paints dry more quickly than others.

Let's make our own samples of paint and compare how long it takes them to dry.

You will need
newspaper
white notebook or typing paper
pencil
rubbing alcohol
water
6 paper cups
holiday egg dye tablets
teaspoon
6 cotton swabs
safety goggles, one per person

1 Put on your safety goggles. Spread newspaper over your work surface. Place one of your dye tablets in the center of a piece of notebook paper. Ask your adult partner to carefully press the side of a can down onto the tablet to crush it into a powder. Pour the dye powder into one of your cups.

2 Crush each of your dye tablets and put the dye powder from each tablet into a separate cup.

3 Divide your cups into two groups. In one group, add 2 teaspoons of *water* and stir. Mark these cups **"W"**. In the other group, have your adult partner add 2 teaspoons of *alcohol* and stir. Mark these cups **"A"**. Be sure to replace the cap on the alcohol bottle.

4 Fold your notebook or typing paper in half. Trace the outline of the *WonderScience* cat on each half of your paper.

5 Use cotton swabs and your *water*-base paints to color in one of your *WonderScience* cats. Quickly use the other cotton swabs to paint your other *WonderScience* cat with the *alcohol*-base paint.

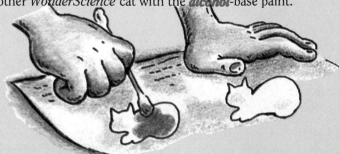

6 Think about what you observed in "Lose Some Weight—EVAPORATE!" and predict whether the alcohol paint or the water paint will dry first. Observe your *WonderScience* cats to see if you are correct.

DISPOSE OF NEWSPAPERS THAT MAY HAVE ALCOHOL ON THEM IN A METAL TRASH CAN

TRY THIS: Did you know that you can even *feel* one liquid evaporate faster than another? Ask your adult partner to wet one clean cotton swab with water and one with rubbing alcohol. Have your adult partner wipe the water on the index finger of your right hand and the alcohol on the index finger of your left hand. Which one feels colder? Which one do you think is evaporating faster? Why do you think evaporation makes your finger feel cold? Be sure to wash your hands when you're finished.

WONDERSCIENCE

This unit focuses on the three main food nutrients: proteins, fats, and carbohydrates and introduces students to a revised food labeling system.

Get the Facts on Fats!

In *Get the Facts on Fats!* students observe some of the major similarities and differences between animal fat and vegetable fat. Animal fats tend to be *saturated* and vegetable fats tend to be *unsaturated*. The saturation of a fat has to do with the chemical structure of the fat. The difference in chemical structure causes saturated fats generally to be more solid at room temperature and unsaturated fats generally to be more liquid. Along with their differences, animal and vegetable fats have several similarities such as being less dense than water and not mixing well with water. Fats are useful in the body for storing energy, as a component of cell membranes, and as insulation for the body.

Starch Search!

In *Starch Search!* students perform a simple iodine test for the presence of starch. Starch is one of several different types of carbohydrates. Another major carbohydrate is sugar in the form of *fructose* (fruit sugar), *maltose* (milk sugar), and *sucrose* (table sugar). Starch is composed of many molecules of the sugar *glucose* connected to one another in a particular way. The activity shows that in addition to detecting the presence of starch, the iodine test can also be used to detect relative concentrations of starch. As the amount of water in the cracker/water samples increases, the concentration of starch decreases. When each sample is tested with iodine, the color change caused by the iodine should be less and less as the concentration of starch decreases.

Proteins: Your Pro Team!

In *Proteins: Your Pro Team!* students investigate the two main functions of proteins. For protein's structural function, gelatin is used to simulate cartilage. Gelatin contains the protein *collagen* and is actually made from either pork or beef cartilage. For protein's enzyme function,

meat tenderizer is used. There is a protein in meat tenderizer that comes from the fruit of the papaya plant. This protein is able to *denature* or break down the collagen in the gelatin. You should have noticed that your gelatin ball with the tenderizer was softer than the ball made with only gelatin and water. Fresh pineapple (not cooked or canned) also contains an enzyme that denatures the protein in gelatin. Try some fresh pineapple juice instead of meat tenderizer and see how it works.

Fact or Fable? Read the Label!

Fact or Fable? Read the Label! introduces students to some of the information that can be gleaned from the new food label. This activity may require extra assistance since the relationship between the words and numbers on the label will not be readily apparent to most students.

RELEVANT NATIONAL SCIENCE EDUCATION STANDARDS

The activities in this unit can be used to support the teaching of the following standards:

✔ Science as inquiry
  Abilities necessary to do scientific inquiry

✔ Physical Science
  Properties and changes of properties in matter transfer of energy

✔ Life Science
  Structure and function in living systems

✔ Science in Personal and Social Perspectives
  Personal health

Get the Facts

Fats *carbohydrates*, and **proteins** are the three main nutrients in the food we eat. Vitamins and minerals are also important, but this *WonderScience* will focus on fats, carbohydrates, and proteins. Fats have a bad reputation because eating too much fat can be harmful to the body. The fats people eat can come from either plants or animals. Fats from plants and animals are similar in some ways but different in others. In the activity below, you can do some simple experiments to learn some fat facts!

You will need

tablespoon of butter	plastic straw
tablespoon of vegetable oil	3 zip-closing
brown paper bag	plastic bags
wax paper	2 clear plastic cups
blunt-end scissors	cotton swabs
water	bowl
masking tape	ballpoint pen

1 Cover your work surface with newspaper. Use your masking tape and pen to label three plastic bags **water**, **butter**, and **oil**. Ask your adult partner to pour hot tap water into a bowl until it is about 1/2 full. Place about 1–2 tablespoons of butter, vegetable oil, and water in 3 separate zip-closing plastic bags.

2 Make sure all three bags are sealed. Place the bags in the bowl of water and leave them there until the butter becomes liquid.

3 Place a piece of a brown paper bag flat on your work surface. Use your pencil to divide the paper into three sections. Label the sections **water**, **butter**, and **oil**.

4 Dip a separate cotton swab into the liquid in each bag and place the wet end of the swab on its labeled area on the paper. Reseal the bags and put them back into the water. Go on to the next step; we'll come back to these cotton swabs later.

on Fats!

5 Tape a piece of wax paper flat on your newspaper. Use separate straws to place a drop of water, a drop of oil, and a drop of butter on the wax paper. Observe each drop for similarities and differences. Try dragging each drop along the paper with the straws. What did you observe?

6 Again on your wax paper, use a straw to try mixing a few drops of oil with a few drops of water. Try the same thing with butter and water. How well did they mix? Now try mixing some oil and butter. Did they mix any better?

7 Pour cold tap water into a bowl until it is about 1/4 filled. Pour about 1/2 the butter and about 1/2 the oil from their bags into separate small plastic cups. Place the cups in the water and hold them there so they do not spill. What do you notice happening to either the butter or the oil?

8 Let's look back at your brown paper bag. Do you see any similarities or differences in the way the liquids look on the brown paper? Do the butter and oil marks look similar, or does either one look like the water?

9 Fill 2 paper or plastic cups about 2/3 full of tap water. Pour the rest of the oil into one cup and the rest of the butter into the other cup. What did you observe about each liquid? How are they similar or different?

★ All activities in *WonderScience* have been reviewed for safety by Dr. Jack Breazeale, Francis Marion University, Florence, SC and Dr. Jay Young, Chemical Health and Safety Consultant, Silver Spring, MD.

FOOD:
What's in it for You?

Like everything else around you, food is made up of chemicals. These chemicals have many different jobs in the body. The three main functions of most of the chemicals in food are (1) to provide the body with energy, (2) to supply raw material for the body's growth and development, and (3) to be used in all the chemical reactions needed to keep our bodies alive and healthy.

There are many different types of chemicals that make up food. But most of the foods we eat have different combinations of the three main food chemicals, **fats**, **carbohydrates**, and **proteins**

The fats we eat come either animals or plants. In the activity *Get the Facts on Fats* the fats you used were butter and vegetable oil. Butter is made from the milk of a cow, so butter is an animal fat. Vegetable oil is made from corn, peanuts, or other plants. In general, the chemicals that make up fats from animals and plants have many similarities but certain important differences. This is why the butter and oil you experimented with were similar in certain ways but different in others. Generally, eating animal fat is considered more unhealthy than eating fats from plants. **There are exceptions**—Fish are animals but fish oil is not considered unhealthy; coconut and palm oil are from plants but are thought to be less healthy than corn and some other vegetable oils.

Carbohydrates are another important nutrient. There are several kinds of carbohydrates. Different types of **sugars** such as table sugar and the sugar in fruit are carbohydrates. Another carbohydrate is **starch**, which is found in potatoes, rice, pasta, corn, bread, beans, and other vegetables. In *Starch Search*, you can do a chemical test to identify starch in foods. Another type of carbohydrate we eat is the material that makes up leaves and stems of plants. This material is called **cellulose**. Cellulose does not give us nutrients like fats, protein, and other carbohydrates, but it has been shown to be important in the health of the digestive system.

Proteins have two major functions in the body. First, proteins make up a large portion of most of your body parts. Skin, muscle, organs, bones, and even blood have large amounts of protein that help make up their structure. In the protein activity *Proteins*, you will be working with the protein in gelatin. This protein is called **collagen**. You also have collagenic you! It's part of your cartilage, tendons, and bones. Aside from helping to make up these body structures, proteins have another major function. Certain proteins help the body's chemical reactions to take place. These proteins are called **enzymes**. Most of the chemical reactions you need for survival would not take place fast enough if it weren't for enzymes. In the activity *Proteins*, you will experiment with an enzyme in meat tenderizer to see whether it has an effect on the collagen in gelatin.

Fact or Fable? you will help you to understand the new food label. Reading the new label on foods you eat should help you choose the right combination of fats, carbohydrates, proteins, and other nutrients for a healthy diet. Bon appetit!

Starch Search!

You will need

crackers (light-colored)

rice

spaghetti

5 paper or plastic cups

masking tape

tincture of iodine

tablespoon

straws

sheet of white paper

ballpoint pen

wax paper

Another major nutrient in the food we eat is carbohydrates. One of the most popular carbohydrates throughout the world is starch. Starch is the major ingredient in bread, potatoes, rice, and pasta. In the activity below, you can use a simple test to see if a food contains starch.

CAUTION:
- **Be very careful when using tincture of iodine.**
- **Read and follow all directions on the label.**
- **When you have finished the activity, rinse out all cups and the straw and throw them away.**
- **Throw away all food items and wash your hands.**

1 Cover your work surface with newspaper. On your sheet of white paper, label three areas as follows: **cracker**, **rice**, and **pasta**. Place a small amount of each food on its area of the paper.

2 Place 1 drop of iodine on each type of food. What do you observe? A dark color shows you that the iodine has reacted with starch in the food. Do all these foods seem to contain starch?

cracker	rice	pasta

The iodine test can tell us whether a food contains starch. Let's see whether another kind of iodine test can tell us if one food sample has more or less starch than another.

3 Use your masking tape and pen to label the cups **1**, **2**, **3**, and **4**. Break a cracker into 4 equal-size pieces. Place one piece in each of your four labeled cups. Add 1 tablespoon of water to cup 1, 2 tablespoons of water to cup 2, 3 tablespoons of water to cup 3, and 4 tablespoons of water to cup 4.

4 Use separate straws to stir and mix your crackers with the water in each cup until the cracker has completely fallen apart and is well mixed with the water.

5 Use a straw to take a few drops from the top of each water/cracker solution. Place 3 drops of each solution on a piece of wax paper as shown. Rinse the straw with water between uses.

6 Ask your adult partner to add 1 drop of iodine to the drops of each solution on the wax paper. Did the color change in any of the solutions? Did all the colors look the same? What explains the difference in color if you saw any?

Proteins:

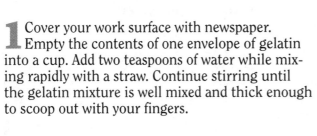

You will need

unflavored gelatin

water

paper or plastic cup

teaspoon

straw

newspaper

As you read earlier, proteins can be separated according to two major purposes. Some proteins help make up important structures in the body such as cartilage and tendons. The other type helps the body's chemical reactions take place. In the following activity, you can experiment with the protein that makes up cartilage and tendons.

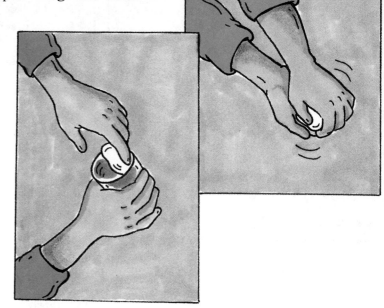

1 Cover your work surface with newspaper. Empty the contents of one envelope of gelatin into a cup. Add two teaspoons of water while mixing rapidly with a straw. Continue stirring until the gelatin mixture is well mixed and thick enough to scoop out with your fingers.

2 Scoop out the gelatin mixture and knead it back and forth between your hands. (Put a little water on your hands so the gelatin will not stick to your hands too much.) Form the gelatin into a ball. Allow the gelatin ball to sit for about 2–3 minutes.

3 Gently squeeze the ball of gelatin. What does it feel like? When you press it, does it go back to its original shape?

Gelatin is made from a protein called *collagen* Collagen is the main protein that makes up your body's cartilage and tendons. Let's see whether there are any similarities between the gelatin you made and your own cartilage and tendons!

4 The outside of your ear is mostly cartilage. Gently bend your ear and let it go. Are there any similarities between your ear and the gelatin ball? Gently push the tip of your nose to the side and let go. Do you think there is cartilage in your nose?

5 How about tendons? Sit in a chair with your feet flat on the floor. Bend down and feel the thick cord behind your ankle. This is your Achilles tendon. Gently press it with your fingers. How does it compare with your gelatin?

Your Pro Team!

Some proteins help your body's chemical reactions take place by helping to form or break apart molecules in the body. Proteins that have this special function are called **enzymes**. In the activity below, you can test the enzyme in meat tenderizer to see whether it will affect the proteins in gelatin.

You will need

unflavored gelatin (2 packets)

meat tenderizer

water

3 paper or plastic cups

teaspoon

sheet of paper

masking tape

ballpoint pen

1 Use your pen and masking tape to label 2 cups **water** and **tenderizer**. Mark two areas on your paper in the same way. Empty one packet of gelatin into each cup.

2 Add 2 teaspoons of water to the gelatin in the **water** cup and stir rapidly. Continue stirring until the gelatin mixture is well mixed and thick enough to pick up.

3 Scoop out the gelatin mixture and knead it back and forth between your hands. (Put a little water on your hands so the gelatin will not stick to you too much.) Form the gelatin into a ball. Allow the ball to sit for 2–3 minutes.

4 Repeat steps 2 and 3, but add the water and 1/4 teaspoon of meat tenderizer to the gelatin in your cup labeled **tenderizer**.

5 After the balls have sat for a few minutes, gently squeeze each one. Do you notice any difference between them? What do you think the tenderizer has done to the proteins in the gelatin? How do you think tenderizer makes meat tender?

FACT OR FABLE?
READ THE LABEL!

Reading the new food labels on cans, boxes, bags, and other containers of food can give you a lot of information about how much fat, carbohydrate, and protein you are eating. The office of the United States government that controls the information on food labels is the Food and Drug Administration (FDA). Recently, the FDA changed food labels to give people a better idea of what is in the food they eat and how much of that food they should be eating. The information on the label is based on an average adult diet.

The new labels can be used in different ways, but we will look only at *Total Fat*, *Total Carbohydrate*, and *Protein*.

Fat

Next to Total Fat it says 6g. This means that if you could weigh only the fat in one average-size serving of this food, it would weigh 6 grams. The number across from 6g and under % Daily Value says 10%. This means that 6 grams of fat is about 10% of the amount of fat the government says is OK to have in your diet each day. Since 10% is the same as 10/100 or 1/10, how would you figure out the total grams of fat that the government says is OK to eat each day? How many grams of fat would this be?

Carbohydrate

Let's look at Total Carbohydrate. Since the label says 15g, there are 15 grams of carbohydrate in an average serving of this food. But the number across from 15g says 5%. This means that 15 grams is only 5% of the amount of carbohydrates the government says you should have in your diet each day. Since 5% is the same as 5/100 or 1/20, how would you figure out the total grams of carbohydrate the government says is OK to eat each day? How many grams of carbohydrate would this be? Does this mean you should have more carbohydrate or more fat in your daily diet?

Protein

The label says 5g. This of course means that there are 5 grams of protein in the average serving of this food. But there is no number in the percent column. This is because the FDA decided that most foods should not be required to state percent daily values for protein. The reason is that the vast majority of Americans get an adequate, if not extra, amount of protein in their daily diet anyway, so the information on the label would not be that useful. The second reason is that the percent daily value for protein is more difficult and costly to calculate than the percentages for fat and carbohydrate. The FDA felt that since we eat enough protein anyway, it is not worth the added cost of making food producers calculate percent daily values for protein. Percent daily values for protein do need to be listed for food intended for children under 4 years of age, and for foods that make a claim about their protein content.

Check the labels on the containers of food you have at home. Look at the percentages of fat and carbohydrate and the grams of protein. Which foods could you eat throughout the day that would give you 100% of the carbohydrates you need, no more than 100% of the fat you should eat.

Nutrition Facts

Serving Size ½ cup (114g)
Servings Per Container 4

Amount Per Serving

Calories 130 | Calories from Fat 60

	% Daily Value*
Total Fat 6g	**10**%
Saturated Fat 0g	**0**%
Cholesterol 0mg	**0**%
Sodium 300mg	**13**%
Total Carbohydrate 15g	**5**%
Dietary Fiber 3g	**12**%
Sugars 3g	
Protein 5g	

Vitamin A	80%	•	Vitamin C	60%
Calcium	4%	•	Iron	4%

* Percent Daily Values are based on a 2,000 calorie diet. Your daily values may be higher or lower depending on your calorie needs:

		Calories	2,000	2,500
Total Fat	Less than		65g	80g
Sat Fat	Less than		20g	25g
Cholesterol	Less than		300mg	300mg
Sodium	Less than		2,400mg	2,400mg
Total Carbohydrate			300g	375g
Fiber			25g	30g

Calories per gram:
Fat 9 • Carbohydrate 4 • Protein 4

WONDERSCIENCE

This unit introduces students to some of the properties and uses of calcium. Because of its atomic structure, calcium reacts very readily with certain other chemical compounds. That's why calcium is always found in nature bonded to other chemicals as part of chemical compounds. One of the most common compounds containing calcium is calcium carbonate, the principal component of limestone. Calcium carbonate is a molecule made up of one calcium atom, one carbon atom, and three oxygen atoms bonded together in a particular way. The chemical formula for calcium carbonate is written $CaCO_3$. Several of these *WonderScience* activities deal with calcium carbonate. There is an enormous amount of calcium in different compounds on Earth. In fact, calcium is the fifth most abundant element in the Earth's crust.

A Plaster Master or a Plaster Disaster?

In *A Plaster Master or a Plaster Disaster?*, students test some of the properties of another common calcium compound, calcium sulfate ($CaSO_4$). The activity investigates the hardening properties of plaster of Paris, which is made mostly of calcium sulfate. When water is added to plaster of Paris, the water molecules and the calcium sulfate form an intertwined network of crystals that makes the plaster of Paris very hard. The salt water used in part of the activity interferes with the normal crystallization process, resulting in a softer product.

The Fate of Calcium Carbonate!

The Fate of Calcium Carbonate! enables students to test different sources of calcium carbonate with vinegar (a weak acid). Students should observe bubbling when vinegar is added. The carbon dioxide gas produced is evidence that a chemical reaction is taking place between the vinegar and the calcium carbonate. The calcium carbonate samples are also tested with water to show that not just any liquid will cause the reaction.

Calcium, The Game

Calcium, The Game is a board game about calcium. The game encourages learning about calcium and using math skills for scoring.

Hard Water—Bubble Trouble?

In *Hard Water—Bubble Trouble?*, students make large amounts of soap scum. When soapy water is added to water with a little plaster of Paris in it, calcium soap or soap scum will form and drop to the bottom of the solution. Since much of the soap is taken out of solution in the process, the liquid is not expected to bubble when air is blown through it with a straw.

RELEVANT NATIONAL SCIENCE EDUCATION STANDARDS

The activities in this unit can be used to support the teaching of the following standards:

✔ **Science as Inquiry**
   Abilities necessary to do scientific inquiry

✔ **Physical Science**
   Properties and changes of properties in matter

✔ **Life Science**
   Structure and function in living systems

✔ **Science in Personal and Social Perspectives**
   Personal health

A Plaster Master or...

T he calcium in your bones and teeth, and the calcium found in most products, is connected to other chemicals. One of the most common chemicals connected to calcium is called **carbonate**. Together, the calcium and the carbonate make a chemical called **calcium carbonate**. Calcium is also often connected to a chemical called **sulfate**, and together they make a chemical called **calcium sulfate**. Both these calcium chemicals are used to make cement, plaster of paris, and similar building materials that need to start off soft and then harden. In the activity below, you can experiment with the hardening of these chemicals in plaster of paris.

You will need

plastic disposable gloves	salt
paper	warm water
masking tape	ruler
pencil or ball-point pen	clock or watch
newspaper or paper towels	tablespoon
plaster of paris (contains calcium carbonate and calcium sulfate)	teaspoon
	4 5-oz paper or plastic cups
	plastic straws

1 Use your sheet of paper to make a chart like the one below. Cover your work area with newspaper or paper towels. Use your masking tape and pen to label your four cups **salt water**, **salt water plaster**, **fresh water**, and **fresh water plaster**.

2 Add 1 tablespoon of salt to the salt water cup. Add 3 tablespoons of warm water and stir until no more salt will dissolve. Place 3 tablespoons of warm water in the fresh water cup.

3 Use your ruler and tablespoon to measure one level tablespoon of plaster of paris powder into each of your other two empty labeled cups. With your adult partner's help, add 1 teaspoon of salt water to the salt water plaster cup and mix thoroughly with a straw. Now add 1 teaspoon of fresh water to the fresh water plaster cup and mix thoroughly with a new straw.

4 Ask your adult partner to help make your mixtures a little thinner or thicker by adding a little more salt or fresh water or a little plaster of paris powder until your mixtures are like dough that can be molded.

TEST	1	2	3	4
Salt water				
Fresh water				

154

a Plaster Disaster?

5 You and your adult partner should put on your gloves and scrape the plaster of paris out of both cups. With the help of your adult partner make 4 small balls from the salt water plaster and four from the fresh water plaster so that they are done at the same time. Try to make all the balls the same size. Place the balls on the sheet of paper as shown.

6 After all the balls are on the paper, wait 3 minutes and then gently place one index finger on the top of the salt water plaster ball and the other index finger on top of the fresh water plaster ball under Test 1.

7 Push down gently on both plaster balls. Does either ball seem to have hardened at all? Continue to push until the plaster balls squish or break apart. Pick up pieces from each ball and see how they feel. Do you notice a difference between them? Write down your observations on your chart.

8 When you finish recording your observations, wait 3 more minutes and then test the salt water and fresh water plaster balls under Test 2 in the same way. Does one feel harder than the other? How do the Test 2 plaster balls compare to the Test 1 plaster balls? Look closely at the balls when they squish or break apart. Pick up some pieces and feel them. Record your observations about the Test 2 plaster balls.

9 Wait another 3 minutes and test your Test 3 plaster balls and then another 3 minutes and test your Test 4 plaster balls in the same way. What is the main difference between them? What do you think causes them to feel the way they do?

---

* All activities in *WonderScience* have been reviewed for safety by Dr. Jack Breazeale, Francis Marion University, Florence, SC and Dr. Jay Young, Chemical Health and Safety Consultant, Silver Spring, MD.

Calcium
The Hard Facts

Calcium is one of those chemicals that's always grabbing onto other chemicals! As you read on page 2, **calcium carbonate** and **calcium sulfate** are very common in cements and other building material. There is also **calcium phosphate**, an important part of bones and teeth, **calcium chloride**, which is used on icy roads, and many others.

The experiment, *A Plaster Master,* with plaster of paris was mainly about calcium sulfate. The calcium sulfate in plaster of paris is made from a rock called *gypsum*. Gypsum is an interesting material because water molecules are part of its structure! It is not wet when you touch it, but the water molecules (H_2O) are connected to the calcium sulfate in the structure of the rock. Paster of paris is made by heating the gypsum and driving off most of the water from the rock. The rock then becomes softer and can be crushed into plaster of paris powder.

When you added water to the plaster of paris, the water molecules and the calcium sulfate molecules began to connect again and the plaster of paris began to harden and become like gypsum again. You may have thought that the balls of plaster of paris were getting harder as the water was evaporating or leaving the plaster of paris. But actually, it was hardening because the water was staying in and reconnecting to the calcium sulfate! Why do you think the plaster of paris didn't harden as well with salt water?

A little experiment can show you that the water does not have to evaporate for the plaster of paris to become hard. Make a plaster of paris ball with fresh water as you did in the first activity. Now fill a paper or plastic cup about half full of water. Gently place the plaster of paris ball in the cup. Take it out after about an hour. Although the water was not able to evaporate from the plaster of paris ball while it was under water, the ball still should have hardened.

Aside from the calcium in plaster and other building materials, calcium is very important in your diet. The calcium you take in as food gets used mostly as material for bones and teeth. In fact, about 99% of the calcium in your body is in your bones. The other 1% is carried around in your bloodstream to do important jobs for the body. The calcium in your blood helps your nerves and muscles work and helps your blood clot when you get a cut. Calcium also helps many of the body's other important chemical reactions to take place. Your body uses the calcium in your diet for all these important functions. Your body also has a way of taking calcium from your bones in tiny amounts when it is not getting enough calcium from your diet. It can also put calcium back in your bones when the calcium in your diet gets back up to where it should be.

Learn more about calcium as you play the calcium board game "Calcium!"

THE FATE OF CALCIUM CARBONATE!

You will need

sheet of paper	water
pencil	vinegar
eggshell	2 straws or droppers
calcium tablet (oyster shell)	egg
white chalk	chicken bone
metal tablespoon	2 jars with lids
2 small paper or plastic cups	aluminum foil

Calcium carbonate is in eggshells, seashells, and chalk. In the activity below, you can make a chemical reaction that causes calcium and carbonate to come apart and produce the gas *carbon dioxide*! You can also see what an egg or bone is like when its calcium is removed!

1 Cover your work surface with newspaper or paper towels. Place your eggshell, 1/4 piece of chalk, and calcium tablet on your work surface.

2 Use the back of a tablespoon to crush each of your samples into small pieces. Make a chart like the one shown. Place half of each sample in the row marked **water** and half of each sample in the row marked **vinegar**.

3 Place a few drops of water on the samples in the water area and observe them very closely. What did you see? Now place a few drops of vinegar on the samples in the vinegar area. What did you observe?

If this chemical reaction causes the calcium and the carbonate to come apart, what do you think would happen to an egg if it were left in vinegar for a few days? How about a bone, which has a lot of calcium phosphate. Let's try it and find out!

Place an egg and a chicken bone in separate jars. Add enough vinegar to cover them completely. Cover the opening of each jar with aluminum foil. Observe the egg and bone over the next three days. What do you notice? At the end of three days, take each one out of its jar. How are they different from when you put them in? What do you think caused them to look and feel the way they do?

	Eggshell	Calcium tablet	Chalk
Water			
Vinegar			

Object of the game:
To get as many points as possible.

Number of players:
2–4 players.

Materials needed:
12 markers, one for each calcium object. You can use pennies.
One die
Playing pieces
Make playing pieces and a die from plaster of paris or use playing pieces and a die from another game.

How to play:
Players begin at "START." First player rolls the die and moves that number of spaces clockwise. If player lands on a numbered space, player checks the key and follows the instructions. If a player lands on a calcium object space, player picks up and keeps the marker and must read and follow instructions in the object box. Player continues following instructions until turn ends. Players take turns rolling the die and moving around the board any number of times.
Game is over when all markers have been picked up.

2

PLASTER OF PARIS

3

4

CHALK

5

1

BROCCOLI

6

5

TEETH

4

3

PLASTER OF PARIS—This useful substance is made from a natural material that's rich in calcium, called gypsum. Plaster of paris isn't really from France, but ooh-la-la, it's magnifique! Add **3** extra points to your score!

BROCCOLI—It may not look like it, but broccoli is an excellent source of calcium. Did you know that the top of broccoli is actually little flower buds? So eat your broccoli for calcium flower power! For not eating enough broccoli this week, your opponents lose **2** points apiece.

CHALK—Chalk comes from tiny microscopic organisms that live in the ocean. These organisms have shells made of calcium carbonate. As the organisms die over millions of years, their shells pile up into large chalk deposits. Chalk one up for you! Take an extra turn!

CALC

TEETH—The enamel on teeth is the hardest substance in the human body. Enamel is made mostly of calcium phosphate. Here's something you can really sink your teeth into—move directly to the next marker!

MARBLE—As a source of calcium, marble is simply marbleous! Marble has been used as a building material and as stone for carving statues for centuries. Don't look now, but you've lost your marble! If the marble marker is there, you must give it to the player who rolls next. If it's gone, you lose **10** points but roll again.

EGGSHELL—Birds, lizards, snakes, and duck-billed platypuses lay hard-shelled eggs. Calcium in eggs makes them hard enough to protect the developing animal from the environment, but gases can also move in and out of the shell! In honor of the eggstraordinary egg, add **10** points to your score.

MARBLE

2

1

EGGSHELL

6

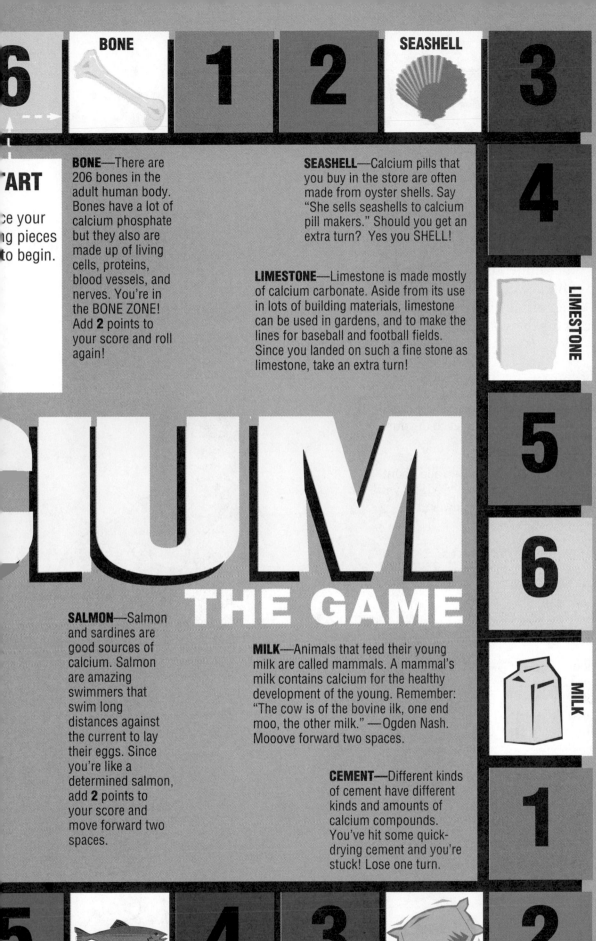

6

BONE

1

2

SEASHELL

3

4

LIMESTONE

5

6

MILK

1

START

ce your
ng pieces
to begin.

BONE—There are 206 bones in the adult human body. Bones have a lot of calcium phosphate but they also are made up of living cells, proteins, blood vessels, and nerves. You're in the BONE ZONE! Add **2** points to your score and roll again!

SEASHELL—Calcium pills that you buy in the store are often made from oyster shells. Say "She sells seashells to calcium pill makers." Should you get an extra turn? Yes you SHELL!

LIMESTONE—Limestone is made mostly of calcium carbonate. Aside from its use in lots of building materials, limestone can be used in gardens, and to make the lines for baseball and football fields. Since you landed on such a fine stone as limestone, take an extra turn!

CIUM

THE GAME

SALMON—Salmon and sardines are good sources of calcium. Salmon are amazing swimmers that swim long distances against the current to lay their eggs. Since you're like a determined salmon, add **2** points to your score and move forward two spaces.

MILK—Animals that feed their young milk are called mammals. A mammal's milk contains calcium for the healthy development of the young. Remember: "The cow is of the bovine ilk, one end moo, the other milk." —Ogden Nash. Mooove forward two spaces.

CEMENT—Different kinds of cement have different kinds and amounts of calcium compounds. You've hit some quick-drying cement and you're stuck! Lose one turn.

5

SALMON

4

3

CEMENT

2

Scoring:
A score sheet is used to keep track of each player's points during the course of the game. When the last calcium marker is picked up, the game is over. Calcium markers are each worth 10 points. Players count their markers, then multipy the number of markers by 10 and add it to their score.

Bonus points:
The player who picks up the last marker to end the game adds 25 points to his or her score instead of the standard marker value of 10.

Key:

1 Add **1** point to your score but give each of your opponents **2** points.

2 Add **2** points to your score then move backward to the nearest calcium marker and take it.

3 Each of your opponents gets **3** points but you move directly to the next marker and take it.

4 Add **4** points to your score but skip your next turn.

5 Each of your opponents gets **5** points. Roll again.

6 You get **6** points but go back to "START."

HARD WATER—
BUBBLE TROUBLE?

Sometimes, when water flows over limestone or other material with a lot of calcium in it, the calcium gets into the water. Water that contains a lot of calcium or other minerals is called *hard water* One characteristic of hard water is that it makes a soap film or soap scum when mixed with soap. It can also make it more difficult for the soap and water solution to bubble.

1 Cover your work area with paper towels or newspaper. Use your masking tape and pen to label your cups **water**, **water and plaster**, and **soapy water**. Pour 1/2 cup of warm water into each of your plastic cups.

2 To the cup labeled water and plaster, add about 1/4 teaspoon of plaster of paris powder. Stir with a straw until the plaster of paris powder is thoroughly mixed with the water.

3 Ask your adult partner to help you use your grater to grate 1–2 tablespoons of soap from your bar of soap. Add about 1 tablespoon of grated soap to the soapy water cup. Stir with a new straw until no more soap will dissolve.

4 Add 1 tablespoon of soapy water from your soapy water cup to each of your other two cups. Do not stir right away. Observe the solutions closely. Do you see a difference between them? What do you see happening in one of the cups? Stir each cup with a separate straw. Do they still look different?

5 Use a separate straw to blow gently into each cup. Do you notice a difference in the bubbling? What do you think is the reason? *Be sure to blow into the liquid. Do not suck the liquid into the straw.*

You will need

warm water	ball-point pen
measuring spoons	bar soap
plaster of paris	grater
3 clear 8 oz plastic cups	sheet of paper
	plastic straws
masking tape	

Food Additives

This unit introduces students to some of the major uses of food additives. The main food additives can be categorized as thickeners, flavorings, coloring agents, nutritional supplements, and preservatives. When dealing with this topic, it is important to point out the many positive contributions food additives have made to the quality and availability of food as well as the negative aspects of health problems associated with some food additives. A balanced approach should help children make intelligent decisions about the food they eat as they grow older.

Through Thick or Thin

In *Through Thick or Thin*, students experiment with the thickening agents flour and cornstarch. In step 6, make sure you point out the strange qualities of the cornstarch mixture as more cornstarch is added. With enough cornstarch, the mixture will seem thicker when stirred quickly than when stirred slowly. Also, when mixing gelatin with milk, at the end of the activity, be sure to mix it very thoroughly to get the desired consistency.

A Coloring Conundrum!

A Coloring Conundrum! deals with the difficulty of coloring an oil-based product, in this case oil itself, with water-based food coloring. Because oil and water do not mix, something must be added to the oil/coloring combination to help mixing take place. The egg yolk acts as an *emulsifier* to help this mixing occur. The emulsifier breaks the oil up into tiny droplets that can more easily mix with the water.

Foiling Spoiling

Foiling Spoiling features an activity on a class of preservatives that prevents foods such as apples and bananas from turning brown. In this activity, students can set up an experiment, control variables, make and record observations, and draw conclusions.

Flavorings: Let Your Taste Buds Blossom

The two activities in *Flavorings: Let Your Taste Buds Blossom* involve sweeteners and spices. In the first activity, students see that tasting is an inexact test but can be used to determine relative sweetness. The spice activity on the bottom of the page can be challenging for students. After doing this activity, you might want to use other activities to explore the close relationship between smell and taste.

WonderScience Chef of the Future

WonderScience Chef of the Future offers an opportunity for some friendly competition in a recipe contest between groups of students. All of the additives discussed in the previous activities are combined to see how they can all work together and to see the effect of a little more or a little less of a particular additive.

RELEVANT NATIONAL SCIENCE EDUCATION STANDARDS

The activities in this unit can be used to support the teaching of the following standards:

✔ Science as Inquiry
   Abilities necessary to do scientific inquiry

✔ Physical Science
   Properties and changes of properties in matter

✔ Science and technology
   Abilities of technological design
   Understandings about science and technology

✔ Science in Personal and Social Perspectives
   Science and technology in society

✔ History and Nature of Science
   History of science

Through THICK

Some additives used in foods are called *thickeners* which, as you might guess, make certain foods thicker. Scientists who work with foods need to be able to measure thickness. Try the following activity and see if you're ready to become a *WonderScience* food scientist!

1 Cover your work surface with paper towels or newspaper. Put 2 tablespoons of milk into each of two cups. With your masking tape and crayon, mark one cup "flour" and the other cup "cornstarch."

2 Add one tablespoon of flour and one tablespoon of cornstarch to their labeled cups and stir each one with a separate spoon. Does the liquid in either cup seem thicker than before? Do you think that looking at the liquid is a good test for thickness?

3 Add one more tablespoon of flour and cornstarch to their labeled cups and stir thoroughly. Do the liquids seem to be getting thicker? Does one liquid seem to be getting thicker than the other?

4 Let's try a common test for thickness. Cut your straw in half and see in which cup a half straw will stand up. In which liquid were you able to keep the straw standing?

162

or THIN

5 Another test for thickness is the **flow test**. Get a piece of cardboard about 30 cm wide and about 60 cm long. Use tape to cover one side of the cardboard with wax paper. Make a ramp from the cardboard by placing one end on a stack of old books about 10 to 15 cm high.

6 Place several sheets of newspaper at the bottom of your ramp. Add 2 more tablespoons of cornstarch to its cup and stir very thoroughly. Now you have two liquids of similar thickness. Let's use the flow test to see which one is thicker! Take one cup in each hand and quickly pour all the liquid from each cup out in separate streams at the top of the ramp. Which liquid flows the fastest? Which liquid is the thickest?

7 Touch the trails left by the liquids on your wax paper. Does one feel thicker than the other? Does the way they feel match how fast they traveled down the ramp?

8 See if you and your adult partner can design your own liquid thickness test based on how fast liquids drip drop by drop. Think about the equipment you will need and how you will set up your experiment. Good luck!

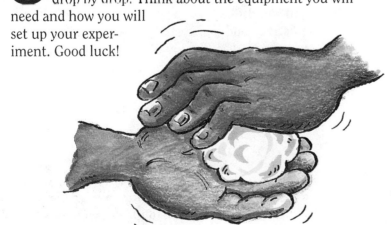

9 And now for something really thick! Place 2 tablespoons of milk in a cup. Add one packet of dry unflavored gelatin and stir. Even though the mixture is getting thicker, keep stirring until it gets **very** thick.

10 When the mixture is like a thick dough, take it out with your hand and roll it into a ball. Try bouncing your milk and gelatin ball. Now that's **THICK!**

---

* All activities in *WonderScience* have been reviewed for safety by Dr. Jack Breazeale, Francis Marion College, Florence, SC; Dr. Jay Young, Chemical Health and Safety Consultant, Silver Spring, MD; and Dr. Patricia Redden, Saint Peter's College, Jersey City, NJ.

Food additives:
Let's sum it up!

As you have already seen, thickeners used as food additives can affect the way a food looks, how it can be shaped, and how it feels. All this has a big effect on how the food can be used and stored and whether or not people will like to eat it.

Food additives have a very long history. Salt has been used as a flavoring and as a preservative for **thousands** of years. Fresh meat and fish were thoroughly salted so that certain *bacteria* could not grow on the food and spoil it. Spices have also been very important throughout history. Many explorers traveled all over the world in search of pepper, salt, and other spices. Spices were once so valuable that wars were fought to control the trading of spices from one country to another.

Food additives have many purposes, but the most important are as *preservatives* and *flavorings*, and to add *nutritional value* to food. Preservatives are important because many foods are not produced near the people who need to eat them. Without certain preservatives, many foods would spoil and be wasted before people could use them. Flavorings such as sweeteners, salt, and spices are needed to give many foods the taste that people like. Believe it or not, even chocolate would taste terrible without sugar added to it! If you don't believe us, you might want to ask your adult partner to let you taste a little unsweetened chocolate. Don't say that we didn't warn you! Many other foods would be very bland or not taste very good without added flavorings. Vitamins and minerals are food additives that make many foods more nutritious. These chemicals are added in very small amounts because our bodies need only a very little, but with vitamins and minerals, a little goes a long way!

Some people don't like the idea of having additives in their food because they say that they don't want to eat "chemicals." But that really doesn't make any sense because all the food we eat, the liquids we drink, and even the air we breathe are **made up** of chemicals! It is true that over the years, there have been some food additives that have been shown to be a health risk for people. But today, laws about the safety of food additives and the improved methods of testing additives for safety help scientists be sure that additives are safe before they can be used in food.

As you and your adult partner do the experiments and activities in this month's *WonderScience*, think about how far scientists have come in helping to make nutritious foods that can be sent to people all over the world. The proper use of food additives is a big part of making this possible.

ILLUSTRATION BY AMY HAYES

A COLORING CONUNDRUM

Some of the most common food additives are chemicals used to color certain foods. You have probably used or helped an adult use food coloring in cake or cookie icing or to color some other food. In this activity, you will see that coloring certain foods isn't as easy as you might think.

1 Place one tablespoon of oil into one of your cups. Add one drop of food coloring and mix thoroughly. How does the food coloring look in the oil? Does the food coloring do a good job of coloring the oil?

2 Let's see if putting food coloring in water and then adding this to the oil will help color the oil. Do you think this will work? Put one tablespoon of water in another cup and add one drop of food coloring. Mix thoroughly.

3 Put one tablespoon of oil into another cup and add the colored water and mix thoroughly. Did adding the water help color the oil? Look closely at the oil and colored water together. Do the two liquids mix?

How about adding a little flour to the oil and then adding some food coloring? Maybe that will work.

4 Put one tablespoon of oil into a separate cup. Add ¼ teaspoon of flour and mix thoroughly. Add one drop of food coloring and mix. Does the oil seem to be getting more colored than before? Put this cup aside and check it again in 5 minutes to see if the oil stays colored.

5 One more try! Put one teaspoon of water into a separate cup. Ask your adult partner to help you separate the yolk from the rest of an egg. Add 3 or 4 drops of yolk to the water and mix. Put one tablespoon of oil into a separate cup and add the yolk and water mixture and stir.

6 Add one drop of food coloring to this mixture and stir thoroughly. Does the mixture seem to get colored? What do you think made the difference?

Foiling Spoiling

Other important food additives are used to preserve foods so that bacteria and fungus will not grow on them as fast as they normally would. Some foods change color because of a chemical reaction they have with the oxygen in the air. This reaction is called **oxidation**. There are certain chemicals that can be added to foods to slow down this chemical reaction. These chemicals are called **antioxidants**

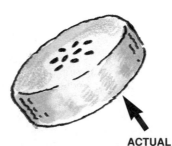

You will need

paper towels
4 sheets of paper
potato
banana
apple
lemon
water
butter knife

Be sure to wash your hands when you finish. Lemon juice can sting your eyes!

1 Spread paper towels over your work area. Ask your adult partner to help you cut three pieces each of potato, apple, and banana to about the size shown. Also, ask your adult partner to cut the lemon in half.

2 Place a sheet of paper on your paper towels and put the pieces of potato, apple, and banana on the paper in rows and label the rows as shown.

ACTUAL SIZE

3 Do nothing to the first piece of food in each row. Squeeze a few drops of lemon juice on the second piece in each row so that the whole surface of the piece has lemon juice on it. Put a few drops of water on the third piece in each row so that the whole surface has water on it.

4 Label the columns on your piece of paper as "**nothing**," "**lemon juice**," and "**water**" as shown.

5 On a separate sheet of paper, make a chart like the one at right but make it big enough to fill the whole sheet. Each box is for you to draw a picture of the food and write down your observations about how it looks.

6 Wait about one hour and look very closely at your pieces of food. In each box, write down any changes you see in the food in that box. See if you can draw what each piece of food looks like and the changes you see happening to each piece, if any.

Make at least two more charts to record your observations at 12 and at 24 hours. Did the lemon juice act as a preservative?

	ADDITIVE		
FOOD	nothing	lemon juice	water
potato			
apple			
banana			

FLAVORINGS: Let your taste buds blossom

One group of food additives we can't leave out is the *flavorings* group. Flavorings that most people like to taste are the *sweeteners.* People who prepare food need to know just how sweet certain sweeteners are. Unlike most scientific testing, food scientists can test a sweetener's sweetness by tasting it. Try the following activity and see how sweet it is!

You will need

sugar
brown sugar
honey
fructose (in grocery near artificial sweeteners)
measuring spoons
water
masking tape
ink pen
4 plastic or paper cups
cotton swabs

1 Mix 1 tablespoon of sugar in ¼ cup of warm water until all the sugar dissolves. This is your *standard* for sweetness. Your job is to find out if brown sugar, honey, or fructose are less sweet, just as sweet, or sweeter than sugar.

2 With your masking tape and pen, label 4 cups "**sugar**," "**brown sugar**," "**honey**," and "**fructose**."

3 Add ¼ cup of warm water to each cup and then add 1 tablespoon of brown sugar, honey, and fructose to its labeled cup. Stir each solution with a separate spoon until it is dissolved.

4 Take a little sip of water to clear your mouth for your first taste test. Dip one end of a clean cotton swab into your standard sugar solution and touch the swab to your tongue.

5 Throw the swab away. Think about how sweet the sugar tasted. Take another sip of water. Dip another swab into the brown sugar solution and touch the tip to your tongue. Does the brown sugar taste sweeter, less sweet, or just as sweet as the sugar standard? Write down what you think. Have your adult partner take the same test.

6 Take another sip of water and taste your standard again. Take another sip of water and taste your honey solution. Record how its sweetness compares to sugar. Does your adult partner agree? Try this taste test with your last sweetener to see which of your sweeteners is the sweetest of them all!

Other popular flavorings are *spices*. Because the senses of smell and taste work together, the smell of a spice is important when it is used as a flavoring. Let's see if you can identify different spices from their smell!

You will need

garlic powder   cinnamon
parsley flakes   pencil
oregano   5 tissues
celery seed   5 pieces of string

1 Open each spice container and smell each spice carefully one by one. *Be careful not to inhale any powdered spice.*

2 Remember the name of each spice. You may need to smell the spices again to **really** remember the smells.

3 Now comes the real test! Ask your adult partner to wrap some of each spice in a tissue and to tie the top with a string. Your adult partner should keep each wrapped spice next to its container hidden from your view.

4 Your adult partner should bring out one wrapped spice at a time to let you smell it and guess what it is. Try it and see how well you do! Let your adult partner take the same test to see who is the **Super Spice Smeller**!

WonderScience
Chef of the Future

In the following activity, you will be able to change the amounts of different food additives to make the food the way you like it best! You will use gelatin (thickener), food coloring (coloring agent), sugar (sweetener), cinnamon (spice), and lemon juice (antioxidant) to make a dessert especially for you!

You will need

unflavored gelatin	measuring cup
food coloring	lemon
sugar	butter knife
bananas	3 small bowls
cinnamon	

1 Pour 1 cup of hot tap water into a bowl. Add 1½ teaspoons of unflavored gelatin and stir until the gelatin dissolves. Add three teaspoons of sugar and stir until dissolved. If you want, add 1 drop of food coloring.

2 Cut up ½ a banana and add the pieces to the gelatin mix. Squeeze in about 4 or 5 drops of lemon juice and sprinkle on a little cinnamon. Place the bowl in the refrigerator for 3–4 hours until the gelatin is firm. Taste your dessert!

3 Maybe your dessert could be a little bit better! Experiment with changing the recipe a little bit. You can make it a little more firm or a little less firm by using a little more or a little less gelatin. If you want to change the sweetness, you could change the amount of sugar. You could also use more or less lemon to change the flavor, or use different food coloring to change the color.

Have a **contest** with your adult partner to see who can come up with the best recipe (have someone else be the judge!).

Blue ribbon CONTEST

Your recipe	**Adult partner's recipe**
_____ cup(s) hot water	_____ cup(s) hot water
_____ teaspoon(s) unflavored gelatin	_____ teaspoon(s) unflavored gelatin
_____ teaspoon(s) sugar	_____ teaspoon(s) sugar
_____ banana	_____ banana
_____ sprinkles cinnamon	_____ sprinkles cinnamon
_____ drop(s) lemon juice	_____ drop(s) lemon juice

WONDERSCIENCE

This unit focuses on some of the science involved in soda pop. Carbonation, sweeteners, and acid content are discussed.

Be a WonderScience Fizz Whiz!

In *Be a WonderScience Fizz Whiz!* students go through a series of steps to determine what causes bubbling in a cup of soda pop when different substances are added. Students should discover that placing sugar, salt, sand, and even a cotton swab into soda makes bubbles appear. The bubbles form because the carbon dioxide molecules dissolved in the soda bump into these substances, slow down, attach, and accumulate to form bubbles.

Racin' Raisins!

In *Racin' Raisins!* students observe the action of raisins placed in soda. The activity works best if the soda used is highly carbonated such as club soda. Students are challenged to use some of what they discovered in the first activity to help their raisin move up and down the most.

All Shook Up!

All Shook Up! introduces students to a method of determining the volume of a balloon filled with carbon dioxide gas by the amount of water it displaces. If students are not familiar with the concept of volume, this should be explained and demonstrated before students try the activity. This activity also requires patience in its step-by-step approach for which students may need extra guidance.

How Sweet It Is!

How Sweet It Is! is a fun way to illustrate the difference in sweeteners between diet and regular soda. When placed in water, the can of diet soda should float and the can of regular soda should sink. Since the volumes are the same, the contents of the regular soda must be more dense than the diet. The last part of the activity should show that because of density differences, the regular soda will stay in a layer under the water and the diet soda will tend to mix with the water.

Sour Power!

Sour Power! uses an indicator from red radish to show that soda contains acid.

RELEVANT NATIONAL SCIENCE EDUCATION STANDARDS

The activities in this unit can be used to support the teaching of the following standards:

✔ Science as Inquiry
   Abilities necessary to scientific inquiry

✔ Physical Science
   Properties and changes of properties in matter

Be a WonderScience

The chemical that really makes soda different from almost all other liquids is **carbon dioxide**. Soda is mostly water (also a chemical) but it's the carbon dioxide that gives the soda its fizz! In the activity below, you can investigate some fizzing phenomena!

You will need

small candy-coated colored candies	sand
	cotton swab
1 small clear plastic cup	small watercolor paint brush (optional)
soda pop (any variety)	steel wool (optional)
salt	ice
sugar	ice cream

1
Pour soda into your cup until it is about 3/4 filled. Place a coated candy in the soda. What do you observe? Where do you think these bubbles came from? What do you think caused them to form?

2
Rinse out your cup and again add soda until the cup is about 3/4 filled. Sprinkle some sugar into the soda. What do you observe? Do you think the candy's sugar and the sugar you just put in somehow caused the bubbles? Let's try something different!

3
Rinse and refill your cup as before. Take a pinch of salt and sprinkle it into the soda. What do you observe? Try it again with a little more salt. What do you think might be causing these bubbles?

4
Rinse and refill your cup again. Take a pinch of sand or gravel and drop it into the soda. What do you observe? Did you think this would happen? How do you think the sand or gravel caused the bubbles to form? Do you think the same thing that caused these bubbles also caused the bubbles with the sugar and salt?

The soda is part of your experiment. Remember, never eat or drink materials you are using in a science experiment.

FIZZ WHIZ!

5

Rinse and refill your cup again. Touch the surface of your soda with a cotton swab, paint brush, or piece of steel wool. Keep the end of the object in the soda. Look closely at the soda around the object. What do you notice? Do you have an idea about why these bubbles have been forming in the different steps of this activity?

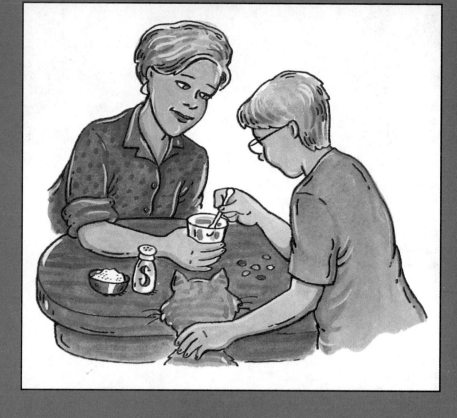

6

Place 2 or 3 new ice cubes from an ice cube tray in a cup. Carefully pour soda over the cubes. What do you notice? What do you think caused this bubbling?

7

Pour off the soda but save the ice cubes. Put a little water in the cup to rinse off the ice cubes. Throw the water away. Carefully pour soda over the cubes again. Do you notice a difference in the amount of bubbling?

8

Place 2 tablespoons of ice cream in a cup. Add some club soda. What do you observe? If you are still bubbling over with curiosity about what causes all this bubbling, just turn the page and find out!

* All activities in *WonderScience* have been reviewed for safety by Dr. Jack Breazeale, Francis Marion University, Florence, SC; Dr. Jay Young, Chemical Health and Safety Consultant, Silver Spring, MD; and Dr. Patricia Redden, Saint Peter's College, Jersey City, NJ.

The Science of Soda!

Soda has something in it that almost no other liquid has: lots of **carbon dioxide**. The carbon dioxide in soda is a **gas** that makes soda bubbly. There are some places in nature where water absorbs lots of carbon dioxide by flowing over rocks and minerals with certain chemicals in them. The sodas we buy at the store have had carbon dioxide added to them at the soda factory. When people say that sodas are "carbonated," they mean that they have had carbon dioxide added to them.

Carbon dioxide, like everything else in the world, is made up of **atoms**. You may know that two or more atoms can combine in a special way to make a **molecule**. Carbon dioxide is a molecule made up of one atom of **carbon** and two atoms of **oxygen**. That's why chemists use the letters and number CO_2 to stand for carbon dioxide. Carbon dioxide is one of the gases in our atmosphere that plants need to survive. When animals breathe, they take in oxygen and give off carbon dioxide.

The soda we drink is mostly water, carbon dioxide, sweetener, and flavoring. When making soda, it is not so easy to get the carbon dioxide to go into the water. At the soda factory, the carbon dioxide is forced into the water with a lot of **pressure** and the bottle or can is immediately sealed. When you open a soda slowly, the "psssssss" you hear is the carbon dioxide gas escaping when the pressure is released.

Also, soda factories use very cold water because more carbon dioxide will go into very cold water than into warmer water. You can see that carbon dioxide also stays in cold water better by doing a simple experiment. Place about 1/4 cup of soda in each of two disposable paper or plastic cups. (Do not use thick plastic or foam.) Ask your adult partner to put one of your cups into a bowl of hot water from the faucet. Put the other cup into a bowl of ice water. You can see that the cold temperature helps keep the carbon dioxide in the soda and that the warm temperature allows the carbon dioxide to escape.

This brings us the activity **"Be WonderScience FIZZ WHIZ!"** Now we can answer the question: Why did the carbon dioxide form bubbles when you put sugar, salt, sand, gravel, and even a cotton swab in the soda? The reason is similar to what happens when you put a straw in soda. Have you ever noticed that a straw gets lots of bubbles on it and sometimes even lifts up out of your cup? This is because the carbon dioxide molecules moving around in the soda hit the straw and slow down. As more carbon dioxide molecules hit the straw, they begin to build up near the straw and attach to it. This is also why you see bubbles form on the sides and bottom of a cup with soda in it. The same thing happens when you put sand or sugar or almost anything in the soda that can slow down the carbon dioxide molecules and give them something to attach to!

Have fun with the rest of your *WonderScience* as you explore the science of soda!

DAVE JONASON

172

Racin' Raisins!

BRUCE VAN PATTER

Challenge your adult partner to the Carbon Dioxide Raisin Rally Championship!

You will need

raisins
clear soda
2 clear plastic cups (8 oz)

1 You and your adult partner should each fill a clear plastic cup about 3/4 full of soda. Place 3 raisins in the soda in each cup. Observe the raisins closely. After sinking to the bottom, the raisins should soon get bubbles on them, lifting them to the surface. Some of the bubbles should break, causing the raisins to sink again.

2 You and your adult partner should observe your raisins for a minute or two. Each of you should choose the raisin that floated to the top of your cup most often. This is your prize raisin! What qualities does your prize raisin have that you think made it go up and down better than the others?

3 Remove the raisins from the cups and save your prize raisin. Put one cup away and place the other cup in the middle as the **Raisin Challenge Cup**! When you say "GO!" you and your adult partner should place your prize raisins in the challenge cup. The raisin that gets to the surface the most times in two minutes WINS! **GOOD LUCK!**

4 Look at the winning raisin closely. Do you think there is anything you could do to your raisin or a new raisin that would improve its chances for victory? You and your adult partner should each pick a new raisin. Mold, dent, cut, or change your raisin in a way that you think will help. Have another Raisin Challenge Cup!

5 See if you can figure out how you could use a candy, salt, sugar, or sand from the activity on pages 2 and 3 to help your raisin climb to the top of the Raisin Cup Challenge!

All Shook Up!

You probably know that you can make carbon dioxide bubble out of a soda by shaking it. If you were a chemist or other scientist, you might need to measure the amount of carbon dioxide released by the soda. In the activity below, you can learn how to measure the amount of gas released by a soda that's all shook up!

1 Carefully open a bottle of soda and have your adult partner quickly place the opening of a balloon over the top of the bottle. Give the bottle a couple of good shakes to get some carbon dioxide gas to enter the balloon. (Some soda will also enter the balloon—let it flow back into the bottle.)

2 Pinch the opening of the balloon and carefully remove it from the bottle. Try not to allow any carbon dioxide to escape. Keep the balloon pinched, and twist it so that no gas escapes. Do not tie the balloon because you will need it again. Put the cap back on the bottle.

If the balloon were a perfect **sphere**, you could measure around the balloon and use a mathematical formula to find out how much gas is in it. This is called the volume of the balloon. Because the balloon is not a perfect sphere, it is very difficult to measure the volume of the balloon by using a measuring tape.

You will need

1 bottle of soda	water
2 round balloons	tray
bucket or other deep container	measuring cup

Before starting this activity, you should inflate and deflate your balloons a few times to stretch them out.

An ancient Greek scientist named ***Archimedes*** discovered a way to use water to measure the volume of an object with an irregular shape. Here's how to do it with your balloon:

3 Fill your bucket or other deep container to the very top with water. Place the container in a tray as shown. Make sure the container is filled to the very top.

4 Take your balloon filled with carbon dioxide and slowly push it down into the water. Keep pushing until the balloon is just under the surface of the water. Do not submerge your fingers, hand, or arm.

5 Water should flow out of the container and into the tray. Carefully take the balloon out of the water and remove the container from the tray. Pick up the tray and pour the water into a measuring cup. The volume of water in the tray should be equal to the volume of the balloon filled with gas!

6 Let the gas out of your balloon. Place the balloon on the bottle and see how much more gas you can get out of the soda. After collecting the gas and twisting the balloon, see if you can predict the volume of water it will displace. Then try Archimedes' method again to see how close you came!

HOW SWEET IT IS!

You will need

can of regular soda	eyedropper
can of diet soda	straw
bucket of water	masking tape
1 plastic or paper cup	ballpoint pen
3 clear plastic cups (at least 8 oz)	

One of the important chemicals that adds to the taste of soda is the *sweetener*. For many years soda was sweetened with sugar. Now there are artificial sweeteners that are used in diet soda. You can do a simple test to see which soda has sugar and which has artificial sweetener.

1 Fill a bucket with water. Place your cans of diet and regular soda in the water. Make sure no air is trapped under the cans. What do you notice? If the only difference between the sodas is the sweetener, what does this tell you about the difference between sugar and artificial sweetener used in the sodas?

2 Label one of your clear cups "regular" and the other cup "diet." Fill each cup about 2/3 full of water. Pour about 1/4 cup of regular soda into another cup. Place your straw on an angle all the way into the cup marked "regular."

3 Use an eyedropper to carefully drip some regular soda through the straw and into the bottom of the cup. Be very careful not to stir the liquids in the cup. What do you notice about where the soda stays in the cup?

4 Rinse out your straw, eyedropper, and soda cup. Repeat step 3 using the cup marked "diet" and the diet soda. Look at both cups closely. Do you notice a difference between them? Do you think this has anything to do with what the cans of soda did in step 1?

SOUR POWER!

Lemonade, orange juice, lime juice, and grapefruit juice all contain **acid** that give the juices a kind of sour flavor. Many sodas also contain acid. Chemists can use special chemicals called **indicators** to find out how acidic a liquid is. In the following activity, you can use an indicator to see how acidic a lemon or lemon-lime soda is.

NOTE: THE TYPE OF INDEX CARD USED WILL AFFECT HOW WELL THIS ACTIVITY WORKS. WE FOUND THAT THE UNLINED SIDE OF A STAN-DARD 3X5 INDEX CARD WORKED BEST.

You will need

3 small paper or plastic cups	ballpoint pen
lemon or lemon-lime soda	3 X 5 index cards
red radishes	cotton swabs
fresh lemon	measuring spoon
masking tape	measuring cup
	water

1 Use a pen to divide and label the unlined side of a 3 X 5 index card as shown. You or your adult partner should hold down your card as one of you rubs a radish on the card. Rub the radish hard enough so that the card becomes a fairly dark pink color. This is your indicator.

2 Use your masking tape and pen to label your cups "lemon," "water," and "soda." Ask your adult partner to cut a lemon in half. Squeeze about a tablespoon of lemon juice in its labeled cup. Place about a tablespoon each of water and soda into their labeled cups.

3 Place a separate cotton swab in each cup. Wipe a streak of lemon juice on your radish indicator in its area on the card. What color did your indicator become?

4 Now wipe separate streaks of water and soda on your indicator. Did the water seem to change the indicator color? How about the soda? From this test, do you think the soda has acid in it?

5 How many tablespoons of water do you think you would need to add to your lemon juice to make it look like the soda looked on your indicator? As you add the water, test your solution on a new area of radish indicator to see how close you are getting!

The activities in this unit explore the properties of chemicals called *polymers*. Polymers are linked chains of smaller, usually identical chemical units. Natural polymers come from plants or animals. For example, leather, wool, cotton, rubber, linen, and starch are polymers that have begun as parts of plants or animals. Artificial polymers are first made by chemists in laboratories, then produced on a large scale by chemical manufacturers. The development of artificial polymers, such as Plexiglas, polyethylene, Dacron, nylon, Teflon, polystyrene, and other plastics have had an enormous impact on modern society.

It's In the Bag!

It's In the Bag! allows students to examine some of the properties of natural and artificial polymers. The object is not to determine whether one of the materials, paper or plastic, is "better" than the other, but to observe the properties of these materials in different situations.

It's A Sticky Subject and From Moo to Glue

The adhesive properties of some natural polymers are examined in two activities. In *It's A Sticky Subject*, two homemade glues are compared for stickiness in various situations. In *From Moo to Glue*, students can make a protein-based glue and see if its properties are the same or different from those of the "Sticky Subject" glues.

WonderScientist Inventors

WonderScientist Inventors includes an interview with an inventor discussing the qualities needed to be a successful inventor. Challenge students to some up with a new invention using one or more of the polymers Teflon, Plexiglas, and polystyrene (Styrofoam).

Polymer Triathlon

Polymer Triathlon challenges students to compare some of the characteristic properties of various polymers including rubber, plastic, and paper by observing their behavior in various tests.

RELEVANT NATIONAL SCIENCE EDUCATION STANDARDS

The activities in this unit can be used to support the teaching of the following standards:

✔ **Science as Inquiry**
   Understandings about scientific inquiry

✔ **Physical Science**
   Properties and changes of properties in matter

✔ **Life Science**
   Structure and function in living systems

✔ **Science in Personal and Social Perspectives**
   Science and technology in society

✔ **History and Nature of Science**
   Science as a human endeavor

Some special chemicals are made of chains of smaller chemical units. Some of these linked chemicals are found in nature, but others can be made artificially. We're going to compare two bags: one a natural material; the other artificial. Can you tell which is which?

You will need

2 paper lunch bags
2 plastic freezer bags
measuring cup
mixing bowl
water
vegetable oil
blunt scissors
paper towels
hand lens (magnifying glass)

1 First, just look at and feel a plastic and a paper bag. Open the two bags and stand them up on a surface. Which stands up best? Now, look at both bags with the lens. Record any **differences** you see between the two bags.

3 Pour out the water and set the bags on a paper towel. Using your hand lens, compare both bags. What has the water done to the paper and plastic? Which material is best to use to carry water? **Why?** Which bag can be used again later?

4 You've seen what happens when plastic and paper are used to hold a liquid (water). Predict what you think will happen when two fresh bags are used to hold another liquid— oil. Record your predictions here:

_____

_____

5 While you hold fresh bags open over the mixing bowl, have your partner add ⅛ cup oil to each bag. Observe what happens to the bags for 3 minutes and record. Carefully pour the oil from the paper bag back into the measuring cup. (You may need to use measuring spoons to measure the oil.) Record the amount. Put the used paper bag aside on paper towels.

6 Discard the oil in the cup (check with your adult partner about the discarding procedure) and wash it. Now measure the oil left in the plastic bag. Record the amount, and discard the oil. Compare the amounts of oil that were left in both bags. Are there any differences?

THE BAG!

2 Next, hold both bags open over the sink while your partner pours 1/8 cup water in each one. **Observe** what happens to the bags for one minute. Now, hold the bags closed and gently shake them for 4 minutes. What happens? Would you choose to carry a goldfish home from the pet store in a paper bag? Why or why not? Record your observations.

7 Compare the oily plastic and paper bags by holding both up to the light. Has the oil had the same effect on the paper and plastic? Can your observations explain any differences in the amounts of oil left in the bags?

8 From what you have observed in this activity, try to answer the following questions:
   a. What are the advantages in using paper bags to pack groceries? What are the advantages in using plastic bags for groceries?
   b. Which bag looks like it would disintegrate (break apart) more easily when thrown away?

OBSERVATIONS

	NAKED EYE	LENS	WATER	OIL
PAPER BAG				Amount left _____
PLASTIC BAG				Amount left _____

SURROUNDED BY POLYMERS!

The linked chemicals that made up the paper and plastic bags with which you experimented in the activity "It's In The Bag!" are called **polymers.** "Poly" means "many"—the linked chemicals are called polymers because they are chains of *many* smaller chemical units linked to make larger chemicals. Many polymers occur in nature. One of these polymers is the basic building block of wood, paper, and cotton—cellulose. Some other polymers that occur in nature are starch (such as flour), protein (such as egg white and meat), rubber (used for tires and boots), and silk (for clothing.) Did you notice that all of these natural polymers come from either animals or plants? What do you think happens to the supply of a natural polymer if the plant or animal from which it comes becomes rare? What could happen to the *cost* of the natural polymer?

As the human population has grown, the demand for more polymers also has grown. The need for rubber in the United States became critical during World War II and led to the development of artificial rubber. To make artificial rubber, polymer chemists needed first to understand what smaller chemical units made up natural rubber. The chemists used tests and instruments to tell which different chemical units made up the polymer rubber. Using this knowledge of the chemicals in natural rubber, the chemists then experimented with the best ways to make artificial rubber. Artificial rubber did not depend on the supply of foreign rubber trees, because it could be made from raw materials that were easily found in this country. Artificial rubber could be made cheaply and in very large amounts.

Other artificial polymers that have changed the way we live are nylon (a substitute for silk), polyethylene (the most common plastic), Teflon (for non-stick surfaces in cookware), Dacron (a fabric), and Bakelite (a hard material used for such items as telephones and billiard balls).

You compared some of the properties of two different polymers in "It's In The Bag." Can you tell now which bag was made of the natural polymer, and which bag of the artificial polymer? Both bags have the same job— to hold something. What was special about the plastic bag that made it best for holding liquids? What was special about the paper bag that allowed it to stand upright? Polymers have many such characteristics that make them special. "It's a Sticky Subject" and "From Moo to Glue" will give you and your partner a chance to experiment with the adhesiveness (stickiness) of some natural polymers. The "Polymer Triathlon" allows you to compare the characteristics of several natural and artificial polymers in three "events."

ILLUSTRATION BY LAUREN MENDELSOHN

IT'S A STICKY SUBJECT

Let's see how two polymers, which are commonly used as foods, can also be used to stick things together. One of the polymers that we'll be comparing is called a starch (flour); the other is a protein (egg white).

Before you start this experiment, touch each type of glue with your fingers. Rub each type of glue between your fingers. Do they feel the same to you? Does one feel *stickier* than the other? Predict which glue might be best for gluing paper to paper or for gluing paper to wood.

1 Cut the half sheet of paper into four pieces. Put two pieces aside for later. You can leave the two remaining pieces of paper as is, or you can decorate *one* side with fancy shapes (hearts, rockets, flowers, etc.).

2 Now, using a cotton swab, brush a thin layer of your flour glue onto the top half of the wide side of a Popsicle stick as shown. Repeat with the egg white glue and the second Popsicle stick. Quickly press the blank sides of your colored pieces of paper onto the gluey sticks to make two "paper lollipops."

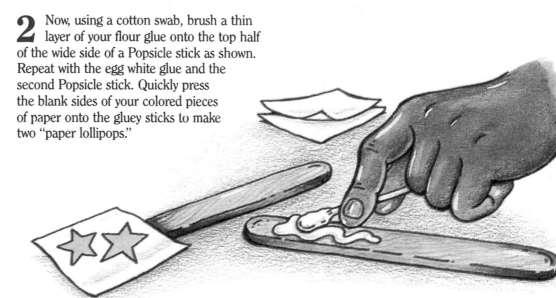

3 Pick the lollipops up by the dry ends of their sticks and hold them upside down. Have your partner time how long it takes for one of the pieces of paper to fall off its stick. Record the time here. _____ (Don't wait any longer than five minutes. If both stick for five minutes, or both fall off at the same time, call it a tie.)

4 Stick the lollipops back together, if necessary, and let both glues dry. Check the glues every five minutes to see which dries fastest. Which polymer would be the best to use to stick paper to wood? *Why?* Set the lollipops aside.

5 Now, cut each of the remaining two pieces of paper in half. (You should have four small pieces of paper.) Write "egg white—protein" on two pieces and "flour—starch" on the other two.

6 Using a swab, cover one side of the "egg white" paper with egg white glue. Place the other piece of "egg white" paper on top of the gluey piece. Press down. You should have a "sandwich" of: paper—egg white glue—paper. Repeat with the flour glue and papers.

7 Check the glues as they dry to see which dries fastest. Try lifting the top sheet on each "sandwich" occasionally to see which glue is working best. Which glue do you think would be the best to use to stick paper to paper? *Why?* Let the sandwiches dry and observe any differences between the two glues. Talk about these two polymers with your adult partner. How are they the same? How are they different?

WONDERSCIENTIST INVENTORS

Here are some of the solutions that our WonderScientists sent to us in response to the WonderScientist Challenge. These young inventors were challenged to come up with different uses for coatings of chemicals enclosed in tiny capsules.

Stinky sneakers—Heart-shaped insert with microencapsulated foot deodorant. *J.J. Kee*, Bethesda, MD.

Stinky sneakers—Microencapsulated deodorant built into the lining of the shoe. *Gustavo Diaz*, San Angelo, TX.

Providing more atmosphere at movies—Scratch and sniff card with smells that go along with what's on the screen. *April Neuwirth*, Wells, ME.

Solving crimes—Microencapsulated indicators for evidence such as blood stains that could be taken to the scene of the crime. *April Neuwirth*, Wells, ME.

Nutrients for plants—Tiny containers that dissolve in water are filled with plant food and placed in soil. *Margaret Hawes*, Fairfax, VA.

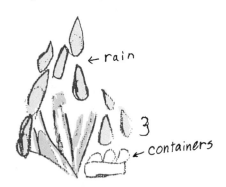

← rain

3 ← containers

Putting on cologne when not at home—Paper towel with perfume in tiny capsules. Instructions: rubbing the towel on your face breaks the capsules and releases the cologne. *Matthew Hawes*, Fairfax, VA.

Rub it on your face, breaking the tiny containers.

Children not eating vegetables—Scratch and sniff plate. Instructions: A fork scratching on the surface of the plate releases chocolaty smells. *Nate Reutter*, East Peoria, IL.

EUREKA! THE RECIPE FOR A GREAT INVENTOR

Artificial polymers are so much a part of our lives now that it is difficult to imagine not having them around. The chemists who discovered many of these polymers, however, sometimes had to wait several years before their discoveries became popular and were used to make everyday items. Teflon, for example, was discovered in 1938 by Roy Plunkett with Jack Rebok, but did not appear in the form of non-stick cookware until about 1960. Plexiglas, which is very widely used today as a light but strong substitute for glass, was first developed in 1932 by Walter Bauer.

The artificial polymer industry has relied on the talents of chemist inventors—such as Wallace Carothers, who developed nylon 66 in 1935—to produce new materials for mass production. What are the qualities of these chemists that make them successful inventors? We interviewed **Dr. Philip Landis,** a chemist who has to his credit more than 70 U.S. patents, to find out.

WS: Why do you like to invent things?
Dr. Landis: I get a great deal of personal satisfaction and a sense of achievement from discovering something that no one else has ever seen before. There's a feeling of excitement when you're "on to something"—a sense of: "Hey, I must be pretty smart to have figured that one out!"

WS: Does it matter to you whether your invention is of practical use?
Dr. Landis: You want your discoveries to be useful and to make money, but it's hard to judge whether they're useful or not. When I first started working for one corporation, I discovered a chemical that was later used to prevent rust inside pipelines and ships. This rust preventer reduced the need to constantly replace the pipes and recoat the ships, thereby saving a great deal of money.

WS: What qualities would you say that inventors have in common?
Dr. Landis: Imagination, patience, and a willingness to share information.

WS: What advice do you have for young inventors?
Dr. Landis:
1. Be patient and understanding.
2. Read a great deal to find out what other people are doing.
3. Practice using laboratory equipment.
4. Concentrate on science and math courses.
5. Get involved with problem-solving contests.
6. Trade ideas with friends.
7. Get a broad background of knowledge.

FROM MOO

TO GLUE

Making Glue from Milk

Glue can be made from a polymer (a protein) found in **milk.** To get the protein out of the milk, you need to curdle the milk by adding a mild acid, vinegar. Try the same tests for stickiness that you used in "It's a Sticky Subject." Is this protein glue as sticky as the other protein glue that you made from egg white?

You will need

2 Tbsp vinegar
½ cup non-fat milk made from non-fat
   milk powder and hot tap water
   (follow package directions)

¼ tsp baking soda
teaspoon for stirring
2 8-oz mugs or cups
funnel

coffee filter or paper towel
paper and Popsicle sticks to make paper lollipops
blunt scissors
crayons (optional)

1 Pour the vinegar into one of the mugs, and stir in the hot milk. Let the mixture sit until the solids are separated from the liquid (about 3 minutes). Carefully pour the liquid from the mixture down the sink drain. Save the solids.

2 Line the funnel with the coffee filter or a circle of paper towel folded to a cone that will fit the funnel. Put the funnel in the second mug.

3 Carefully pour the damp solids into the funnel. Pour any liquid that collects in the mug down the sink, but save the solids in the funnel. Wash both mugs.

4 Scrape the solids from the funnel into one of your clean mugs, and stir in the baking soda and 1½ teaspoons of water. The mixture in the cup is your completed glue. How does it compare with your egg white or flour glues? Experiment with some paper lollipops to find out!

IN SEARCH OF: POLYMERS

See how many natural and artificial polymers you can find in this kitchen. Put an N on each natural polymer and an A on each artificial polymer. (Can you always tell which is which? Why or why not?)

Now, imagine that artificial polymers had never been discovered. Make a list of the natural polymers (or other materials) that would be used in place of the artificial polymers in the picture. For example, if there were no plastic, what material would be used to make the milk container?

Or you can imagine what this picture would be like if there were no more natural polymers available. Make a list of the artificial polymers that could be used to replace the natural polymers.

POLYMER TRIATHLON

FIRST EVENT
Rubber (Natural) vs. Plastic (Artificial)

You will need

wide rubber band (¼″ in width)
roll of heavy-duty plastic wrap

blunt scissors
ruler

pencil and paper to record

1 Cut the rubber band and open it out to its full length. Measure its length and width and record them on a sheet of paper. (Don't stretch the band yet!)

2 Now, cut a piece of plastic wrap the exact length and width of the rubber band. Record its measurements on your piece of paper.

3 On a flat surface, have your partner stretch the rubber band as far as it will go. Measure the stretched length and width of the band and record them. What happens to the length and width when your partner gently releases the rubber band? Record your observations on the sheet.

4 On the same flat surface, have your partner stretch the strip of plastic wrap as far as it will go without tearing. Measure and record the stretched length and width. What happens to the length and width of the plastic wrap when your partner lets go? Record your observations. What characteristics do the rubber and the plastic have in common? What characteristics are different?

SECOND EVENT
Paper (Natural) vs. Plastic (Artificial)

You will need

a paper sandwich bag
a plastic freezer storage-size bag

blunt scissors
a ruler

paper and pencil for recording
(from First Event)

1 Cut each bag in half crosswise. Save the bottom halves for the Third Event. Cut a 10″ by 2″ strip out of the top halves of each bag.

2 On a flat surface, have your partner stretch each strip as far as it will go without tearing. Measure and record each stretched length and width. Which stretched the farthest? _____ Did the width of the strips change?

3 Now, stretch each strip until it breaks. Look at the torn edges of each strip. How are they the same? How are they different?

THIRD EVENT
Paper (Natural) vs. Plastic (Artificial): A Rematch

You will need

bottom halves of the paper and plastic bags from Second Event
pencil and paper to record observations (from First and Second Events)

1 Crumple the bottom halves of both bags into tight balls. Place the balls on a flat surface and watch what happens. Record your observations.

2 Which material stayed in the ball form the longest? Is this what you expected, based on your other experiences with plastic and paper?

This unit introduces students to some of the characteristics of plastics. Plastics are so much a part of our daily lives that it is important for students to recognize their usefulness as well as the problems associated with them. A better understanding of what plastics are, where they come from, and how they are used will help put the advantages and disadvantages of plastics into perspective.

Which Plastic Is Most Fantastic?

In *Which Plastic Is Most Fantastic?*, students investigate the properties of two different types of plastic. Clear plastic sandwich bags and thinner plastic grocery bags should show significant differences when tested as described. Because plastics are long chains of connected molecules, plastic sheets often tear more easily along the chains of molecules than across them.

A WonderScience Incrediblob!

In *A WonderScience Incrediblob!* students create a plastic material that can be molded and will bounce off a hard clean surface. Students should work quickly with this material as it dries out fairly rapidly during use. Students also measure length and diameter in millimeters and centimeters.

Recycling: The Shape of Things To Come!

In *Recycling: The Shape of Things To Come!* students are challenged to think of new products that could be produced from recycled plastic foam. Plastic foam can also be shrunk in the oven to produce a more dense and brittle material. You might also try the clear plastic from grocery store salad bar containers. Follow the same directions for shrinking the plastic foam and see which plastic shrinks the most. An interesting point is that plastic foam and the clear plastic container material are actually the same type of plastic called polystyrene. The process used to form each product is what accounts for their very different final properties.

A Plastics Breakthrough!

A Plastics Breakthrough! demonstrates how some plastic is so flexible that it can be punctured but still form a water-tight seal around the object that punctured it. Students will be surprised to see the pencil go all the way through the bag and water with no leakage. This activity should be done over a sink just in case. Also, water will flow from both holes when the pencil is removed.

RELEVANT NATIONAL SCIENCE EDUCATION STANDARDS

The activities in this unit can be used to support the teaching of the following standards:

✔ **Science as Inquiry**
   Abilities necessary to do scientific inquiry

✔ **Physical Science**
   Properties and changes of properties in matter

✔ **Science in Personal and Social Perspectives**
   Science and technology in society

✔ **History and Nature of Science**
   Science as a human endeavor

Which Plastic is

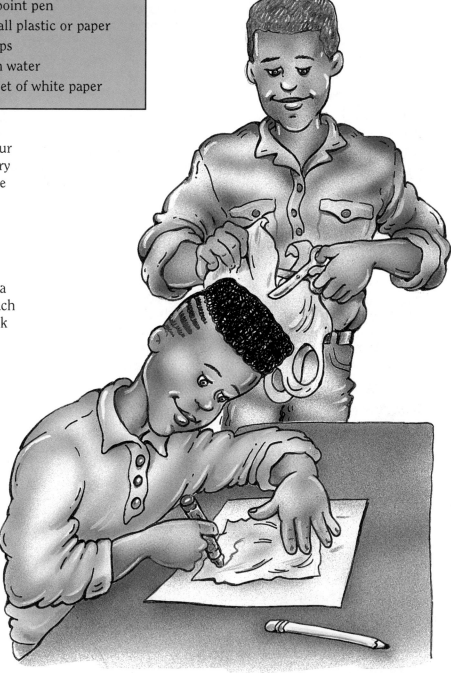

1 Cut a rectangle of plastic from your sandwich bag and from the grocery bag which are the same size as the strip of polyvinyl alcohol plastic (about 10 cm x 15 cm).

2 Put each piece of plastic on the sheet of white paper. If you use a pencil to print your name on each piece of plastic, which one do you think will be easiest to see? Try it!

3 Now try to print your name using a crayon and a pen. Which do you think will work best on which plastic? Was your prediction correct? Do you think that companies need to think about what type of plastic to use for packaging if they want to print a design or message on the package?

4 Does the plastic keep its shape? You and your adult partner should take each piece of plastic and crunch it up into a small ball. Let each ball go and see which type of plastic stays in a ball and which one uncrunches the fastest.

Most Fantastic?

5 How ***strong*** is the plastic? Some plastics are stronger in one direction than another. Take each plastic and try tearing it in the long direction. Now try tearing it across the width. Did the plastic seem to be easier to tear in one direction than the other?

6 Try pulling each plastic slowly from opposite ends to see which plastic stretches the most. Does it matter whether you pull it lengthwise or widthwise?

7 Ask your adult partner to hold one of your plastics tightly over a paper or plastic cup. Use your finger to slowly push through the plastic. Try it with the other two plastics. Which one was the easiest to push through? Which was the most difficult?

8 Put about 1/2 cup of warm water into each of three cups. Cut a 5 cm x 5 cm square from each piece of plastic. Place one square in each cup. Move each piece of plastic between your fingers to see how the different pieces feel. What do you notice about each one?

9 Take each piece out of the water and pull it in opposite directions. Does the water change the way the plastic stretches? What do you notice about the polyvinyl alcohol piece of plastic. Put that piece back in the water and move it between your fingers again to see how much more it changes!

---

* All activities in *WonderScience* have been reviewed for safety by Dr. Jack Breazeale, Francis Marion College, Florence, SC; Dr. Jay Young, Chemical Health and Safety Consultant, Silver Spring, MD; and Dr. Patricia Redden, Saint Peter's College, Jersey City, NJ.

PLASTICS:
Breaking out of the Mold!

There are so many different kinds of plastics and so many products made from plastics that it is almost impossible to list them all. In fact, plastics show up so often and in so many different forms that we sometimes forget what an amazing material plastic really is. Here is a short list of some products that are made of plastic or have plastic in them: plates, cups, utensils, straws, bottles, food containers, plastic wrap, plastic bags, buttons, zippers, parts of shoes, non-stick counter tops, the inside of refrigerators, microwaves, coffee makers, alarm clocks, radios, televisions, CDs, CD players, videocassettes, VCRs, plastic insulation, underground pipes, telephones, computers, furniture, football helmets, tennis rackets, beach balls, Ping-Pong balls, combs, toothbrushes, paint brushes, credit cards, lunch boxes, rulers, notebooks, table cloths, camera film, skateboard wheels, artificial grass, skis, fishing rods, surfboards, toys, and even parts of automobile engines.

Plastics have many qualities that make them so useful. They are lightweight and strong, can be flexible or rigid, can be made almost any color, and can be molded into almost any shape! Plastics are made from oil, natural gas, or coal—all materials found in nature. Plastic companies break these materials down into the small ***molecules*** they are made of and then use heat, pressure, and other chemicals to connect the molecules together into long chains. The types of molecules in the chains and how the chains are connected to each other are what give different plastics their different qualities. The final step is to form the plastic into shapes such as thin sheets for plastic wrap or garbage bags, hollow shapes for soda bottles and other strong containers, or complicated shapes such as the outsides of telephones or computer keyboards.

One of the problems with many plastics is that after they are thrown away, they don't break down naturally in the environment. But the good news is that people are beginning to recycle many different types of plastic. Plastic soda bottles and milk jugs are recycled to produce products such as the fiber in carpeting, the stuffing in bed comforters, plastic lumber, and park benches. There are many companies looking for new ways to recycle plastics. In *Recycling*, we give you a chance to recycle a type of plastic and challenge you to think of new ways!

One of the items you need to obtain is a strip of ***polyvinyl alcohol*** (POLLY VINE-UL ALKA-HALL). This type of plastic is very special because unlike most plastics, it can dissolve in water! An important use for polyvinyl alcohol is for the bags hospitals use to store laundry that might have germs on it. The whole bag can simply be thrown into a washing machine without ever being opened! This way, fewer people have to handle the laundry so fewer people will touch or breathe in the germs. See if you and your adult partner can think of some other uses for this incredible plastic that dissolves in water! There are other important uses for plastics in hospitals and in the medical field. Artificial body parts such as hip joints, heart valves, and arms and legs are now made of plastic and help people live longer, healthier lives. Contact lenses, glasses, X-ray film, and many other medical products are made from plastics.

Plastics are a truly amazing material which we use every day in many helpful ways.

Adapted from "PLASTICS, At Your Service Every Day In Every Way" with permission from The Society of the Plastics Industry, Inc.

A WonderScience
Incrediblob!

You can use chemistry in the following activity
to make your own plastic ball like the one the *WonderScience* cat
is using on the cover of your *WonderScience!*

1 Cover your work surface with a double layer of paper towels. In a small cup, place 1 tablespoon of Elmer's® glue.

2 In a separate small cup, add 1/2 teaspoon of Epsom salt and 1/2 teaspoon of water. Swirl the cup until no more Epsom salt will dissolve. (There may be a little Epsom salt left at the bottom of the cup).

3 Pour all the contents from the Epsom salt cup into the glue cup and stir. What do you notice happening to your mixture? What does your mixture look like?

4 Scoop the mixture out onto a double thickness of paper towels. Fold the towels over the mixture and press down to absorb the extra water.

You will need

paper towels	plastic spoon
measuring spoons	2 small paper or plastic cups
Elmer's® white liquid glue	
Epsom salt	wax paper
water	metric ruler

5 Pick up your plastic and form it into a long roll. Measure it to see how long you can make it without it breaking. (Try to work quickly because your plastic material will dry out as you use it).

6 Form your plastic into a ball and press it down on a piece of wax paper until it is like a pancake. Measure the diameter of the pancake to see how large you can make it and still be able to lift it off the wax paper in one piece.

7 Form it back into a ball and try bouncing it off a hard clean surface. Congratulations on creating an incredible incrediblob incrediball!

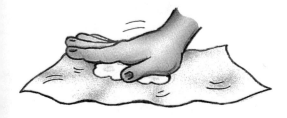

Recycling:

Did you know that the foam cups used for hot coffee, tea, and other drinks are made from plastic? Instead of dissolving away like your special plastic from page 3, this plastic will build up in the environment if we don't find ways to recycle it. We thought of an easy way to recycle plastic foam to make a coaster for mugs. Can you think of other products you could make from recycled plastic foam?

You will need

1 16-oz plastic foam cup	clear plastic tape
1 paper or plastic cup	wax paper
white liquid school glue	blunt-end scissors
spoon	thin cardboard/poster board

1 Ask your adult partner to help you break up a plastic foam cup into small pieces about 1 cm long. Place all the pieces in a cup.

2 Add 2 tablespoons of white liquid glue and a drop of red, blue, or yellow food color. Mix thoroughly.

3 Cut a strip of cardboard about 30 cm long and about 2 to 3 cm wide and curve it into a circle as shown. Tape the ends of the cardboard together. (If you like, you may make another shape, like a square or a diamond!)

4 Put your cardboard shape on wax paper and scoop all of your glue/plastic mixture into it. Level the mixture out with the back of a spoon and let it dry overnight. Decorate the outer cardboard part of your coaster with crayons, paint, or glitter to make a beautiful recycled *WonderScience* coaster!

The Shape of Things To Come!

Another interesting thing about plastic foam is that it shrinks and hardens when you heat it. In fact, another way to recycle plastic foam is to shrink and harden it to form new products. But before you can decide what new products you can make from it, you first need to find out how much it shrinks!

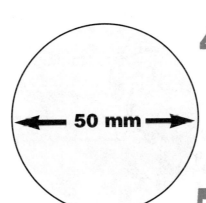

You will need

2 plastic foam sheets
   (from a meat tray or
   disposable container)
cookie sheet
oven mitt

spatula
metric ruler
blunt-end scissors
ball point pens (different
   colors)

50 mm

◄— 50 mm —►

1 Use your scissors to cut out a plastic foam square and circle the size of the pictures shown.

2 Record the length of the sides of the square and the *diameter* of the circle in the chart under **BEFORE**.

3 Ask your adult partner to preheat your oven on bake to 200 degrees F. Place your shapes on a cookie sheet and place the cookie sheet in the oven for three to five minutes.

4 Use an oven mitt to take the cookie sheet out of the oven and set it aside for 10–15 minutes. Use a spatula to remove your plastic foam shapes. How do they look? How do they feel? Measure the sides of the square and the diameter of the circle and record the measurements in your chart under **AFTER**.

5 To find out how many times longer the sides of the square and the diameter of the circle were before they were shrunk compared with after they were shrunk, do the division shown at the bottom left of this page.

6 One possible recycled product from shrinking plastic foam could be glue-on decorations for cards, presents, or key chains. Use different colored ball point pens to draw pictures on different shapes of plastic foam and have your adult partner help you shrink them!

	BEFORE	*AFTER*
SQUARE	mm	mm
CIRCLE	mm	mm

BEFORE ÷ AFTER = How many times longer the sides of the square and the diameter of the circle were *before* they were shrunk compared to *after*.

What other products can you and your adult partner create by shrinking plastic foam?

A Plastics Breakthrough!

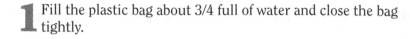

The flexibility and moldability of plastics allows them to cling to surfaces and to fit tightly around or inside many different shapes. In this activity, you will see how tightly plastic can fit around the shape of a pencil.

You will need

1 zip-closing plastic
   sandwich bag

1 pencil

water

paper towels

1 Fill the plastic bag about 3/4 full of water and close the bag tightly.

2 Get your adult partner and hold the bag over the kitchen or bathroom sink. While holding the bag, have your adult partner slowly push the point of the pencil through one side of the plastic bag and into the water. Did any of the water spill? ***Warning: The point of the pencil may be sharp; please handle it with care.***

3 Look closely at the plastic bag around the pencil. How would you describe the way the plastic bag fits around the pencil?

4 Do you think the pencil can go all the way through the water and out the other side of the bag without any water spilling? Ask your adult partner to slowly push the pencil all the way through the other side of the bag! Did any water spill?

5 Can you think of any special uses for this type of plastic? What products do you think could be made from this plastic so that the contents wouldn't leak even if it got punctured?

If you were a plastics researcher and were trying to invent a new plastic, what special quality would your plastic have? How would it be used? How would it make people's lives better without harming the environment?

Andrea Hazlitt is a scientist who invents new plastics and new ways for using plastics. Some plastics she has helped invent have ***carbon*** fibers in them, making the plastics lightweight and stronger than steel! These plastics are used in racing bicycles, tennis racquets, and even airplane bodies. Andrea also worked on a plastic coating for jet plane windows so that they wouldn't get scratched by particles in the air and on a plastic that had enough carbon in it to conduct electricity! She says that working with plastics is fun because there are so many types of plastics and so many different uses for them. To be a plastics inventor, she says, "be creative and use your imagination!"

WONDER SCIENCE

Rubber

This unit introduces students to some of the properties of rubber. The main point of the unit is that rubber's stretchy and bouncy properties are related to the chemicals that compose it.

Get A Grip!

In *Get A Grip!* students investigate one of the properties of rubber that makes it so valuable as material for shoe soles. The traction or grip that rubber soles seem to have for certain surfaces such as a cement sidewalk, an asphalt road, or a tile floor is a result of the force of friction between the rubber and the surface. The interaction between the rubber and the surface against which it is rubbed makes rubber a useful material for shoes.

Make Tracks with Rubber!

Make Tracks with Rubber! explains some of the chemistry that makes up this interesting material. The main molecule in rubber is called *isoprene*. It is composed of 5 carbon atoms and 8 hydrogen atoms. Many isoprene molecules are connected in a long chain to make a polymer called polyisoprene, which is natural rubber. These long polymer molecules are twisted, coiled, entangled, and flexible, giving rubber its ability to stretch or be compressed and then to return to its original shape.

A Stampede!

A Stampede! illustrates rubber's ability to pick up ink and then to lay it down on paper or another surface. Rubber's ability to do this is based on the interaction between the atoms and molecules in rubber and the atoms and molecules that compose the ink and the surface being inked. You might ask students why rubber is able to erase pencil marks from paper. (The attraction between rubber and the material in pencil must be stronger than the attraction between paper and the material in pencil.)

Rubber Band Racer!

In *Rubber Band Racer!* students create a little vehicle which gets its power from a twisted rubber band. Your racer works well when the eraser end of the pencil is not touching the surface on which the racer is traveling.

A WonderScience Boing Bat!

A WonderScience Boing Bat! offers an opportunity for some friendly competition between students. Changing the tension of the balloon should produce different results. You could compare these results to changing the tensions on a drum or trampoline.

Rubber is Amazing—Get the Point?

Rubber is Amazing—Get the Point? looks at rubber's ability to seal around an object such as a nail, tack, or pin. Practice doing this activity so you know what to expect. A slow, patient pressure of the pin against the balloon while twisting the pin should work. Remember to add just enough water to fill the balloon's shape without stretching it.

RELEVANT NATIONAL SCIENCE EDUCATION STANDARDS

The activities in this unit can be used to support the teaching of the following standards:

✔ Science as Inquiry
  Abilities necessary to do scientific inquiry

✔ Physical Science
  Properties and changes of property in matter
  Transfer of energy

✔ Life Science
  Diversity and adaptations of organisms

✔ Science in Personal and Social Perspectives
  Science and technology in society

✔ History and Nature of Science
  Science as a human endeavor

GET A GRIP!

Did you ever notice how your sneakers or other shoes with rubber soles grab the floor or ground better than shoes with other kinds of soles? When a material kind of sticks to the ground to let you grip and push off better, we say that the material gives you good *traction*. In the activity below, you can test the traction of different materials and see which you would use if you were designing a pair of shoes.

1 Use your scissors to cut a balloon into two sections as shown. **Save the round end of the balloon for step 6.** Now cut out a square piece from the other end of the balloon that is approximately 5 cm × 5 cm. Cut a 5 cm × 5 cm square from your paper and a 5 cm × 5 cm square from your plastic.

2 Put your index finger on the paper. Slide the paper across a smooth hard surface as you push down harder and harder on the paper. Was it difficult to keep the paper sliding as you pushed down on it? Try the same thing with your piece of plastic. Did it feel any different from the paper?

3 Now try the same thing you did in step 2 with your piece of rubber from the balloon. Were you able to push it along as easily as the other materials? Does this give you any ideas about why rubber is used for tires and the soles of shoes?

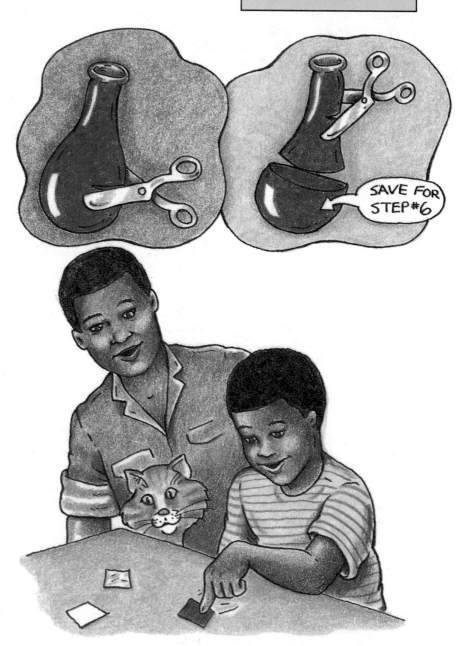

SAVE FOR STEP #6

Remember to throw out your balloon pieces after doing these activities!

4 Cut out circles from your paper and plastic that are about 20 cm in diameter. Ask your adult partner to tape the paper on the front of your shoe as shown. Push off with the front of your foot as if you were starting a race. Does the paper give you good traction?

5 Repeat step 4 using your piece of plastic. Did you get better traction with the plastic? Do you think your traction will improve if you use the rubber from the balloon on your shoe? Let's try it and see!

6 Take the round part of the balloon and stretch it over the front of your shoe. Try pushing off with the front of your shoe as you did before. Does your traction improve when you use the rubber from the balloon?

> **Be sure to keep your balance while trying steps 4 and 5!**

---

* All activities in *WonderScience* have been reviewed for safety by Dr. Jack Breazeale, Francis Marion University, Florence, SC; Dr. Jay Young, Chemical Health and Safety Consultant, Silver Spring, MD; and Dr. Patricia Redden, Saint Peter's College, Jersey City, NJ.

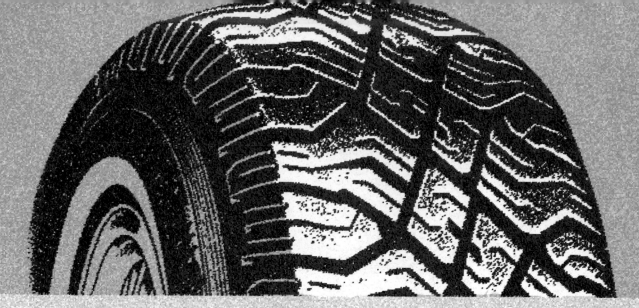

MAKE TRACKS WITH RUBBER!

Cars, buses, airplanes, and bicycles would have a lot of trouble working as well as they do without tires made of rubber. The inside of many basketballs, golf, tennis, and super bouncing balls, and even bowling balls would not have the bounce, flight, or impact they need if they weren't made of rubber. Many engines and other machines wouldn't work as well or as long without the rubber hoses, belts, and washers as important rubber parts. Erasers, balloons, the elastic in clothes, rubber bands, life rafts, the soles on sneakers and other athletic shoes, wet suits, and of course, baby buggy bumpers, all have special qualities and uses because they are made of rubber.

Rubber is an amazing material. Rubber was named by a scientist named Joseph Priestley who discovered, in the late 1700s, that it could *rub* out pencil marks.

Natural rubber is produced from a milky material found in a few different types of tropical trees. This white liquid is called *latex*. The latex is collected by making circular cuts around the trunk of the tree. The latex flows down the cuts and is collected in cups. The cuts stop flowing in about a day and need to be reopened if more latex is needed. The cutting doesn't seem to hurt the trees. The best trees for gathering latex grow wild in Brazil. These trees are now grown on large farms in the country of Malaysia. In fact, Malaysia is the world's largest producer of natural rubber.

There are different ways to process the latex into usable rubber. One of the oldest methods is to drip the latex onto a stick over a fire. The latex changes from a loose liquid to its more familiar rubbery texture. Another method is to mix the latex with an acid.

There is a particular molecule in latex that forms rubber. In the 1950s, scientists discovered how to make this molecule in the laboratory! Rubber produced from this laboratory-made molecule is called *synthetic* rubber. In both natural and synthetic rubber, this molecule is connected to itself over and over again in a long chain called a *polymer*. Because of the special qualities of the molecule, the chains become coiled and tangled with each other. The flexibility of these coiled and twisted polymers is what gives natural rubber and synthetic rubber its bounciness.

The majority of the rubber sold in the world is used to make car tires. The rubber used in tires must go through a special process called *vulcanization*. In this process, the chemical *sulfur* is used to connect the long rubber polymers together at different places along their chains. Vulcanization improves the strength of the rubber so that tires will perform better and last longer. The vulcanization process was invented by Charles Goodyear in the early 1840s.

Rubber has come a long way since those early days. Today we see rubber all around us. So the next time you are running in your favorite sneakers, riding your bike, bouncing a ball, or erasing a rare mistake, remember that the chemistry of rubber makes it possible!

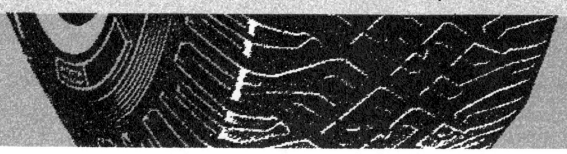

A Stampede!

You will need

2 rectangular pink school erasers
ball point pens (red, blue, green)
cardboard
white paper
blunt-end scissors

Because of the chemicals that make up rubber, rubber has a way of picking up ink and then releasing the ink to paper. Printing presses still use rubber rollers to pick up ink and to apply it to the surface that needs to be printed. In the activity below, you can see that rubber makes a great stamp.

1 Cut a piece of cardboard into a square that is about 5 cm on each side. Now take your eraser and draw a line to divide it in half.

2 Draw a simple shape such as a star or heart on your cardboard and on the eraser. Fill both of them in with a lot of ink to make them very dark.

3 Turn the eraser and the cardboard upside down on a piece of paper. Press down hard on both of them and then lift them off the paper. Which one printed better? Why do you think one worked better than the other?

4 On the other half of your eraser draw another star or other simple picture like a flower. You could use different colored pens for different parts of the flower. Remember to color each part very dark. See how many good clear prints on your paper you can make without re-inking your eraser.

5 You can use the other eraser to make a stamp of your name. This is not as easy as you might think. To have your name come out correctly when you print it, you have to write it backwards on the eraser. Here are two examples of how you would have to print a name to make it come out correctly when you print it:

Add some designs around your name!
Use different colors, be creative, and have fun!

ꓤOBEꓤT

MAꓤIA

RUBBER BAND RACER!

One of the useful things about rubber is its ability to store *energy*. When you use your energy to stretch or twist a rubber band, the stretched rubber band has some of that energy stored in it. When you let a stretched rubber band go, it can use the energy stored in it to do some kind of work. A stretched rubber band can propel toy airplanes or, in the activity below, a Rubber Band Racer!

You will need

large sewing thread spool (with or without thread)

2 paper clips

tape

plastic drinking straw

rubber band (about twice the length of your spool)

unsharpened pencil

blunt-end scissors

1 If your spool still has thread on it, use a piece of tape to tape down the thread so it will not unravel. Do not remove the paper from the ends of the spool. If the paper has been removed, cut two circles of paper to the correct size and glue each to the ends of the spool.

2 Use a pencil to poke through the paper at the center holes on the ends of the spool. Stand a straw next to your spool and cut a piece of straw that is about 1 cm longer than your spool.

3 Take a rubber band and push it as far as you can into the straw. Ask your adult partner to help you unbend a paper clip. Use the paper clip to reach into the straw to pull the rubber band through until some rubber band is sticking out of both ends of the straw.

4 Put the straw through the spool. About 1 cm of straw should be sticking out. Thread the rubber band at one end of the spool through the paper clip as shown. Use several pieces of tape to securely tape the paper clip to the paper at the end of the spool.

5 Slip a pencil through the rubber band at the other end of the spool. Wind the rubber band by twirling the pencil around as if you were winding up a toy propeller. Wind the rubber band a lot. Make sure that all the twisting in the rubber band is inside the straw.

6 Place the rubber band racer on the floor as shown with the eraser end of the pencil pointing up. Let it go! Try other size spools, rubber bands, pencils, and straws until you have a design that goes the farthest and fastest!

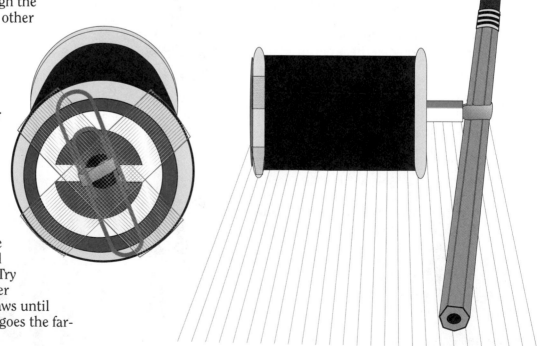

A WonderScience Boing Bat!

You will need

aluminum foil	rubber band
plastic bag	ruler
balloon	tape
blunt-end scissors	table tennis ball
sturdy plastic cup	

Another great thing about rubber is its bounciness. Many toys are made with rubber because of rubber's ability to bounce. Already you read about the molecules in rubber that make it bounce. In the activity below, you can test certain materials for bounciness and make your own bounce toy!

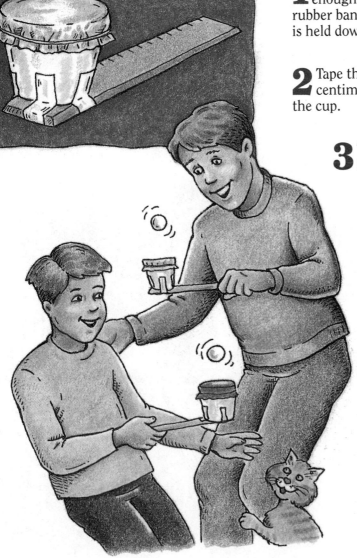

1 Cut out a square or circle of aluminum foil large enough to easily cover the top of your cup. Place a rubber band around the rim of the cup so that the foil is held down securely.

2 Tape the cup to a ruler so that at least 1 or 2 centimeters of the ruler is sticking out beyond the cup.

3 Take your table tennis ball and try bouncing it off the aluminum foil while holding the end of the ruler as a handle. How elastic was your aluminum foil?

4 Repeat steps 1–3 using plastic from a plastic bag. Was the plastic elastic enough to bounce the table tennis ball well?

5 Use scissors to cut your balloon in half. Repeat steps 1–3 by stretching the round part of the balloon over your plastic cup. Try bouncing the table tennis ball on your balloon surface. Does the rubber make the ball bounce better than the other two materials?

6 Try stretching the balloon more tightly or more loosely over your cup to see which gives a better bounce. See how many times in a row you can bounce the ball. Challenge your adult partner to an elasticity bouncing competition!

Rubber Is Amazing—
Get the Point?

Another important quality of rubber is its ability to seal things tightly. When a nail goes into a tire, rubber's elasticity allows it to squeeze itself around the nail. Sometimes a nail can stay in a tire for a long time with no air escaping! Try the activity below to see what we mean.

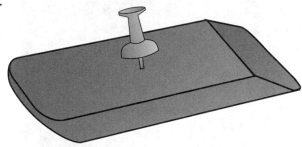

> ### Be careful when handling pins; they are very sharp!

1 Place your pink eraser on the table in front of you. Poke a push pin all the way into the eraser. Pull the push pin out. What do you notice about the size of the hole and the size of the push pin that went into the eraser? Why do you think the hole looks as small as it does?

Let's try something different!

You and your adult partner should do this activity outside or over a sink.

1 Put just enough water in your balloon to fill the shape of the balloon without stretching it.

2 Pour a few drops of vegetable oil into a small cup. Take a straight pin and dip the tip into the oil.

3 Take the pin and slowly push it into the balloon while twisting the pin between your fingers. Push the pin into the balloon so that about half the pin is in the balloon and half is sticking out. The rubber that makes up the balloon should seal around the pin and no water should leak out of the balloon.

4 Push a few more pins into the balloon. With some practice, you should get better at it. Try pushing a pin into the balloon without putting oil on it. If you are outside or over a sink, take one of the pins out to see what happens. This is similar to the way air escapes from a tire when a nail is removed.

You will need

rectangular pink school eraser

push pin

balloon

water

straight pins

vegetable oil

small cup or other small container

WONDERSCIENCE

Metals

This unit introduces students to some of the properties of metals. On the atomic level, different metals have certain similarities because the structure of their atoms is similar. In metal atoms, the electrons on the outermost part of the atoms come off relatively easily. This makes metals react in a particular way with other chemicals and gives metals the properties that are so useful in everyday life.

Corrosion—Metals' Chemical Enemy!

In *Corrosion—Metals' Chemical Enemy!* the greatest amount of rust should form on the steel wool exposed to both water and air. For rust to form, oxygen in the air and water must react with the iron in the steel. Stainless steel doesn't rust because the metal nickel, chromium, or manganese is added to the steel which prevents rusting.

In the short activity about removing tarnish from pennies by using lemon juice, citric acid in the lemon juice reacts with the chemical compounds that make up the tarnish causing the tarnish to break apart and to detach from the copper.

Shape Up With Metal Malleability!

In *Shape Up With Metal Malleability!* students work together on an art project while exploring metals' malleability.

Magnetism and Metals—Maybe Yes, Maybe No

In *Magnetism and Metals—Maybe Yes, Maybe No*, students can dispel a widely held misconception that all metals are magnetic.

Metals in Music—They're Instrumental!

In *Metals in Music—They're Instrumental!* a metal cooling rack for cookies or a metal rack from a toaster oven can be used instead of a hanger. Be sure these objects are not hot when you are about to use them in an activity.

Metals Can be Hot Stuff!

In *Metals Can be Hot Stuff!* the property of metals as heat conductors is explored. Make sure that the two plastic cups used are exactly the same type. Also be sure the students hold the cups so that the paper and the aluminum foil are flush against the sides of the cups. The cup with the aluminum foil should feel hotter because aluminum conducts heat better than paper.

Metals are Electrifying!

Metals are Electrifying! shows that aluminum is better than paper for conducting electricity. While doing this activity, students will learn the origin of Morse Code and how to use it.

RELEVANT NATIONAL SCIENCE EDUCATION STANDARDS

The activities in this unit can be used to support the teaching of the following standards:

✔ **Science as Inquiry**
Abilities necessary to do scientific inquiry

✔ **Physical Science**
Properties and changes of properties in matter
Transfer of energy

✔ **Life Science**
Structure and function of living systems

CORROSION —METALS'

When certain chemicals touch certain metals, a *chemical reaction* can happen which changes some of the metal into a new substance. If this happens for a long enough time, the metal will begin to get weaker and may begin to change the way it looks. This process is called *corrosion*.

One type of corrosion is *rust*. Rust is the orange-colored chemical you sometimes see on metal parts of toys, bicycles, cars, and other objects. Only substances that contain the metal *iron* can rust.

Steel wool aluminum foil are both made of metal, but only the one that has iron in it will rust. Do you know which one it it? In order for it to rust, iron must come in contact with two other chemicals. Do you know what They are?

Let's do an experiment to find out whether steel wool or aluminum foil contains iron and which two chemicals make iron rust.

1 If you have steel wool with soap in it, ask your adult partner to put on rubber gloves and to wash the steel wool in warm water until all the soap is removed. Your adult partner should cut off a piece of steel wool and dry it as completely as possible with paper towels.

2 Place the piece of dry steel wool in the bottom of one of the paper cups. Use your tape and crayon to label this cup **Steel Wool Plus Air**.

3 Place an equal amount of steel wool in a second cup and add 1/4 cup of water. Mark this cup **Steel Wool Plus Air Plus Water**.

You will need
rubber gloves
steel wool (with or without soap)
Paper towels
Plastic wrap
water
aluminum foil
6 paper cups
masking tape
crayon
blunt-end scissors

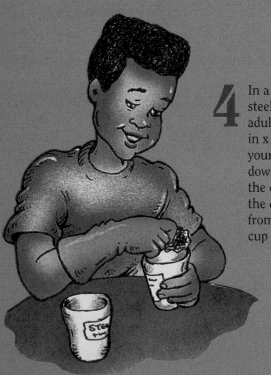

4 In a third cup, place the same amount of steel wool, plus 1/4 cup of water. Ask your adult partner to cut a 12.5 cm x 12.5 cm (5 in x in) square piece of plastic wrap. Have your adult partner push the plastic wrap down onto the surface of the water and tape the edges of the plastic wrap to the inside of the cup. This should keep as much air away from the steel wool as possible. Mark this cup **Steel Wool Plus Water**.

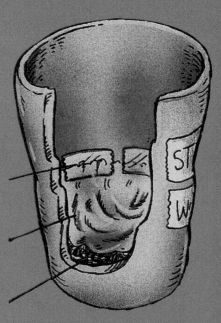

CLEAR PLASTIC TAPE

PLASTIC WRAP

STEEL WOOL +WATER

---

* All activities in *WonderScience* have been reviewed for safety by Dr. Jack Breazeale, Francis Marion College, Florence, SC; Dr. Jay Young, Chemical Health and Safety Consultant, Silver Spring, MD; and and Dr. Patricia Redden, Saint Peter's College, Jersey City, NJ.

CHEMICAL ENEMY!*

5 Take a piece of aluminum foil and cut it into 15 very thin strips (about .5 cm wide and 15 cm long)(1/8 in x 6 in). Set up three cups with 5 aluminum foil strips in each, just like the ones you set up for the wool. Label these cups Aluminum Foil Plus Air, Aluminum Foil Plus Air Plus Water, and Aluminum Foil Plus Water?

6 Allow the cups to stay in one spot for about three days. Check the cups at the end of each day. Did any of the steel wool cups or any of the aluminum foil cups get rusty? Does steel wool or aluminum foil contain iron.

7 Look at the steel wool cups. In which cup did the steel wool become the most rusted? What two chemicals do you think make iron rust?

Try this *corrosion* experiment:
You know that some pennies are bright and shiny and some are dull and dark. Pennies become dark because of the process of *corrosion*. *Water*, *oxygen*, and a chemical called *sulfur* cause some of the *copper* metal on the pennies to change into another darker chemical. People call this dark chemical *tarnish*. You can use chemistry to help remove the tarnish from your pennies and make them shiny again!

1 Line up three dull dark pennies on a paper towel.

2 Press down on a lemon while rolling it on a kitchen counter to make the lemon juicy.

3 Have your adult partner cut the lemon in half.

4 Take a lemon half and squeeze it over one of the pennies so that *one* drop of lemon juice falls on the date on the front of the penny.

5 On the next penny, put a drop of lemon juice on Abraham Lincoln's profile. On the third penny, put a drop on the back of the penny on the Latin words *E PLURIBUS UNUM* (that means "One Out of Many").

6 Let the drops stay on the pennies for about 10 minutes, then wash them off. WOW! Maybe lemons could be used to shine up the Statue of Liberty!

TO ALL WONDERSCIENTISTS— YOU DESERVE A *METAL!*

You wake up in the morning and turn *metal* handles to make water run out of a *metal* faucet so you can wash and get ready for school. While getting dressed, you probably close a *metal* buckle, zip a *metal* zipper, and put on a *metal* watch or other *metal* jewelry. You might look in a mirror, which is usually a piece of glass coated with *metal* on the back. In the kitchen, you could get something from a *metal* refrigerator; put bread in a *metal* toaster; or eat breakfast with a *metal* knife, fork, or spoon. You could wrap your sandwich in *metal* foil and put it in a *metal* lunch box or put *metal* coins in your pocket to buy lunch at school. You probably use a *metal* doorknob to open a door on *metal* hinges to walk to the bus stop to get into a *metal* bus. On the way, you might pass some *metal* signs and *metal* mail boxes or see a *metal* airplane flying overhead. It's still early and you have already seen, touched, and used a lot of *metal*.

Metals are a group of chemicals that have certain things in common. Most can be formed into different shapes, some are magnetic, most allow heat and electricity to move through them easily, and many are a shiny silvery color. The reason why many metals have so much in common is that the *electrons* in the *atoms* that make up the metals are arranged in a similar way.

Sometimes, a metal can be made stronger, lighter, or better for a certain job if another metal or some other chemical is mixed with it. The mixture that results is called an *alloy*. *Bronze* is an alloy of *copper* and *tin*. *Brass* is an alloy of *copper* and *zinc*. In "CORROSION—Metals' Chemical Enemy," the steel wool rusted because steel has iron in it. *Steel* is an alloy of *iron* and *carbon*. Because steel contains iron, it can rust. In this experiment you should have observed that the steel wool in the cup with water and air became the most rusted. *Water* caused *oxygen* from the air to mix with the iron causing a *chemical reaction* to take place. This reaction formed the new chemical, *rust*.

Some metals are used in very interesting ways: *Gold* can be used to make the tiny electrical circuits on computer microchips. *Silver* is an important part of X-ray film and other film used in photography. *Mercury*, the only metal that is a liquid at room temperature, is used in thermometers and barometers. *Lead* is often used to line the huge safes in banks and can be used in shields to protect people from X-rays. The metals *magnesium, sodium,* and *potassium* are needed, in very tiny amounts, in your own body; they are also used, in a different form, in fireworks!

Illustration by Tina Mion

SHAPE UP
WITH METAL MALLEABILITY!

You will need

aluminum foil
metal clothes hanger
string
blunt-end scissors
cardboard
white liquid school glue
coins
metal paper clips
metal bottle caps
safety pins
keys

THE WORD **MALLEABILITY** MEANS THE ABILITY OF A MATERIAL TO BE BENT OR POUNDED INTO DIFFERENT SHAPES. MOST **METALS** ARE MALLEABLE AND CAN BE MOLDED INTO ALMOST ANY SHAPE. YOU CAN BECOME A WONDERSCIENCE ARTIST BY USING MALLEABILITY TO CREATE A METAL SCUPLTURE FROM YOUR OWN BODY!

1 Put your hand and arm flat on a table with your fingers spread far apart. Have your adult partner take a piece of aluminum foil and mold it over your fingers, thumb, wrist, and part of your arm. Your adult partner should now carefully lift up the aluminum foil sculpture and put it aside.

2 Ask your adult partner to mold aluminum foil to your other hand and arm in the same way. Take off your shoes and socks and have your adult partner mold a piece of aluminum foil to your toes, feet, ankles, and part of your legs.

3 For your sculpture's face, cut apiece of cardboard into a circle about the size of your own face.

4 Glue coins, paper clips, metal bottle caps, safety pins, and an old key to your cardboard to make a face for your sculpture.

5 You and your adult partner can use scissors to cut the extra aluminum foil from between the fingers and from around the models of your hands and feet.

6 Take a clothes hanger and hang it from the top of a door. use a pen or pencil to make a hole in each body part. Tie one end of a piece of string through the hole and the other end to the hanger so that the body part hangs at the right level for your body.

7 Make a statue of your adult partner—it's *FUN!*

MAGNETISM AND METALS— MAYBE YES, MAYBE NO

You will need

refrigerator memo magnet
wood or stiff plastic ruler
clear plastic tape
key
metal paper clip
metal spoon
aluminum foil ball
hair pin
safety pin
penny
nickel
dime
quarter
metal jar lid
nail
metal bottle cap

1 Use the tape to attach your refrigerator magnet to the end of the ruler so that the magnet is facing *away* from the ruler. It is not necessary to remove the magnet from its decorative casing.

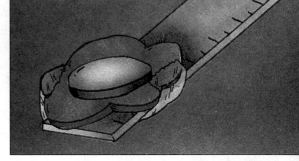

2 Place your metal objects in a row and predict which ones are magnetic and which ones are not. If you think the object *is* magnetic, write *YES* in the box next to the object under *Prediction*. If you think it *is not* magnetic, write *NO* in the same box.

Illustration by Lori Seskin-Newman

3 Put all your metal items in a pile and move the magnet through the pile. Take the magnet out and see which items were attracted to the magnet. Put these in one area and put the magnet back into the pile to pick up any magnetic objects you may have missed.

4 Look at the chart under *Result* and write *YES* if the object *was* attracted to the magnet and write *NO* if it *was not* attracted. Were your predictions usually correct? Is there any way of telling if a metal is magnetic just by looking at it?

METAL OBJECT	PREDICTION	RESULT
KEY		
METAL PAPER CLIP		
METAL SPOON		
ALUMINUM FOIL BALL		
HAIR PIN		
SAFETY PIN		
PENNY		
NICKEL		
DIME		
QUARTER		
METAL JAR LID		
NAIL		
METAL BOTTLE CAP		

5 Take one of the objects that was magnetic and place it on the magnet for about a minute. Now take it off the magnet and see if it can attract your other magnetic objects. Metals that are magnetic can be made into magnets themselves!

METALS IN MUSIC— THEY'RE *INSTRUMENTAL!*

Metals are often used to make musical instruments, such as cymbals, triangles, xylophones, and bells that you hit to make a sound. Metals make good musical instruments because different sizes, shapes, thicknesses, and types of metals vibrate differently and make different sounds. Make your own instrument from metals and become a *WonderScience* Metals Musician!

You will need
a metal coat hanger
three metal spoons of different sizes
string
pen

1 Get a piece of string about 2/3 meter (about 2 feet long). Tie a metal coat hanger to the center of the string as shown.

2 Tie the three spoons separately along the string.

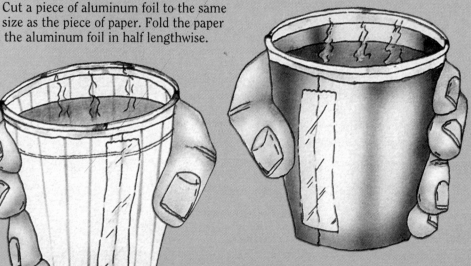

Illustration by Lori Seskin-Newman

3 Make a loop at each end of the string. Put your index fingers through the loops and put the ends of your index fingers in your ears.

4 Ask your adult partner to gently strike the hanger with the pen. How does it sound Have your adult partner strike the other metal objects at different times and in different order to see how the metals sound.

5 Let your adult partner listen while you play your new *WonderScience* metals instrument! Tie some other metal objects on your string and see how the sound changes!

Metals Can Be *HOT STUFF!*

You will need
two clear plastic cups
1 piece of notebook or typing paper
aluminum foil
clear plastic tape

1 Cut a piece of aluminum foil to the same size as the piece of paper. Fold the paper and the aluminum foil in half lengthwise.

2 Wrap one cup with the paper and one cup with the aluminum foil. Use a piece of tape to keep the wrappings on the cups.

3 Ask your adult partner to put hot water from the faucet into both cups and to hand the cups to you immediately (be careful not to spill the water).

4 With your hands around each cup, see if you can tell whether the paper or the aluminum foil allows the most heat to pass from the cup to your hand.

5 If a material allows heat to travel through it easily, it is called a good *conductor* of heat. Is the aluminum foil or the paper a better conductor of heat?

Illustration by Lori Seskin-Newman

METALS ARE *ELECTRIFYING!*

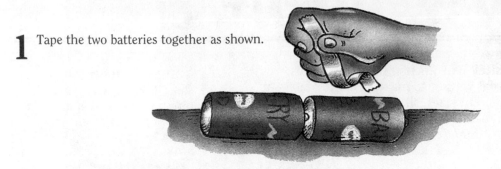

1 Tape the two batteries together as shown.

You will need
2 flashlight batteries (size D)
1 flashlight bulb
masking tape
aluminum foil
1 piece of typing or notebook paper

2 Cut two strips of aluminum foil about .5 cm wide and 18 cm long (approx. 1/4 in x 7 in). Cut two strips of paper to the same size.

3 Tape one end of each aluminum strip to opposite ends of the batteries.

4 Wrap the free end of one of the aluminum strips around the metal casing of the light bulb.

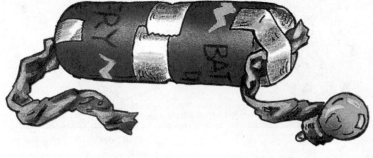

5 While your adult partner holds the taped aluminum strips firmly to the ends of the batteries, you hold the aluminum strip around the metal casing of the bulb and touch the very bottom of the bulb to the other aluminum strip. **Note: Do not let the aluminum foil strips touch each other, or your bulb will not light.**

6 Do exactly the same experiment using your paper strips instead of the aluminum strips. Does the paper or the aluminum allow the electricity to flow? If electricity can flow through a material, the material is said to be a *conductor* of electricity. Is paper or aluminum a better conductor of electricity?

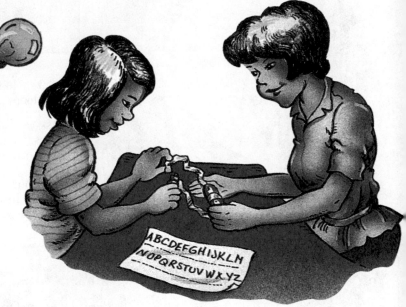

7 You can use the batteries, aluminum strips, and bulb to make a *WonderScience* Code Signaler!

A famous code was invented in 1838 by a scientist and painter Samuel Morse. The code is called **MORSE CODE** and was used to send messages over *telegraph* wires or by flashing lights. The code, which was changed a little and called The International Morse Code, looks like this:

A	B	C	D	E	F	G	H	I	J	K	L	M
•−	−•••	−•−•	−••	•	••−•	−−•	••••	••	•−−−	−•−	•−••	−−

N	O	P	Q	R	S	T	U	V	W	X	Y	Z
−•	−−−	•−−•	−−•−	•−•	•••	−	••−	•••−	•−−	−••−	−•−−	−−••

A dot (•) means that you make a very quick flash of the light by touching the bulb to the aluminum strip and lifting it up very quickly. A dash (−) means that you leave the light on a little longer.

When you are done with the letter, wait a bit longer before starting the next one.

Think of a word and flash it in International Morse Code. Give your adult partner the International Morse Code decoder on this page and see if he or she can figure out the word you are sending. Send your name! Send the name of a metal! Let your adult partner send you words and see if you can figure them out!

This unit introduces students to some of the basic properties of insulators. The unit deals only with heat insulators, not sound, electrical, or other types.

The purpose of a heat insulator is to inhibit the transfer of heat. Heat is the energy that is transferred through a material or from one material to another when there is a difference in temperature. The heat energy is always transferred from the area of high temperature to the area of lower temperature. In order for this to happen, there must be a medium of atoms or molecules that can vibrate or otherwise move to transfer the energy. The types of atoms and molecules and their arrangement in a material determines how well the material will act as an insulator. The atoms and molecules in some materials, such as rubber and many plastics, do not transfer heat well and make these materials good insulators. The particles in other materials, such as most metals, do transfer heat well, making them generally poor insulators.

Cold or Hot—Insulation Helps A Lot!

Cold or Hot—Insulation Helps A Lot! can be used to emphasize that insulation has the ability to keep cold things cold and hot things hot. It should be stressed that insulation does these seemingly different functions in the same way: by slowing down the transfer of heat. A coat keeps you warm in the winter because it helps prevent the flow of heat out from the surface of your body. A plastic foam cup keeps a drink cold because it slows down the flow of heat into the cup.

Ice should form most slowly in the cups insulated with cotton and with foam. After the ice forms, it should also be slowest to melt in the cotton and foam cups. In all of the cups, there is a significant amount of trapped air between the pieces of material in the cup. Trapped air is a good insulator because the molecules that make up the gases in air are far enough apart to be relatively poor at transferring heat.

Heat's In—You Win!

Heat's In—You Win! illustrates that because hot air rises, a significant amount of heat may flow through the roof of a house if it is not well insulated. Insulating the roof of your model house should help students see why it is important to use insulation between the ceiling and roof of a real house.

Cool Ways to Stay Warm!

Cool Ways to Stay Warm! offers a series of related activities on insulation that can slow down the transfer of heat from your fingers to cold water. The lard or vegetable shortening can be compared to the fat on walruses and seals. The activity with the balloon and cotton shows that the insulating ability of each material is due to a combination of the characteristics of the material itself and the presence of trapped air.

Insulation: Nature's a Natural

Insulation: Nature's a Natural illustrates the similarities between the way people use insulation and how insulation is used in nature.

RELEVANT NATIONAL SCIENCE EDUCATION STANDARDS

The activities in this unit can be used to support the teaching of the following standards:

✔ **Science as Inquiry**
Abilities necessary to do scientific inquiry

✔ **Physical Science**
Properties and changes of property in matter
Transfer of energy

✔ **Life Science**
Diversity and adaptations of organisms

Cold or Hot

Insulation helps keep cold things from warming up and warm things from cooling down. Insulators do this by slowing down the loss of heat from warm things and the gaining of heat by cool things. In the following activity, you can test different substances to see which ones seem to be the best insulators.

1 Break up your foam cup into small pieces. Tear your aluminum foil into pieces and loosely crunch the pieces up. Pull your cotton balls apart a little and flatten them so the cotton is more like a pancake. These are your insulating materials.

2 Place a little of each insulating material into its own large cup so that it just covers the bottom of the cup. Do not put anything in one of the cups because air will be the insulator for that cup. Place a small cup in the center of each large cup as shown.

3 Fill the space between the cups with the same insulating material you put on the bottom. Put 3 tablespoons of warm tap water into each small cup. Cover each large cup with plastic wrap held on with a rubber band.

4 Place the cups in the freezer. Check the cups every 15 minutes to see which cup begins to form ice first. Which one do you think it will be? After you see the first ice form, keep checking until you see ice forming in all four cups.

5 In which cup did ice form first? How about second, third, and fourth? Which insulator was best at slowing down the loss of heat from the warm water? Which was the worst?

Insulation Helps A LOT!

6 Allow the cups to sit in your freezer until the water in all four cups is frozen solid. Take the cups out of the freezer and place them into a small metal baking pan.

7 Place a book or magazine on the cups so they don't float and tip over. Ask your adult partner to pour very warm tap water into the pan.

8 Check the ice in your cups every 15 minutes to see which one seems to be melting first. Which one do you think it will be? Keep checking until you see melting in all four cups.

9 In which cup did the ice begin to melt first? How about second, third, and fourth? Which insulator was the best at slowing down the movement of heat from the water to the ice? Which was the worst? Do your results make sense with the results from step 5?

---

* All activities in *WonderScience* have been reviewed for safety by Dr. Jack Breazeale, Francis Marion University, Florence, SC; Dr. Jay Young, Chemical Health and Safety Consultant, Silver Spring, MD; and Dr. Patricia Redden, Saint Peter's College, Jersey City, NJ.

The word "insulator" is used in different ways. As you saw in *Cold or Hot—Insulation Helps Alot!*, an insulator can help slow down the movement of heat into cool things or out of warm things. The word "insulator" can also be used when talking about electricity. A material used as an electrical insulator helps prevent the movement of electricity through that material. Wood, rubber, and plastic are good electrical insulators because it is difficult for electricity to pass through them. There are also sound insulators. The wall between two movie theaters needs good sound insulation so that sound cannot travel easily from one theater to the other. In this *WonderScience* unit, we have picked one type of insulator to study—the kind that helps slow down the movement of heat.

When thinking about insulators, remember that it is the heat that is transferred, not the cold. When you put warm water in the freezer, heat moves out of the water, making the water cold. Cold does not move into the water. When you put cold water in a warm room, heat moves into the water, making the water warm. Cold does not move out of the water. An insulator's job is to slow down this movement of heat.

What makes a good heat insulator? There are two important qualities that make a good heat insulator. You can figure them out by reading the paragraphs below.

Imagine that you have two pans on the stove. One pan is all metal, including the handle. The other pan has a handle made of wood. If both pans were on the stove for the same amount of time, which handle would be hotter? The handle made of metal would be much hotter because heat moves more easily through metal than it does through wood. So a good heat insulator must be made of a material that does not allow heat to move through it easily.

Something can be done to a material that will make it an even better insulator. Think about what the following insulators have in common: a fluffy down jacket and that stringy spongy fiberglass material used between the inner and outer walls of houses. The answer is air! Feathers and glass can be pretty good insulators by themselves, but the way they can be used to trap air makes them even better! Heat does not travel easily through still or trapped air. So feathers fluffed up with air and glass threads with lots of trapped air make excellent insulators.

HEAT'S IN—YOU WIN!

You will need

stiff paper such as manila file folder or index card stock

tape

blunt-end scissors

metric ruler

pencil

paper or plastic cup

zip-closing plastic bag

inexpensive thermometer

clock or watch with second hand

hot tap water

Insulation materials such as: cloth, paper towel, or plastic foam tray from meat or chicken package

Insulation is used between the walls of houses to help keep the inside of the house cool in the summer and warm in the winter. In the activity below, you can use a model of a heated house to find out where the heat is lost and to insulate it to help keep the heat in.

1 Cover your work area with newspaper. Fill the plastic bag with cool water and close it securely. Lay the bag down on the newspaper. Ask your adult partner to help cut your folder or card stock and to make a house that will fit around the plastic bag as shown.

2 Make sure that the roof of your house is the same distance (approx. 3–5 cm) from the top of the bag as the walls are from the sides of the bag. Tape your walls and roof together so that the house can be easily lifted from the bag in one piece.

3 Fill a cup with water from your bag. Discard any extra water. Ask your adult partner to fill the bag with hot tap water. Close the bag securely and lay it down. Put your house over the bag.

4 Dip the thermometer into the cup of water which should be about room temperature and record that temperature. Hold the thermometer against the side of the house for 2 minutes. Make sure you hold the thermometer from the end and that you do not touch the bulb of the thermometer. Check the temperature and record it.

5 Dip the thermometer in the water again until it shows the water temperature you had before. Now hold the thermometer on the roof of the house. Let it stay there for 2 minutes. Check the temperature and record it.

6 Was more heat being lost from the wall or the roof of the house? Tape a piece of insulating material such as cloth or paper towel to the inside of the part of the house that lost the most heat. Repeat your temperature test to see if your insulation helped slow down the loss of heat.

There are several different types of insulation that protect living organisms from severe temperatures. In the activity below, you can see how fat and trapped air can help insulate another living creature,...YOU from cold temperatures.

FAT

Walruses, seals, whales, and other animals that live in very cold water have a thick layer of fat beneath their skin to help insulate their bodies from losing heat. This fat is called blubber. In the activity below, you can make your own blubber finger!

1 Fill 2 cups about 3/4 full of cold water. Place 2 ice cubes in each cup. Ask your adult partner to place about 1/2 inch layer of lard or vegetable shortening completely around the index finger of one of your hands.

2 Place your covered finger and your uncovered index finger into the cups of water. Can you feel the difference in temperature between your two fingers? Is the lard a good insulator?

3 Fold a piece of aluminum foil a few times so that you have a strip of foil about 30 cm long and a width about an inch longer than the length of your finger. Have your adult partner wrap your bare index finger with the foil so that you have a thick covering of aluminum foil. Fold the end of the foil up so that water will not get in when your finger is placed in water.

4 Place your lard-covered finger and your foil-covered finger in the cups of cold water. Can you feel the difference in temperature between your two fingers? Is aluminum foil a good insulator when used in this way?

stay warm!

AIR

Feathers, fur, and hair protect many animals from the cold. These materials have good insulating qualities themselves, but they also insulate well because they trap a lot of air. In the activity below, you can see how air is a good insulator.

1 Take 2 cotton balls and pull them apart a little so they become fluffier. Form the cotton around one of your index fingers. Place a piece of plastic wrap over your finger. Ask your adult partner to tape the plastic wrap so that the cotton remains fluffy on your finger.

2 Repeat step 1 on your other index finger except this time, have your adult partner tape the plastic wrap tightly so that the cotton is pressed close to your finger.

3 Place each index finger in a cup of cold water. Can you tell the difference in temperature between your two fingers? Which finger is better insulated? Why does the cotton insulate one finger better than the other?

You can also see what a good insulator air is by doing the following activity.

1 Ask your adult partner to help you place a balloon over one of your index fingers. After you have the balloon on, try to squeeze out any air that is in the balloon.

2 Blow some air into the other balloon. Ask your partner to help you place it on your other index finger so that the air stays in the balloon. You can squeeze some air out so that you have a tube of air around your finger as shown.

3 Place both index fingers into the cups of cold water. Can you feel the difference in temperature between your fingers? Can you think of other ways that air is used as an insulator?

Insulation: Nature's a Natural

Half of the pictures on this page show insulation as it is used in nature. The other half of the pictures show insulation as it is used by people.

See if you can match each picture of insulation in nature with a picture of insulation used by people.

Explain to your adult partner how the types of insulation that match work in similar ways.

You can make a chart like the one shown to record your answers.

A

1

2

B

C

3

D

4

E

5

		A	B	C	D	E	F
Natural							
Manufactured							

This unit introduces students to some of the principles involved in recycling. In most of the activities, a technological view of recycling is taken so that students will get a better understanding of scientific and technological factors concerning the recycling process on a large scale.

The Great Divide!!

In *The Great Divide!!*, the problem of separating recyclable materials is addressed. Students use magnetism, static electricity, and density differences to separate materials, and are encouraged to imagine how these methods could be used to separate trash for recycling at large recycling plants. The following are answers to the activity's "challenge": the *shaker* makes the glass marbles roll away, the *blower* gets rid of the wood pencil shavings, and the *grabber* picks up the rubber bands, leaving the pennies behind.

Instant Re-Ply!

In *Instant Re-Ply!*, students make paper in a way that closely models how recycled paper is really made. When you have made a piece or two, you might have students draw or paint on it and assess the paper's quality.

Be a WonderScience Re-Cycler!

Be a WonderScience Re-Cycler! gets students thinking about the items they throw away that can be used for other purposes. The activity is presented in a competitive game format so that students can have fun while learning together. You might also explain that many "disposable" items such as plastic utensils, paper and plastic bags, and aluminum foil can be used many times for the same purpose and don't have to be thrown away even though they are "disposable."

Filtering: Slow and Steady Wins the Race!

Filtering: Slow and Steady Wins the Race! deals with the recycling of water, a topic often ignored in discussions of recycling. When the dirty water is filtered in this activity, be sure students do not taste it since it has not been purified.

RELEVANT NATIONAL SCIENCE EDUCATION STANDARDS

The activities in this unit can be used to support the teaching of the following standards:

✔ **Science as Inquiry**
   Abilities necessary to do scientific inquiry

✔ **Physical Science**
   Properties and changes of properties in matter

✔ **Life Science**
   Populations and ecosystems

✔ **Earth and Space Science**
   Structure of the Earth system

✔ **Science and Technology**
   Abilities of technological design
   Understandings about science and technology

✔ **Science in Personal and Social Perspectives**
   Populations, resources, and environments
   Natural hazards
   Science and technology in society

THE GREAT DIVIDE*!!

You may see people separating trash so that the different materials can be recycled. Paper, glass, plastic, and metal each has its own way of being recycled, so each needs to be separated from the others before recycling. Many people are beginning to separate their garbage, but most still mix all their waste paper, plastic, metal, and glass in one trash container. This costs the recycling companies a lot of time and money trying to separate all the trash.

If you were the owner of a recycling company, you would need to find a fast and easy way to separate the trash for recycling. We thought of a good way to separate plastic straws, paper balls, steel paper clips, and small pieces of aluminum foil!

1 Cut the plastic straw into five pieces. Cut or tear the paper towel and the aluminum foil into 5 pieces each. Roll each piece of paper towel into a little ball between your thumb and index finger. **DO NOT** roll the aluminum foil.

2 Place the plastic, paper, aluminum foil, and paper clips together in a pile on the screen.

You will need
metric ruler
1 plastic straw
1 square of aluminum foil (5 cm x 5 cm)
1 square of paper towel (5 cm x 5 cm)
5 metal paper clips
blunt-end scissors
1 piece of window screening (20 cm x 30 cm)
1 balloon
1 refrigerator magnet
rectangular cake pan (approx. 32 cm x 23 cm x 5 cm)

3 Take your magnet and run it through the pile so that it attracts anything magnetic. What did you separate from the pile? Put these objects aside. Do you think this could work at a big recycling plant? How strong do you think the magnet would have to be?

4 Take your balloon and rub it on your hair. Bring the balloon down close to the pile and see what happens to the objects. How could a large recycling company make enough static electricity to pick up even heavier pieces of trash? Recharge your balloon and move it over the pile again. You should now have two piles of separated material.

---

* All activities in *WonderScience* have been reviewed for safety by Dr. Jack Breazeale, Francis Marion College, Florence, SC; Dr. Jay Young, Chemical Health and Safety Consultant, Silver Spring, MD; and Dr. Patricia Redden, Saint Peter's College, Jersey City, NJ.

5 How can we now separate the last two types of objects? Fill the cake pan with water. Take the screen with the remaining objects on it and dip it into the water so that the screen touches the bottom of the pan. Now you can pick off the floating material and put it in a third pile. Do you think this could also be done at a big recycling company? How?

6 Lift the screen out of the water. What is left on the screen? Make this into a fourth pile. All the materials are now separated!

Fill in this *flow chart* to show what materials you started with, what you used to separate each material, and which materials were left after each step.

EXAMPLE: The first box shows everything you started with. In the box labeled **ATTRACTED TO MAGNET**, write in **PAPER CLIPS**, because they were the only objects attracted to the magnet. In the box labeled **NOT ATTRACTED TO MAGNET**, write **PLASTIC STRAWS, PAPER BALLS, ALUMINUM FOIL PIECES**. Now, using only the objects in the **NOT ATTRACTED TO MAGNET** box, move on to the next level and write in which ones jumped to the balloon and which ones did not jump to the balloon. Then fill in the last level.

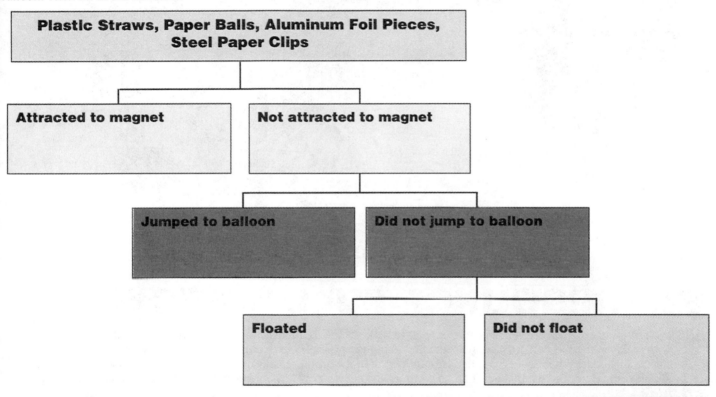

Plastic Straws, Paper Balls, Aluminum Foil Pieces, Steel Paper Clips

- **Attracted to magnet**
- **Not attracted to magnet**
  - **Jumped to balloon**
  - **Did not jump to balloon**
    - **Floated**
    - **Did not float**

Challenge: Now try to separate some different materials that can be recycled.

On a piece of cardboard, place four pennies (**COPPER**), some pencil shavings (**WOOD**), four rubber bands (**RUBBER**), and three marbles (**GLASS**) in one pile.

Your job is to figure out a good way to separate them. You may use the following actions or equipment, but not necessarily in this order:

    THE BLOWER—Use short, gentle bursts of air from your mouth to blow air at the pile.

    THE GRABBER—Hold a piece of tape (25 cm long) from one end and lower the other sticky end down onto the pile.

    THE SHAKER—Shake the cardboard back and forth in short fast movements.

Experiment with these methods to figure out in what order to do them so the materials can be separated easily. Our answer is on the adult letter that comes with your *WonderScience*.

REMEMBER, RECYCLING HELPS YOUR COMMUNITY, YOUR COUNTRY AND THE WHOLE EARTH!

Illustration by Tina Mion

BE "RESOURCE-FULL:" RECYCLE!

Did you ever wonder where the material comes from to make all the useful products around us? Where did the paper come from to make your notebook, for example? And how about the plastic wrap or aluminum foil you used to wrap your sandwich for lunch? What about the metal in your bicycle frame or in the body or engine of a car? The question is not only where does it all come from, but where does it all go when we throw it away? All these questions are important when learning about *recycling*

The materials in our environment that are used to make products are called *raw materials* or *natural resources*. Underground material such as oil, natural gas, coal, and minerals found in rocks are all natural resources. Other natural resources include wood from trees; clay; the nutrients in soil; and the water in lakes, rivers, and the oceans. When we make a product, we use up a part of our natural resources. When we throw the product away, that natural resource can be lost forever. The idea behind *recycling* is to use a product *more than once* so that natural resources can be saved and so that we won't need so many garbage dumps and landfills.

There are different ways that products can be recycled. One of these ways is simply to find another use for the product. One example of this could be to use empty cans as pencil holders, or empty egg cartons to hold a shell or rock collection. To get into the recycling mood, try making a list of things you normally throw away and at least two ways of re-using each one. Share this information with your adult partner to see how many uses the two of you can invent together, and "Be a *WonderScience* Re-Cycler."

A second way of recycling our resources is to use heat, chemicals, or pressure to break a product down into its basic materials, and then to form these materials into the same or a different product. You will be able to try some of the steps in this kind of recycling by doing the activities in this unit of *WonderScience*. The paper-making *Instant Re-Ply!* will give you a good idea of how paper recycling works as you make your own paper. The process that you use is very similar to what is really done in paper recycling plants.

When people think about recycling, many of them think *paper!* The reason paper recycling is so important is that paper is made mostly from wood. Because wood comes from trees, to make paper, you have to cut down trees. Although new trees are planted to replace the ones cut down, this is not the same as having the original old trees. Forests of large old trees are a special environment for many plants and animals, so it is better not to cut down forests of bigger, older trees.

About 40% of all trash in the United States is paper. That's a lot of trees just being thrown away. If you use paper over again instead of throwing it away, fewer trees will need to be cut down. Recycling paper is a great way to save trees!

The most common types of paper that are recycled are newspaper and cardboard boxes. In the recycling factory, used paper is put in a huge blender with water and beaten until the paper is broken down into tiny fibers. The mixture of water and fibers is fed onto a screen where the water is pressed out and the mixture is flattened with rollers. When the flattened mixture is dried and cut, you have paper! You can do the same thing on a smaller scale!

You will need

1 piece of window screening
   (20 cm x 30 cm)
toilet tissue (approx. 1 meter)
rectangular cake pan
   (32 cm x 23 cm x 5 cm)
metal fork
rolling pin
6 paper towels

Illustrations by Lori Seskin-Newman

NOTE: This activity uses toilet paper because it is easy to break down in water. In reality, toilet paper is not recycled since most of it ends up in the sewage system where it breaks down but is not used again.

1. Fill the cake pan about 3/4 full of warm water. If your toilet paper is double-ply, separate the layers; tear the paper into small pieces and put them in the water.

2. Beat the paper and water mixture hard and fast with the fork, as if you were beating an egg. Beat it until the paper is broken down into fine fibers.

3. Take the screen and slide it from the side of the pan down into the water, under the paper fibers. Lift the screen up so that it is covered with the fibers.

4. Put the screen down on a pile of three paper towels and place three paper towels on top.

5. Press down on the paper towels and roll with a rolling pin to flatten the wet fibers and to squeeze water out of them.

6. Carefully remove all the paper towels and allow the paper to dry on the screen for a day or two. When it is *completely* dry, peel the paper from the screen and you will have a new sheet of paper!

How do you think colored paper is made from recycled paper? Try to make some by using food coloring!
DON'T FORGET—Let your paper towels dry and use them again!

Be a *WonderScience* Re-Cycler!

In "Be Resource-Full: Recycle!", you learned that there is more than one way to recycle. Products can be broken down and formed into new products or a used product can simply be used for another purpose. Let's see how resourceful you and your adult partner can be at finding new and different uses for old products!

You will need
1 piece of white paper
metric ruler
1 piece of thick cardboard
   (20 cm x 30 cm)
1 piece of thin cardboard
   (12 cm x 3 cm)
blunt-end scissors
white liquid glue
1 tack
assorted crayons or colored pencils
pen

1 Trace the Re-Cycler Wheel on a piece of paper. Cut the wheel out and glue it to your piece of thick cardboard.

2 Use a pen to write the name of each product between the spokes of the Re-Cycler Wheel. Color each of the 10 sections.

3 Using your thin cardboard, cut out an arrow like the one shown.

4 Ask your adult partner to attach the arrow to the wheel by pushing a tack through the center of the arrow and into the center of the wheel. Spin the arrow and adjust the tack until the arrow spins easily.

LET'S PLAY!
The object of the game is to spin the arrow and to think of another use for the product in the space where the arrow lands.

EXAMPLE: If the arrow lands on **SHOE BOX**, you could use it to store a chess or checker set or to make a Valentine box or for many other uses. You wouldn't want to just throw it away.

You and your adult partner can see who can think of a new use for the product the fastest! **OR** You could see how many different uses you could each think of in two minutes and write them down. You could even try the ones you think of!

FILTERING: SLOW AND STEADY WINS THE RACE!

Did you ever wonder where all the water goes after you take a shower or a bath or brush your teeth or wash clothes or flush the toilet? Do you think we recycle that water and use it again? *WE DO!*

Most of the water that we use every day in so many different ways eventually finds its way to a *water treatment plant* where it is filtered and cleaned and put into a river or stream. This water flows to the ocean, where it evaporates and rains down to eventually be used again.

One common way to help *purify* water is to use a filter. In most large water purification plants, some form of filtering is used. Certain filtering systems work better than others. Let's see what works best for *you!*

1 Ask your adult partner to use the point of a pencil to make a small hole (about the diameter of the end of the point) in the center of the bottom of the three foam cups. With the masking tape and crayon, label the cups **A**, **B**, and **C**.

2 Put the cotton balls in cup **A**. Press them down into the bottom of the cup. This is Filter **A**.

3 In cup **B**, pour in about 1/2 cup of sand and then about 1/2 cup of gravel so that the gravel is on top of the sand. This is Filter **B**.

4 In cup **C**, push a paper towel down into the cup so that it touches the bottom. Tape the extra paper towel to the outside of the cup. This is Filter **C**.

> **You will need**
>
> 1 paper towel
> 10 cotton balls
> small gravel (aquarium-size 1/2 cup)
> sand (about 1/2 cup)
> 3 12 oz plastic foam cups
> 1 sharpened pencil
> 3 clear reusable plastic cups
> soil (about 1 1/2 cups)
> bowl
> masking tape
> crayon

> **Warning:** Do not drink the water even if it looks clear. It has not been purified and is not safe to drink.

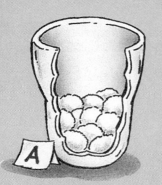  

5 Put 1/2 cup of soil into a bowl. Add about 1 cup of water and stir until the water is very dirty. Have your adult partner hold Filter A over a clear glass or plastic cup. *Slowly* pour the dirty water into Filter A. Observe the water as it drips into the cup below. Is the filtered water dirtier or cleaner than you expected?

6 Make another bowl of dirty water as you did before. Have your adult partner hold Filter B over another clear cup while you pour the dirty water *slowly* into Filter B.

7 Observe the filtered water as it drips into the cup. Compare the water from Filter B with the water from Filter A. Which filter made the water clearer? Why do you think one filter works better than the other?

8 Make another bowl of dirty water. With your adult partner holding Filter C over another clear cup, *slowly* pour the dirty water into Filter C. How does the water dripping out of filter C compare to the water from the other two filters?

Which filter worked the best? Which filter took the *longest* time for the water to drip through? Do you think that the time it takes for water to run through a filter has anything to do with how clean the water will come out? Why?

CHALLENGE: By combining the materials you just used, try to make a filter that allows the water to run through quickly but that cleans the water very well.

THE TRUTH ABOUT TRASH

An average American family produces 100 pounds of trash every week!

About 14 billion pounds of trash is dumped into the sea every year!

We throw away enough iron and steel to supply all of America's car makers with all the metal for all the cars they need to make!

Every three months the United States throws away enough aluminum to build all the airplanes of all the U.S. airlines!

About one third of your garbage is packaging that you throw out immediately!

Over a billion trees are used to make disposable diapers every year.

A small drip from a leaky faucet can waste over 50 gallons of water per day!

At the rate Americans now produce garbage, we need places for 500 new garbage dumps every year!

RECYCLING—IT'S A NATURAL

Nature uses its natural resources *very* efficiently. The natural environment has used recycling to keep itself going ever since there has been life on Earth! Two of the most important recycled materials in nature that allow living things to survive are *water* and the *nutrients* in the soil.

The water that plants and animals need is always being recycled. Water from oceans, lakes, and rivers evaporates to form clouds and then rains down onto the land where plants and animals can use it. Much of the water finds its way back to streams, rivers, and oceans where it evaporates, and the cycle repeats again.

The nutrients in the soil are also recycled. Plants use the nutrients to grow and to produce fruit. When an animal eats the plant or fruit, it uses the nutrients to live and grow. When the animal or plant dies, tiny organisms called *bacteria* break each of them down and return the nutrients to the soil where plants can use them again.

SOURCE: *50 Simple Things You Can Do To Save the Earth;* The EarthWorks Group; Earthworks Press: Berkeley, CA, 1989.

Illustrations by Tina

WONDER SCIENCE

Chemical Particles

The activities in this unit stress the concept that all substances are made up of tiny particles. Activities involving dissolving and evaporating are used to demonstrate some of the particulate characteristics of substances.

Chemical Detectives

Chemical Detectives illustrates that different solid substances dissolve to different extent. The term scientists use to discuss a substance's tendency to dissolve is solubility. Students discover that sugar, salt, and softdrink mix have different solubilities. When students evaporate the solutions they have made, they see that the particles reappear but in a somewhat different form than they looked originally.

Now You See Them...Now You Don't!

In *Now You See Them...Now You Don't!*, students make a model of what happens to a substance when it dissolves. Students should understand that the substance breaks apart and that the particles making up the substance spread apart but do not vanish.

Chem-Mystery

Chem-Mystery is a short story that requires students to solve a science-related mystery. The activity involving a balloon and vanilla extract that follows, shows students that although a balloon is tied tightly, the air inside will escape through the balloon itself.

Particle Carnival

In *Particle Carnival*, students design a simple experiment to see if water temperature or stirring has a greater effect on the rate at which a substance dissolves. Students explore the particle nature of water and watch crystals slowly form from a solution of sugar or salt dissolved in water.

RELEVANT NATIONAL SCIENCE EDUCATION STANDARDS

The activities in this unit can be used to support the teaching of the following standards:

✔ Science as Inquiry
   Abilities necessary to do scientific inquiry

✔ Physical Science
   Properties and changes of properties in matter

✔ Earth and Space Science
   Structure of the Earth system

✔ History and Nature of Science
   History of science

CHEMICAL DETECTIVES

What You and Your Partner Will Need:

1 teaspoon sweetened KOOL-AID or other dry soft-drink mix

1 teaspoon sugar

1 teaspoon salt

3 pencils or pens

a paper towel cut into 4 squares or a coffee filter cut in half

3 wire TWIST-TIES

3 clear plastic glasses filled halfway with room-temperature water

newspaper or towels to cover the work area

4 shiny metal pie pans or cookie sheets

magnifying glass (hand lens) OPTIONAL

What To Do:

1 Look closely at the dry KOOL-AID and sugar and salt. What shapes and colors do you see? Use a hand lens to look closer. Write down what you see.

2 Place a teaspoon of KOOL-AID in the center of one of the paper towel squares. Tie the corners of the square together with a TWIST-TIE. Tie the bag to a pencil with one end of the TWIST-TIE.

Make a bag for sugar and one for salt in the same way.

3 Shake and squeeze each bag. Can you make the food come out of the bags without breaking or tearing the bags open? Why o why not?

4 Write down what you think will happen when you soak the bags in water. Then test your predictions.

I predict that . . .
KOOL-AID® will _____
_____

Salt will _____
_____

Sugar will _____
_____

Gently lower each bag into a glass of water. Adjust the bag so it hangs just touching the water. Watch closely. Describe what you see happening. Is this what you thought would happen?

5 After several minutes, lift the bags out of the water. Open each bag and look closely at what is left inside. Did anything get inside the bag? Write down what you see. Compare what you see now to what you saw in step one.

6 How is the water in the glass different now? Dip your finger into the water and taste it. How did the food get out of the bag?

MY OBSERVATIONS	KOOL-AID®	Sugar	Salt	Other
Dry				
Wet				

7 Pour the water from each glass into a shiny pie pan. Fill a fourth pan with the same amount of tap water. Label each pan so you will remember what was in it. Set all four pans onto a sunny windowsill or porch for a few days. Wait until all the water dries up (evaporates).

What is left behind on the bottom and sides of the pans? Use your hand lens to look closer. Where do you think this substance came from? Note: You and your adult partner may try speeding up the evaporation by putting the pie pans inside a warm oven.

8 You and your partner may want to make more bags and test other food you find in the kitchen. You can try brown sugar, flour, cornstarch, coffee, tea, or baking soda but Caution: Never taste chemicals unless an adult partner says it is safe to do so.

Which of the foods act the same way as KOOL-AID, sugar, and salt? Which ones act in a different way? How do you explain what happened?

Act the same	Act differently
_____	_____
_____	_____
_____	_____
_____	_____
_____	_____

WONDERSCIENCE

© WONDERSCIENCE, AMERICAN CHEMICAL SOCIETY, 1986

Leaking Particles Found in Kitchen

When you looked closely at the dry salt, sugar, and KOOL-AID, the shapes you saw were **crystals.** The sugar and salt crystals were colorless and the KOOL-AID crystals were mixed with a food color. The crystals were too big to go through the tiny holes in the bag when dry. But when wet, the crystals broke into **smaller particles** that leaked through the bag and **dissolved** in the water.

Although you couldn't see the salt or sugar anymore (you may have seen the color from the KOOL-AID) you knew the **food chemicals** were in the water because you tasted them. Very small particles of each food chemical were outside the bag, dissolved in the water. How did your experiment show that water particles also leaked into the bags while the sugar and salt particles leaked out of the bags?

When you let the water **evaporate** on the windowsill, the dissolved particles were left behind. The particles were big enough to see but were not the same shape or size as the dry crystals you started with. What do you think caused their shape and size to change?

You may have found some other food chemicals that did not dissolve and leak through the bag into the water. Can you think of reasons why these foods could not leak through the bag?

227

Now You See Them . . .
Now You Don't!

Use a balloon and a colored marking pen to help you picture what happens when chemical particles dissolve in water.

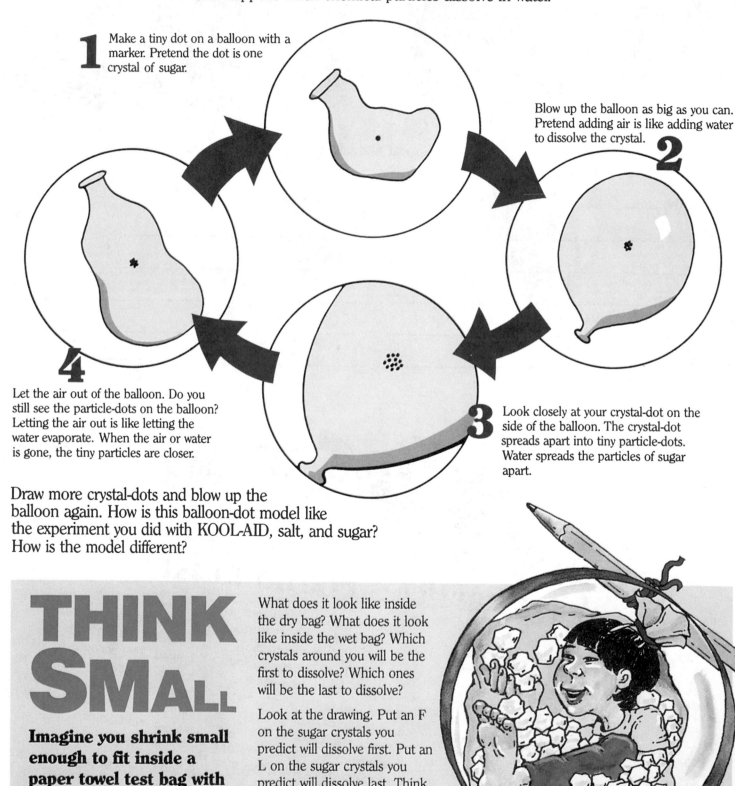

1 Make a tiny dot on a balloon with a marker. Pretend the dot is one crystal of sugar.

Blow up the balloon as big as you can. Pretend adding air is like adding water to dissolve the crystal. **2**

3 Look closely at your crystal-dot on the side of the balloon. The crystal-dot spreads apart into tiny particle-dots. Water spreads the particles of sugar apart.

4 Let the air out of the balloon. Do you still see the particle-dots on the balloon? Letting the air out is like letting the water evaporate. When the air or water is gone, the tiny particles are closer.

Draw more crystal-dots and blow up the balloon again. How is this balloon-dot model like the experiment you did with KOOL-AID, salt, and sugar? How is the model different?

THINK SMALL

Imagine you shrink small enough to fit inside a paper towel test bag with one teaspoon of sugar crystals.

What does it look like inside the dry bag? What does it look like inside the wet bag? Which crystals around you will be the first to dissolve? Which ones will be the last to dissolve?

Look at the drawing. Put an F on the sugar crystals you predict will dissolve first. Put an L on the sugar crystals you predict will dissolve last. Think of a way to test your predictions—then try it!

228

Write Your Own Endings to This Sentence

Chemicals are made of particles like . . .   . . . houses are made from bricks.
                                               . . . necklaces are strung with pearls.
                                               . . . ?
                                               . . . ?

How many more can you think of? Challenge your partner to a contest. The partner with the longest list wins!

My List

1. _____
2. _____
3. _____
4. _____
5. _____
6. _____

My Partner's List

1. _____
2. _____
3. _____
4. _____
5. _____
6. _____

?????CHEM-MYSTERY?????

The Case Of The Pooped Balloons

There it was in the store window. "Look at that skateboard!" cried Pete.

"Wow! That's just what we need to win the summer skateboard race," answered Joe.

"That's hot, really hot!" exclaimed Pete. "But look at the price. How are we going to get $35.00?"

"Maybe we can earn it," said Joe as he looked at a sign in the window. "We can sell balloons at the fair on Saturday. Our scout troop did it last fall. The troop made a lot of money."

"Yeah! My Aunt Judy owns a flower shop that sells helium balloons. I bet she would loan us the helium and rubber balloons and let us pay her after we sell them all," said Pete.

By Tuesday night, the boys had worked out all the details. Aunt Judy loaned them a gross of balloons and a tank of helium. On Wednesday, Joe's father filled all 144 balloons with helium and the boys tied them with ribbon. They then covered them with a heavy blanket so they wouldn't float around inside Pete's garage and get popped. They wanted to sell every single one!

Thursday and Friday after school, Joe and Pete built their booth for the fair. They painted it as bright as the skateboard they hoped to buy with their profits.

Early Saturday morning, the boys raced to Pete's garage. They threw off the blanket and looked at their balloons with wide eyes. "Oh no! What happened?" they cried. All 144 balloons were limp on the floor. ➡

229

"I bet someone sneaked in here and popped all our balloons!" yelled Pete angrily.

"But who would do such a thing?" asked Joe.

Just then Pete's twin sister Molly peeked in to see what had happened. "Those aren't popped balloons; they're pooped balloons," Molly told them. "I'll prove to you that leaky chemical particles caused your problem, not some sneaky balloon popper."

With that, she went over to the kitchen and came back with a bottle of vanilla and a glass of water. Molly picked up one of the pooped balloons and untied it. She poured two capfuls of vanilla into the balloon and then filled the balloon up again with air. She set the

balloon on the glass so that the knot was under water. Turning to the curious boys, Molly said, "Okay, lock the garage. We'll go to the fair for a few hours. I think your noses will help you solve this mystery when we come back."

Now You Finish the Story!

What kind of experiment was Molly setting up? You can use a balloon to help you set up an experiment like Molly's and smell what she was up to. Try it! (If you don't have any vanilla, you can try a different flavor like almond or orange.)

How does the result of your experiment prove there were chemical particles leaking through the walls of the balloon? After you and your partner have tried the experiment write an ending for this story.

The Rest of the Story:

_____

_____

_____

_____

_____

_____

_____

_____

_____

_____

Particle Problems:

1. The boys must pay $64.95 to the flower shop for the tank of helium and the 144 balloons they needed. What is the least amount they could sell each balloon for and still make a $35.00 profit?

2. How many balloons would they have to sell at this price, just to pay for their supplies?

Answers to Particle Problems: 1.) 70¢ 2.) 93 balloons

NO LEAKS

Leaking helium particles are a real problem for people who deliver helium balloon bouquets to parties. Their customers often call to complain that the helium balloons droop after only 24 hours. Can you think of some ways to slow this leaking down and make the balloons last longer?

Who Are You Going To Call? *LEAK BUSTERS!*

DON BURCHETTE IS A *LEAK BUSTER* FROM KENTUCKY. HE WORKS AS A CHEMICAL ENGINEER FOR A LARGE CHEMICAL COMPANY.

DON'S WIFE'S BALLOON DELIVERY SERVICE WAS IN **TROUBLE** BECAUSE OF LEAKY HELIUM PARTICLES!

SOOO... DON INVENTED A CHEMICAL CALLED *HI-FLOAT* TO SLOW DOWN THE LEAKS.

HELIUM BALLOONS COATED WITH *HI-FLOAT* STAY FULL 5 TIMES LONGER THAN UNCOATED BALLOONS!

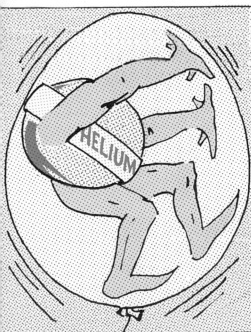

SOME WILL FLOAT AS LONG AS *15 DAYS!*

HI-FLOAT COATS THE INSIDE OF BALLOONS WITH A SPECIAL STRETCHY FILM. IT MAKES IT HARDER FOR THE HELIUM PARTICLES TO LEAK THROUGH THE WALLS OF THE BALLOON.

SHINY, FOIL BALLOONS MADE FROM *MYLAR* ARE ALSO *LEAK BUSTERS.* FIND OUT HOW LONG A MYLAR HELIUM BALLOON LASTS COMPARED TO AN UNCOATED BALLOON.

231

Illustration by Amy Hayes

HERE ARE SOME MORE ACTIVITIES WITH CHEMICAL PARTICLES YOU AND YOUR PARTNER MIGHT WANT TO TRY

Particle Carnival

Particle Races

Do you think the shape and size of a chemical makes any difference as to how fast it will dissolve?

Design a race to find out which dissolves faster in water:
a cube of sugar,
a teaspoon of table sugar,
or a teaspoon of powered sugar.

(use a hand lens to compare the shape and size of each form of sugar.)

Design another race to find out if the temperature of the water makes any difference. Will stirring the water speed up or slow down the race? Find out!

Particle Boogie

Fill a clear plastic glass with tap water. Set the glass of water on a table where it won't get moved. Wait until the water is still, then gently drop a few drops of food color onto the water. Watch what happens!

Leave the glass and come back for a look later. What does this show you about how particles move? How does this movement compare to the movement you saw when the KOOL-AID, sugar, and salt dissolved?

Particle Gardens

With an adult partner's help, heat 1 cup of water in a pan. Stir salt (or sugar) into the very hot water until no more will dissolve. Wait until it cools, then pour this very salty (or sugary) water into a clean jar.

Tie a string onto a pencil. Attach a paperclip to the other end of the string. Wet the string; then roll it in some dry salt (or sugar). Lower the string into the jar. Set the jar in a place where it won't be moved for several days. By then, you should have a string of crystals!

What do you think makes this garden grow? Use a hand lens to look closely at the crystals that grew on the string. Compare them to the sugar or salt crystals you started with. How do they compare?

Particle "Price Is Right"

Get a small bag of nuts or candies. Pretend the bag is a crystal of sugar and the nuts inside are the particles that make up the crystal. Challenge your partner to an estimate contest.

The partner that estimates closer to the correct number of "particles" inside the "crystal" gets to keep the bag!

How many ways can you find to estimate the correct number before you actually count each candy? Which way gives the closest answer?

(Hint: Try weighing, measuring size with a ruler, counting a small sample, and so on.)

Density

The activities in this unit introduce students to the concept of density. The main point is that even though two objects contain the same amount of material, one can be more dense if the material occupies a smaller space in one than in the other.

Density Dilemma

Density Dilemma addresses a common misconception among children that, given two objects, the larger, heavier one will always sink when placed in water. Students discover that a factor (density) that cannot be directly observed determines whether objects float or sink in water.

Density Tower, Density Dessert, and The Mystery of the Stubborn Aquarium

The two activities *Density Tower* and *Density Dessert* as well as *The Mystery of the Stubborn Aquarium*, all allow students to apply their knowledge of density to solve problems. You will want to discuss with your students the purpose of the control (unshaken) jar in the *Density Tower* experiment as a means of comparison with the experimental (shaken) jar.

How Dense Can It Be?

Students need to measure accurately and to divide using decimals to do the activity *How Dense Can It Be?* Students gain experience determining both the volume and the weight of a solid and calculating the density of

that solid. Students discover that a solid that floats in water has a density less than that of water (1 g/cm^3 at room temperature). The "sink or float number line" included in the activity reinforces the link between the calculated value for density and the predicted behavior of the solid in water.

RELEVANT NATIONAL SCIENCE EDUCATION STANDARDS

The activities in this unit can be used to support the teaching of the following standards:

✔ Science as Inquiry

Abilities necessary to do scientific inquiry

✔ Physical Science:

Properties and changes of properties in matter

DENSITY

You will need:

1 stick of butter or margarine
1 thick chocolate bar
2 bouillon cubes
2 sugar cubes
1 large bowl of cold water
paper towels
1 table knife
pencil

1 Unwrap the stick of butter and the bouillon cube. "Weigh" the two materials in your hands. Which material appears to weigh more?

2 Record a prediction in the chart: What do you think will happen to the butter and to the bouillon cube when you put them into the bowl of water? Will they sink or float? What evidence do you have for making that prediction?

_____
_____
_____

3 Now, test your prediction by putting first the stick of butter, then the bouillon cube, into the water. **What happens?** Record your observations in the chart below. Was this what you expected to happen? _____ How can you explain what you observed?

_____
_____
_____

4 Maybe size has something to do with the behavior of the materials in the bowl of water. Let's see what would happen if the piece of butter were the **same size** as the bouillon cube. Put a fresh, unwrapped bouillon cube next to the butter, and cut a cube of butter the same size as the bouillon cube. Record another prediction: What will happen to these same-sized cubes when put into water? Do you have any evidence for your prediction?

	Butter stick
Prediction (sink or float)	
Observation (sank or floated)	

DILEMMA

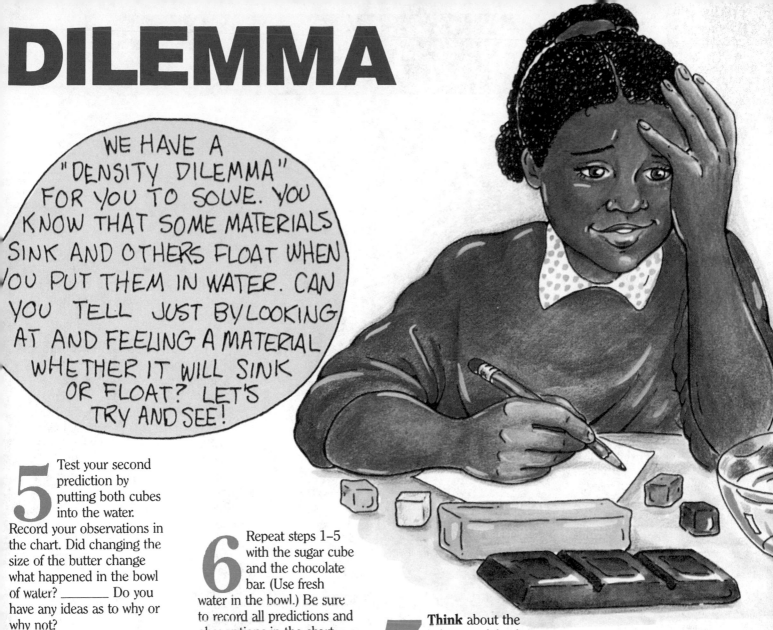

WE HAVE A "DENSITY DILEMMA" FOR YOU TO SOLVE. YOU KNOW THAT SOME MATERIALS SINK AND OTHERS FLOAT WHEN YOU PUT THEM IN WATER. CAN YOU TELL JUST BY LOOKING AT AND FEELING A MATERIAL WHETHER IT WILL SINK OR FLOAT? LET'S TRY AND SEE!

5 Test your second prediction by putting both cubes into the water. Record your observations in the chart. Did changing the size of the butter change what happened in the bowl of water? _____ Do you have any ideas as to why or why not?

_____

_____

_____

6 Repeat steps 1–5 with the sugar cube and the chocolate bar. (Use fresh water in the bowl.) Be sure to record all predictions and observations in the chart below. Note: The chocolate will need to be at room temperature for you to cut a cube from it. You may want to chill your chocolate cube slightly before you test your predictions.

7 **Think** about the behavior of the four materials that you have been placing in water. Could you tell by feeling or looking at the materials whether they would sink or float?

_____

_____

_____

8 It seems pretty obvious that whether a material sinks or floats in water depends upon something about the material that we can't see. That "something" is called a material's **DENSITY**. To find out what density is, read "Dateline: Density"

DATA CHART

	Bouillon cube	Chocolate bar	Chocolate cube	Sugar cube

DATELINE: DENSITY

You probably noticed in the "Density Dilemma" that it is difficult to tell, just from looking at an object, whether that object will sink or float when put into water. Some small objects, such as the sugar cube, the bouillon cube, and the chocolate cube, sank when they were put into water, as did the large chocolate bar. This means that these materials were MORE DENSE than the water into which they were placed. The butter, whether it was a whole stick or a small cube, floated in the water. It was LESS DENSE than the water in which it floated.

What do we mean when we talk about an object's DENSITY, or how DENSE something is? Let's try an experiment to see. Tear off two sheets of aluminum foil, each 1 foot in length. LOOSELY crumple both sheets into balls of about the same size. Do the sheets still take up the same amount of space? Does each sheet still contain (approximately) the same amount of foil? Now, put one of the foil balls aside and crumple up the other ball as much as you possibly can. Do both balls still contain the same amount of foil? Do both balls take up the same amount of space? The smaller of the two balls has become more DENSE—it contains the same amount of foil that you started with, but it takes up less space.

Density can be defined as the amount of material that takes up a certain amount of space. The more material—whether a solid, a liquid, or a gas—that you have in a particular space, the more dense that material is

For example, at room temperature, the amount of 1 gram of pure liquid water takes up 1 cubic centimeter of space. We say, then, that the density of pure liquid water is 1 gram per cubic centimeter. If a material has a density that is MORE than 1 gram/cubic centimeter, that material will SINK when it is put into water. A material with a density of LESS than 1 gram/cubic centimeter will FLOAT when it is put into water. You can figure out the densities of some of the solid objects with which you experimented in the "Density Dilemma" by doing the activity called "How Dense Can It Be?"

You can investigate the densities of different liquids when you make your "Density Tower," and you can think about the densities of gases by remembering how balloons behave when filled with air and when filled with helium gas. Would you say that helium gas is more or less dense than air? Why? Which of the clown's balloons do you think is filled with helium?

Put your density knowledge to work when you solve the "Mystery of the Stubborn Aquarium"

TINA MION

DENSITY TOWER

You will need:

- 2 clean 16-oz clear plastic jars with lids
- blue and yellow food color
- vegetable oil
- light corn syrup
- 3 clear plastic cups
- 2 spoons
- paper towels
- measuring cup

1 Cover your work surface with a layer of paper towels. Add ⅓ cup of water to two of your plastic cups. Add 2 drops of blue food color to each cup of water and stir.

2 Now add ⅓ cup of corn syrup to the first cup of water, and ⅓ cup of vegetable oil to the second cup of water, by pouring these liquids over the back of a spoon and into the cups. Record your observations in the Cup Chart below. Does the corn syrup appear to be above or below the water? _____ Is the corn syrup more or less dense than the water? _____ How can you tell?_____
_____

3 Look at the cup containing the water and the oil. Is the oil above or below the water?_____ Can you tell if the oil is more or less dense than the water?_____ How? _____
_____

4 Make a prediction: What do you think will happen when you put some corn syrup and some oil in the third cup? _____ Why? _____
_____

5 Test your prediction by putting ⅓ cup of oil in the third cup. Next add 2 drops of yellow food color to ⅓ cup of corn syrup, and add this mixture to the oil in the third cup. Is the corn syrup above or below the oil? _____ Was your prediction accurate? _____ Record your observations in the Cup Chart.

6 You should now have enough information to be able to make your Density Tower. Carefully dispose of the liquids in your three plastic cups with the help of your adult partner. Wash the cups and dry them. Put ⅓ cup of oil into one of the clean plastic cups, ⅓ cup of water into the second cup, and ⅓ cup of corn syrup into the third cup.

7 Add 2 drops of blue food color to the water, and 2 drops of yellow food color to the corn syrup. Now, stir the liquid in each cup and pour the liquid that you think will remain on the bottom into one of the plastic jars. Carefully add the second liquid that should float on the bottom liquid. (Don't stir!) Now, pour in the third liquid that should float on the other two liquids. You've created your first Density Tower! Now repeat steps 6 and 7 to make a second tower using the other plastic jar.

8 Put the lids tightly on both jars, and shake up the contents of **one** of the jars. What happens to the three liquids in the shaken jar? Compare the two jars. Using your knowledge of density, what can you explain about the behavior of the liquids in both the jars? _____
_____
_____
_____

CUP CHART

	Cup 1	Cup 2	Cup 3
Contents	⅓ cup blue-colored water + ⅓ cup corn syrup	⅓ cup blue-colored water + ⅓ cup oil	⅓ cup oil + ⅓ cup yellow-colored corn syrup
Observations			

HOW DENSE CAN IT BE?

YOU KNOW FROM READING "DATELINE DENSITY" THAT DENSITY MEANS THE AMOUNT OF MATERIAL IN A PARTICULAR AMOUNT OF SPACE. IF WE DIVIDE THE AMOUNT OF MATERIAL BY THE SPACE IT FILLS, WE GET THE **DENSITY** OF THAT MATERIAL. LET'S SEE IF WE CAN FIND THE DENSITY OF A STICK OF BUTTER OR MARGARINE!

You will need

1 stick of butter or margarine with the wrapper on
metric ruler
large mixing bowl ⅔ filled with cold water
pencil and paper for figuring

1 You will first need to find out how much butter or margarine is in the stick. This amount (in grams) is printed on the wrapper of the butter. Round this amount to the nearest whole number and record it here: _____ g.

2 To find the space that the stick of butter fills is a little trickier. Since the butter is a rectangular-shaped solid, we can find this amount of space by measuring the butter's length, width, and height, and multiplying those three numbers together.

3 First take the wrapper off the butter, then measure the three edges of the butter using centimeters. Record the three measurements here:

Length: _____ cm
Width: _____ cm
Height: _____ cm

Now multiply Length × Width × Height and record the number here: _____

Space the butter fills = _____ cubic cm (or cm³)
(cm × cm × cm = cm³)
Round your answer to the nearest whole number: _____ cm³

4 You are now ready to find the approximate density of your stick of butter. Divide your amount number (in grams) by your space number (in cubic centimeters). Record the answer here: _____ g/cm³

The above number is the approximate density of your stick of butter. Check your answer against the "sink or float numberline" below to see if your butter should sink or float when you put it in water.

Try to find the densities of the bouillon cube, the sugar cube, and the chocolate that you experimented with in the "Density Dilemma." This method of finding the densities of rectangular solids is not very accurate or precise, since you are rounding off the measurements to the nearest whole numbers, but it does give you an idea of how some densities can be found. What are some reasons that you can think of why it might be important to know the density of a material? Which industries might be concerned with making materials that float?

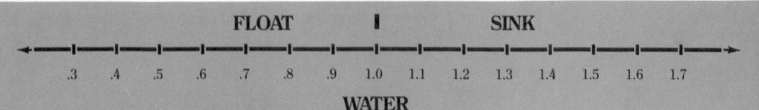

FLOAT | SINK

.3 .4 .5 .6 .7 .8 .9 1.0 1.1 1.2 1.3 1.4 1.5 1.6 1.7

WATER
(in g/cm³ at room temperature)

THE MYSTERY OF THE STUBBORN AQUARIUM

Jack was doing his homework on density when he heard angry yells from his little brother Danny's room. Jack ran down the hall to see what the matter was, and there was Danny, red-faced with frustration, yelling at his new aquarium. Plastic plants, two divers, and a little castle were all bobbing around the surface of the full tank.

"This stuff is driving me crazy!" Danny hollered when he saw Jack. "I put all the decorations and gravel and plants and stuff into the dry aquarium first, but now look at it! As soon as I put the water in, everything except the gravel floats to the top! Nothing ever stays put! What's the matter with this stuff, anyway?"

Can you tell why Danny is having so much trouble with his aquarium? How can Jack use what he knows about density to get Danny's aquarium to look the way Danny wants it to look?

DENSITY DESSERT

You will need

- 1 4-oz box of lemon gelatin
- 1 8-oz container of whipped cream cheese at room temperature
- 1 8-³⁄₄-oz can of fruit cocktail (drained)
- measuring cup
- mixing bowl
- 4 8-oz clear plastic cups
- mixing spoon

1 Put the dry lemon gelatin into the bowl. Add 1 cup of hot tap water (Get your adult partner to help with this!) to the gelatin, and stir until the gelatin is completely dissolved.

2 Add half of the container of cream cheese and stir. (The cream cheese won't blend in with the gelatin, but it will break into little bits.) Does the cream cheese sink or float in the gelatin? _____ Why? _____
_____

3 Add 1 cup of cold water to the gelatin and stir.

4 Now add the fruit to the gelatin/cream cheese mixture. Stir. Does the fruit sink or float in the mixture? _____ How can you explain that? _____
_____
_____
_____

5 Pour the gelatin mixture into the 4 cups and refrigerate them until the gelatin is set (several hours). Observe any changes in the dessert as it chills. Where does the cream cheese end up in the cup? _____
_____

How about the fruit? _____
_____

When the dessert is completely chilled, eat it!

Try some different types of Density Desserts using different-flavored gelatins, chopped nuts, fresh fruits, marshmallows and maybe some non-dairy whipped topping.

WONDERSCIENCE

This unit introduces students to some of the basic properties of mixtures. The factors effecting the ability of substances to mix and techniques for separating the components of mixtures are investigated.

Master a Mixing Mystery!

In *Master a Mixing Mystery!*, students conduct a simple activity with the potential for very interesting observations and discussion. The activity focuses on investigating what happens when different liquids are brought together. Students should be encouraged to make detailed observations. You may want to give students yellow, blue, and green pencils to better record their observations.

When blue water is mixed with yellow water, an area of green will probably appear where the two liquids meet with outer areas remaining blue and yellow. But when blue water is mixed with yellow salt water, the mixing will be faster and the entire liquid will become green more quickly. The liquids mix faster because of the difference in concentration between them. The blue water has a higher concentration of water molecules than the yellow salt water. When the two liquids are brought together, water molecules will move from an area where they are in high concentration to an area where they are in lower concentration, and rapid mixing will occur.

Another important factor that influences the abilities of different liquids to mix is a characteristic of molecules called *polarity*. A polar molecule is a molecule whose electric charges are unevenly distributed in the structure of the molecule. (See Water Unit) Polar molecules tend to mix well with other polar molecules. Non-polar molecules tend to mix well with other non-polar molecules. Polar and non-polar molecules tend to mix poorly.

Water is very polar. Alcohol is polar, but not as polar as water. Water and alcohol molecules are similar enough in polarity to mix but different enough in polarity so that their mixing is affected. Differences in viscosity and surface tension also affect the mixing of water and alcohol.

The experiment with water and detergent should have given you a different result from the others. Detergent breaks the surface tension of water and should have caused fairly rapid mixing and spreading out of the water/detergent mixture.

Oil and water do not mix well because water is polar and oil is non-polar. They can be made to mix by adding detergent. Detergent has a polar end which mixes with the water and a non-polar end which mixes with the oil, allowing the oil and water to form an emulsion—droplets of oil surrounded by water.

Candy Chromatography!

In *Candy Chromatography!*, different pigment molecules can be separated from a mixture by using paper chromatography (See Mixtures Unit). Because of the different shape, weight, size, and electric charges on the different pigment molecules, the molecules separate as they move up the paper at different rates.

A Soapy Separation!

A *Soapy Separation!* enables students to begin to separate a mixture of soap and water by adding different salts. The salts should bind onto the soap to different degrees, causing a different amount of separation when filtered.

A WonderScience Centrifuge!

A *WonderScience Centrifuge!* shows that mixtures can be separated by spinning them. The pennies should immediately move to one or both ends of the bottle while the paper disks should remain in the middle.

Inflate and Separate!

Inflate and Separate! illustrates how a gas can be separated from a liquid.

RELEVANT NATIONAL SCIENCE EDUCATION STANDARDS

The activities in this unit can be used to support the teaching of the following standards:

✔ Science as Inquiry
   Abilities necessary to do scientific inquiry
✔ Physical Science
   Properties and changes of properties in matter
✔ Earth and Space Science
   Structure of the Earth system
✔ Science in Personal and Social Perspectives
   Science and technology in society

Master a Mixing Mystery!

Mixtures can be made by combining two or more different liquids, solids, or gases. Solid with liquid, solid with solid, gas with gas, gas with liquid, etc., can all combine to make mixtures. In the activity below, you will observe what happens when certain liquids are used to make mixtures.

You will need

newspaper	liquid dish detergent (clear or yellow)
wax paper	
water	vegetable oil
6 paper or plastic cups (7 oz)	2 sheets white unlined paper
food coloring (blue and yellow)	pencil
	straws
salt	tape
rubbing alcohol	tablespoon

1 Cover your work area with newspaper. Use your pencil and one sheet of unlined paper to make a chart like the one below. Make the chart large enough to fill the entire paper. Cover the chart with a piece of wax paper and tape down the corners as shown.

2 Fill a cup about 1/2 full of water. Add one drop of blue food coloring to the cup. Gently swirl the cup to mix the food coloring with the water.

3 Place about two tablespoons of water in a separate cup and add about 1/2 teaspoon of salt. Stir with a spoon until no more salt will dissolve. Use your masking tape and pencil to label this cup **salt water**.

4 Place about two tablespoons each of **water**, **alcohol**, **dish detergent**, and **oil** in separate cups. Label the cups. Add 1 drop of yellow food coloring to all your labeled cups and mix with separate straws. (What did you notice about the food coloring and the oil?)

5 Pour a small amount of blue colored water onto the upper circle under number 1. The pool of water should be about the size of a quarter. Pour about the same amount of yellow-colored water onto the lower circle under number 1.

WARNING!
Rubbing alcohol is flammable and is poisonous if swallowed. Read and follow all precautions on the label.

1	2	3	4	5
WATER (Blue)	WATER (Blue)	WATER (Blue)	WATER (Blue)	WATER (Blue)
○	○	○	○	○
○	○	○	○	○
WATER (Yellow)	SALT WATER (Yellow)	ALCOHOL (Yellow)	DETERGENT (Yellow)	OIL (Yellow)

242

6 Put the end of a straw in the blue water and slowly move the water toward the yellow water directly below it. Bring them very close and then allow them to touch.

7 Observe very closely the way the two liquids mix. Write down your observations for area 1 on a separate sheet of paper.

8 Now add blue water to the upper circle and yellow salt water to the lower circle under number 2. Bring them close together and let them touch. Write down your observations. Repeat the same process for the blue water and each yellow liquid in experiment areas 3–5. Record your observations for 3–5 on your paper.

9 You probably noticed that the oil and water did not appear to mix very well. Try mixing the two liquids by using your straw to gently stir the oil and water together. Could you get them to mix a little?

10 Add one drop of detergent from your detergent cup to the oil and water mixture. Now try using your straw to mix them again. Did adding the detergent help in the mixing?

∗ All activities in *WonderScience* have been reviewed for safety by Dr. Jack Breazeale, Francis Marion University, Florence, SC and Dr. Jay Young, Chemical Health and Safety Consultant, Silver Spring, MD.

Get the Mixture Picture!

What do saltwater, air, concrete, mud, milk, hot cocoa, tea, oil and vinegar salad dressing, and soda have in common? They're all *mixtures*! Saltwater is a mixture of sodium chloride (table salt) and water. Air is a mixture of nitrogen, oxygen, and other gases. Mud is a mixture of soil, clay, sand, and water. A mixture may consist of solids, liquids, or gases mixed with themselves or with one another. A mixture is made when two or more substances are combined but the *molecules* that make up the substances do not change, they just get mixed.

Scientists study the way things mix and also how to separate mixtures. Scientists have developed different ways of separate the substances that make up mixtures. The simplest method is called *sedimentation*. This is what happens when dirt mixed with water sits for a period of time. The dirt and water will separate. Most of the dirt will sink to the bottom. Most of the water will be on top.

Another method commonly used by scientists is called paper *chromatography*. In this type of chromatography, a mixture is absorbed onto a special type of paper. As the mixture moves up the paper, the substances in the mixture separate based on their size, weight, shape, and other characteristics.

Sometimes, scientists add other chemicals to a mixture to help them separate the substances in the mixture. The new chemical may be able to react with or attach to one of the substances, creating clumps of material. Scientists call the clumps a *precipitate* and the whole process *precipitation*. If the precipitate sinks to the bottom, the liquid at the top can be poured off and separated. Scientists often pour the whole mixture, precipitate and all, through filter paper. This step is called *filtration*. The precipitate will stay on the filter paper and be separated from the rest of the substances which go through.

Another way mixtures can be separated is called *centrifugation*. The mixture to be separated is first placed in a test tube or other container, and then into a device called a *centrifuge*. The centrifuge spins the mixture at a very high rate of speed. Heavier substances in the mixture are forced to the bottom of the container, and lighter substances remain near the top.

You'll see that *gases* can also be separated from mixtures. Heating a mixture is one way to make the gas come out. Try the other ways in the activity and think about how you could separate gas from liquid on a large scale.

Candy Chromatography!

You will need

coated chocolate candy (brown)

coated peanut butter candy (brown)

coated fruit jelly candy (brown)

pencil

coffee filter (cone type)

cotton swabs

water

paper or plastic cup (at least 7 oz)

blunt end scissors

As you read, gases, liquids, and solids can be mixed with themselves or with one another in different ways. You also know that there are different ways in which mixtures can be separated. In the activity below, you can separate the substances used to color candy by using *chromatography!*

1 Use your scissors to cut 3 strips of coffee filter about 10 cm long and about 3 cm wide. Write the name of each candy on a separate strip. The name should be written near one end of the strip.

2 Pour about 1/4 cup of water into a cup. Dip one end of a cotton swab into the cup and gently wet one side of one of your candies. Gently rub the candy's wet side onto its filter strip about 2 cm from the end to make a dark dot on the paper. **Do not put the used end of the cotton swab back in the water.**

3 Repeat step 2 for your other two candies and paper strips. Use a clean end of a cotton swab each time. Be sure to make your dot dark, on the opposite end of the strip from the name of the candy, and about 2 cm from that end of the strip.

4 Carefully place your strips in the cup of water so that only a small portion of the bottom of each strip touches the surface of the water. Be sure your colored dot is above the surface of the water. Bend the rest of the strip over the rim of the cup to keep the strip in place.

5 Observe each strip as the water moves up through the dot. What do you notice happening? Was the brown color on the candies a mixture of other colors? What are these other colors? Compare the colors used in each candy. In what ways are they the same or different?

Check the ingredients listed on the candy wrapper to see whether the colors you see were actually used to color the candies!

A Soapy Separation!

Many times, a solid is so well mixed in a liquid that it is very difficult to separate them. Sometimes a chemical can be used to help the solid separate from the liquid. In the activity below, you can try two different kinds of salt to help you separate a mixture of soap and water.

You will need

bar soap	Epsom salt
grater	coffee filters
water	(cone-shaped #4)
7 clear plastic cups	measuring spoons
(at least 7 oz)	masking tape
table salt	ball-point pen
straws	

1 Ask your adult partner to grate a bar of soap onto a piece of paper so that you have at least 3 tablespoons of grated soap. Place about 3/4 cup of water in a plastic cup. Add the 3 tablespoons of soap and stir with a straw to mix thoroughly.

2 Use your masking tape and pen to label 2 cups **control,** 2 cups **table salt,** and 2 cups **Epsom salt.** Pour 1/4 cup of your soap and water mixture into one of each pair of labeled cups.

3 Add 1 teaspoon of table salt and 1 teaspoon of Epsom salt to the soap and water mixture in its labeled cup. Do not add anything to the control cup. Stir each cup with a separate straw for about one minute.

4 Place a coffee filter in each of the three empty labeled cups as shown. Make sure there is a space of about 5 cm between the bottom of the coffee filter and the bottom of the cup.

5 Pour the mixture from each cup into its matching filter. Observe the liquid that drips through the filter and into the cup. Do you notice a difference in the way the liquids look in each cup? When the dripping slows down, look into the coffee filters and compare what you see.

6 If the materials in the filters look different, try to explain why. Do you think the way the materials look in the different filters has anything to do with how clear the different filtered liquids are?

Cent rifuge!

Another way a mixture can be separated is by a process called ***centrifugation.*** Centrifugation requires that a mixture be spun around very quickly. If the centrifuge is set up correctly for a particular mixture, the different materials that make up the mixture will be able to separate themselves based on size, weight, shape, and other factors. You can make a simple model of a centrifuge in the activity below!

You will need

clear plastic bottled-water bottle (1 liter)

coffee filter (cone type)

ball point pen

blunt end scissors

masking tape

string (strong)

5 pennies

1 Fill the bottle with water and put the cap on securely. Ask your adult partner to tie a piece of string around the middle of the bottle so that when you hold the string as shown, the bottle is balanced.

2 After you have adjusted the string so that the bottle is balanced, tape the string down securely with the masking tape.

3 Use your pen to color an area of your coffee filter. Use a penny and your pen to trace five circles the size of a penny on the colored area of your paper. Cut out these five disks.

4 Open the bottle and place five pennies and your five paper disks in the water. Screw the cap back on securely. Gently tip the bottle back and forth to mix the disks and the pennies in the water.

5 Allow the pennies and disks to rest along the bottom of the bottle as it hangs sideways. While your adult partner holds the string, grip the bottle under the center and give it a quick twist so that it spins around quickly.

6 After the bottle has spun for a few seconds, place your hand beneath the center of the bottle and gently touch the bottle to slowly stop its spinning.

7 Did the pennies and the disks separate? Where did the pennies go? Did the disks seem to move much? Why do you think the pennies moved more than the disks?

INFLATE
AND
SEPARATE!

A mixture can also be made from a gas and a liquid. Soda pop is a good example of a mixture of the gas *carbon dioxide* with water. The carbon dioxide is added to very cold water using a lot of pressure. To help separate the carbon dioxide from the water, you can release the pressure or warm the soda!

You will need

1 plastic bottle of soda	paper
round balloon	pencil
hot tap water	baking pan

Before starting this activity, you or your adult partner should inflate and deflate your balloon a few times to stretch it out.

1 Carefully open your soda bottle and ask your adult partner to quickly place the opening of a balloon over the bottle. Notice how long it takes the balloon to fill up with enough gas to stand upright.

2 Ask your adult partner to pour hot water into a pot or pan until it is about half full. Remove the balloon from the bottle, allow it to deflate, then quickly place the bottle in the water and put the balloon back on. Watch the balloon as it inflates. Did the balloon fill up faster or more slowly than before? (Remember, the soda has less gas than it did when you first opened it.)

3 Take the bottle out of the water and remove the balloon. Let the gas out of the balloon. Quickly put the balloon back on and shake the bottle a few times. How fast did the balloon fill up this time?

If you owned a factory that separated carbon dioxide from soda, what kinds of machines and equipment would you invent to do it? Draw a picture of your equipment and explain to your adult partner how it would work.

248

Activities in this unit deal with substances whose properties interfere with their readily mixing with each other. An example of two such substances are oil and water. Methods used to help these substances mix are also investigated.

Mixable Unmixables

In *Mixable Unmixables*, students place drops of food coloring into two different kinds of milk with different fat contents. Students see that the drops do not mix very much with the milk. This is because the water-based food coloring and the fat in the milk do not tend to mix. Students then see that adding a drop of dish detergent causes the coloring to spread out on the surface of the milk and begin to mix. Because of its chemical structure, detergent has the ability to help oil and water mix.

A Real Chemistry Brainteaser

As a follow-up to *Mixable Unmixables*, in *A Real Chemistry Brainteaser*, students mix food coloring in water and food coloring in oil. Detergent is then added to each to see which one the detergent helps mix the most. Students use their observations to draw conclusions about what caused the behavior they observed in *Mixable Unmixables*.

Mix Tricks

In *Mix Tricks*, students experiment with the action of stabilizers to see how they effect the time it takes for certain mixtures to separate. Students control variables such as the amount of each liquid used and the number of times each container is shaken.

The Chemistry of Color Film and Food for Thought

The Chemistry of Color Film and Food for Thought both illustrate how science and technology have been used to develop dispersions that are used to make products we use every day.

RELEVANT NATIONAL SCIENCE EDUCATION STANDARDS

The activities in this unit can be used to support the teaching of the following standards:

✔ **Science as Inquiry**
  Abilities necessary to do scientific inquiry

✔ **Physical Science**
  Properties and changes of properties in matter

✔ **Science in Personal and Social Perspectives**
  Science and technology in society

✔ **History and Nature of Science**
  Science as a human endeavor

SAFE SCIENCE TIP:
WASH AND DRY YOUR HANDS
SPOONS, AND CONTAINERS BEFOR
DOING ANY FOOD EXPERIMENTS.
EVERYTHING THAT TOUCHES FOOD
YOU MIGHT TASTE MUST BE
KEPT VERY CLEAN!

What to Do

1 Pour each of the milk samples into a saucer. Label each saucer so you will know which type of milk it holds. What differences between the milks can you see, taste, or smell? Write your **observations** in the chart on this page.

2 Add three drops of food color to the milk in each saucer. Put the different color drops anywhere yo like. Watch to see whether the color spreads out or stays together in eac milk. **Record any differences** you notice in the chart.

4 What happens if you add a drop of detergent to each saucer? **Compare** the milks and record any differences you see.

Milk Test Results

Types of milk I test	How each milk looks, tastes, and smells	What happens when I add food color drops	What happens when I touch with a dry swab	What happens when I add detergent
Sample 1				
Sample 2				
Other samples I test				

NMIXABLES

What You Will Need

- samples of two different fat content milks (about 50 ml of each type—you can use whole, low-fat, skim, half-and-half, or cream)
- 2 clean, shallow saucers, pie pans, or bowls
- 1 teaspoon liquid dish detergent
- 2 cotton-tipped swabs
- food color (any colors you like)
- dropper
- paper and pencil for labeling the saucers

Special thanks to Christine Esposito, Eastman Kodak Co., Dr. Londa Borer, California State University, Dr. Jay Young, and Dr. Jack Bulloff, chemical consultants, for suggesting parts of this issue.

3 Touch a dry cotton swab to a food color drop in each saucer. What happens? Wet a swab with detergent and touch it to the food color drops. Caution: Don't taste the milk after you add detergent to it!

5 Do you think the fat content of the milk affects what you see happening? **Predict** whether other types of milk might act the same if you tested them. Which milks might let the food color drops spread more? Which milks might swirl longer when detergent is added? If you can get more kinds of milk, test your predictions! Remember to keep track of your observations in the chart.

6 Think about the differences you observed between the milks in this experiment. What differences might explain why the food color drops and detergent act a bit differently in each milk sample?

_____

_____

_____

What do you think causes the milk to swirl the food color when detergent is added?

_____

_____

_____

Detecting Dispersions

Milk is a **mixture** of oil (cream or butterfat) and water (skim milk). Shortly after a cow is milked, globs of the oily part join together and float to the top of the watery part. When this happens, a layer of cream floats to the top of the skim milk just like cooking oil floats on colored water in the wave bottle you see below. Ask some older adults if they remember buying fresh milk that separated into two layers.

But the milk you like to drink doesn't separate into layers! That's because modern dairies **homogenize** the milk so the oily part is mixed **permanently** into the watery part. A homogenizer is a machine that forces fresh milk at high speed and pressure through tiny holes. This breaks the big oily globs into tiny droplets that spread (**disperse**) throughout the surrounding water.

When the droplets are very small, they get coated by a layer of the protein dissolved in the milk. This protein coat prevents the oil droplets from sticking together again to make larger blobs that would float to the top. The protein is a **stabilizer**, because it helps the oily droplets stay **permanently dispersed** throughout the milk.

Try making your own wave bottle. Shake it quickly back and forth in a rocking motion, then set it on a table and look at it closely. If you see droplets of oil and water instead of two layers, then you've made an **oil-and-water dispersion**! Is your **dispersion temporary or permanent**? (HINT: Watch to see if the droplets separate again.) Homogenized milk contains protein (a stabilizer) that coats the tiny dispersed droplets of oil so they can't join together again. Is there a stabilizer in your wave bottle?

Detergent is a stabilizer, too. You use it to mix oil and water when you wash your hands or your greasy dishes. If you added one teaspoon of detergent to your wave bottle, what would happen? Try it! Think about how the detergent might also work on the dispersed oil droplets in homogenized milk. What do you think causes the milk to swirl the food color when detergent is added?

Dispersions are everywhere, not just in milk! Many other foods, paints, cosmetics, polishes, and even photography films are made by adding stabilizers to some usually unmixable materials. Read some labels on food containers to see if you can detect some food dispersions. If the label says the food contains a stabilizer (or an **emulsifier**), then it probably is a dispersion. Some stabilizer ingredients to look for are: agar, gums, alginate, carageenen, lecithin, pectin, egg, or gelatin. How many dispersions do you detect in your kitchen cupboard?

List all the dispersions you detect:

_____

_____

**one-third-filled
with cooking oil**

wave bottle

**two-thirds-filled
with colored water**

A Real Chemistry Brainteaser

So why does food color swirl in milk when you add detergent? This is a real puzzle to most scientists! If you asked some scientists this question, they would need to do more experiments to help them figure out an answer. If you want to understand more about what is going on in the milk, you can do some more tests, too.

Test 1:

You will need 2 clear plastic 8 oz. cups.
Fill one cup ⅔ full of water, and the other cup ⅔ full of cooking oil
Add one drop of food color to each cup, then stir.

Does the food color mix with
the water? ☐
the oil? ☐

When you add food color to milk, does it mix in the watery part, the oily part, or both parts?

cooking oil   water

Test 2:

Add one drop of dish detergent to the mixture in each cup. Stir again.

After adding dish detergent, does the food color mix with
the water? ☐
the oil? ☐

What evidence does this test give you that adding detergent to milk changes how the food color mixes into the milk?

_____

If you didn't add food color to the saucers, would the milk still swirl when you added detergent? _____ Find out!

cooking oil and color

oil

water and color

MIX TRICKS

If you shook a wave bottle in outer space, would the dispersion of oil and water separate again like it does on Earth? Scientists wondered about this during the 1974 Skylab mission. They wanted to find out if zero-gravity would act like a stabilizer on an oil and water mixture. To find out, they made a wave bottle to test on Earth and one to test on the Skylab. They shook the bottles to make good dispersions and then timed how long each mixture took to separate.

In space, the bottles showed no signs of separating, even after 10 hours. How long did it take a bottle on Earth to separate? Time one and find out! Does zero-gravity act as a good stabilizer?

You can do some earthly mix tricks with stabilizers. Make the following mixtures in any clear container with a lid. (Ask a photo store to give you the clear, 35-mm film containers they throw away—they make great test tubes and they're free!)

Shake each mixture, and observe the size of the droplets and how long the dispersion takes to separate.

Add a stabilizer and shake the mixture again. Find out if the stabilizer changes the size of the droplets or the separation time.

Do any of these stabilizers work as well as zero-gravity?

SAFE SCIENCE TIP: DO NOT SMELL OR TASTE THE MUSTARD POWDER OR ALUM. MAKE SURE AN ADULT HELPS YOU GET ONLY THE SMALL AMOUNTS NEEDED FOR EACH TEST. CLOSE THE CONTAINERS AND WASH YOUR HANDS IMMEDIATELY. THESE SUBSTANCES CAN IRRITATE YOUR SKIN, EYES, AND NOSE!

| Mixtures | | | | Stabilizers | |

Trick 1

1. Fill a clean, clear container ⅓ full of water and ⅓ full of cooking oil. Put the lid on the container.

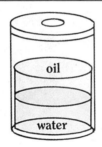

2. Mix by shaking the closed container 10 times.

3. Ob e and measure the time it takes for the mixture to separate. Time: _____.

4. Add 5 drops of detergent or bits of soap.

5. Shake the mixture 10 times.

6. Observe and measure the time it takes for the mixture to separate again. Time: _____.

Trick 2

1. Fill a clean, clear container ⅓ full of vinegar and ⅓ full of cooking oil. Put the lid on the container.

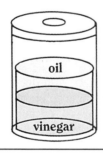

2. Mix by shaking the closed container 10 times.

3. Observe and measure the time it takes for the mixture to separate. Time: _____.

4. Add 5 drops of egg yolk or ⅛ teaspoon of mustard powder.

5. Shake the mixture 10 times.

6. Observe and measure the time it takes for the mixture to separate again. Time: _____.

Trick 3 You will need 3 clear plastic 8 ounce cups labeled A, B, and C for the solutions below:

Solution A: Mix 3 teaspoons of baking soda in an 8 ounce plastic cup half-filled with tap water

Solution B: Mix 3 teaspoons of powdered alum in an 8 ounce plastic cup half-filled with tap water

Solution C: Mix one envelope of unflavored gelatin in an 8 ounce plastic cup one-fourth-filled with tap water.

Now, use Solutions A, B, and C to make your mixtures for Trick 3.

1. Mix ¼ cup of Solution A (baking soda water) and ¼ cup of Solution B (alum water) in a clean, plastic 8 ounce cup.

2. Observe and measure the time it takes for the mixture to separate. Time: _____.

3. Add 3 teaspoons of the Solution C (gelatin water) to the cup which contains the remainder of Solution A (baking soda water).

4. In a clean jar mix the remaining ¼ cup of Solution B (alum water) with the soda and gelatin water mixture you made in Step 3. DO NOT PUT A LID ON THE JAR!

5. Observe and measure the time it takes for the mixture to separate again Time: _____.

The Chemistry of Color Film

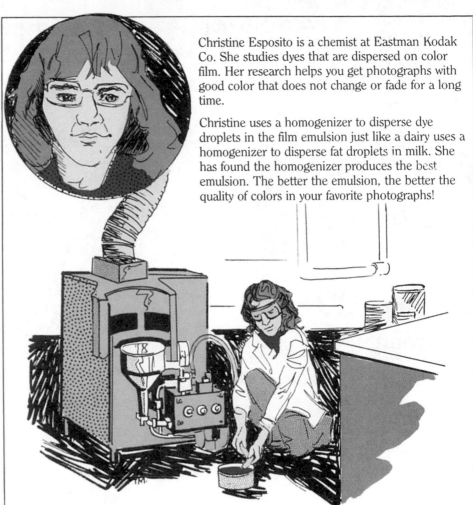

Christine Esposito is a chemist at Eastman Kodak Co. She studies dyes that are dispersed on color film. Her research helps you get photographs with good color that does not change or fade for a long time.

Christine uses a homogenizer to disperse dye droplets in the film emulsion just like a dairy uses a homogenizer to disperse fat droplets in milk. She has found the homogenizer produces the best emulsion. The better the emulsion, the better the quality of colors in your favorite photographs!

A color photograph is made of three layers of dye droplets dispersed in a gelatin that coats the paper. One layer holds cyan droplets, another holds magenta droplets, and the last holds yellow droplets. All three layers are needed to reproduce the colors you see when you take a picture. You may have heard this coating on film called an emulsion.

Search for Dispersions

Circle the letters found at the following chart coordinates:

(6,13)	(7,9)	(5,9)	(9,10)	(11,2)
(1,1)	(1,3)	(1,12)	(12,3)	(13,2)

Note: The coordinates stand for (X,Y). The first number inside each set of parentheses is found on the **"X" or horizontal axis** of the chart. The second number is found on the **"Y" or vertical axis** of the chart. An example is done for you.

Each letter marks the beginning of a word that relates to **dispersions**. The words may be printed in any direction. What words are **dispersed** in this puzzle?

"Y" axis

```
13  b  m  r  t  o  w  f  x  u  a  p  z  e
12  s  a  u  n  r  a  e  j  b  o  i  n  w
11  p  t  l  b  f  t  a  x  l  d  w  o  p
10  m  r  a  o  l  e  n  i  g  r  h  i  f
 9  e  y  f  b  d  r  o  p  l  e  t  s  a
 8  l  g  k  t  i  u  v  a  o  b  f  r  t
 7  b  w  d  i  n  l  x  a  b  j  l  e  b
 6  a  m  g  n  r  o  i  d  s  m  y  p  r
 5  x  v  o  b  q  c  f  z  b  d  k  s  v
 4  i  a  d  k  w  f  p  b  e  o  l  i  m
 3  m  i  x  t  u  r  e  x  o  r  i  d  e
 2  n  p  d  e  z  i  n  e  g  o  m  o  h
 1  u  r  q  a  f  k  o  m  t  e  w  z  p
    1  2  3  4  5  6  7  8  9 10 11 12 13
```

"X" axis

HERE ARE SOME DISPERSIONS YOU CAN MAKE AND EAT. REMEMBER TO ONLY WORK WITH CLEAN HANDS AND KITCHEN SUPPLIES. **BON APPETIT!**

Food for Thought

Dispersion Recipes from the WonderScience Kitchen

French Salad Dressing

Put 3 tablespoons oil, 1 tablespoon vinegar, 1/2 teaspoon sugar, 1/2 teaspoon mustard powder, 1/2 teaspoon salt, some freshly ground pepper, and 1 crushed garlic clove in a screw-top jar. Shake. Store the dressing in the refrigerator. Use it on salads or vegetables.

What is the stabilizer in this recipe? _____

Mayonnaise

Separate the yolks from two eggs. Put the yolks in a mixing bowl with 1/2 teaspoon salt, 1/2 teaspoon sugar, and 1/2 teaspoon mustard powder. Mix with a fork, whisk, or mixer until smooth. Add 2 tablespoons oil by dropping it into the mixture two or three drops at a time and mixing constantly. Slowly add 1 tablespoon lemon juice or vinegar and about 1 1/4 cups more oil—beating the mixture all the time. You can add a bit more lemon juice or vinegar if the mixture gets too thick. **Store the mayonnaise in the refrigerator no longer than one day.** Use it on salads or sandwiches.

What are the stabilizers in this recipe? _____

Vanilla Ice Cream Bags

For this recipe you'll need two sandwich-size and two gallon-size zip-lock bags to make into double-thickness bags to prevent leaks!

Make sure everything is cold, including the mixing bowls. Mix 1/2 cup cream or half-and-half, 1/4 cup milk, 2 tablespoons sugar, 1/8 teaspoon vanilla, and 1 beaten egg in a cold bowl. Pour this ice cream mix into the doubled sandwich-size zip-lock bag. Seal the bags tightly. Put about 3 cups of crushed ice and 1/2 cup of rock salt into the doubled large zip-lock bag. Place the small bag of ice cream mix inside the large bag of ice and salt. Make sure everything is sealed tightly. Watch what happens while you gently rock the bag for about 5 minutes. (Don't rock too hard, or you'll end up with salty ice cream!) When the ice cream looks frozen enough, remove the small bag and rinse it in cold water to remove any salt on the outside. This makes about one big scoop of ice cream. You can eat the soft ice cream right away or put it in a freezer to let it get even harder. (Throw away the large bag of salty ice.)

What's the stabilizer in this recipe? _____

Why do you have to rock the mixture as it freezes? _____

WONDER SCIENCE

Diffusion

The activities in this unit introduce students to a physical process called diffusion. Diffusion is the movement of particles (usually atoms or molecules) from an area where they are in high concentration to an area where they are in lower concentration.

An example of diffusion is the spreading of odor from perfume or air freshener from one location throughout an entire room. The reason the perfume molecules spread out is because all molecules, whether in a solid, liquid, or gas, are constantly moving. The movement of the perfume molecules themselves plus the continual impact from molecules in the air, results in the perfume molecules spreading out away from each other or diffusing.

Molecules on the Move! and Colliding Clouds of Color!

In *Molecules on the Move!* and *Colliding Clouds of Color!*, students discover that molecules tend to diffuse more quickly at higher than at lower temperatures. Heating molecules makes them move faster, resulting in more rapid diffusion.

Sweet, Sweeter, Sweetest!!

In *Sweet, Sweeter, Sweetest!!*, students observe that diffusion takes place slowly throughout a liquid if the liquid is not stirred and allowed to sit for a long enough period of time. Students should understand that the molecular motion within the liquid causes diffusion to take place.

The Case of the Missing Bananas

The Case of the Missing Bananas challenges students to solve a mystery by deciding whether molecules can diffuse through containers which appear to be closed. Students can discuss examples of smelling odors through certain containers and not others.

What is That Cologne You're Wearing?

What is That Cologne You're Wearing? describes the difference between cologne, toilet water, and perfume, and shows that our ability to smell odors depends very much on the process of diffusion.

Diffusion Designs

In *Diffusion Designs*, students make colorful designs and pictures using the process of diffusion.

RELEVANT NATIONAL SCIENCE EDUCATION STANDARDS

The activities in this unit can be used to support the teaching of the following standards:

✔ Science as Inquiry
  Abilities necessary to do scientific inquiry

✔ Physical Science
  Properties and changes of properties in matter

✔ Life Science
  Structure and function in living systems

✔ Earth and Space Science
  Structure of the Earth system

MOLECULES
ON THE MOVE!*

1 Have your adult partner put two cups of hot water in a bowl. Add two envelopes of unflavored gelatin to the water in the bowl and stir until the gelatin is dissolved.

2 Divide the clear gelatin between the two cups. Put the cups into the refrigerator until the gelatin is firmly set (about 1 1/2 hours.)

3 Remove one cup from the refrigerator and put it on the counter or table until it reaches room temperature (about 1/2 hour.) Label this cup: **ROOM TEMPERATURE.**

4 Take the chilled cup from the refrigerator and place it on the counter next to the room temperature cup. Label this cup: **CHILLED.**

* All activities in *WonderScience* have been reviewed for safety by Dr. Jack Breazeale, Dr. Jay Young, and Dr. Patricia Redden.

5 Carefully sprinkle 1/2 tsp of dry drink mix in a circle against the inside rim of each cup of gelatin. Mark a point on the rim of each cup with a crayon and measure the width of the drink mix at that point. Record the width of the drink mix for each cup in the chart below. Also record any observations you have about the way the drink mix looks in the gelatin. Put the chilled cup back in the refrigerator.

6 Every ten minutes, for the next thirty minutes, record the width of the drink mix from the mark on the edge of the cup, and any observations you have on the appearance of the drink mix in both cups. Be sure to leave the room temperature cup out and to return the chilled cup to the refrigerator each time you make your measurements.

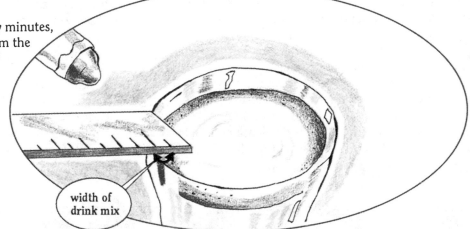

width of drink mix

	TIME	WIDTH OF DRINK MIX	OBSERVATIONS
CHILLED CUP	Start (0 Minutes)		
	10 Minutes		
	20 Minutes		
	30 Minutes		
ROOM TEMPERATURE CUP	Start (0 Minutes)		
	10 Minutes		
	20 Minutes		
	30 Minutes		

7 Does the dry drink mix move more quickly in the room temperature gelatin or in the chilled gelatin? Why do you think that the drink mix doesn't stay at the edge of the cup where it was first put?

DIFFUSION:
MOVIN' ON OUT!

How can you tell when you're getting close to a bakery? You can smell it, of course! At first, when you are some distance from the bakery's doors, you just get a whiff— just a hint of good smells. As you get closer and closer, though, those odors get stronger and stronger, until *finally*, you're *there* and you just *have* to go in.

Did you ever wonder how those great bakery smells could travel so far, even on a windless day? The answer is a process called *diffusion*. When particles (usually molecules) *diffuse*, they end up moving from a place where they are very closely crowded together to a place where they are less crowded. In the bakery, the molecules that carry the baking smell are very crowded right where the baking is going on. As these molecules move in different directions and bump into each other, they naturally spread out away from the bakery where they were most crowded. The molecules *diffuse* through the air and bring the smell of the bakery to where your nose can sense it, even some distance away.

You saw some evidence of how particles diffuse through one another when you put the dry drink mix in the gelatin in "Molecules on the Move." Did you notice that the drink mix was able to move more quickly through the room temperature gelatin than through the chilled gelatin? When molecules move more quickly, either by being heated or by being stirred or shaken, diffusion can happen more quickly also. You can see how different temperatures change the speed of the diffusion of liquids when you do "Colliding Clouds of Color."

You will be able to use your sense of taste to check for the diffusion of sugar in tea in "Sweet, Sweeter, Sweetest." Your sense of smell will help you solve a diffusion mystery in "The Case of the Missing Bananas."

SWEET, SWEETER, SWEETEST!!
or A TASTE FOR DIFFUSION!

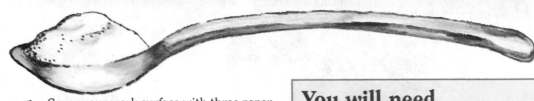

1 Cover your work surface with three paper towels. Put a cup of tea or fruit drink with no sugar in it on the left paper towel and label it **NO SUGAR.**

2 Put a second glass of tea or fruit juice on the middle paper towel. Add 2 teaspoons of sugar to this glass but **DO NOT STIR.** Label this glass **UNSTIRRED SUGAR.**

3 Put a third glass of tea or fruit drink on the right paper towel. Add 2 teaspoons of sugar and stir until the sugar dissolves. Label this glass **STIRRED SUGAR.**

You will need
3 8-oz glasses of unsweetened decaffeinated tea or unsweetened fruit drink mix
4 tsp sugar
spoon
pencil
cards for labeling
paper towels

4 Taste the drink in the unsweetened glass first, then look at the scale below. The drink with no sugar in it should be ranked as a "1" since it is unsweetened. Next, taste the tea in the **stirred sugar** glass. It should be a "5" since it is our sweetest sample.

5 The glass labeled **unstirred sugar** should be tasted every five minutes for the next 30 minutes. Judge where the drink fits on the Sweetness Scale every time you taste, then record the number on the chart. Be careful not to shake or swirl the drink in the glass when you are doing your tastings. (You may need to taste your other two glasses each time to remind yourself of the tastes at the opposite ends of the Sweetness Scale.)

•••••••••••••• **SWEETNESS SCALE** ••••••••••••••

1	2	3	4	5
NOT SWEET		MEDIUM SWEET		VERY SWEET

6 Record each of your "sweetness numbers" in the chart below for the **unstirred sugar** glass. (We filled in the **no sugar** and **stirred sugar** boxes for you since those numbers stay the same.)

7 What happens to the sweetness of the **unstirred sugar** glass as time goes by? Use what you know about diffusion to explain what happened in the **unstirred sugar** glass. How could you change the temperature of the tea to speed up the diffusion of the sugar?

Time	No Sugar	Unstirred Sugar	Stirred Sugar
START (0 Minutes)	1		5
5	1		5
10	1		5
15	1		5
20	1		5
25	1		5
30	1		5

The Case of the Missing Bananas

Mike and his mom got up early on Saturday to make banana breads for Mike's class' bakesale. Mike was in charge of banana-mashing and measuring the flour, so he got out a measuring cup and spoons; and a fork and bowl for mashing the bananas.

As Mike watched his mom mixing the sugar and butter together in a large bowl with her electric mixer, she said, "Mike, why don't you go ahead and get the bananas mashed so they'll be ready for me. I've been saving those last two bananas just for your bakesale."

"Okay, Mom," said Mike. "Where are they?"

"Look next to the bread keeper. That's where they were yesterday," she replied. Mike looked, but couldn't find the bananas anywhere. "Where could they have gone?" said his mother with a puzzled glance around the kitchen. "I wonder if your grandma could have moved them when she was staying with you yesterday?"

"Let's call her and ask," suggested Mike.

"No, she's teaching a class at the college this morning, Mike. We'll just have to find them on our own."

"Wait a minute, Mom. Just stand here and smell for a second. Can't you smell bananas?"

"I *CAN* smell bananas! Now where could they be?"

How can Mike and his mother use their powers of smell to find the missing bananas? Where are the most likely places for the bananas to be? A sealed metal tin? In a zip-closing plastic bag? In a paper bag? Wrapped in a paper towel? Why are some of these places very *un*likely hiding places for the bananas?

COLLIDING CLOUDS
OF COLOR!

You will need
2 8-oz clear plastic cups
hot and cold water
1 dropper bottle of red food
coloring
1 dropper bottle of blue food
coloring

1 Have your adult partner fill one cup 3/4 full of hot tap water, and the other 3/4 full of cold water.

Illustrations by Lori Seskin-Newman

2 At the same time, you and your adult partner should put two drops of red and two drops of blue coloring gently into the water in each cup.

3 Observe what happens in each cup over the next ten minutes. What differences in the speeds of diffusion do you notice between the two cups?

4 In which cup do the colors diffuse into the water more quickly? Compare what happened to the liquid food color in this activity to what happened with the dry drink mix and gelatin in "Molecules on the Move." In which experiment did the color move more quickly? Come up with an explanation for why the diffusion of the color happened more quickly in one experiment than in the other.

WHAT *IS* THAT COLOGNE YOU'RE WEARING?

Illustration by Tina Mion

Have you ever walked into a department store and smelled perfume even before you got to the perfume counter? Or maybe you could smell perfume on your grandmother at lunch but when she hugged you at bedtime, you couldn't smell it anymore. What makes perfume smell and why doesn't the smell last all day?

Certain kinds of plants, like cinnamon and rose, have tiny sacs that make special good smelling oils. These oils, called *essential oils*, can be mixed with alcohol to make perfume. The reason why you are able to smell the perfume is because of *diffusion*. The perfume molecules your grandmother puts on her skin in the morning diffuse slowly out into the air where you breathe them in through your nose and smell them. The molecules keep diffusing all day until there are so few left that you can't smell them anymore.

There are different types of perfumes. If the alcohol has only a small amount of essential oils, it is called *cologne*. If it has more essential oils it is called *toilet water,* and if it has the most essential oils, it is called *perfume*. Getting essential oils out of plants is difficult, so perfume costs more than cologne or toilet water. Just one ounce of a certain perfume can cost up to $600.

One way to get the essential oils out of plants is to pass steam through a plant part, like the petal of a rose, so that the liquid oils turn into a gas. The perfume maker collects the gas in a tube and cools it so that the gas turns back into a liquid. The essential oils are then mixed with alcohol, coloring, and chemicals to make the oils last longer, and the perfume is ready to go!

by Jennifer Snyder

DIFFUSION DESIGNS

REMEMBER WHAT HAPPENED IN "MOLECULES ON THE MOVE" WHEN YOU PUT THE DRY DRINK MIX ON THE GELATIN? YOU CAN USE THIS SAME TYPE OF DIFFUSION TO MAKE GREAT WORKS OF WONDERSCIENCE ART!!

1 Have your adult partner pour the cup of hot water into the bowl. Add the gelatin to the water and then stir the mixture until the gelatin is dissolved.

You will need

2 white pressed foam meat trays (8 in x 10 in)
1 envelope of unflavored gelatin
1 cup of hot tap water
3 colors of dry drink mix
2 teaspoons
small bowl
mixing spoons
3 paper cups

2 Pour the gelatin into the meat trays to form two thin layers. Refrigerate the two trays until the gelatin is firmly set (about 30 minutes).

3 Remove the trays from the refrigerator and put them on your work surface.

4 You and your adult partner can make designs and pictures by carefully sprinkling different colors of drink mix onto the gelatin with the tip of your spoon. Watch how the colors "develop" as they begin diffusing from where they are sprinkled.

5 You can save your finished Diffusion Designs by putting them back into the refrigerator or freezer.

6 When you are ready to do some new art, your adult partner can clean off your trays with hot tap water.

This unit introduces students to some of the basic properties of crystals. Students model the regular repeating pattern of the atoms within a crystal and investigate how crystals grow and some of the modern technological uses for crystals.

A Closer Look at Crystals

In *A Closer Look at Crystals*, students observe some interesting properties of three common household crystals. Students discover that crystals have certain geometric shapes, dissolve to different extent in water and recrystallize differently when a solution of the crystal is evaporated.

Table Salt Crystals

In *Table Salt Crystals*, students make a model of a crystal of common table salt (sodium chloride). You can explain to students that although atoms, and the bonds between them, look nothing like gum drops and toothpicks, scientists can still learn a lot from making models. A three-dimensional crystal model shows the distances from one part of the crystal to another, what the crystal looks like from many different angles, the shape that would result if the crystal were cut in a certain way, and other pieces of information.

The Many Facets of Crystals

The Many Facets of Crystals points out some of the modern technological uses of crystals that students should find fun and interesting.

Captain Ice. . .Commander Expander!

In *Captain Ice. . .Commander Expander!*, students investigate the phenomenon of water expanding when it crystallizes to become ice. The article on potholes at the bottom of the page illustrates a common problem caused by water's expansion when it crystallizes to form ice.

Crystals and Ice Cream Just Don't Mix!

Crystals and Ice Cream Just Don't Mix! emphasizes the point that sometimes we want crystals to grow and sometimes we don't. Tasting the two types of ice cream shows students that texture of ice cream is better when the crystals are prevented from growing too large by beating the ice cream while it freezes.

RELEVANT NATIONAL SCIENCE EDUCATION STANDARDS

The activities in this unit can be used to support the teaching of the following standards:

✔ Science as Inquiry
   Abilities necessary to do scientific inquiry

✔ Physical Science
   Properties and changes of properties in matter
   Transfer of energy

A CLOSER LOOK AT CRYSTALS*

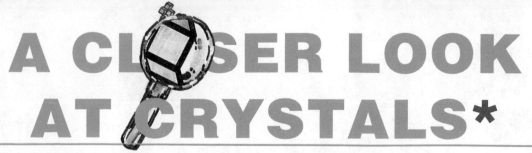

You will need

table salt
Epsom salt
sugar
three disposable clear plastic cups
4 cotton swabs
notebook paper (1 piece)
black construction paper (2 pieces)
blunt-end scissors
metric ruler
pencil
masking tape
teaspoon
magnifying glass (optional)

Warning: Do not use household drinking cups for this activity. The cups will be discarded after the activity.

1 Use your ruler and pencil to divide one piece of black paper into three equal sections. With the masking tape and pencil, label the top section *"salt,"* the middle section *"sugar,"* and the bottom section *"Epsom salt."*

2 Put about 10 crystals each of table salt, sugar, and Epsom salt in its labeled area. Look very closely at the crystals. If you have a magnifying glass, use it to observe the crystals.

3 How would you describe the shape of the *salt* crystals? What have you seen in your house or somewhere else that is bigger than the salt crystals but has the same shape?

4 Look at the *sugar* crystals. How does their shape compare to the shape of the table salt crystals? Can you see any differences? Now look at the *Epsom salt* crystals. How would you describe the shape of these crystals? Have you ever seen larger crystals with this shape before? Where? Discard the table salt, sugar, and Epsom salt crystals.

5 Take your three clear plastic cups and label them *"salt,"* *"sugar,"* and *"Epsom salt."* Ask your adult partner to put 1/4 cup of hot tap water in in the salt cup, and place it in its area on the black construction paper.

6 Put one level teaspoon of table salt into the cup and stir with a spoon or swirl the cup until the salt crystals dissolve (until you can't see any crystals against the black background). Add another teaspoon and stir or swirl until these crystals dissolve.

* All activities in *WonderScience* have been reviewed for safety by Dr. Jack Breazeale, Francis Marion College, Florence, SC; Dr. Jay Young, Chemical Health and Safety Consultant, Silver Spring, MD; and Dr. Patricia Redden, Saint Peter's College, Jersey City, NJ.

7 Repeat this process, counting the number of teaspoons of crystals used, until the water cannot dissolve any more crystals (when you still see crystals after stirring or swirling). In the chart, record the number of teaspoons used.

8 Repeat steps 6 and 7 using the sugar cup and then the Epsom salt cup. Record the number of teaspoons of each type of crystal that dissolved in the water. Which type of crystal were you able to dissolve the most of in water? Of which did you dissolve the least?

	Table salt	Sugar	Epsom salt
Number of teaspoons dissolved			

NOT ONLY WILL CERTAIN CRYSTALS DISSOLVE IN WATER, BUT THEY WILL TURN BACK INTO CRYSTALS AGAIN WHEN THE WATER IS REMOVED BY EVAPORATION!

9 Dip a cotton swab in the table salt cup. Use the liquid to write your name in the salt area on the black construction paper. Do the same thing with the other two liquids using separate cotton swabs. Allow the water to evaporate (15 minutes–1/2 hour) and you should see crystals again!

❄ ❄ ❄ ❄ ❄ CRYSTAL SNOWFLAKES! ❄ ❄ ❄ ❄ ❄

Cut a circle from your notebook paper that is about 15 cm in diameter.

Fold the paper in half and then fold it in thirds, along the dotted lines as shown.

Cut out the colored areas of the folded paper, as shown in the drawing.

Open the paper to reveal a beautiful snowflake pattern!

Tape the pattern to a piece of black construction paper. Use your table salt or Epsom salt liquid to paint in all the openings with another cotton swab.

Allow the liquid to evaporate. Remove your snowflake pattern to reveal a *WonderScience* crystal snowflake design!

Remember to discard your plastic cups when you are finished.

LET'S MAKE THIS CRYSTAL CLEAR!

What do you think of when you hear the word *crystal?* When some people talk about very fancy glass, they call it *crystal*. Other people might look at a plastic or glass prism that breaks up light into colors and call it a *crystal*. So what *IS* a crystal?

Well, the word *crystal* is used in different ways by different people, but scientists mean something very special when they talk about crystals.

You have probably learned that everything in the world is made of very tiny particles called *atoms*, and that atoms can join with each other to make *molecules*. Atoms and molecules connect to each other to form all the things around you, even your own body! But when atoms or molecules join together to form a *crystal*, they naturally join to each other only in a certain pattern that repeats itself over and over again, making a certain shape. This repeating pattern and particular shape are what make crystals so special! Scientists would say that the glass and plastic mentioned above are *not* real crystals in the scientific meaning because their atoms and molecules *do not* have an exact repeating pattern, and exact shape.

A crystal is able to grow by adding the same number of atoms or molecules to all its sides, in the same pattern as the ones added before. In this way, the sides of the crystal, called *facets*, and the crystal itself get bigger but keep the same shape!

A very common crystal that you see almost every day is table salt. In the first activity, you saw that a table salt crystal is shaped like a *cube*. You and your adult partner can make a model of the atoms in a cubic crystal by doing the first activity. You can learn about some of the important uses of crystals in modern technology!

There are many different types of crystals with many different qualities. You probably know that a diamond is a crystal, and that ice is a crystal, but did you know that all *metals* are crystals? The atoms that make up metals are connected to each other in the same way over and over again, so even though they may not look like it, all metals are crystals!

Not only do many crystals look different from each other, they also act differently. Most metals allow electricity to flow through them easily, but electricity will not flow well through many other crystals. Many crystals allow light to pass through them, but light will not pass through many metals. Water will dissolve table salt, sugar, and some other crystals, but will not dissolve diamonds, quartz, or most metals.

Now that the basics are *crystal clear*, have fun learning more about *crystals*!

TABLE SALT CRYSTALS . . .

MODEL 'EM!

To get an idea of the pattern and connections of atoms in a **cubic** crystal, you and your adult partner can make a model of a crystal using gum drops and toothpicks!

The gum drops represent **atoms** or **molecules**, and the toothpicks represent the place where the atoms or molecules join together to form the shape of the crystal.

You will need
27 gum drops
toothpicks

WARNING: *Wash your hands before doing this activity. If you plan to eat the gum drops, remove the toothpicks first.*

1 Use your toothpicks to connect nine gum drops in a square as shown. Push the toothpicks well into the gum drops so that the connections are strong.

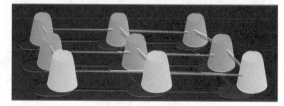

2 Build two more squares of nine gum drops like the first one and stack them to make a model of a cubic crystal like the picture to the left.

3 Because this is a model of a **cubic** crystal, what does each side or **facet** of the crystal have in common with the others? Are they the same size? Are they the same shape? What shape is each facet?

4 If you could see the atoms of a table salt crystal, they would **not** look like gum drops and toothpicks, so why do you think scientists build models to learn more about crystals?

You will need
cup
paper clip
pencil
table salt or Epsom salt
string
teaspoon

1 Ask your adult partner to fill your cup 3/4 full of hot tap water.

2 Dissolve as much table salt or Epsom salt in the water as you can and then add another teaspoonful.

GROW 'EM!

3 Tie a paper clip to one end of a string; to the other end, tie a pencil and place it on the cup as shown.

4 Place the cup in a spot where it will not be disturbed. As the water slowly evaporates, salt crystals will form on the string.

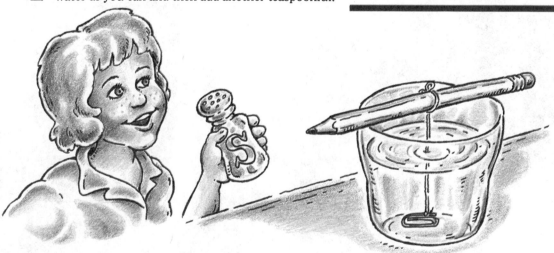

In about one to two weeks, you should have salt crystals near the top of the string in the table salt solution or the bottom of the string in the Epsom salt solution. If you want to keep your crystals growing, make up another salt water solution and add it to the cup every few days as the water evaporates.

THE MANY FACETS OF CRYSTALS

When a thin layer of quartz crystal is squeezed, electricity can be produced!

Crystals are used in photovoltaic cells, special devices that change light into electricity!

A thin quartz crystal vibrates at a constant ra so it can be used in a watch to keep time!

Crystals are used in transistors, an important part of radios, TVs, and other electronic devices!

Crystals grown in space, in low gravity, will have a more perfect shape for use on Earth!

CAPTAIN ICE...
COMMANDER EXPANDER!

When water freezes, it crystallizes to become ice. When most liquids get cold enough to form crystals, the crystals almost always take up *less* space than the liquid did before it crystallized. But water is different. When water freezes to form ice crystals, the ice takes up *more* space than the water did. You can prove it to yourself by doing these two activities!

> **WARNING:** *Do not try these activities with glass or metal containers.*

You will need
balloon
metric tape
pencil

Have your adult partner partly fill a balloon with water. Tie the balloon making sure that no air gets in. Use a metric tape measure to measure the largest area around the balloon. Record your measurement.

Place the balloon in the freezer and take it out the next morning. Measure the largest part of the balloon again. Is it bigger or smaller than before? Did the water or the ice take up more room inside the balloon?

Have you ever heard of water pipes breaking in the winter because the water in them freezes? Why do you think the pipes break when the water freezes? What could happen to some engine parts if you didn't use *antifreeze* in the water you put in your car engine?

Illustrations by Tina Mion

You will need
plastic margarine tub

Fill a plastic margarine tub to the very top with water. Put the lid on tightly and put the tub in the freezer. Take it out the next morning and look at the tub. What happened to the water when it crystallized to become ice? When water freezes to form ice, do you think the water molecules get further from each other (*expand*) or get closer together (*contract*)?

If you had a rock with a crack in it and you couldn't break it by hitting it or by dropping it, how could you use water to help you break it?

While riding in a car, have you ever said or heard someone yell, "Watch out for that pothole!" What do you think causes these holes in the road to appear where the road seemed fine before? The answer has a lot to do with crystals! When a road has been in use for a long time, it may get a small crack in it. During the winter, rain or melting snow gets into the crack and freezes. Ice crystals take up more space than the water, so the ice pushes against the sides of the crack, making the crack bigger. Then, more water gets in and freezes, making the crack even bigger and causing more cracks. The new cracks get water in them and the whole process continues until the road is very weak. When trucks and cars drive over the weak spot, pieces of road break loose and a pothole is formed.

CRYSTALS AND ICE CREAM JUST DON'T MIX!

Crystals are useful for many purposes but sometimes it's best *not* to have them. You don't want ice crystals to form in the radiator or hoses of your car. When salt crystals form inside water pipes, the pipes can become clogged or damaged. Crystals are allowed to form in certain foods but in some foods, like ice cream, we try to stop the crystals from forming. Try this experiment and see why crystals and ice cream just don't mix!

You will need

2 cups half and half
1/2 cup sugar
1 tsp vanilla
2 aluminum foil pie pans
mixing bowl
2 cereal bowls
spoon
wire whisk
can opener
masking tape
pencil

NOTE: *Be sure to wash your hands and all utensils before doing this activity.*

1 Mix the half and half, sugar, and vanilla in a mixing bowl. Use the tape and pencil to mark one aluminum pan "A" and the other "B."

2 Pour half of the mixture into each pie pan. Put both pans in the freezer. Leave pan A completely alone.

3 Take pan B out of the freezer after about 30 minutes. Beat the mixture thoroughly with the wire whisk and then return pan B to the freezer.

4 Beat the mixture thoroughly with the wire whisk every 15 minutes for 1 hour. Then let the mixture freeze without touching it for one hour.

5 Scoop some ice cream from the edges of pan A and pan B into separate cereal bowls. Taste some of each. Compare the *texture* and the taste of each. Does ice cream A or ice cream B taste creamier? Which had larger ice crystals in it?

When ice cream is made in a special ice cream maker, what do you think is the job of the *dasher* (the big paddle in the middle)? Is it good to have large crystals in ice cream? Why or why not?

WONDERSCIENCE

Chemicals and Chemical Reactions

This unit introduces students to some of the principles involved in chemical tests that chemists do in a chemistry laboratory. The objective is to help students discover that they can perform real chemical tests that they can observe, analyze, and understand.

Become a WonderScience Chemist and Test Your Reactions!

Become a WonderScience Chemist and *Test Your Reactions!* shows that there can be more than one chemical test to learn about the substance being tested. Of the five liquids tested, vinegar, lime juice, and lemon juice should be the most acidic, and should bubble the most when dripped on baking soda. Orange juice should be less acidic, and water should be the least.

In the red cabbage juice indicator test, vinegar, lime juice, and lemon juice should again be the most acidic and should cause the indicator to turn the most pink, while orange juice will have less of an effect and water should produce no color change.

Solve a WonderScience Mix-tery

In *Solve a WonderScience Mix-tery*, students use a popular chemical test called chromatography. Paper chromatography involves placing a mixture of chemicals on a piece of paper and allowing the chemicals to move up the paper. Different chemicals will move up the paper at different rates. The different size, shape, electrical charge, and weight of different chemicals makes them move at different rates so a mixture of chemicals can be separated using chromatography.

Chemistry Can Be Gobs of Fun!

In *Chemistry Can Be Gobs of Fun!*, students explore the concept that a small amount of a substance can have a large effect. One variable which is difficult to control is the actual amount of cornstarch in 1/2 cup due to unintended packing. After making your three cornstarch and water mixtures and adding the 1, 2, and 3 teaspoons of extra cornstarch, check the consistency of the material in your third bowl. It should be thick enough to be taken out and formed into a ball. If it is not, you will probably need to add a little extra cornstarch to each bowl.

Carbon Dioxide...What a Gas!

In *Carbon Dioxide...What a Gas!*, students discover that there are ways of analyzing not only solids and liquids, but gases as well. When carbon dioxide is bubbled through the blue indicator solution, the liquid should turn a purplish color. When you bubble your own breath into the indicator, there should be a less perceptible color change or no change at all. This is because the concentration of carbon dioxide in your breath is not as high as that in the club soda.

Do These Liquids "Stack" Up?

Do These Liquids "Stack" Up? shows that dissolving a chemical in water makes a solution with a greater density than the original water. When the salt water is dripped into the fresh water, the salt water should sink, making two distinct layers. When the water with the most salt is added, it should stay below the other two layers, resulting in three distinct layers.

RELEVANT NATIONAL SCIENCE EDUCATION STANDARDS

The activities in this unit can be used to support the teaching of the following standards:

✔ Science as Inquiry
   Abilities necessary to do scientific inquiry

✔ Physical Science
   Properties and changes of properties in matter

BECOME A WONDERSCIENCE CHEMIST

Chemists do many interesting and important jobs. One big part of being a chemist is being able to figure out what chemicals are in certain substances. Another important job of a chemist is to combine the right chemicals in the right way to make useful new substances!

To find out what chemicals are in a substance, chemists have learned to do many different types of tests. Some tests tell the chemist what chemicals are in the substance; other tests tell how much of each chemical there is.

In the next two activities, you can do two different chemical tests on drops of five common liquids to learn which drops have the most *acid.*

You will need:

paper towels	water	eye dropper
11 3-oz paper	tablespoon	teaspoon
or plastic cups	baking soda	1 butter knife
1 lemon	1 piece of black con-	masking tape
1 lime	struction paper	crayon
1 orange	red cabbage	2 sheets of white paper
white vinegar	zip-closing plastic bag	pencil

1 Cover your work surface with paper towels. Ask your adult partner to cut open your lemon, lime, and orange. Squeeze 2 tablespoons of each fruit juice into separate cups. Also put 2 tablespoons of vinegar and water into separate cups and label all 5 cups with your masking tape and crayon.

2 Line up your 5 cups along the black paper and put 1/4 teaspoon of baking soda in front of each cup. Starting with the vinegar, use your dropper to put three drops of each liquid on the baking soda in front of each cup. *Be sure to wash out the dropper with clean water between uses.*

3 Observe what happens very closely. Was the reaction with orange juice the same as that with vinegar? How do the reactions with the other liquids compare? The reactions you saw were *chemical* reactions!

4 Use a blank piece of paper to make a chart like the one below on the right. Think about what you observed and write the name of the liquid in the area of the chart where you think it belongs. Like a real chemist, do each test again to make sure where to put each liquid in your chart.

5 Which liquid caused the biggest reaction? Which caused no reaction? Which caused a medium reaction? Which drops do you think had the most acid? Which drops do you think had the least?

6 What do you think you could do to the liquid that caused the *strongest* reaction to make it cause only a *medium* reaction? Use any of your 5 liquids to experiment and see if you're right!

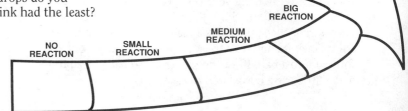

274

AND TEST YOUR REACTIONS!

In chemistry, there is often more than one way for a chemist to find the information he or she needs. Here is a **completely different** way to find out which drops of liquid have the most acid!

1 Take your cups of vinegar, water, lemon juice, lime juice, and orange juice away from the black paper and line them up at the edge of a white piece of paper.

2 Tear up two leaves of red cabbage and place the pieces in a zip-closing plastic bag. Add 1 cup of warm water and close the bag tightly. Use your hands to press the leaves inside the bag until the water becomes a medium blue color. This is your **indicator** for acid.

3 Pour an equal amount of indicator into 6 small cups. Place each indicator cup in front of each test liquid. The one extra cup is your **control** cup.

4 Starting with the vinegar, use your dropper to place one drop of each liquid into the indicator in front of each cup. **Be sure to wash out the dropper with clean water between each use.** Swirl the indicator and observe the color of the liquid. Compare this color to the color in the control cup. If none of your indicator changed color, add one more drop of each test liquid to its indicator cup.

THE MORE ACID IN A DROP OF TEST LIQUID, THE PINKER THE COLOR OF THE RED CABBAGE INDICATOR!

5 Observe the colors closely. Which liquid turned the indicator most pink? Which left it the most blue? Which turned it a medium color between blue and pink? Which drop had the most acid? Which had the least?

6 Use a clean sheet of paper to make a chart like the one below. Look at your cups and write the name of the liquid that best fits in each area on the chart.

Did your liquids end up in the same order along the arrow from this test as they did in the baking soda test? Is the test on this or the previous page better for testing for acid? Why?

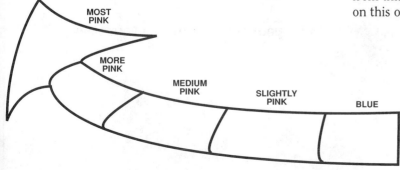

Control cup

MOST PINK
MORE PINK
MEDIUM PINK
SLIGHTLY PINK
BLUE

* All activities in *WonderScience* have been reviewed for safety by Dr. Jack Breazeale, Francis Marion College, Florence, SC; Dr. Jay Young, Chemical Health and Safety Consultant, Silver Spring, MD; and Dr. Patricia Redden, Saint Peter's College, Jersey City, NJ.

CELEBRATE NATIONAL CHEMISTRY WEEK!

If you like experimenting with chemicals the way a chemist does, you should know that there is a **NATIONAL CHEMISTRY WEEK!** During this week, people from all over the United States will be doing chemical demonstrations, experiments, and other activities to teach and learn about chemistry.

Chemistry is a very important science because chemists are able to study the things around us down to the very tiny particles called *atoms* and *molecules.* Chemists can figure out what atoms or molecules are in a substance and can combine atoms or molecules in different ways to make new substances. Another name that people use for these atoms and molecules is the word *chemicals.* Everything around you, including your own body, is made up of these chemicals. In fact, anything you can touch, see, hear, smell, or taste is a result of chemicals. The water you drink, the air you breathe, and the food you eat are all made of chemicals. Chemicals make up the paper and pencils you use in school, the clothes you wear, the trees in your neighborhood, your parents' car, and the gasoline they put in it.

Another good way for you and your adult partner to celebrate National Chemistry Week is to set aside an area or cabinet in your kitchen for a *WonderScience* Chemistry Laboratory! Each time you get a new *WonderScience* that has chemistry activities in it, you and your adult partner can use the equipment in your kitchen lab to do the experiments and then add any new equipment as you need it.

IMPORTANT:

1. *Always* have your adult partner with you when doing *WonderScience* experiments in your *WonderScience* chemistry lab.

2. Only add equipment to your laboratory that is in the "you will need" section of a *WonderScience* activity.

Ask your adult partner to help you begin to supply your *WonderScience* Chemistry Lab! Here are some things from your new *WonderScience* and from some past *WonderScience* issues that you will need to get your lab started:

Protective goggles, paper towels, small and medium plastic or paper cups, zip-closing plastic bags, baking soda, table salt, sugar, flour, cornstarch, vinegar, food coloring, unflavored gelatin, small bowls, metric ruler, measuring cups, measuring spoons, eye dropper, aluminum foil, round balloons, string, dish detergent, paper, masking tape, blunt-end scissors, crayon, and water.

Have fun doing *WonderScience* chemistry activities with your adult partner in your new *WonderScience* kitchen laboratory!

Solve a WonderScience
Mix-tery

Sometimes chemists have a mixture of chemicals and need to know what each chemical in the mixture is. One way chemists can separate chemicals in a mixture is by a process called ***chromatography.*** In this activity, your adult partner will make up three ***mystery mixtures*** and you will try to figure out what is in the mixture by using chromatography!

You will need:

three 8-oz paper or plastic cups
white coffee filter
metric ruler
blunt-end scissors
food coloring
water
three pencils
clear plastic tape
tablespoon

Since this is a mystery that you need to solve, your adult partner should do steps 1 and 2 without you watching.

1 Your adult partner should fill each cup with 3 tablespoons of water and put 3 drops of ***red*** and ***blue*** food coloring into one cup, 3 drops of ***red*** and ***yellow*** in another cup, and 3 drops of ***red, blue,*** and ***yellow*** in another cup.

2 Ask your adult partner to write the colors in each cup on a piece of masking tape and tape it to the ***bottom*** of the cup so that you cannot see it.

Now you can use
chromatography
to figure out what colors
are in which cups!

3 Take an unused coffee filter and cut three strips about 10 cm long and about 2 cm wide.

4 Wrap one end of a strip around a pencil and lower the other end so that it goes about 1/2 cm into the water. Tape the filter paper to the pencil and place the pencil on the rim of the cup.

5 Repeat step 4 for your 2 other cups. Watch as the water and food coloring move up the filter paper. Can you tell which cup contained which food coloring? If you get a green color on any of your paper strips, how do you explain this?

Try your own color combinations and have fun with ***chromatography!***

Chemistry can be
GOBS OF FUN!

Chemists not only test substances to find out what chemicals they are made of, they also put chemicals together in a certain way to make new substances with special characteristics. Sometimes, a very small amount of a chemical can make a very big difference in the qualities of the final product. Try the following activity and see that a little bit more or a little bit less can make a big difference!

You will need:

cornstarch
warm water
three small bowls
three teaspoons
paper towels
masking tape
crayon

1 Cover your work area with paper towels. Place 1/2 cup of cornstarch in each of the three bowls. Add 1/4 cup of water to each bowl and stir until smooth. Use your masking tape and crayon to label the bowls A, B, and C.

2 Add 1 extra teaspoon of cornstarch to bowl A and stir until smooth. Add 2 extra teaspoons to bowl B and stir until smooth. Add three extra teaspoons to bowl C and stir until smooth.

Try this *WonderScience* tongue-twister:

A little extra makes a mixture with extra texture!

3 Use your fingers to scrape up a handful of material from bowl A. As you scrape it up, does the material at the bottom of the bowl feel different than the material in the rest of the bowl? Does the material feel different when you squeeze it quickly between your fingers than when it just sits in the palm of your hand?

4 Rinse off your hands and dry them and repeat step 3 with the material in bowl B. Gather the material into a glob in one area of the bowl. Does your finger go further into the glob if you poke it hard or if you push your finger gently into it? Quickly pull some material out of the bowl and hold it. Does it feel and act differently when you hold it than when you pulled it out?

5 Rinse and dry your hands and make a ball out of the material in bowl C. Does it stay in a ball if you leave it in the palm of your hand? Is it difficult to make it stay in one shape? How does it act when you pull it apart slowly and when you pull it quickly? Close your fist quickly around it and then close slowly and observe the difference.

6 You can see that a little more or a little less of the chemicals in cornstarch and water make a big difference in the qualities of the final product. Experiment to see if you can find the **exact** amount of water and cornstarch to make the material you like best!

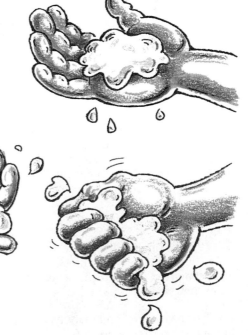

Carbon Dioxide... What a
GAS!

I n the activity on page 3, you used red cabbage juice as an *indicator* to test how much acid there was in drops of different *liquids.* We can also use red cabbage juice to help find out something about *gases.* In this activity, you will find out if a sample of your breath or a sample of gas from a bottle of club soda has more of the gas *carbon dioxide.*

You will need:

1-liter bottle of club soda or seltzer water

2 large round balloons

2 straws

red cabbage

warm water

zip-closing plastic bag

3 3-oz plastic or paper cups

1 Tear up two leaves of red cabbage and place the pieces into a zip-closing plastic bag. Pour 1/2 cup of warm water into the bag and close it tightly.

2 Use your hands to press the cabbage inside the bag until the water becomes a medium blue color. This is your *indicator* solution for carbon dioxide. Pour an equal amount of indicator into each of the three cups. Put one cup aside as your *control* cup.

3 Slowly open your bottle of seltzer and put a balloon over the opening. Allow the balloon to fill up as much as it can with carbon dioxide gas.

4 Twist the bottom of the balloon while it is still on the bottle so that when you remove the balloon, no gas will escape.

5 Remove the balloon and put the balloon opening around the end of a straw. Now pinch the balloon opening tightly against the straw and put the other end of the straw into your blue indicator liquid.

6 Slowly untwist and squeeze the balloon so that the gas goes through the straw and into your indicator solution. Compare the color of the indicator to your control cup. Did the color of your indicator change?

7 Take your other balloon and inflate it with your own breath with the same amount of gas as there was in the first balloon. Using a straw, repeat steps 5 and 6 with your other cup of indicator.

8 Compare this cup with your control cup. Can you see any difference between them? If a *change in indicator color* means that more carbon dioxide is present, which had more carbon dioxide, the balloon with your breath or the one with gas from the soda?

See if you can design an experiment to test the air around you for carbon dioxide. Remember, you need to get the same amount of air in the balloon as you had with the seltzer water and your own breath.

DO THESE LIQUIDS "STACK" UP?

You will need:

3 3-oz clear plastic cups
food coloring (red, yellow, and blue)
eye dropper
measuring spoons
warm water
table salt
1 straw

Sometimes a chemist may need to change a substance so that it will float or sink in another substance. You've probably seen a boat float on water, but did you know that by adding a common chemical like table salt, you can make *water* float or sink in **water?**

1 Place 1 tablespoon of warm water into each cup. Put 2 drops of yellow food coloring in the first cup, 2 drops of red in the second, and 2 drops of blue in the third.

2 Place 1/2 teapoon of salt in the red cup and stir until the salt dissolves. Place 1 teaspoon of salt in the blue cup and stir until as much dissolves as possible. Do not put any salt in the yellow cup.

3 Put a straw into the yellow cup so that it touches the bottom at an angle. Using your dropper, drip all of your red liquid into the yellow cup through the straw. Without stirring the liquid, carefully remove the straw.

4 Look at your cup from the side. Did the liquids mix or is one floating on the other?

5 Put your straw back into the bottom of the cup. Now, slowly drip the blue liquid into the straw until the blue cup is empty. Look at your cup from the side. Why do you think the liquids stay where they do?

6 Repeat steps 1 and 2 to make up a new set of liquids. Use your straw to add them in a different order. What do you think will happen?

Unit 36
More Chemical Reactions

This unit introduces students to some of the observable results of chemical reactions. The unit explores the different clues scientists look for to tell that a chemical reaction may have occurred. These clues include color changes, gas production, two liquids forming a solid, and a change in temperature when two or more substances are combined.

Lose the Indicator Blues!

In *Lose the Indicator Blues!*, students prepare an indicator solution from red cabbage and water. When vinegar (an acid) is added to the indicator, the solution turns from blue to pink. When detergent (a base) is added, the solution turns from blue to green. Students are challenged to make the chemical reaction go in reverse and change the solution back to its original blue color.

Liquids to Lumps!

In *Liquids to Lumps!*, students combine an Epsom salt-and-water solution with a detergent-and-water solution. These two liquids undergo a chemical reaction to produce a solid, called a **precipitate**. A precipitate is a solid that is produced from the combination of two or more liquids. Epsom salt solution contains magnesium, which combines with the detergent to form the precipitate.

Heat Up to Some Cool Reactions!

In *Heat Up to Some Cool Reactions!*, students add yeast to water and to hydrogen peroxide. A chemical in the yeast causes a chemical reaction in which the hydrogen peroxide breaks apart to form oxygen gas. By measuring the temperature every 10 seconds, students will observe an increase in temperature. In the WonderScience Challenge, reducing the amount of water added to the cup will make the temperature increase more quickly.

In the next part of the activity, students add baking soda to vinegar and again record temperature changes. Baking soda reacts with vinegar to produce carbon dioxide gas. This reaction causes a rapid drop in temperature. Students must be ready to take these temperature readings very quickly — every 3 seconds! In the second *WonderScience* Challenge, adding water will dilute the vinegar causing the reaction to slow down and not get as cold as quickly.

A Gas Sudsation!

In *A Gas Sudsation!*, students add baking soda to a vinegar, water, and dish detergent solution. After adding the baking soda, students should continually swirl the solution so the reaction will continue for as long as possible. The challenge at the end of the activity encourages students to experiment with adding more or less water, vinegar, baking soda, or detergent to cause the reaction to foam to a precise height.

RELEVANT NATIONAL SCIENCE EDUCATION STANDARDS

The activities in this unit can be used to support the teaching of the following standards:

✔ **Science as Inquiry**
   Abilities necessary to do scientific inquiry

✔ **Physical Science**
   Properties and changes of properties in matter
   Transfer of energy

✔ **Life Science**
   Structure and function in living systems

✔ **Science and Technology**
   Abilities of technological design

YOU WILL NEED:

red cabbage (1 leaf)

warm water (about 3/4 cup)

measuring spoons

plastic zip-closing bag

eye dropper

3 small cups (paper or plastic)

vinegar (about 1 teaspoon)

laundry detergent powder
  (about 1 teaspoon)

1 flat toothpick (as a tiny scoop)

masking tape

ballpoint pen

Everything in the world is made of **chemicals!**

One of the most amazing things about chemicals is the way they can j
together to make different new chemicals. That's why chemicals can
make up all the zillions of different things in the world! When two or
more chemicals come together and make a new chemical, a
chemical reaction has happened!

There are different ways that scientists can get clues that a chemical
reaction has happened. One thing that scientists may look for is a cha
in color! Sometimes scientists use special chemicals called
indicators that change color when a certain chemical reaction h
occurred. Try this activity and see what we mean!

FIRST STEP:
MAKE YOUR INDICATOR SOLUTION

1 **Tear up** the red cabbage leaf into small pieces.

2 **Place** the pieces in a zip-closing plastic bag.

3 **Add** 3/4 cup of warm water and **close** the bag tightly

4 **Squish** the cabbage and water until the water turns dark blue (about 3 minutes).

THIS IS YOUR INDICATOR SOLUTION

ACTIVITY

1 **Label** your cups vinegar, detergent, and control using your masking tape and pen.

2 **Open** your plastic bag. Use a tablespoon
to **place** 2 tablespoons of indicator
solution into each cup. **Close** the bag
tightly. You will need the extra liquid late

3 Use your dropper to **place** 1 drop of
vinegar in the vinegar cup. Gently
swirl to mix.
*What did you observe in your
vinegar cup? How does it
compare with the control?*

4 Use a toothpick to **add** a very small
amount of detergent to the detergent
cup. Gently **swirl** to mix. *What
did you observe in your
detergent cup? How does it
compare with the control?*

Blues!

TRY TO CHANGE THE COLOR IN YOUR VINEGAR CUP BACK TO BLUE

5 Use your toothpick to **put** a tiny amount of detergent in the vinegar cup and **swirl.**

Compare the color in the vinegar cup with the color of your control cup.
How close did you get?

Be careful; if it ends up looking green, you've added too much detergent.

TRY TO CHANGE THE COLOR IN YOUR DETERGENT CUP BACK TO BLUE

6 **Add** one drop of vinegar to the detergent cup and **swirl.** Try to think of a way to add less than a drop at a time so you don't accidentally add too much. Compare the color you get to the control cup.

How close did you get?

✓ WONDERSCIENCE CHALLENGE 1

1 Rinse out your vinegar and detergent cups thoroughly.

2 Place 2 tablespoons of indicator solution in each cup.

3 In one cup, add 5 drops of vinegar. In the other cup, add 5 tiny scoops (using a toothpick) of detergent.

4 Use what you learned in steps 3–5 above to change the colors in these two solutions back to their original blue!

✓ WONDERSCIENCE CHALLENGE 2

1 Rinse out either the vinegar or the detergent cup thoroughly.

2 Add 2 tablespoons of indicator solution to one of the cups.

3 Have your partner add a mystery amount of 1 to 5 drops of vinegar OR 1 to 5 tiny scoops of detergent to the cup.

4 Your partner should write down the exact amount added but not show you.

5 Your job is to change the color back to blue and to figure out the amount of either vinegar or detergent that your partner must have added. See how close you can get! *GOOD LUCK!*

Chemical Reactions: The Main Attraction

As you know, everything in the world is made of chemicals. And all chemicals are made up of tiny particles called **atoms.**

A **chemical reaction** happens when atoms join together or break apart to form new and different combinations of atoms.

Do this first!

Chemical reactions are part of what we see and do every day.

Can you figure out which chemical reactions are described below? Try to match them up with the answers on the right.

▶ **This chemical reaction takes place in the sun**
And can leave you looking quite overdone!

▶ **Curly hair can be quite an attraction,**
Get it with this chemical reaction!

▶ **The stuff that you eat will do you no good**
If this chemical reaction doesn't work on your food!

▶ **Shiny metal can turn disgusting**
With this chemical reaction that causes crusting!

▶ **Bright streaks of color up in the sky,**
This chemical reaction is in early July!

▶ **A chemical reaction that turns black to gray,**
Food is extra-good when cooked this way!

▶ **Those flashes you see as day becomes night**
Are tiny chemical reactions in flight!

Permanents

Hair is made up of a chemical called **protein.** In a permanent, chemicals are applied to the hair that break connections or **bonds** in the hair's protein. After rollers are put in, more chemicals are added that rejoin the hair's protein in a different way. Permanents can make straight hair curly or curly hair straight!

Rusting

Some metals, such as steel, contain the chemical **iron.** When iron comes in contact with water and oxygen from the air, another chemical called **iron oxide** is formed. Iron oxide is the substance we call rust.

Tanning

When the ultraviolet rays of the sun strike the skin, it causes chemicals in the skin to react and form a new chemical called **melanin.** It is the buildup of melanin, a dark-colored chemical, that gives skin a tan.

Charcoal burning

Charcoal is actually made from wood. Wood is made up mostly of the chemicals **carbon, hydrogen,** and **oxygen.** When we burn charcoal, a chemical reaction occurs between the chemicals in the charcoal and oxygen in the air, resulting in heat, fire, and ashes.

Fireflies flashing

The flashing light of a firefly is produced when chemicals in the firefly's body combine to form a new chemical that glows. But unlike most light sources, the firefly's light gives off no heat, because nothing is burning. Fireflies do not use their light to see but to attract mates or prey.

Fireworks

Some chemicals produce a bright color when they are heated. The different colors and patterns you see in a fireworks display are the result of heating different mixtures of these chemicals. Sometimes another chemical is added that makes a loud booming sound when it explodes.

Digestion

The food we eat is made up of chemicals. Our bodies are made of chemicals. In order for our bodies to use the chemicals in food, a chemical reaction must take place. **Digestion** is a process in which the chemicals in food combine with chemicals in your mouth, stomach, and intestines to make new chemicals that your body can use.

LIQUIDS TO LUMPS!

Scientists also get clues that a chemical reaction may have happened when two or more **liquids** are added together and a **solid** is produced! This solid is called a **precipitate**.

1 Place 1/2 cup of warm water into the large cup. **Add** 1 teaspoon of laundry detergent and **stir gently** until no more detergent will dissolve.

2 Place 2 tablespoons of warm water into one of your smaller cups. **Add** 1 tablespoon of epsom salt and **stir** until no more epsom salt will dissolve.

3 Add 3 drops of blue food coloring to the epsom salt cup and **stir.**

4 Use an eye dropper to **pick up** some of the colored epsom salt solution. Put the end of the dropper Into the detergent solution and **squeeze gently.** Look from the side so you can see the epsom salt solution going into the detergent solution. **What do you observe?**

5 Make two more epsom salt solutions as you did in step 2. **Color** one red and the other yellow. Use your dropper to make a layered colorful precipitate design in your cup.

ROD LITTLE

WONDERSCIENCE CHALLENGE

See if different laundry detergents make different-looking precipitates. See how much of a different detergent it takes to get the same kind of precipitate you got in your experiment above!

Heat up to some c

A CHANGE IN **TEMPERATURE** IS ANOTHER TIP-OFF THAT A CHEMICAL REACTION MAY BE GOING ON. IN SOME CHEMICAL REACTIONS THE TEMPERATURE GOES UP AND IN OTHERS THE TEMPERATURE GOES DOWN.

LOEL BARR

Teachers:
Before doing these activities, have your students practice using and reading their thermometers

1 Make a chart like the one below or use the chart on your worksheet.

Time (sec.)	0	10	20	30	40	50	60	70	80	90	100	110	120
Temp (°F)													

2 Pour 2 tablespoons of hydrogen peroxide into a cup. Add 1 tablespoon of water. Place the thermometer into the cup. Hold the thermometer and the cup so they do not fall over. Read the temperature and record it in the chart under "Time 0".

3 Measure out 1 teaspoon of yeast. Have one partner watch the thermometer and another look at the second hand on a watch.

4 Dump all the yeast into the cup. Gently swirl the cup while one partner calls out the time every 10 seconds. When each 10 seconds is called, another partner should call out the temperature. The third partner should record the temperature in the chart. What did you observe?

5 Make a graph like this or use the graph on your worksheet. Use the information in your chart to graph your results. During what period of time did the temperature change the most? How about the least?

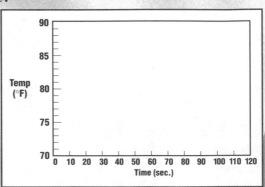

CHALLENGE!

Of your three ingredients, yeast, water, and hydrogen peroxide, which do you think you could use less of to make the temperature get hotter more quickly?

Experiment to test your prediction. Make a chart and a graph and fill them in to show if you were right!

ol reactions!

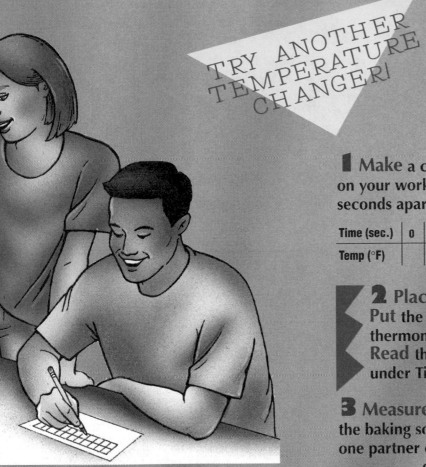

TRY ANOTHER TEMPERATURE CHANGER!

YOU WILL NEED:

vinegar

baking soda

measuring spoons

water

cup (paper or plastic)

thermometer
(use thermometers with red liquid only)

1 Make a chart like the one below or use the chart on your worksheet. Notice that the times are only 3 seconds apart!

Time (sec.)	0	3	6	9	12	15	18	21	24	27	30
Temp (°F)											

2 Place 2 tablespoons of vinegar in the cup. Put the thermometer in the cup. Hold the thermometer and cup so they do not fall over. Read the temperature and record it in the chart under Time 0.

3 Measure 1 teaspoon of baking soda. Dump all the baking soda in the cup. Gently swirl the cup while one partner calls out the time every 3 seconds. When each 3 seconds is called, another partner should call out the temperature. Another partner should record the temperature in the chart. What did you observe?

BE READY TO CALL OUT AND RECORD THE TEMPERATURE EVERY 3 SECONDS!

4 Make a graph like the one below or use the graph on your worksheet. Use the information in your chart to graph your results. During what period of time did the temperature change the most? How about the least?

CHALLENGE!

Think about the yeast activity you did earlier. What liquid could you add to your vinegar and baking soda so that the temperature does not get as cold as quickly?

Do an experiment like the one you did above to test your prediction. Make a chart and a graph and fill them in to show if you were right!

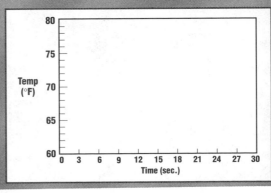

YOU WILL NEED:

- vinegar
- baking soda
- liquid dish detergent
- measuring spoons
- soda bottle (empty)
- 2 cups (paper or plastic)
- paper
- tape
- student scissors

A GAS SUDSATION!

The release of a **gas** is another piece of evidence that a chemical reaction may have happened.

In the activity and challenge below, see how well you can control this gas-producing chemical reaction!

1 **Cover** your work area with paper towels or newspapers. Use your masking tape and pen to **label** one cup **vinegar** and one cup **baking soda.**

2 **Pour** 3 tablespoons of vinegar and 3 tablespoons of water into your vinegar cup.

3 **Pour** the vinegar and water into the soda bottle. **Add** 1/2 teaspoon of detergent. **Swirl** very gently to mix the detergent with the vinegar and water.

4 **Cut** a piece of paper in half widthwise. **Curve** one of the pieces into a cone and **tape** it to make a funnel as shown.

5 **Place** 3 teaspoons of baking soda into its cup. **Use the funnel to dump** all the baking soda into the soda bottle. **Swirl** the mixture. **What do you observe?**

6 Even if you think the reaction has stopped, **Continue** to swirl because there may be a lot more bubbling still to come!

CAN YOU DO IT?

SEE IF YOU AND YOUR PARTNERS CAN USE **TWO** MORE TRIES TO FIGURE OUT THE EXACT AMOUNT OF INGREDIENTS THAT WILL MAKE YOUR FOAM GO TO THE VERY TOP OF THE BOTTLE BUT NOT OVERFLOW!

VINEGAR   BAKING SODA

ILLUSTRATIONS BY ROD LITTLE

This unit contains a variety of activities based on the theme of color-changing chemicals found in common plants. These color changing chemicals are known as *indicators*. When an indicator is combined with an acid or a base, a new compound is formed and a different color is produced.

Indicator Indi-Gator

In *Indicator Indi-Gator*, grape juice is used as the indicator. Baking soda (a base) should turn the indicator greenish and vinegar (an acid) should turn it bluish. Students are challenged to use their observations to create a striped Indi-Gator.

Inside Indicators

In *Inside Indicators*, students are told that ammonia is a base and that vinegar is an acid. Based on their observations in Indicator Indi-Gator, students are asked to predict what color change will occur when flower petals are placed in ammonia and vinegar. The connection between flower petal color and the concentration of acid or base in the soil is made.

How To Lose The Red Cabbage Blues

In *How To Lose The Red Cabbage Blues*, students use carbon dioxide gas to create an acid (carbonic acid) that will change the color of red cabbage indicator. It is important

to point out that nothing was done to one cup of indicator (cup #2). This was the "control". The control is used to compare the results of adding a substance to the indicator with the original indicator.

RELEVANT NATIONAL SCIENCE EDUCATION STANDARDS

The activities in this unit can be used to support the teaching of the following standards:

✔ **Science as Inquiry**
   Abilities necessary to do scientific inquiry

✔ **Physical Science**
   Properties and changes of properties in matter

INDICATOR INDI-GATOR

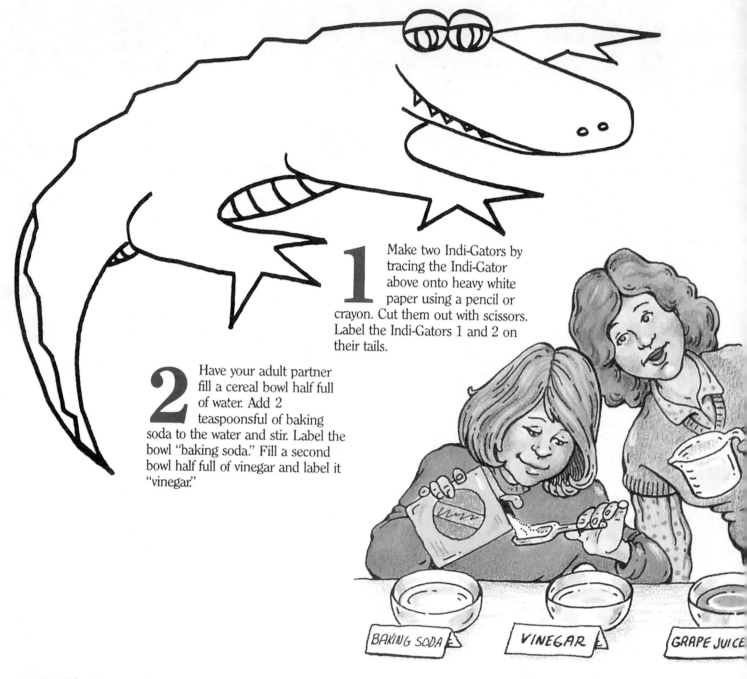

1 Make two Indi-Gators by tracing the Indi-Gator above onto heavy white paper using a pencil or crayon. Cut them out with scissors. Label the Indi-Gators 1 and 2 on their tails.

2 Have your adult partner fill a cereal bowl half full of water. Add 2 teaspoonsful of baking soda to the water and stir. Label the bowl "baking soda." Fill a second bowl half full of vinegar and label it "vinegar."

BAKING SODA   VINEGAR   GRAPE JUICE

5 What do you think will happen to the Indi-Gator when it is dipped into baking soda water?

Record your **predictions** in the chart. Now, carefully dip the Indi-Gator (except for the tail!) into the baking soda water.

Record any **changes** to Indi-Gator 1 in the chart.

6 Will Indi-Gator 1 change when dipped into vinegar? **Predict** what you think might happen and record. Now, dip Indi-Gator 1 into the vinegar. Record any changes in the chart.

7 Repeat Steps 4, 5, and 6 using Indi-Gator 2. Start with vinegar this time. What do you think will happen to the Indi-Gator?

Based upon what you've observed so far, what do you expect to happen when you dip Indi-Gator 2 into the baking soda solution? Try it, and record your results in the chart.

Can you make your Indi-Gator have stripes? **Hint:** use the swab and some vinegar. Can you make the stripes disappear? Try it!

AN **INDICATOR** SHOWS OR POINTS OUT SOMETHING TO YOU. A SMILE CAN BE AN INDICATOR OF A HAPPY FEELING. IN CARS, A NEEDLE INDICATES HOW FULL THE GASOLINE TANK IS. CHEMICAL COLOR-CHANGERS INDICATE SOMETHING BY CHANGING COLOR. MY FRIEND, THE **INDI-GATOR** WILL HELP YOU DISCOVER WHAT THAT SOME-THING IS!

You will need

1 can frozen grape juice concentrate
white drawing or construction paper
blunt scissors   3 plastic teaspoons
baking soda   measuring cup
vinegar   cotton swab
3 cereal bowls   paper towels
pencil and paper to label bowls

3 Add ¼ cup of thawed grape juice concentrate to ¼ cup of water in the third bowl. Mix and label the bowl "grape juice."

4 Holding Indi-Gator 1 by the tail, dip it in the grape juice bowl. Take the Indi-Gator out of the juice letting the extra juice drip into the bowl.
    Record the color of the Indi-Gator on the chart below.

Grape Juice

INDI-GATOR DATA CHART

	INDI-GATOR 1		INDI-GATOR 2	
	Prediction	Color of Indi-Gator	Prediction	Color of Indi-Gator
GRAPE JUICE	✕	✕	✕	
BAKING SODA				
VINEGAR				

8 Now that you have experimented with a grape juice Indi-Gator, what do you predict will happen with Indi-Gators dipped in other juices such as raspberry, blackberry, cherry, or blueberry juice? Make a chart and record the colors that the juices become with baking soda water and vinegar. Do you think that you would get the same color changes if the paper that you dipped into the juices were different shapes and sizes? Try some!

Pear Skin

Blueberry Juice

Tomato Skin

Hibiscus Petals

Peach Skin

Grape Juice

Red Apple Skin

Hydrangea Petals

Plants with a Plus

Did you wonder why the Indi-Gator in the first activity was pointing with one foreleg? When you point to something, you are *indicating* (or *showing*) where or what that something is. Your Indi-Gator was actually *indicating* a difference between the two substances, vinegar and baking soda. The grape juice on the Indi-Gator changed color when it was put into baking soda, one of a group of chemicals called BASES. It changed color again when put into vinegar, a chemical known as an ACID. You may have other acids and bases in your house. For example, lemon juice is an acid. A base that many people use for cleaning is ammonia.

Many plant parts such as leaves, flowers, and fruits contain colorful chemicals. Many of these chemicals are nature's *indicators*, because acids and bases make them change color. The pictures on this page show plant parts that have indicators. As you experiment with some of the indicators made from these plant parts, you can keep a record of the colors that each indicator becomes. You can use markers, crayons, or colored pencils to color each inside border the color that the indicator turns when dipped in an acid such as vinegar or lemon juice. Color the outside border the color that each indicator turns when dipped in a base such as baking soda water.

Some plant parts, flower petals for example, can change color merely when dipped in a base or an acid. Other plant parts such as leaves, fruit pulp, and fruit skin work best when made into indicator solutions. You can make indicator solutions by putting the chopped-up plant part in a bowl or a zip-closing plastic sandwich bag and having your adult partner cover the plant parts with hot water. You will then need to carefully mash the water/plant part mixture together until the water that you have added is cool and colored. Strain the indicator before you use it. The juices that are found with canned cherries, blackberries, and blueberries also work very well as indicators.

The Indi-Gators that you made for the first activity in this issue were a type of indicator paper. The great fictional detective, Sherlock Holmes, also used indicator papers to help solve crime mysteries. Other detectives, such as water chemist Timothy Clark of Oklahoma Gas and Electric, use indicators to test for acids and bases in water samples. You can use your Indi-Gators to test some other liquids in your house to see if they are acids or bases. See the last page of *WonderScience* for a list of these liquids. *Do not test any liquids without the permission and supervision of your adult partner!*

Red Cabbage Juice

Raspberry Juice

Turnip Skin

INSIDE INDICATORS

Some of the chemicals that give flower petals their colors also are indicators for acids and bases. Let's see what happens to the color of a flower petal when we put it in an acid or a base.

You will need:

5 drops of household ammonia
1 dropper
vinegar
tweezers
red or pink carnation petals
2 zip-closing plastic sandwich bags
1 popsicle stick
paper towel
masking tape and pencil to label

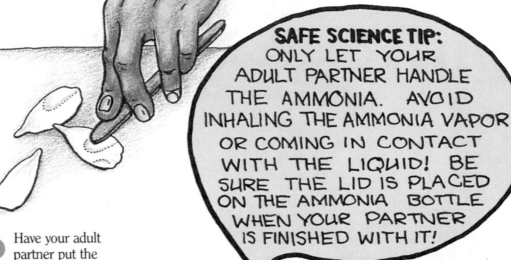

1 Make a design on two carnation petals by pressing on them in different places with the popsicle stick.

2 Have your adult partner put the five drops of ammonia in the plastic sandwich bag and close the bag.

SAFE SCIENCE TIP: ONLY LET YOUR ADULT PARTNER HANDLE THE AMMONIA. AVOID INHALING THE AMMONIA VAPOR OR COMING IN CONTACT WITH THE LIQUID! BE SURE THE LID IS PLACED ON THE AMMONIA BOTTLE WHEN YOUR PARTNER IS FINISHED WITH IT!

3 Fill the second sandwich bag ¼ full of vinegar and close the bag. Label both bags with tape.

4 Before placing the flower petals in the ammonia bag, make a **prediction**. What do you think will happen to the petals when they touch the base, ammonia? Have your adult partner place the designed petals in the ammonia bag. Be sure that the ammonia touches the petals. What happens? Leave the petals in the bag for 10 minutes, then have your partner remove both of them with the tweezers. Rinse the petals in running water and place them on the paper towel. Observe any changes in both of the petals. Have your partner close the ammonia bag.

5 What do you think will happen to a petal that is placed in the acid, vinegar? Using tweezers, put one of your two petals into the vinegar bag for 10 minutes. Observe any changes. Take the petal out of the bag, rinse in running water, and place on the paper towel next to the petal that was only in the ammonia bag. What differences do you see? How could you get your "vinegar petal" to look like your "ammonia petal?"

6 The color of some flower petals depends upon how much acid or base is in the soil in which the flower grows. Soil testing kits that can be bought from garden supply stores often use indicators that show how much acid or base is in a soil sample.

ChemMystery

THE CASE OF THE PETAL PUZZLER

"I don't understand this!" cried Mr. Davis. "When I bought this plant at the nursery last spring, the flowers were blue. But now that it's been growing here beside the porch, the flowers have changed to pink. What's been going on here? Polly! Come out here, please!"

Polly Davis came running out of the house. "What's the matter, Dad?" she asked. "Did you hurt yourself?"

"No, I'm not hurt," replied Mr. Davis. "I'm perfectly fine. Wait, I take that back—*my brain does hurt*. I can't figure out why this hydrangea plant, that used to have blue flowers when I bought it, now has pink flowers! Have you been watering it regularly?"

"Yes, I have, Dad, but I don't think that not watering it could cause this to happen. The flowers don't look limp or anything."

"Maybe it's not getting enough light," suggested Mr. Davis. "Maybe the blue flowers just fade away to pink."

"But don't you remember, Dad?" reminded Polly. "We read the tag on the plant and planted it exactly where it would get the right amount of light. So I don't think that's it either. Maybe there is something in the soil that caused the flowers to change color. We made flowers change color in science class last week. I think I know an experiment that we could do to **help solve this mystery!**"

What might be special about where the hydrangea is planted that could cause the petals to change from blue to pink? How could Polly and Mr. Davis find out why the hydrangea petals might have changed color? Explain your experiment on a sheet of paper. Tell what things are needed to do the experiment and what you would do to solve this Petal Puzzler.

294

HOW TO LOSE
THE RED CABBAGE BLUES

What puts the fizz in sodas? What makes the holes in bread as it bakes? Carbon dioxide gas, that's what! When carbon dioxide gas is combined with water, an acid called CARBONIC ACID is formed. You can make this acid and test for it using a color-changing indicator made from red cabbage leaves. *Here's how!*

You will need

baking soda
14″ round balloon (inflated size)
plastic soda straw
3 8-oz clear plastic cups
measuring spoons
pencil and paper to label cups
vinegar
1 clean 16-oz plastic soda bottle
1/8 head red cabbage at room temperature, torn into small pieces
1 zip-closing plastic sandwich bag
base solution: cup with 1 tsp baking soda stirred into 1/8 cup water
funnel (optional)
cereal bowl

STEP 1: Make the Indicator

Fill the sandwich bag half full of cabbage, and set the bag in the bowl. Have your adult partner cover the cabbage with hot tap water. Close the bag, wait until the bag is cool enough to handle, then mash it gently with your hands. Strain the indicator liquid into one of the plastic cups. Throw the cabbage bag away.

LAUREN MENDELSON

STEP 2: Set Up Experiment

1. Label the cup containing the indicator "1—Base + Acid." Label the other cups "2—Indicator Only" and "3—Base." Pour half of the indicator from Cup 1 into Cup 2 and add 1/4 cup of tap water to each. Leave Cup 3 empty for now.

Add 1/4 teaspoon of base solution to Cup 1. Stir. Record the colors in Cups 1 and 2 in the chart.

2. Pour half of the liquid from Cup 1 into Cup 3 for later. Record the color in Cup 3 in the chart.

STEP 3: Add Carbon Dioxide to the Indicator + Base

1. To fill your balloon with carbon dioxide gas:

a.–Add one heaping teaspoon of baking soda to the empty soda bottle. (You may need a funnel for this.)

b.–Fill the balloon half full of vinegar and attach it tightly to the mouth of the bottle so the balloon hangs down the bottle's side. Now, lift the balloon so the vinegar flows into the bottle. What happens to the balloon?

c.–Pinch the neck of the balloon to keep the carbon dioxide that you have just made inside. CAREFULLY remove the balloon from the bottle.

2. To make carbonic acid from the carbon dioxide gas:

a.–Ask your partner to help you put one end of the soda straw into the balloon. (DON'T RELEASE THE PINCH YET!) Wrap the end of the balloon closely around the sides of the straw to make a tight seal.

b.–Put the other end of the straw into the liquid in Cup 1. Now, SLOWLY release the pinch on the neck of the balloon, letting all the carbon dioxide bubble into the liquid. What happens? Record what you see in the chart. (You may need to repeat Step 3 to get the best results.)

	STARTING COLOR	COLOR WITH BASE	COLOR WITH CARBONIC ACID
CUP 1 BASE AND ACID			
CUP 2 INDICATOR ONLY			
CUP 3 BASE ONLY			

STEP 4: Think About What Happened

Look at the cups. What caused the changes in Cup 1? Could you make Cup 1 look like Cup 3? How?

TIM CLARK—Water Analyst

Tim Clark is a chemist who uses different indicators to test water samples for the Oklahoma Gas and Electric Company. Water is important in the making of electricity because water turns the turbines that produce electricity. Indicators are used to test the water for too much base and for calcium. When calcium and base are together in a water sample, a hard deposit is formed that can coat the inside of water pipes. This deposit makes the room inside the pipes smaller, and the water has less space to flow through. Therefore, more energy is needed to pump the water to the generating plant and the plant will not work as efficiently. This means that Tim uses indicators to keep water quality high and make the electricity cheaper for the person watching television or using electric lights.

TINA MION

BE AN INVESTI-GATOR

Activity one: *Petals Revisited*

Carnation petals are not the only flower petals that contain indicators. You can do the Inside Indicator activity with petals from hibiscus, petunias, dianthus, roses, violets, or irises, to name a few. Just be sure to follow the directions for the activity carefully, and have your adult partner present.

Activity two: *Loads of Liquids*

Dip a fresh Indi-Gator in grape juice, then use it to test the following household liquids: (Be sure to get permission and supervision from your adult partner first!) milk, lemon juice, grapefruit juice, liquid dish detergent, water, and carbonated sodas. You can make a chart like the one used in the Indi-Gator activity to keep track of your results. Which liquids are acids, which are bases, and which are neither?

Activity three: *Indicator Art*

Paint a picture using different indicator fruit juices (such as grape, blackberry, cherry, raspberry, or blueberry) in different parts of the picture. Tell a friend that you can completely change the colors in the picture just by painting over the colors with a clear solution. Paint over the picture with a solution of 1 teaspoon of baking soda stirred into $\frac{1}{2}$ cup of water. Try changing the picture to its original colors by painting over the picture with vinegar or lemon juice.

296

Unit 38
Plant Chemistry

This unit introduces students to several of the uses of some of the chemicals in plants. Substances in plants can be used as chemical indicators, as flavorings and scents, and for many products we use every day.

Be an Indicator Investigator!

In *Be an Indicator Investigator!*, students observe the color changing qualities of plant pigments. Plant pigments are large molecules made up of many atoms. When placed in water, the pigment molecule takes on a certain shape based on its own structure and the way it interacts with water. The characteristics of the pigment molecule determine the color that we perceive the pigment to be. When an acid or a base is added to a pigment solution, the chemicals in the acid or base can change the structure of the pigment molecule. When the structure of the pigment molecule changes, it may appear to be a different color. This ability to change color under the influence of an acid or a base, makes certain plant pigments excellent indicators for the presence of acids or bases.

Starch: A Popular and Plentiful Potent Plant Product!

Starch: A Popular and Plentiful Potent Plant Product! uses tincture of iodine as a test for starch. Be sure to read the warning on the tincture of iodine label. Also, tincture of iodine will stain clothes, so be careful when making your iodine solutions.

Plant Parts: Common Scents and Good Taste!

Plant Parts: Common Scents and Good Taste! shows students the plant parts from which some common flavorings and scents are made. You could also have students smell some fresh basil, parsley, or other fresh herbs.

Plant Stems—Totally Tubular!

Plant Stems—Totally Tubular! encourages students to make very close observations of a common celery stick. The purpose of the activity is to discover how water moves up through a plant stem. The vast majority of plants have a series of tube-like cells that bring water up the plant to the leaves and another set of tubes that takes nutrients produced in the leaves down the plant. When removing the tubes from the celery, try to take them out without stripping the outside of the celery. After 24 hours, the celery without the tubes should be much more limp than the piece with the tubes intact.

A Plant Panorama!

A Plant Panorama! illustrates the many uses of plants in students' daily lives.

RELEVANT NATIONAL SCIENCE EDUCATION STANDARDS

The activities in this unit can be used to support the teaching of the following standards:

✔ Science as Inquiry
   Abilities necessary to do scientific inquiry

✔ Physical Science
   Properties and changes of properties in matter

✔ Life Science
   Structure and function in living systems

✔ Earth and Space Science
   Structure of the Earth system

BE AN INDICATOR

Plants and their chemicals have been used throughout history for many different purposes. In the following activity, you can use the roots, leaves, and fruit from three different plants to make chemical *indicators*!

ROOT

1 Use your paper and pencil to draw a chart like the one below. Ask your adult partner to help you grate the skin off 4 or 5 radishes. Place the skin into one of your cups. Add 1/2 cup of warm water. Stir the water until it turns a pink color. Allow the skin to color the water for at least 5 minutes. This is your **radish** indicator solution.

2 Divide your indicator equally between 3 cups. Label one cup as your *control*. Do not add anything to your control. Add a very small amount of vinegar (a few drops) to one of your cups of indicator and swirl. Compare the color of this indicator to the color of your control. Write in and draw the color in the chart.

3 Now add a small amount of baking soda (a small pinch) to your other indicator cup and swirl. Compare the color in this cup to your control. Record the color in your chart.

4 If either of your indicators changed color, see if you can figure out what to add to it to make it turn back to the color of the control. Try it!

LEAF

5 Draw a new chart like the one in step 1. Tear up two leaves of red cabbage and place the pieces in a zip-closing plastic bag. Add 1/2 cup of warm water and close the bag tightly. Use your fingers to press the leaves inside the bag until the water becomes a deep blue color. This is your **red cabbage** indicator solution. Repeat steps 2, 3, and 4.

FRUIT

6 Draw your last chart like the one in step 1. Place 2 teaspoons of concentrated grape juice in a cup. Add 1/2 cup of warm water. This is your **grape juice** indicator solution. Repeat steps 2, 3, and 4.

You will need

radishes	measuring spoon
red cabbage	water
grape juice (concentrate)	white unlined paper
vinegar	grater
baking soda	masking tape
5 plastic cups	pencil
crayons or colored pencils	cotton swabs

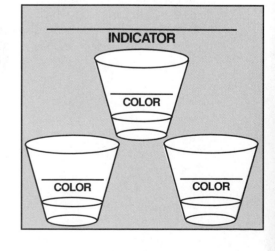

INDICATOR

COLOR

COLOR   COLOR

INVESTIGATOR!

ANOTHER WAY TO MAKE INDICATORS!

7 Get three pieces of white paper. Label them individually "Radish," Red Cabbage," and "Grape Juice." Rub a radish on its paper so that an area on the paper becomes pink. Rub a cabbage leaf on its paper until it becomes purple. Use a cotton swab to rub concentrated grape juice into a thin layer on its paper.

8 Add 1 teaspoon of baking soda to 3 tablespoons of water in a cup. Put a little vinegar in another cup. Use a new cotton swab to put a little baking soda solution onto the color on each paper indicator. You could make a dot or draw a line or squiggle.

9 Use a separate cotton swab to put a little vinegar onto the color on each paper indicator. Which indicator reacts most to vinegar? Which reacts most to baking soda? Do any of the indicators react to both? Watch them for a few more minutes. Do they change?

10 Cut your colored indicator papers into strips. Dip one end quickly in and out of your baking soda solution. Dip the other end quickly in and out of the vinegar. Could these papers be used as a kind of "litmus" paper?

---

* All activities in *WonderScience* have been reviewed for safety by Dr. Jack Breazeale, Francis Marion University, Florence, SC; Dr. Jay Young, Chemical Health and Safety Consultant, Silver Spring, MD; and Dr. Patricia Redden, Saint Peter's College, Jersey City, NJ.

Plant Chemicals:
They're Plantastic!

You used the chemicals from different plant parts to make *indicators*. Scientists use indicators to help them learn about the substances they are testing. Adding vinegar to your indicators made them change color because chemicals in the vinegar had a *chemical reaction* with the chemicals in the indicator. The chemical in the vinegar that did this is called an *acid*. Adding baking soda to your indicators made them turn a different color because the chemicals in baking soda caused a different chemical reaction with the indicator. The chemical in baking soda that caused the reaction is called a *base*. When you know that an indicator turns one color with an acid and another color with a base, you can test other substances with your indicator to see if they contain acid or base. If the indicator turns one color, the substance contains acid, if it turns the other color, it contains a base. (Never test a substance unless you check with an adult first.)

The chemicals in plants have many other uses. The most important use is for food for people and other animals. In fact, all animal life on Earth depends on these plant chemicals. Animals get these chemicals by eating plants or by eating other animals that ate plants. Think about it. If you had cereal for breakfast, it was probably made from corn, wheat, oats, or rice, all plants. If you had a sandwich for lunch, the bread was made from wheat. If the sandwich was peanut butter and jelly, the peanuts are seeds from the peanut plant and the jelly is made from the fruit of a plant. If you had a hamburger, the meat came from a cow that ate plants to live. You can trace all the food we eat back to plants!

The chemicals in plants have also been used to make other important products. For many years, people have used the chemicals in plants to make medicines. The sap from the aloe plant helps soothe burns. The medicine *quinine* is made from the bark of the cinchona tree. Quinine is very useful in curing a sickness called malaria. Chemicals in garlic have been shown to kill bacteria. Chemicals from the sweet gum tree can kill certain parasites. A new medicine called taxol helps fight certain kinds of cancer. This medicine is made from chemicals in a tree called the Pacific yew. The use of plants as a source of medicines is one reason we need to protect the wide variety of plants on our planet!

Plants are used to make many other products. Rubber was first made from the sap of the rubber plant. All paper products are made from trees. In a way, even plastic is made from plants! Plastic is made from petroleum which is found under the surface of the Earth. Petroleum was formed millions of years ago from decay PLANTS!

Look at the last picture in the unit and see how many different things you can find that are made from plants or plant products. Good luck and enjoy the rest of your *WonderScience*!

ANSWERS FOR A PLANT PANORAMA!: HOUSEPLANTS, BOOKS, DOORMAT, LOGS IN FIREPLACE, BAMBOO SHADES, PENCIL, WOOD FURNITURE, WICKER CHAIR, NEWSPAPER, PANCAKE FLOUR, MAPLE SYRUP, FRUIT, LETTUCE, SUGAR, CEREAL GRAINS, TEA, ORANGE JUICE, PLASTIC CONTAINER, LINEN TABLE CLOTH AND COTTON CLOTHES, LIPSTICK

STARCH: A Popular and Plentiful Potent Plant Product!

You will need

tincture of iodine
5 disposable plastic cups
water
samples of starch such as:
   white bread
   flour
   rice
   noodle
   lima bean or peanut
straw
butter knife

Plants produce chemicals that people and other animals need to survive. A very important chemical that people get from plants is **starch**. Starch is a basic part of the diet for people in almost every culture. Bread, potatoes, rice, corn, beans, and pasta all contain large amounts of starch from plants. In the following activity, you can use **tincture of iodine** to test some common foods for starch. Then you can use the starch in white bread as a test for how much iodine there is in a drop of solution of iodine and water!

CAUTION: Be very careful when using tincture of iodine. Read and follow all directions on the label. When you have finished the activity, rinse out all cups and the straw and throw them away. Throw away all food items and wash your hands.

1 Cover your work area with a double layer of newspaper. Put one teaspoon of water into a plastic cup. Ask your adult partner to add one drop of iodine to the water. This is your starch test solution. Use a straw to put one drop of the test solution on a piece of white bread. What happens? A blue color means that the sample contains starch.

2 Place a little flour on a piece of newspaper. Place a drop of your test liquid on the flour. What happens? Try testing a few grains of rice and a noodle in the same way. Do all these samples contain starch?

3 The seeds from rice, bean, corn, and wheat plants all contain starch. Why do you think plant seeds contain starch?

REMEMBER, ALWAYS HAVE AN ADULT WORK WITH YOU ON ALL WONDERSCIENCE ACTIVITIES.

Just as you can use a drop of iodine solution to test for starch, you can use starch to compare the amount of iodine in drops of different solutions of iodine and water.

1 Line up four cups. Use your tape and pen to mark them "1," "2," "3," and "4." Place one teaspoon of water in cup 1, two teaspoons in cup 2, three teaspoons in cup 3, and four teaspoons in cup 4.

2 Ask your adult partner to place one drop of iodine in each cup. Use your straw to place one drop of each iodine solution on your slice of white bread. Be sure to wash out the straw with clean water between each test. Can you see how the starch in the bread acts as an indicator for the amount of iodine in the drop of solution?

CHALLENGE: Have your adult partner put one drop of one of your iodine solutions on the bread. Can you guess which solution it is from?

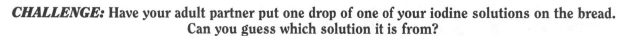

Plant Parts:
Common Scents and Good Taste!

The chemicals in some plants are used to make our food taste and smell better, to make perfumes, and to make other products smell better. The chemicals usually used for these flavorings and scents can come from the flower, fruit, stem, leaf, or root of the plant. Let's investigate some of these chemicals in the activity below!

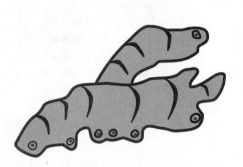

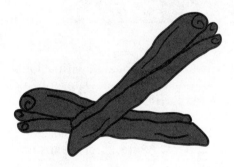

ROOT

1 Break off a little piece of ginger root. Smell the part where you broke it off. Now take a little sip of ginger ale. Can you tell that ginger root is used to flavor ginger ale?

LEAF

2 Tear a mint leaf and smell it. Can you think of anything you eat that smells like this leaf? Smell or taste a piece of mint gum or a candy mint. Do you think mint leaves were used in some way to make the gum or candy? What other foods or products can you think of that use mint?

STEM

3 Smell your cinnamon stick. Do you know where this cinnamon comes from? Believe it or not, it is from the inner bark of a tree! Taste a cinnamon bun or a piece of cinnamon raisin bread. Can you tell that it was made with this bark?

FRUIT

4 Take a lemon and scrape the peel a little with your fingernail. Smell the part that you scraped. Can you think of any products that have this smell? Try to think of ones that are not for eating.

FLOWER

5 The flowers of many plants are used for their scent. Rose, lilac, lavender, and other flowers are used for perfumes and air fresheners. Next time you go to the store, check the label on some air fresheners to see what flowers they use as ingredients.

In the summer, you can get a few of these flowers, dry the petals in the sun, and wrap them in thin cloth or tissue paper. Keep them in your room for a nice smell or give them as gifts!

Plant Stems—
Totally Tubular!

As you know, plants need **water** to live. You also probably know that water goes from the root, up the stem, and into the leaves. But how is the stem specially made so that water can travel up it? Let's do an experiment and find out!

1 Have your adult partner help you cut a 12-cm-long piece of celery. Put about 1/4 cup of water into a glass. Add 5 drops of blue food coloring to the water. Place the wide end of the piece of celery into the water.

2 After three or four hours, you should be able to see blue coloring at the top of your celery stick. What does the coloring look like? Is it spread out over the top or is it in little dots? Why do you think the blue color shows up the way it does? How did it get there?

3 Use your fingernail to start pulling away one of the blue structures at the top of the celery. Grab the blue piece between your thumb and index finger. Pull it down and away to remove it from the celery stick. Were you able to pull it all the way out? What does it look like? What do you think it does?

4 Have your adult partner cut two more pieces of celery to 12 cm each. Look at the narrow end of these celery sticks. Compare them with the stick with the blue top. Can you see the tops of the long tubes in these new celery sticks even though they are not colored?

5 Carefully remove all the tubes from one of the new sticks. Do not change the other new stick in any way. Place both new celery sticks in the blue water with the wide end down. How do you think removing the tubes will affect the celery? Compare the celery sticks in 24 hours and find out.

When finished the activity, be sure to throw your celery away.

A Plant Panorama!

After reading and doing the activities in this month's *WonderScience*, you know that plants are used to make all sorts of products. Look carefully at the picture below. Write down as many objects from the picture as you can that are made from plants. Good luck!

WONDER SCIENCE

The activities in this unit introduce students to several sources of carbon dioxide and its uses. The activities stress good experimental design with an emphasis on controlling variables.

Fizz-Bubble-Pop!

In *Fizz-Bubble-Pop!*, students learn to control variables by placing the same amount of baking soda into the same amount of three different solutions. Students are encouraged to predict, observe, and then draw conclusions based on their observations. The most bubbling should be in the vinegar bag, the least in the water bag, and an intermediate amount in the bag with a mixture of vinegar and water. Students should be able to conclude that the vinegar is most responsible for the bubbling.

Fast Get-Aways

Fast Get-Aways enables students to explore how temperature effects the escape of carbon dioxide gas from soda pop. Carbon dioxide gas should escape from the bottle in hot water the fastest, the next fastest from the bottle in room temperature water, and the slowest from the bottle in ice water.

Chem-Mystery

In *Chem Mystery*, students read a short story with a science-related mystery at the end. The story connects the problems of gas escaping from soda pop with the technology of plastic bottles that resist expanding and help prevent the soda's gas from escaping. The story illustrates how science and technology solve everyday problems to which students can relate.

Gas Gallery

In *Gas Gallery*, students try some entertaining uses of carbon dioxide. In each activity, students are encouraged to try some suggested design modifications. This process should help students better understand the experimental process and give them additional opportunities to learn more about how carbon dioxide behaves.

RELEVANT NATIONAL SCIENCE EDUCATION STANDARDS

The activities in this unit can be used to support the teaching of the following standards:

✓ **Science as Inquiry**
  Abilities necessary to do scientific inquiry

✓ **Physical Science**
  Properties and changes of properties in matter

✓ **Earth and Space Science**
  Structure of the Earth system

✓ **Science in Personal and Social Perspectives**
  Science and technology in society

FIZZ–BUBBL

What You and Your Partner Will Need

3 zip-lock sandwich bags
vinegar
baking soda
tap water

marker for labeling bags
   (or marker and masking tape)
a paper towel cut into four equal s
a teaspoon

What to Do:

1 Put one level teaspoon of baking soda in the center of a paper towel square. Roll the paper up and twist the ends closed like a wrapper. Make two more of these roll-ups.

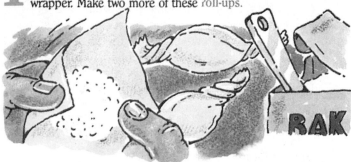

2 Use the marker and ruler to draw a line 2 cm from the bottom of each zip-lock bag. Label one bag "vinegar," one bag "water," and one bag "vinegar and water."

5 **Predict** what **changes** you will observe in each bag if you drop in one baking soda roll-up. In the chart, write what you think will happen.

I predict . . .

the vinegar bag will _____.

the water bag will _____.

the vinegar and water bag will _____.

8 Empty the bags and rinse them with tap water so you can use them again. Here are some more tests you can try.
CAUTION: Do not test any other mixtures unless an adult says it is safe.

Try These Experiments:	
Pour into the bag up to the 2-cm line	**Add and seal**
Warm water	½ Teaspoon dry yeast and ½ teaspoon sugar
Lemon juice or vinegar	1 Teaspoon crushed eggshell
Water	1 Teaspoon baking powder
Water	1 Alka Seltzer Tablet
Lemon juice or vinegar	A few small pieces of seashell, white garden pebbles, limestone, or chalk

pOp!

... dishpan
... newspaper to cover the work area
... ruler (marked in centimeters—cm)

HERE'S A SAFE SCIENCE TIP: WHEN YOU TRY **SMELLING,** KEEP YOUR NOSE AND FACE AWAY FROM THE BAGS. INSTEAD, **USE YOUR HAND TO FAN THE ODOR TOWARD YOU.** YOU'LL STILL SMELL IT, BUT YOU WON'T GET A STRONG ENOUGH WHIFF TO BURN YOUR NOSE OR EYES.

3 While your partner holds the vinegar bag, pour in ... negar up to the 2-cm ... ne. Seal the bag.

... the same way, pour ... ater to the line in the ... ater bag. In the last ... ag, pour vinegar half- ... ay to the line and then ... ish filling to the line ... th water.

4 Use your senses of sight, touch, and smell to observe each bag closely. Write all your **observations** in the chart below.

6 Now test your **predictions.** Work over the ... nk for this step!

... rop one roll-up into ... e vinegar bag ... d quickly seal the ... g tightly.

... hat happens? ... ecord any changes ... u observe. Is this ... hat you predicted ... uld happen?

7 Repeat step 6 with the other two bags. In which bags do you observe the most changes? What do you think happened inside these bags? Why didn't the same thing happen in all three bags?

MY OBSERVATIONS

Bag labeled	What I see, feel, and smell before adding one roll-up	Changes I observe after adding one roll-up
Vinegar		
Water		
Vinegar and water		
Other bags I make:		

WONDERSCIENCE

Seeing Is Not Always Believing

Here's the answer to the riddle on the front page:

carbon dioxide gas

Some of the **chemicals** you mixed together in the zip-lock bags fizzed, bubbled, and made the bags puff up like a balloon. You may have felt some of the bags change temperature. The changes you observed in some bags probably made you think a **new substance** was being made, but you couldn't see or smell any new substance inside the bags!

The **invisible** new substance you made was **carbon dioxide gas.** Carbon dioxide gas is **colorless** and **odorless.** That is why you do not see it or smell it. You observed it being made when you saw bubbling, or when you squeezed the bag and noticed it was getting fuller.

You may have noticed that some mixtures you tested made more carbon dioxide gas than other mixtures did. Some of these mixtures may have filled the bag so full that it popped open and let the carbon dioxide gas **escape.** It is easier to study carbon dioxide gas when it is trapped inside a container like a zip-lock bag. If you had not sealed the bags tightly, would you have been able to tell a new gas was made?

Out-of-Sight but NOT Out-of-Mind

Even though **carbon dioxide gas** is **invisible,** you can tell it is present by **observation.** Carbon dioxide gas is just one of many things that you cannot see but that you know about from other **evidence.** Brainstorm with your partner to make a list of other invisible things. Think hard, there are lots of them! Here are some to get you started:

Invisible things	Evidence or proof
Carbon dioxide gas	Bubbles, puffing bags
Wind	Waving flags, shaking leaves
Friendship	Smiles, kindness, sharing
Robbery	Missing items, fingerprints

_____   _____   _____   _____

_____   _____   _____   _____

_____   _____   _____   _____

Keep adding to the list for at least five minutes. Don't judge your answers—just keep writing them down as you and your partner think of them. After five minutes, count how many you listed and give yourself a score for your brainstorming efforts!

Scoreboard

Number listed	Your thinking was
0–3	Out-of-gas
4–7	Just warming up
8–11	Bubbling and fizzing
12 or more	**Great gases! Nothing escapes you!**

FAST GET-AWAYS

Did you know that soda pop gets its fizz from **carbon dioxide gas?** Carbon dioxide gas is added to the soda before the bottle is sealed. As soon as you open a **carbonated soda,** the gas starts to **escape.** The tiny bubbles that pop and tickle your face when you drink a soda are really bubbles filled with carbon dioxide gas! What do you think causes a soda to lose all its gas and **go flat?**

Try this experiment to find out whether **temperature** affects the **speed** at which carbon dioxide gas escapes from soda pop.

Circle the answer you predict:

I predict that warm soda will lose its **carbon dioxide gas**   faster / slower / at the same speed   as cold soda.

Open three bottles of room-temperature soda. Quickly cover each bottle with a balloon. Set the balloon-covered bottles in bowls of ice water, room-temperature water, and hot tap water.

Wait five minutes.

Wrap a string around the widest part of each balloon.

Measure the length of the string with a metric ruler.

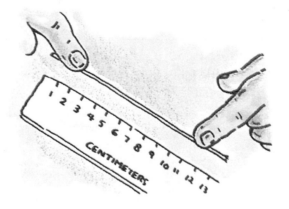

Compare the size of each balloon.

Bottle in	Size of widest part of balloon after 5 minutes (in cm)
Ice water	
Room-temperature water	
Hot tap water	

Which **temperature** caused the carbon dioxide gas to have the "fastest get-away" from the soda?

Which of these sodas would lose its gas (go flat) the quickest?
☐ an open soda in the refrigerator?
☐ a sealed soda on the counter?
☐ an open soda left on a picnic table in the sun?

Discuss the reasons for your answer with your partner.

?????CHEM-MYSTERY?????

The Case of the Plastic That G I V E S

"Gee thanks, Mom and Dad! You never buy us soda to drink. What's the special occasion?" asked Maria when she was helping unpack the groceries her parents brought home.

"Well, we thought you might like to take some with you on your school field trip tomorrow. Don't you have to pack your lunch for the trip?" questioned Maria's mother.

"Yes I do. But Mom, our teacher said we can't bring any glass bottles on the school bus. May I drink it now instead?"

"No," replied her mother, "we'll pour some into a bottle that isn't glass so you can take it on the bus."

Maria searched in the cupboard and pulled out an old Thermos bottle. She asked, "How about this?"

"It is not safe to put carbonated drinks into a glass-lined Thermos jug," Maria's father said. "The glass might crack from the pressure of the gas escaping from the soda."

"Well, how about this instead?" suggested Maria's mother as she got a small plastic juice bottle from the refrigerator. "If we drink this little bit of orange juice and rinse out the bottle, we could put the soda in it!"

That sounded like a good solution. Together they refilled the plastic bottle with soda, packed Maria's lunch, and closed her lunch box.

Maria didn't open her lunch box again until lunch time the next day. She and her friends sat around the picnic table so they could share their lunches with each other. But when Maria pulled out her plastic bottle of soda, everyone started to giggle!

"Look at that bottle," they laughed, "it sure is out of shape! What did you do to it?"

Maria called her teacher over to look at her drink. "Do you think my soda spoiled?" she asked her teacher.

"No," said her teacher, "your soda is fine. It's the plastic bottle that's causing the problem." With that, he picked up a two-liter soda bottle from a nearby table and showed it to Maria. "See the difference between the bottle you used and this plastic bottle? If you had used a bottle made from this kind of clear plastic instead of this frosted-looking plastic, you wouldn't have had this problem."

Maria looked puzzled and said, "But I thought all plastic bottles were the same!"

Use this space to draw
what you think Maria's out-of-shape plastic bottle looks like.

Now You Finish the Story

What do you think caused the problem with Maria's plastic bottle?

_____

_____

_____

_____

_____

_____

See for yourself what the problem was by repeating what Maria did. Pour some soda into a clean plastic juice bott or milk jug. Close the bottle and let it sit five minutes or more. Does your drawing look similar to what happens i your test?

PUMPING PLASTIC

Compare a plastic juice bottle or milk jug with a two-liter plastic soda bottle. How are they different? How are they similar? Do you think that all plastic bottles are the same? Why or why not?

NATHANIEL WYETH IS A **MECHANICAL ENGINEER.** WHEN HIS BOSS TOLD HIM THAT PLASTIC BOTTLES COULDN'T HOLD THE GAS INSIDE CARBONATED DRINKS, HE WANTED TO **SEE THE PROBLEM HIMSELF.**

AT HOME, HE FILLED A CLEAN PLASTIC JUG WITH GINGER ALE AND LEFT IT IN THE REFRIGERATOR OVERNIGHT.

THE NEXT DAY, THE BOTTLE WAS SO **SWOLLEN** HE COULD HARDLY GET IT OUT OF THE REFRIGERATOR!

TO SOLVE THIS PROBLEM, HE HAD TO **MAKE THE PLASTIC STRONGER.** HE DISCOVERED THAT JUST LIKE STRETCHING A FIRE BLANKET IN ALL DIRECTIONS MAKES IT TIGHT, **STRETCHING THE PLASTIC** USED TO MAKE SODA BOTTLES **MAKES IT STRONGER.**

THE NEW PLASTIC SODA BOTTLES HE INVENTED ARE CALLED **PET* BOTTLES** BECAUSE OF THE KIND OF PLASTIC USED TO MAKE THEM. IN 1985, MORE THAN 6 BILLION TWO-LITER **PET** BOTTLES WERE MADE. THIS NUMBER SHOULD **DOUBLE BY 1990.**

*PET STANDS FOR **POLYETHYLENE TEREPHTHALATE** (POLY-ETHEL-EEN TARE-A-THAL-ATE)

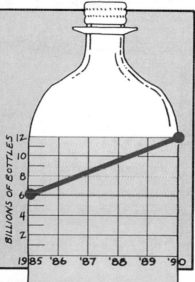

PET BOTTLES ARE **CHEAPER** AND **LIGHTER** THAN GLASS BOTTLES, AND THEY CAN BE USED TO PACKAGE MANY OTHER PRODUCTS. IN THE FUTURE, WE WILL BE ABLE TO **RECYCLE PET** PLASTIC BOTTLES THE WAY WE CAN RECYCLE GLASS TODAY. RECYCLED PLASTIC COULD EVEN BE USED TO MAKE CAR PARTS!!

YOU CAN TELL **PET** PLASTIC FROM OTHER KINDS BECAUSE IT IS **CLEAR**, NOT CLOUDY LIKE A MILK JUG. SOMETIMES **PET** BOTTLES ARE TINTED GREEN OR AMBER. COUNT HOW MANY **PET** PLASTIC BOTTLES ARE IN YOUR HOUSE TODAY. ARE YOU SURPRISED BY THE NUMBER?

NATHANIEL WYETH IS A MEMBER OF A FAMOUS FAMILY OF ARTISTS. TRY TO FIND OUT ABOUT N.C. WYETH, ANDREW WYETH, JAMIE WYETH, HENRIETTE WYETH, CAROLYN WYETH, AND OTHER MEMBERS OF THIS VERY CREATIVE FAMILY. A LIBRARIAN CAN HELP YOU WITH THIS.

GAS GALLERY

You and your partner may want to try these activities that use carbon dioxide gas.

Gas Bubble Boat

Pour a mixture of vinegar and water to a depth of two or three centimeters inside a plastic bottle that has a reclosable spout. (An old shampoo or dish detergent bottle is fine.) Make a baking soda roll-up.
Partially fill a deep sink or bathtub with water. Drop the roll-up into the bottle of vinegar and water. Quickly put the top on the bottle (make sure the spout is closed). Lower the bottle into the water, open the spout, and let go. When the gas and foam escape from the spout, what happens to your bottle? Experiment with different amounts of vinegar, water, and baking soda. Which combination makes the boat move best?

Gas Dancing

Pour some colorless soda (like 7-Up or Sprite) into a tall, clear glass. Drop a teaspoon of dry rice into the glass of soda. What happens? Try to explain what makes the rice dance. See whether raisins, macaroni, broken spaghetti, or uncooked popcorn will dance too!

Gas Painting

Cover your work area with cardboard or newspaper. Put small pools of nontoxic watercolor paint on a piece of paper. Point the end of a straw at the paint pools and gently blow in the direction you want the paint to move. Try blowing at pools of different colors to mix and blend them together on the paper. Draw in details when the paper dries. Experiment with different kinds of paper and with different sized straws. Try making your own paint by mixing a teaspoon of cornstarch, a little water, and a few drops of food coloring.

WONDERSCIENCE

This unit introduces students to some of the fundamental properties of rocks. Students will consider the wide variety of ways in which rocks are used as well as some of the ways scientists test them.

Let's Rock!

In *Let's Rock!*, students run a series of tests on seven different kinds of rocks they have collected. Students closely examine and describe the rocks, recognize that rocks that have similar appearances may have other characteristics that are different, and see how the characteristics of rocks can be used to classify and identify them.

Be sure to follow the safety precautions when doing the Break Test. Also, be careful when handling rocks that have sharp points or edges. The Streak test calls for a piece of unglazed porcelain, such as the back side of a porcelain bath tile. It is not unusual for the color streak a rock makes on the unglazed porcelain to be different from the color of the rock itself.

Before conducting the Hardness Test, you might challenge students to predict the order of hardness of their rocks.

Panning for Gold!

Panning for Gold! uses the principle of density to separate "gold" from sand and water. Gold panning works because pieces of gold metal are very heavy for their size, or very dense. In order for this activity to similarly work, the bits of metal that are substituted for gold must also be very dense. We suggest using small nuts and bolts. These usually contain iron which is only slightly less dense than gold.

Japanese Garden!

Japanese Garden! illustrates how rocks are used for aesthetic, as well as practical purposes. Some of the instructions are intentionally a bit open-ended to promote students' artistic creativity.

Fabricate Some Fabulous Fossils!

In *Fabricate Some Fabulous Fossils!*, students learn about two different kinds of fossils, mold fossils and cast fossils. Instructions are provided for making samples of each of these two fossil types. Museums sometimes make artificial casts of real fossils from plaster of Paris so they can be displayed in other museums.

Rocks and Their Roles!

In *Rocks and Their Roles!*, students are challenged to identify things made of rock or from materials produced from rocks.

RELEVANT NATIONAL SCIENCE EDUCATION STANDARDS

The activities in this unit can be used to support the teaching of the following standards:

✔ **Science as Inquiry**
   Abilities necessary to do scientific inquiry

✔ **Physical Science**
   Properties and changes of properties in matter

✔ **Life Science**
   Diversity and adaptations of organisms

✔ **Earth and Space Science**
   Structure of the Earth system
   Earth's history

LET'S ROCK!

There are lots of different rocks. When scientists find a rock and are not sure what it is, they do different tests on the rock to discover its characteristics in order to classify and identify it. In this activity, you will try some of these same tests on different rock samples you find around your home or school. If you have trouble finding enough rocks, you can use aquarium pebbles, gravel, rock salt, marble chips, or small stones you find in broken concrete. At the end of the activity, you will use the results of your tests to try to classify a "mystery" rock.

Be sure to wear safety glasses while rocks are being hit.

You will need

Safety glasses for all participants	small hammer
empty egg carton	magnifying glass
7 rock samples that look different	unglazed porcelain tile (back of porcelain bath tile)
masking tape	nail
sheet of white notebook paper	penny
	glass marble
old hand towel or dish rag	white vinegar

1 Get your adult partner to help you collect one or more small samples of seven different kinds of rocks. Put six of the samples in the six compartments on one side of your egg carton. Save the extra sample for step 5. Write numbers on small pieces of masking tape to label each compartment. You are now ready to run tests on your rock samples to describe and classify them.

2 Copy the chart below onto your paper. Make the chart large enough to record the results of the following tests:

	1	2	3	4	5	6
BREAK TEST						
APPEARANCE TEST						
STREAK TEST						
HARDNESS TEST						
ACID TEST						

BREAK TEST—Wrap a towel or dish rag completely around one of your rock samples. Ask your adult partner to place the wrapped sample on a hard surface outdoors. Ask your adult partner to hit the rock a couple of times with a small hammer until it breaks. Open the towel and look at your sample. What does it look like now? Did it break in a smooth or jagged way? How hard was it to get the rock to break? Get your adult partner to try the Break Test on each of the other rock samples. Write the results on your chart. Be sure each sample is completely wrapped.

APPEARANCE TEST— Study each kind of rock with the magnifying glass. Look at the freshly broken surface. Is the surface rough or smooth? Shiny or dull? Does it look like it is made of one kind of material or more than one material? What color is it? Is it made of crystals? Write a description of each rock on your chart.

STREAK TEST—Try to draw a line on a piece of unglazed porcelain with each kind of rock. Which rocks make a streak? What does the streak look like?

HARDNESS TEST—Use the tests on the Hardness Scale to figure out how hard each rock sample is. The higher the number, the harder the rock. Write the hardness number you get for each sample on your chart. Scientists use a scale a lot like this one to test the hardness of rocks.

HARDNESS SCALE

Can be scratched with a fingernail	(1 pt)
Can be scratched with a penny	(2 pts)
Can scratch a penny	(3 pts)
Can scratch a glass marble	(4 pts)
Can be scratched with an iron nail	(5 pts)
Can scratch an iron nail	(6 pts)

ACID TEST—Put one or two pieces of each rock sample into the empty compartment directly behind the sample. Pour a little vinegar, which is a weak acid, over the rock. Observe the rock closely. If you see bubbles, the rock probably contains a substance called **calcite**. Calcite reacts with acid to produce bubbles of carbon dioxide gas.

4 After you have filled in your chart, compare the information you have written about the different rock samples. Are any of the rocks a lot alike? How? Do you think they are the same kind of rock?

5 Have your adult partner give you a rock that is different from the ones you tested. Run all of the tests on this new rock. Which of your six rock samples is this new rock most like? Explain how they are alike.

---

* All activities in *WonderScience* have been reviewed for safety by Dr. Jack Breazeale, Francis Marion University, Florence, SC; Dr. Jay Young, Chemical Health and Safety Consultant, Silver Spring, MD; and Dr. Patricia Redden, Saint Peter's College, Jersey City, NJ.

SANDSTONE

DIAMOND

Rocks Around the Clock!

Since ancient times people have used rocks and materials that come from rocks to make tools, weapons, utensils, jewelry, and other important items. Early humans used rocks like *granite* to make crude hammers, *obsidian* to make sharp blades, and flint to strike together to produce fire. Throughout history people have used *clay* to mold pottery and make stoneware and other kinds of dishes or containers. Today rocks such as *sandstone*, granite, and *marble* are used to build banks, museums, hotels, post offices, and large office buildings. *Limestone* is crushed to make cement for constructing roads, dams, sidewalks, swimming pools, and bridges. *Silicon* from sandstone is used to produce computer chips, which are used in everything from satellites to video games.

As you can see from the pictures on this page, there are many different kinds of rocks. Rocks can be hard or soft, dull or shiny, rough or smooth. Metals such as *iron*, *aluminum*, *gold*, *copper*, and *lead* come from rocks called *ores*. Gems such as *diamonds*, *saphires*, *emeralds*, and *amethysts* also come from rocks.

HEMATITE (IRON ORE)

In fact, the whole crust of the Earth is made of rock. In some places the Earth's crust may be covered with soil, but soil is just tiny rocks mixed with decayed plant and animal material called *humus*.

Some scientists spend their entire careers studying rocks to learn more about the history of the Earth. By examining fossils of plants and animals found in rock formations, scientists can tell what life on Earth was like millions of years ago.

Have fun with the activities in your new *WonderScience* as you learn just how important rocks are!

BASALT

URANIUM ORE

AMETHYST

Panning for GOLD!

During Gold Rush days of the mid-1800s, miners could be seen along the banks of streams, panning for gold. Where did this gold come from? Gold and other valuable metals are contained in rocks called **ores**. Mines are usually dug to remove these ores from the Earth's crust so the metal can be separated from the ore. But sometimes water in streams washes over ore at the Earth's surface, picking up tiny bits of metal. Panning is one of the simplest ways to get the bits of metal out of the stream. It works because the metal is heavier (or scientists would say more dense) than the water, sand, dirt, and other materials in the stream.

You can try panning for "gold" in this activity. Gold is very expensive, so you will have to use other small metal objects as your "gold."

1 Pour your sand into the large plastic container. Mix 15 to 20 pieces of "gold" into your sand. Add water until the container is about 2/3 full.

2 Place a brick or some old books underneath one end of the container so the container tilts and the sand piles up at the bottom of the other end.

3 Take your aluminum pie pan and scoop up some sand from the bottom of the container. Keeping the pie pan under the water, raise it a little bit and begin to swirl it in a circle. As you swirl it, gradually tilt the pie pan. Take your time and go slowly!

4 The sand in the pan should begin to swirl in the water and pour out over the lower edge of the tilted pie pan. The "gold" pieces stay in the pan because they are heavier than the sand.

5 After almost all of the sand has poured out, lift the pie pan out of the water. Can you see the "gold" in the bottom? If not, you may need to scoop up some more sand and try again.

6 Panning for gold takes practice! Find out if it is better to swirl the pie pan quickly or slowly. Does it matter how much sand you put in the pan? What happens if you tilt the pan too much or too little? See how good you can get at panning for gold and then challenge your adult partner to see who can pan the most gold in 2 minutes!

JAPANESE GARDEN!

In Japan, rocks are used in a special way in the art of making a Japanese garden. In a traditional Japanese garden, rocks are arranged by the garden maker to give the viewer a certain feeling when looking at the garden. Rocks may be used in groups to give the feeling of mountains, valleys, islands, or shorelines. The garden artist may rake sand, gravel, or pebbles into a design to create the idea of water. Rocks may also be used to make a garden path or to bring to mind the idea of an animal such as a bird or a fish. Sometimes the rocks are placed to give a feeling of balance and peacefulness to the overall garden. In the following activity, you can arrange different types of rocks and sand to create a model of a Japanese garden.

You will need

shoe box lid or other shallow rectangular tray	gravel
	pebbles
	fork
rocks (different sizes and shapes)	jar lid
	popsicle stick
sand	water

1 Pour sand in your shoe box lid so that it is nearly level with the top of the sides. Use a popsicle stick to make the sand smooth.

2 Use two or more rocks to make an arrangement in one area of your garden. Garden artists must decide whether to place each rock in a horizontal, vertical, or diagonal position. An example of a common Japanese garden rock grouping is shown below. Once you have placed your rocks, look at them from all sides to decide if a different arrangement would look better.

JOAN M. FERGUSON

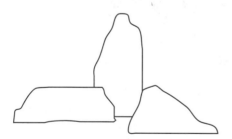

3 You can use a fork to rake the sand into designs between or around your rocks as shown.

4 You can use pebbles to surround your rocks or use them in another area to make a path or a shape like a pond of water.

5 You might want to put a jar lid or plastic lid upside down in the sand and fill it with water to create a pond. You can surround the pond with pebbles or place one or more rocks in the water.

Use your imagination and creativity to make a Japanese-style garden that you really enjoy!

JOAN M. FERGUSON

FABRICATE SOME FABULOUS FOSSILS!

A *fossil* is the remains or imprint of an animal or plant that lived long ago. Fossils found in layers of rock let scientists know what plants and animals were like millions of years ago. It may be a footprint or the outline of a leaf, tooth, or shell. This kind of fossil is called a *mold* fossil. A mold fossil is a rock that has a hollowed-out space shaped like the organism that was once trapped in the rock. Sometimes water will pass through a mold fossil and deposit minerals in the hollow space. This makes another kind of fossil called a *cast* fossil. Scientists can tell when certain plants and animals lived by knowing how old the layer of rock is where fossils are found. In this activity you will make both a mold fossil and a cast fossil.

You will need

small twig, shell, or chicken bone

small plastic margarine tub or
     similar disposable plastic bowl

play dough

vegetable oil

plaster of Paris

measuring cup

mixing bowl

1 Work the play dough with your hands until it is soft and can be easily molded. Pack the play dough in the margarine tub until the tub is about half full. Make sure the surface of the play dough is very smooth.

2 Coat your twig, shell, or chicken bone with a thin film of vegetable oil. Carefully press your plant or animal part into the play dough to make a clear, deep imprint. Remove your item from the play dough and throw it away.

3 Let the play dough harden for a day or two. You have just made a fossil! This kind of fossil is called a mold fossil.

4 Leave your hard mold fossil in the tub and coat it lightly with oil. Measure 1 cup (250 mL) plaster of Paris and 1/2 cup (125 mL) water and mix them together in the mixing bowl. Pour the mixture on top of your mold fossil and let it dry.

Be sure to follow all precautions on the plaster of Paris label.

5 When the plaster of Paris has hardened, carefully separate it from your mold fossil. You now have a cast fossil of your object. A cast fossil has the outward shape of the original plant or animal part.

Scientists working at museums sometimes pour plaster of Paris into a mold fossil to make an artificial cast fossil (just like you did). Look for mold fossils and cast fossils the next time you visit a natural history museum.

Rocks and Their Roles!

You don't have to live in the mountains or the countryside to find rocks. Even in the middle of a big city, you are surrounded by different kinds of rocks. See how many things you can find in the picture below that are made from rocks or from materials that come from rocks. We know of at least 27. Turn the page upside down for a list of the things we found.

Things we have found: clay flower pot, window glass, china, porcelain vase, silverware, paint on a store window sign, sidewalk, road pavement, metal parking meter, nickel, zinc, copper coins, chrome car bumper, car door handles, metal body of car, auto paint, car windshield and windows, metal dolly, granite buildings in background, copper dome, jewel necklace, aluminum garbage can, iron grate in street, metal street sign, metal bell, clay bricks, gold-leaf picture frames, metal dog tags, metal refrigerator.

This unit introduces students to some of the scientific principles related to earthquakes. The cause of earthquakes is briefly discussed, but the emphasis of the unit is on the ways scientists determine the severity and location of earthquakes and some precautions to take against them.

Earthquake City!

In *Earthquake City!*, students will discover that the amount of damage done to a building during an earthquake depends on the intensity and duration of the earthquake, how the building is constructed, and how far away the building is from the earthquake's epicenter. These factors are tested by using different cubes to build model buildings, by tapping a pencil at various distances from the buildings, and by tapping for different lengths of time.

Shake, Rattle...and Record!

In *Shake, Rattle...and Record!*, students can make a simple seismograph to detect earthquakes. Shaking the table (the simulated earthquake) causes the paper to move from side to side as it is pulled beneath the stationary pen. In order for the seismograph to work, be sure that the suspended pen is sufficiently weighted so that it remains relatively still as you shake the table. A real seismograph is extremely sensitive and can detect the smallest vibrations in the Earth's crust.

Earthquakes: The Mercalli Tally

In *Earthquakes: The Mercalli Tally*, a scale of earthquake damage is introduced called the Mercalli scale. A more familiar scale called the Richter scale describes the intensity of an earthquake by how much energy it releases. The Mercalli scale is used to describe the amount of damage an earthquake causes in a particular place. The correct ranking of the jumbled up Mercalli scale is given here.

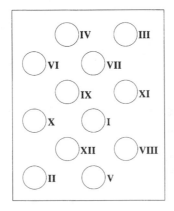

Quake Quest!

In *Quake Quest!*, students learn and practice a mapping process called *triangulation* to locate the epicenter of a hypothetical earthquake.

Earthquake Hazard Hunt

Earthquake Hazard Hunt gives students an idea of how some indoor damage might be avoided during an earthquake.

RELEVANT NATIONAL SCIENCE EDUCATION STANDARDS

The activities in this unit can be used to support the teaching of the following standards:

✔ **Science as Inquiry**
  Abilities necessary to do scientific inquiry

✔ **Physical Science**
  Motions and forces
  Transfer of energy

✔ **Life Science**
  Populations and ecosystems

✔ **Earth and Space Science**
  Structure of the Earth system

✔ **Science in Personal and Social Perspectives**
  Natural hazards

EARTHQUAKE

The movement of the ground during an earthquake can cause serious harm to buildings and other structures. The damage caused to a structure depends on its *design*, the *materials* used to make it, and the *strength* and *duration* of the vibrations from the earthquake. You can test different structures and materials for their ability to withstand earthquakes in your *WonderScience* **Earthquake City!**

Gelatin cubes

Follow the recipe on the gelatin box but use only ⅓ as much water as the recipe calls for. Chill until very firm. Have your adult partner cut the firm gelatin mixture into small cubes about the size of sugar and bouillon cubes.

1 Turn the empty box upside down. Use your pencil and ruler to draw *vertical* lines and *horizontal* lines to make a grid on the bottom of the box. Each line on the grid should be 5 cm apart. Each line is a street in Earthquake City! Label the vertical streets 1st Avenue, 2nd Avenue, 3rd Avenue, etc. Label the horizontal streets A Street, B Street, C Street, etc.

2 When there is an earthquake, *energy* travels through the Earth and can cause damage to buildings and other structures far away. To show this, build three sugar cube skyscrapers, each five sugar cubes tall. Build the skyscrapers at the following corners: A and 1st, B and 2nd, C and 3rd.

3 Now make an earthquake by tapping with the eraser end of a pencil on the box at the corner of D and 4th. Continue tapping until at least one cube from each of the skyscrapers falls. Which skyscraper falls first? In a real earthquake, do you think more damage would happen in one place than another? Where would most of the damage happen?

4 The amount of damage caused by an earthquake depends on the strength of the earthquake and on how long it lasts. Build your three skyscrapers again in the same locations as before. See how many *hard* vibrations it takes to knock at least one cube from each building. Find out how many *softer* vibrations it takes to cause the same amount of damage.

CITY!

5 Whether a building has heavy objects at the top or bottom has a lot to do with the amount of damage done during an earthquake. Build one skyscraper by stacking three sugar cubes on top of a bouillon cube, and another by stacking a bouillon cube on top of three sugar cubes. Since the bouillon cube is heavier than the sugar cube, one building has something heavy at the bottom and the other has something heavy at the top.

6 Place one building at the corner of A and 1st and the other at the corner of A and 3rd. Create an earthquake by tapping at the corner of C and 2nd until at least one cube falls. Repeat this test two or three times. **Be sure to tap the box the same way each time.** Does the same building fall each time?

7 Today, some skyscrapers are made more flexible so that they actually bend and sway and do not fall down as easily. Stack four or five gelatin cubes on top of each other to make a flexible building. Put it at the corner of C and 2nd and create an earthquake at the corner of B and 4th. Watch the flexible skyscraper bend and sway! How long do you have to tap before it falls?

> **Do not eat sugar, bouillon, or gelatin cubes after handling them.**

8 Use the sugar, bouillon, and gelatin cubes to build a complete Earthquake City! Make some buildings tall and some short. Construct buildings made from a combination of different kinds of cubes. Place them at different locations around the city. Pick a spot anywhere in the city to create an earthquake. The spot you choose is the *epicenter* of your earthquake. Predict which buildings will collapse first and which will not be affected at all and then **make your quake!**

WonderScience would like to thank the American Geophysical Union for their assistance in creating this issue.

* All activities in *WonderScience* have been reviewed for safety by Dr. Jack Breazeale, Francis Marion College, Florence, SC; Dr. Jay Young, Chemical Health and Safety Consultant, Silver Spring, MD; and Dr. Patricia Redden, Saint Peter's College, Jersey City, NJ.

Curious about
QUAKES?

What is an earthquake?

You probably know that the Earth's crust is made up of rock that is many kilometers thick. But you may not already know that huge sections of the Earth's crust are always moving! This movement of the crust causes the rock in some places to become squeezed or stretched. When this happens, a lot of energy gets stored in the rock, just like energy is stored in a squeezed or stretched spring. If there is too much force on the rock, it breaks, and the energy stored in the rock is released. The energy then travels through the Earth, causing a sudden, rapid shaking of the Earth's surface.

Where do earthquakes occur?

An earthquake can happen almost anywhere, but some places are much more likely than others to have an earthquake. The map in *Quake Quest* shows you the areas of the United States where earthquakes are most likely. Many times earthquakes occur where there is a break in the rock, or a fault, from a previous earthquake. Usually you cannot see faults because they are below the surface of the Earth. The place where an earthquake starts is called the **seismic focus.** The point on the Earth's surface directly above where an earthquake starts is called the **epicenter** of the earthquake. People located near the epicenter are the first to feel the vibrations from the earthquake.

What kind of damage can an earthquake do?

Earthquakes can damage or destroy buildings, roads, bridges and other structures. People can be hurt or killed as these structures fall during an earthquake. The amount of damage from an earthquake depends on several different things such as the strength of the earthquake, how long it lasts, and where it happens. There are thousands of earthquakes every year but most are so small that people living nearby do not even notice them or feel only a very small vibration of the ground. Every once in a while, there is an earthquake so strong that it destroys hundreds of buildings and kills or injures thousands of people. On page 6, you can learn how scientists describe the amount of damage caused by an earthquake.

How can you protect yourself in an earthquake?

In an earthquake, the best thing to do is to stand in a doorway or to crawl under a desk or table. This will help protect you if the roof of the building you are in collapses. Do not go outside. There are too many heavy objects outside that could fall on you.

There are several things you can do to make your home a safer place in an earthquake. Check large and heavy objects to make sure they cannot easily fall over in an earthquake. Do not hang heavy objects over places where people may sit or stand. Do not place things made of glass where they could hurt people if they were broken during an earthquake. Make sure that all cabinet and closet doors are fastened shut so that things cannot fall out of them. Keep flammable objects far away from sources of heat. The home pictured on page 8 is full of earthquake hazards! How many can you find?

How do scientists detect earthquakes?

Scientists called **seismologists** are always watching for earthquakes so that they can tell as soon as they happen. Using an instrument called a **seismograph**, they can detect an earthquake thousands of kilometers away! In *Shake, Rattle. . .and Record!*, you can make your own seismograph to detect earthquakes. Then, with *Quake Quest!*, you can learn how scientists tell where an earthquake occurred. Unfortunately, seismologists cannot tell exactly when or where the next major earthquake will be. But they are doing research to find ways to predict earthquakes in the future!

Shake, Rattle...
and Record!

1 Tape a felt-tip marker to a can so that the tip of the marker sticks out beyond the can. *Caution: The vapor from some felt-tip markers is dangerous if breathed. Be sure that the labeling on the pen indicates that it is safe to use.*

2 Cut 6 pieces of notebook paper into thirds, lengthwise (you should have 18 strips). Take six strips of paper and tape them end to end to make a long strip. Do this two more times with your remaining 12 strips of paper, so that you have a total of three long strips.

3 Use your paper strip to measure the width you need and then tape down 4 popsicle sticks as shown so that the paper will fit between them. Now tape down two popsicle sticks across your other sticks as shown. This is your paper track. Slide your strip of paper under the paper track as shown.

4 Pile two stacks of books on opposite sides of the paper track. Place a ruler under the top book on each stack. Tie one end of a string around the top of the can and tape the string down so that it does not come loose. Tie the other end to the ruler so that the point of the marker gently touches the paper.

5 Pull the paper *very slowly* through the track as your adult partner shakes the table in quick little vibrations, then with bigger vibrations, and then with really big vibrations.

6 Look at the marks on your paper. Can you tell which marks were made from the different kinds of shaking by your adult partner? Try the same activity again with a new strip of paper. This time have your adult partner do the same type of shakes but in the opposite order.

7 By looking at your new marks, were you able to tell the order of the shaking and when it changed?

8 Now for a **mystery quake!** Ask your adult partner to get someone else to pull the paper while you leave the room. Ask them to use the same types of shakes as before, but to do as many of them and in any order as they want. By reading your earthquake detector paper (or **seismogram**), tell them the order and type of shakes in their earthquake!

You will need

6 popsicle sticks	blunt end scissors
felt-tip marker	8-10 large heavy
masking tape	books
6 sheets of notebook	ruler
paper	string
unopened food can	

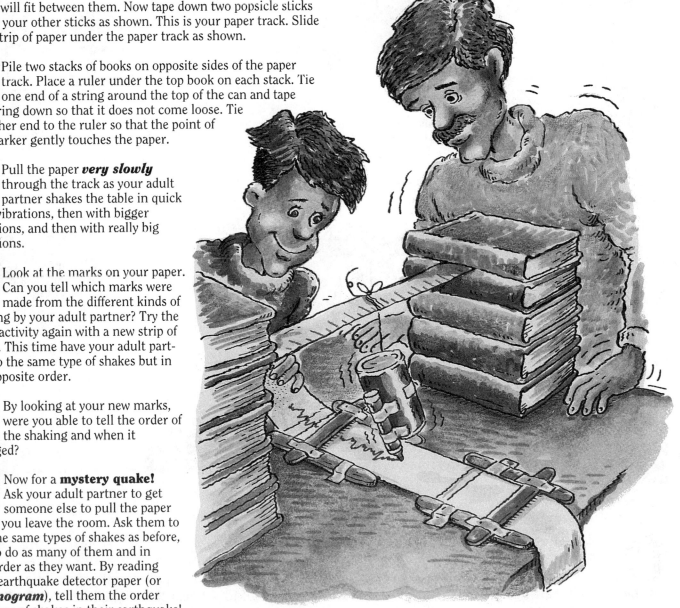

Earthquakes:
The Mercalli Tally

People indoors will feel it, but people outdoors may not.

It's hard just to stand.

People on upper floors can feel it.

Everyone feels it, and it is hard to walk.

Foundations are damaged. The ground cracks.

Bridges are put out of service.

Buildings are destroyed, and water is thrown out of rivers.

Only instruments can detect it.

Most things are leveled. Large objects are thrown into the air.

It's hard to drive cars. Chimneys may fall.

People lying down can feel it.

Everyone feels it and will wake up if sleeping.

ILLUSTRATIONS BY BOB BORDEAUX

One way scientists describe earthquakes is by how much damage is caused. A scale called the ***Mercalli*** scale is used to rank an earthquake from I to XII based on how much damage the earthquake causes. Here are pictures of the Mercalli scale that are out of order. Look at the pictures and read the descriptions. Try to put the Mercalli scale in order by writing a ***roman numeral*** from I to XII next to each picture, with I being the least damage and XII being the most damage.

QUAKE QUEST!

When an earthquake happens, scientists can *detect* the earthquake on a *seismograph* Scientists can tell the strength, or *magnitude*, of the earthquake and how far away it happened, but they cannot tell what direction the earthquake vibrations came from. In order to locate the earthquake, at least *three* seismographs in different places must detect the earthquake. Scientists then use a method called *triangulation* to locate the earthquake. Let's try it!

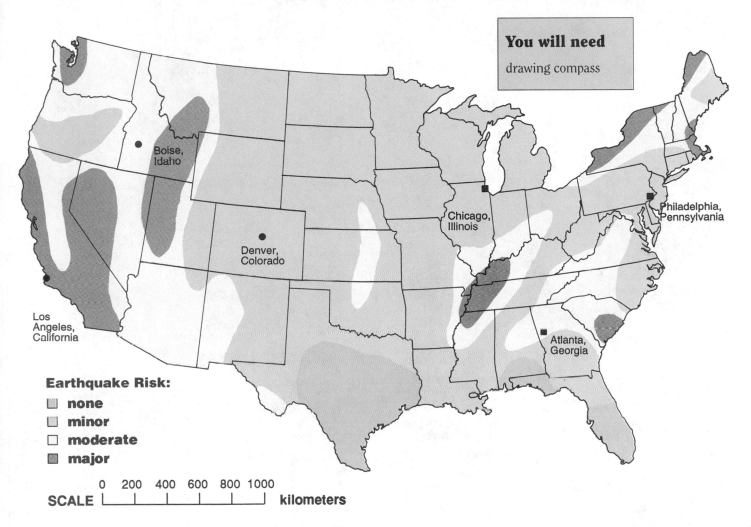

You will need

drawing compass

Earthquake Risk:

- none
- minor
- moderate
- major

```
        0   200  400  600  800 1000
SCALE   |___|___|___|___|___|___|   kilometers
```

Seismographs in three different cities detected an earthquake at these distances from each city.

Boise, Idaho—600 kilometers   Denver, Colorado—400 kilometers   Los Angeles, California—1000 kilometers

Use your scale to open your compass to 600 kilometers. Place the point of your compass on Boise, Idaho and draw a circle on your map. The earthquake happened somewhere along that circle but you can't yet tell where. Now measure and draw circles for Denver (at 400 kilometers) and Los Angeles (at 1000 kilometers). Where the three circles *intersect* is where the earthquake actually happened. In what state is the *epicenter* of the earthquake? Why do you think scientists call this method triangulation?

Try another one! If the epicenter is 800 km from Philadelphia, PA, 400 km from Atlanta, GA, and 600 km from Chicago, IL, in what state is the epicenter? You and your adult partner can use your scale, map, and compass to make up your own **earthquake hunts!**

Earthquake Hazard Hunt

There are certain things in your house that might be dangerous to people during an earthquake. Look at the picture below and see if you can figure out the **earthquake hazards**. See how many hazards you can list on a separate piece of paper.

This unit introduces students to some of the basic techniques of weather measurement. The unit does not stress the different factors related to the causes of various weather conditions. Instead, its focus is on making and understanding devices to measure different aspects of the weather.

Be a Weather Watcher!

In *Be a Weather Watcher!*, students observe and measure three common weather phenomena—rain, temperature, and wind. Making a rain gauge is relatively simple and is a close approximation to an actual rain gauge that meteorologists use. A meteorologist's rain gauge may have a funnel at the top that is 10 times the diameter of the opening of the collection tube. This way, if 1 inch of water collects in the tube, it means that .1 inch has actually fallen, which might be a difficult amount to measure without a funnel.

The temperature activity gives students a chance to record data in a chart and to create a graph based on the data. It may also be the first introduction to the Celsius scale, which is used extensively in scientific work. There is a relatively simple formula to convert Fahrenheit to Celsius and vice versa.

To convert to Celsius to Fahrenheit: $F = 9/5\ C + 32$
To convert Fahrenheit to Celsius: $C = 5/9\ (F - 32)$

Since establishing a scale is essential to the process of measurement, the wind speed activity gives students an opportunity to create their own scale and to use it to make relative wind speed measurements.

Swirl & Twirl

In *Swirl & Twirl*, students make an instrument that creates a vortex of water as a model of the wind activity in a tornado. Make sure to use wide tape such as duct tape or some other very sticky wide flexible tape.

Humidity, Don't Sweat It!

Humidity, Don't Sweat It! introduces the concept of relative humidity. Understanding that warmer air can hold more water than colder air may be helpful in explaining why hot summer days in certain places can feel so moist. The activity is a bit more sophisticated than most other *WonderScience* activities in that an indirect method of measuring humidity is used.

A Jarometer Barometer!

In *A Jarometer Barometer!*, students construct a working barometer. When the balloon is placed over the jar and sealed with rubber bands, the air pressure inside the jar should be about equal to the atmospheric pressure. If the atmospheric pressure drops, then the air inside the jar is at a higher pressure and the balloon will be pushed up. Because of the way the straw is attached, when the balloon moves up, the pointer goes down. When the air pressure increases, it is higher than the pressure in the jar so it pushes the balloon down. Again, due to the design, the straw will tilt up.

RELEVANT NATIONAL SCIENCE EDUCATION STANDARDS

The activities in this unit can be used to support the teaching of the following standards:

✔ Science as Inquiry
　Abilities necessary to do scientific inquiry
✔ Physical Science
　Motions and forces
✔ Earth and Space Science
　Structure of the Earth system

BE A WEATHER WATCHER!

Three common things about the weather that most people notice are the **rain**, **temperature**, and **wind**. In the following activities, you can make a *WonderScience* weather station to measure all three!

Rainfall

The amount of rain that falls in a particular spot is measured with a simple instrument called a **rain gauge**. A rain gauge measures the *depth* of rain that falls on a flat surface in a certain period of time.

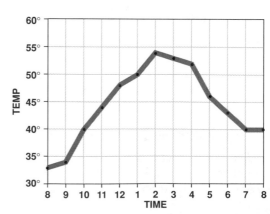

1 Use your ruler and pen to mark a strip of tape in centimeters. Stick the tape to the side of the jar so that the numbers increase as you move up the jar. This jar is your rain gauge.

2 Place your rain gauge outside on flat ground on a day when rain is expected. Make sure you place your gauge away from bushes, trees, or buildings. Leave your rain gauge there for 24 hours.

3 If your rain gauge has collected any rainwater, measure the amount using the masking tape scale. Try this for several days in a row and record your results to see how much rainfall your neighborhood is getting. Listen to the weather report or check the newspaper to see if your results match the experts'! Why might your results be different?

Temperature

Temperature is measured with an instrument called a **thermometer**. Many outdoor thermometers have two **scales**, labeled "F" and "C." The F stands for **Fahrenheit** and the C stands for **Celsius**. These scales are two different ways of measuring the same temperature, just as inches and centimeters are two different ways of measuring the same distance.

1 Place your thermometer outside in a shady spot. What is the temperature on your thermometer on the Celsius scale? What is the temperature on the Fahrenheit scale? Which scale gives you a higher reading? If you knew that water freezes at 0° C, can you tell the temperature at which water freezes on the Fahrenheit scale?

2 Make a chart for time and temperature like the example below. Look at your thermometer at 8:00 am and record the temperature using the Fahrenheit scale. Record the temperature every hour as in the example. Use your information to make a graph like the example shown. (You may need to use different temperatures on your graph.)

TIME	8:00AM	9:00AM	10:00AM	11:00AM	12:00PM	1:00PM	2:00PM	3:00PM	4:00PM	5:00PM	6:00PM	7:00PM	8:00PM
TEMP	33°	34°	40°	44°	48°	50°	54°	53°	52°	46°	43°	40°	40°

You will need

Rainfall:

wide-mouth jar
  with straight sides
masking tape
ball point pen
metric ruler

Temperature:

outdoor thermometer
  with C and F scales
sheet of paper
pencil

Wind Speed:

piece of cardboard
string (about 50 cm)
piece of aluminum foil
  (about 30 cm × 30 cm)
tape

pencil
metric ruler
paper clip
blunt-end scissors

Wind Speed

Your rain gauge used a scale of centimeters to measure rainfall. Your thermometer used the scale of Fahrenheit and Celsius to measure temperature. In the activity below, you can make your own scale to measure wind speed!

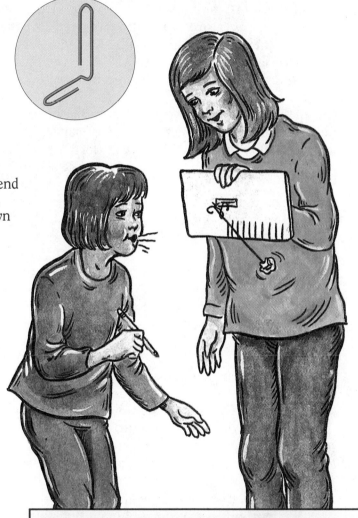

1 Crinkle the aluminum foil into a ball around one end of the string so that the ball holds onto the string. Ask your adult partner to unbend a paper clip as shown and tape it to the center of a large piece of cardboard.

2 Tie the free end of the string to the paper clip so that the foil ball hangs straight down. Put a pencil mark on your cardboard directly behind the string. Label this point "0."

3 Ask your adult partner to hold the cardboard. Blow the ball with a soft, medium, then hard burst of air. Put a dark mark on the highest point the ball reached.

4 Use a ruler to draw a line straight down from your mark. Label this mark "10." Ask your adult partner to help you divide the space between your two marks into 10 equal parts. You have now made your own wind speed gauge! You can name the scale the "Brian" scale, the "Susan" scale, or any name you like.

5 Take your wind gauge outside on a breezy day. Position the gauge so that the wind will be able to push the ball. At one time the wind might be a 3 on the "Danny" scale or a 7 on the "Kathy" scale. If the ball is blown past your 10 mark, how can you change your gauge to measure these high winds?

It is our policy that all activities in *WonderScience* are reviewed to assure their safety for children under adult supervision. However, in the January 1994 issue on rocks, in the "Panning For Gold" activity on page 5, the option to use **lead shot** was inadvertently added to the materials list after safety review had taken place. **Lead is toxic and should not be used.**

* All activities in *WonderScience* have been reviewed for safety by Dr. Jack Breazeale, Francis Marion University, Florence, SC; Dr. Jay Young, Chemical Health and Safety Consultant, Silver Spring, MD; and Dr. Patricia Redden, Saint Peter's College, Jersey City, NJ.

WEATHER—YOU LIKE IT OR NOT!

The study of weather is called *meteorology*. Meteorologists collect information about the weather using instruments similar to the ones you have been making in this unit. Collecting weather information is important because meteorologists need to have weather data from all over a country to make an accurate weather forecast for just one city! To get all this information, countries with good weather forecasting have weather stations set up in many places.

One of the most common pieces of weather data is *temperature*. As you saw in *Be a Weather Watcher!*, temperature is usually measured in either the Fahrenheit scale or the Celsius scale. Gabriel Fahrenheit, a German physicist, developed the Fahrenheit scale. The Celsius scale was developed by Andes Celsius, a Swedish astronomer. The Celsius scale, also called the *centigrade* scale, is used in many scientific formulas where temperature needs to be measured.

One of the most common parts of a weather report is the rain forecast. *Raindrops* form when water molecules in clouds collect on tiny dust particles to make tiny water droplets. The droplets become larger and the cloud usually begins to form in a certain shape that tells the weather people that rain may be on the way. What else do you notice about clouds that makes you think it might rain?

People also want to know how hard the *wind* is or will be blowing. Wind may be produced when cool and warm areas of air meet. As air is warmed by passing over land or water, it begins to rise. Cooler air that was above this air moves down to take its place and causes wind.

Some of the most violent storms on Earth are caused by the tremendous winds of *tornadoes*. Tornadoes usually occur when moist warm air meets cold dry air. These conditions also may cause severe thunderstorms. In fact, tornadoes usually drop down from huge thunderclouds in which the cold and warm air began to swirl to form the tornado.

The *barometric pressure* is something you hear about on almost every weather report. The barometric pressure measures how hard the air presses down on the Earth at a particular spot. Barometric pressure is often measured with a "U"-shaped glass tube with the shiny liquid metal *mercury* in it. One end of the tube is open, and the other is closed. Air pressure pushes down on the mercury in the open end, causing a rise in the mercury in the other side of the tube. The pressure is measured by how high or low the mercury goes. A drop in pressure may indicate an approaching storm; an increase in pressure usually means good weather is on the way.

Humidity is a measure of the amount of water in the air at a certain temperature. The temperature is important in measuring humidity because air at different temperatures can hold different amounts of water. When weather people talk about humidity, what they really mean is *relative humidity*. Relative humidity is the amount of water in the air at a certain temperature compared with the maximum amount of water the air could hold at that temperature. Warm air can hold more water than cold air. When the weather report ways that the humidity is 40%, it means that the air is holding 40% of the maximum amount of water that it can hold at that temperature. Can you see why 50% humidity on a cold day may feel dryer than 30% humidity on a hot day?

Once meteorologists collect all these data, they can predict or forecast what will happen next. But forecasting the weather is not always easy. Even highly trained meteorologists get it wrong because of the ever-changing nature of nature.

Swirl & Twirl

You will need

2 clear plastic soda bottles that are the same size

wide tape

water

A *tornado* is the most violent of all the Earth's storms. Hurricane winds can bend and break trees, but tornadoes can uproot them and fling them into the sky. Tornadoes can have wind speeds of over 300 miles per hour and have been known to carry away cars, buses, and even trains. A tornado is a violently rotating column of air that stretches from a cloud to the ground.

1 Fill one of the bottles about two-thirds full with water.

2 Turn the second bottle over and place its opening on the opening of the bottle with the water. Tape the two bottles together very securely as shown. Check the seal between the two bottles for any leaks.

3 To create a model tornado of water, invert the bottles and swirl the top bottle containing the water in a circular motion. After swirling for a couple of seconds, stop and watch the water flow into the lower bottle.

4 The shape you see should look kind of like a long twirling funnel. This is called a *vortex.* Try swirling the top bottle with the water in a larger or smaller circular pattern. Try swirling it faster or more slowly. Does this affect the shape of your model tornado? Try larger or smaller plastic bottles and different amounts of water. See if you can discover a combination that makes the best model tornado!

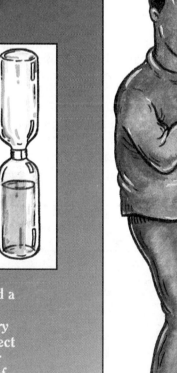

Humidity Don't Sweat It!

Humidity is an important weather fact because it has a lot to do with how fast water *evaporates* from our bodies and other surfaces. When there is a lot of water in the air, or high humidity, water evaporates slowly. When there is little water in the air, or low humidity, water evaporates more quickly.

You can use the rate of evaporating water to measure humidity in an interesting way by using a thermometer! When water evaporates from an object, the temperature of the object goes down. The lower the humidity, the faster the evaporation and the lower the temperature. In this activity, you will be able to measure humidity by measuring the drop in temperature as water evaporates from a paper towel.

1 Place about 1/2 cup of cool water in a bowl. Allow the water to come to air temperature for about 1 hour in the area where you are going to measure the humidity.

2 Use your thermometer to take the temperature of the air in degrees Fahrenheit. Write this number down. Tear a paper towel in half and dip it in the bowl of water. Squeeze out the excess water.

3 Wrap the damp paper towel around the bulb of the thermometer and hang the thermometer in a place where it won't be disturbed. Check the temperature every 10 minutes for about a half-hour to see if the temperature drops. When the temperature stops dropping, record this number. Subtract this reading from the air temperature. Use this number in the chart below to find the humidity of the air.

You will need

- thermometer
- paper towel
- water at air temperature
- small bowl

Temperature Drop	Temperature of Air °F							
	30°	40°	50°	60°	70°	80°	90°	100°
1	90	92	93	94	95	96	96	97
2	79	84	87	89	90	92	92	93
3	68	76	80	84	86	87	88	90
4	58	68	74	78	81	83	85	86
6	38	52	61	68	72	75	78	80
8	18	37	49	58	64	68	71	71
10		22	37	48	55	61	65	68
12		8	26	39	48	54	59	62
14			16	30	40	47	53	57
16			5	21	33	41	47	51
18				13	26	35	41	47
20				5	19	29	36	42
22					12	23	32	37
24					6	18	26	33

Example:

Air temperature is 70° F. Evaporating paper towel causes temperature to drop to 64° F. The temperature drop is 6°. Go to 6 under "Temperature Drop" and look across under 70° and you will see that the humidity is 72%.

A Jarometer Barometer!

A **barometer** measures something called **atmospheric pressure**. Atmospheric pressure is a measure of how much the air is pressing down on the Earth's surface. The temperature and movement of air masses cause the barometric pressure to rise or fall. These changes in air pressure help meteorologists to predict if the weather will be stormy or fair. In the activity below, you will make your own barometer! You can set your barometer up inside your house since the air pressure is the same inside the house as it is outside.

You will need

two identical glass jars
scissors
balloon
popsicle stick
glue
straw
rubber bands
pencil
tape

1 Ask your adult partner to cut a balloon in half. Stretch the round piece of balloon tightly over the opening of one of the jars. Wrap a rubber band around the rim to hold the balloon in place.

2 Cut the end of the straw so that it forms a tip. Glue or tape the other end of the straw to the center of the balloon. Hold the straw gently in place until it dries completely. The straw will be the pointer of the barometer that will show changes in air pressure.

3 Use your rubber bands to fasten the popsicle stick to the outside of the other jar. The popsicle stick will be the scale for your barometer. Position the stick and the jars so that the straw points to the center of the stick. Place a mark on the stick where the pointer is pointing.

4 Now call the weather service or watch the TV weather report for the current barometric pressure. With your pencil, write in that number beside your mark.

5 During the next few days, check a weather report any time you notice a change in the position of the pointer and write the new reading on the barometer. Once you have a range of readings filled in on the scale you may use your barometer to make readings any time!

Hint: Put your barometer in a room where the temperature doesn't change much. Changes in the air temperature can also cause changes in the barometer readings. Why do you think that happens?

Wild Weather Wonders!

■ As lightning streaks to the Earth, its path through the air can heat up to 30,000 °C or 54,000 °F — 6 times as hot as the surface of the sun!

■ Highest air temperature ever recorded on Earth was 58 °C or 136.4 °F in Al'azizyah, Libya, on September 22, 1922.

■ Hottest place in North America is Death Valley, California, which reached 56.7 °C or 134 °F on July 10, 1913.

■ Lowest air temperature ever recorded on Earth was in Vostok, Antarctica; it was −89.2 °C or −128.6 °F on July 21, 1983.

■ Coldest spot in the U.S. was Prospect Creek Camp in the Endicott Mountains of northern Alaska with a temperature of −62.1 °C or −79.8 °F on January 23, 1971.

■ Rainiest place on Earth is Tutenendo, Columbia, where it rains about 11,770 mm (about 460 inches) a year.

■ Driest place in the world is the Atacama Desert of Chile. Over a 50-year period it got only 0.7 mm (0.02 inches) of rain.

■ The United States leads the world in the number of tornadoes per year. All 48 states of mainland America have had a tornado touch down.

■ It is estimated that at any given moment nearly 2000 thunderstorms are in progress over the Earth's surface, and lightning strikes the Earth 100 times each minute.

■ The largest hailstone officially measured in the U.S. fell in Coffeyville, KS, on September 3, 1970. It weighed almost 3/4 of a kilogram (about 1-3/4 pounds) and was about the size of a cantaloupe.

Unit 43
Solar Energy

This unit introduces students to some of the scientific concepts underlying solar energy. While there are a variety of uses for solar energy, the activities in this unit primarily focus on the use of solar energy for heating.

Warm up to your WonderScience Solar Greenhouse

Warm up to your WonderScience Solar Greenhouse provides instructions for building a solar greenhouse. The difference between this greenhouse and an ordinary greenhouse is the use of black water-filled cans to store heat and radiate it back into the greenhouse after dusk. As an extension to this activity, you might help students investigate why the cans are black and why they are filled with water:

Black works best because it absorbs almost all of the light energy falling on it and converts this energy to heat. Other colors only absorb a portion of the light energy and reflect the rest. Water is an excellent substance for storing heat. For every degree increase in temperature, water absorbs and stores more heat energy than the same amount of air, soil, or almost any other materials. In conducting these investigations, be sure students change only one variable at a time. They should not change both the color and contents of the cans at the same time.

Soaking up the Rays

In *Soaking up the Rays*, students compare different materials to find which is best for converting sunlight to heat. The black-covered cup should have the greatest rise in temperature. If there is no significant difference in the temperatures of the cups, try leaving the cups in the sun for either a shorter or longer period of time before reading the temperatures. You might have students take the temperatures in the cups at regular intervals, such as every two minutes, and show the results on a graph like the one in the first activity.

Solar-Power Plants!

In *Solar-Power Plants!*, students use their greenhouse as a place to grow plants. If covering the greenhouse with a dark cloth for two days does not seem to affect the plants, this suggests that the plants have stored energy reserves. You can then leave the cloth on until you do see results.

Be a Sun-sational Chef!

In *Be a Sun-sational Chef!*, students make a solar cooker that converts sunlight to heat for warming food. Success at marshmallow warming will depend on location, time of year, time of day, and weather conditions. You should notice that the brown marshmallow warms up more than the white one. This is because the white color reflects the sun's energy while the darker color absorbs more of the energy, converting a portion of it to heat.

The final maze activity shows how the sun's energy is part of many more processes than students might realize. Ask students to think of other processes in which the sun's energy has an important role.

RELEVANT NATIONAL SCIENCE EDUCATION STANDARDS

The activities in this unit can be used to support the teaching of the following standards:

✔ **Science as Inquiry**
Abilities necessary to do scientific inquiry

✔ **Physical Science**
Transfer of energy

✔ **Life Science**
Populations and ecosystems

✔ **Earth and Space Science**
Earth in the solar system

✔ **Science in Personal and Social Perspectives**
Science and technology in society

Warm up to your WonderScience

Solar greenhouses and simple solar homes work in much the same way. With an hour of work, you can build your own solar greenhouse and experiment to find out how it works!

Adult Safety Note

After opening the cans, carefully press down any jagged edges with the back of a spoon and cover the rim of the can with 2 layers of adhesive tape.

Making Your Greenhouse:

1 Cover your work surface with newspaper. Along with your adult partner, use your water-based paint to paint the cans and the outside of the box black. Let the paint dry overnight.

2 Cover the inside of the box and lid with a layer of aluminum foil, shiny side showing, and secure it with tape. The aluminum foil will reflect the Sun's rays into the greenhouse. Put the bottom and lid of the box together as shown.

3 Fill the black cans with water and cover them tightly with plastic wrap and rubber bands. Place the cans inside your greenhouse, against the back wall. Tape the thermometer to an inside wall of the greenhouse.

4 Cover the front of the greenhouse with plastic wrap. Stretch the wrap tightly and tape it down. If you have to use more than one piece of plastic wrap, be sure to tape any seams.

Solar Greenhouse

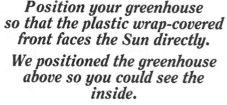

5 On a separate piece of paper, make a graph like the one shown below. Make it large enough to fill up your entire paper.

6 Place your greenhouse in a spot where it will receive direct sunlight. Read the temperature inside the greenhouse and record it on your graph. Continue to read and record the temperature every five minutes until it stops rising.

7 Now put the greenhouse in the shade and record the temperature every five minutes for at least half an hour.

8 What was the purpose of the black cans of water? How would your results be different without the black cans in your greenhouse? Try it and find out! You might want to record new temperatures on the same graph, but in a different color.

> **Caution**
> The cans could become too hot to touch.
> Use pot holders.

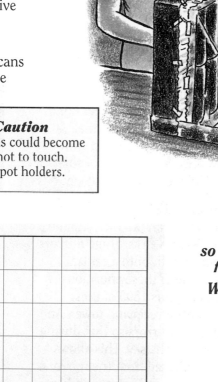

Position your greenhouse so that the plastic wrap-covered front faces the Sun directly.

We positioned the greenhouse above so you could see the inside.

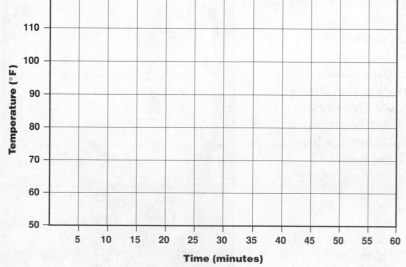

* All activities in *WonderScience* have been reviewed for safety by Dr. Jack Breazeale, Francis Marion University, Florence, SC and Dr. Jay Young, Chemical Health and Safety Consultant, Silver Spring, MD.

S☀lar Energy

Almost all of the energy we use on Earth comes from the Sun. The Sun gives us energy as light, and gives us heat that keeps the surface of the Earth warm. Energy from the Sun, or *solar energy*, can be used in several ways.

The simplest use of solar energy is to change that energy directly to heat. When you built the solar greenhouse described on pages 2–3, you were using solar energy in this way. When sunlight strikes the black cans inside your greenhouse, light energy is changed into heat and raises the temperature of the water inside the cans. The energy is "stored" inside the black cans of water, keeping the greenhouse warm even after the Sun goes down.

A solar house works in much the same way. Instead of black cans, a solar house usually has a *solar collector* that absorbs the Sun's heat. This heat is transferred to air or water (like the water inside your black cans), which circulate in pipes inside the collector. The heated air or water then travels through pipes to a storage tank. From the storage tank, fans or pumps are used to send heated air or water to various parts of the house where it is needed.

Another way to use solar energy is with a *solar cell*. A solar cell absorbs energy from the Sun and changes it to electricity. Solar cells are used to power everything from calculators to street lights to automobiles like the one pictured here. Did you know that many unmanned spacecraft use solar cells to provide them with electricity? A picture on this page shows two huge panels of solar cells that provide all the power for the Hubble Space Telescope.

A third way to use solar energy is a process called *Solar Thermal Energy Conversion*, or STEC. This process can produce enough electricity for an entire city. Here's how STEC works. Huge mirrors are all turned so that they reflect the Sun's light onto a central receiver. The picture on this page shows one of these enormous mirrors. A 72-acre field in Barstow, CA, contains 1800 of these mirrors, or *heliostats*, surrounding a central receiving tower. An automatic control system keeps turning the mirrors so that during the day they track the path of the Sun across the sky. This allows the maximum amount of sunlight to be reflected from the mirrors. The concentrated sunlight from the mirrors supplies enough heat at the central receiver to turn large amounts of water into superheated steam. The steam is piped to ground level and used to turn turbines, which drive the big generators that produce electricity.

Solar energy is also used by green plants to make food in a process called *photosynthesis*. People and other animals then eat the plants to obtain the energy that they need. Some scientists think that one day we may have big farms where special plants will be grown to be used as a source of energy. We would get energy from the plants either by burning them as we do with wood, or by changing them into a chemical to substitute for gasoline!

Soaking up the Rays

You will need

paper and pencil

blunt-tip scissors

a shoe box

insulating material (packing foam, crumpled newspaper)

foam drinking cups

cover materials (aluminum foil, clear plastic wrap, a square from dark green or black plastic garbage bag)

rubber bands

2 thermometers

Some materials absorb the Sun's energy better than others. When you built your greenhouse, you painted the outside black and lined the inside with aluminum foil. Why do you think it was important to do this? What do you think would have happened if you had covered the outside of the greenhouse with foil and painted the inside black? After finishing this activity you should be able to answer these questions. You'll know what makes a good *solar collector!*

1 Have your adult partner trim the sides of the shoe box down until they are the same height as the foam cups. While your partner trims the box, fill two cups with cold water.

2 Put the two cups in the box, and pack crumpled newspaper into the box around them. Measure the temperature of the water in both cups. Make a chart like the one below and record your results.

3 Cover one cup with aluminum foil, shiny side up. Leave the other uncovered. Set the box in bright sunlight for ten minutes. Measure the temperature in both cups again. Record your results.

4 Empty the cups and fill them with fresh cold water. Repeat the experiment but this time cover one cup with clear plastic wrap and the other with dark green or black plastic. Record your results on your chart.

5 Which cup had the greatest temperature increase? Why? In which cup was there the least change in temperature? Why?

	initial temperature	temp. after 10 minutes	temp. difference
uncovered			
aluminum foil			
black plastic			
clear plastic			

Solar-Power Plants!

Plants use the Sun to get the energy they need to live, grow, and reproduce. Plants use the Sun's light in a process called *photosynthesis*. Photosynthesis uses the sun's energy, water, and carbon dioxide to produce stored energy for the plant. Use your solar greenhouse to grow your own *Solar-Power Plants.*

You will need

your solar greenhouse

blunt-end scissors

potting soil

a pack of bean seeds

small clay plant pots (or small milk cartons with tops cut off and a hole in the bottom)

water

1 First you'll need to make changes to your greenhouse to keep the inside from getting too hot and to let fresh air inside. Ask your adult partner to cut two flaps, about 10 cm inches wide and 3 cm tall, in the plastic wrap on each side of your greenhouse.

2 Following the directions on the seed packet, plant your seeds. Place your planted pots inside the greenhouse. Be sure to open the greenhouse every few days to water your plants!

3 When your seeds start to grow, you should notice that they don't grow straight up and down. Which way do they lean? Why do you think they do this? What would happen if you turned the plants so that they pointed at the back wall?

4 What would happen if you took away the plants' energy source by covering the greenhouse with black plastic or a dark cloth? Try it! After two days, remove the cover and look at the plants. How have they changed? Why?

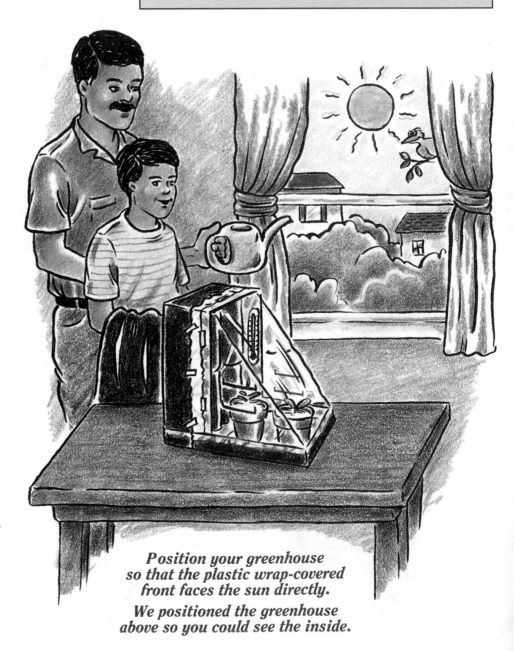

Position your greenhouse so that the plastic wrap-covered front faces the sun directly.

We positioned the greenhouse above so you could see the inside.

Be a Sun-sational Chef!

You don't need solar cells or large power stations to cook with solar energy! There are parts of the world where heating fuel is scarce and people use solar cookers to prepare their meals. You can be a Sun-sational Chef when you cook marshmallows with your own *WonderScience* **solar cooker!**

You will need

blunt-end scissors   aluminum foil
tape   2 straws
empty shoe box   marshmallows
file folder   cocoa powder
books or magazines

Making Your Cooker

Before making and using your cooker, there are some important things to remember:

● *Never look directly at the Sun.* ● *Never look directly at any really bright areas in your cooker.* ● *Wash your hands before handling or eating the marshmallows.*

1 Tear or cut the file folder in half along the fold. Place one of the halves in the shoe box so that it curves into the shape of a tube cut in half lengthwise. Tape the folder to the box as shown.

2 Line the folder with aluminum foil with the shiny side showing, and tape the foil to the box. Ask your adult partner to cut a slit about 1 cm wide and 6 cm long in each end of the box. Make marks along the slit at 2 cm, 4 cm, and 6 cm starting from the top to make your solar cooker adjustable!

3 Place about one teaspoon of powdered cocoa on a piece of aluminum foil. Roll a marshmallow in the cocoa and rub the cocoa onto the marshmallow until the marshmallow is brown.

4 Join two straws together by pushing the end of one straw into the end of another. Push this long straw through a brown cocoa-covered marshmallow and through a white marshmallow so that the marshmallows are near the middle as shown. Your solar cooker is ready to use.

Using Your Cooker

5 Find a sunny outdoor spot with a table or chair on which you can put the cooker. Rest the ends of the straws in the slits at the 6-cm mark. With your adult partner's help, try to aim the cooker directly at the Sun. Leave the marshmallows at the 6-cm point for 10 minutes. Did either marshmallow warm up?

6 Put a new brown and a new white marshmallow on the straws and move the straws up to the 4-cm mark. Place a piece of tape under the straws to keep them at the mark. Allow the marshmallows to cook for 10 minutes. Did either get warmer than before? Now try two new marshmallows at the 2-cm mark. How warm did they get? See if you can find the best level for cooking marshmallows on your *WonderScience* solar cooker! If one of your marshmallows got warmer than the other, can you explain why?

Did you know that the Sun's energy is needed to make something as simple as a pencil? Use a pencil to try to trace your way through the different steps, in the correct order, that connect the Sun's energy with you using the finished pencil.

Sun
1

2
Trees

4
Logs being made into pencils

5
You using a pencil to do your *WonderScience* maze

3
Logs

This unit introduces students to several important aspects of our solar system. The relative sizes of the planets, their distances from the sun, and their characteristics are explored. The apparent motion of the moon and sun are also investigated.

Scaling the Solar System!

In *Scaling the Solar System!*, students learn and practice the important math concept of representing distances to scale. Not only will students discover that large distances can be represented on a smaller scale, they will be able to appreciate the relative distances from planet to planet as well as the distance from each planet to the sun.

Planet Quest!

Planet Quest! gives students some interesting information about each of the planets in our solar system while challenging them to figure out which planet matches each set of five clues. The pictures of the planets in this activity are not to scale.

Space Trek!

Space Trek! is an original solar system game intended to give some information about objects in the solar system, develop some new vocabulary, and introduce some interesting aspects of space travel to students while they have fun playing the game.

Sun-Sational Shadows!

Sun-Sational Shadows! shows that shadows change their length and position as the day and year go on. The shadows change at different times during a single day because of the Earth's rotation. The shadows change their length and position during the year because of the Earth's movement around the sun. Be sure students understand that it is the movement of the Earth that causes the shadows to change.

Moon Diary

In Moon Diary, students make detailed observations of the phases of the moon and record some general surface features. Watching the moon for an entire month helps make changing phases of the moon make more sense.

The Voyager II article adds a little history and technology lesson about amazing real-life space exploration!

Be A WonderScience Crator Creator!

In *Be A WonderScience Crator Creator!*, students simulate the process of crater formation. The reason why there are so many craters on the moon and so few on Earth is that the Earth has an atmosphere that causes meteors to heat up and disintegrate as they fly through it. The moon has no atmosphere so meteors can travel directly to the moon's surface. Another important factor is that many of the craters on the Earth have been washed away by rain, erosion, and other weathering which does not occur on the moon.

RELEVANT NATIONAL SCIENCE EDUCATION STANDARDS

The activities in this unit can be used to support the teaching of the following standards:

✔ **Science as Inquiry**
  Abilities necessary to do scientific inquiry

✔ **Physical Science**
  Motions and forces

✔ **Earth and Space Science**
  Earth in the solar system

✔ **Science in Personal and Social Perspectives**
  Science and technology in society

SCALING THE SOLAR SYSTEM!*

The distances from planet to planet and across our Solar System are so large that it is hard to even imagine them! Often, when scientists want to study very large distances, they make a smaller *scale model*. A map is a good example of a scale model. A map can show many of the rivers, mountains, and distances between places, but everything on the map is made smaller according to a certain *scale*. The scale might be 1 centimeter (cm) on the map stands for 10 kilometers (km) in real distance, or 1 cm stands for 100 km, or 1 cm stands for 1,000 km or whatever scale is needed to reduce the real distances to a map of a certain size.

In this activity, you will make your own scale model of the Solar System to get an idea of the distances between the planets. Since our Solar System is so huge, we will use a scale in which 1 cm stands for 10,000,000 km!

You will need

paper strip at least 6 meters long
   (cash register tape
   or adding machine tape)
metric tape measure or ruler
colored pencils or crayons

The chart below shows the *real* distance from the *sun* to each of the *planets* in kilometers (km) and the same distance in centimeters (cm) if we use a scale in which 1 cm stands for 10,000,000 km.

1 Draw a small picture of the sun near one end of your paper strip. Look at the *scale* distances in the chart to find out how far from the sun to draw each planet. Measure each distance from the center of the sun and draw a small picture of each planet at its correct distance.

2 Write the name of each planet next to its picture. Put your strip on the wall in your room at home or at school.

PLANET	REAL Distance from SUN	Distance in SCALE (1 cm stands for 10,000,000 km)
Mercury	60,000,000 km	6 cm
Venus	110,000,000 km	11 cm
Earth	150,000,000 km	15 cm
Mars	230,000,000 km	23 cm
Jupiter	780,000,000 km	78 cm
Saturn	1,430,000,000 km	143 cm
Uranus	2,880,000,000 km	288 cm
Neptune	4,590,000,000 km	459 cm
Pluto	5,900,000,000 km	590 cm

Your paper strip scale model only shows how the *distances between* the sun and the planets compare. Look at the *scaled* pictures below to see how the *sizes of the planets* compare.

The scale for these pictures is 1 millimeter (mm) stands for 2,000 km. You can figure out the *real diameters* of the planets by measuring the dotted line on each planet in millimeters and then multiplying the number of millimeters by 2,000. Write your answer on the line under each planet. **EXAMPLE:** The picture of Venus is 6 mm in diameter. 6 × 2,000 = 12,000 so Venus is about 12,000 km in diameter.

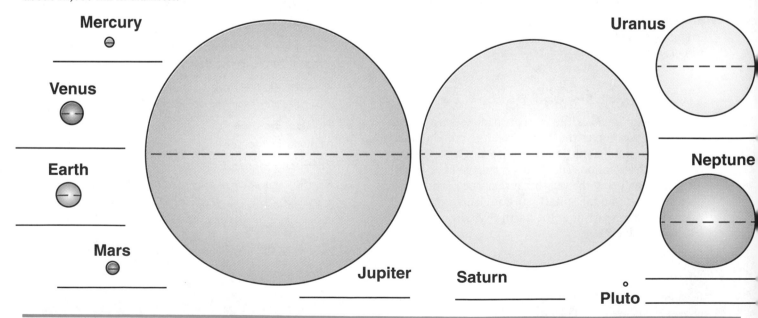

* All activities in *WonderScience* have been reviewed for safety by Dr. Jack Breazeale, Francis Marion College, Florence, SC; Dr. Jay Young, Chemical Health and Safety Consultant, Silver Spring, MD; and Dr. Patricia Redden, Saint Peter's College, Jersey City, NJ.

PLANET QUEST!

Each set of clues below describes one of the planets pictured on this page. Start with the first clue in each set and see if you can identify the planet using the fewest number of clues. Use some of the information in *Scaling the Solar System* to help you. (**Beware!** The sizes of the planets on this page are ***not to scale.***) The answers can be found on the bottom of *Be A WonderScience Crater Creator*.

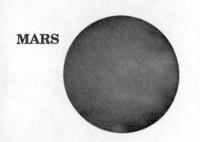

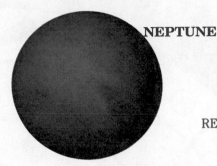

NEPTUNE

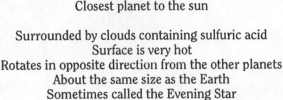

SATURN

Ten moons
Could float on water
Colored bands of clouds
Rings made of rocks and ice
Second largest planet

A little bigger than the Earth's moon
Wrinkled surface
REALLY HOT on side facing sun (about 840 °F)
No moons
Closest planet to the sun

Surrounded by clouds containing sulfuric acid
Surface is very hot
Rotates in opposite direction from the other planets
About the same size as the Earth
Sometimes called the Evening Star

MARS

MERCURY

Polar ice caps
Two space probes have landed here and checked for life
Huge and powerful dust storms
Looks like a reddish star in the sky
Often called the Red Planet

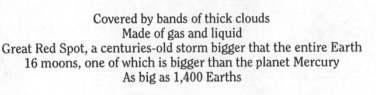

Covered by bands of thick clouds
Made of gas and liquid
Great Red Spot, a centuries-old storm bigger that the entire Earth
16 moons, one of which is bigger than the planet Mercury
As big as 1,400 Earths

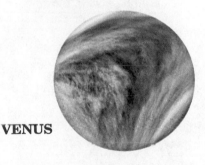

VENUS

JUPITER

15 times more massive than Earth
Clouds of poisonous methane gas
Rotates on its side
Greenish color
15 moons

Medium-sized planet
Atmosphere is mostly nitrogen
2/3 of surface covered by water
Third planet from the sun
Supports life

PLUTO

May have been a moon of Neptune
243 years to travel around the Sun
Coldest planet
Smallest planet
Last planet discovered

EARTH

About the same size as Uranus
Very cold
Blue skies like Earth
165 years to travel around the Sun
8 moons

URANUS

SPACE TREK!

OBJECT OF THE GAME:

To advance outward, from planet to planet, until you are the first Solar System traveler to reach the planet Pluto!

HOW TO PLAY:

Use a small colored eraser, piece of candy, or a player piece from another game as your *space traveler* playing piece.

All travelers begin on the sun, the center of the Solar System.

Travelers roll the die to see who goes first (highest roll goes first).

The first traveler rolls the die and moves that number of spaces onto Mercury's orbit with Mercury's *orbit arrow* as the first space.

After rolling the die, travelers must always move in the direction of the *orbit arrow*.

After landing on a space, check the *Solar System Key* and follow the instructions given in the key. It is then the next traveler's turn.

HOW TO ADVANCE FROM PLANET TO PLANET:

A traveler who ends up on a *planet space* at the *end* of a turn advances *directly* to the *next planet's orbit arrow* and *rolls again*.

A player can end up on a planet space by moving *forward* after rolling the die or by moving *forward* or *backward* after a Solar System Key instruction.

Travelers must advance from planet to planet, in the following order, *Mercury, Venus, Earth, Mars, Jupiter, Saturn, Uranus, Neptune, Pluto.*

The first traveler to land on Pluto's planet space *wins!*

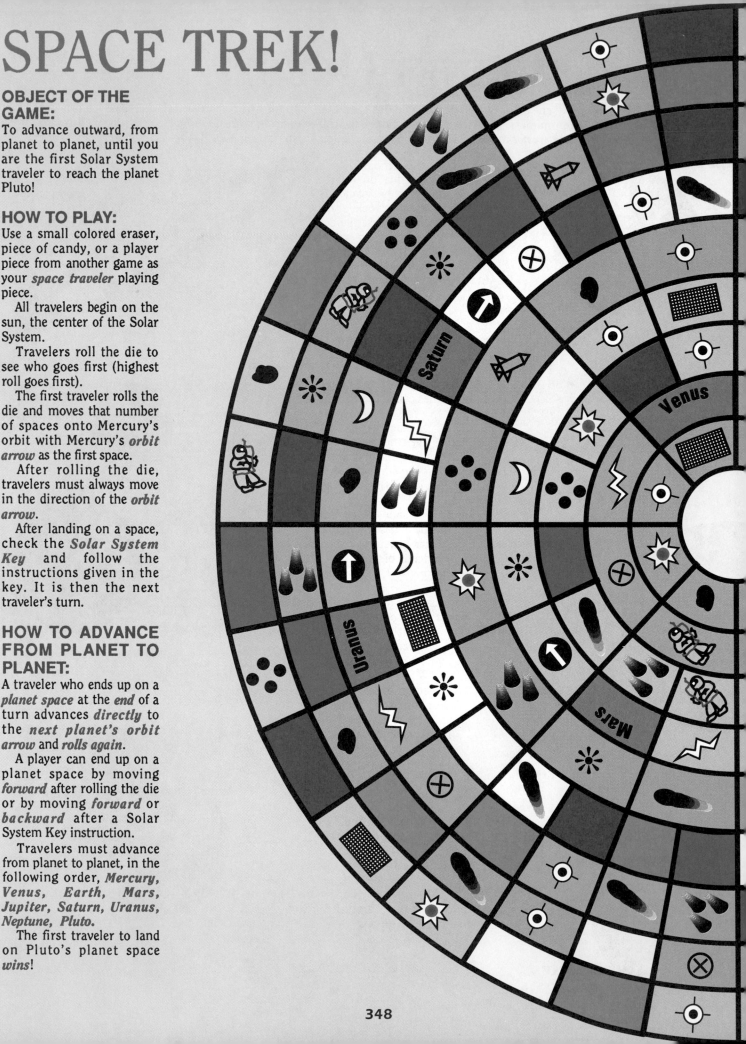

349

SOLAR SYSTEM KEY:

Planet Name

PLANET SPACE—Your destination in each orbit—land here and move onto the next planet's ORBIT ARROW.

ORBIT ARROW—first space of each orbit—shows direction traveler must move. **ROLL AGAIN.**

METEOR SHOWER up ahead—**SLOW DOWN!**—Move BACK 1 space.

PLANET'S GRAVITATIONAL PULL is too strong for you—return to ORBIT ARROW.

ASTEROID coming straight at you—**ESCAPE!**—Move BACK 3 spaces.

COMET spotted in the distance—**INVESTIGATE!**—Move FORWARD 2 spaces.

COSMIC DUST clogs your fuel lines—**ROLL AGAIN** and move BACK that many spaces.

PLANET'S MOON is nearby—**GRAVITATIONAL PULL** increases your speed—Move FORWARD 3 spaces.

SOLAR PANEL MALFUNCTION slows you down—Move BACK 1 space.

SATELLITE information says all clear—Move FORWARD 3 spaces.

SOLAR FLARE causes your space compass to malfunction—Move BACK 2 spaces.

SPACE WALK fixes your broken antenna—**ROLL AGAIN** and move FORWARD that many spaces.

STAR on your star map explodes—**YOU'RE OFF COURSE!**—Move BACK 2 spaces.

STORM IN PLANET'S ATMOSPHERE—USE EXTRA POWER!—Move DIRECTLY to planet.

SPACE JUNK nearby—Stop to clean it up—Move BACK 1 space.

BLUE—One of your opponents is running **LOW ON FUEL**—Pick the opponent who must move BACK 2 spaces.

RED—COMPUTER PROBLEM caused by **MAGNETIC FIELD**—Pick opponent who must move BACK 3 spaces.

YELLOW—PLANET'S GRAVITY increases speed of opponents—All of your opponents move FORWARD 3 spaces.

GREEN—UNIDENTIFIED OBJECT! —all opponents must move FORWARD 3 spaces to investigate.

SUN-SATIONAL SHADOWS!

Every day we see the sun rise in the east, travel across the sky, and set in the west. No wonder for almost 2,000 years people thought the sun traveled around the Earth. Today we know that the *Earth* travels around the *sun*. The rotation of the Earth just makes it *look* like the sun is moving across the sky. Although it is dangerous to ever look directly at the sun, you can learn a lot about it by watching the shadows it makes on the Earth.

You will need

1 large sheet of white poster paper
1 sharpened pencil
modeling clay
clock
colored pencil or crayon
metric ruler
compass

1 Draw a horizontal and a vertical line across the middle of the poster board. Write the directions *north, south, east,* and *west* on the poster as shown.

2 Use modeling clay to stand a pencil straight up at the center of the poster board where the two lines cross. You have now made a *SUN TRACKER!*

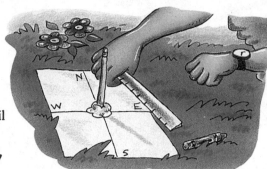

3 Go outside early in the morning on a sunny day and find a flat space in a large open area to place your *SUN TRACKER*. Ask your adult partner to help you use a compass so that you can lay your tracker down with the *north, south, east,* and *west* labels pointing in their actual directions. Can you see the shadow of the pencil on the paper?

4 At exactly 8:00 a.m., use your ruler and crayon to draw a line directly on the shadow from the bottom of the pencil to the end of the shadow. Measure the length of the shadow in centimeters. Write down the length of the shadow and the time of day next to the line and also record it in the Sun-Sational Shadows chart below. Repeat this step every hour on the hour.

5 You can use your *SUN TRACKER* to tell where the sun is in the sky at different times of the day. The sun is always opposite from the direction in which the shadow points. If the shadow points to the northwest, then the sun is in the southeast. What is the position of the sun at noon?

6 In a few weeks, take your *SUN TRACKER* back outside and place it in the same position as before. Use a different color crayon and mark the shadows every hour on the hour as before. Why do you think the shadows have changed? Do you think you could use your *SUN TRACKER* to tell time like a sun dial? Why or why not?

Length of Shadow (in cm)	8:00 am	9:00 am	10:00 am	11:00 am	12 noon	1:00 pm	2:00 pm	3:00 pm	4:00 pm	5:00 pm	6:00 pm	7:00 pm	8:00 pm

7 The pictures to the right show *you* standing in the sun in the morning, around noon, and in the late afternoon. Can you correctly draw your shadow in each of the pictures?

MOON DIARY

You can learn a lot about the moon just by observing it every day and keeping a record of what you see. Use a calendar to make a moon diary like the example you see here.

Sunday	Monday	Tuesday	Wednesday	Thursday	Friday	Saturday

1. Go outside when the moon is easy to see and draw a picture of the shape of the moon and any dark areas on it. These dark spots are large flat areas called "seas," but they do not have any water in them!

2. Keep your moon diary for one month. At the end of the month, look at the dark areas on your moon pictures. Do these areas seem to change position or do they always seem to stay in the same place? Does this mean that we always see the same side of the moon in the same position in the sky?

3. On the days when it was too cloudy and you were not able to see the moon, write "cloudy" in small letters in the lower corner of that day in your diary. Guess what the moon looked like on those days and draw in what you think.

Look at the phases of the moon below. Write in the dates from your moon diary that look most like these pictures. How long did it take your moon to go from a half to a full moon, or from a crescent to a half, or from a full moon to a half?

How long does it take the moon to go through a complete cycle of phases?

SPACE VOYAGER!

In 1977, a space probe called Voyager II was launched on a long and difficult journey to explore the four largest planets in the Solar System. Voyager II's mission was to reach Jupiter, Saturn, Uranus, and Neptune and to send pictures of them back to Earth. It took Voyager II almost two years to reach Jupiter and then a little over two more years to reach Saturn! The pictures Voyager sent back to Earth by radio signals were even better than astronomers had expected. Space scientists designed Voyager II and set its path so that it could use the gravity from Jupiter and Saturn to increase its speed to send it flying toward the planet Uranus. The plan worked perfectly: Voyager II flew past that planet about five and a half years after visiting Saturn, and then flew past Neptune about three and a half years after that. By 1989, Voyager II had traveled more than 6 billion kilometers in our solar system and was right on schedule. Sometime after the year 2000, Voyager II will leave the solar system and begin its journey into interstellar space!

Be A *WonderScience* CRATER CREATOR!

Have you ever seen a shooting star streaking through the night sky? A shooting star is not really a star at all! It is a chunk of metal or rock from outer space called a *meteor*. As a meteor falls through the Earth's atmosphere, heat caused by air friction causes the meteor to become very hot. Most meteors disintegrate before they ever reach the Earth's surface. *Meteors* that *do* hit the Earth are called *meteorites*.

This picture shows a big hole or *crater* that was made by a meteorite that struck the Earth in the Arizona desert. It is about 1 mile wide and 600 feet deep! Try the following activity to make your own *WonderScience* crater!

1 Cover the floor of your work area with newspapers. (You might even want to do this activity outside). Completely fill the bowl with flour then use the ruler to scrape across the flour surface to make it very smooth. Be careful not to inhale the flour.

2 Sprinkle paprika over the surface of the flour.

You will need

newspaper
small plastic butter or margarine tub or paper bowl
ruler
flour
paprika
small stones (a little larger than a pea)

3 Stand directly over the bowl, and drop a small stone "meteorite" into the bowl. Did the stone make a crater in the flour's surface? If not, try dropping a different size stone or dropping it from a different height.

4 Can you still see the stone after it hits? Many meteorites also disappear, but in a different way. Meteorites have so much energy when they collide with a planet or a moon, that they explode, creating giant craters that can be several miles wide! Some meteorites even vaporize when they hit.

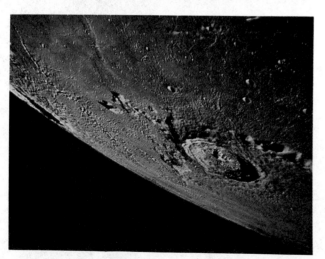

There are very few craters on Earth, but the moon's surface is covered with them. Can you figure out why?

Answers to *Planet Quest!*, from top to bottom: Saturn; Mercury; Venus; Mars; Jupiter; Uranus; Earth; Pluto; Neptune

Stars and Constellations

This unit introduces students to groups of stars known as *constellations*. The activities in the unit integrate language and creative arts along with mathematics to look at constellations from several different viewpoints.

Search for the Stars!

In *Search for the Stars!*, students are challenged to locate several familiar constellations on the star chart pictured. Please note that this chart has been included to use with activities in this unit but is not a good aid for trying to locate stars in the actual sky at night because: 1) the chart shows only a portion of the sky. The Big Dipper, for example, does not appear on the chart, 2) the relative brightness of the stars is exaggerated on the chart, and 3) some of the stars on the chart are too faint to be easily seen in the sky at night.

An actual star chart can be obtained at many bookstores or can be ordered from: The Astronomical Society of the Pacific, 1290 24th Ave., San Francisco, CA 94122.

Canned Constellations

Canned Constellations provides instructions for using old 35-mm film canisters to make constellation viewers and then using the viewers to play a constellation-naming game. Almost any photo development store will gladly give you as many empty film canisters as you want. Be sure to get the black plastic, not the clear ones.

Count Your Lucky Stars!

In *Count Your Lucky Stars!*, students use math skills as they practice the scientific technique of sampling to try to estimate the number of stars that appear on the star chart. In reality, because the stars in the sky are not uniformly distributed, this type of sampling may not be a good method for trying to count stars. Suggest this problem to students and ask them to think of objects whose numbers could be estimated using this sort of sampling.

Constellations: Another Point of View

Constellations: Another Point of View shows students that the apparent arrangement of stars in a constellation depends on the position from which the stars are viewed. It also points out that although the stars in a constellation may appear to be in a single plane, there are actually enormous differences in distance between stars. Students can measure the distance from the center of one foil ball to another and when the scale of 1 cm represents 20 light years is applied, a sense of the distance between stars can be appreciated. Remember, 1 light year equals about 6,000,000,000,000 miles.

Hercules

Hercules includes the science and the myth concerning the constellation Hercules. Students are encouraged to write a myth and to create a constellation from the pattern of seven stars given.

RELEVANT NATIONAL SCIENCE EDUCATION STANDARDS

The activities in this unit can be used to support the teaching of the following standards:

✔ **Science as Inquiry**
Understandings about scientific inquiry

✔ **Physical Science**
Motions and forces

✔ **Earth and Space Science**
Earth in the solar system

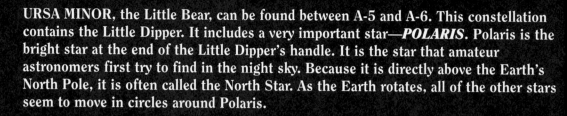

Search for

What do you think people did for entertainment before there were radios, televisions, video games, and computers? For thousands of years, people told stories called myths. They also gazed at the stars to find patterns that looked like the animals, persons, and other objects in their myths. They called these star patterns *constellations*. Some of the best known constellations that you can see at this time of year are described below. Can you find them in the picture of the early winter sky? (Hint: The constellations in the sky chart may appear upside down, at an angle, or facing a different direction than in the drawings.)

URSA MINOR, the Little Bear, can be found between A-5 and A-6. This constellation contains the Little Dipper. It includes a very important star—*POLARIS*. Polaris is the bright star at the end of the Little Dipper's handle. It is the star that amateur astronomers first try to find in the night sky. Because it is directly above the Earth's North Pole, it is often called the North Star. As the Earth rotates, all of the other stars seem to move in circles around Polaris.

ORION, the Great Hunter, can be found between C-2 and D-2. Two of the very brightest stars in the sky are part of Orion. The star Betelgeuse is his right shoulder and the star Rigel marks his raised right foot. Orion holds a club in his right hand. Outside at night, you can locate Orion by the three bright stars that form his belt.

CASSIOPEIA, the Queen of Ethiopia, can be found between B-4 and B-5. According to myth, because of jealousy Cassiopeia had her daughter, Andromeda, chained to a rock in the sea. In the constellation, Cassiopeia is sitting in a chair. It is easy to find her in the sky because five of her brightest stars make a zigzag letter W.

PEGASUS is the Winged Horse. In the Greek myth about Pegasus, the god Zeus cut off the head of Medusa, and Pegasus was born from the blood. He flew up to join the gods where he was tamed by the goddess Athena with a golden bridle. Pegasus is a really large constellation. Look at the stars that make up Pegasus at the left. See if you can find him in the star chart. (Hint: Pegasus looks upside down—look for four fairly large stars in a square.) What are the number and letter where Pegasus is located?

Can you find the above constellations in the sky on a clear night? For safety at night, be sure to take an adult partner with you. You may also want to take a flashlight with you to light your path.

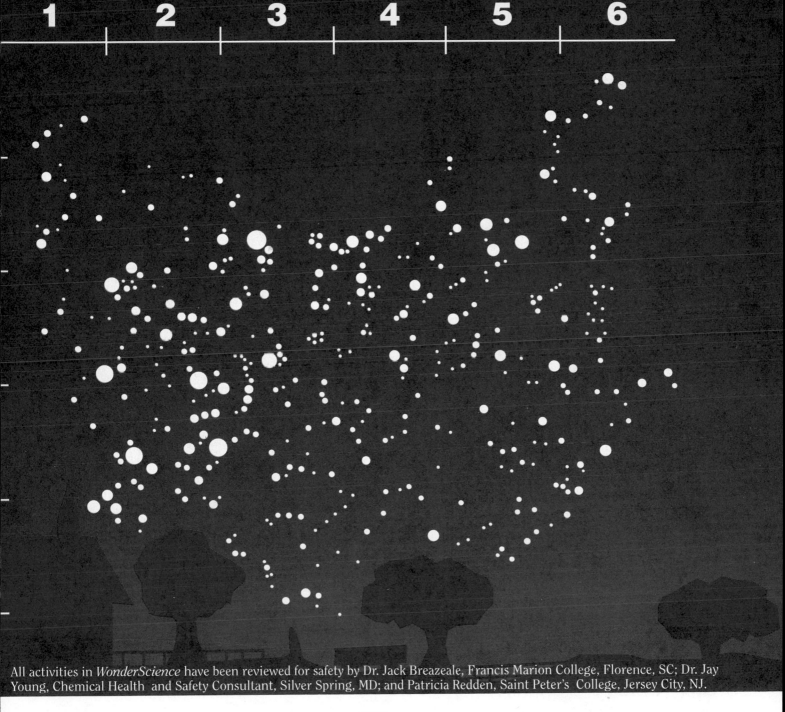

All activities in *WonderScience* have been reviewed for safety by Dr. Jack Breazeale, Francis Marion College, Florence, SC; Dr. Jay Young, Chemical Health and Safety Consultant, Silver Spring, MD; and Patricia Redden, Saint Peter's College, Jersey City, NJ.

BE A BACKYARD ASTRONOMER !

People young and old are finding you don't need a telescope to be an amateur astronomer. You don't even need binoculars! All you need are your own two eyes, a clear night, and a place far enough away from the city lights to see the starry sky. Get comfortable and let your eyes get used to the dark. You might even want to lie down on a blanket. If you use a flashlight, cover the end with a brown paper bag so that the light doesn't make it harder for you to see the stars.

There are lots of things to observe. See if you can find the Little Dipper and Polaris, the North Star. A star chart can help you. Try to locate some of the other constellations and some of the brighter stars in the sky. Notice how stars twinkle, and that stars nearer the horizon appear to twinkle more than those high in the sky. Look carefully and you will observe that stars are not all the same color.

Watch over a few hours and you will see most of the stars move across the sky. Pick out a really bright star and find out how its location changes compared to a fixed object like the top of a tall tree. See how the position of the Little Dipper changes. Look to the east and you will see some stars slowly come up over the horizon. If you stay outside long enough, you will see these same stars rise across the sky and eventually drop below the horizon to the west. This east-to-west motion occurs not because the stars are really moving, but because the Earth is rotating on its axis beneath the stars. The Earth's rotation makes it look like all of the stars are moving in circles about the North Star.

The stars may not look really far away or very far apart from one another, but they are. Besides our own sun, the closest star to us is Proxima Centauri, which is about four light years away. A light year is the distance light travels in one year, or about 5,900,000,000,000 miles! Traveling in a space capsule at a speed of 25,000 miles per hour, it would take over 100,000 years to reach Proxima Centauri!

The sun and almost all the stars you can see with your naked eye are part of a huge system of stars known as the Milky Way Galaxy. This galaxy contains over 100 billion stars! And there are at least 100 billion other galaxies in the universe! The farthest galaxy detected so far is more than 5 billion light years away!

Enjoy your new *WonderScience* as you learn more about stars and constellations. You may even decide that you want to become a professional astronomer!

Pegasus is between C-5 and D-6.

Canned Constellations

You will need

black plastic 35-mm film canisters
(camera and film developing stores will
usually give them to you)
pushpin
white paper
pencil
blunt-tip scissors
clear tape

You can use the patterns on this page to make your own constellation viewers. Then you don't even have to go outside at night to see what the constellations look like! Use your viewers to play a game to see who can name the most constellations.

1 Use the white paper to trace and cut out the constellation patterns at the right. (The constellations in the patterns are the reverse of the way they appear in the sky but will appear correctly when observed through the viewer you will make.)

2 Hold each pattern on the outside bottom of a film canister. Have your adult partner use a pushpin to poke a hole through the canister bottom for each star in the constellation pattern. Make the brighter stars have larger holes by wiggling the pushpin around a little.

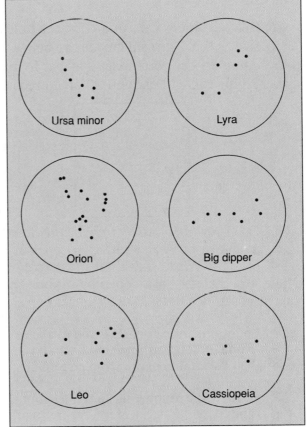

Ursa minor

Lyra

Orion

Big dipper

Leo

Cassiopeia

3 Write the name of the constellation on a small piece of paper and tape it to the inside lid of the film canister.

4 Remove the lid from the film canister. (Don't peek at the name on the lid.) Look through the open end of the canister toward a light source to see the constellation. Replace the lid when you are through.

5 Play a game to identify the constellations. Take turns with your adult partner picking out constellations for the other to view and try to name. Can you name them all correctly?

Count Your Lucky Stars!

You will need

index card
blunt-end scissors
Search for the Stars!
   of this unit
sheet of paper
pencil

How hard do you think it would be to count every star you see in *Search for the Stars*? Sometimes when scientists have a really large number of objects and they want to get an idea of how many objects there are, they use a method called *sampling*. Try the activity below to see if you think sampling is a good way to find out approximately how many stars you can see in the sky.

1 Get your index card and cut out a hole in the middle that is the same size as the 3 cm x 3 cm square below. You have just made a Star Sampler! Use your sheet of paper to make a chart like the one at the lower right. You will use your chart to record your results.

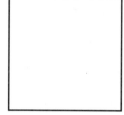

2 Open your book to *Search for the Stars!* and lay it on a table or other flat surface. Drop your Star Sampler onto the Winter sky chart in *Search for the Stars!*. Make sure that the entire opening of your sampler lands on the chart. If it doesn't, drop it again.

3 Count the number of stars you can see inside your star sampler. Write the number under "Number Counted" in your chart. (If your sampler cuts through a star, count the star if more than half of it is in the sampler. Don't count it if it's less than half a star.)

4 Multiply the number of stars you counted by 30 because the area of the winter sky chart is 30 times larger than the area of your sampler. This is your first estimate of how many stars there are on the entire chart. Record this number in the chart.

5 Scientists who use sampling as a method for counting objects usually take several samples and **average** their results. This gives them the best estimate of the total number of objects. Repeat steps 3 and 4 above and record your results for the 2nd Try and 3rd Try in your chart.

Try	Number Counted	Multiply by 30
1st		
2nd		
3rd		

6 To average your results, add the numbers in the right column of your chart. Then divide the answer by three because this is the number of samples you added together. This is your new estimate of the number of stars in the Winter Sky Chart.

7 To find out how many stars are shown in *Search for the Stars!*, turn this page upside down. How close did you come? Do you think sampling is a good method for counting the visible stars in the sky? Why or why not? Do you think you would have better results if you averaged more samples? Try it and see!

There are 406 stars pictured in *Search for the Stars!*.

Constellations: Another point of view

A constellation is the pattern you see in a group of stars when you look at them from here on Earth. But what if you were located somewhere else in space and looked at the same stars? Do you think you would see the same pattern? Make a model of the constellation Orion and find out!

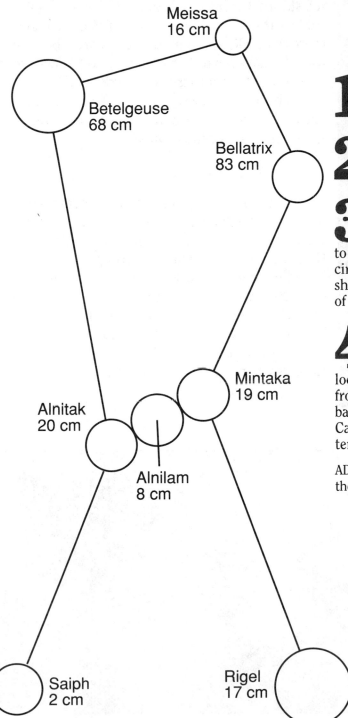

Meissa
16 cm

Betelgeuse
68 cm

Bellatrix
83 cm

Mintaka
19 cm

Alnitak
20 cm

Alnilam
8 cm

Saiph
2 cm

Rigel
17 cm

1 Trace the pattern of Orion onto the paper and then tape it to the piece of cardboard.

2 Make small balls out of aluminum foil to represent the stars in Orion. The balls should match the sizes of the circles on the pattern.

3 Ask your adult partner to use a small nail to poke a hole through the cardboard in the center of each circle. Thread your string down through each hole to hang your foil balls the correct distance below their circles on the pattern. The number next to each circle shows the length of the string in centimeters. Use a piece of tape to attach the ends of the string to the cardboard.

4 Ask your adult partner to hold the cardboard so that the foil balls hang down. To see the way Orion looks from Earth, sit or lie down on the floor and look directly up at the model. To see the way Orion looks from somewhere else in space, stand up and view the foil balls from the side. Does the pattern still look the same? Can you think of an animal or object for the way the pattern looks now?

ADULT NOTE: This model shows the actual relative position of the stars in Orion using the scale 1 cm = 20 light years.

359

HERCULES:

The Constellation

The star marking the head of Hercules is a giant red star that is hundreds of times larger than our sun. Near the right foot of Hercules is a cluster of more than 100,000 stars that can barely be seen with the naked eye. The cluster is so far away that it takes light from these stars over 300,000 years to reach the Earth! Scientists have discovered that one of the stars in Hercules has exploded! An exploding star is called a *nova*.

The Myth

Hercules was the son of a mortal princess named Alcmene. The goddess Hera didn't like Alcmene, so she tried to make Hercules' life miserable. Since Hera was a goddess, she had strong powers. She forced Hercules to do 12 extremely dangerous tasks during his life. The first was to kill a savage lion. The second was to fight a deadly serpent that had many heads. The heads would grow back as soon as they were cut off. The constellation shows Hercules' battle with the serpent.

As you can see from the Hercules constellation, ancient people really used their imaginations to dream up an elaborate picture from the simple pattern of a few stars. Here's your chance to let your imagination run wild! Copy the pattern of seven stars at right onto a separate sheet of paper. Draw a picture of the person, animal, or object that you see in the star pattern. Be creative! Give your constellation a name and then write your own myth about it.

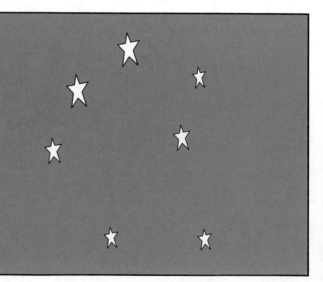

WONDERSCIENCE

This unit introduces students to some of the basic principles involved in the concept of energy. This unit focuses on three energy ideas that are appropriate for elementary school children to investigate: Energy is the ability to do work or to make things go. Energy comes in different forms, including mechanical, light, electrical, chemical, sound, and heat. Energy can be transformed, or converted, from one form into another.

Energy to Go!

Energy to Go! provides examples of how different forms of energy can make things go. Encourage students to think of other ways these forms of energy make things go. The cartoon shows a series of energy conversions. The correct order for the pictures is 1) tomato plant, 2) eating tomato, 3) pedaling bicycle/generator, 4) hot plate, 5) tea kettle. Students are challenged to draw their own cartoon design of a crazy way of performing an ordinary task that uses at least two energy conversions. There are no "right" answers for their drawings, but students should correctly identify the form of energy before and after each conversion.

Go for the Glow

In *Go for the Glow*, students make an incandescent light bulb. An incandescent bulb (not fluorescent) works because its filament is made of metal that is a poor conductor of electricity. Poor conductors offer resistance to the flow of electricity. As a result, instead of efficiently flowing through the filament, some electrical energy gets converted to heat and light. In this activity, the filament is steel; in a real light bulb, it is made of tungsten. Be sure to try this activity before doing it with students.

If your light bulb does not "glow," there are several things you should check: 1) See that all of the batteries are lined up the correct way and that their metal ends are firmly touching. Be sure that the wires are making good contact with the ends of the filament and with the terminals of the battery, 2) Look for a "short circuit." This happens when two bare wires touch. Most likely a short circuit will be in the coiled filament, 3) Another twist tie may work better. The thinner the wire, the better it will work. You could also try one strand from multistranded hanging wire. Remove a single strand from the wire, then follow the instructions for making the filament. This filament will glow very brightly and may even burn out.

The Hot Spot

In *The Hot Spot*, students need to be reminded of safety. For the first activity, make sure the end of the hanger is taped. Caution students to handle the hanger carefully and sensibly. In the second activity, make sure the lamp and its cord are positioned so that students can't knock the lamp over easily.

Energy—Its All in the Cards!

In *Energy—Its All in the Cards!*, some of the cards have the same picture. This is because some pictures can be correctly labeled in more than one way. In a light bulb, for example, electrical energy is converted into light and heat. Therefore two light bulb cards can be labeled "electrical to light" and "electrical to heat." You and the students should examine the cards and fill in the blanks the same way.

More Conversion Diversions!

In *More Conversion Diversions!*, students try different approaches to blocking the light from a calculator's solar cells, such as holding a hand at various distances between the calculator and the light source. For the radio activity, music works better than talking.

RELEVANT NATIONAL SCIENCE EDUCATION STANDARDS

The activities in this unit can be used to support the teaching of the following standards:

✔ **Science as Inquiry**
  Abilities necessary to do scientific inquiry
✔ **Physical Science**
  Transfer of energy
✔ **Earth and Space Science**
  Populations and ecosystems

Energy to Go!

Energy makes things go. There are lots of different kinds of energy.

LIGHT

The energy in light makes plants grow and allows solar cars and solar calculators to work.

CHEMICAL

The chemical energy in gasoline makes cars, trucks, buses, and other vehicles go.

MECHAN-ICAL

This is energy from motion such as water pouring over a waterfall to turn a water wheel or wind blowing to make a windmill or a sail boat go.

ELEC-TRICAL

Electrical energy makes washers, driers, radios, TVs, and battery-powered toys work.

HEAT

Heat can boil water to make steam engines go or drive generators to make electricity.

ALL THIS ENERGY MAKES ME WANT TO GO, GO, GO!

SOUND

Some sounds, such as an opera singer's voice or a powerful clap of thunder, have so much energy that they can break glass or make your body vibrate.

One of the most important things about energy is that one kind of energy can be changed into another kind of energy. A good example is a lightbulb. Electrical energy coming into the bulb is changed into light energy and heat energy. Another example is the food we eat. Our bodies change the chemical energy in food into heat energy to keep us warm. We also change this chemical energy into mechanical energy when our organs and muscles move. These changes are called **energy conversions**

The picture below shows some examples of energy being changed into other kinds of energy. It's a kind of roundabout way of making a whistle blow. See if you can explain which parts of the picture show the energy changes listed below:

LIGHT ➡️ CHEMICAL _____

CHEMICAL ➡️ MECHANICAL _____

MECHANICAL ➡️ ELECTRICAL _____

ELECTRICAL ➡️ HEAT _____

HEAT ➡️ SOUND _____

Challenge:

Use what you know about energy conversions to draw a cartoon of your own energy conversion device. Show at least two energy conversions that work together to make:

1) an alarm clock.

2) a door knocker.

3) an egg cracker.

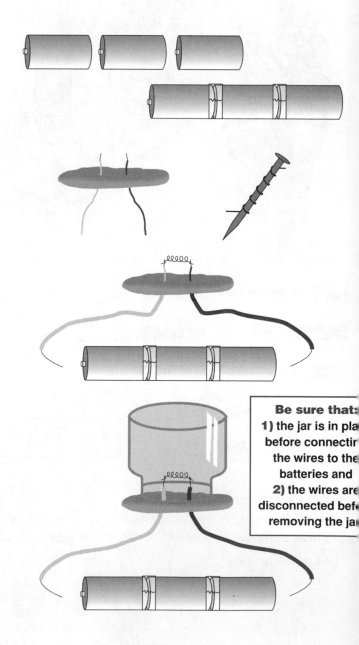

YOU WILL NEED:

3 fresh flashlight batteries
(D cells, 1.5 volt)

metric ruler

tape

2 insulated copper wires
(25-cm long)

nail

1 wire twist tie
(from a plastic bag)

modeling clay

small glass jar

Go for the Glow!

You learned in *Energy to Go* that one kind of energy can be changed into another. This change is called an energy conversion. In the activity below, you can convert electrical energy from batteries into other kinds of energy by making a model of a lightbulb.

TEACHER PREPARATION:

Cut enough 25-cm pieces of insulated wire so that each group of students will have 2 pieces. Use a pair of scissors or wire cutters to strip about 2 cm of insulation from both ends of each wire.

STUDENT ACTIVITY:

1 Lay three batteries end-to-end as shown. The positive ends of the batteries should all point in the same direction. You and your partner should tape the batteries together.

2 Mold some clay into a patty a little bigger around than the mouth of your jar. This will be the base of your lightbulb. Poke your two wires up through the modeling-clay base. The wires should stick out about 5 cm and be about 3 cm apart.

3 Peel off the paper or plastic from the twist tie so that only the bare wire remains. Wind the wire around the nail as shown. Leave a little bit of the wire straight at both ends. Take the wire off the nail. The wire is the **filament** for your light bulb.

4 Twist the ends of the copper wires around the ends of the filament to attach the filament to the wires. Do not let the coils of the filament touch each other. Turn the glass jar upside down over the wires and filament. Press the jar down into the clay. Your light bulb is now ready to light!

5 Darken the room. Touch the ends of the wires to ends of your batteries as shown. Hold them on tightly. Watch the filament. What happens? The *electrical* energy in the batteries is converted to what other kind of energy?

6 Experiment to make a better lightbulb. You might change the length, thickness, or kind of metal used for the filament or for the connecting wires or change the strength or number of batteries. What kinds of changes do you think may make the bulb burn more brightly?

Be sure that:
1) the jar is in pla
before connectir
the wires to the
batteries and
2) the wires are
disconnected befe
removing the ja

The Hot Spot!

In these two activities, you will change one form of energy into another. After doing each activity, write down the first kind of energy and then write down the energy it was changed into after the conversion.

Before beginning this activity, wrap the entire hook of the hanger with masking tape so that the end is completely covered.

1 Hold the bottom section of the hanger with both hands as shown.

2 Bend a section of it back and forth five times. Gently touch the bent part. What do you notice?

3 Bend it back and forth five more times, but faster than you did before. Touch the bent part again. What do you notice? Where did some of the energy go that you used to bend the hanger?

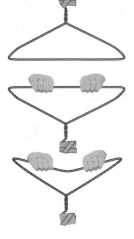

CESAR CAMINERO

ENERGY **BEFORE** CONVERSION

_____

ENERGY **AFTER** CONVERSION

_____

1 Cut a spiral from a sheet of aluminum foil. Carefully poke a small hole in the aluminum foil with a push pin. Put a piece of thread through the hole and use a small piece of tape to hold the thread in place.

2 Hang the spiral by the thread, and hold it about 5 cm above a lamp. What happens? How might you change the spiral to make it spin faster? List as many ways as you can think of.

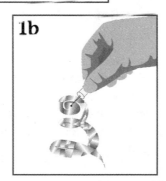

1a

1b

2

CESAR CAMINERO

ENERGY **BEFORE** CONVERSION

_____

ENERGY **AFTER** CONVERSION

_____

Answer Key

1 **Lightbulb:** Electrical -> Light or Heat
2 **Lightbulb:** Electrical -> Light or Heat
3 **Candle:** Chemical -> Light or Heat
4 **Candle:** Chemical -> Heat or Light
5 **Toaster:** Electrical -> Heat
6 **Hand generator:** Mechanical -> Electrical
7 **Windmill:** Mechanical -> Electrical
8 **Rubbing hands:** Mechanical -> Heat
9 **Battery:** Chemical -> Electrical
10 **Hair dryer:** Electrical -> Mechanical (fan)
11 **Hair Dryer:** Electrical -> Heat or Mechanical or Heat
12 **Radio:** Electrical -> Sound
13 **Whistle:** Mechanical -> Sound
14 **Running:** Chemical -> Heat or Mechanical
15 **Running:** Chemical -> Heat or Mechanical
16 **Steam locomotive:** Heat -> Mechanical
17 **Rocket:** Chemical -> Heat or Mechanical
18 **Rocket:** Chemical -> Mechanical or Heat
19 **Opera singing:** Sound -> Mechanical
20 **Solar calculator:** Light -> Electrical
21 **Solar Car:** Light -> Mechanical
22 **Lightning:** Electrical -> Heat or Sound
23 **Lightning:** Electrical -> Sound (thunder) or Heat (thunder)
24 **Plant facing the sun:** Light -> Mechanical
25 **Telephone:** Sound -> Electrical
26 **Telephone:** Electrical -> Sound
27 **Record player:** Mechanical -> Sound
28 **Tea kettle:** Heat -> Sound
29 **Thermostat:** Heat -> Mechanical
30 **Microphone:** Sound -> Electrical
31 **Voice-activated computer:** Sound -> Electrical
32 **Photosynthesis:** Light -> Chemical

Energy—
It's All in the Cards!

Teacher Preparation:

Photocopy all of the cards and distribute them. You could conduct this activity so that each student has a copy of the cards or each pair or group of students has a copy.

The first stage is to ask students to come up with the kind of energy that should go on the right side of the arrow on each card. It could be a competition, or group, or class activity. Discuss the answers with the students.

Have students write in the correct answer for each card. The answer key can be found on the previous page. Students should then cut out each card and tape or glue it to an index card.

When all the cards are made, students can use them to play an *Energy Conversion Card Game!*

RULES OF THE GAME

Number of Players:
Three or four.

Object of Game:
The first person to get rid of all of his or her cards is the winner.

How to Play:
Deal out the entire deck. Extra cards should be put to the side and not used. Cards with **chemical** energy on the left side of the arrow are **BONUS** cards. Players holding these cards should place them, face down, in a pile in front of them to be added to their score later. This reduces the number of cards in their hand and makes it easier to win.

The first player plays **any** card, and names out loud the energy conversion on the left and right sides of the arrow. For example, if you are the first player, you could lay down one of the lightbulb cards and say "Electrical to Light." Then the second player has to play a card that converts "Light" into another form of energy. If Player 2 does not have a "Light to Something Else" card, he or she must pass. Play moves to Player 3, who might put down a solar-powered car card and say "Light to Mechanical." Player 4 must then play a card that has "Mechanical" to another form of energy. If all players must pass, the original player who passed may play any card so that play continues.

Scoring:
The first player who runs out of cards gets 5 points plus 1 additional point for each card in the other players' hands. Each player receives 1 point for any bonus card with **chemical** on the left hand side of the arrow.

There is one **SUPER BONUS** card. This card is the "Photosynthesis" card. It is the only card with **chemical** on the right side of the arrow. Whoever is dealt the super bonus card should put it face down in front of them, like a regular bonus card, before play begins. Whoever has the super bonus card at the end gets to add 5 points to his or her score.

1 Lightbulb
Electrical → _____

2 Lightbulb
Electrical → _____

3 BONUS! Candle
Chemical → _____

4 BONUS! Candle
Chemical → _____

5 Toaster
Electrical → _____

6 Hand generator
Mechanical → _____

7 Windmill/Power lines
Mechanical → _____

8 Rubbing hands together

Mechanical → _____

9 BONUS! Battery

Chemical → _____

10 Hair dryer

Electrical → _____

11 Hair dryer

Electrical → _____

12 Radio

Electrical → _____

13 Whistle

Mechanical → _____

14 BONUS! Running

Chemical → _____

15 BONUS! Running

Chemical → _____

16 Steam locomotive

Heat → _____

17 BONUS! Rocket

Chemical → _____

18 Rocket

Heat → _____

19 Opera singing

Sound → _____

20 Solar calculator

Light → _____

21 Solar car

Light → _____

22 Lightning

Electrical → _____

23 Lightning

Electrical → _____

24 Plant facing the sun

Light → _____

25 Telephone

Sound → _____

26 Telephone

Electrical → _____

27 Record player

Mechanical → _____

28 Tea kettle

Heat → _____

29 Thermostat

Heat → _____

30 Microphone

Sound → _____

31 Voice-activated computer

Sound → _____

32 SUPER BONUS! Photosynthesis

Light → Chemical

367

7

More Conversion Diversions!

Here are two more energy conversion activities to think about. After doing each activity, write down the first kind of energy and then write down the kind of energy it was converted into.

YOU WILL NEED:

solar-powered calculator

paper

1 Use a solar-powered calculator to add some numbers.

2 Try covering different amounts of the solar cell with paper. Is there a certain amount that must be uncovered for the calculator to work? What other things might affect how well the calculator works?

ENERGY **BEFORE** CONVERSION

_____

ENERGY **AFTER** CONVERSION

_____

YOU WILL NEED:

radio

wax paper

scissors

salt

1 Place a radio on a table. Cut a square of wax paper about 6 cm x 6 cm. Place the wax paper over the speaker.

2 Sprinkle a few grains of salt on the paper. Turn the radio on and observe the salt. What happens when you change the volume? What does this have to do with the amount of energy converted from one form to another?

PEGGY CORRIGAN

ENERGY **BEFORE** CONVERSION

_____

ENERGY **AFTER** CONVERSION

_____

This unit introduces students to the phenomena of static electricity. Static electricity is based on the structure of the atom. An atom contains tiny positively charged particles called protons in its core and much smaller negatively charged particles called electrons revolving around the outside. In most atoms, the number of protons equals the number of electrons, so the positive and negative charges cancel each other, leaving the atom with no total or overall charge.

When certain materials are rubbed together, some electrons may move from one material and collect on the surface of the other. The material that *gained* the electrons now has more negative charges than positive charges. The material that lost some of its electrons now has more positive charges than negative charges. Since one is now negative and the other positive, the materials attract because opposite charges attract.

Make a Balloon Ec-Static Today! and The Great Electron Rip-Off.

In *Make a Balloon Ec-Static Today!*, the balloon gains some electrons from rubbing it on hair. The balloon now has extra electrons and a negative charge, and the hair has more protons than electrons and a positive charge. The balloon and hair should attract each other because opposite charges attract. When both balloons are rubbed on hair, the balloons each have a negative charge and should repel each other because like charges repel. You can further explore these same concepts in *The Great Electron Rip Off*.

Static Elec-Fish-ity!, Toe Dancing Tinsel, and The Mysterious Moving Ping-Pong Ball

The next three activities are examples of a different property of static electricity. In these activities, only one object is rubbed and charged with static electricity and is then used to attract an uncharged or *neutral* object. In *Static Elec-Fish-ity!* for example, the balloon is given a negative

charge by rubbing it on a garment or on hair. The fish are not rubbed at all and are electrically neutral. When the charged balloon is brought near a fish, the electrons on the balloon's surface repel electrons from the area of the fish that is closet to the balloon. The fish doesn't actually lose electrons; instead, some of its electrons simply move away from the part of the fish that is closest to the negatively charged balloon. This area of the fish now has a positive charge. The positive area of the fish is attracted to the negative balloon and the fish should jump to the balloon. This same principle applies to the activities *Toe Dancing Tinsel!* and *The Mysterious Moving Ping-Pong Ball*.

RELEVANT NATIONAL SCIENCE EDUCATION STANDARDS

The activities in this unit can be used to support the teaching of the following standards:

✔ Science as Inquiry
   Abilities necessary to do scientific inquiry
✔ Physical Science
   Properties and changes of properties in matter
   Transfer of energy
✔ Science in Personal and Social Perspectives
   Natural hazards

MAKE A BALLOON _EC-STATIC_ TODAY!*

RUBBING BALLOONS WITH CERTAIN MATERIALS CAN CAUSE THE BALLOON _AND_ THE MATERIAL TO BECOME CHARGED WITH _STATIC ELECTRICITY!_

You will need

2 round balloons (inflated and tied)
2 20-in pieces of string (approx. 50 cm)
1 wool or acrylic sock (not cotton)

1 Tie a string to each of the balloons. Rub one of the balloons for about 15 seconds on your hair. Be sure to rub around the whole balloon. What happens to your hair? What happens when you bring the balloon back close to your hair?

2 Rub the balloon on your hair again and have your adult partner do the same thing with the other balloon. Hold the strings and let the balloons hang freely but don't let them touch each other or anything else.

3 Slowly move the two balloons toward each other by moving your hand closer to your adult partner's hand. (Do not touch the balloons.) What do you observe? Do the balloons push away from each other or do they pull together?

* All activities in _WonderScience_ have been reviewed for safety by Dr. Jack Breazeale, Dr. Jay Young, and Dr. Patricia Redden.

4 Place your hand between the two hanging balloons. What do you see?

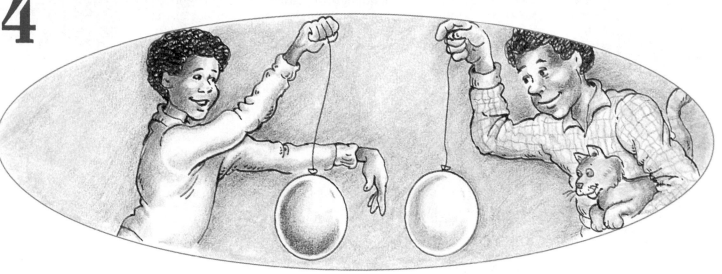

5 Place a sock over one hand and rub one of the balloons with the sock. Let the balloon hang freely. Bring your sock-covered hand near the balloon. What happens?

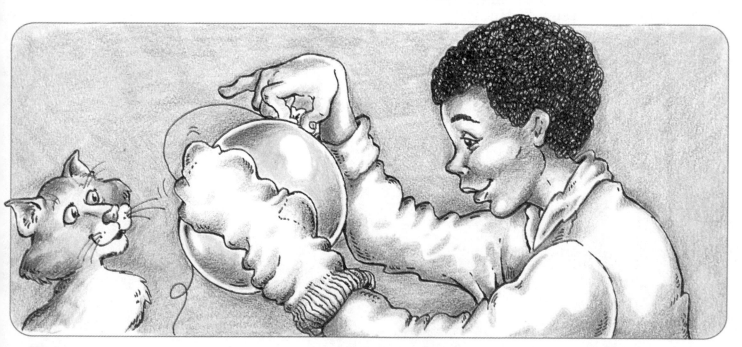

6 What do you think would happen if you rubbed both balloons with the sock and then let them hang near each other? Try it and see! Do the balloons push away from each other or pull together?

Have you ever felt a shock when you reached for a metal doorknob on a cold winter day? Or seen a bolt of lightning flash across the sky? Or noticed that sometimes your clothes stick together when you take them out of the dryer, and crackle when you pull them apart? These things have a lot in common. They are all examples of a special kind of electricity called *static electricity*.

While wearing a pair of hard-soled shoes, try shuffling your feet across a wool or nylon rug on a cool dry day. When you do this, tiny particles called *electrons* are rubbed off the rug and onto you. If you then touch something, especially metal, the electrons will jump from you to the metal. This is the shock that you feel. You may even see a tiny spark and hear a zap!

All materials contain millions of electrons. Electrons are so small that people cannot see them even with the most powerful microscopes. Along with electrons, all things also contain tiny particles called *protons.* Electrons and protons both have electrical charges. Electrons have a *negative* charge and protons have a *positive* charge. Usually, a material has the same number of electrons as protons so the negative and positive charges balance each other.

Sometimes when two materials are rubbed together, the electrons from one material get rubbed onto the other. When this happens, both materials become charged with static electricity. The one that gained electrons will have a negative charge and the one that lost electrons will have a positive charge. Two materials that have *opposite* charges (positive and negative) will move *toward* each other or *attract*. Two materials that have *like* charges (positive and positive *or* negative and negative) will move *away* from each other or *repel*.

In most of the activities in this unit, *Static Electricity*, you will begin by rubbing two different kinds of material together. Remember that when you do this, you are rubbing electrons off one material and onto the other. One material will then have a *positive* charge and the other will have a *negative* charge.

REMEMBER: *OPPOSITE* charges *ATTRACT*.
 LIKE charges *REPEL*.

NOTE: In the pictures on this page of the boy with the doorknob, the girl brushing her hair, and the girl with the clothes dryer, static electricity is pictured as little yellow lightning bolts. The actual flashes from static electricity caused by these activities would be much smaller, thinner, and harder to see.

Illustration by Tina Mion

THE GREAT ELECTRON
— · — RIP-OFF — · —

You will need
2 one-foot pieces of clear plastic tape (approx. 30 cm)

Illustration by Lori Seskin-Newman

1 Stick the length of each piece of tape to a smooth hard kitchen counter top. Allow about 1/2 in (approx. 1.5 cm) of each piece to hang over the end of the counter.

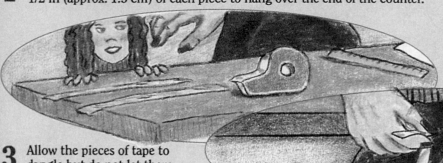

2 In each hand, grab the end of one of the pieces of tape. Quickly rip the pieces of tape off the counter.

3 Allow the pieces of tape to dangle but do not let them touch anything or each other. Slowly bring the pieces of tape near each other. What do you observe? Can you explain why this happens? (The name of this activity should give you a clue!)

4 Try another experiment! Stick one of the pieces of tape to your work surface again. Although tape is sticky, rub the entire length of the other strip of tape by pulling it between your thumb and index finger.

5 Now rip the the first piece from the counter and let the two pieces hang near each other. What happens? Do the pieces attract or repel each other? Do you think the pieces of tape have *like* charges or *opposite* charges?

6 What do you think would happen if both pieces were pulled between your fingers and then hung next to each other? Try it and see!

> OPPOSITE CHARGES _ATTRACT!_ AND LIKE CHARGES _REPEL!_

TOE DANCING TINSEL!

1 Hold the ends of the tinsel strands together in one hand. Trim the bottom of the tinsel so that the strands are all the same length.

2 Rub the meat tray back and forth with the piece of paper to charge the tray with static electricity.

3 Slowly lower the strands of tinsel until their tips just touch the center of the meat tray. Slowly move the tinsel up and down over the tray. What do you observe? How can you explain what you see?

You will need
4 strands of holiday tinsel

1 pressed foam meat tray (clean and dry)

1 piece of notebook or typing paper

blunt end scissors

4 Rub the tray again to recharge it with static electricity. Hold the tray to the side or above the tinsel and see what happens. Move the tray around and see how the tinsel reacts. Try different lengths of tinsel to see what they do!

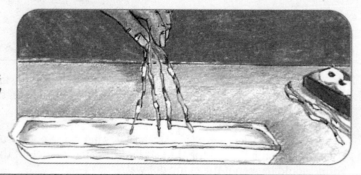

Illustration by Lori Seskin-Newman

THE MYSTERIOUS *MOVING* PING-PONG BALL

1 Place the ping-pong ball on a smooth flat table-top. Run a comb through your hair about 10 or 15 times. Now the comb should be charged with static electricity. (If your hair is too short, you can rub the comb with a piece of wool.)

You will need

one unbreakable or rubber comb
one ping-pong ball
one tape measure

2 Bring the back of the comb near but not touching the side of the ping-pong ball. Slowly move the comb away from the ping-pong ball. Can you get the ping-pong ball to follow the comb across the table? Do you think the ball would follow the comb if you had not run the comb through your hair?

3 See how far you can make the ping-pong ball travel this way. Measure the distance with your tape measure. Have a contest with your adult partner! Using separate combs, see who can make the ping-pong ball go the farthest!

4 If you have two ping-pong balls and two combs, you can have a race! Mark a finish line about 1 yard away from a starting line. Put both ping-pong balls on the starting line.

5 When you say **"GO,"** you and your adult partner should start combing your hair. Quickly use your comb to get your ping-pong ball moving! If your ball stops before the finish line, comb your hair again for some extra static electricity and finish the race!

TRY THIS! Make a *very* thin stream of water come out of your kitchen faucet. Comb your hair a few times and slowly bring the back of the comb toward the thin stream of water (do not let the comb touch the water). What does the water do? What do you think would happen if the comb got wet?

STATIC ELEC-FISH-ITY!

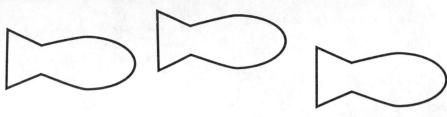

You will need

2 large round balloons,
  inflated and tied
2 18-in pieces of string
  (each approx. 50 cm)
1 sheet of notebook paper
blunt end scissors
pencil
2 rulers or plastic drinking straws
clear plastic tape
wool, wool-blend or cotton
  garment

1 Cut out 30 fish from the note-book paper using the fish above as a model. (Fold the paper so you can cut out more than one fish at a time.)

2 Spread all your fish out on a flat surface such as a table, uncarpeted floor or counter top.

3 Tape one end of a piece of string to the side of a balloon. Tie the other end of the string to a ruler or drinking straw.

4 Your fishing pole should look like this:

5 Holding the fishing pole in one hand and the balloon in the other, rub the untaped side of your balloon against one of your garments or your hair. Your balloon should now be charged with static electricity.

6 Hold your fishing pole and slowly lower your balloon until it is almost touching the fish. See if any fish jump up to your balloon. If no fish come to your balloon, try charging it with some more static electricity. How many fish can you catch?

7 Try pushing one of the fish that are "attached" to the balloon with your finger. As you push the fish along, what does the fish do?

8 *HAVE A FISHING CONTEST!* Make another fishing pole just like your first one. Spread the fish out again. You and your adult partner can charge your balloons by rubbing them on your garments or your hair. When you say *"GO!"* lower both balloons down close to the fish. Whoever catches the most fish, **WINS!**

MAKE A LIGHTNING SAFETY POSTER!

Lightning is a powerful and dangerous kind of electricity. Every year about 2 billion lightning bolts flash across the Earth's skies. The Empire State Building in New York City is struck by lightning at least 30 times each year.

During a storm, clouds and objects on the ground become charged with static electricity. When this happens, electrons can jump from an area that has a negative charge to a positively charged area. This is a bolt of lightning. Lightning can jump between two clouds, between different parts of the same cloud, or from a cloud to the ground. When lightning travels toward the ground, it will usually strike the tallest object around. This is why the Empire State Building has been struck by lightning so many times. That is also why you do not want to be swimming or boating during a storm—**YOU** are probably the tallest object around!

Below is a list of lightning safety rules. Choose one of the rules and draw and color a poster that shows the rule. Write the rule on your poster.

During a lightning storm:
- Do not stand under a tree.
- Do not stand on top of a hill—move to low ground.
- If you are caught outside, lie down.
- Do not swim or go boating.
- Do not use the telephone.
- Do not touch the radio or television.
- Do not use electrical appliances.
- If you are in a car, stay inside with windows and doors shut.

Illustration by Lori-Seskin-Newman

Electric Circuits

This unit focuses on some of the basic principles of electric circuits. The activities have been designed to require only a standard working flashlight, about 2 meters of copper wire that can be purchased cheaply at almost any hardware store, and a few other regular household items such as tape and aluminum foil. Use only the equipment specified and follow the instructions given. Please warn students NOT to try these same activities with any other type of batteries or with electricity supplied from wall or other outlets.

Get It Right and See the Light!

In *Get It Right and See the Light!*, students explore different ways of connecting a battery, bulb, and wires to make a complete circuit. The goal is for students to see the complete path of the circuit. They should be able to understand that the electricity flows from the negative terminal of the battery, through the wire, through the filament of the bulb, and into the positive terminal of the battery. If there is a gap in any part of the circuit, the circuit is not complete and the bulb will not light.

Fabulous Flashlights

In *Fabulous Flashlights*, students examine the circuit in a flashlight. Students should look closely at the contacts made by the batteries both at the bottom of the flashlight and at the bulb. Also, students should carefully note the movement of the metal piece along the inside of the flashlight when the switch is shifted to the "on" position. Students should try to determine the complete circuit in the flashlight when all the necessary components are making contact.

WonderScience Secret Circuits!

In *WonderScience Secret Circuits!*, teachers create a hidden circuit that students try to discover through trial and error using wires, a battery, and a bulb. A related challenge is presented in the second part of the activity where stu-

dents are challenged to connect 3 wires in different ways to create the greatest number of complete circuits when connected to a wire, battery, and bulb.

Another Bright Idea!

Another Bright Idea! was featured in the Inventions Unit but is very instructive when doing activities involving electric circuits. After constructing the flashlight, encourage students to review all the contracts that create the complete electric circuit.

RELEVANT NATIONAL SCIENCE EDUCATION STANDARDS

The activities in this unit can be used to support the teaching of the following standards:

✔ Science as Inquiry
  Abilities necessary to do scientific inquiry

✔ Physical Science
  Properties and changes of properties in matter
  Transfer of energy

✔ Science in Personal and Social Perspectives
  Science and technology in society

GET IT RIGHT AND

All you need to test batteries is some wire and a flashlight bulb. But you have to be sure that the battery, bulb, and wire are arranged in the right way. In the activity below, you will explore different ways of arranging a battery, bulb, and wires to make a working battery tester!

1 The pictures below show some different ways you can arrange a battery, flashlight bulb, and wire. In which of the arrangements do you think the bulb will light? Do you think you can use only one wire to make the bulb light, or do you need two wires?

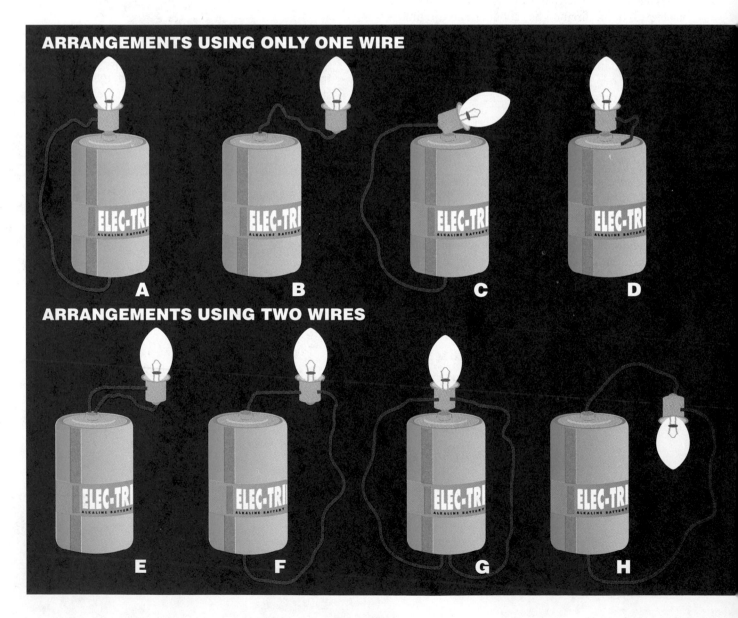

ARRANGEMENTS USING ONLY ONE WIRE

A   B   C   D

ARRANGEMENTS USING TWO WIRES

E   F   G   H

SEE THE LIGHT!

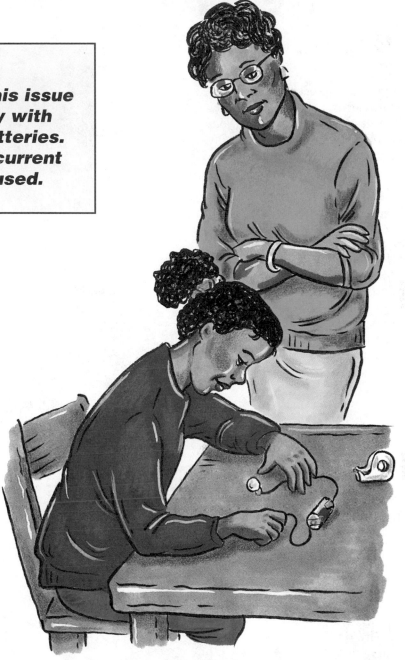

2 Once you have made your predictions, arrange your battery, wire, and bulb in each of the ways shown in the pictures. Remember to use a battery that you know is good. Ask your partner to help you hold the wires and bulb and to use tape where it is helpful. Which of the arrangements worked? How many of your predictions were correct?

3 Look at all the diagrams that worked to light the bulb. Can you find at least three ways all of these arrangements are alike? Turn this page upside down for answers.

ANSWERS: All of the arrangements that worked were alike in the following ways: (1) There was a complete loop for the electricity to travel through. Scientists call this loop an **electric circuit**. (2) There were two special places on the bulb that had to be contacted. One place was on the side of the base of the bulb. The other place was the tip at the bottom of the bulb base. (3) Contact had to be made with both ends of the battery.

The pictures showing arrangements in which the bulb should light are A, C, G, H.

★ All activities in *WonderScience* have been reviewed for safety by Dr. Jack Breazeale, Francis Marion University, Florence, SC and Dr. Jay Young, Chemical Health and Safety Consultant, Silver Spring, MD.

BATTERIES AND BULBS— GET THE CONNECTION?

For electricity to make lights, buzzers, motors, and other electrical devices work, the electricity must travel through the device. In this light bulb, the electricity enters through the bottom of the bulb base, travels through the *filament* of the bulb, and exits through the side of the bulb base. Whenever a light bulb or other electrical device is put in a circuit, there are always two special places that must be connected to the circuit—a place where the electricity enters the electrical device and a place where it exits.

To have a continuous flow of electricity there must be a closed loop, or an electric *circuit*, through which the electricity can travel. Can you trace your finger around the complete path through which the electricity flows in this diagram?

Electricity is the flow or movement of tiny charged particles. The charged particles that move through circuits like the one here are *electrons*

The electricity in this circuit travels through wires made of *copper* as well as through the bulb. Materials like copper, through which electricity can move easily, are called *conductors*. There are other kinds of materials through which electricity cannot easily move.

These are called non-conductors or *insulators*. If the copper wires in this circuit were replaced with plastic fishing line, do you think the bulb would still light? What if they were replaced with strips of aluminum foil?

A battery stores electrical energy. A battery always has two terminals: a *positive* terminal and a *negative* terminal. The terminals are at opposite ends of this battery. When a battery is connected in an electric circuit like the one here, electrons in the circuit move away from the negative terminal of the battery through the wire and bulb and back to the positive terminal of the battery.

ELEC-TRI

ALKALINE BATTERY

FABULOUS FLASHLIGHTS

You will need

standard 2-battery flashlight

blunt-end scissors

pencil

quarter, nickel and penny

paper, aluminum foil, and
plastic wrap

In this activity, you will use a simple flashlight to learn more about electric circuits and to discover different kinds of materials through which electricity can travel.

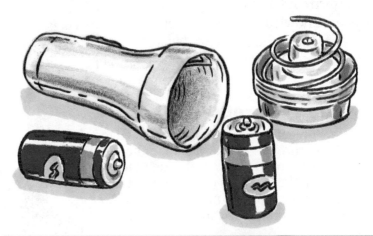

1 Have you ever looked inside a flashlight to figure out how it actually works? Ask your adult partner to help you take your flashlight apart. See whether you can figure out the complete circuit through which the electricity flows to make the bulb light. How do you think the switch works?

2 The electric circuit in your flashlight includes two batteries. Look at one of the batteries. It has a bump on one end, and the other end is flat. These are the **terminals** of the battery. Look carefully and you should find that one terminal is marked **positive** (+) and the other is marked **negative** (–). What kind of terminal is the end of the battery with the bump?

3 Do you think it matters how the two batteries are arranged in your flashlight? Try arranging the batteries in different ways and see whether the flashlight will still work.

4 What do you think will happen if you put the two batteries in the flashlight the correct way, but you put a quarter between them? Do you think the bulb will still light when the flashlight is turned on? Try it and see! Was the electricity able to travel through the quarter? What about a penny or a nickel?

5 With the help of your adult partner, cut circles the size of a quarter out of paper, aluminum foil, and plastic wrap. What happens when you place each of these between the batteries in your flashlight?

6 Separate all the materials you tested into **conductors** and **insulators**. Was the bulb brighter with some conductors than with others?

WonderScience

Get your adult partner to help you make a Secret Circuit Board! Your partner will connect wires to make a hidden pattern underneath the board. You can use your knowledge of electric circuits to figure out where the wires are located without looking under the board!

You will need

piece of cardboard (about 15 cm × 20 cm)

8 brass paper fasteners

pen or pencil

20–26 gauge bare copper wire

flashlight bulb

flashlight battery

tape

blunt-end scissors or wire cutters

Making Your Secret Circuit Board

1 Ask your adult partner to use a pen or pencil to poke 8 small holes through the cardboard in the pattern shown. Place a brass paper fastener through each hole. Open the leaves of the fasteners on the underside of the cardboard to hold them tightly in place. Number the fasteners 1–8 on the top of the cardboard as shown.

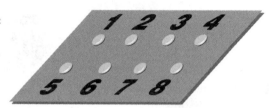

2 Cut three of 18-cm-long pieces from your copper wire. Now close your eyes while your adult partner attaches each wire between two brass fasteners on the underside of the cardboard. (Don't peek!) None of the wires should cross. Your partner should then place the cardboard on your work surface so that you cannot see the pattern of wires underneath.

Making Your Secret Circuit Tester

3 Cut two 25-cm-long pieces from your copper wire. Wrap one end of one wire snugly around the metal bulb casing and twist the wire closed. Securely tape the other end of this wire to the positive terminal of the battery. Tape one end of your other wire to the negative terminal of the battery. This is your Secret Circuit Tester!

Using Your Secret Circuit Tester

4 Touch the free end of the wire from the battery to any brass fastener on the top of your Secret Circuit Board. Then touch the bottom tip of the bulb to any other fastener. The battery, wires, and bulb of the tester must make a complete circuit with the hidden wires in order for the bulb to light. If the bulb lights, there must be one or more wires connecting these two fasteners.

5 Test other pairs of fasteners with your Secret Circuit Tester. Make a drawing of the Secret Circuit Board to record your results. Can you figure out the pattern of the three hidden wires under your secret circuit board?

Secret Circuits!

Note: If your bulb NEVER lights, even when touching two fasteners that are connected,

- check to make sure that your tester wires are securely attached to the battery terminals and to the metal bulb casing.

- check to be sure that the secret circuit wires are securely attached to the brass fasteners.

- make sure that the wires do not accidentally cross and touch each other in the circuit. This could create a short circuit that might cause the electricity to bypass the bulb and/or the Secret Circuit.

- If all else fails, check to see if the bulb is burned out or the battery is dead.

Y ou can use your Secret Circuit Board for another battery and bulb brain challenge!

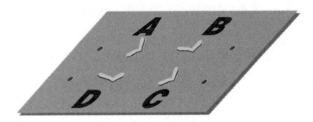

1 Turn your secret circuit board over and take out all the fasteners except for the middle four. Label these four fasteners **A**, **B**, **C**, and **D** as shown.

2 Connect your wires from A to B, then from B to C, and then from C to D. Now you can use your Secret Circuit Tester from page 6 to find out how many different complete circuits you can make with this pattern of wires and your tester.

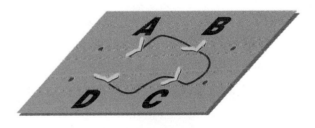

3 Touch the end of the wire to A and the bulb to B. The bulb should light. This is complete circuit A–B. Now touch A and C. The bulb should light again. This is complete circuit A–C. There are four more possible complete circuits, for a total of six, with this pattern of wires on your board. Can you find them?

4 Can you find other patterns of three wires that will also give you six different complete circuits? What are these patterns?

Another Bright Idea!

You will need

flashlight	tape
2 D cell batteries	plastic bottle
aluminum foil	blunt-end scissors
paper	metric ruler
pencil	

You can use a lot of what you have learned about batteries and bulbs to make your own flashlight!

1 Take the batteries and bulb from a flashlight. Tape the two batteries together with the plus and minus ends touching as shown. Lay the batteries on a piece of paper and roll them up in the paper to form a paper tube around the batteries. Tape the tube closed. Trim off the extra paper so that the paper tube is the same length as the batteries.

2 Cut a rectangle of paper that is about 10 cm long and 5 cm wide. Cut off a strip of aluminum foil that is about 5 cm wide and about 30 cm long. Wrap the aluminum foil around the center of the paper until the whole strip of aluminum foil is used up and both sides of the paper are covered with several layers of aluminum foil.

3 Place the paper and aluminum foil on the open end of an empty bottle. Have your adult partner use a sharpened pencil to poke a hole all the way through the aluminum foil and paper. The hole should be the same diameter as the pencil.

4 Push the glass part of the flashlight bulb up through the hole until the aluminum foil is firmly pressed against the metal collar of the bulb base. Hold the bulb so that the bottom tip of the bulb sits on the bump on the top of the battery. Tape the paper and aluminum foil to the sides of the paper tube to hold the bulb in place.

5 Tear off a strip of aluminum foil about 5 cm wide and about 20 cm long. Keep folding it in half lengthwise until you have a long thick wire. Tape one end of the wire firmly to the end of the bottom battery.

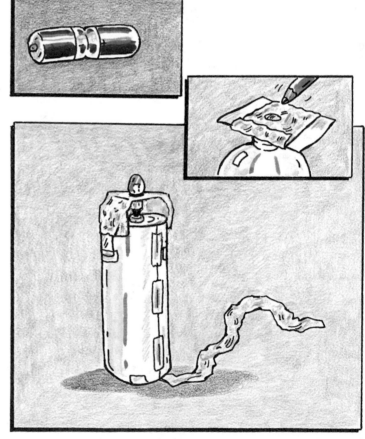

6 Test your homemade flashlight by touching the free end of your aluminum foil wire to the aluminum around the bulb. The bulb should light! If it does not, check to make sure that the aluminum foil is touching the metal part of the bulb, that the bottom of the bulb is touching the top of the battery, and that the aluminum foil wire is firmly attached to the end of the bottom battery.

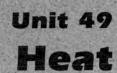
This unit introduces students to some of the physical processes involved when gases and liquids are warmed and cooled. Students will see that both liquids and gases expand and become less dense when warmed and become more dense when cooled.

WonderScience Balloon Bath

WonderScience Balloon Bath shows how the gases in air expand when heated and contract when cooled. Before starting the activity, you should inflate and deflate the balloons several times to make them more flexible. In the activity itself, it is important not to inflate the balloons too much. Be very careful when letting hot water flow onto the balloon. Let the water come out in a slow to medium flow and be sure the water runs away from students' hands after the water hits the balloon. The difference in balloon size due to temperature changes may be only a few millimeters, so accurate measuring is important.

Full of Hot Air

In *Full of Hot Air*, students easily see the balloon inflating and deflating when the air inside the bottle is warmed and cooled, respectively. In the other activity on the page, students see that what appears to be a small amount of warmth from their hands is enough to expand the air inside the bottle. This activity requires patience because it may take a few minutes for the air in the bottle to warm sufficiently and expand enough to lift the inverted cap.

Warm Air Whizzers!

In *Warm Air Whizzers!*, students make a pinwheel-type toy that turns when held over a hot lighted incandescent bulb. Make sure students hold the Whizzer at least 15 cm above the bulb so there is no fire hazard. Be sure that students understand that it is the warm rising air that causes the Whizzer to turn, and not the light.

Up, Up, and Away!

Up, Up, and Away! offers some historical and technical information about hot air balloons. Many students mistakenly believe that a hot air balloon, like a helium balloon, is filled with a special type of gas. They do not realize that the balloon is filled with air that has been heated by a propane gas burner.

A Current Affair

In the top activity in *A Current Affair*, the hot red water will flow upward and the cold blue water will flow downward when the push pins are removed. This is because the hot water is less dense than the surrounding water and the cold water is more dense than the surrounding water. In the activity on the bottom of the page, because the hot red water is less dense, it will stay in the upper jar when the plastic square is removed. When the jars are switched, and cold water is on the top, the result is different. The less dense hot red water rises as the more dense cold water sinks. The result is a complete mixing of the water in the two jars.

RELEVANT NATIONAL SCIENCE EDUCATION STANDARDS

The activities in this unit can be used to support the teaching of the following standards:

✔ **Science as Inquiry**
   Abilities necessary to do scientific inquiry

✔ **Physical Science**
   Properties and changes of properties in matter

✔ **History and Nature of Science**
   History of science

WONDERSCIENCE

Imagine you are blowing up balloons for an outdoor party. You start early in the morning when the temperature outside is still cool. What will happen to the inflated balloons as the temperature rises during the day? What will happen to the balloons that evening as the temperature begins to drop again?
Try this activity to find out what happens when party balloons are heated and cooled!

1 Blow up your balloons and release the air a few times to stretch them out. Now blow up both of your balloons until they are less than half-filled and still very flexible. They should be about the same size. Tie them closed. Use your pen to carefully mark one balloon "hot" and the other "cold."

2 Measure the distance all the way around the fattest part of each balloon with the measuring tape. This is called the *circumference* of the balloon. Record your measurements on the chart below.

3 What do you think will happen if the air inside one of your balloons gets warmer? To find out, have your adult partner turn on the hot water in your kitchen sink.

> **CAUTION:**
> **Hot tap water can
> be very hot.
> Make sure your child's hand
> does not come in
> direct contact
> with the hot tap water.**

4 Hold the balloon by the tied end and let hot water run over it. Move the balloon out of the water and measure its circumference again. Record your measurement on the chart. Was your prediction correct?

Circumference			
	At start	**After water runs over it**	**Back to room temperature**
Hot water			
Cold water			

BALL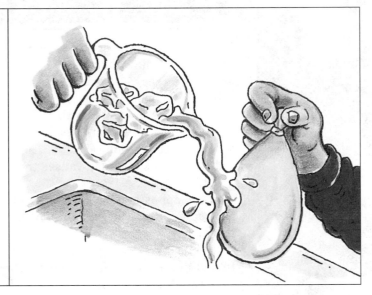N BATH

5 What do you think will happen to your other balloon if you pour cold water over it? Fill a large cup or bowl with ice and water. Hold your balloon by the tied end over the sink. Ask your adult partner to slowly pour cold water over your balloon.

6 Measure the circumference of the balloon and record it on the chart. Was your prediction correct?

7 Put the balloons down for about ten minutes to let them return to room temperature. As the balloons return to room temperature, will their sizes change again? Which one do you think will get bigger and which one do you think will get smaller? Why?

8 When the balloons have returned to room temperature, measure the circumference of each one again. Was your prediction correct?

See what happens to the circumference of your balloon if you put it in a warm sunny spot or inside your refrigerator or freezer!

---

* All activities in *WonderScience* have been reviewed for safety by Dr. Jack Breazeale, Francis Marion University, Florence, SC; Dr. Jay Young, Chemical Health and Safety Consultant, Silver Spring, MD; and Dr. Patricia Redden, Saint Peter's College, Jersey City, NJ.

Warm Up
and
Cool Down

Why does a balloon get bigger when you warm it? To understand this, you have to think about what happens to the air inside the balloon. As you may already know, air (and other matter) is made of tiny particles called molecules that are too small to be seen. These molecules are constantly moving. When air is heated, its molecules gain energy and begin to move faster and spread farther apart from each other. As the air inside the balloon *expands* in this way, it pushes on the inside walls of the balloon and causes the balloon to expand, too.

Just the opposite happens when a balloon is put in a colder place. The molecules of air inside the balloon slow down and the balloon gets smaller or *contracts*.

In addition to expanding or contracting, something else can happen to air when it is heated or cooled. The air may rise or sink! You have probably seen smoke-filled hot air rising from a chimney or a candle, or a huge balloon filled with hot air rising into the sky. As heating causes air molecules to move farther apart, the heated air becomes lighter than an equal volume of cooler air. (Scientists say that the hot air is less dense.) If the heated air is free to move, it will rise above heavier, colder air. If you live in a house with more than one story, you may have noticed that the upper floor is sometimes much warmer than the lower one. This is because warmer air rises while cooler air sinks.

Even in a single room in your house, warmer air rises and cooler air sinks. Imagine that you have a floor furnace in your bedroom. Heated air from the furnace will quickly rise toward the ceiling. As it begins to cool, it becomes heavier and will sink toward the floor to be warmed by the furnace 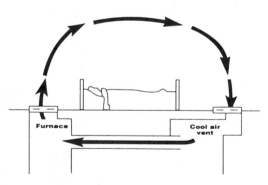 again. At the same time, newly warmed air is already rising toward the ceiling. This pattern of rising hot air and sinking cooler air, called a *convection current*, is shown above.

There are convection currents outside your house as well as inside. Worldwide wind patterns and gentle ocean breezes are both just convection currents caused by the movement of giant warm and cold air masses.

Other gases and liquids can also rise when heated, sink when cooled, and create convection currents for the same reasons that air does. In *A Current Affair*, see for yourself what happens when warmer water meets cooler water!

Full of Hot Air

Here are two quick activities that let you see what happens when air is warmed.

You will need

2 liter plastic soda bottle
large round balloon
hot and cold tap water

1 Attach the end of a balloon onto the opening of your bottle. Hold the bottle near the balloon and let hot tap water run over the end of the bottle as shown. What do you observe? Why does this happen?

2 Switch the water to cold. What did you observe? Is this what you thought would happen?

You will need

empty glass soda bottle
(with plastic twist-off lid)
water

1 Place the bottle on your work surface. Remove the lid and wet the top of the lid with a little water. Place the lid upside down on the top of the bottle. Make sure that it covers the opening completely.

2 Hold the bottle with both hands so that you warm the air in the bottle as much as possible. Do not move the bottle. Watch the lid closely. Be patient, this may take a few minutes. What did you see?

Warm Air Whizzers!

1 Trace the mug or glass onto the manila folder and cut out the disk. Fold the disk in half, then open it up and fold it in half in the other direction. Fold it in half two more times so that the creases look like Figure 1.

Figure 1

2 cm

Figure 2

2 Cut along each of the creases about 2 cm as in Figure 2. Fold the left side of each individual fin down and the right side up so that it looks like Figure 3. You have now created your *WonderScience* Warm Air Whizzer!

Figure 3

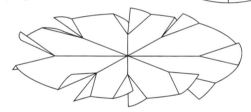

3 Have your adult partner help you use a tack or pencil point to make a small hole in the center of your Whizzer. Put a piece of thread (about 45 cm long) through the hole and tie a knot in the thread so that the Whizzer hangs level at the end.

4 Ask your adult partner to go over to a table lamp with you. Try to choose a lamp that is not near any vents or drafts. Make sure the lamp bulb is turned off and cool. Hold the thread so that the Whizzer hangs over the lamp shade at least 15 cm above the lamp bulb. The Whizzer may spin a little because of twist in the thread, air currents, or your own movements. Wait for the Whizzer to stop spinning.

5 Ask your adult partner to turn the lamp on while you hold the hanging Whizzer. What do you observe? What do you think causes the Whizzer to turn? Can you make the Whizzer spin in the opposite direction? Can you make a Whizzer that spins faster than your first Whizzer? Try it and see!

UP, UP, AND AWAY!

Can you identify the parts of a hot air balloon that are highlighted in the story? Write the name of each part in the blank. Turn the page upside down to check your answers!

Some of the earliest hot air balloons were launched in France in the late 1700's by two brothers, Jacques and Joseph Montgolfier. The Montgolfier brothers began making balloons by filling small paper bags with smoke. They thought the smoke made the bags rise. Later, they discovered that it was the hot air inside the bags that caused them to rise. One of their first large hot air balloons carried a duck, a sheep, and a rooster! The flight was only about eight minutes long and all of the animals landed safely. Soon, people began to take rides in hot air balloons too!

Today, when hot air balloons are launched, the balloon **bag** is first spread evenly over the ground. The **basket** is attached so that it lies on its side facing the balloon. A huge fan is used to blow air into the balloon until it is about half-filled. The pilot then turns on a **propane gas burner** mounted underneath the **mouth** of the balloon. The flame from the burner heats the air inside the balloon. As the air inside the balloon is heated, it expands and begins to fill the balloon. Because the heated air in the balloon is lighter than the same volume of surrounding outside air, the balloon slowly rises off the ground and pulls itself upright. As the burner continues to supply heat, the air inside the balloon becomes so much lighter than the outside air that the entire balloon and its contents lift off! The pilot can make the balloon rise higher by burning more propane fuel. To descend, the pilot can either burn less fuel or pull the **vent cord,** which opens a slit near the top of the balloon. This slit is called the **cooling vent** and it lets some of the hot air escape. After the balloon has safely landed, the pilot pulls the **rip cord.** This opens the circular **rip panel** at the very top of the balloon and causes the balloon to deflate.

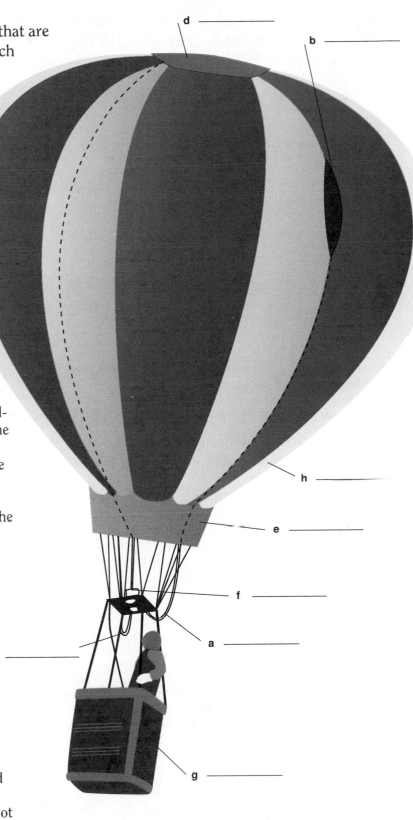

ANSWERS: a. vent cord **b.** cooling vent **c.** rip cord **d.** rip panel **e.** mouth **f.** propane gas burner **g.** basket. **h.** bag

A Current Affair

You will need

2 paper cups (same size)
2 push pins
red and blue food coloring
clear plastic shoebox, aquarium, or bowl
metric ruler
ice
hot and cold tap water

Just as winds are caused by the movements of warm and cold air masses, ocean currents are caused by the movements of warm and cold water. In the activities below, you can see for yourself how streams of warmer or colder water move through the ocean!

1 Pour room temperature water into the large container. This is your "ocean." The depth of your ocean needs to be about 2 cm lower than the height of your cups.

2 Completely fill one cup with ice water and add 8 drops of blue food coloring. Have your adult partner completely fill the other cup with hot tap water. Add 8 drops of red food coloring to the hot water.

3 Insert a push pin into each cup about 1/4 the distance from the bottom. Ask your adult partner to help you carefully lower each cup into your ocean so that the cups sit on the bottom. In which direction do you think the blue and red water will move when the push pins are taken out of the cups?

Warning: Push pins have sharp points. Be careful not to jab your finger.

4 Carefully remove each of the push pins and observe through the side of the container. What happens? (If no colored water comes out of the holes, use one of the push pins to make the holes a little larger.)

See whether you can predict what happens when hot water and cold water meet in the activity below.

You will need

2 identical small, clear, glass jars (baby food jars work well)
hot tap water
ice water
thin stiff plastic square to cover mouth of jar (cut from yogurt or cottage cheese lid)
red food coloring

1 Fill one jar completely to the brim with ice water. (Remove any ice cubes before pouring the water into the jar.) Have your adult partner completely fill the other jar with hot tap water and color the water dark red with several drops of food coloring. Place both jars in a shallow pan to catch any water that may spill.

2 What do you think would happen if you could turn the jar of hot red water upside down on top of the jar of cold clear water without any water spilling? Do you think the clear and colored water would mix or stay separated?

3 Slide the plastic square over the jar of hot water so that there are no air bubbles in the jar. Ask your adult partner to hold the plastic square on the jar and to turn the jar upside down directly on top of the other jar. Make sure the openings of the two jars are perfectly lined up. Then, as your adult partner holds both jars steady, quickly pull out the plastic square! What happens?

4 What do you think would happen if you turned the jar of cold clear water upside down on the jar of hot red water? Try it and see!

Warning: Hot tap water may be very hot.

This unit introduces students to some of the basic properties of magnetism. The fundamentals of magnetism at the atomic level are too abstract for elementary school children but here are some basic concepts you may want to know: The electrons that move around the nucleus of an atom also spin on their own axes. Scientists believe that the direction of spin of an atom's electrons is an important factor in giving the atom its magnetic properties. In the atoms of iron, nickel, cobalt, and a few other materials, the effect of the spinning electrons gives these atoms a net magnetism. When iron, nickel, and cobalt are placed near a magnet, they will be attracted to the magnet because of their own atoms' magnetic properties. Also, when iron, nickel, and cobalt are placed near a strong enough magnet, the atoms in these metals align themselves in such a way that the material itself becomes a magnet.

Electricity and Magnetism— A Powerful Pair!

In *Electricity and Magnetism—A Powerful Pair!*, students make a magnet based on an electric current (electromagnet). Students should notice that the more coils of wire in the electromagnet, the greater the magnetic effect. Students should also see that increasing the current with the extra battery should produce a stronger magnet.

A WonderScience Magnetic Mystery Map!

A WonderScience Magnetic Mystery Map! can be used by students at home to discover which common objects in a kitchen are magnetic. This activity can be easily adapted to the classroom. Students could be asked to draw their own magnetic map of the classroom and to predict what materials are magnetic and then to experiment to verify their predictions.

Magnet-Making Marvels!

In *Magnet-Making Marvels!*, students observe one of the basic laws of magnetism: that when like poles of a magnet are brought near each other, they will repel and that when opposite poles are brought near each other, they will attract.

Magnets Are Amazing, Through and Through!

In *Magnets Are Amazing, Through and Through!*, students observe that magnets attract magnetic materials through gases, liquids, and solids. This activity could be extended by adding more pieces of paper to see how thick the pile could be before the magnet stopped attracting the paper clip.

Pointing the Way...With a WonderScience Compass!

In *Pointing the Way...With a WonderScience Compass!*, students discover that the Earth itself acts like a magnet. There are some difficult concepts regarding the Earth's magnetism which are not discussed in the unit. One is that the *magnetic* poles of the Earth are not exactly at the Earth's *geographic* poles. Another confusing fact is that the Earth's magnetic north pole is near its geographic *south* pole and its magnetic *south* pole is near its geographic *north*.

RELEVANT NATIONAL SCIENCE EDUCATION STANDARDS

The activities in this unit can be used to support the teaching of the following standards:

✔ Science as Inquiry
   Abilities necessary to do scientific inquiry

✔ Physical Science
   Properties and changes of properties in matter

ELECTRICITY AND MAGNETISM— A POWERFUL PAIR!*

You've probably seen a **horseshoe** magnet like this . . .

. . . or a **bar** magnet like this . . . but there is another interesting kind of magnet like the one on the cover called an **electromagnet**. . .

An electromagnet uses electricity to make a magnet!

You will need

2 "D" size batteries
3 meters insulated wire
  (22 gauge or thinner)
blunt-end scissors
3 nails (approx. 5 cm long)
10 metal paper clips
masking tape
metric ruler

1 Ask your adult partner to cut three lengths of wire that are 50 cm (1/2 meter) long, 100 cm (1 meter) long, and 150 cm (1 1/2 meters) long. Also, ask your adult partner to place a small piece of masking tape over the point of each of the three nails.

2 Have your adult partner use the scissors to "strip" about 1 cm of insulation off both ends of all three wires and twist the exposed wire if it is frayed.

3 Coil the 1/2 meter wire around one of the nails. Make sure that the coils are close together and that you leave about 5 or 6 cm of wire uncoiled at the beginning and end of the wire.

4 Repeat step 3 using the other two nails and the other two lengths of wire to make two more electromagnets.

* All activities in *WonderScience* have been reviewed for safety by Dr. Jack Breazeale, Francis Marion College, Florence, SC; Dr. Jay Young, Chemical Health and Safety Consultant, Silver Spring, MD; and Dr. Patricia Redden, Saint Peter's College, Jersey City, NJ.

5 Take your nail with the 1/2 meter of wire and connect the ends of the wire to the battery as shown. You have just made an *electromagnet*! Use the head of the nail to pick up as many paper clips as you can. Record the number you picked up in the chart.

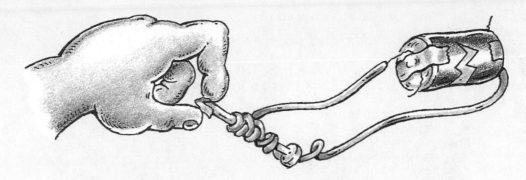

6 While the paper clips are still attached to your electromagnet, disconnect one of the ends of the wire from the battery. What happens?

7 Repeat steps 5 and 6 using the nail with 1 meter of wire and then the nail with 1 1/2 meters of wire. Record the number of paper clips that each was able to lift. Which one was the strongest magnet? Which was the weakest?

8 Tape your two batteries together as shown. Since it is hard to reach from the top of one battery to the bottom of the other, tape one end of the wire to the negative end of the battery (flat end) and hold the other end of the wire to the positive end of the other battery.

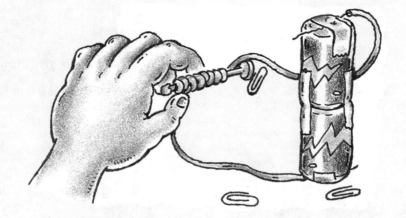

9 See how many paper clips each of your three electromagnets can pick up using two batteries instead of one. Fill in the chart with your results. Did the extra electricity make your electromagnets stronger?

	NUMBER OF PAPER CLIPS	
	ONE BATTERY	**TWO BATTERIES**
1/2 METER WIRE ELECTROMAGNET	S	S
1 METER WIRE ELECTROMAGNET	S	S
1 1/2 METER WIRE ELECTROMAGNET	S	S

MAGNETS: WHAT MAKES THEM SO ATTRACTIVE?

1. Are big magnets always stronger than smaller magnets?
   NO! There can be large magnets that are weak and small magnets that are strong. The size of the magnet, by itself, does *not* control how strong it is.

2. What materials can be made into magnets and what materials are attracted by magnets?
   Most common magnets are made from the metals *iron*, *cobalt*, and *nickel* and some other materials that contain these metals. These are also the most common materials that can be attracted by a magnet, so they are called *magnetic* materials. At very high and very low temperatures, the magnetic qualities of many materials can change! Some common nonmagnetic materials are wood, aluminum, and glass. Can you think of some others?

3. What causes magnetism anyway?
   Scientists believe that magnetism is actually caused by *electric currents*! In *Electricity and Magnetism*, you saw that an electric current in a wire could be used to make a magnet. The *electrons* in the *atoms* of all materials make tiny electric currents. In magnetic material, the electric currents act together in a special way that makes these materials magnetic. **REMEMBER:** Where there is an electric current, there is magnetism!

4. Why do we call the two poles of a magnet the NORTH pole and the SOUTH pole?
   The poles of a magnet are called "north" and "south" because when a magnet is allowed to hang freely, one end will always point to an area near the Earth's **NORTH** pole and the other end will always point to an area near the Earth's **SOUTH** pole. The end that points toward the north is called the **NORTH** pole of the magnet and the end that points toward the south is called the **SOUTH** pole of the magnet. A *compass* needle, which helps you find directions, is actually a small magnet!

5. Is it the Earth that somehow makes a hanging magnet, such as a compass needle, point the way it does?
   YES! The Earth itself is like a huge magnet! Scientists believe that hot liquid material moving deep within the Earth makes electric currents in the Earth's core. They think that these electric currents cause the Earth to act like a magnet with north and south poles. It's the Earth's magnetism that attracts and repels the poles of a hanging magnet, making it point toward the north and south.

6. When the poles of two magnets are brought near each other, what happens?
   If two **NORTH** poles are brought close together, they will move away from each other or *repel*. If two **SOUTH** poles are brought near each other, they will also *repel*. If a **NORTH** pole and a **SOUTH** pole are brought near each other, they will move toward each other or *attract*. **REMEMBER:** The same or *like* poles *repel*; opposite or *unlike* poles *attract*.

7. How do people use magnets?
   Magnets are used in all electric motors and in generators that produce electricity. They also help produce the pictures on television and computer screens. Magnets are used in door bells, car ignitions, tape players, video cassette recorders, record players, microphones, telephones, stereo speakers, electric guitars, and in many other pieces of equipment.

A WonderScience Magnetic Mystery Map!

Magnets are attracted to some types of materials but not to others. You can detect the magnetic materials in your kitchen at home by using your magnet and following your *WonderScience* Magnet Map!

You will need

1 **strong** refrigerator-door magnet

Note: Use a refrigerator magnet that is made from a traditional round, square, or rectangular magnet. Do not use the flat sheet-type magnetic material in this or any of the following activities.

Take your magnet, your map, and your adult partner into your kitchen. Use your magnet to test the objects listed below, to see which ones are magnetic.

After testing each object along the map route, put a check in the box next to the name of the object. Color in the objects that are magnetic and leave the nonmagnetic objects blank. When you are finished, look at your map to see how magnetic your kitchen really is!

☐ **Refrigerator door**	☐ **Plastic wrap and box**	☐ **Metal utensils**
☐ **Refrigerator handle**	☐ **Food cans**	☐ **Glass cup**
☐ **Metal pitcher**	☐ **Aluminum foil and box**	☐ **Screws in tables and chairs**
☐ **Cabinet doors**	☐ **Faucet spout**	☐ **Table and chairs**
☐ **Cabinet hinges**	☐ **Faucet handles**	☐ **Pots and pans**
☐ **Cabinet handles**	☐ **Sink**	☐ **Lids to pots and pans**
☐ **Paper towel dispenser**	☐ **Plate**	☐ **Door knob**

MAGNET-MAKING MARVELS!

You learned that all magnets have two poles. You also learned that if you bring the same or *like* poles from two magnets near each other, they will move apart or *repel*. Also, when you bring opposite or *unlike* poles near each other, they will come together or *attract*. As a *WonderScience* Magnet Maker, you can make your own magnets and even test them to make sure they have opposite poles!

You will need

two paper clips
clear plastic tape
sewing thread (approx. 15 cm)
popsicle stick
1 **strong** refrigerator-door
    magnet

1 Have your adult partner straighten out two paper clips. Wrap a small piece of tape around one end of each of these wires.

2 Slowly rub the magnet down each wire from the taped end to the other end. Do this about 30 times for each wire. **MAKE SURE THAT YOU RUB THE WIRES ONLY IN THIS ONE DIRECTION EACH TIME!**

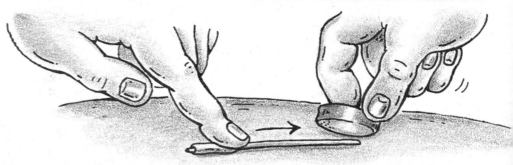

Since you rubbed both wires in the same direction, your two wires should now be magnets, and the taped ends of the magnets should have the same poles. The untaped ends should have the same poles as each other, but opposite from the poles of the taped ends. Let's test them to find out!

3 Tape one of your new magnets to a popsicle stick as shown. Tie a piece of thread around the popsicle stick so that the stick hangs level when held from the other end of the thread. Ask your adult partner to hold the thread.

4 Wait for the popsicle stick to stop moving. Take your other wire magnet and bring its *taped* end near the *taped* end of the hanging magnet. Did the taped ends of the magnets *repel* or *attract*? Does this mean that the taped ends have the *same* poles or *opposite* poles?

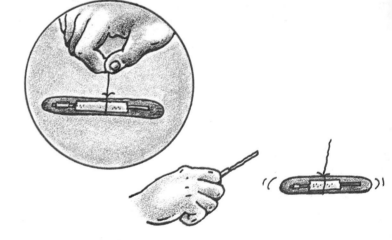

5 Let the hanging magnet stop moving again and then bring the *untaped* end of your magnet near the *untaped* end of the hanging magnet. Did these ends *attract* or *repel*? Are the untaped ends the *same* or *opposite* poles?

6 What do you think will happen if you bring the *taped* end of your magnet near the *untaped* end of the hanging magnet? Try it and see! Did these ends *attract* or *repel*? Are these ends the *same* or *opposite* poles?

MAGNETS ARE AMAZING, THROUGH AND THROUGH!

O ne of the most amazing things about magnetism is that a magnet can often attract magnetic material even when there are certain gases, liquids, and solids between the magnet and the material.

MAGNETISM THROUGH GASES

T he air around us is made of different types of *gases*. You can't see these gases but they are made of very tiny particles called *molecules*. These molecules are made up of even smaller particles called *atoms*. Let's see if your magnet can attract a magnetic material even though gas molecules are in the way!

1 Tie one end of the string to a paper clip. Have your adult partner hold the string while you move the magnet *very slowly* toward the paper clip.

2 As you get closer and closer, think about the gas molecules that are between the paper clip and the magnet. Was your magnet able to attract the paper clip even though gas molecules were in the way?

You will need

strong refrigerator-door
    magnet
two metal paper clips
string (approx. 15 cm)
large bowl
piece of paper
    (approx. 10 cm x 10 cm)
aluminum foil
glass jar or drinking
    glass
popsicle stick
lid from plastic food
    container
uninflated balloon
paper

MAGNETISM THROUGH A LIQUID

A *liquid*, such as water, is also made up of atoms and molecules. In a liquid, the molecules are closer together than they are in a gas. Do you think your magnet will be able to attract the paper clip with water molecules in the way?

1 Fill a large bowl about half full of water. Ask your adult partner to lower the paper clip below the water's surface.

2 Lower your magnet down into the water and move it *slowly* toward the paper clip. Was the magnet able to attract the paper clip even though water molecules were in the way?

MAGNETISM THROUGH A SOLID

A *solid*, such as plastic or wood, is also made of atoms and molecules. These particles are much closer to each other in a solid than they are in a gas or a liquid. Do you think your magnet will be able to attract the paper clip through different solids?

1 Ask your adult partner to hold the string and paper clip again. Hold a piece of paper over the front of your magnet.

2 Slowly move the magnet and paper toward the paper clip. Was your magnet able to attract the paper clip through the solid paper?

3 Try the same experiment with a lid from a jar (metal), a popsicle stick (wood), an uninflated balloon (rubber), the plastic lid to a food container (plastic), and a drinking glass (glass). Was your magnet able to work through all these solids or only through some of them?

Do you think the *thickness* of the solid affects whether magnetism can work through it or not? What experiment can you make up that would help answer this question?

POINTING THE WAY . . . WITH A *WONDERSCIENCE* COMPASS!

You will need
1 12-oz foam cup
1 ***strong*** refrigerator-door magnet
1 metal paper clip
large bowl of water
blunt end scissors
clear plastic tape

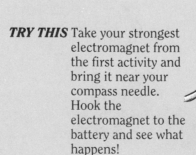

You learned that a compass needle is actually a magnet! You can make your own compass and use it to detect the Earth's ***magnetism***!

1 Ask your adult partner to straighten a paper clip so that it is a straight piece of wire.

2 Hold one end of the wire down with your finger and slowly run your magnet along the wire from your finger to the other end. Do this about 30 times. **BE SURE THAT YOU RUB THE WIRE ONLY IN THIS ONE DIRECTION EACH TIME!** Your wire is now a magnet!

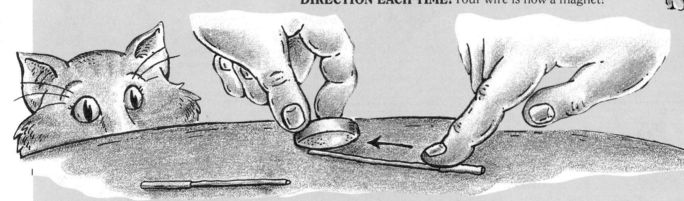

3 Use your scissors to cut the base off your foam cup. Fill the bowl about half full with water. Tape your wire magnet to the cup base and float it in the bowl of water as shown. You have now made a ***compass*** with the magnet as your compass needle! What happens to the needle when you float it in the water?

4 Use two pieces of tape to mark the opposite sides of the bowl where the two ends of the compass needle point. Turn the needle to another direction in the water and let it go. Do the ends of the needle return to point in the same direction as before?

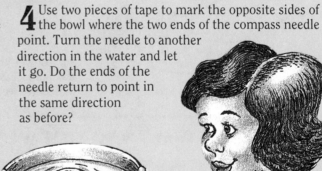

5 Ask your adult partner which end of the needle is pointing north and which end is pointing south. Since your compass needle is a magnet, the end of the needle that points ***north*** is the _____ pole of the magnet and the end of the needle that points ***south*** is the _____ pole of the magnet.

TRY THIS Take your strongest electromagnet from the first activity and bring it near your compass needle. Hook the electromagnet to the battery and see what happens!

6 Take the tape off the bowl and look at something in the room that one end of the needle is pointing at. Carefully pick up the bowl and look down at the needle. ***Slowly*** turn around in a circle while watching the needle. Does the needle keep pointing at that same thing in the room? Try it again to make sure.

WONDERSCIENCE

This unit introduces students to the fundamentals of the concept of force. This is a difficult topic and for the purposes of this unit, force is treated as a push or a pull.

A WonderScience Bubble-O-Meter

In *A WonderScience Bubble-O-Meter*, students observe a small air bubble in a water-filled, 2-liter bottle as the bottle is pulled across a level surface. (If your 2-liter bottle has a dark plastic base, be sure to remove it before starting the activity.) When the bottle is pulled across a level surface, there are two forces acting on the bottle that affect the bubble's behavior. One, obviously, is the force exerted by the person pulling on the bottle. As the bottle slides across the table, there is also the force of friction acting in the opposite direction. What happens to the bottle, and also to the bubble, depends on how the sizes of these two opposing forces compare. You can tell whether the two forces are balanced (the same size) or unbalanced by watching the air bubble and referring to the chart at the bottom of the activity. Be sure to watch the bubble carefully, especially as the bottle slows down, because the bubble can very suddenly change its position or the direction in which it is moving.

You will notice that the term *friction* is not used in the Bubble-O-Meter activity. In deciding whether you should use it in your own discussions about the activity, consider the developmental level of your child or student. It is probably best to not use it at this point unless a child asks a question that cannot simply and honestly be answered otherwise.

May The Force Be With You

May The Force Be With You illustrates that almost any action that involves a force can be described in terms of a push or a pull.

Science Friction

In *Science Friction*, students should begin to understand that whenever an object rolls or slides across a surface, there is a force called friction that causes the moving object to slow down and stop. The amount of friction depends on (among other things) the kind of surface across which the object moves. Generally, if the surface is rough, then the friction force is stronger and the moving object will be brought to rest more quickly.

Gravity: It Can Really Get You Down

Gravity, the attractive force between the Earth and objects at or near the Earth's surface, is explored in *Gravity: It Can Really Get You Down*. Instructions are provided for making a simple instrument to measure the force of attraction between the Earth and small items such as pennies, dried beans, etc. The amount of stretch of the rubber band indicates the size of the Earth's attractive force for whatever is in the cup. It is also a measure of the weight of the items in the cup, although this idea is not introduced in the activity.

The Great Tablecloth Trick!

The Great Tablecloth Trick! shows students what can happen, or not happen, when a force suddenly acts on an object under a certain situation. The idea of inertia is introduced, and is defined as the tendency of objects at rest to remain at rest. (It is also the tendency of objects in motion to remain in the same state of motion.)

RELEVANT NATIONAL SCIENCE EDUCATION STANDARDS

The activities in this unit can be used to support the teaching of the following standards:

✔ Science as Inquiry
  Abilities necessary to do scientific inquiry

✔ Physical Science
  Motions and forces

✔ Earth and Space Science
  Earth in the solar system

A WonderScience Bubble–O–Meter

Imagine you are standing still, minding your own business, when a friend grabs your right hand and starts pulling you to the right. At the same time, another friend grabs your left hand and starts tugging you to the left. Can you feel the forces on you? You bet! What happens to you? Well, that depends on how hard each friend is pulling. If the two friends are pulling with the same strength, you won't move at all! This is because the forces on you are **balanced** forces. But if one friend is pulling harder than the other, then there is an **unbalanced** force on you, and you will be pulled toward the friend who is pulling harder. In the activity below, you can make your own WonderScience Bubble-O-Meter to study balanced and unbalanced forces!

You will need

2-liter clear plastic soda bottle with cap (Adult partner should remove any dark plastic bottom)

sheet of white paper

pen or pencil

transparent tape

metric ruler

2 drops of food coloring (optional)

1 Fill the bottle with water so that when it is capped and turned on its side you see only a small air bubble (about the size of a nickel). If there is more than one bubble, tap on the side of the bottle until they join into a single bubble. You may add a drop or two of food coloring to the water to make the bubble more visible.

2 Lay the bottle on its side on a level surface like a table or counter. Tap on the bottle until the air bubble comes to rest.

3 Cut a strip of paper about 2 cm wide and 25 cm long. Draw marks, one centimeter apart, along the edge of the strip.

4 Tape the paper strip to the side of your bottle, making sure that the air bubble is directly above one of the marks. Label this mark 0. (This may or may not be in the center of the bottle.) Number the other marks in both directions.

5 You have just made a Bubble-O-Meter! You can use it to detect unbalanced forces on the Bubble-O-Meter bottle as you pull it across the table. It will also show you the direction and size of any unbalanced force you find! See the box "How to Read Your Bubble-O-Meter."

6 Lay your Bubble-O-Meter on a flat surface. Make sure it is level and that the air bubble is on the zero mark. What do you think will happen to the air bubble if you pull the bottle to the right? Try it and see! What is the largest number the bubble reaches on your Bubble-O-Meter force scale?

7 Find out what happens if you pull the bottle to the right more quickly than before. How does the maximum reading on the force scale change?

8 Try slowly pulling the bottle across a smooth level surface at a constant speed (without slowing down or speeding up as you pull it). Which of the pictures in the chart below shows the position of your bubble?

9 Observe the air bubble as the bottle slows to a stop. In what direction does the bubble move? Does it cross the zero mark?

10 Have your adult partner hold the Bubble-O-Meter horizontally, making sure the bubble is over the zero mark. What do you think the bubble will do if your adult partner spins around in a circle? Try it and find out!

11 If you have a bicycle, you might have your adult partner help you mount your Bubble-O-Meter on the bicycle so that you can study the forces acting on it when you walk your bike forward or backward. How can you use your Bubble-O-Meter to tell when you are walking your bike with a constant speed?

HOW TO READ YOUR BUBBLE-O-METER

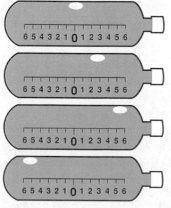

NO UNBALANCED FORCE.
(There may be forces present but they balance one another, so the result is the same as no force at all.)

UNBALANCED FORCE PUSHING OR PULLING TO THE RIGHT.

LARGER UNBALANCED FORCE PUSHING OR PULLING TO THE RIGHT.

UNBALANCED FORCE PUSHING OR PULLING TO THE LEFT.

Remember: Make sure your Bubble-O-Meter lies level on its side when you use it. When it is not moving, the air bubble should always be directly above the zero mark.

All activities in *WonderScience* have been reviewed for safety by Dr. Jack Breazeale, Francis Marion College, Florence, SC; Dr. Jay Young, Chemical Health and Safety Consultant, Silver Spring, MD; and Dr. Patricia Redden, Saint Peter's College, Jersey City, NJ.

FORCES

Force describes an action, or really an interaction, between two things like between a bat and a ball or between a first baseman's hand and a runner's jersey. **Forces are interactions between two things!**

Some people define a force as a *push* or a *pull*. If you think about it, you can't have a push (or a pull) without two things being involved—one thing being pushed and the other thing doing the pushing. Your finger pushes a doorbell, moving air pushes against the sail of a boat, the North pole of one magnet pushes away the North pole of another magnet, a small child pulls a toy wagon, a dropped handkerchief is pulled toward the Earth. All of these are examples of interactions between two things.

There are several different kinds of interactions, or forces. Two kinds of interactions you will learn about in your new WonderScience are *friction* and *gravity*

Whenever two materials rub against one another, there is a force between them called *friction*. There is friction when the tires of a speeding car rub against the road, when a towel rubs against your wet skin, when air rubs against a falling apple, and when water rubs against a swimming fish. You can feel the difference in the amount of friction when you wave your hand through the air compared to when you move it through water or thick mud. Sometimes friction is undesirable because it slows things down or makes things more difficult to move. At other times, friction is very helpful! It helps start things moving and is also used to make things stop moving. In "**Science Friction**" you can compare the amount of friction between a marble and different materials.

What happens if your math book accidentally slips out of your hands? It will drop to the ground, of course! All objects on or near the surface of the earth are pulled toward the earth. This attraction is called *gravity*. Because of gravity, when you jump up you come back down, water always flows downhill, and balls that are dropped or even pitched forward will fall to the ground. Learn more about the interaction of different objects with the earth in "**Gravity: It Can Really Get You Down!**"

Forces are an important part of our everyday life. They push and pull on us and on all of the objects around us. What happens when a force pushes or pulls on an object, such as a car? Well, it depends on whether or not there are other forces present, such as friction and gravity. If all the forces on the car balance one another, you probably won't see anything different about the car or the way it moves. But an unbalanced force will cause the car either to start moving, to move faster, to change direction, or to slow down and even stop. In "**A WonderScience Bubble-O-Meter**," anytime you made the bottle speed up or slow down or turn around, your scale should have indicated there was an unbalanced force on it.

Scientists often use arrows to represent forces. The **length** of the arrow shows the size of the force. A longer arrow means a stronger force. The **direction** that the arrow points shows the direction in which the force is pushing or pulling on an object. Look at the arrows on this page. Which one represents the strongest force? Which shows balanced forces?

FORCES

May The FORCE Be With You

L ook at the pictures below. Each shows an interaction between two things. See if you can use the word "pushes" or "pulls" in a sentence to tell what is happening in each picture. Then think of a more creative **FORCE WORD** (like the ones we used on the cover) which better describes what is happening. Write this word in the blank. Check your answer by seeing if you can use it to replace the word "pushes" or "pulls" in your sentence.

_____

_____

_____

On a blank sheet of paper draw your own pictures to show examples of interactions, or forces, that may be described by the following words: Stretch, Crush, Bang, Shove, Bounce.

SCIENCE FRICTION

1 Find a long flat surface like a smooth floor or long counter top. Make an inclined track by leaning two rulers next to each other on a book as shown below. Be sure there is plenty of flat space at the end of the track.

2 Place the length of wax paper at the end of the track. Release a marble (don't push it!) from a point near the top of the track and watch as it rolls down the track and along the wax paper. How did the speed of the marble change as it rolled across the wax paper? How far did it go?

3 Measure the distance from the bottom of the track to the place where the marble stopped, and write it in the chart. Roll the marble down the track two more times, measuring the distance the marble travels each time. Be sure to release the marble from the same place each time. Write your measurements in the chart.

4 Add your distance measurements together and divide this answer by three to find the *average* distance the marble rolled. When scientists do experiments, they always make several measurements like this and then average their results. Why is it a good idea to do this?

You will need

two rulers

yardstick, meter stick, or measuring tape

one marble

book (about 3-4 cm thick)

wax paper, about 60 cm long

several sandpaper sheets taped together. about 30 cm long

bath towel

aluminum foil, about 30 cm long

5 Do you think the distance the marble travels will change if you replace the wax paper with a towel? Try it and see! Repeat three times, writing down and averaging your distance measurements like you did before. What is the name of the force that stops the marble? All forces have a direction. What is the direction of this force?

6 Try placing other materials such as sandpaper or some aluminum foil that has been crumpled and then flattened out at the end of the track. With which material is the force of friction the greatest?

NAME OF MATERIAL	TRIAL 1	TRIAL 2	TRIAL 3	AVERAGE
Wax Paper				
Aluminum Foil				
Sandpaper				
Towel				

GRAVITY

1 Cover the outside of your box lid with white paper. Use a ruler to draw a straight line on the paper down the center length of the lid. Ask your adult partner to use a small nail to punch a hole near one end of the lid on the line you have just drawn.

2 Cut a rubber band open and tie one end to the middle of a paper clip. Thread the other end of the rubber band through the back of the lid so that the rubber band sticks out the front. (The paper clip will keep the rubber band in place.) Tape the lid securely on the box. Tie another paper clip to the end of the rubber band.

3 Have your adult partner poke three holes directly below the lip of the cup and spaced about equal distances apart. Thread each of three pieces of string through the holes in the cup and pull through and tie a knot in each. Place tape over the holes to keep them from tearing.

4 Hold the ends of the three strings together and tie them to the end of another piece of string as shown. Tie the end of this string to the paper clip. Have your adult partner hold the box so the cup hangs freely. Place a mark on the center line of the box lid right where the bottom of the paper clip is, and write the number zero next to it.

5 Use your ruler to make marks one centimeter apart below the zero mark. Number your marks. You have just made a force scale! You can use it to measure the *gravitational* pull between the Earth and anything you put in the cup.

6 Have your adult partner hold the box while you put five pennies in the cup. To read your force scale, look at the number beside the bottom of the paper clip. What is it? How many pennies do you think you need to put in the cup to make the gravitational force twice as large? Try it!

7 Guess how many dried beans you would need to put in the cup to get the same reading as you did for five pennies. Try it and find out!

8 Place 10–15 pennies in the cup. Have your adult partner hold the box in the air and drop it as you watch the force scale reading. What is the reading on the scale as the box falls? Can you explain this?

You will need

shoe box with lid	2 metal paper clips
white paper	rubber band (medium size)
tape	string
small nail	paper or plastic cup, 9 oz.
blunt-tip scissors	10-15 pennies
ruler	30 dried beans
pen or fine-line marker	

THE GREAT TABLECLOTH TRICK!

Have you ever seen a magician pull a tablecloth out from under a set of dishes? There is really no trick to it. The magician is just using a little physics to fool the audience! You see, the magician knows that the dishes will tend to remain in place when the tablecloth is quickly jerked away. This tendency of dishes and other objects to remain at rest, even when there is suddenly a brief force on them, is called *inertia*. Find out about inertia in the great tablecloth trick below!

You will need

unbreakable plastic cup or small bowl with smooth bottom

metal washers, coins or other small heavy objects

sheet of plain white paper

table or counter with smooth surface

1 Lay the paper on the table so that about 5 cm extends from the table edge. This is your tablecloth.

2 Examine the bottom of your unbreakable cup or bowl to make sure it doesn't have any rough edges. If it looks okay, fill it at least half-full with washers, coins, or other heavy objects. Then place it in the center of the sheet of paper.

3 Using both hands, grab the edge of the sheet of paper that hangs over the end of the table. Quickly, without hesitating or stopping, jerk the paper downward and out from under your dish!

4 Try repeating the stunt with an empty cup or bowl. Does it work as well?

5 Magicians often put food on the plates and water in the glasses when they do the tablecloth trick. Do you think this makes the trick easier or harder to perform? Why?

WONDERSCIENCE

This unit introduces students to some of the basic principles of air pressure. We live at the bottom of an ocean of air called the Earth's atmosphere. Since gravity pulls down on the atmosphere, air near the Earth's surface is "squashed" by the weight of all of the air above it. This means that there are actually more molecules in the air at sea level then there are just one mile above sea level, and a lot more than there are at the top of a high mountain. At any point in a column of air, the motion of the molecules at that point causes what we call air pressure. Since molecules move in all directions, the air pressure at any point is considered to be equal in all directions. Whenever there is a *difference* in air pressure between two places, the air will tend to move from a place of higher pressure to a place of lower pressure.

There's Air in There!

There's Air in There! features several examples of air pressure phenomena: In Steps 1-4, water does not enter the inverted soda bottle because the bottle is already occupied by air. Poking a hole in the side of the bottle allows the air inside, which is under pressure due to the water around it, to flow outside the bottle, where the pressure is lower. As air leaves, water can enter. If water enters the bottle very slowly, the hole should be made a little larger.

In Step 5, the air pressure on the water at the top of the bottle pushes the water out of the hole in the side. When the bottle is capped, air can no longer press on the water's surface, and the water stops coming out. When students stretch a balloon across the mouth of the bottle, and uncover the hole, water will come out and air will leave the balloon. As water pours out of the bottle, no outside air can come in to replace it. This causes the air pressure in the space between the balloon and the water surface to be lowered. Since the outside air pressure is now higher than the inside, air can push the balloon into the bottle.

Air Pressure Rules!

Air Pressure Rules! offers several important ideas about air pressure, along with corresponding activities. These concepts are ones that can be applied in other activities in the unit.

The Ins and Outs of Air Pressure!

In *The Ins and Outs of Air Pressure!*, the plastic liner cannot be lifted out of the trash can (unless there is an air leak). The bag has air in it and above it but very little air below it to equalize the pressure. This large air pressure difference makes it very difficult to pull the bag out of the can. In the second activity, instead of going into the bottle, the piece of paper will fly out. Blowing increases the air pressure inside the bottle. Because pressure always equalizes when it can, air rushes out of the bottle and carries the paper with it.

The Difference Makes the Difference!

In *The Difference Makes the Difference!*, you may want to minimize the number of bottles needed by dividing students into groups or having them rotate through activity centers. If students work in groups, each group might be assigned one type of bottle (A, B, or C) and then share their results.

Take the Plunge!

In *Take the Plunge!*, students discover that the way a plunger works is related to the trash can liner activity. Pushing the plunger down forces air out from beneath it. This creates a large air pressure difference between the inside and outside of the plunger, making it very difficult to lift. In the second part of the activity, if the two plungers don't hold together well, try wetting their rims with water.

Toying Around With Air Pressure

In *Toying Around With Air Pressure*, students make an air pressure-powered rocket and try to find ways to make it go as far as possible. Students can try changing the size, shape or weight of the paper cone, the length or diameter of the straw, or the size or shape of the plastic soda bottle.

RELEVANT NATIONAL SCIENCE EDUCATION STANDARDS

The activities in this unit can be used to support the teaching of the following standards:

✔ Science as Inquiry
   Abilities necessary to do scientific inquiry

✔ History and Nature of Science
   Nature of science

There's Air in There!

YOU WILL NEED:

2 identical empty clear plastic soda bottles (with screw-on caps)

push pin

water

clear deep container for water (aquarium, sink)

balloon

pencil

Although you can't see it and normally can't feel it, air pressure affects us every day, all day long, and in many different ways. The air is made up of zillions of atoms and molecules moving around in every direction and constantly bumping into everything around them. There are so many of these little particles bashing into things so often that they end up pressing on things pretty hard. That's air pressure. In the activities that follow, you will see some surprising things about air pressure!

Do this activity with a partner.

1 Remove the cap from one of the bottles and place the open bottle upside down in your large container of water. Push the bottle down about 8–10 cm. Don't let the water in the large container overflow.

2 Look closely at the mouth of the bottle. Did any water enter the bottle? What do you think is keeping more water from entering the bottle? Tilt the bottle to the side to allow some air to escape. What happened to the level of the water inside the bottle?

3 Use your push pin to carefully poke a hole in the side of the bottle near the bottom as shown. Place the bottle upside down in the water again. What do you observe about the level of water in the bottle now?

4 If you want to observe the process again, empty the bottle into the large container. Cover the hole with your finger and place the bottle upside down in the water again. Take your finger off the hole and observe the water level in the bottle.

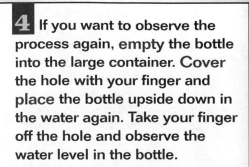

5 Working on the counter at the edge of your sink, **fill** the bottle with water and **observe** the water coming out of the hole into the sink in a thin stream. After a few seconds, **cover** the mouth of the bottle with the palm of your hand. What happened to the water coming out of the hole?

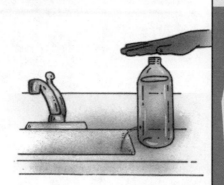

6 Screw on the bottle cap. **Hold** the bottle sideways with the hole facing down. Does the water still stay in the bottle? Stand the bottle upright again. **Loosen** the cap a little. What do you observe? **Tighten** the cap again.

7 Remove the cap and **place** a balloon over the opening of the bottle. Does the water come out of the hole with the balloon on the bottle? Describe what happens to the balloon as the water comes out. What does the balloon look like when the water stops?

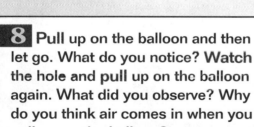

8 **Pull** up on the balloon and then let go. What do you notice? **Watch** the hole and **pull** up on the balloon again. What did you observe? Why do you think air comes in when you pull up on the balloon?

9 Use a pencil to **make** your pin hole the same diameter as your pencil. **Put** your finger over the hole and fill the bottle with water. Your partner should **fill** the other bottle with water. When you say "go," take your finger off the hole while you each turn your bottle upside-down. Which one empties first?

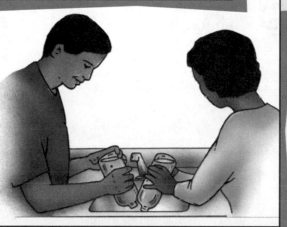

Try this!

10 Try steps 5 and 6 again to see what happens now that your bottle has a larger hole!

Air Pressure Rules!

YOU WILL NEED:

bucket

cup

paper towel

cardboard (smooth piece)

balloon

Air takes up space.

Place a wad of paper towel in the bottom of a glass. Turn the glass upside down and push it straight down into a deep bowl of water. The paper towel stays dry. Water cannot fill the glass because it is already filled with air. But, if you tilt the glass, some of the air will escape and water can then enter.

Air pushes on things in all directions.

Fill a glass to the rim with water. Place a square of cardboard over the the glass, making sure there are no air bubbles trapped inside. Holding the card in place, turn the glass upside down over a sink or bowl. Take your hand off the card. Air pushing up keeps the card and water in place. Because air pushes in all directions, you can even turn the glass sideways and the water won't pour out.

When air is squashed or compressed, its pressure increases.

When a pump is used to inflate a tire, a lot of air is squashed into the small amount of space inside the tire. The air pressure inside the tires of a car is strong enough to hold up the entire car and the people and things inside it!

Air always tries to move from a place of higher pressure to a place of lower pressure.

Blow up a balloon and hold it shut. The pressure of the compressed air inside the balloon is greater than the pressure of the air outside. Let go of the balloon, and the air will rush out.

ILLUSTRATIONS BY LOEL BARR

The **ins** and **outs** of air pressure!

When used in different ways, air pressure can keep some things in and other things out. In the first activity below, see how air pressure keeps something in when you think it should come out. In the second activity, see how air pressure can keep something out when you think it should go in!

1 Place the plastic liner inside the trash can. Fold the top of the liner over the can as shown. Press all around the inside of the liner so that you push as much air as possible out from between the can and the liner.

2 Use a piece of string to tie the top of the liner tightly against the can under the lip of the rim.

3 Reach into the can and grab the center of the bottom of the bag. Try to pull the trash can liner straight up out of the bag. Can you do it?

4 Have a partner hold the trash can sideways or upside down. Try to pull the bag out. Is it any easier?

YOU WILL NEED:

kitchen or classroom
plastic trash can
(with lip around upper edge)

clean plastic trash can liner
(with no holes)

string

YOU WILL NEED:

glass soda bottle (with narrow neck)

small piece of paper napkin
(or tissue)

What's going on here?

1 Cut or tear the piece of tissue paper so that it is slightly larger than the opening of the bottle. Place the piece of paper on the opening.

2 Try to blow the paper into the bottle! What happens? Why do you think its so difficult?

3 Give yourself a little head start by pushing the paper partially into the bottle as shown. Try blowing it in again.

413

The *Difference* makes the Difference!

Air will flow from an area of high air pressure to an area of lower air pressure. It is this difference in air pressure that causes air to move. For air pressure, it's the difference that makes the difference!

In the activity below, see how many ways you and your partners can use air pressure to inflate or deflate the balloons in the bottles. You might want to blow into the bottles, squeeze the bottles, and use other parts of the bottles in different ways. Be creative!

Teacher preparation:

1 Blow up the balloons a few times to stretch them out. Place each balloon inside a plastic bottle and stretch the opening of the balloon over the mouth of the bottle as shown. Use the masking tape to label the bottles **A, B,** and **C**. Do nothing else to bottle A.

2 Carefully use a push pin to poke a hole in bottle B. Use a pencil to make the hole the same diameter as the pencil. Do nothing more to bottle B.

3 Carefully use scissors to cut off the bottom of bottle C. Cover the cut edge with masking tape. Cut the top off the fourth balloon. Stretch the balloon over the bottom of the bottle and secure it with masking tape. Do nothing else to bottle C.

Student activity:

Inflate the balloon

How many different ways can you and your partners think of to inflate the balloons either inside or outside the bottles? Have one person inflate the balloon and one person write down how it was inflated.

Deflate the balloon

How many different ways can you and your partners think of to deflate the balloons? You should record your results as you did before.

Take the Plunge!

1
Press a plunger straight down on the floor until it sticks. Try lifting the plunger. Is it hard to lift? What do you think this has to do with air pressure?

2
If you can't pick up the plunger, push a spoon against the rubber edge to pry it loose. What does the spoon do that allows the plunger to be moved?

3
Try pushing the plunger down on different surfaces. Why does it work better on smoother surfaces?

4
Wet the rims of both of the plungers and press them together. Have a person hold the handle of each plunger and try to pull them straight apart.

If you think the plungers are hard to separate, read the true story below!

In 1654 in Magdeburg, Germany, a scientist named Otto von Guericke did an amazing demonstration to show everyone how hard air pushes on things. He took two copper hemispheres which together formed a sphere about 35 cm in diameter. He ground their rims very smooth and covered them with grease.

He put the two rims together and used a vacuum pump to remove the air inside. The air pressure on the outside was so great that two teams of horses were unable to pull the hemispheres apart.

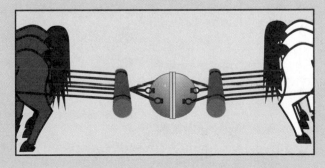

TOYING AROUND

WITH AIR PRESSURE

You can make a fun toy using air pressure. Earlier, you learned that air can be compressed and that as air is compressed, it has a higher and higher pressure. You also learned that air will always move from an area of high pressure to an area of lower pressure. You can use these two air pressure facts to make an air pressure rocket!

YOU WILL NEED:

cotton swab

paper

blunt-end scissors

tape

straw

empty plastic soda bottle

1 Cut a circle about 4 cm in diameter from your paper. Cut a slit to the center as shown then shape into a cone. Trim the point to make a small hole at the top.

ILLUSTRATIONS BY ROD LITTLE

2 Pull off the cotton from one end of a cotton swab. Push the cotton on the other end of the swab up through the hole so that the cone stays on the swab snugly. This is your **air pressure rocket**.

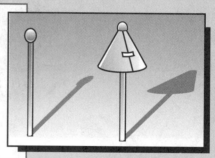

Caution: Be sure to point the rocket away from yourself and anyone else.

3 Place a straw into the empty bottle and hold it in place. Use the same hand to seal the opening of the bottle as much as possible. Place the rocket into the straw.

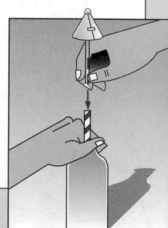

4 Point your rocket away from your face and away from any one else. Give the bottle a hard squeeze. Your rocket should zoom!

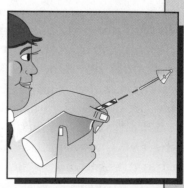

Challenge

Try using a different bottle, straw set-up, or rocket design to create an air pressure rocket that goes the farthest!

This unit introduces students to a branch of physics called *aerodynamics*. Although most of the unit concerns the application of aerodynamics to airplanes, the science actually relates to the effect that air has on any moving object including, for example, cars, boats, footballs, skiers, and skateboards.

Welcome to WonderScience Flight School

In *Welcome to WonderScience Flight School,* make sure the activity is done in an open area so that the balsa wood plane will not crash into any walls or other objects. Groups of students should work with each plane. Groups can compete against each other for flight accuracy, distance, and maneuverability.

Take a Whirl with a Wonderwhirler!

In *Take a Whirl with a Wonderwhirler!*, students are asked to discover a way to make the whirler spin in the opposite direction. The way to do it is to bend the two blades in the opposite direction from the way shown in the activity.

3...2...1...Lift Off!

3...2...1...Lift Off! has a long set of instructions but is not very difficult to understand. The most important part is to be sure that the weight on the back straw almost exactly balances the weight of the plane so that the slightest pushing up on the plane will make it lift off the table.

The Return of the Boomerang

The Return of the Boomerang includes a little history and culture from Australia. You might want to show students a map of the world and let them find Australia and determine whether it is easier to go east or west to get there from the United States.

RELEVANT NATIONAL SCIENCE EDUCATION STANDARDS

The activities in this unit can be used to support the teaching of the following standards:

✔ **Science as Inquiry**
 Abilities necessary to do scientific inquiry

✔ **Physical Science**
 Motions and forces

✔ **Science in Personal and Social Perspectives**
 Science and technology in society

✔ **History and Nature of Science**
 Science as a human endeavor

WELCOME TO WONDERSCIENCE FLIGHT SCHOOL *

One of the areas in which the science of *aerodynamics* is important is in making and flying airplanes. You can learn how air affects the flight of an airplane by entering—*WonderScience* **Flight School!**

Step up and learn to pilot your very own *WonderScience* plane. Master stunts like dives, loop-the-loops, and curls! Test your accuracy and distance but most of all have a **GREAT FLIGHT!**

You will need

1 small balsa wood plane (without propeller)
2 index cards
metric ruler
blunt-end scissors
white school glue
clear plastic tape

1 Cut five small rectangles from the index card. Each rectangle should be about 5 cm long and about 3 cm wide. These are your airplane flaps.

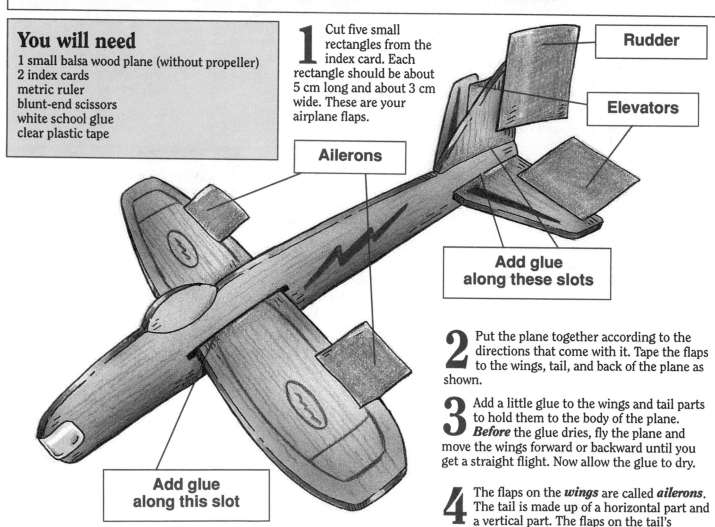

Rudder

Elevators

Ailerons

Add glue along these slots

Add glue along this slot

2 Put the plane together according to the directions that come with it. Tape the flaps to the wings, tail, and back of the plane as shown.

3 Add a little glue to the wings and tail parts to hold them to the body of the plane. *Before* the glue dries, fly the plane and move the wings forward or backward until you get a straight flight. Now allow the glue to dry.

4 The flaps on the *wings* are called *ailerons*. The tail is made up of a horizontal part and a vertical part. The flaps on the tail's **horizontal section** are called *elevators* and the flap on the **vertical section** is called a *rudder*.

5 Bend the *right* aileron *up* and see how the plane flies. Why do you think it turned the way it did? Try bending the *right* aileron *down*. Now what does the plane do? What do you think will happen if one aileron is raised and the other is lowered? Try it and see!

---

* All activities in *WonderScience* have been reviewed for safety by Dr. Jack Breazeale, Francis Marion College, Florence, SC; Dr. Jay Young, Chemical Health and Safety Consultant, Silver Spring, MD; and Dr. Patricia Redden, Saint Peter's College, Jersey City, NJ.

Bend different flaps up or down or left or right and see how many different ways you can make your plane fly!

7 Put a piece of paper on the ground as a landing strip or target and see if you can land your plane on it from different distances. Take turns with your adult partner and see who is the champion *Wonderpilot!*

EARN YOUR WONDERSCIENCE WINGS!

Master each of the following maneuvers to become an official *WonderPilot* !

___ Fly straight ahead
___ Turn right
___ Turn left
___ Nose upward
___ Nose dive
___ Loop-the-loop
___ Curl (flip over sideways)
___ Longest flight
___ Landing accuracy

Wilbur Wright and Orville Wright

Said Orville Wright to Wilbur Wright
"These birds are very trying.
I'm sick of hearing them cheep-cheep
About the fun of flying.
A bird has feathers, it is true,
That much I freely grant.
But must that stop us, W?"
Said Wilbur Wright, "It shan't."

And so they built a glider first,
And then they built another.
—There never were two brothers more
Devoted to each other.
They ran a dusty little shop
For bicycle-repairing,
And bought each other soda-pop
And praised each other's daring.

They glided here, they glided there,
They sometimes skinned their noses.
—For learning how to rule the air
Was not a bed of roses —
But each would murmur, afterward,
While patching up his bro,
"Are we discouraged, W?"
"Of course we are not, O!"

And finally at Kitty Hawk
In Nineteen Three (let's cheer it!),
The first real airplane really flew
With Orville there to steer it!
-And kingdoms may forget their kings
And dogs forget their bites,
But not till [we forget our] wings
Will [we] forget the Wrights.

by Stephen Vincent Benét

IT'S A BIRD, IT'S A PLANE . . .
. . . IT'S AERODYNAMICS!

Anyone who has ever ridden a bicycle knows that the faster you go, the harder you feel the air pushing against you. This pushing of the air against you is called *air resistance* or *drag*. Can you imagine how hard air pushes against airplanes that travel at hundreds of miles per hour? The study of how air pushes against moving objects is called *aerodynamics*. Aerodynamics applies to airplanes, flying birds, cars, sailboats, kites, footballs, and any other objects that move through the air.

To have the least possible drag, bicycle racers bend down low over the handle bars so less air hits their bodies as they ride. They even wear special tight-fitting clothing so that air moves past them more smoothly and with less drag.

When an object is shaped so that air passes over it smoothly with little drag, it is called a *streamlined* shape. Most of today's cars are streamlined. Airplanes and birds have a streamlined shape. Streamlining saves energy because not as much energy is needed to fight against drag.

Sometimes air pushing on objects is helpful. In "Welcome to *WonderScience* Flight School," you saw how air pushing against the flaps of an airplane was used to steer the plane. When you use your WonderWhirler on the next page, you will see how air can make the blades of a helicopter turn. Air helps slow down the fall of many objects like parachutes, leaves, and special kinds of seeds.

The more spread out an object is, the more air can slow it down as it falls. This is easy to see by doing a simple experiment. Take two pieces of paper the same size and crumple one of them into a ball. Drop them at the same time, from the same height. Why do you think the uncrumpled paper falls to the ground more slowly? What does this experiment show you about air resistance?

Air is also important in keeping flying objects like birds and airplanes from falling down from the sky. A plane can only stay up in the air if its wings are the correct shape and are held at a certain angle as it moves through the air. The shape and angle of the wings cause air to move more quickly over the wings than under them. This causes air to push up on the bottom of the wings. This upward push is called *lift* and helps the plane take off and stay in the air.

Find the puzzle solutions on page 8.

ACROSS

3. Another word for air resistance
4. It surrounds the earth and moving things must pass through it
5. The smooth slim shape that allows things to move easily through the air
8. The upward force underneath the wing that keeps the plane in the air
10. It must be the right shape and at the right angle for the plane to stay in the air
12. The part of the plane made of the horizontal stabilizer and the vertical stabilizer
13. It spins in the front of some planes to make them go

DOWN

1. The last name of a woman pilot whose plane disappeared in 1937
2. Wilbur and Orville _____. They built the first plane that had a motor and a propeller.
4. Movable flaps on the wing of an airplane
6. The force that slows down an object as it moves through the air is called air _____.
7. The flaps on the horizontal part of the tail that make the nose of the plane go up or down
9. The flap on the vertical part of the tail that helps turn the plane right or left
11. What humans have wanted to do ever since they saw a bird soar through the air
13. The person who flies the airplane

Illustration by Tina Mion

TAKE A WHIRL WITH A WONDERWHIRLER!

You will need

1 piece of notebook or typing
  paper
metric ruler
blunt-end scissors
paper clip
1 piece of string (about 40 cm)
crayons or colored pencils

1 Cut a rectangle out of the paper that is 17 cm long and 6 cm wide.

2 Cut along the dotted lines as shown in the drawing.

3 Fold blade "A" toward you and blade "B" away from you so that your whirler looks like this:

Illustration by Lori Seskin-Newman

4 Place a paper clip on the end of your wonderwhirler, hold it high over your head, and drop it. What does it do as it falls? Does it always spin in the same direction? Experiment with the wonderwhirler to see if you can make it spin in the opposite direction.

5 What happens if you take the paper clip off? How about adding an extra paper clip? Try making the blades longer or shorter. How do these changes affect the way the whirler moves? Try different types of paper. Which paper works better?

6 Tape or tie a piece of string to the paper clip. Hold the end of the string and swing your wonderwhirler through the air in a figure 8 pattern. You can run with your whirler or take it outside on a windy day and see how well it spins.

7 Use crayons to decorate your whirler. Put designs on the blades and see how it looks when your whirler whirls!

3...2...1... LIFT OFF!

You will need

2 sheets of notebook or typing
  paper
clear plastic tape
metric ruler
blunt-end scissors
8 flexible plastic straws
6-8 thick books
** hair dryer
aluminum foil
a few pennies
pencil

You learned that the wings of an airplane must be the right shape and at the right angle for a plane to take off and stay in the air. Scientists can test the shape and angle of airplane wings by putting a model of the plane in a wind tunnel.

Normally, when an airplane flies, it is the ***plane*** that moves through the air at a certain speed. But in a wind tunnel, the plane does not move. Instead, air is blown at the plane at the same speed the plane would go if it ***were*** moving. You can test the shape and angle of airplane wings by experimenting with a *WonderScience* Wind Tunnel and a Test Plane. Get your adult partner and **LET'S TAKE OFF!**

1 Cut each piece of paper in half lengthwise. With a metric ruler, draw a line along the length of one of the half sheets of paper about 2 cm from the edge.

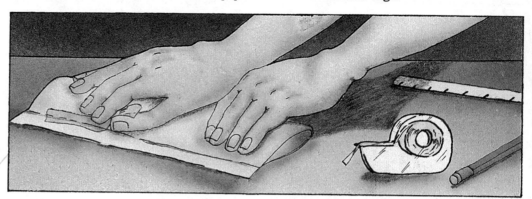

Illustrations by Lori Seskin-Newman

2 Bend the paper over lengthwise (do not crease) until the edge of the paper meets the line. Tape the edge of the paper to the line. Do exactly the same with another half sheet of paper. These are your test plane's wings.

3 Roll another half sheet of paper lengthwise into a tube and tape it. Fold and tape one end of the tube into a point. This is the front of the body of your plane.

4 Place the wings on both sides of the body about 3/4 of the way toward the front of the plane. Make sure that the wider part of the wing is facing toward the front of the plane. Put two pieces of tape connecting the top of the wings and body of the plane together. Turn the plane over and put two pieces of tape on the bottom of the plane to also hold the wings and body together.

5 From your 8 straws, make 4 double-length straws by pushing the end of one straw into another. (Make sure you connect each pair of straws at the ***non-flexible*** end.) Make a frame from the four long straws as shown. Reinforce each straw intersection with tape. Snip off the ends of the back straw as shown. Attach your plane to the straw frame by taping the end of the straws to the underside of each wing.

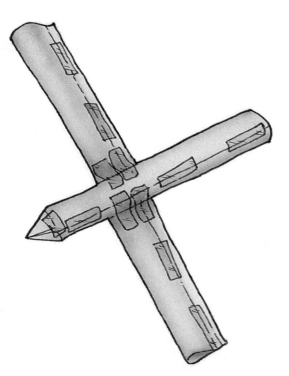

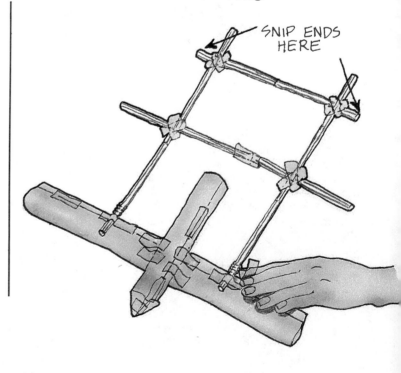

SNIP ENDS HERE

6 Turn the plane over so it is right-side up. Bend the flexible ends so they are almost an "L" shape and place a piece of tape between the top of the wing and the straw as shown.

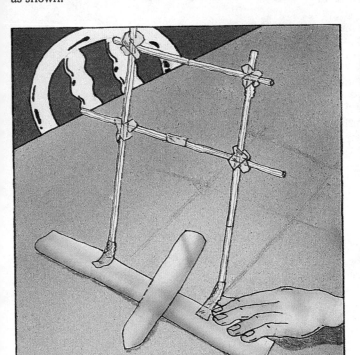

7 Place the straws and airplane on two stacks of books about 15 cm high. Wrap 3 to 5 pennies in a piece of aluminum foil and tape the aluminum foil to the back straw so that it *almost* balances the weight of the plane and the plane rests *very* lightly on the table.

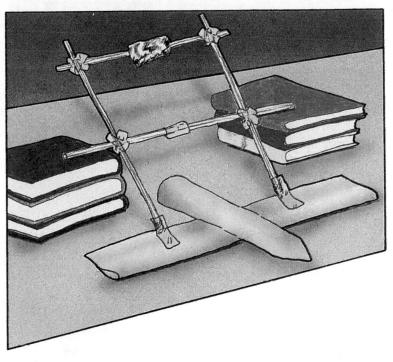

8 To make your wind "tunnel," hold a hair dryer about 2 meters in front of the plane. Turn the hair dryer on medium and aim a stream of air about a half-meter above the plane. Slowly lower the dryer until the air passes right over the top of the wings. Your plane should lift off.

9 If your plane does not go up, try putting the dryer on high or adding a little more weight to the back straw.

** Make sure the hair dryer you use has a plug with a wide prong and a narrow prong.

WOMEN ON WINGS!

One of the most famous pilots in American history is Amelia Earhart. She was born in 1898, almost 100 years ago. She worked as a military nurse in Canada during World War I and then as a social worker in Boston, Massachusetts. She became very interested in airplanes and decided to become a pilot. Ms. Earhart took her flying lessons during the 1920s, and because very few women were flying airplanes at that time, her decision to become a pilot took a lot of courage. In 1932 she became the first woman to fly a plane across the entire Atlantic Ocean! She later made several long-distance flights on her own across the United States. In 1937, she and her navigator attempted to fly around the world, but after finishing over two-thirds of the trip, the plane disappeared in the southern part of the Pacific Ocean. To this day, the plane has never been found, and no one knows what went wrong.

Another woman involved in aerodynamics is Christine Dardin. Ms. Dardin works at the National Aeronautics and Space Administration (NASA) facility in Hampton, Virginia. Her job is to change the shape of different parts of jet planes so that the planes can fly faster and faster without creating the loud blast of noise called a sonic boom. Some jets are not allowed to fly over the United States because they make so many loud sonic booms. Ms. Dardin uses computers to figure out the right design for the plane and then orders a model to be made according to her design. The model is put in a wind tunnel to see if air flows over it the right way so that sonic booms can be reduced or even eliminated.

THE RETURN OF THE BOOMERANG

A BOOMERANG is a specially shaped object that returns to you when you throw it. Some of the first boomerangs were banana-shaped pieces of wood made by the Aborigines in Australia. The Aborigines used them as hunting weapons to kill animals for food. These early boomerangs did not return to the thrower. In fact, the first boomerang that did return was probably discovered by accident. Scientists have found ancient fragments of boomerangs that are at least 10,000 years old!

Today, boomerangs come in different shapes and sizes and most are made from wood or plastic. The boomerang pattern on this page has three wings. Using this pattern, trace the boomerang on a piece of cardboard and cut it out.

Take your boomerang outside to a large open area. Grasp the end of one wing between your thumb and index finger. Hold it shoulder high and tilted a little bit away from you. Throw your boomerang with a quick snap of the wrist. You may have to try it a few times to get the perfect throw that brings your boomerang right back to you!

See how many times you can throw the boomerang and catch it without letting it hit the ground.

Throw your boomerang and have your adult partner try to catch it! Let your adult partner throw the boomerang and you try to catch it! Boomerangs are so much fun that *you* will always come back to *it!*

Illustration by Lori Seskin-Newman

BOOMERANG BRAIN BOGGLERS

Can you explain how each of the following bizarre and baffling boomerang tales is possible? (Turn the page upside down for the answers.)

1. In a single flight, a boomerang flew across four states before returning to the thrower.

2. A boy in Georgia threw a boomerang that didn't return until the next year.

3. A 10-year-old girl got a new boomerang on the day of her birth and for each of the rest of her birthdays, but now she has only three boomerangs.

Puzzle solution from page 4.

Brain Boggler Answers

1. The boomerang was thrown across Colorado, New Mexico, Arizona, and Utah where the four corners of these states meet.
2. The boy threw the boomerang at 11:59 pm on December 31st.
3. The girl was born on February 29th, in a leap year.

The activities in this issue stress designing a product (a hovercraft) from simple materials that will work well under specific conditions. Students are introduced to the concepts of air pressure and surface area. Students alter variables in the design to find modifications that create the best hovercraft.

Hovercraft Test Pilots

Hovercraft Test Pilots gives students instructions on making a hovercraft. Students are then encouraged to modify the design in different ways to produce the best hovercraft they can. Students learn to change one variable at a time and to test, observe, draw conclusions and make further modifications.

U.F.H.'s (Unidentified Flying Hovercrafts) Sighted Racing on Kitchen Table

U.F.H.'s (Unidentified Flying Hovercrafts) Sighted Racing on Kitchen Table explains that the gases in air are composed of tiny particles and that, in a hovercraft, the air pressure caused by the force of these particles on the bottom of the hovercraft, is what makes the craft hover.

Get a Better Feel for Air Pressure

In *Get a Better Feel for Air Pressure*, students make a model to simulate the different forces that make hovercraft hover.

It's the Area that Counts

It's the Area that Counts is an introduction to the concept of area and how to measure it. The relationship between the surface area of the bottom of a hovercraft and how well it hovers is explored. If the weight of a hovercraft remains the same, a larger surface area should make for better hovering.

Other Hovers

In *Other Hovers* students design ways of using air pressure to lift heavy objects and to make a hovercraft that can lift the most weight. The emphasis is on students designing their own solutions and on modification of design and testing.

RELEVANT NATIONAL SCIENCE EDUCATION STANDARDS

The activities in this unit can be used to support the teaching of the following standards:

✔ Science as Inquiry
  Abilities necessary to do scientific inquiry

✔ Physical Science
  Motions and forces

✔ Science and Technology
  Abilities of technological design

✔ Science in Personal and Social Perspectives
  Science and technology in society

HOVERCRAF

Your Mission

Here are some plans for building two **hovercraft** test models. Your first goal is to compare the models to see if the **weight** of the hovercraft affects how it hovers. But weight may not be the only thing that affects hovering. Your mission is to discover what other factors are important. **You can design more test models with materials you find at home or at school.** Just remember to change only one part at a time on each new model so that you can tell which changes make the hovercraft work best. Keep track of your test findings in a chart. At the completion of your mission, you will challenge your partner to a hover race with your very best designs.
Good luck and happy hovering!

What to Do

1 Stand a paper tube in the center of each paper plate or tray. Trace around it with a pencil. Carefully cut out the circles.

2 Turn the plates upside down and gently push one end of a paper tube in the openings. Make sure the tubes fit snugly.

3 Make a "heavy skirt" for one plate by cutting a 5-cm strip of grocery bag and taping it around the sides of a plate.
Make a "light skirt" for the second plate by cutting a 5-cm strip of plastic bag and taping it around the sides.

6 If you have a blow dryer, you can compare blowing air from your lungs to blowing air from the dryer down the tube of one of the models. How does the amount of air affect hovering? Write the results you observe for test 2 in the chart.

7 What would happen if you changed the shape of a model? How about comparing long and short tubes? Think of **improvements** you can make and then change one of the models so you can test if it improves hovering. There are lots of changes you can make. Just remember to compare only one change at a time! Keep track of your changes and test results in the chart.

SAFE SCIENCE TIP: NEVER USE BLOW DRYERS OR ANY OTHER ELECTRIC TOOLS NEAR WATER OR SINKS. YOU COULD GET A DEADLY SHOCK!

'EST PILOTS

5cm

What You Will Need

For the first test:

2 paper plates or Styrofoam trays (same shape and size)

2 toilet paper or paper towel tubes (or make tubes from cardboard)

1 brown paper grocery bag (or sheet of stiff paper or posterboard)

1 thin plastic trash bag (or frozen food bag)

masking tape

metric ruler

pencil

scissors

smooth, flat table, counter top, or uncarpeted floor

blow dryer (optional)

For other tests:

You may want different sizes or shapes of plates and trays, plastic margarine tubs, aluminum pie plates, longer or shorter tubes, foil, wax paper, or other such items.

Special thanks to Audrey Brainard, Council for Elementary Science International, and Chris Fitzgerald, Hoverclub of America, Inc., for suggesting parts of this activity.

4 Set the plates on a smooth, flat table or floor. Adjust the tubes so that their bottoms don't touch the table. Blow two or three times into each tube and see what happens.

5 Compare how each plate moves. How does the weight of the skirt affect how the hovercraft hovers? In the blanks in the chart below, write the test results that you observed.

Test Number	I Compared Hovering Using Different	Test Results I Observed
1	weight of skirts	the heavy skirt _____.
		the light skirt _____.
2	amounts of air blown into the tube	less air _____.
		more air _____.
3	_____	
4	_____	

Fill these in for other tests you do!

8 Challenge your partner to a hover race with your very best test models. Which pilot hovers the model to the far side of a table the fastest? Think about the race results. What other **improvements** can you test on your model?

9 Look at your test results chart. What did you find out about hovercraft? List four things you found that make a big difference in how **hovercrafts hover.**

1. _____   2. _____

3. _____   4. _____

BRAVO! YOU ACCOMPLISHED YOUR MISSION.

U.F.H.'s (Unidentified Flying Hovercrafts) Sighted Racing on Kitchen Table

Try to explain to your partner how a hovercraft hovers. Could a hovercraft lift off the table and hover out to space? Why or why not?

Hovercraft have no wheels or wings. They **float** over the ground or water on a cushion of air trapped inside the skirt. **Hovercraft** are also called **air-cushion vehicles.** Why did using a blow dryer affect hovering?

Did you notice that some hovercraft shapes lifted better than others? **Gases,** like air, are made of tiny **particles.** When these particles are trapped inside a container (like a balloon or a hovercraft skirt), they fill the container and push against the walls. This pushing force is called pressure. **Air pressure** is the **force** all the tiny **gas particles** make on the walls of a container.

Real hovercraft use large fans to move air under the craft. The **shape** of the hovercraft is important. The bottom must be very long and wide to make a big container for the air particles to push against and lift the craft. Air particles pushing against a **large area** can exert a lot of **lift.** Air pressure makes the hovercraft hover. Which of your models had the largest area for the air to push against?

Car tires and bicycle tires are also air cushions that lift up vehicles. You may have noticed that it takes more air pressure to fill a bike tire than it does to fill a car tire, even though the car is much heavier to lift. Why is that? (Hint: Which tire has the smallest **area** touching the ground?) A hovercraft has a much larger **air cushion area** touching the ground than a car or bike does. Of the three, which probably needs the least **air pressure** to lift it? (Hint: Can you fill a tire with a fan?)

Have you ever seen a real **hovercraft?** You may have heard about a famous hovercraft that is used to ferry cars and people across the English Channel. Other hovercraft are used by the military and by people who must move heavy loads over rough, soggy, or icy surfaces. Piloting a hovercraft is like flying a plane very close to the surface of the water or ground. Since the vehicle doesn't touch the surface, it can move much faster than similar-sized boats or cars.

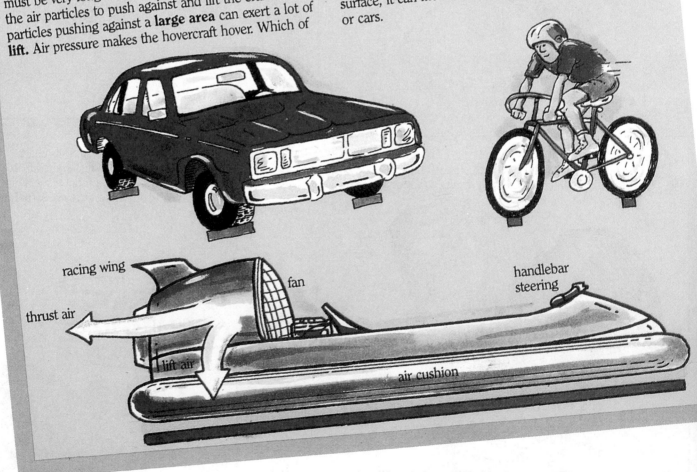

racing wing

thrust air

fan

lift air

air cushion

handlebar steering

Get a Better Feel for *Air Pressure*

Try to push the bag down.

Feel the <u>air cushion</u> push up when you try to push down.

In a hovercraft, fans blow air into the skirt. **Air particles** trapped inside the skirt fill the space inside the skirt. Air particles push against all sides of this space. The air particles that push up on the craft's bottom **lift** it off the ground. The hovercraft begins to **hover**!

hand (acts like hovercraft bottom)

plastic bag

rubber band or tape securely

wide-mouthed can or jar (acts like hovercraft skirt)

FUNKY WINKERBEAN   **BY TOM BATIUK**

DEFINE THE FOLLOWING:

(1.) HOVERCRAFT

Needlepoint done in a helicopter!

10-22

It's the *Area* that Counts

Find out which shape has the most **area**.
Trace each shape onto a piece of clear plastic or wax paper. Lay the shapes over the grid and count how many squares are covered by each shape. Count squares that are only partly covered by the shape as ¹⁄₂, or **estimate** how much of the square is covered.

Write your square area count beside each shape.

Which shape would be best to use for a hovercraft? Explain why!

From an idea submitted by Dr. Dorothy Gable, National Science Foundation.

Square count _____

Square count _____

Square count _____

Square count _____

Square count _____

FANTASTIC HOVER VOYAGE

Find a quiet, relaxing spot. Have your partner read you this story while you close your eyes and try to imagine the trip. Your partner should pause for several seconds after each slash mark. This will give you time to picture each part of the trip in your mind. This is your very own fantastic voyage. If something sounds impossible, remember, everything is possible in your imagination. *Bon voyage!*

Put yourself in a hovercraft./ Make the hovercraft red./ Make the hovercraft yellow./ Make the hovercraft striped./ What color are the stripes?/ Turn the hover fans on./ Hear the fans whir./ Turn the hover fans off./ Hear that there is no sound./ Put a passenger in the hovercraft with you./ Who is there?/ Put more passengers in the hovercraft./ Put some cars in the hovercraft./ Make the hovercraft bigger./ Fill the hovercraft with people and cars./ Turn the hover fans on again./ Have the people clap their hands and the cars honk their horns./ Make the hovercraft hover./ Make it hover higher./ Make the hovercraft speed across a lake./ Make the hovercraft speed across a beach./ Make it hover in one spot./ Stand under the hovercraft./ Touch the bottom of the hovercraft./ Stand in front of the hovercraft./ Make the people disappear./ Make the cars disappear./ Make the hovercraft smaller./ Make it even smaller./ Change the hovercraft to a helicopter./ Make it hover above some trees./ Have it hover even higher./ Change the hovercraft to a flying saucer./ Make the saucer green./ Make the saucer purple./ Put polka-dots on the saucer./ Put a robot in the saucer./ Have the robot wave good-bye to you./ Have the flying saucer zip out to space./ See that the flying saucer is gone./ See that everything is gone./ Open your eyes.

Tell your partner about your hover voyage. What kind of cars were on your hovercraft? How many people were on your hovercraft? What did it look like underneath the craft? What did the robot look like? What was your favorite part of the trip?

Now, read the story to your partner. Compare your trips.

HOVERING HAPPENINGS

If you visit Disney World's EPCOT Center in Florida, you'll see 10 hovering dragons! The hoverdragons perform during the air and water show, Skyleidoscope®. The dragons were built from hovercraft made by Chris Fitzgerald's company in Indiana.

Chris is an aeronautical engineer who designs and develops hovercraft recreation vehicles. He is president of the Hoverclub of America, Inc. The club hosts hover rallies and races, shares light hovercraft building plans, and publishes *Hovernews*.

The first hovercraft was invented in 1953 by Britain's Sir Christopher Cockerell. He built the first working model with an old vacuum cleaner and two coffee cans. Since then, many engineers have worked on improving hover designs.

Hovercraft can move over land, water, ice, and even snow. They are useful in places where regular boats or cars can't go. Some oil companies use them to get to oil rigs located in frozen or swampy places. The first European explorers of the upper Amazon River used a hovercraft to get there. A Swedish company even sells an air cushion lawnmower called Flymo!

In the future, high-speed hovertrains may be common. These trains could travel on air in a concrete-lined trench dug in the ground instead of running on rails. The trenches would be cheaper than roads because they wouldn't be as thick. What other uses for hovercraft do you think might be possible?

Illustration by Tina Mion

Other Hovers

Now that you know more about hovercraft, try to make a model that hovers over water. CAUTION: Don't use electric fans or dryers near water! You'll need to design a new air supply that's safe to use near water. Have fun!

Give Me a Lift

Pretend you work at a zoo. An elephant is ill and laying on its side. The zoo's vet says you must get the elephant to stand up and walk around or it will never get well. The elephant is too heavy to lift. How can you get the elephant to stand?

Here's one way you might try—make an air cushion! heavy book as your "elephant." Design an air cushion to slide under the elephant and lift it. What does your **invention** look like? How many "elephant books" can it lift? What if you made the air cushion as big as an air mattress you use at the beach? How many books could it lift then? How big do you think your air cushion would need to be to lift a real elephant?

Gliding Glasses

Try this the next time it's your turn to wash the dishes! Wash a dinner plate but do not dry it. Set it right-side-up on the counter. Make sure there is a very thin film of water on its surface. Wash a small plastic cup. Empty it and quickly drop it upside down on the plate. It should start to skate on the plate! You can make it glide with a gentle breath. How is it like a hovercraft? Would it still work if you washed with cold water? Can a hovercraft travel uphill? Can a hovercraft travel over big rocks? Why or why not?

It's Not Heavy . . . It's My Hover

What's the heaviest load your hovercraft can carry? Try taping paperclips, pennies, or other items to your best model to find out. How can you improve your model so that it will carry even more? Design a hoverpad that could be used to move really heavy loads in a warehouse or factory. What would your hoverpad look like?

Want to Learn More?

HERE ARE SOME BOOKS YOU MAY WANT TO GET FROM A LIBRARY OR BOOK STORE.

The Future World of Transportation: Walt Disney World EPCOT Center Book, by Valerie Moolman and Editors of Grolier; Franklin Watts, Inc.: Danbury, CT, 1984.

The drawings and descriptions in this book show K–8 grade level students how hovercraft and other types of transportation vehicles might be used in the future.

How It Works: The Illustrated Science and Invention Encyclopedia, 3rd edition; Marshall Cavendish Corporation: Freeport, NY, 1983.

This encyclopedia's index can be used to locate volumes that explain how hovercraft, air-cushion vehicles, ground-effect vehicles, or surface-effect vehicles work.

Inventor's Workshop, by Alan McCormack; David S. Lake Publishers: Belmont, CA, 1981.

Students in grades 3–8 can use this workbook to help turn on their creativity so they can design new gadgets and machines.

Amazing Air, by Henry Smith; Lothrup, Lee, and Shepard Books: New York, 1983.

This book is from the Science Club Series. It gives students in grades 3–6 directions for more experiments with air.

If you are a hovernut, you can join the Hoverclub of America, Inc. Write to them at Box 216, Clinton, IN 47842-0216.

WONDERSCIENCE

This unit introduces students to some of the fundamentals of the concept of balance. Balancing an object depends on the object's *center of gravity*. Center of gravity refers to the point on an object where there is exactly the same amount of weight on one side as there is on the opposite side. This must be true for every direction around that point. For an object with a uniform shape and weight distribution, such as a ruler, the center of gravity is in the exact center. For objects with irregular shapes or with their weight spread out unevenly, the center of gravity will not necessarily be in the center of the object.

Achieve the Power of Balance

In *Achieve the Power of Balance*, students should work in pairs or groups of three. One can balance the ruler, another can place pennies on the ruler, and another can record data. Students see that for each penny added to the ruler, the finger will need to move a similar distance toward the pennies. Students can use their data to make a graph.

In the second part of the activity, instead of adding pennies and finding the new center of gravity, the location of the center of gravity can be kept the same by adding pennies and then moving the pennies. Students should discover that for each penny added, the pennies will need to be moved different distances toward the finger. Students can use their data to make a graph.

Bring Balance to Life!

In *Bring Balance to Life!*, students see that it is almost impossible to stand directly up from a sitting position without first leaning forward. Leaning forward helps put the body's center of gravity over the feet. In the second activity, students see that it is impossible to stand on one foot without shifting the body's center of gravity over that foot.

The next activities investigate the human sense of balance. Specialized mechanisms in the inner ear constantly monitor changes in the orientation of the head in relation to the body's center of gravity. Every time the head moves, nerves in the inner ear send messages to the brain. This way, the body can respond to changes in orientation immediately. Be sure students let go of the bat after spinning around and getting dizzy.

Center of Gravity-On the Move!

In *Center of Gravity-On the Move!*, students challenge their partner to locate the center of gravity on an object whose weight distribution can change in many ways. Let students know that certain combinations of weights (paper clips) may significantly move the center of gravity while other combinations will only move it a little. You might want to ask students whether it is the amount of weight or where the weight is placed that most effects the location of the center of gravity. The answer is that both are important. More weight close to the original center of gravity can have the same effect as less weight placed further away.

A WonderScience Balancing Act!

In *A WonderScience Balancing Act!*, students discover that tall objects are easier to balance than short objects when supported vertically on the palm of the hand. Because a taller object's center of gravity is higher than that of a shorter object, it takes a longer time for its center of gravity to move beyond its base of support when it begins to fall. This gives the hand more time to react and place itself under the center of gravity again.

Balancing: Short and Simple *and* Balancing Bernie

In *Balancing: Short and Simple*, students should experiment with longer or shorter wire, with the wire attached at different heights on the pencil, and with different numbers of washers to discover which combinations make for the best balancing pencil. In *Balancing Bernie* be sure students create a figure that has two places to place weights, such as ears, legs, wings, or horns that act like Bernie's hands.

RELEVANT NATIONAL SCIENCE EDUCATION STANDARDS

The activities in this unit can be used to support the teaching of the following standards:

✔ Science as Inquiry
   Abilities necessary to do scientific inquiry

✔ Physical Science
   Motions and forces

✔ Life Science
   Structure and function in living systems

Achieve the Power of Balance

You've probably balanced a ruler, or something like it on your finger before. You may have noticed that the slightest little movement causes the ruler to tilt and fall off. When you find the exact spot where your finger needs to be to balance the ruler, you have found the ruler's **center of gravity**.

Center of gravity is the exact spot on an object where there is the same amount of weight on one side of the spot as there is on the opposite side. Once you change the weight anywhere on the object, the center of gravity changes too.

In this activity, you can use your finger to chase the changing center of gravity of your ruler as you add weight to one of the ends.

YOU WILL NEED:

metric ruler
   (wood or stiff plastic)
pennies
pencil
paper

1 Make a chart like the one below. Take a ruler and place it on your finger as shown. Find the place where your finger needs to be so that the ruler is perfectly balanced. Record that number in your chart under 0 pennies.

2 Work with your partner to place one penny exactly on the 1 cm mark of the ruler.

3 Now move your finger so that the ruler is balanced again. Look to see exactly where your finger is on the ruler. Record that number in your chart under 1. Did you move your finger toward, or away from the penny?

4 Now place another penny on top of the first and again find the spot where your finger perfectly balances the ruler. Record this number in your chart. How does this number compare with the number for one penny?

5 If you put three pennies on the 1-cm mark, where will your finger need to be to balance the ruler? Try it to see if you were right.

6 Continue experimenting and filling in your chart for 4, 5, and 6 pennies. Can you predict each time where your finger needs to be to balance the ruler? Were your predictions correct? How many pennies can be placed at 1 cm and still be balanced by moving your finger?

number of pennies	0	1	2	3	4	5	6
finger position							

ROBERT BOURDEAUX

434

On the previous page, you searched for the center of gravity by moving your finger along the ruler. This time, instead of moving your finger, you can keep the center of gravity where it is, directly over your finger, by moving different numbers of pennies along the ruler.

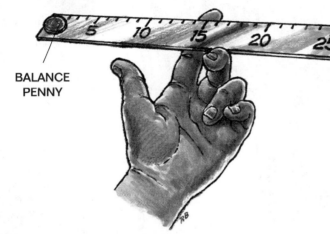

BALANCE PENNY

BALANCE PENNY

1 Make a chart like the one below. Take a ruler and place it on your finger as shown. Find the place where your finger needs to be so that the ruler is perfectly balanced.

2 Work with your partner to place one penny exactly on the 1 cm mark on your ruler. This is your "balance penny." You will not move this penny or your finger for the rest of the activity. Place another penny on the opposite end of the ruler from the balance penny. Move this penny until the ruler is perfectly balanced. Record the position of the penny in the chart under 1.

3 Have your partner place another penny on top of the first on the side of the ruler opposite the balance penny. Find the place where the two pennies need to be to balance the one balance penny on the other side. Write this number in the chart.

4 Is it possible to balance three pennies on one side with one on the other? See if you and your partner can find the number on the ruler where the three pennies need to be to make it work.

5 Can you predict where four pennies would need to be to balance the one balance penny on the other side? Try it to see if you were right.

6 What is the greatest number of pennies that can be balanced on one side of the ruler with only one penny on the 1-cm mark on the other? On what number does this stack of pennies need to be?

This time, try to balance different amounts of pennies on one side with **two** pennies on the 1-cm mark on the other. Make a chart to record your results. Compare the answers to your first chart. In what ways are they similar and different?

number of pennies	1	2	3	4	5	6	7
position of penny stack							

435

Bring Balance

We don't think about balance very often, but we use it every day, all day long. Many of our most basic actions such as standing and getting out of a chair depend on how we balance our bodies.

1 Sit in a chair with your back against the back of the chair and your hands at your sides.

2 Without using your hands and without leaning forward, try to stand up. Can you do it?

3 Try again. This time, keep your back straight and bend at your waist to lean forward a little bit. Try standing up again. If you could not stand up, keep leaning forward until you can do it. Notice how far forward you need to lean to stand up. What do you think this has to do with center of gravity?

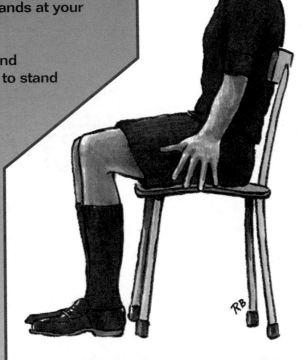

ROBERT BOURDEAUX

Place your left shoulder and left foot against a wall as shown. Try to raise your right foot and keep it raised. Can you do it?

It is impossible because to stand on your left foot only, you need to shift your center of gravity over your left foot, but the wall won't let you shift your weight.

You can see this by doing a simple experiment. Stand with your feet about a half meter apart. Without shifting your weight, lift your right foot straight up. It will probably go back down immediately. Now shift your weight so that you will be able to lift your right foot up and keep it up. Describe how you changed your body position to be able to balance yourself on your left foot.

To Life!

As people and other animals move their arms, legs, and body parts, their center of gravity is always changing. We have a special way of sensing where our center of gravity is and then responding by moving our bodies so they stay balanced. This is called the sense of balance. Most people talk about hearing, seeing, tasting, smelling, and touching as the five senses. But our balance is another important sense.

YOU WILL NEED:

masking tape
baseball bat

1 Use masking tape to make a straight line on the floor about three meters long.

2 Hold a baseball bat and place your forehead on the handle of the bat as shown. To make yourself dizzy, walk quickly around on the bat about 10 times. Let the bat fall and have your partner help you find the line.

3 Try walking along the line. Could you do it? What do you think happened to your sense of balance?

Dizziness—It's All In Your Head!

When you spin around and make yourself dizzy, you are confusing your body's system for keeping itself balanced. This balancing system involves the **inner ear** and the **brain**. Look at this picture. It shows the outer ear on the left and the many different parts of the inner ear on the right. Notice the three tubes called the **semicircular canals** of the inner ear. At the ends of these tubes are bulb-like structures that each contain a little sack called an **ampulla**. Just below the three ampullas is another larger bulblike structure, which contains another sack called the **utricle**.

The ampullas and utricle help your body keep its balance by sending nerve messages to the brain about the position and movement of your head. Here's how it works: The ampullas and utricle are filled with a thick fluid. They also have tiny fine hairs attached to their inner walls that stick into the fluid. The hairs are attached to nerves that go to the brain. When you tilt or rotate your head in a certain direction, the fluid pushes against the hairs and causes nerve signals to go to the brain. The brain recognizes the signals as meaning that the head has moved in a particular way and is in a particular position. You use this information to adjust the movements of your body to maintain your balance.

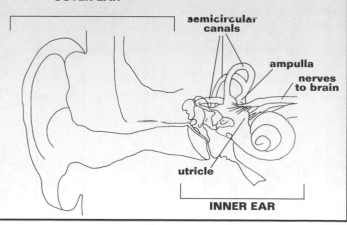

OUTER EAR

semicircular canals

ampulla

nerves to brain

utricle

INNER EAR

Center of Gravity— On the Move!

One way to find an object's center of gravity is to move the object around on the tip of your finger until it balances nice and flat without tilting in any direction. As you saw previously, the center of gravity can change when weight is added somewhere on the object. In the activity below, you and your partner can have some friendly competition to see who is better at predicting center of gravity.

YOU WILL NEED:

3 x 5 index card
paper clips
metric ruler
pencil

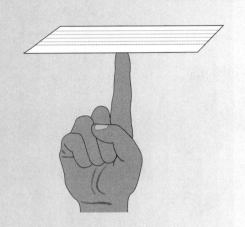

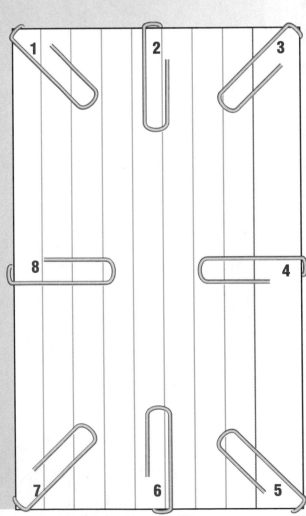

Teacher Preparation:

Use the picture of the index card to show students how to mark their index cards for paper clip positions.

1 Look at your index card. Think about where the center of gravity might be. (Remember: this is the spot where the card would balance flat on your finger tip.)

2 Use your pencil to make a small dot exactly where you think the center of gravity is. Hold the card up so that you can see the dot. Place the dot on the tip of your index finger to see if it balances. If it does, congratulations—you found the center of gravity! Now it's your partner's turn to repeat step 2.

3 If the card does not balance, observe how much it tilts. Also observe in what direction it tilts. Use this information to move the card on your finger tip while you watch it from below. When the card balances, your finger is on the center of gravity. Have your partner help you mark that spot.

Who is better at finding a moving center of gravity?

4 Attach a paper clip to weight spot 1 on the card. You and your partner should each put a dot on the card where you think the new center of gravity will be. Put your initials next to your dots.

5 Place one of the dots on your finger tip and find the center of gravity as you did before. Now try the other dot. Mark the new center of gravity. Use your ruler to see if you or your partner was closer. Whoever was closer scores a point.

6 Add a paper clip to any one or more weight spots in any combination. You and your partner should predict where you think the center of gravity is. Mark the card with a dot and your initials and then find the center of gravity to see who was closer.

438

A *WonderScience* Balancing Act!

Have you ever tried to balance something long and thin on the palm of your hand or on the tip of your finger? Some skinny objects are easier to balance than others. The length of the object and the way its weight is spread out makes a big difference in how easy it is to balance. In the activity below see if you can get into the balancing act!

YOU WILL NEED:

unsharpened pencil
ruler
meter stick
ball of clay
(about the size of a golf ball)

1 Place the eraser end of the pencil on the palm of your hand and let go. Try to balance it. It is not easy.

2 Now take a ruler and try to balance it on the palm of your hand. Is it easier, harder, or about the same as balancing the pencil?

3 Now try balancing a meter stick on the palm of your hand. Is it easier, harder, or about the same as balancing the ruler? How about compared to the pencil?

4 Try balancing the pencil again. Now place a ball of clay on top of the pencil and try balancing it again. Is it easier or harder with the clay?

5 Try balancing the ruler again. Now place the ball of clay on top of the ruler and try balancing it again. Was it easier or harder? Move the clay down to the middle of the ruler and try balancing it again. Was it easier or harder than before?

6 Try balancing the meter stick again. Now place the clay ball at the top of the meter stick and try balancing it again. Was it easier or harder? Move the clay ball near the bottom of the meter stick and try balancing the stick. What do you notice?

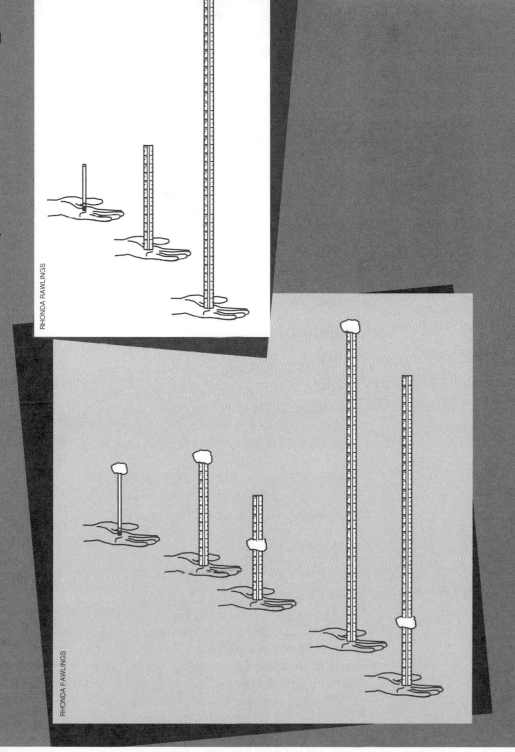

RHONDA RAWLINGS

RHONDA RAWLINGS

YOU WILL NEED:

unsharpened pencil

wire (20-22 gauge)

metal washers

tape

Balancing: Short & Simple

There is a way to make short things such as the pencil you used easier to balance. If you can add some weight to the pencil in the right way, you could balance it all day long! Try the activity below to see what we mean!

Teacher Preparation:

Cut a 25-30 cm length of wire for each pair of students.

1 Wrap the middle of your wire once or twice around the pencil as shown. You should have about the same length of wire on each side of the pencil. Tape the wire to the pencil to make sure the wire doesn't slip down the pencil.

2 Add a washer to each end of the wire. Place the eraser end of the pencil on your finger tip to see if it will balance.

3 See if you and your partner can find the best position for the wires and washers so that the pencil stands as straight up as possible. Adjust the position of the washers to see the different ways the pencil will balance on your finger.

Balancing Bernie

YOU WILL NEED:

card stock or manila folder

scissors

paper clips

Teacher Preparation:

Photocopy Balancing Bernie and distribute to the class.

1 Cut out Bernie and trace his outline onto a piece of card stock or manila folder. Cut Bernie out of the card stock.

2 Place a paper clip on each of Bernie's hands as shown. Place Bernie's head on your finger tip to see if he balances.

Challenge:

Make your own figure that balances better than Bernie!

Draw your own balancing figure, and cut it out from card stock or a manila folder. You could make your figure taller or shorter than Bernie. You could make it with longer or shorter arms or with arms in a different position than Bernie's. You could use more or less weight than you did with Bernie.

When you are done, try balancing each one on its head for a head-to-head contest!

440

This unit introduces students to some of the principles involved in the motion of wheels. The activities encourage students to look closely at the behavior of different wheels to get a deeper understanding of some of the factors that influence the way wheels work.

Round, Round, Get A-Round. .

In *Round, Round, Get A-Round. .*, students use juice cans to explore how factors such as mass and size affect the motion of a wheel down a ramp. Students should discover that an empty can will reach the bottom of the ramp before a full can of the same size and that a larger can will reach the bottom before a smaller can filled with the same material. Other cans can be substituted for juice cans, but if this is done be sure to cover the edges of any opened ends with tape for safety purposes.

Merrily We Roll Along

In *Merrily We Roll Along*, students see how wheels help make heavy objects easier to move. The second activity shows how ball bearings work. Both activities deal with the central role of wheels in reducing friction.

Make a Wonder Wheel-a-rang!

The *Make a Wonder Wheel-a-rang!* activity is a fun application of wheels to create a simple toy. When the Wheel-a-rang is rolled, energy becomes stored in the twisted rubber band on the inside. When the rubber band starts to unwind, the stored energy is released and the Wheel-a-rang rolls back again. If the Wheel-a-rang is not working, make sure that the washers are securely tied to the rubber bands and that they do not flop over when the can rolls.

This Wheel Really Measures Up!

In *This Wheel Really Measures Up!*, students find the circumference of a bicycle wheel, and then use the wheel as a distance measuring tool. Math skills are further developed through problems provided at the end of the activity.

Get a Lift with a WonderScience Windlass

In *Get a Lift with a WonderScience Windlass*, students make a device called a windlass to lift a cup of pennies. Although it doesn't look like it, the windlass is actually a wheel and axle. A wheel and axle can reduce the amount of force required to lift a heavy object. In the case of the windlass, when you turn the handle, you exert only a small force as you move your hand through a large circle. By contrast, lifting the cup of pennies directly (or by twisting the axle with your fingers) requires that a much larger force be exerted through a shorter distance.

RELEVANT NATIONAL SCIENCE EDUCATION STANDARDS

The activities in this unit can be used to support the teaching of the following standards:

✔ Science as Inquiry
  Abilities necessary to do scientific inquiry

✔ Physical Science
  Motions and forces

✔ Science in Personal and Social Perspectives
  Science and technology in society

✔ History and Nature of Science
  History of science

ROUND, ROUND,

What do all wheels have in common? They are all *round!* In this activity, you can use juice cans as wheels and race them down a ramp to see how different wheels move!

You will need

1 table
several old books
2 small unopened frozen juice cans with zip-off top (6 oz)
1 large unopened frozen juice can with zip-off top (12 oz or larger)
clear plastic tape
modeling clay

1 Ask your adult partner to prop up one end of a table with old books of the same thickness to make a ramp.

2 Empty one of your small cans (you could make some juice), and put its top back on. You may need a little tape to hold the top in place.

3 If you race a full can and an empty can of the same size, which do you think will reach the bottom first? Try it and see! (Be sure you start the cans from the same height, don't give either can a push, and catch the cans at the end of the ramp so they don't hit the floor!) Which can wins? Why do you think that can won?

4 Fill the bottom half of the empty can with modeling clay so that one half of the can is heavier than the other half. Before letting the can roll down the ramp, explain to your adult partner how you think the clay will change the way the can rolls. (Hint: Think about what happened when the small empty can and the small full can rolled down the ramp).

5 Try rolling the small unopened can and the large unopened can down the ramp at the same time. Which can reaches the bottom first? Is this because of the size of the can or how heavy it is? (Hint: Think again about what happened in step 3!)

6 Have a ramp race with your adult partner! See who can find an unopened food can that will reach the bottom of the ramp first! What kind of can should you try to find?

GET A-ROUND..

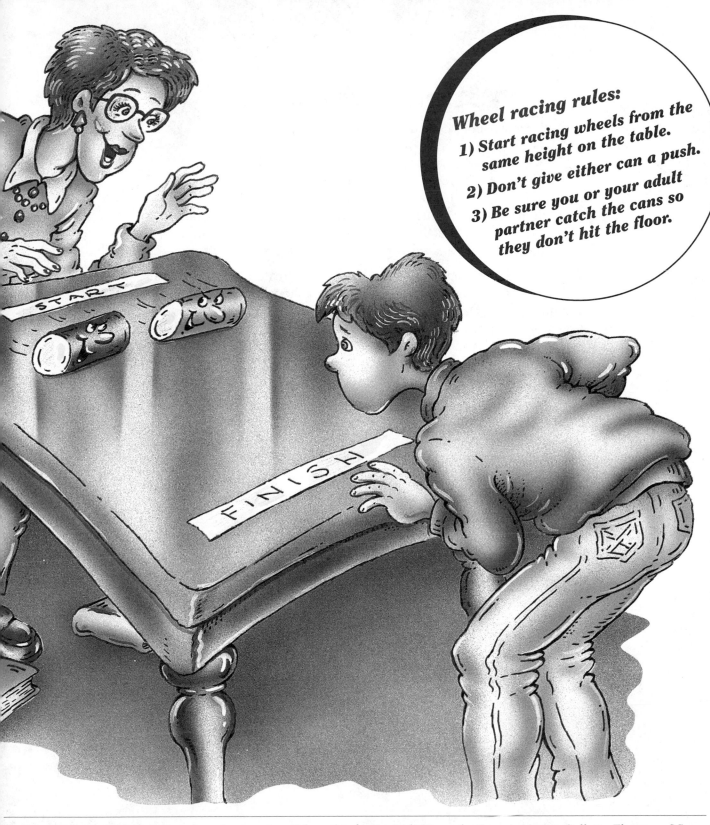

Wheel racing rules:

1) Start racing wheels from the same height on the table.

2) Don't give either can a push.

3) Be sure you or your adult partner catch the cans so they don't hit the floor.

---

* All activities in *WonderScience* have been reviewed for safety by Dr. Jack Breazeale, Francis Marion College, Florence, SC; Dr. Jay Young, Chemical Health and Safety Consultant, Silver Spring, MD; and Dr. Patricia Redden, Saint Peter's College, Jersey City, NJ.

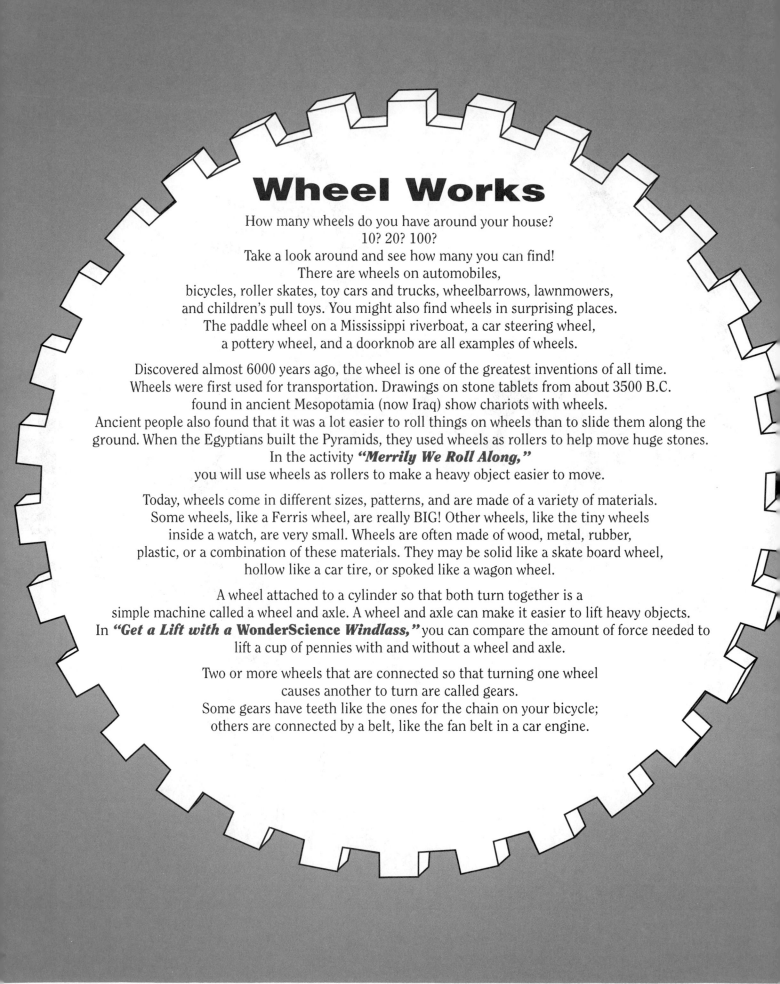

Wheel Works

How many wheels do you have around your house?
10? 20? 100?
Take a look around and see how many you can find!
There are wheels on automobiles,
bicycles, roller skates, toy cars and trucks, wheelbarrows, lawnmowers,
and children's pull toys. You might also find wheels in surprising places.
The paddle wheel on a Mississippi riverboat, a car steering wheel,
a pottery wheel, and a doorknob are all examples of wheels.

Discovered almost 6000 years ago, the wheel is one of the greatest inventions of all time.
Wheels were first used for transportation. Drawings on stone tablets from about 3500 B.C.
found in ancient Mesopotamia (now Iraq) show chariots with wheels.
Ancient people also found that it was a lot easier to roll things on wheels than to slide them along the
ground. When the Egyptians built the Pyramids, they used wheels as rollers to help move huge stones.
In the activity **"Merrily We Roll Along,"**
you will use wheels as rollers to make a heavy object easier to move.

Today, wheels come in different sizes, patterns, and are made of a variety of materials.
Some wheels, like a Ferris wheel, are really BIG! Other wheels, like the tiny wheels
inside a watch, are very small. Wheels are often made of wood, metal, rubber,
plastic, or a combination of these materials. They may be solid like a skate board wheel,
hollow like a car tire, or spoked like a wagon wheel.

A wheel attached to a cylinder so that both turn together is a
simple machine called a wheel and axle. A wheel and axle can make it easier to lift heavy objects.
In **"Get a Lift with a WonderScience Windlass,"** you can compare the amount of force needed to
lift a cup of pennies with and without a wheel and axle.

Two or more wheels that are connected so that turning one wheel
causes another to turn are called gears.
Some gears have teeth like the ones for the chain on your bicycle;
others are connected by a belt, like the fan belt in a car engine.

merrily we roll along

You will need

heavy book
15 plastic straws
flat table top

Make your own model of the way builders in ancient times moved huge, heavy stones!

1 Lay the book on the table. Gently start pushing against the book with the tip of one finger. Increase the force of your push until the book starts to move.

2 Now lay the straws down next to one another, about 2 cm apart. Place the book on the straws and give the book a gentle push with one finger. Were you able to move it more easily with the rollers than without them?

Builders and engineers in ancient times sure had the right idea!

Did you know that the wheels of many cars, trucks, and even bicycles have small hard steel balls inside them? These steel balls are called *ball bearings.* These balls help a wheel spin more easily by reducing friction between the wheel and the axle. Try the following activity to see how ball bearings work!

You will need

plastic coffee can lid
6–8 marbles
large heavy book

Turn the plastic lid upside down and place 6–8 marbles in the ridge along the inside edge of the lid. Place the book on the marbles. Using one finger tip, see how easy it is to make the book spin. Watch the marbles move as the book spins. Do you think the book will spin as easily without the marbles? Try it and see!

Just as the marbles keep the book and lid from rubbing together, ball bearings keep a wheel and axle from rubbing together and slowing the wheel down.

Make a Wonder Wheel-a-rang!

Astonish your friends with this mysterious WonderWheel that returns to you like a boomerang when you roll it away!

You will need

13-oz coffee can with both ends removed
2 plastic coffee can lids
hole punch
3 or 4 long thick rubber bands

6 metal washers (about the size of a quarter)
2 short pieces of string (each about 10 cm)
adhesive tape

1 Use a hole punch to make 2 holes in each plastic lid. The two holes should be on opposite sides of the lid, the same distance from the center.

2 Cut the rubber bands, and tie their ends together to make one long rubber string about 45 cm long.

3 Ask your adult partner to help you run the rubber band through the four holes in the plastic lids as shown and then tie the rubber band together on the outside of one of the lids.

4 Tie the rubber band together in the center with a piece of string as shown and then tightly tie five or six washers to this center spot.

5 Your adult partner should now bend one of the lids and push it through the can so that the lids can be attached to opposite ends of the can. Your rubber band should be stretched a bit but not tight.

6 Lay the can on its side on a smooth uncarpeted surface. Give it a gentle push so that it rolls away from you. What happens?

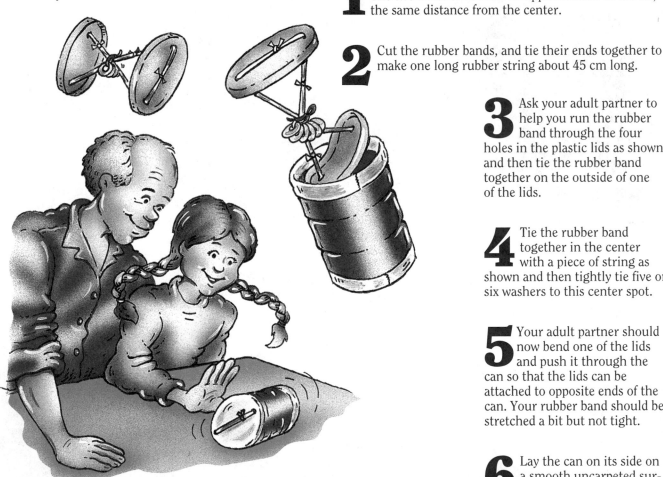

Adult safety tip: After opening the coffee can, carefully press down any jagged edges with the back of a spoon and cover the rim of the can with adhesive tape.

WHEEL-A-RANG DESIGN CHALLENGE!

Find out what happens if you tie a different number of washers to the rubber band or if you use a rubber band of different length or thickness. See if you can design a WonderWheel that:

- Goes the longest distance before returning.
- Rolls back at the fastest speed.
- Rolls back at the slowest speed.
- Will roll back up a ramp after you roll it down!

This Wheel Really MEASURES UP!

Another important use for wheels is to measure distances. The wheels on a car are used to measure the distance that the car has traveled, and the distance is recorded on the car's *odometer.* If you know the distance around the car tire and the number of times the tire has turned, you can figure out the distance that the car has traveled. Try this activity and see if you can go the distance!

You will need

bicycle (or wagon or large toy truck)

masking tape

cloth tape measure

1 Wrap the measuring tape snugly around the front tire of the bicycle. The distance around the tire is called its *circumference.* Write down the circumference of the tire in the chart below.

2 Find a long flat surface, like a sidewalk, that you can roll your bicycle along. Have your adult partner help you mark a Starting line and, at least 20 paces away, a Finish line.

3 Position your bicycle so that the front tire is right on the starting line. Ask your adult partner to put a piece of masking tape on the side of the wheel where it touches the starting line and to count how many times the wheel turns as you slowly roll your bicycle toward the finish line.

4 To find the distance that your bike traveled, multiply the circumference by the number of turns of the wheel. Write your answer in the chart under "Distance."

5 You and your adult partner can check your result by measuring the distance using only your tape measure. How accurate was the wheel measuring method?

Circumference	X	Number of turns	=	Distance
_____	X	_____	=	_____

Let's see if your math skills are "wheely" good!

1) If your wheel has a circumference of 2 meters, and it turns 25 times, how far will it travel? _____ meters
2) If your wheel has a circumference of 2 meters and it turns enough times to travel 20 meters, how many turns did it make? _____ turns
3) If you traveled 100 meters and your wheel turned 50 times, what was the circumference of your wheel? _____ meters

You and your adult partner can make up and answer your own wheel questions until your math skills "wheely" measure up!

Get a Lift with a WonderScience Windlass

You will need

2 unopened soda cans
2 flexible straws
4 paper clips
small paper cup (3 oz)

string or thread
adhesive tape
20 pennies

A *windlass* is a special kind of wheel and axle that is used to lift heavy objects. Old fashioned wells often used a windlass to raise a large wooden bucket of water. In this activity, you will make your own windlass, and discover how using this special wheel system can make it a lot easier to lift heavy things.

1 Open the paper clips into an "S" shape. Use two of the paper clips to make a handle for the small cup, and tie the string to this handle.

2 Place 20 pennies in the cup. Lift the cup by the string. Feel how much force you use to lift the cup this way.

3 Tape the two soda cans together, one on top of the other. Tape two paper clips on opposite sides of the upper can. The large end of each paper clip should stick up above the edge of the can.

4 Place the long end of a flexible straw through the paper clip loops so that the straw rests on top of the can. This straw is the *axle* of your windlass. Bend the short end of the flexible straw upward.

5 Bend the second straw at the flexible joint. Attach the long end of the second straw to the short end of the first. The second straw is the handle or *wheel* of your windlass.

6 Now you can hang your cup of pennies from the windlass. Tape the end of the string to the straw about 2-3 cm from the end opposite the handle.

7 Turn the handle of your windlass and watch the cup of pennies rise! How does the force needed to lift the pennies this way compare to lifting the cup of pennies before?

8 Try lifting the cup by using your fingers to turn the straw axle at the end near the string. Is it easier or harder than using the handle?

9 Experiment with your windlass to see how many pennies you can lift!

448

Unit 57
Sound and Hearing

This unit introduces students to some of the basic concepts of sound and hearing. Students examine sources of sound, how sound travels through different materials to their ears, and how their ear-brain system has the ability to recognize and locate sounds. All sounds are produced from something that is vibrating. Vibrating objects cause adjacent air molecules to begin vibrating, which in turn cause other air molecules to vibrate, which cause still other air molecules to vibrate. In this manner, the vibrations travel to our ears.

Two important characteristics of a sound that help us recognize and describe it are *pitch* and *loudness*. The pitch of a sound relates to the rate of vibration (or number of vibrations per second). The faster something vibrates, the higher the pitch of the sound it makes. The loudness of a sound is related to how large the vibrations are. Larger vibrations produce louder sounds.

Let Your Ears Be The Judge!

In *Let Your Ears Be The Judge!*, students become aware of the subtle differences in the sounds they hear and of their ability to detect and analyze these very minor sound differences. A list of possible items that might be used has been provided, but you should feel free to replace these with whatever small safe objects you have available.

Good Vibrations!

Good Vibrations! provides a concrete model for showing how sound vibrations travel from a sound maker to our ears. Students discover that in order for there to be a sound there must be 1) a vibrating source (the coat hanger), 2) a material through which the sound vibrations travel (string), and 3) a sound receiver (our ears). Students should experiment by replacing the coat hanger with other metal objects suggested. You might also have them try replacing the string with plastic fishing line or thread.

Hearing in 3-D

In *Hearing in 3-D*, students discover the value of having two ears as opposed to one. You may notice that students have the hardest time telling the difference between a sound that comes from directly in front of them and one that comes from directly behind even when listening with both ears. This is because, in both cases, the distance to both ears is the same.

A WonderScience Pitch Switcher

A WonderScience Pitch Switcher is similar to an activity in the Physics of Music Unit, but has been revised to allow students to get a better feeling for the relationship between the length of the plucked rubber band and the pitch of the sound. Students should discover that increasing the length of the vibrating part of the rubber band causes it to make a lower-pitched sound. Decreasing the length of the vibrating part of the rubber band causes it to make a higher-pitched sound. Before doing the activity, be sure to lay down some ground rules about the safe handling of rubber bands.

The Many States of Hearing

In *The Many States of Hearing*, students discover that not only can they hear through solids and liquids, but they can hear even better through these materials than through air! This is because sound travels faster through liquids and solids than through air. This is why old Western movies often showed someone placing an ear to the ground to listen for approaching horses. You may want to try some shredded newspaper, a book, a piece of wood, or "packing peanuts" in the bag.

RELEVANT NATIONAL SCIENCE EDUCATION STANDARDS

The activities in this unit can be used to support the teaching of the following standards:

✔ Science an Inquiry
   Abilities necessary to do scientific inquiry

✔ Physical Science
   Transfer of energy

✔ Life Science
   Structure and function in living systems

Let Your Ears Be

Do you think you can guess what an object is just by the sound you hear when the object is dropped?

1 Place a cookie sheet flat on a table. You and your partner should **each** make a list of the items you have collected. One of you will be the **Dropper**; the other will be the **Guesser**. The Dropper decides in what order to drop the objects and then numbers his or her list to match the order. The Guesser will take the other list without the numbers and turn around, away from the cookie sheet.

2 The Dropper then drops the objects, one at a time, from a height of about 1/2 meter onto the cookie sheet in the order on the list. After each object is dropped, the Guesser tries to figure out which object it was and writes a number next to the name of the object. For example, the number "1" will be the first object dropped.

3 When all of the objects have been dropped, check how well the Guesser did. Then switch so that the Dropper is Guesser and the Guesser is Dropper. The new Dropper renumbers the list and drops the items in the new order.

NOTE: After an object is dropped, remove it from the cookie sheet. Do this before the next object is dropped.

4 Once each partner has had a turn being the Guesser, discuss how the sound of the objects hitting the cookie sheet helped you identify the objects. Next to each object, write one or two words that describe the sound made by the object.

BOB BOURDEAUX

the Judge!

5 Do you think you can identify the items by hearing them move around inside a box? This time, there is still a Guesser, but the Dropper becomes a **Shaker**. The Shaker makes a list as before and numbers each item in the order that it will be shaken.

6 The Shaker places the first object on the list in the box so that the Guesser cannot see it. The Shaker then slowly tilts and gently shakes the box so that the Guesser can hear the object moving around inside. After each object is shaken, the Guesser tries to figure out which object it is. The Guesser then writes a number next to the name of the object. For example, the number "1" will be the first object shaken.

NOTE:
After an object is shaken, remove it from the box. Do this before the next object is placed in the box.

7 When all of the objects have been shaken, check how well the Guesser did. Then switch so that the Shaker is the Guesser, and the Guesser is the Shaker. The new Shaker renumbers the list and shakes the items in the new order.

8 Once each partner has had a turn being the Guesser, discuss how each sound from inside the box helped you identify the objects. Next to each object, write one or two words that describe the sound the object made.

Was it easier to identify the object in the drop test or the shake test? Explain why you think one was better at helping you identify the objects than the other.

Hear! Hear!

You may think that those two things sticking out on the sides of your head are what let you hear sounds. But your outer ears don't really hear at all. They are just "sound catchers." Your real hearing organs are located **inside** your head.

In fact, you hear through a system made up of two ears, two paths to the brain, and two brain halves. This "double" system lets you tell the direction a sound is coming from and how far away it is. It also lets you hear **stereo sound**. Just as sound from a stereo system comes from two speakers, sound comes to your brain from your two ears.

Your two ears are almost identical. The picture below shows what one of your ears looks like.

Sound collected by the **outer ear** travels through the air in your **ear canal** to your **ear drum**. Three small bones are connected to the eardrum. These bones are called the **hammer**, **anvil**, and **stirrup**

because of their shapes. Next to these bones is a large snail-like shell called the **cochlea**. The stirrup touches the cochlea at a small membrane-covered opening called the **oval window**. The space inside the cochlea is filled with a thick fluid. Along the inside wall of the cochlea are more than 10,000 very sensitive hair cells that stick into the fluid. Attached to these hair cells are nerves that come together at the back of the cochlea and go to the brain stem.

Here's how it all works: Sound makes the ear drum vibrate. The vibrating ear drum makes the hammer, anvil, and stirrup vibrate. The vibrating stirrup causes the oval window to vibrate. The vibrating oval window causes the fluid in the cochlea to vibrate. The hair cells sense the vibrating fluid and send nerve signals to the brain stem. The nerve signals from both ears are combined in the brain stem and sent up to the brain, which interprets the signals as sound.

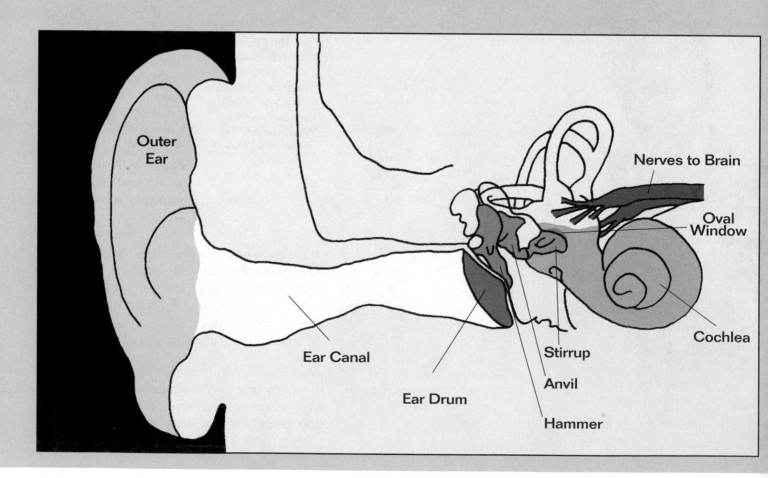

GOOD VIBRATIONS!

Here's a neat activity you can do to help you better understand sound and hearing.

1 Hold the coat hanger upside down. Tie a piece of string to each end of the bottom of the coat hanger. Wrap the other ends of the strings a couple of times around the ends of your index fingers. Place your index fingers in your ears.

2 Have your partner use a pencil to lightly tap the hanger. Describe the sound you hear.

3 Try it again, but this time, after your partner taps the hanger, your partner should very gently touch the string. Can your partner feel the string vibrate?

4 As other sound sources, instead of the hanger, use other metal objects, such as spoons of different sizes or keys to hear how they sound.

5 One thing that works really well is an oven rack from a toaster oven or kitchen oven. Tie the strings to the oven rack and let it hang down like the hanger. Have your partner tap it with a pencil. Describe the sounds you hear.

CAUTION:
If you are using an oven rack, be sure that the oven has not been used for several hours and that the rack is not hot.

Once the sound reaches your ear, it makes your ear drum and other parts of your ear vibrate. The vibrations cause nerve messages to go to your brain. Your brain interprets these messages as sounds.

There must always be some material for a sound to travel through to get to your ear. Here the material is the string and your finger. Usually the material is air.

If you touch the string very gently, you can feel it vibrating as sound travels through it. When sound travels through air, it makes particles of the air vibrate, but they are too small for you to see or feel.

All sounds you hear are produced by vibrating objects like this vibrating coat hanger. The coat hanger is the sound source.

BOB BOURDEAUX

Hearing in 3-D

You are riding your bike down a busy street. A motorcycle roars up behind you. A bus honks its horn. A man coughs. A radio blares from somewhere nearby. A trash can lid bangs on the sidewalk. A bird sings. You have the amazing ability to hear all of these sounds at the same time. You can also tell, without looking, where each sound is coming from. You can do this because you have two ears. This activity will help you figure out why two ears work better than one.

YOU WILL NEED:

no special materials

1 Stand in the middle of the room surrounded by your classmates. Close your eyes and plug up one ear. Your teacher (or someone else) should silently point to one of your classmates. This person should clap once.

2 Listen carefully for the sound and point your finger in the direction it seemed to come from. Your teacher then silently points to another classmate in another part of the room. This new classmate claps once, and you try to point toward the sound. Your teacher continues to point to other classmates to make sounds for you to try to locate.

3 Keep your eyes closed, but unplug your ear. Your teacher will repeat the activity, but this time you will use both ears to locate the sound. Are you more successful?

THE KEY TO HEARING IN 3-D:
Your brain can tell which direction a sound is coming from in two ways:

(1) By which ear hears the loudest sound: Your ear that is closest to the sound source will hear the sound a little louder than the other ear. Your brain interprets the extra loudness to mean that the sound source must be in the direction of the ear that hears it the loudest!

(2) By the difference in the time that the sound reaches each ear: Sounds coming from the side will reach your closest ear a tiny fraction of a second before they reach your other ear. Your brain interprets this time difference to mean that the sound source must be in the direction of the ear which heard the sound slightly sooner!

STAFF ILLUSTRATION

A *WonderScience* Pitch Switcher

Humans can hear a wide range of loudness, from the very quiet sounds of a whisper to the loud roar of a jet engine. We can also hear extremely small differences in the highness and lowness of sounds. This characteristic of sound is called pitch. Some musical instruments, such as a piano or harp, have strings, each of which plays a different pitch. Try the activity below to see what makes some strings produce a high-pitched sound and others a low-pitched sound.

1 Use your push pin to carefully poke a hole in the center of the bottom of a cup.

2 Cut a rubber band. Thread one end through the cup and out the hole. Tie two or three knots in the end of the rubber band inside the cup as shown.

3 Tape the cup to the ruler so that the bottom of the cup is on about the 2 centimeter line. Tie a paper clip to the free end of the rubber band. Stretch the rubber band to the end of the ruler. Tape the rubber band down as shown so that the paper clip helps the rubber band stay securely attached to the end of the ruler.

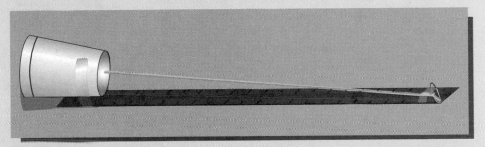

4 Hold the cup to your ear as shown. Pluck the rubber band once. Press the rubber band down onto the ruler near the end opposite the cup. Pluck the rubber band again. Was the sound different than before?

5 Press the rubber band down as you move your finger closer and closer to the cup. Pluck the rubber band each time you press down the rubber band. How does changing the length of the vibrating part of the rubber band change the pitch of the sound?

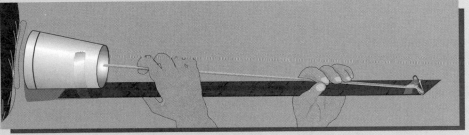

RHONDA RAWLINGS

6 How do you think the sound will change if, instead of pressing the rubber band down closer and closer to the cup, you press the rubber band down farther away from the cup? Try it and see! How is this similar to the way a guitar player can change the pitch of a string on a guitar? Can you use this idea to make a homemade guitar?

The Many States of Hearing

To reach your ear, sound usually travels through the air. But sound can travel through other things too. Try the activity below to see how well sound travels through the different states of matter: liquids, gases, and solids.

1 Put sand or dirt in a plastic bag so that it is about half full. Push the extra air out and then seal it so that no sand or dirt will leak out. Lay the bag on its side.

2 Fill another plastic bag with water so that it is as full as the bag of dirt. Push the extra air out and then seal it so that no water will leak out. Lay the bag on its side.

3 Blow into one of your plastic bags so that it is inflated. Let some air out until the bag is as full as the bags of dirt and water. Seal it so that no air will leak out. Lay the bag on its side.

4 Clear off a table and place one of the bags on the table. Put one ear gently on the bag and put your finger in your other ear. Lightly tap or rub the table with the eraser end of a pencil from about an arm's length away. How well can you hear the sound? Lift your ear off the bag and tap or rub the pencil again. Do you hear it better with or without the bag?

5 Repeat step 4 with the other two bags. Through which bag did you hear the sound best? Through which bag was the sound hardest to hear?

People who lived on the great plains in the early days of the United States put an ear on the ground to tell if buffalo or horses were coming. Can you see why they didn't simply listen in the air?

Dolphins and whales communicate through great distances under water. Do you think they could communicate from so far away if they lived on land?

YOU WILL NEED:

3 zip-closing
   plastic bags

water

sand or dirt

pencil

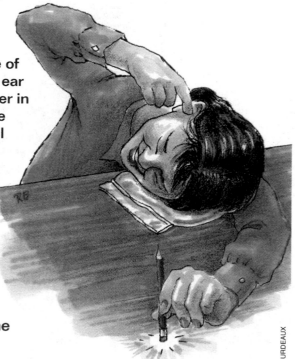

BOB BOURDEAUX

456

WONDER SCIENCE

Physics of Music

This unit introduces students to some of the physics behind musical instruments and the sounds they make. Students should discover that all the musical sounds we hear are produced by something vibrating, that the greater the rate of vibration, the higher the pitch of the sound, and that changing the length of an object changes the rate at which the object vibrates and the pitch of the sound it produces.

Bottled Music!

In *Bottled Music!*, students notice that when tapping on the bottles, the bottles with the most water have the lowest pitch and those with the least water have the highest pitch. When blowing over the bottles, the results should be reversed. The reason for this is that when tapping on the bottles, it is the bottle and water together that are vibrating. Adding water adds mass to this bottle/water system, causing the rate of vibration to decrease which lowers the pitch. When blowing across the bottle, it is the air inside the bottle that vibrates first, which then causes the bottle to vibrate. When water is added, the length of the column of air inside the bottle is reduced. This shorter air column vibrates faster, causing the bottle to vibrate faster, increasing the pitch.

Good Vibrations!

Good Vibrations! illustrates that as an object is made longer, it vibrates more slowly and makes a sound of lower pitch. To emphasize this point, make sure there is a large difference between the length of the ruler that extends beyond the edge of the table in the different steps in the activity.

Pluck-A-Cup Strummer

In *Pluck-A-Cup Strummer*, students are challenged to discover the range of pitches that can be played by plucking a rubber band attached to a paper or plastic cup. The length of the rubber band is the main factor effecting the pitch of the sound. Holding the rubber band at different points along its length should produce lower pitched sounds with greater lengths and higher-pitched sounds with shorter lengths. Length has a much greater impact on pitch than does degree of stretch.

Singing Trees

Singing Trees discusses a recent scientific discovery that some trees, during drought conditions, emit ultrasonic sounds. Ultrasonic sounds refer to noises that are beyond the range of human hearing. These sounds are produced by something vibrating more than 20,000 times per second. Dogs, bats, and as you will learn in this article, certain insects can hear ultrasonic sounds.

A Straw Whistle Symphony!

A Straw Whistle Symphony! is another fun way to illustrate the relationship between length of a vibrating object and its pitch. Students will see that a very small change in the length of the straw creates an audible difference in pitch.

A Vibration Sensation!

A Vibration Sensation! enables students to indirectly see the vibrating air caused by the music or talking from a radio speaker. The key to this activity is to hold the soap film very close to the speaker and to change the volume and station until you hit a combination that makes the film vibrate. It also helps if the viewer looks at the film at an angle rather than straight on.

RELEVANT NATIONAL SCIENCE EDUCATION STANDARDS

The activities in this unit can be used to support the teaching of the following standards:

✔ Science as Inquiry
  Abilities necessary to do scientific inquiry

✔ Physical Science
  Transfer of energy

Bottled Music!

Parent/adult note: It is important to clean bottles thoroughly, in a dishwasher or with very hot soapy water, before anyone blows into them. Also, bottles should be rewashed prior to a new person placing his or her mouth over the opening.

1 Pour different amounts of water into each bottle so that the heights of the water in the bottles are 2 cm, 5 cm, 7 cm, 9 cm, 12 cm, and 17 cm.

2 If you gently tap the side of each bottle with a spoon, do you think the sounds you hear will be different? How do you think they will differ? Try it!

3 Arrange your bottles in a row according to the types of sounds you heard. Start your row with the lowest sounding bottle on the left and moving to the highest sounding bottle on the right. Then look at your bottles and fill in the level of water in each bottle in the chart below.

lowest pitch   highest pitch

4 Predict what will happen if, instead of tapping each bottle with the spoon, you blow across the top of each bottle. Which bottle do you think will make the highest pitched sound? The lowest pitched sound? Try it and find out! Were your predictions correct?

lowest pitch   highest pitch

5 After blowing across the top of each bottle, rearrange your bottles in a row, putting the lowest sounding bottle on the left and moving to the highest sounding bottle on the right. Fill in the level of water in each bottle in this new bottle chart. Now compare your two charts. What do you find?

6 Are you surprised by the results of your experiment? Can you explain them?

7 Line up the bottles in order from the highest water level to the lowest. Number the bottles from 1 to 6. You are now ready to play some of the songs below, or to make up tunes of your own! Just use the spoon to gently tap the sides of the bottles in the order shown!

Mary Had a Little Lamb

3 2 1 2 3 3 3   2 2 2   3 5 5
3 2 1 2 3 3 3   3 2 2   3 2 1

Frère Jacques (Are You Sleeping?)

1 2 3 1   1 2 3 1   3 4 5   3 4 5
5 6 5 4 3 1   5 6 5 4 3 1
1 2 1   1 2 1

8 Did "Mary Had a Little Lamb" sound right when you played it on your bottles? If not, try changing the amount of water in the bottles until you get the pitch that you want.

9 How would you rewrite the notes of the above songs if you were going to blow across the bottles instead of tapping them with the spoon? Try it and see if it works!

---

* All activities in *WonderScience* have been reviewed for safety by Dr. Jack Breazeale, Francis Marion College, Florence, SC; Dr. Jay Young, Chemical Health and Safety Consultant, Silver Spring, MD; and Dr. Patricia Redden, Saint Peter's College, Jersey City, NJ.

Tune In!

Do you play a musical instrument? If you do, you probably know that when an instrument makes a sound, some part of the instrument vibrates back and forth very quickly. In fact, all sounds that you can hear are made by objects vibrating at least 20 times each second! You may have seen the top of a drum vibrating or felt the vibrations against your lip when you blew on a trumpet or other horn. The faster something vibrates, the higher the pitch of the sound it makes. You can discover this yourself in "Good Vibrations."

Some musical instruments, such as violins and guitars, have strings that vibrate when you pluck or rub them. Did you know that even a piano has strings? For each piano key there is a string hidden inside the piano. Whenever the key is played, a little hammer attached to the key strikes the string causing it to vibrate. If you raise the lid of the piano and look inside, you will see that the strings are all of different lengths. If you try playing different keys, you will find that hammers hitting the shortest strings make the highest pitched notes. Hammers hitting the longer strings make notes of lower pitch. A guitar player makes the vibrating part of a guitar string shorter by pressing the string against the neck of the guitar. When the shortened string is plucked, it will vibrate faster and make a higher pitched sound. Changing the thickness or tightness of a string also changes the pitch. If you look at a guitar, you will see that some of the strings are thicker than others. Tuning screws at the end of the neck allow a player to change the tightness of the guitar strings. In "Pluck-A-Cup Strummer" activity , you can find out how changing the length, tightness, or thickness of a vibrating string changes the pitch of the sound it makes.

Musical instruments like trumpets, harmonicas, flutes, tubas, saxophones, and even wind chimes do not have strings. But if you gently touch one of these instruments as it makes a sound, you can feel it vibrating. Many instruments are hollow. When hollow instruments are played, the air inside of them vibrates first, which then makes the rest of the instrument vibrate.

When you blew over each of the soda bottles in "Bottled Music," you were making the air inside each bottle vibrate. The bottle with the most water had the shortest column of air, and produced the highest pitched sound when you blew over it. When you tapped this same bottle with the spoon, the pitch of the sound was the lowest because it was the tallest column of water that was vibrating! Just remember:

Longer objects vibrate more **slowly** and make sounds of **lower pitch!**

Shorter objects vibrate **more quickly** and make sounds of **higher pitch!**

Have fun with your new *WonderScience* as you investigate the physics of music!

GOOD VIBRATIONS!!

GOOD VIBRATIONS!!

1 Extend most of the ruler over the edge of the table, pressing the other end against the table with the palm of your hand. Lightly thump the extended end, and listen carefully to the sound the vibrating ruler makes.

2 Again thump the end of the ruler lightly, but this time watch the ruler to see how fast it is vibrating.

3 What do you think will happen if you thump the ruler harder? Will the ruler vibrate more quickly or will the vibrations just be larger? How will the sound the ruler makes change? Try it and find out! Make sure the same amount of ruler extends over the table edge each time.

4 How do you think the sound will change if you thump the ruler with only a small amount extended over the edge of the table? Try it and see! Watch the ruler to see if the rate at which it is vibrating has changed.

5 See how many sounds you can make with the ruler. Can you use it to play a song? If you had several rulers, how could you make an instrument out of them?

You will need

flexible ruler (1 ft)
table

What's All the Buzz About?

D id you know that a bee makes a buzzing sound only when it is flying? The buzz is made by the bee's wings flapping through the air very fast. A bee's wings vibrate several hundred times every second! Can you make your hands flap back and forth that fast?!!

Match each insect below with how fast you think its wings vibrate back and forth. Here's a hint: The insect that makes the highest pitched sound has wings that vibrate the fastest!

1. Honeybee   A. 580 vibrations each second
2. Beetle   B. 352 vibrations each second
3. Housefly   C. 200 vibrations each second
4. Mosquito   D. 440 vibrations each second

Answers are after "A Straw Whistle Symphony."

PLUCK-A-CUP STRUMMER

1 Cut the rubber band to make it a single long rubber string. It should be at least 15 cm unstretched. If not, you may need to tie two or more cut rubber bands together.

2 Have your adult partner use a pencil or other sharp object to poke a very small hole in the center of the bottom of the cup.

3 Tie a knot in one end of your rubber string, then run the string through the hole in the cup bottom. Place a piece of tape across the knot inside the cup.

4 Hold the cup up to one ear, and gently pluck the rubber string!

5 Discover how many differently pitched sounds you can produce with your Pluck-A-Cup Strummer. Does holding the rubber band closer or further from the cup change the pitch? What other ways can you change the rubber string to make different pitched notes?

You will need	
disposable plastic or paper cup	tape
long rubber band	sharpened pencil or nail

Singing Trees

Did you know that sometimes trees sing? Yes, indeed! During a drought, when trees do not get enough water, they chirp and cheep! The sounds trees make are called ***ultrasonic*** sounds. They are too high-pitched to be heard by humans, although they can be detected with special instruments. The bad news is that many insects can hear the ultrasonic sounds made by a thirsty tree.

A Straw Whistle Symphony!

You will need

blunt-tipped scissors
plastic straws

1 Wash your hands and make sure they are clean. Flatten one end of a straw by biting down on it and then pulling it between your closed teeth. Cut the flattened end into a point as shown. You have now made a straw whistle!

2 Place the pointed end of the straw whistle in your mouth, press down gently with your lips, and blow. With a little practice, you should be able to get your straw whistle to produce a loud buzzing sound! (If you have trouble, make sure your lips are not pressed together so hard that air cannot pass through the straw. You might also try flattening the end some more, or placing your lips further down on the straw.)

3 How do you think the sound will change if you make your straw whistle shorter? Cut off about 1/4 of your straw from the unflattened end and find out!

4 Make a new straw whistle. Then, while you are blowing on it, have your adult partner use the scissors to cut the straw shorter and shorter. How does the pitch of the sound change?

5 Make straw whistles of different lengths. Get some friends to join you for a straw whistle symphony! Give each person a different length straw whistle. Try using the whistles to play some of the tunes learned, or make up a tune of your own!
Never run or play with a straw in your mouth.

Scientists have discovered that these sounds even attract harmful tree-boring insects, like the bark beetle. The bark beetle bores into a tree that is weak because of drought or disease. This makes the tree even weaker, and often kills it. Scientists are now trying to use other sources of ultrasonic sounds to "fool" the bark beetle so they can trap it. Can you explain how this might work?

Answers: 1. (D), 2. (C), 3. (B), 4. (A)

Adapted from "Science Report," a publication of the American Institute of Physics

A Vibration Sensation!

The music and talking that you hear on the radio is also caused by vibrations. In the following activity, you will use a radio and a **WonderScience** *Sound Vibration Detector* to help you "see" these musical vibrations!

You will need

liquid dish detergent (yellow, blue, or green)
16-oz plastic-foam cup
sugar
small plate
small cup
measuring spoons
radio

1 Take the rim off of your plastic foam cup so that you have a plastic foam ring.

2 Pour 1 tablespoon of dish detergent into a small cup. Add 1 teaspoon of sugar and stir until the sugar dissolves.

3 Pour your solution onto a small plate. Dip the ring into the solution and gently lift it out to form a thin film inside the ring.

4 Turn a radio on to music at a medium volume. Ask your adult partner to hold the ring as ***close as possible*** to the radio speaker without touching it.

(Adult note: It is best to rest your hand on a table so that you can hold the ring with as little vibration from your own hand as possible).

5 Watch the film from the side to see if it vibrates with certain sounds in the music. If you don't see the film vibrating, change the volume. If you still cannot see the vibrations, you should try changing the station to other music. You may also get good vibrations from people talking on the radio.

What kind of music gives you the best vibrations?

WONDERSCIENCE

In this unit, students investigate the topic of echoes. Echoes are the result of sound bouncing off an object and returning to the source of the sound or some device capable of detecting the sound. A sound will produce a good clear echo only under certain conditions:

1. the sound must be strong enough to reach the object and to bounce off without dissipating too much;
2. the reflecting object must be large enough so that most of the sound will bounce off rather than go around it;
3. the reflecting object must be far enough away so that the original sound and the echo don't combine to make one sound or a garbled sound; and
4. the reflecting object must be hard and smooth enough so that most of the sound will bounce off rather than be absorbed.

Sounds Good to Me!

In *Sounds Good to Me!*, a student should do the yelling *and* the listening for the activity to work well. In this activity, a clear echo will not be produced because the source of the sound is too close to the inside of the can. But the reflected sound from the bottom and sides of the can should make the total sound appear louder than the same yell without using the can. When holes are punched into the can, the yell should seem quieter. With the bottom missing completely, the yell should seem quieter still. Throughout this activity, be sure not to allow a student to handle the edges of the can or to reach into the can. It may be very sharp.

Make an Echo...Echo...Echo!

In *Make an Echo...Echo...Echo!*, students communicate by sending words through tubes and bouncing them off a smooth hard surface.

Echoes Are Everywhere!

In *Echoes Are Everywhere!*, students develop map skills while learning how echoes are used in nature and in modern technology.

Bats? We're All Ears!

In *Bats? We're All Ears!*, students combine art and mathematics to make a pair of bat ears while learning why some bats have such large ears.

RELEVANT NATIONAL SCIENCE EDUCATION STANDARDS

The activities in this unit can be used to support the teaching of the following standards:

✔ Science as Inquiry
   Abilities necessary to do scientific inquiry

✔ Physical Science
   Properties and changes of properties in matter
   Transfer of Energy

SOUNDS GOOD TO ME!*

You will need

2 identical large metal cans
    (such as 2-lb coffee cans)
hammer
large nail
can opener
dish towel
aluminum foil

Adult Partner Safety Tip: Each time you use a can opener to remove an end of a coffee can, look around the edge for any sharp points. If you find any jagged edges, use a screw driver or the back of a spoon and carefully press the sharp edges down against the inside of the can. Whether you notice sharp edges or not, cover the rim of the can with two layers of adhesive tape for safe handling.

1 Place the open end of one of the cans about 5 cm (approx. 2 in) in front of your mouth. Yell *"HELLO!"* into the can. How does it sound? Now yell *"HELLO!"*, with the same loudness, *without* using the can. Is there a difference? Which one seems louder? Why do you think one is louder than the other?

2 Place a dish towel on a work-bench, or on the ground and put the can on the towel with the bottom side up. Ask your adult partner to use the hammer and nail to make 10-15 holes in the bottom of the can.
WARNING!: DO NOT PUT YOUR HAND INSIDE THIS CAN! THE BOTTOM IS SHARP AND DANGEROUS!

---

* All activities in *WonderScience* have been reviewed for safety by Dr. Jack Breazeale, Francis Marion College, Florence, SC; Dr. Jay Young, Chemical Health and Safety Consultant, Silver Spring, MD; and Dr. Patricia Redden, Saint Peter's College, Jersey City, NJ.

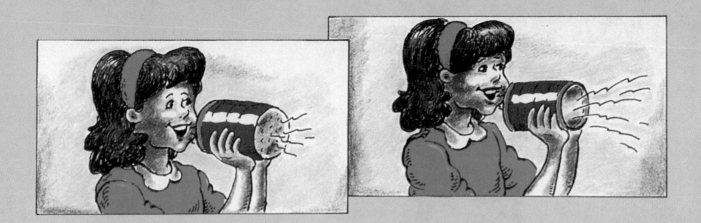

3 Yell the same thing you did before into this can. Try to yell with the same loudness *(volume)* as you did before. How is the sound different from the sound you heard using the can with the solid bottom? Why do you think the holes make a difference in the sound you hear?

4 Ask your adult partner to use a can opener to remove the bottom of the can (the can should now be open at both ends). Now yell into the can as you did before. Is the sound that you hear louder or not as loud as before? Why?

5 Take the other can (with the bottom still on it) and yell into it as you did before. Now line the inside of the can with a small dish towel or wash cloth so that it covers as much of the bottom and sides of the can as possible. Yell into the can with the same volume as before. Does the sound seem louder with or without the cloth? Why?

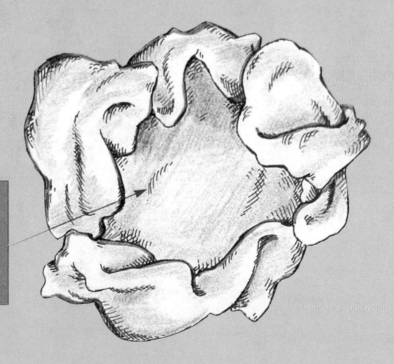

INSIDE VIEW OF DISH TOWEL-LINED CAN

6 Take the cloth out of the can and yell into the can again. Now spread aluminum foil around the inside of the can. Yell into the can. Did cloth or aluminum foil make the sound quieter? Why?

LET'S HEAR IT FOR ECHOES!

Imagine that you are standing in a large open field facing the side of a huge brick building. The building is about 100 meters (approx. 110 yards) away from you and there is nothing else around. "Yahoo!" you yell in your loudest voice. You first hear the sound of your voice as you yell, and a moment later you hear your voice again. What makes this happen?

When you yell, the sound of your voice travels outward in all directions. When some of the sound reaches the smooth hard wall of the building, it bounces off and travels back to your ear.

This *reflected* sound is called an *echo*. An echo is a sound you hear after it is reflected from some object.

If you move nearer to the building and yell again, the sound of your voice and the sound of the echo will be heard closer together. In fact, if you get near enough, the two may almost run together. And if you get closer than about 15 meters (approx. 50 ft) from the building, you won't hear an echo at all! This is because the sound gets back to you so quickly that your ear can't tell it apart from your original yell. This is why you can't hear an echo in an ordinary room even though sounds are reflected from the walls, ceiling, floor, and even from some of the furniture.

When you yelled into the can with the bottom on it in "Sounds Good To Me!", you could not hear a clear echo because you were too close to the can. Instead, what you heard was the sound of your voice plus the sound of your voice bouncing back at you at almost the same time. These two sounds added together made the whole sound much louder.

When you yelled into the can with holes in it, some of the sound passed through the holes instead of bouncing off the bottom. Since not as much sound could bounce back, the sound you heard was not as loud as before. When you yelled into the can with the bottom missing, there was even less surface from which the sound could bounce, so the volume of this yell should have seemed lowest of all. You may have also noticed that sound is reflected best from surfaces that are smooth and hard like aluminum foil. Materials that are soft such as a dish towel usually *absorb* a lot of the sound that strike them, so very little is reflected.

Usually sound reaches your ear by many paths. If you are sitting in the school auditorium, some of the sound from the stage travels directly to your ear. But some of the sound is reflected from the ceiling, walls, floor and other objects that are good sound reflectors. Some of the sound may even reflect off more than one surface before it finally reaches your ear. Because the direct sound and the reflected sound reach your ear at slightly different times, the sound in an auditorium might not always seem clear and easy to understand.

In your new *WonderScience* you will discover how to produce and detect echoes and how people and animals use echoes in important ways.

Illustration by Tina Mion

468

MAKE AN *ECHO* . . . *ECHO* . . . *ECHO!*

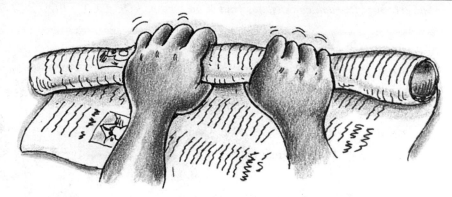

You will need

6 sheets of newspaper
1 large book
metal cookie sheet
masking tape
pen

1 Hold 3 sheets of newspaper on top of each other and roll the newspaper to make a long tube with a 1-1/2 in diameter. Use about 6 pieces of tape along the tube to hold it together. Use the other 3 sheets to make another tube like the first one. Use your pen to label one tube "A" and the other tube "B"

2 If you have a table next to a wall, stand a cookie sheet against the wall at the end of the table. If your table is not against a wall, stand a hard-cover book on the table and lean the cookie sheet against the book.

3 Place tubes "A" and "B" at the same angle to the cookie sheet as shown. Keep the ends of the tubes about 2.5 cm (approx. 1 in) away from the cookie sheet.

4 Have your adult partner whistle into tube "A" while you listen through the opening in tube "B". Your ear should touch the opening of tube "B" so it is as close to the opening as possible. How well do you hear the whistle through tube "B"? How do you think the sound gets from tube "A" to tube "B"?

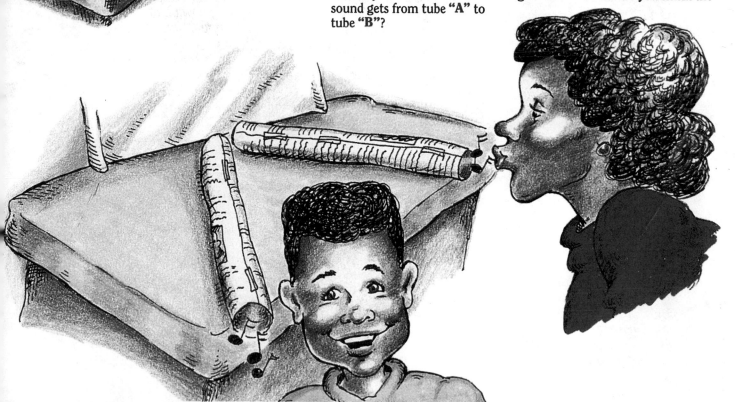

5 Now *you* can whistle or talk very quietly into tube "B" while your adult partner listens at the end of tube "A". You and your adult partner can talk and listen back and forth through your new *WonderScience* Echo Communicator! See if you can make even longer tubes to bounce sounds and messages over even longer distances! Hey, *sounds* like fun!

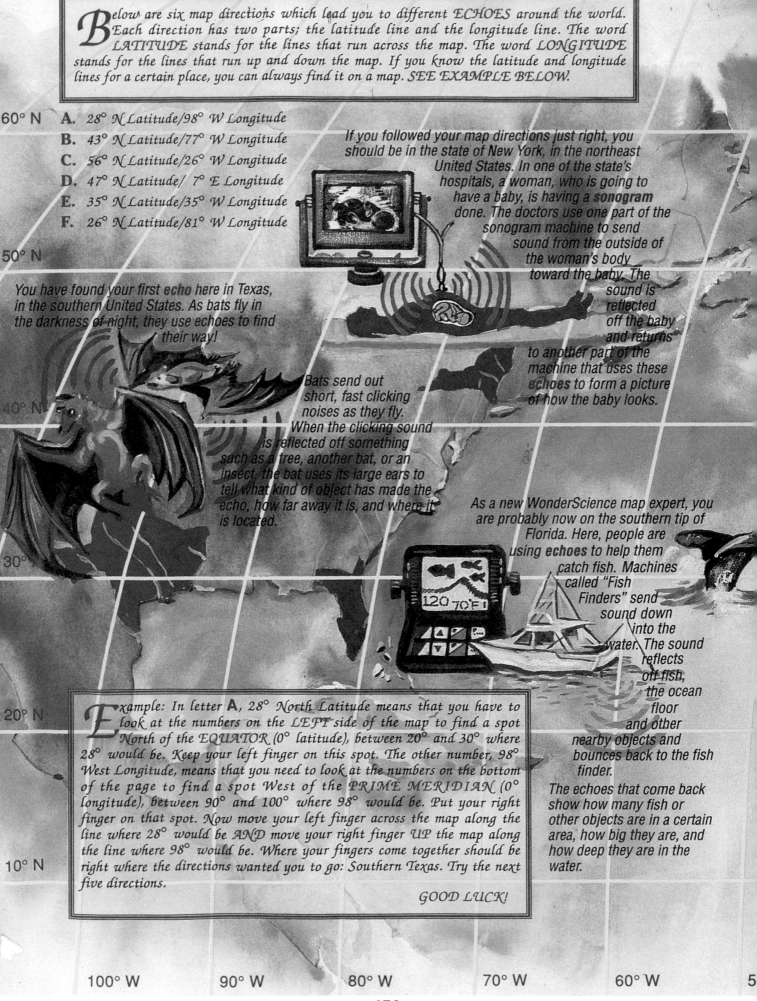

Below are six map directions which lead you to different ECHOES around the world. Each direction has two parts; the latitude line and the longitude line. The word LATITUDE stands for the lines that run across the map. The word LONGITUDE stands for the lines that run up and down the map. If you know the latitude and longitude lines for a certain place, you can always find it on a map. SEE EXAMPLE BELOW.

60° N

A. 28° N Latitude/98° W Longitude
B. 43° N Latitude/77° W Longitude
C. 56° N Latitude/26° W Longitude
D. 47° N Latitude/ 7° E Longitude
E. 35° N Latitude/35° W Longitude
F. 26° N Latitude/81° W Longitude

50° N

If you followed your map directions just right, you should be in the state of New York, in the northeast United States. In one of the state's hospitals, a woman, who is going to have a baby, is having a **sonogram** done. The doctors use one part of the sonogram machine to send sound from the outside of the woman's body toward the baby. The sound is reflected off the baby and returns to another part of the machine that uses these echoes to form a picture of how the baby looks.

You have found your first **echo** here in Texas, in the southern United States. As bats fly in the darkness of night, they use echoes to find their way!

40° N

Bats send out short, fast clicking noises as they fly. When the clicking sound is reflected off something such as a tree, another bat, or an insect, the bat uses its large ears to tell what kind of object has made the echo, how far away it is, and where it is located.

As a new WonderScience map expert, you are probably now on the southern tip of Florida. Here, people are using **echoes** to help them catch fish. Machines called "Fish Finders" send sound down into the water. The sound reflects off fish, the ocean floor and other nearby objects and bounces back to the fish finder.

30°

120 70 F

20° N

Example: In letter A, 28° North Latitude means that you have to look at the numbers on the LEFT side of the map to find a spot North of the EQUATOR (0° latitude), between 20° and 30° where 28° would be. Keep your left finger on this spot. The other number, 98° West Longitude, means that you need to look at the numbers on the bottom of the page to find a spot West of the PRIME MERIDIAN (0° longitude), between 90° and 100° where 98° would be. Put your right finger on that spot. Now move your left finger across the map along the line where 28° would be AND move your right finger UP the map along the line where 98° would be. Where your fingers come together should be right where the directions wanted you to go: Southern Texas. Try the next five directions.

The echoes that come back show how many fish or other objects are in a certain area, how big they are, and how deep they are in the water.

10° N

GOOD LUCK!

100° W   90° W   80° W   70° W   60° W   5

ECHOES ARE EVERYWHERE!

Illustration by Tina Mion

The longitude and latitude lines have led you right to our submarine in the middle of the Atlantic ocean. This submarine is traveling at 200 meters (220 yds) below the water's surface.

Submarines use sonar to travel in their underwater darkness without hitting coral reefs, icebergs, underwater mountains, or other submarines.

The sonar sends sound into the water where it is reflected off objects and comes back to the sonar system as an *echo*. From the type of echo and the time it takes to return, the sonar can tell the size, shape, distance, and location of the object.

Your map skills are good If you found your way to the Alps, a mountain range along the border of France, Italy, and Switzerland.

Some people in the Alps do a special type of singing called *yodeling*. The yodeler sings in a loud voice switching back and forth from low to high notes. If the yodeler stands in the right place, the singing will echo from mountain to mountain, making a unique sound.

If you are a good navigator, you are back in the Atlantic ocean again. Here we find porpoises, dolphins, and killer whales using *echoes* in the ocean as bats do in the air. These underwater animals make sounds at a higher *pitch* than bats, but use the echoes that come back in a similar way. From their use of echoes, they can tell one object from another and where to swim to go toward the object or away from it.

N
W E
S

PRIME MERIDIAN

40° W   30° W   20° W   10° W   0°   10° E

BATS? WE'RE ALL EARS!

In "Echoes are Everywhere!", you learned how bats use echoes to fly and catch insects in the dark. To do this, bats need large and sensitive ears to collect the echoes from the insects and other objects around them. If you were a bat, how big would your ears be?

CAUTION: When putting your bat ears up to your own ears, be sure *not* to push the ends into your ears. It will hurt!

1 Measure the length of *the opening of the bat's ear* as shown in the drawing. Record that number in the square, on the *left* side of the "+".

2 Measure the length of the *bat's face* from its forehead to its chin, as shown, and record that number in the square, on the *right* side of the "+".

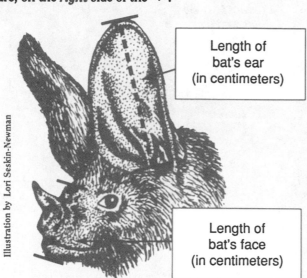

Length of bat's ear (in centimeters)

Length of bat's face (in centimeters)

Illustration by Lori Seskin-Newman

3 To find out how big the bat's ears are compared to its face, solve the math problem, and record your answer in the circle. The number in the circle tells you how many times bigger the bat's ears are than its face.

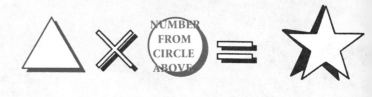

4 Have your adult partner measure the length of *your* face from your forehead to your chin. Record that number in the triangle. Multiply this number by the number in the circle above to find out how big your bat ears need to be if you were a bat. Record that number in the star.

5 To make your bat ears, roll each piece of poster board into a cone with the *small* end about 1-2 cm (1/2-3/4 in) in diameter. For your bat ears to be the right size for *you*, make the diameter of the *large* opening equal to the number you put in the star above.

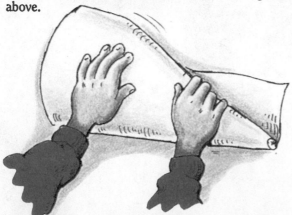

6 Use 3 or more pieces of tape to hold each bat ear together.

7 Put the small end of the bat ears up to your ears and see how well they collect the sound around you. Make sure you have the large opening facing out away from you and not down at the floor. Have your adult partner speak to you very quietly near one of your bat ears. Can you hear better with or without your bat ears?

8 Ask your adult partner to go into another room and to speak in a normal voice. Can you hear the words well? Turn on the TV or radio in another room and see how well you can hear it even if the volume is low. Have fun with your *WonderScience* bat ears!

This unit introduces students to some of the basic aspects of human vision. The complexities of the process of human vision are enormous. This unit seeks to familiarize students with the primary structures of the human eye and their functions. The other important concept for students is that vision is a process involving the eyes and the brain.

The Eyes Have It!

The Eyes Have It! shows students how well-coordinated their eyes are at working together. Students should notice that the left and right eye follow the finger in exactly the same pattern and at exactly the same time even when one eye is closed. Students should also discover that most people depend more on one eye than the other when pointing at an object. Most students should find that, regardless of the hand they use when pointing, one eye will line up their finger closer to the object than the other. Steps 7-10 deal with the eyes' ability to focus on objects at different distances and the effects of looking into the distance while an object is in the foreground.

Be a Receptor Detector!

In *Be a Receptor Detector!*, students examine the common experience of continuing to sense the effect of light even after the eyes are closed. The image seen after the eyes are closed is called an "afterimage."

Letter-perfect Vision

In *Letter-perfect Vision*, students can recreate a visit to the eye doctor by testing their vision with the help of a partner. The rating for this type of vision test is based on seeing at a distance. A vision rating of 20/40 means that what someone with normal vision can see at 40 feet, a person with 20/40 vision can only see at 20 feet. 20/60 vision is worse, 20/80 vision is worse, and so forth.

Two Eyes Are Better Than One!

In *Two Eyes Are Better Than One!*, students should discover that it is much easier to put the end of the straw in or very near the container when they have both eyes open. The key to judging distance is depth perception, and the key to depth perception is binocular vision, or the use of both eyes. When conducting the activity, have students walk toward the cup and then come straight down with the straw rather than gradually feeling their way down.

See a Sea in 3-D!

The illustration in *See a Sea in 3-D!* is created by a computer program developed by N.E. Thing Enterprises in Bedford, Massachusetts. Illustrations like these are contained in the "Magic Eye" series of books published by N. E. Thing Enterprises. Photocopies of the illustration will give the same 3-D effect as the color illustration. The technique for seeing these illustrations in 3-D takes time and patience to develop. Some students may not be able to do it but in time, most should.

ANT NATIONAL SCIENCE EDUCATION STANDARDS

The activities in this unit can be used to support the teaching of the following standards:

✔ **Science as Inquiry**
   Abilities necessary to do scientific inquiry

✔ **Life Science**
   Structure and function in living systems

THE EYES

From tiny particles of dust to giant mountains thousands of meters high. From the light of a distant star to the detailed pattern of a butterfly wing. From a speeding race car to the slowly moving turtle, your eyes can see it all! Your eyes and your brain work together to give you your amazing sense of vision. Try the activities that follow to SEE some of the wonders of vision!

1 Look closely at your partner's eyes. Hold your index finger about 20 cm in front of your partner's nose. Move your finger very slowly from one side of your partner's face to the other. Your partner should follow your finger tip with his or her eyes without using any head movement.

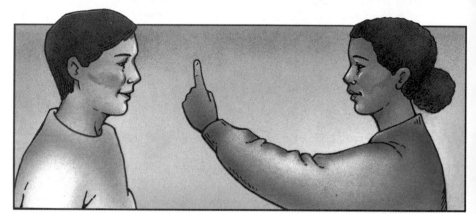

LOEL BARR

2 Do your partner's eyes move in exactly the same way? Slowly move your finger up and down. Do the eyes move up and down as far as they move from side to side? Why do you think this might be?

3 Ask your partner to close one eye and to follow your finger tip with the open eye as you move your finger slowly from side to side. Watch the eyelid of the closed eye. What do you notice?

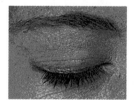

4 Repeat steps 1–3, except this time, *you* follow your partner's finger tip while your partner watches *your* eyes.

5 With both eyes open, use your right arm and index finger to point to a small object such as a light switch at the other side of the room. While still pointing at the object, close your left eye. Now switch eyes. Which eye makes your finger look closer to the object?

6 Repeat step 5 using your left arm and index finger. Which eye makes your finger look closer to the object? Is it the same eye as before? Do you think one of your eyes is more **dominant** than the other?

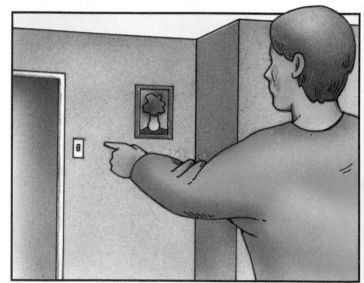

LOEL BARR

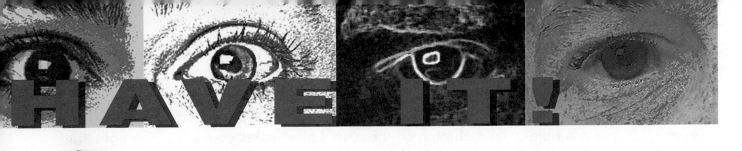
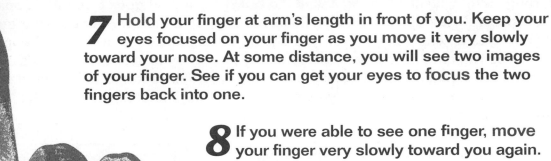

7 Hold your finger at arm's length in front of you. Keep your eyes focused on your finger as you move it very slowly toward your nose. At some distance, you will see two images of your finger. See if you can get your eyes to focus the two fingers back into one.

8 If you were able to see one finger, move your finger very slowly toward you again. Try to find the exact distance where you can no longer get the two finger images to focus into one. Your partner should measure this distance between your finger and your nose.

Now, your partner should do the activity while you measure the distance. Compare these distances to others' in your class.

9 Hold one index finger to the side and slowly move it toward your nose. As soon as you see two images of your finger, bring your other index finger over and touch finger tips. You should see something between your two fingers. What does it look like?

10 Look over your fingers while aiming your eyes into the distance. Can you still see the thing between your fingers? Separate your fingers a little. What do you see now? Hold your fingers at arm's length in front of you. Can you still see the thing between your fingers?

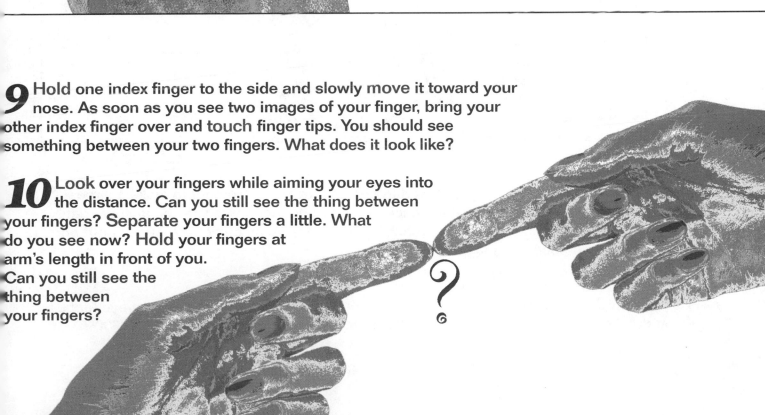

In order to see any object, light coming off the object must enter your eyes. The light first goes through a thin, clear covering called the **cornea**. It then goes through an opening called the **pupil**. The pupil looks like a black round spot in the very front of your eye. If you look at your eyes up close in a mirror, you should be able to see your pupils. (People with very dark eyes will have to look very closely). Close your eyes for a few seconds and then open them. You should be able to see the size of your pupils change with the different amount of light. The colored part of your eye, surrounding the pupil, is called the **iris**. The iris is made of muscles that control the size of the pupil.

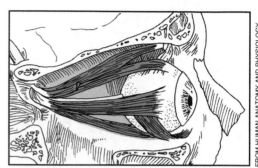

After the light enters the pupil, it passes through the **lens**. The lens is a clear structure that focuses the light toward the back of the eye. The lens has muscles attached to it that change the shape of the lens to bring objects into focus. As you moved your finger toward you during the activity on page 3, you saw two images, but your lens changed shape to focus the two images into one.

MUSCLES THAT MOVE THE EYEBALL

FROM HUMAN ANATOMY AND PHYSIOLOGY, SECOND EDITION, BY SPENCE AND MASON. COPYRIGHT © 1983 BY THE BENJAMIN/CUMMINGS PUBLISHING COMPANY.

The lens focuses light on the **retina**, which makes up the inside back of the eyeball. The retina is made up of tiny structures called **light receptors**. Some light receptors help you see the **brightness** of light, while others help you see the **colors** of light. The image on the retina is upside-down but your brain is able to understand it as right-side up!

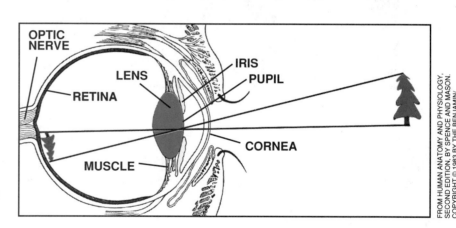

FROM HUMAN ANATOMY AND PHYSIOLOGY, SECOND EDITION, BY SPENCE AND MASON. COPYRIGHT © 1983 BY THE BENJAMIN/CUMMINGS PUBLISHING COMPANY.

The receptors on the retina are connected to nerves that come together to make a large nerve, called the **optic nerve**, at the back of the eye. In fact, there is a "blind spot" right where the optic nerve connects to the retina. If the light from an object is focused right on that spot, you can't see the image.

Blind Spot Activity:
Position yourself directly above the dot. Close your left eye, then with your right eye focus on the dot while moving closer to and farther from the page. What happens to the "X"?

The optic nerve sends nerve signals to the part of the brain that deals with vision. Your brain takes the signals from each eye and puts them together giving you your amazing sense of vision!

476

Be a Receptor Detector!

The retina at the back of the eye is made up of receptors that detect light. In most cases, you can see the effect of light hitting your receptors even after your eyes are closed! Try the activity below and be a receptor detector!

YOU WILL NEED:

flashlight

white or light-colored wall
(or piece of paper)

Teacher:
Leave the lights on in the room. Turn on a flashlight, and place it shining out toward your students.

Students:

1 From about 3 meters away from the flashlight, **close** one eye and use the other eye to **look** directly into the light from the flashlight for about 3 to 5 seconds.

You have now activated the receptors on your retina!

2 Now **close** both eyes. Leave them closed for a while. **Describe** what you see. What is its shape? Does it have a color? Is it moving? Does it change shape or color?

3 Keep your eyes closed, and **place** your hands over your closed eyes. **Describe** any changes in what you see.

4 Open your eyes so that you are looking at a white or light-colored wall or piece of paper. **Describe** what you see now. Did it change color? Close and open your eyes very slowly. What did you notice?

RENATA ROBERTS

5 If you can still see your spot with your eyes open, slowly **move** toward the wall or piece of paper you are looking at. What happened?

6 If you are interested in what you saw, try the whole activity again for another look!

Letter-perfect vision

Our sense of vision allows us to see the details of things from far away. But how much detail, and from how far, is the question. One way the eye doctor tests your ability to see details from a distance is to have you read letters from an eye chart. Here is a way you can compare your vision with your partner's and with other students' in your class!

Teacher Preparation:

Photocopy this page so there is one page for each pair of students.

If you wear eyeglasses, you may keep them on for this activity!

A

A-1	**ARNTS**
A-2	**BLDPC**
A-3	**FTLRG**
A-4	**EOSYT**

B

PCQVM	B-1
HWJVN	B-2
IKBZL	B-3
QNRGI	B-4

Student Activity:

1 Cut out the strips of letters, and keep the four strips in column A. Give your partner the 4 strips in column B. You should each keep your strips secret from each other.

2 Make a chart like the one below. Tape strip A-1 on a wall at one end of the room. Stand near the strip so that you can read the letters clearly. Your partner should stand at the other end of the room.

	Distance from the letters		Distance from the letters
A-1		B-1	
A-2		B-2	
A-3		B-3	
A-4		B-4	

3 Ask your partner to read the letters out loud from left to right. If any mistakes were made, your partner should move a little closer and try again. When all the letters are read correctly, use your meter stick measure the distance between your partner and the strip. Record that distance in the chart next to A-1.

4 Now your partner should tape B-1 on the wall and *you* try to read the letters. Move closer if you get any wrong. When you get them right, your partner should measure the distance between you and the strip. Your partner should record the distance in the chart next to B-1.

5 Repeat steps 2 to 4 using A-2 and B-2, then A-3 and B-3, and then A-4 and B-4. From the information in your chart, how does your vision compare to your partner's? Which of you could see big letters from further away? Was this same person also better at seeing the small letters?

Compare your results with other students in your class. What did you discover?

TWO Eyes are Better Than ONE!

YOU WILL NEED:

5 straws (at least one must be flexible)

1 empty film container or similar small container

metric ruler

paper

pencil

One of the most important things about vision is our ability to tell which things are close to us and which are far away. This is called **depth perception**. One of the keys to depth perception is using our two eyes at the same time. Because our eyes are separated from each other, each eye looks at a scene from a slightly different angle and gets a slightly different view of the scene. Your brain puts these two views together. This process in the brain allows us to tell which things are close to us and which are far away. Try the following activity to see that two eyes are better than one.

1 Use your ruler to find the center of your paper. Mark the center with a dot. Place your container on the center dot, and use your pencil to draw a circle around it.

2 You and your partner should each make a chart like the one below. Connect 5 straws by placing one straw inside the other as shown. Be sure the last straw has a flexible end sticking out. Point the flexible end down as shown.

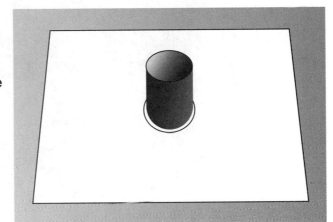

3 Stand about 2 meters from the container. Close one eye, extend your arm, and walk forward until you think the end of the straw is directly over the container. Lower the straw and see where the tip lands.

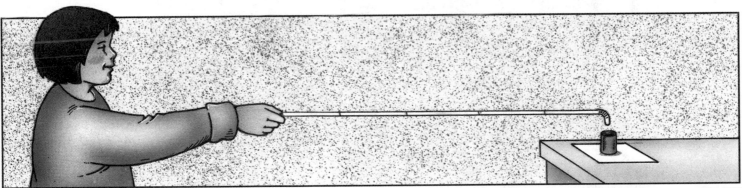

LOEL BARR

	Distance from container		
	1st try	2nd try	3rd try
Right eye open			
Left eye open			
Both eyes open			

4 Your partner should use a ruler and measure from the side of the container to the place where the straw landed. Record the distance in centimeters in the chart.

5 Try it three times with just your right eye open and three times with just your left eye open. Then try it three times with both eyes open. Look at your chart when you are done. What are all the things your measurements tell you?

479

See a Sea in 3-D!

Hold the picture at arm's length in front of you. Allow your eyes to relax.

Although the picture is in the way, focus your eyes on something in the distance as if your eyes could see right through the picture. This should make the two eyes at the top of the page move toward each other. When they meet, you should see the sea in 3-D!

Here's another way to try it: Focus your eyes on some object in the distance. Hold the picture with your arms extended down around your knees. While keeping your eyes focused in the distance and the picture at arm's length, slowly raise the picture until it is in front of you. Remember to keep your focus into the distance even though you see the picture in front of you. You should see the sea in 3-D!

WONDERSCIENCE

The activities in this unit introduce students to the concept that light is made up of different colors. The effects of mixing colors and a technique for separating colors are also investigated.

Making Rainbows!

In *Making Rainbows!*, students use a clear plastic cup of water and a flashlight to produce a spectrum. Please note the angle at which the flashlight must be held to get the best results. The light should be held slightly below the edge of the table at the angle pictured in the drawing. The cup of water should be at the edge of the table or counter.

Spin Those Colors! *and* Make Your Own Color Mix Chart

In *Spin Those Colors!*, a simple color wheel is used to explore how our eyes interpret colors as "mixing" when they are spun on a color wheel. As a follow-up to *Spin Those Colors!* students can investigate what colors look like when they actually are mixed in *Make Your Own Color Mix Chart*. Have students combine the same colors as in *Spin Those Colors!* and compare the results.

Break It Up!

In *Break It Up!*, students use a technique known as paper chromatography to separate mixtures of colored inks. The different colors which make up black ink are carried by the water traveling up the coffee filter strip at different rates. Students should be able to tell which colors of ink travel faster than others by examining the finished strips.

Prism in a Pan

In *Prism in a Pan*, students make prisms from gelatin. The prisms can be made in various sizes to meet your needs in the classroom, but the shape should be similar to the one in the drawing. As with the "cup of water" prism, the position of the gelatin prism at the edge of the table, and the angle of the flashlight are crucial.

RELEVANT NATIONAL SCIENCE EDUCATION STANDARDS

The activities in this unit can be used to support the teaching of the following standards:

✔ Science as Inquiry
  Abilities necessary to do scientific inquiry

✔ Physical Science
  Properties and changes of properties in matter
  Transfer of energy

MAKING RAINBOWS!

You will need

clear plastic cup (8 oz.)
water
flashlight
food color (red, green, and blue)
white poster board (small size)
dark room
crayons or nontoxic markers
ruler

1 Fill the cup almost full of water. Make a screen by folding the poster board in half and standing it up like a tent. Put the cup of water at the edge of the table. (Be careful not to knock it over!) Move your screen so that it is about 3 in. from the base of the cup.

2 Turn on the flashlight and darken the room completely. Shine the flashlight through the side of the plastic cup at the angle shown in the picture.

3 Change the angle of the flashlight slightly until you see a band of color on the screen. What colors do you see? Make a copy of your color band here with crayons or markers. Label each color.

4 Now, experiment with the way that you hold the flashlight. If you move the flashlight toward the table, what happens to the bands of color? Try moving the flashlight back to where you first held it and watch the color band. What happens? Record your observations here _____

_____

_____.

What could the water be doing to the beam of light to cause the colors to appear?

5 You have been using plain water in your cup so far. Let's see what might happen if you use red water in the cup. To change the color of your water, add three drops of red food color to the water in your cup. Now, make a color band on the screen using the red water. What colors do you see now? Record your observations here. _____

_____

6 Now, predict what will happen to the color band if you make it with blue, then with green water. _____

_____

Test your predictions with the other two colors of water. (Start with fresh water each time.) What happens? Record your observations here. _____

_____

_____

7 Was the water necessary to make the color band? Pour out the water in your cup and try to make a color band with the cup alone. Did it work? What part does water play in causing a color band to be formed?

8 Turn the page to read more about light and color. You can find another color band activity on the last page of this unit.

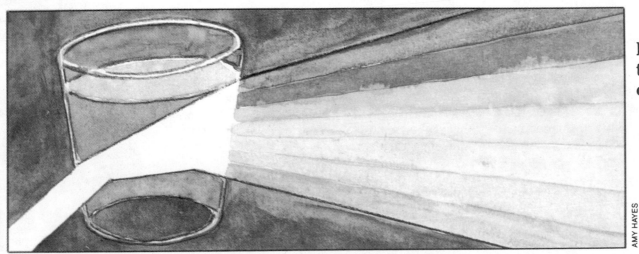

Label the bands of color!

AMY HAYES

COLOR
What Goes In; What Comes Out

Color is a very important part of our lives. Colors help identify many plants and animals. We expect lemons to be yellow, for example, and male cardinals to be red. Some living things even have their particular colors attached to their names: black bears, red raspberries, bluebirds, redheaded woodpeckers, bluets, yellow-bellied sapsuckers, green snakes, violets, and many others. Color also plays a part in our enjoyment of food. Do you think that blue mashed potatoes would be as appetizing as white ones? Would you be happy about biting into a *dark green* chicken leg? We expect certain things to be certain colors, but what makes us see color in the first place?

To answer the above question, try this experiment. Look closely at the colors of the clothes that you're wearing. Now, go into a dark room and look at your clothes again. Can you still see the colors? It is quite clear that we need to have light to see colors. Our eyes have special structures in them called cones that enable us to see the colors around us. The color message goes from the cones to our brains. We both see and understand that a tomato that we are looking at is red, for example.

The colors that we see are part of what is called the visible (because we can see it) light *spectrum*. When you see a rainbow in the sky (or the color band that appeared on your screen) you are seeing a spectrum. A spectrum is made when white light traveling through the air is slowed down by going through a clear material such as water, glass, or plastic. This "slowing down" causes the white light to break into the colors of the spectrum. Red light is slowed down the least when this happens, and violet light the most. The first letters of the colors of the visible light spectrum spell out ROY G. BIV. These letters stand for the colors Red, Orange, Yellow, Green, Blue, Indigo, and Violet. It is possible to filter out colors from the spectrum by using colored cellophane filters over a flashlight lens. You tried a similar experiment when you made your color band using different colors of water.

Both chemists and physicists work with color, but in different ways. A physicist can break white light into colors by slowing the light down, just as you have already done. A chemist can separate a colored ink, such as green ink, into its different colors by using chemicals and special paper. You have already had a chance to make rainbows by slowing down light. Try separating colored inks with the activity called "Break It Up."

Mix colors of light as the physicists do when you "Make a Color Wheel." Mix different food colors as a chemist does when you "Make Your Own Color Mix Chart." Compare these two ways of mixing color. How are they the same? How are they different?

Think about a world without color. List some ways in which your life would be different if there were no color. Talk about these ways with your adult partner.

TINA MION

SPIN THOSE COLORS!

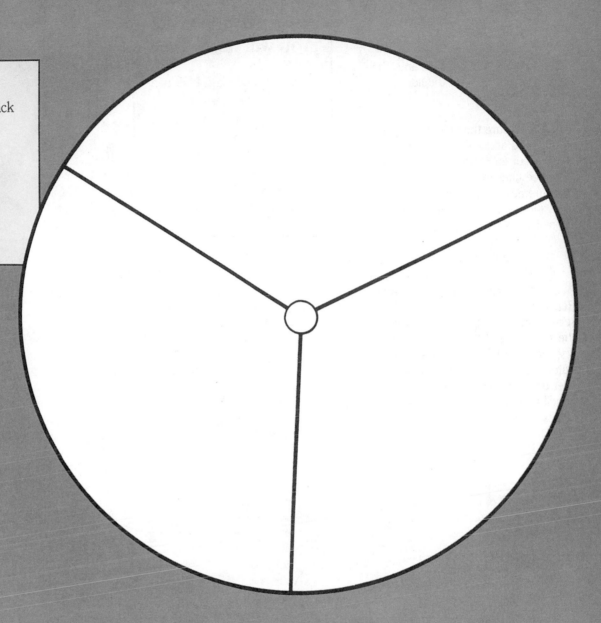

You will need

red, blue, green, and black crayons or nontoxic markers

blunt scissors

unsharpened pencil

rubber band

stiff paper or cardboard

white paper

1 Mix colors by making a color wheel! Trace this three-part circle onto your white paper with your black crayon or marker. Color one part of the circle red, one blue, and the third green. Cut the circle out with blunt scissors and tape the back of it to stiff paper or cardboard.

2 Cut the stiff paper in the same shape as the color wheel. Have an adult make a hole in the center of the wheel and push the pencil through. Wind the rubber band on the end of the pencil to keep the wheel from spinning off. Hold the other end of the pencil and spin the wheel!

3 What happens to the different colors when you spin the wheel? Try using other colors instead of red, green, and blue to make another wheel. Can you get the same results as when you spun the red/green/blue wheel?

ANN BENBOW

BREAK IT UP! (How to Separate Colors)

1 Pour 1/4-in. of water into the jar and replace the lid.

2 Measure the height of the jar and add 2 in. to the height. Cut four strips of paper towel or coffee filter to the above measurement. Each strip should be 1 in. wide. Cut a point at one end of each strip as shown.

3 Using the black pen, make a 1/4-in. dot of ink 1 in. up from the point on one of the strips. Repeat with the blue pen and a second strip. Let the dots dry. Place the strips carefully in the jar so that just the point of each strip is in the water. Bend the other end of the strip over the Popsicle stick or unsharpened pencil and place the stick or pencil across the top of the jar.

You will need
water
dark blue and black Flair pens
1 clean 16-oz. plastic jar
paper coffee filters or white
    paper towels
ruler
blunt scissors
1 Popsicle stick or
    unsharpened pencil

4 Observe what happens to the dots of color as the water moves up the strips of paper. Record your observations here. _____

_____

When the ink has traveled up to the stick or pencil, remove the strips and place them on a paper towel.

5 What did you find out about the black and blue inks? Would you have suspected this from the color of the dot when you started? You can find more "Break It Up" adventures at the end of the activity "Make Your Own Color Mix Chart"

Make Your Own Color Mix Chart

You know from making your color bands and by just looking at the different colors of your crayons or markers, that there are more colors around than just red, yellow, and blue. How can we make some of these colors? Let's experiment and see!

BE SURE TO WORK ON A PAPER TOWEL-COVERED SURFACE AND TO WIPE UP ANY SPILLS IMMEDIATELY TO STOP ANY STAINS! ALSO, WHEN YOU ARE POURING THE COLORED WATER OUT, RINSE THE SINK AND CUPS THOROUGHLY, AND WASH YOUR HANDS WITH LOTS OF SOAP AND WATER.

You will need

3 dropper containers of food color (red, blue, and yellow)

3 clear plastic cups—labeled 1, 2, and 3—half-filled with water

crayons or nontoxic markers

paper towels

several flat toothpicks

1 Place all three cups in a row on a double thickness of paper towels before you begin.

2 Add two drops of red food color to Cup 1, two drops of yellow to Cup 2, and two drops of blue to Cup 3. Gently swirl each cup to mix the colors with the water. Record the color of water in each cup in the "1 COLOR" row of the chart below.

3 Now, add two drops of yellow food color to the water in Cup 1, two drops of blue color to Cup 2, and two drops of red color to Cup 3. Swirl all three cups and record the colors in the chart in the "2 COLORS" row.

4 Next, add two drops of blue food color to Cup 1, two drops of red color to Cup 2, and two drops of yellow color to Cup 3. Swirl all three cups and record the colors in the chart in the "3 COLORS" row.

5 Did you notice anything special about the final color in each cup? Did the order in which you added all three colors make any difference in the final color? Why or why not?

6 Now you know what happens when you mix certain colors to get new colors. You can separate mixed colors the same way that you separated the black ink in the activity, "Break It Up!" Mix two or three drops of the food colors of your choice in a clean cup. Transfer the dot of mixed food color to a strip of filter paper with the blunt end of a flat toothpick. Place the strip in the jar of water as before and watch your colors move!

Compare the colors that you mixed to make orange water with the colors that are on either side of the orange band in the spectrum chart you made in the first *WonderScience* activity. What do you notice?

COLOR MIX CHART			
	CUP 1	**CUP 2**	**CUP 3**
1 COLOR	red = red	yellow =	blue =
2 COLORS	red + yellow =	yellow + blue =	blue + red =
3 COLORS	red + yellow + blue =	yellow + blue + red =	blue + red + yellow =

COLOR HAIKU FOR YOU

Haiku (pronounced "hi koó") is a form of unrhymed Japanese poetry that is special because each poem is only three lines! The first line must be five syllables, the second line seven syllables, and the last line five again. The finished poem should allow the reader to imagine or experience a simple but powerful image or feeling expressed by the poet. Several examples of haiku using color follow here. You get a chance to finish the last one, and then to write one of your own. Be sure to include *colors* in your haiku and remember, the syllable counts for the lines are 5, 7, 5.

Red light stops your car	5
Beside masses of roses.	7
Look quickly! Green light!	5

Black and white cows watch.	5
The farmer opens the gate.	7
Home for yellow hay!	5

Hot sand under foot.	5
Golden beaches meet blue sea.	7
(You finish this one!)	5

PRISM IN A PAN

When you did the first activity in this unit, you were able to make color bands by shining a beam of light through a cup of water. The cup of water acts as a *prism* by making a spectrum. You may have used a glass prism at home or in school to make a spectrum. Many prisms are shaped like this:
Light passes through a prism to form color bands.

It is possible for you to make a prism yourself with the help of your adult partner. This prism won't last very long, so work quickly and carefully!

1 Put the hot water in the mixing bowl and sprinkle the gelatin over it. Stir until the gelatin is completely dissolved. Lightly oil the inside of the loaf pan.

2 Pour the gelatin in the loaf pan and allow to cool to room temperature. Place the loaf pan in the refrigerator until it is very firm. (Overnight is best.)

3 Loosen the edges of the gelatin with the knife, shake the pan gently, then turn the gelatin out onto a square of foil.

4 Have your adult partner use the knife to cut the gelatin into a prism shape as shown. Set up a poster board screen and move the gelatin prism to the edge of the table or counter as you did with your water prism. Darken the room, and repeat the "Making Rainbows" experiments with your gelatin prism. Were the color bands sharper with your water prism or your gelatin prism? Try making gelatin prisms in different colors by adding food color to the hot water before you add the gelatin. What kinds of color bands do you think that you will get from *these* prisms?

You will need
1 envelope of unflavored gelatin	spoon
poster board (small size)	table knife or wire cheese cutter
1 cup of hot tap water	aluminum foil
1 16-oz. foil loaf pan	flashlight
oil	small mixing bowl

WONDERSCIENCE

This unit introduces students to the principle that light is composed of different colors. Most of the activities in this unit concentrate on observing the spectrum of colors produced when light is viewed, under different conditions, through a diffraction grating supplied with the original *WonderScience* issue. Inexpensive plastic diffraction gratings are available through many science-oriented stores or science supply companies.

Light is an electromagnetic wave. Some electromagnetic waves have high energy, some have low energy, and some are in between. This range of electromagnetic waves is called the *electromagnetic spectrum*. Waves in the electromagnetic spectrum include X-rays, microwaves, radio waves, the waves of visible light, and others. The waves of visible light, or the light that we can see, have lower energies than X-rays and higher energies than microwaves and radio waves. Visible light is kind of in the middle of the electromagnetic spectrum.

A useful way to talk about the different energies of electromagnetic waves is through the concept of *wavelength*. *High-energy* waves like X-rays have short wavelengths. *Lower energy* waves like microwaves and radio waves have long wavelengths. This relationship between energy and wavelength also applies to visible light.

When you see the spectrum of colors through your diffraction grating, you are seeing light of different wavelengths. The series of colors you see is called the *visible spectrum*. The colors appear in order according to wavelength. From longest wavelength to shortest wavelength, the colors appear as red, orange, yellow, green, blue, and violet. The waves in the electromagnetic spectrum just beyond red are called *infrared* and are longer than we are able to see. The *waves* just beyond violet are called *ultraviolet* and are shorter than we can see.

The diffraction grating is able to separate light into its different wavelengths because the different wavelengths of light are bent at slightly different angels as they pass through the diffraction grating. Shorter wavelength light is bent more than longer wavelength light. This causes the different wavelengths of light to separate from each other, which allows them to be seen individually as different colors.

RELEVANT NATIONAL SCIENCE EDUCATION STANDARDS

The activities in this unit can be used to support the teaching of the following standards:

✔ Science as Inquiry

   Abilities necessary to do scientific inquiry

✔ Physical Science

   Properties and changes of properties in matter
   Transfer of energy

The Colors of Light—

You've probably seen the beautiful colors made by a rainbow or by light passing through a prism. But rainbows are usually not so easy to find, and prisms are a little bulky to always have with you when you need one. That's why you will need a diffraction slide available from science or teacher supply catalogs. It's a slide made from *diffraction* film. You can use it in the following activities to see the colors in light!

Most of the activities in this issue call for a darkened room. Be sure to turn the lights back on before setting up the next activity.

1 Have your adult partner help you turn off the lights in a room to make the room as dark as possible.

2 Turn on one light without a lampshade so that you can see the lit bulb. Stand a few meters away from the light. Hold the slide up to your eye as you look at the bulb. What do you see?

3 You should see many bands, each made up of different colors. Pick one of the bands and look closely at its colors. What colors do you see? If you think you see only 3 or 4 colors, look again. Do some of the colors take up more room on the band than others? Which colors take up the most room? Which take up the least? Name the colors you see in order, starting with red.

4 Ask your adult partner to turn on a flashlight. Turn off the other light in the room. With the flashlight a few meters away, look directly into the light through your diffraction slide. What do you see?

5 How is what you see with the flashlight different from what you saw with the larger light bulb? How is it similar? Do the colors in the bands always appear in the same order? Turn your slide around clockwise and counterclockwise as you look through it. What do you observe?

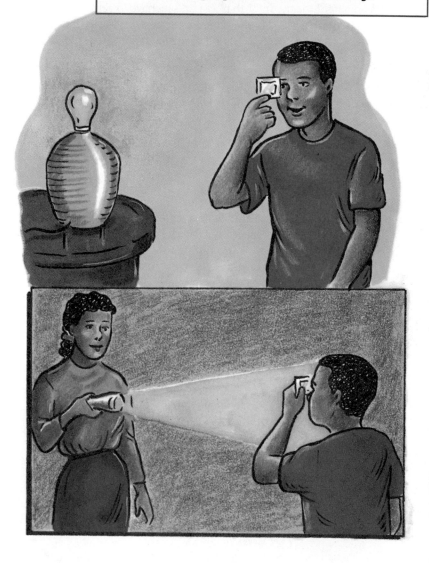

What a Sight!

6 Cover the front of the flashlight with a piece of aluminum foil. Use a pushpin to make a small hole in the center of the foil. Turn off all lights in the room and turn on the flashlight.

7 Hold the flashlight at arm's length and look directly at the light with the diffraction slide up to your eye. Does this look different than the flashlight without the aluminum foil? While looking through the slide, slowly move the slide back and forth between your eye and the flashlight. What do you observe?

8 Use the pushpin to make several more holes in the aluminum foil. Use your diffraction slide to look at the light coming through the aluminum foil. Turn your slide clockwise and counterclockwise as you look through it. How do the bands of color appear to move?

9 Cover the bottom of a clear plastic cup with marbles. Ask your adult partner to hold the cup on top of the flashlight as shown. Turn on the flashlight and look down into the cup through your diffraction slide. Describe what you see.

10 Pour water into the cup so that the water just covers the marbles. Ask your adult partner to shine the light up through the marbles and the water. Look into the cup through your slide. Have your adult partner shake the flashlight and cup while you look at the light. Try looking into the cup from close up and from farther away. How do the two look different?

---

* All activities in *WonderScience* have been reviewed for safety by Dr. Jack Breazeale, Francis Marion University, Florence, SC and Dr. Jay Young, Chemical Health and Safety Consultant, Silver Spring, MD.

SEEING
IN A WHOLE NEW LIGHT!

You looked at light through a piece of **diffraction** film. What you should have seen were bands of different colors. If you looked closely at the colors, you probably saw red, orange, yellow, green, blue, and violet. These colors that you see in this order form a **spectrum**. A spectrum is produced when diffraction film, a prism, or water drops "break up" light into its different colors.

The light from the light bulb you were looking at is actually made up of different colors of light. Your diffraction film separates these different colors so you can see them individually.

Your diffraction film is made from a special material etched with about 15,000 to 30,000 tiny lines per inch. The lines are equally spaced and all running in the same direction. When light hits the diffraction film, these tiny lines cause the light to bend. The different colors of light bend by different amounts. This causes the colors to separate from each other, which allows you to see them individually.

Most objects look the way they do because of the light that reflects or bounces off of them. On the other hand, materials such as colored glass or colored water look the way they do because of the light that is able to pass through them.

Light not only allows you to see objects, but it also allows you to see *color*. For example, when light shines on an apple, certain properties of the apple will cause some colors of the light to reflect off the surface of the apple so you can see them. Other colors of the light will not be reflected. A red apple will look red to you because of the colors of light that reflect off the apple and into your eyes.

A Dot of a Different Color!

You will need

2 sheets of white unlined
  paper
4 clear plastic cups (8–10 oz)
water
food coloring (red, blue,
  green, and yellow)

cotton swabs
pencil
metric ruler
flashlight

You learned that most objects appear as a certain color because of the colors in the light that strike and reflect off the object. In the activity below, you can see how different colored light can change the way colors appear.

1 Fill each of your cups to about 3 cm high with water. Add 3–5 drops each of red, blue, green, and yellow food coloring to separate cups. These are your colored filters.

2 Carefully place a few drops of red food coloring on one end of a cotton swab. Use the swab to make a dark red dot about 2 cm in diameter on a white piece of paper. Use separate swabs to make the same size dots of blue, green, and yellow food coloring.

3 On your other sheet of paper, make a chart like the one below. Ask your adult partner to turn on a flashlight and to turn off all the other lights in the room to make it as dark as possible.

4 Ask your partner to shine the flashlight straight down on the red dot. As you look at the dot, your partner should move the red water beneath the light so that red light shines on the red dot. Does the color of the dot look different? Write down the color you see in the chart where the red dot color and red filter color intersect.

5 Next, your partner should shine the light directly on the blue dot and then move the red filter under the light as before. Does the color of the dot seem to change? Record the color you see in the chart where the blue dot color and red filter color intersect.

6 Next, use the flashlight and red filter as before on the green and yellow dots. Repeat the activity with the remaining colored filters and each different colored dot. Record all of your results. Which filters seemed to cause the greatest change in which colored dots? Did any filter seem to make a dot very faint or even disappear? What else did you notice?

		Dot color		
		red	**blue**	**green**	**yellow**
Filter color	**red**				
	blue				
	green				
	yellow				

INSPECT A SPECTRUM!

Some things around the house can be used to make a spectrum. The colors that you see will not be as brilliant as those you saw with the diffraction slide. If you are patient and work in a very dark room, you should be able to make a faint spectrum with a cup of water and a brighter one with a cassette tape case!

You will need

clear plastic cup
water
flashlight
clear plastic cassette tape case
books
white unlined paper
shoe box

1 Stand a shoe box on a table and against a wall as shown. Place a few books in the bottom of the shoe box to make it sturdy. Fill a clear plastic cup 1/4–3/4 full of water.

2 Place the cup on the box, so that a small portion of the cup extends beyond the edge of the box. Turn on the flashlight and darken the room completely. Stand the flashlight directly under the overhanging bottom of the cup.

3 You may already see a faint spectrum on your wall. If you don't, slowly and carefully move the bottom of the flashlight away from the box. As you move the flashlight, watch for a faint spectrum to appear on the wall. To help you see the colors, tape a piece of white paper to the wall to act as a screen. You could also change the amount of water to see if that helps. Look closely at the spectrum. What colors do you see? Do you see as many as you did with the diffraction slide? Are they in the same order?

Try a different spectrum maker!

1 Hold a clear plastic case from a cassette tape about 1/2 meter from the front of a flashlight. Make sure the room is darkened as before.

2 Turn on the flashlight and slowly rotate the plastic case with the light shining through it. At some point as you rotate the case, you should see a spectrum appear on the wall. Is this spectrum easier to see than the one with the cup of water? Can you see all of the colors you saw with the diffraction slide?

Filter & Diffraction Action!

You will need

6 clear plastic cups (8-10 oz)
water
food coloring
  (red, blue, green, yellow)
flashlight
diffraction slide

Colored filters allow some of the colors to pass through but not others. You can make your own colored filters and use your diffraction slide to see which colors the different filters let through.

1 Fill five of your cups about 3/4 full of water. Put 5–8 drops each of red, blue, green, and yellow food coloring, separately, into four of the cups. Do not add anything to the water in one of the cups.

2 Ask your adult partner to hold a flashlight straight up, to turn it on, and to hold the cup of colorless water on top of the flashlight as shown. Hold the diffraction slide up to your eye and look down through the water at the light. Note the colors that you see.

3 While you continue looking, your partner should take off the cup of colorless water and replace it with a cup of red water. Now what colors do you see? Does it appear that some colors did not get through the red filter? Which ones?

4 Ask your adult partner to put the colorless water back on the flashlight. Again use the diffraction slide to look through the water at the light. Now ask your partner to put the blue water on the flashlight. What colors do you see? Does it appear that some colors did not get through the blue filter? Which ones?

5 Repeat the activity for the remaining two colors. Which filter gave you results you did not expect? Try mixing two colors in a separate plastic cup. Predict what colors you will be able to see.when looking through your diffraction slide. Was your prediction correct?

Your Own Rainbow Show!

You will need
garden hose
sunny day

Y ou may have seen a rainbow on a day when the sun came out while rain was still falling. You may also have seen one at a waterfall where the water splashed up into a mist, or even in the water from a lawn sprinkler on a sunny day. In the activity below, you can try making your own rainbow!

1 With your adult partner, turn on a hose and use your thumb or a nozzle to produce a fine spray.

2 Move so that you are looking at the water with the sun behind you. Can you see a rainbow? If not, spray harder or softer and higher or lower.

3 If you still can't see a rainbow, try changing your position so that the sun hits your water from a different angle. You might also try letting your partner spray the water while you look from farther away and from different angles.

4 When you do see the rainbow, look at the colors carefully. Are they the same ones that you saw using the diffraction film? Are they in the same order?

WONDERSCIENCE

This unit deals with the fun and interesting topic of optical illusions. Many students may be familiar with optical illusions but this unit has some examples that may surprise even your experienced student optical illusionist.

Wonder Spinners

Wonder Spinners introduces students to a type of interesting optical illusion in which a drawing has to be spun for the illusion to work. Some of these illusions depend on a phenomenon called persistence of vision which is explained later in the unit.

It's Fun to See in 3-D!

It's Fun to See in 3-D! is an activity that requires red/blue 3-D viewing glasses. These glasses are inexpensive and can be purchased from most science-related toy stores. The combined effect of the blue and red leaves with the blue and red lenses in the 3-D glasses makes the leaves appear to be different distances from your eyes. To understand how this illusion is achieved, we must first look at how our eyes and brain ordinarily work together to judge the relative distances of the objects around us.

Because your eyes are separated by the distance between them, each eye looks at an object from a slightly different perspective. Your left and right eye each see a separate image of an object and your brain combines them into one. Your brain also analyzes the angle formed by the two views of the object to determine how far away the object is. In the diagram, you can see how the angle is different when the object is different distances away. The larger the angle, the nearer the object; the smaller the angle, the further the object.

How does this apply to the 3-D leaves? Because the leaves are all printed on the same plane, at the same distance from your eye, they have to artificially be made to appear different distances from your eyes. The separation between the blue and red leaves and the fact that you see the red leaves through the blue lens and the blue leaves through the red lens determine the angle at which your eyes see the leaves. Based on this angle, your brain determines how far away the leaves looks. The diagram here illustrates how this works. It also shows why reversing the glasses changes how far away the leaves appear. Pick a leaf and use your glasses to see how it works.

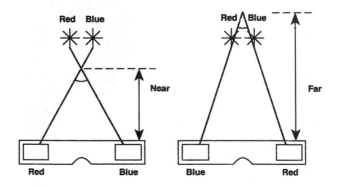

The other illusions throughout the unit deal with several different aspects of the way our eyes and brain work together to see color, length, size, and shape.

RELEVANT NATIONAL SCIENCE EDUCATION STANDARDS

The activities in this unit can be used to support the teaching of the following standards:

✔ Science as Inquiry
   Abilities necessary to do scientific inquiry

✔ Life Science
   Structure and function in living systems

Take these illusions for a spin!

Wonder Spinners

You may think that seeing is believing. But is it really? Try making the WonderSpinners below, and you will find out that sometimes you see things very differently from the way they really are!

1 Use your cup to draw a circle on the blank side of an index card, and use a ruler to make the wedges. Use red and blue crayons to color in the wedges of the design. Cut out your disk.

2 Ask your adult partner to help you make a hole in the center of your disk with a pushpin. Use the pushpin to connect the disk to the eraser end of a pencil.

3 Spin the pencil rapidly back and forth between your hands. What color do you see? Why do you think this happens? Try making disks with different color combinations, like red and yellow, or blue and yellow. Try different designs to see how they look when they spin!

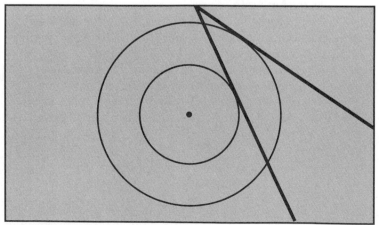

4 Here's another illusion to try! Trace the circles and lines at the right and glue your drawing to an index card. Connect it through the center dot to the eraser end of a pencil with a pushpin. Loosen the pushpin a little and hit the index card on the edge so that it spins very quickly. What happens to the two lines that touch the circles?

5 Cut an index card into a rectangle the size shown below. Find the exact center and draw a line down the middle. Draw the bird on one side of the line and a bird cage on the other so that they are in the exact center of their area on the index card.

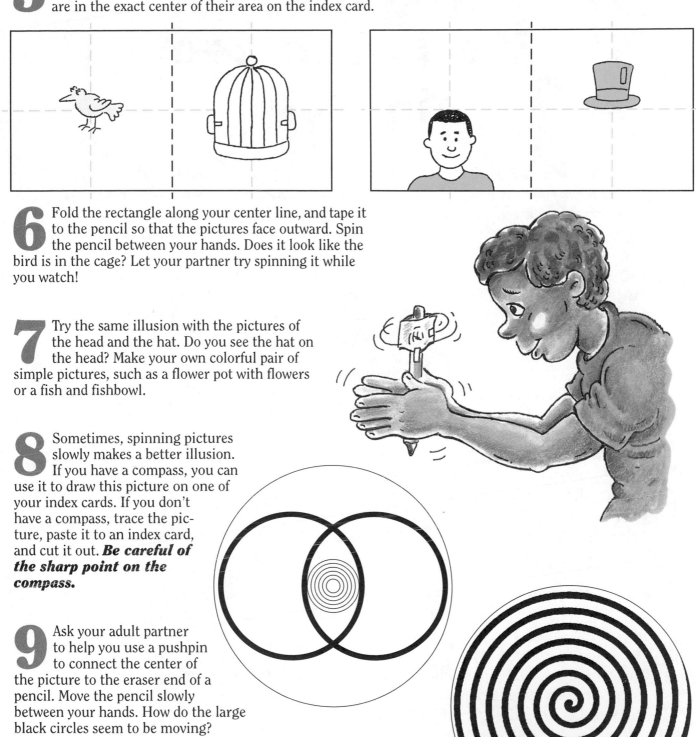

6 Fold the rectangle along your center line, and tape it to the pencil so that the pictures face outward. Spin the pencil between your hands. Does it look like the bird is in the cage? Let your partner try spinning it while you watch!

7 Try the same illusion with the pictures of the head and the hat. Do you see the hat on the head? Make your own colorful pair of simple pictures, such as a flower pot with flowers or a fish and fishbowl.

8 Sometimes, spinning pictures slowly makes a better illusion. If you have a compass, you can use it to draw this picture on one of your index cards. If you don't have a compass, trace the picture, paste it to an index card, and cut it out. ***Be careful of the sharp point on the compass.***

9 Ask your adult partner to help you use a pushpin to connect the center of the picture to the eraser end of a pencil. Move the pencil slowly between your hands. How do the large black circles seem to be moving?

10 Trace the spiral drawing and paste it to an index card. Attach it to a pencil and spin it slowly. Where does it look like the spiral is going? How about if you spin it the other way?

---

* All activities in *WonderScience* have been reviewed for safety by Dr. Jack Breazeale, Francis Marion College, Florence, SC; Dr. Jay Young, Chemical Health and Safety Consultant, Silver Spring, MD; and Dr. Patricia Redden, Saint Peter's College, Jersey City, NJ.

It's fun to see in 3-D!

Have you ever seen something that is not really there? Or maybe seen something look different from the way it actually is? These are called *optical illusions*. We see illusions either because our eyes are tricked by them or because what our eyes see is real but the message sent to our brain gets muddled up.

There are several different kinds of optical illusions. Many optical illusions are drawings that seem to be a different shape or size than they really are. This is often done by fooling our eyes with a background of a certain design or color which makes the main drawing look longer or shorter or a different shape or color than it actually is.

Another kind of illusion is caused by the ability of our eyes to remember something we have seen for at least a fraction of a second after it is gone. This is called *persistence of vision*. Our eyes still see one picture while looking at another and can put the two pictures together. This is why the color wheel looked purple and why the bird looked like it was in the cage.

Some really surprising illusions happen because we have two eyes that each see things a little differently. This is part of what makes this page look 3-D! An explanation of 3-D vision is on the first page of this unit. You can read it with your teacher or parent.

Some optical illusions are caused by the way our eyes see color and by the way our eyes react after they have looked at the same color for a long time. Learn about this interesting type of color illusion in "Ghostly Illusions."

There are many other optical illusions throughout your *WonderScience* that are interesting and amazing! Have fun with your *WonderScience* and remember—don't always believe everything you see!

Ghostly Illusions

Our eyes see color with tiny structures called *cones.* Cones are found in a part of the eye called the *retina.* We have three kinds of cones— green, red, and blue—with different chemicals in them that let us see different colors. In this activity, see what happens when one kind of cone gets tired!

> ## You will need
>
> crayons
>
> white paper

1 Stare at the picture of the green ghost for about 30 seconds. Now look at the white piece of paper. Keep staring at it. What do you see?

2 When you look at the green ghost, your green cones get tired. Then, when you look at the white paper, they do not respond and so you see a ghost of a different color. The color of the ghost should be the opposite, or *complement*, of the color of the real ghost. What color is it?

3 What do you think will happen if you stare at the orange pumpkin and then look at the white piece of paper? Try it and see!

4 Use crayons to draw a butterfly or other colorful design and make your own ghostly illusions!

Mind and LINE *Benders*

Have you ever seen a line that looks bent but really is straight? Or an object that looks a different size, shape, or color than it really is? Try these next illusions and see if you can believe your eyes!

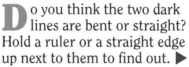

Do you think the two dark lines are bent or straight? Hold a ruler or a straight edge up next to them to find out. ▶

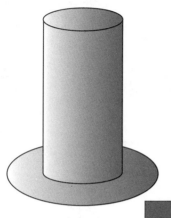

Is the bottom rim of this hat as wide as the hat is tall? Measure and see! ▲

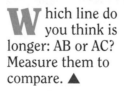

Which line do you think is longer: AB or AC? Measure them to compare. ▲

Look at the drawing above. Does it seem to move or shimmer? Tilt it from side to side and see if it shimmers even more. ▲

Look at the picture at left. Do you see anything where the white lines intersect? Look closely at one intersection. Does anything seem to happen? ◀

Illusions—A "Hole" new world!

Our eyes each look at an object from a slightly different view and give us two different pictures of the object. Our brain then takes these two pictures and combines them into one. You can see how this works by studying a familiar object—your finger!

1 Close your left eye and hold up your index finger at arm's length so that it blocks out some small item across the room. Now switch eyes while looking at your finger. Does it look like your finger moved? Try switching eyes again. What happens? Do you agree that each eye sees your finger from a different view?

2 Now hold your index finger only a few centimeters in front of your face. Close one eye and then the other like before. Do the views of your finger seem to be closer together now or further apart? Our brain can tell the distance away an object is by how close together or far apart the views are from each eye. The closer together the views, the greater the distance the object is from our eyes.

3 To see how your brain can take the different views from each eye and combine them into one, try this optical illusion. Roll a piece of paper into a tube and tape the tube closed.

4 Look through the tube with your right eye while keeping both eyes open. Bring your left hand against the side of the tube near your face. Let the view of the hole and the view of your hand come together and it should look like you have a hole in your hand!

Have you ever noticed that the moon looks really big when it is down near the horizon and much smaller when it is high in the sky? This is an optical illusion, too. The buildings and the trees that are down on the horizon give a background for the moon that makes it look big because they are very small by comparison. But when the moon is high in the sky, the background is the whole sky so the moon looks very small.

You can prove to yourself that this is just an illusion. Cut out a little round piece of paper so that when you hold it at arm's length, it just covers the moon when it is low on the horizon. You will need to trim the paper to make it match the moon exactly. Then try matching them up later, when the moon is high in the sky, holding the paper disc the same distance from your eye as before. Even though the moon looks much smaller, the moon and the disc should still match up.

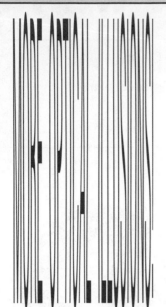

CAN YOU READ THIS TITLE??

If not, hold the magazine flat and almost level with your eye and try to read it again.

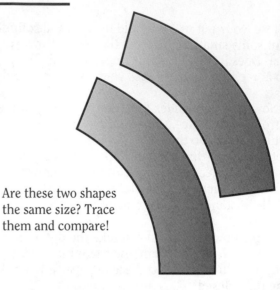

Are these two shapes the same size? Trace them and compare!

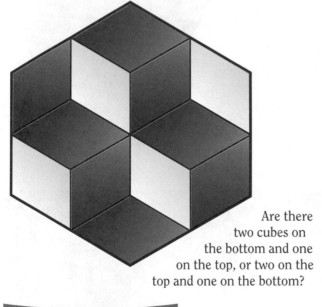

Are there two cubes on the bottom and one on the top, or two on the top and one on the bottom?

This may seem to be a normal picture of Elvis printed upside down, but turn the page upside down and see what happens!

From Explorabook, by John Cassidy and the Exploratorium, © Klutz Press 1991

What do you see here? Two people or a birdbath?

Which do you see? An old lady or a young girl?

Originally drawn by W. E. Hill in 1915

This unit introduces students to some of the basic principles of magnification. A magnifying lens is a convex lens. Convex lenses may vary somewhat in shape, but all are thicker at the center than at the edges. A convex lens is also called a *converging* lens because it causes parallel rays of light that enter the lens to bend toward one another, or converge. The point toward which these light rays converge is the focal point of the lens. Depending on the position of the object, lens, and eye, the image of an object may look upside down and small or right side up and large.

The diagram below illustrates the upside-down reduced image you see when you hold the lens at arm's length and look through it at an object such as a tree. The diagram shows how two different light rays from the top of the tree coverage to form an image of the tree top. Two different light rays from the bottom of the tree converge to form an image of the tree bottom.

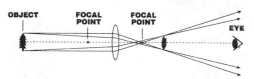

The diagram below shows what happens when you look at an object (a small nail) that is inside the focal point of the lens. Although the rays were bent while passing through the lens, your eye and brain interpret the rays as having travelled in a straight line (dotted line extension of rays) from the direction at which they entered your eye. You perceive the nail as being larger than it really is and right-side up.

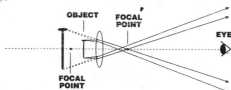

Magnificent Magnifiers!

In *Magnificent Magnifiers!*, students examine a picture of a colorful butterfly through an ordinary magnifying glass. Students should notice that the apparent size and clarity of the butterfly changes as the lens is moved closer and farther from the picture. Students make magnifiers from several objects which act like magnifying lenses because they are clear and have smooth surfaces that curve or bulge outward.

Magnifiers, How Do They Measure Up?

In *Magnifiers, How Do They Measure Up?*, students learn to determine the magnification of a lens. The worm segments must be viewed through the lens at their greatest magnification while clearly in focus. Then, the hole in the card must be exactly the same size as the lens, and must be held in exactly the same position as the lens was. The distance from the eye to the card and from the card to the tapeworm must be the same as with the lens.

Say Cheese!

In *Say Cheese!*, students observe images of outdoor objects on paper "film" on the back of the camera. The image of the object will be small and upside down on the camera's paper "film." By taping an opaque object to the window, students can see how close they can get to the object and still bring it into focus. Students should relate this to the minimum distance a camera lens can be from an object to take a focused picture.

And Now For Something Really Big!

In *And Now For Something Really Big!*, students make a crude but effective projector. To find how much the projected image is magnified, students use a ruler to measure the height of their original drawing and the height of the image on the wall. Dividing the height of the image by the height of the drawing gives the magnification.

What's For Lunch?

The *What's For Lunch?* activity might be extended by having students illustrate their ideas of what certain objects might look like through a scanning electron microscope.

RELEVANT NATIONAL SCIENCE EDUCATION STANDARDS

The activities in this unit can be used to support the teaching of the following standards:

✔ **Science as Inquiry**
   Abilities necessary to do scientific inquiry

✔ **Physical Science**
   Properties and changes of properties in matter

✔ **Science in Personal and Social Perspectives**
   Science and technology in society

MAGNIFICENT M

YOU WILL NEED:

1 or 2 magnifying glasses
(preferably different in size or magnification)

clear plastic soda bottle
(any size, washed and label removed)

clear glass marble

index card

hole punch

transparent tape

straw

water

When you want to see something clearly that's really small, like a bug or some other tiny thing, what can you do to make it look bigger? Use a magnifying glass and BOOM—A BIGGER BUG! Try the following activity to learn about making things look bigger with the power of **MAGNIFICATION!**

1 Look at the picture of the butterfly through your magnifying glass lens. Move the lens closer and farther from the picture until the insect looks as big as possible and you can still see it clearly. Study it carefully.

2 Look at the picture without the lens and then with the lens again. List all of the things you can see with the lens that you cannot see without it. Hold the lens at different distances from your eye.

How does this change what you see? Does the butterfly ever look upside down?

3 If you have another magnifying glass, use it to Look at the butterfly. (If not, skip this step.)

Is one lens a better magnifier than the other?

How can you tell?

How do the size and shape of the two lenses compare?

How does the butterfly look if you use both lenses together?

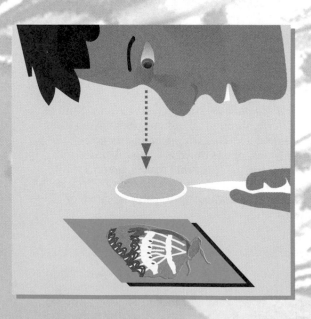

4 Fill the clear soda bottle completely with water so no air is left inside. Replace the cap. Look at the butterfly through the bottle.

Does the butterfly look as big as it did with the magnifying glass?

Can you make the butterfly look upside down?

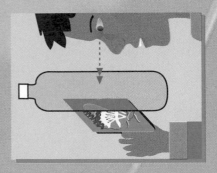

5 Use the hole punch to make a hole near the center of the index card. Stick a piece of clear tape across the hole. Turn the card over. Use a straw to put a drop or two of water on the tape. Observe the butterfly through the water drop.

Does it look bigger?

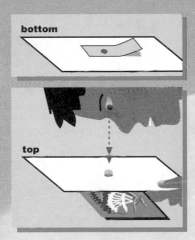

6 Experiment with different sizes of water drops.

What is it about the water drop that makes it a good magnifier?

Is it the size, shape, or something else?

Experiment to figure it out!

7 Place a clear marble on the paper and slowly move it over the butterfly.

How does its magnification differ from the other magnifiers you have used?

Lift the marble away from the insect very slowly while looking through the marble.

What do you notice?

In what ways were all of the objects you looked through alike?

Why do you think some were better magnfiers than others?

Try looking at some other small things like salt crystals, pepper, grains of sand, your fingerprints, hairs on your arm, and letters on a page!

LENSES...THEN AND NOW—WOW!

TELESCOPES

Early telescope

Invented by Isaac Newton in 1668

Uses a lens and a flat and a curved mirror

Magnification: 20-30x

Newton used telescopes such as this to observe the motion of the moon, comets, and planets.

PHYSICAL SCIENCES COLLECTION, NMAH, SMITHSONIAN INSTITUTION

NASA

Hubble Space Telescope

Placed in orbit around Earth in April, 1990

Orbits about 600 km (about 370 miles) above Earth

Equipped with 2.4 meter reflecting telescope

Added set of lenses to correct a misshapened mirror in 1993

Hubble's position above Earth's atmosphere allows it to see about 10 times better than the best ground telescope under the best conditions.

Can detect objects 10-20 billion light years away

MICROSCOPES

Early microscope

Built by Antonie van Leeuwenhoek (lay-vun-hook) in the Netherlands in 1673

Made with one high-quality lens (the lens is the small blue dot at left-center)

Magnification: about 250x

MEDICAL SCIENCES COLLECTION, NMAH, SMITHSONIAN INSTITUTION

Could see bacteria and other organisms about 2 thousandths of a millimeter in diameter (about 250 times smaller than a period on this page)

Scanning Electron Microscope

Developed in late 1940s at Cambridge University, England

Uses beam of electrons instead of light

Electron beam is focused with magnets instead of lenses.

Object to be magnified is covered with super-thin layer of gold.

Magnifies up to 200,000 times—could make a human hair appear about 16 meters (about 50 feet) wide.

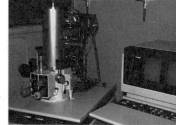

DENNIS KUNKEL, UNIVERSITY OF HAWAII

MOVIE PROJECTORS

Early Movie Projector

Earliest movie projector for viewing by an audience was used in 1895 in Paris, France.

Although ingenious in design, it was noisy and caused a flickering image on the movie screen.

Light source was an electric arc amplified by a mirror and focused through a lens.

No sound

PHOTOGRAPHIC HISTORY COLLECTION, NMAH, SMITHSONIAN INSTITUTION

IMAX CORPORATION

IMAX Movie Projector

Premiered at EXPO '70, Osaka, Japan, 1970.

Projects huge, bright, detailed image on screens over 80 feet high and 100 feet wide

Film is 10 times wider than film in standard movie projectors.

Super-sharp focus by holding film against the lens with a vacuum

Light source: High-voltage xenon gas lamp

Used with powerful digital audio sound system

GLASSES

Early glasses

First use of lenses to improve vision is believed to go back about 1,500 years to China and other ancient civilizations.

First lenses are believed to have been made from quartz.

Earliest lenses in frames as glasses were probably made sometime during the 1200s.

MEDICAL SCIENCES COLLECTION, NMAH, SMITHSONIAN INSTITUTION

Earliest glasses were used to see things close up and later ones for seeing things further away.

Ben Franklin combined the two when he invented bifocals in 1784.

Intraocular Lens

Modern lens produced to replace natural eye lens damaged by cataracts (a clouding of the lens)

Made from super-clear highly polished plastic

Surgery used to remove natural lens and to implant intraocular lens

The loops help hold the lens in place.

After eye heals, vision is greatly improved in the vast majority of patients.

AMERICAN ACADEMY OF OPTHAMOLOGY

Magnifiers

HOW DO THEY MEASURE UP?

You will need:

magnifying lens   scissors

index card   *WonderScience*
           measuring tape worm (below)

pencil

Some lenses make things look a bit bigger, and other stronger lenses can make things look a whole lot BIGGER! The strength of a magnifying lens is called its **magnification**. For example, a lens that makes things look three times bigger has a magnification of 3. Try the activity below to figure out the magnification of your lens.

1. Use your pencil to draw the outline of your magnifying lens on the middle of an index card. Cut along this line to make a hole in your card. (Carefully poke a pencil through the card to help you start cutting.)

ROD LITTLE

2. To find the magnification of your lens, hold it over your measuring tape worm (below) so that the sections appear as large as possible and still clearly in focus; then follow the steps below.

ROD LITTLE

Step A:
Count the number of sections you can see through the lens. Don't count the tapeworm's head. Record this number as A below.

A= _____
(Number of sections through the lens.)

ROD LITTLE

Step B:
Hold the card the same distance from your eye and from the paper as you did with the lens. Look through the hole and count the number of sections you can see. Record this number as B.

B= _____
(Number of sections without the lens.)

Magnification = B divided by A

Measuring tapeworm

Tapeworms are pretty disgusting, but you can use this picture of one to measure the magnification of your lens. The tapeworm can be used to measure magnification because its segments are all the same width. To learn some interesting facts about tapeworms, look up "tapeworm" in an encyclopedia or biology book!

Challenge:
A ruler or lined paper can also be used to measure the magnification of your lens. Can you figure out how? Try it, and see if you get the same answer as using the measuring tapeworm.

A VERY IMPORTANT PART OF A CAMERA IS THE LENS IN THE VERY FRONT. THE CAMERA IS ABLE TO WORK BECAUSE THE LIGHT GOES THROUGH THE LENS AND MAKES A SMALL FOCUSED IMAGE ON THE FILM AT THE BACK OF THE CAMERA. SEE HOW IT WORKS IN THE ACTIVITY BELOW!

YOU WILL NEED:

magnifying lens
construction paper (1 piece)
metric ruler
tape
safety scissors
pencil
paper (1 piece, white copier or notebook)

1 Cut a 6 cm wide strip from the top of your construction paper. Roll the strip of paper into a tube so that the opening of the tube fits the size of your magnifying lens. Tape the tube closed. Tape the magnifying glass to one end of the tube as shown. This is the **lens** for your camera.

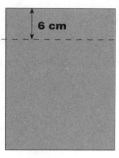

2 Cut squares out of the corners of the construction paper that are each 6 cm x 6 cm. Use the other end of the tube and your pencil to draw a circle in the middle of your construction paper. Use the pencil to carefully poke a hole through the paper so that you can cut out the circle.

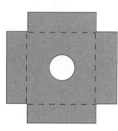

3 After cutting out the circle, fold the sides of the paper toward each other to form a box with one open side. You and your partner should tape the sides together to make a box. This is the **body** of your camera.

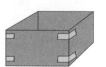

4 Measure the length and width of the open side of your box. Cut the white paper so that it is slightly larger than this open side. Tape the paper to the open side of the box as shown. This is the **film** for your camera. Place the tube inside the hole in the camera body and your camera is ready to use!

5 Turn the lights off in the room. Stand about 10 feet from a window and aim your lens at objects outside such as buildings, cars, and trees. Make sure there is plenty of light on the objects. Look at the paper "film" on the back of the camera.

6 You can focus your camera by moving the lens tube in and out. Focus your camera until you can see a clear picture of the objects on your film. This picture is called an **image**.

LOEL BAF

What are some of the things you notice about the image? Can you see color? Tape a small object to the window. How close can you get to the object and still have it in focus?

AND NOW FOR SOMETHING REALLY

BIG!

IN A CAMERA, LIGHT FROM **OUTSIDE** GOES THROUGH THE LENS AND MAKES A **SMALL** FOCUSED IMAGE ON THE FILM INSIDE. IN A SLIDE OR MOVIE PROJECTOR, LIGHT FROM INSIDE THE PROJECTOR GOES THROUGH THE LENS AND MAKES A **LARGE** FOCUSED IMAGE ON A SCREEN **OUTSIDE**. IN THIS ACTIVITY, YOU CAN MAKE A PROJECTOR FROM A FLASHLIGHT AND A MAGNIFYING GLASS!

1 Fold your paper in half and in half again to make four equal sections. Use your scissors to cut out the four sections.

2 Use a black marker to draw a small design or picture in the center of one of the pieces of paper.

3 Place your drawing over the front of the flashlight. Secure it with a rubber band. Turn on the flashlight and darken the room. Stand about two or three feet from the wall. Aim the flashlight at the wall.

4 Slowly move a magnifying glass back and forth in front of the flashlight until an image of your drawing is clearly in focus on the wall. How does the image compare with the drawing?

YOU WILL NEED:

magnifying glass	**rubber band**
black marker	**scissors**
paper (white copier or notebook)	**metric ruler**
flashlight	**white wall** (or screen)

RENATA ROBERTS

CAN YOU DO IT?

Can you and your partner figure out how much your drawing is being magnified?

What measurements would you need to make with your ruler to figure this out?

Can you move farther from the wall and still make your image clearly focused on the wall?

Is it a bigger or smaller image?

Can you make the image of your drawing appear right side up?

511

WHAT'S FOR LUNCH?

You've heard the saying "You are what you eat"? Well, get an up-close look at what you really eat! These pictures of common foods—strawberry, rice, broccoli, and chicken—were taken through a **scanning electron microscope (SEM)**. Can you match each food with its SEM picture? See bottom of page for answers.

Care for some cheese sauce?

Would you like whipped cream?

X 200

X 1000

X 5000

X 1500

A little salt and pepper, perhaps?

Could I interest you in a little butter?

This unit introduces students to the phenomenon of the reflection of light. The activities deal with observable characteristics of the reflection of light and not at all with the underlying theory of light as a wave or as a particle.

Be a Reflector Detector!

In *Be a Reflector Detector!*, students can use a flashlight and a mirror to observe the basic law of reflection: The angle of incidence always equals the angle of reflection. This means that when light strikes a perfectly reflecting surface at a particular angle, it will reflect off the surface at exactly that same angle. Students will not actually measure the angles, but by observing the direction of the incoming and reflected light, they should be able to see the relationship described in the law of reflection. This activity calls for use of a "*WonderScience* mirror" which was supplied with the original issue. You can use a silver reflective piece of Mylar available at most art supply stores.

There Are Two Sides to Everything!

There Are Two Sides to Everything! shows how reflection can be used to determine whether a picture is symmetrical.

Mirror Myths

In keeping with the *WonderScience* practice of integrating science into other subject areas, *Mirror Myths* offers an example of how reflection has had a prominent place in certain famous stories, mythological tales, and superstitions.

Fun House Mirrors

In *Fun House Mirrors*, the reflections from convex and concave mirrors are analyzed by using a metal spoon. The "mirror tester" allows students to see which side of the spoon stretches or condenses the image either vertically or horizontally. When looking at the concave side of the spoon, the mirror tester's image should be upside down, but when brought very close to the spoon (about 1 cm away) it should turn right side up.

Mirror Mania

Mirror Mania offers five short activities that demonstrate some of the unexpected characteristics of reflection.

RELEVANT NATIONAL SCIENCE EDUCATION STANDARDS

The activities in this unit can be used to support the teaching of the following standards:

✔ Science as Inquiry
  Abilities necessary to do scientific inquiry

Be a REFLECTOR DETECTOR!*

When light from a certain direction hits a smooth, shiny surface, the light will "bounce," or *reflect* off that surface in another particular direction.

B   D

F   A

E   C

You will need

flashlight
small mirror
white unlined paper
tape
pencil
2 pieces of cardboard (14 cm x 8 cm each)

1 Cut two pieces of cardboard and one piece of white paper to the same size as your small mirror. Tape the mirror to one piece of cardboard and the paper to the other, using two small pieces of tape each. The mirror is your *reflector* and the white paper is your *screen*

2 Lay a pencil down the middle of the cardboard side of the reflector so that the tip of the pencil point just sticks out beyond the edge of the cardboard. Use two or three pieces of tape to fasten the pencil firmly to the cardboard.

3 Put the front of your flashlight at the bottom of the page as shown. Stand the pencil point and mirror on the dot in the center of the page.

4 Have your adult partner stand the screen, along the dotted line, at target area A. Turn on the flashlight but do not move it out of position.

5 Rotate the screen until you can reflect the light right at the center of the screen. Ask your adult partner to move the screen to target area B and C and so on until you can quickly rotate the mirror and hit each target screen right in the middle!

Put front of flashlight here

514

6 Now, you and your adult partner should shut off most of the lights so that the room is pretty dark.

7 Hold the flashlight in one hand and your reflector in the other. Ask your adult partner to call out an object in the room, such as a doorknob, a picture on the wall, or a light switch. Shine the light on the object by bouncing light from your flashlight off your reflector and onto the object! Good luck and have fun **REFLECTING!**

8 What did you notice about the path the light took from the flashlight to the screen when you were being a **"Reflector Detector?"** Talk this over with your adult partner, then try the **"Reflector Detector"** again to check your ideas.

---

* All activities in *WonderScience* have been reviewed for safety by Dr. Jack Breazeale, Francis Marion College, Florence, SC; Dr. Jay Young, Chemical Health and Safety Consultant, Silver Spring, MD; and Dr. Patricia Redden, Saint Peter's College, Jersey City, NJ.

REFLECT ON *THIS* . . .

Did you know that you have never really seen your own face? What you have always seen are *images* of your face in photographs or reflected from mirrors or other surfaces.

If you look around, you can see your image in many different objects such as a shiny wood table top, a microwave oven door, a shiny apple or a calm lake. The surfaces of these objects act like a mirror because they are so smooth and shiny that light can bounce off them very well. When light bounces off a smooth shiny surface, we say the light is *reflected* or that the surface caused a *reflection*

For you to be able to see an object in a mirror or other smooth surface, light from the object must reflect off the surface and into your eyes without spreading out.

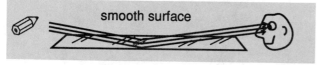

smooth surface

The light that is reflected from rough surfaces like crinkled aluminum foil spreads out, making the image harder to see.

rough surface

Try the activity **"Be a Reflector Detector"** with a wrinkled piece of aluminum foil as your reflector. Compare the reflection you get with the wrinkled aluminum foil to the reflection you got from the mirror. You can see that there is a big difference between a reflection made by a smooth surface compared to a wrinkled surface.

As you will discover in **"Mirror Myths,"** reflection and mirrors have fascinated people throughout history. Today, mirrors have important uses in modern technology. The dentist uses a tilted mirror to see the back of your teeth, which would be impossible to see without the mirror. Cars, trucks, buses and even some bicycles use special mirrors to help drivers see behind them and to the sides. Periscopes on submarines, lasers, cameras, telescopes, and microscopes all use mirrors.

In this unit of *WonderScience* you can learn about curved mirrors like the fun house mirrors at carnivals; you can work you way through a mirror maze; and you can try your skill at decoding some mirror writing!

GOOD LUCK and **HAVE FUN!**

Illustration by Tina Mion

THERE ARE *TWO SIDES* TO EVERYTHING!

> AN OBJECT IS SYMMETRICAL IF ONE HALF OF IT IS THE MIRROR IMAGE OF THE OTHER HALF. YOU CAN USE A MIRROR TO TEST WHETHER OR NOT SOMETHING IS SYMMETRICAL!

Stand your mirror along the dotted line in each of the pictures below. Look into the mirror. If what you see, made partly from the picture and partly from the reflection, is the same as what you see without the mirror, then the picture is symmetrical.

Under each picture, write **YES** if it is symmetrical or write **NO** if it is not symmetrical.

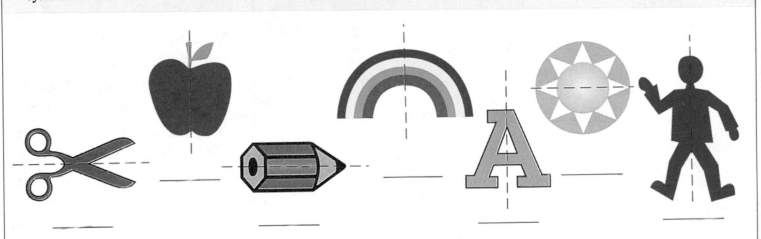

In the pictures below, use your mirror to find the symmetry line which divides each picture into halves, which are mirror images of one another. Do any of the pictures have more than one symmetry line?

Illustrations by Amy Meyer Phifer

Use crayons or colored pencils to draw your own symmetrical picture on a separate piece of paper. Make it as detailed and as colorful as you want and then check it with the mirror to make sure it is symmetrical.

MIRROR MYTHS

Reflection has had a special place in certain ancient stories called **MYTHS**. These tales are usually about heroes and villains with special powers of good and evil. Reflection is also an important part of certain scary stories and superstitions.

One look at the evil and dangerous Medusa, who had live snakes for hair, would turn a person to stone. But Perseus looked at her reflection in his shield and was able to fight and defeat her.

Mythical vampires, like Dracula, can stand directly in front of a mirror and make no reflection at all.

Narcissus liked looking at his reflection so much that he fell in love with his own image. For being so conceited, he was turned into a flower forever.

A famous superstition says that breaking a mirror brings seven years of bad luck.

The traditional sign for woman is a hand mirror used by the goddess Venus.

Illustration by Sherrell Medbery

You will need

shiny tablespoon (or larger spoon)
sheet of construction paper
blunt end scissors
tape
metric ruler
mirror
pencil

Have you ever seen yourself in a fun house mirror? You might appear to have a tall skinny head on top of a short fat body, a short round head on a long skinny body or almost any other combination. These mirrors are actually made of two kinds of curved mirrors—**convex** and **concave**. The two sides of a spoon are like these two types of mirrors. When you look at the back of a shiny spoon, you are looking in a **convex** mirror. When you look into the bowl of the spoon, you are looking in a **concave** mirror.

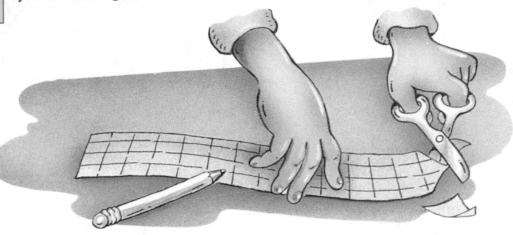

1 To make your mirror tester, cut a strip of construction paper about 15 cm long and about 4 cm wide. Draw three lines along the length of the tester each 1 cm apart. Now draw 14 lines across the tester, each 1 cm apart. At one end of the tester, cut the tip into a point.

2 Hold the spoon, **convex** side facing you, about 20 cm away from your eye, with your left hand. With your right hand, hold your mirror tester, with the point up, directly in front of and almost touching the spoon.

3 Slowly bring the tester toward you, while leaving the spoon where it is. Watch the image of the tester in the spoon and observe whether the spaces between the lines get bigger or smaller. Does the image of the the tester appear to change in any other way?

4 Repeat steps 2 and 3 with the **concave** side of the mirror facing you. Observe how the image of the tester changes.

5 Cut a hole in the construction paper the same shape and size as your spoon. Tape the paper to your mirror so that its reflecting area is the same size as your spoon mirror.

6 Move the tester closer and farther from the mirrors and compare the way it looks in the concave, convex and flat mirrors. In which mirror can you see more of the tester and the scene around you? Why do you think the large round mirrors, high in the corner of many stores, are convex, rather than concave, or flat?

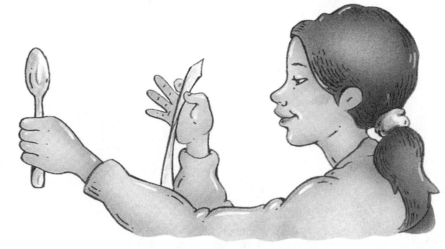

You and your adult partner can check your house for shiny round doorknobs, a shiny metal pitcher or coffeepot, a faucet spout or handle, a shiny ceramic bowl (inside and out), a shiny Christmas tree ball, or a full plastic cola bottle. Use your mirror tester to look for strange effects from these concave and convex reflectors. Maybe your house is really a **FUN HOUSE**!

MIRROR MANIA

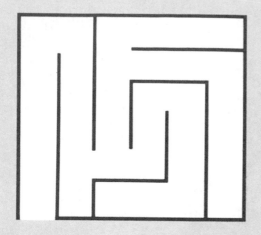

Have your adult partner stand the mirror along the dotted line at top of the maze. Lean the mirror a little forward so that you can see the maze clearly in the mirror. Looking *only* in the mirror, use a pencil to find your way from the *start* to the *finish*.

Can you use a mirror to make this *stop* sign read correctly?

Write the letters of your name on this line so that when seen in a mirror, your name will look the way it should.

Get five people to sit in a row directly in front of a mirror. Whom does each person see in the *middle* of the mirror?

After you take a shower or bath, the bathroom mirror gets all steamed up. Use your finger to wipe a spot just big enough for you to see your whole face. Do you think your face will take up less room in the spot if you move away from the mirror? How about more room if you move toward it? Try it and see!

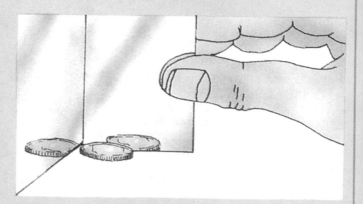

Stand two mirrors side-by-side and lay a dime down so that it touches the place where the mirrors meet. Slowly rotate the mirrors toward each other and watch your money multiply!

Illustrations by Lori Seskin-Newman

Science Fair Projects

rown-ups

Which peanut butter is the stickiest?

Are guppies attracted to mirrors?

Which animals in a zoo are kept in families?

The school year has hardly begun, it seems, when it's once again time for...the science fair project. Many parents approach science fair time with a great deal of uncertainty. You want to help your child with the project, but you don't want to actually do the project for your child! How can you deal with this dilemma?

This unit answers some of the most commonly asked questions about science fairs. Here, you'll discover how to help your child:

• select a topic,

• collect materials, and

• create a display.

You'll also discover how a science fair experience helps your child. To start your child thinking about a science fair project, we've included dozens of possible science fair questions throughout this unit. Remember: The best project is one that really interests your child—not you!

Why do schools assign science fair projects?

Your child can benefit in many ways from doing a science fair project—and not just in terms of improved science knowledge and skills. Science fair projects teach problem-solving skills, enhance written and oral communication skills, make your child an expert on a topic which interests him, and provide the satisfaction of accomplishment that comes with the completion of a worthwhile project.

WHOSE PROJECT IS IT, ANYWAY?

It's still your child's project, even if you've helped plan and guide it. As you make suggestions and coach your child, remember that the main purpose of doing a science fair project is for your child to explore and learn.

How much should I help?

Of course you want your child's project to succeed. However, as a parent, your best role is to guide and assist—*not* to do the project for your child.

More than anyone else, you know your child's strengths, weaknesses, and level of understanding. Don't be afraid to challenge, but be prepared to offer help if needed. Think of it as teaching a child to ride a bike. She may need your help getting started, or after a fall. But it's just as important to let go and let her ride on her own when she's able.

ARE WE HAVING FUN YET?—Science fair projects involve wondering, observing, inventing—activities children love to do!

522

One of the best ways to help your child is to know the project guidelines set up by the teacher. Find out the date of the science fair, any due dates for interim assignments, safety rules, specifications for the display, and the grading or judging criteria. When you have all of this information, sit down with your child and help make up a project timetable. Allow for unexpected delays by suggesting "due dates" to aim for in advance of the school's.

It's OK to *suggest* possible topics and approaches, but let your child make the final decision. You can check on your child's progress by reviewing preliminary ideas and outlines or helping to find material at the library. See if your child wants help with constructing the display. Play the role of a science fair judge to help your child prepare answers to questions about her project. *And always offer encouragement and praise!*

WHEN IN DOUBT, CHECK·IT OUT—Your child can become knowledgeable about a science fair topic with just a trip or two to the local library.

How do you pick a topic?

Here's a good rule of thumb: If your child is interested in the topic, he'll be motivated to do a good job on the project and will benefit most.

Encourage your child to think about his favorite things to read, watch, or do (see list at left for ideas). Are there science questions in any of these areas of interest?

Urge your child to look in science books in your community library for possible ideas. Other sources of information include science publications (such as *WonderScience*), government agencies, and private businesses. And don't forget your child's teacher. He or she may be the biggest source of help in doing the project.

Once my child picks a topic, what's next?

Which kinds of fabrics are best for keeping you warm?

Which kinds of cereal get soggy the fastest and stay crunchy the longest?

Design a city where all the children can walk to school without crossing streets.

Which kind of vinegar makes the best reaction (loudest, longest, most bubbly) with baking soda?

The next step is for your child to think of a specific **question** about the topic that the project will try to answer. The question chosen will depend on the type of project she wants to do. Many science fairs require projects to be either **exploratory** or **experimental**. Some schools may allow a third type: **invention or design projects**.

In an **exploratory** project, your child might collect or observe certain objects or events in nature and try to draw a conclusion from her observations.

For example:

Topic: Stars and Planets

Question: Why do the stars seem to change their position in the sky during the year?

Your child could observe the stars over a few months and track their apparent movement by comparing them to a fixed point and making star charts and other written observations. By combining observations with research about the rotation of the Earth, your child could form a conclusion about why the stars appear to move during the year.

Another type of project involves setting up an **experiment** to answer a question. Setting up a good experiment begins with asking a very specific question.

"How do we prevent global warming?" would *not* be a good question for a science fair experiment on the environment. The question is not specific enough to design an experiment that can answer it. A better question might be, "How does increasing temperature affect plants that normally grow in cool places?" It would be easier to design an experiment to attempt to answer this question.

MORE EXPLORATORY PROJECTS

TOPIC: The Earth
QUESTION: Are there different living things in different soils?

TOPIC: Weather
QUESTION: Are temperature and barometric pressure good predictors of rainfall?

TOPIC: Plants
QUESTION: Is there a relationship between the size of a tree and the size of its leaves?

Which kind of sponge is better, natural or synthetic? (and how do you define "better?")

What combination of water, liquid soap and sugar make the best bubble-blowing liquid?

Design a soup bowl and spoon that allow you to finish the last bit of soup without tipping the bowl.

How will changing the type of food in a bird feeder affect the types of birds that feed?

MORE EXPERIMENTAL PROJECTS

TOPIC: Music
QUESTION: What is the relationship between the length of a plucked rubber band and the sound it produces?

TOPIC: Animals
QUESTION: Does the amount of food given to a gerbil affect how long it sleeps?

TOPIC: Food
QUESTION: Do different-colored hard candies dissolve at the same rate?

TEAM EFFORT—Working as a team can be fun and interesting. See if your child's school allows group science fair projects!

Make sure that your child doesn't pick a question that is specific but is too difficult to answer. Consider the question, "Do larger gills allow fish to swim faster?" This question is specific—but getting fish with different gill sizes and measuring how fast they swim would not be easy! Keep in mind that the question must lend itself to an experiment that can be conducted with available time and resources.

Help your child think ahead, and try to avoid any problems that might arise in designing an experiment to answer the question. Before setting up an experiment, your child should do some research to see what's already known about the question. This research may also help your child decide if the question needs to be narrowed down. Or, it could help him discover a related topic with its own potential questions for a science fair project.

In an **invention** or **design** project, a child devises and demonstrates a new tool or system with which to accomplish a task or process. Like the types of projects mentioned above, invention and design projects still require research, testing, and detailed observations. For example, your child might devise and demonstrate a system for waking someone up without noise, or a new utensil for eating spaghetti. Because not all schools allow invention and design projects, your child should find out what the rules say *before* starting.

Safety first—Make sure your child's project is safe by checking with the teacher before you begin.

Do babies prefer certain colors or shapes of blocks?

Which colors can be seen from the greatest distance?

Do members of the same family tend to have the same favorite color?

Is there a relationship between the length of people's hands and the length of their feet?

Can you train an earthworm to do something?

Which brand of cotton balls is the best (number per price, or rate of absorption, or total absorption, or strength)?

Do larger batteries (D and C cells) last longer than smaller ones with the same voltage (AA and AAA)?

Can male grasshoppers jump farther than female grasshoppers?

TO MEASURE UP, GO METRIC

Any measurements your child makes in his experiment should be in metric units because scientists have agreed to use this measurement system in scientific experiments.

TO FIND SUPPLIES, BE RESOURCEFUL

Here are some possible sources of free or inexpensive supplies and equipment. Make sure your child starts lining up supplies early!

- science teachers
- hobby shops
- labs
- hospitals
- suppliers of scientific equipment

What materials are needed?

Good science fair projects should **not** be expensive. If your child can't find needed materials around the house, he may be able to find them at a local supermarket, pharmacy, or hardware store. Keep in mind that creative projects using basic materials make for the most impressive science fair projects.

How should my child record what happens?

Your child should make detailed observations—either with **descriptions** or **measurements**. A descriptive observation could be noting the color of leaves on trees in different seasons. A measurement could be recording how many centimeters tall a plant was at the beginning of an experiment and at the end. All observations should be recorded accurately in tables, charts, drawings, or graphs or organized clearly in another way for later reference.

Which dishwashing liquid produces the most suds?

What's the smallest portion of a potato needed to start the growth of another potato?

What surfaces do mealworms prefer?

Which paper plates will hold more weight without buckling?

How long can people hold their breath? What characteristics might affect it?

Where do seeds sprout best?

Will a seed grow if part of it has been removed?

What kinds of plants will and will not grow from cuttings?

How does too much of a good thing (water, fertilizer, light) affect plants?

Does fertilizer affect the amount of algae growth in water?

Do taller people have bigger feet?

Do solutions of different kinds of salt and sugar produce different crystals when they evaporate?

Does a light object REALLY fall at the same rate as a heavy object?

Which non-flying insects, if any, will walk across a water barrier?

Can you make a painting using only pigments from the plants, soils, and minerals in your neighborhood?

Is the hatching time of brine shrimp affected by the amount of salt in the brine solution?

Are snails attracted or repelled by light?

Which kind of soil will hold more water?

How many different living and non-living thins are in soil?

NINE TIPS FOR MAKING A GREAT DISPLAY

1
Keep the display simple; include only the essentials

2
Don't go into lengthy description. Let the headlines tell the story.

3
Be accurate— no misspelled words.

4
Use color to clarify data (graphs, charts, and diagrams).

5
Include photographs or drawings to help show what was done.

6
Protect the display in some way so that it can be handled by others.

7
Make sure that the display will fit into the space available for it at the fair.

8
Let the teacher or science fair chairperson know early if the display needs electricity or other special arrangements.

9
Use safe, durable materials. If your child is going to display any equipment or items, make sure that they meet the school's safety requirements.

What should the display look like?

Have your child begin by sketching his display on paper. It should feature a large, easy-to-read title and clear subtitles such as Topic, Question, Materials, Procedure, Data, and Conclusions or Explanation.

The display should be as neat as possible. If your child can use a computer to make labels, graphs, and charts, that's fine—but not essential. If he can't use a computer, your child can still make an attractive and effective display. He should use a pencil first and then carefully go over the pencil lines with a dark marker. Letter stencils and a ruler should be used wherever possible.

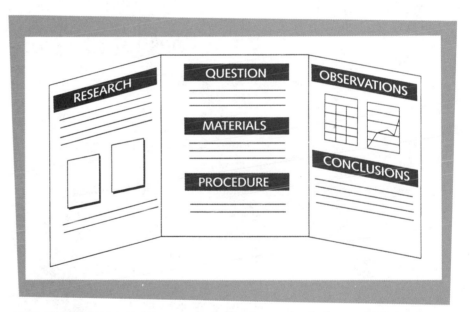

A TYPICAL SCIENCE FAIR DISPLAY—Generally, the simpler the layout, the better. Try to mark clearly the different sections of your project, and be sure to include the most useful or interesting photos, illustrations, and observations.

What if the results are not as expected?

Design a vehicle which can travel 10 feet by itself powered only by rubber bands or balloons.

Don't panic! In the world of science, things don't always turn out as expected. But there's no need to scrap the project. Have your child think carefully about what she did. Was a step forgotten? Can your child repeat the experiment or observations? If she still gets the same results, ask her to explain why her observations didn't fit her expectations. Have her suggest better ways to test her question next time.

Remember, science fair projects are **learning experiences**. If your child learned something, then she was successful. A thorough understanding of a science fair project that *didn't* turn out as expected is more valuable than a less thorough understanding of one that *did*.

HAS THE PROJECT BEEN DONE BEFORE? Originality and creativity are among the qualities judges look for in science fair projects. So it's generally best not to do a project that's been done before—unless your child is really interested in the project and will be discovering something new. Still, it may be possible to make some changes and improvements in the project so it becomes uniquely his own.

Are paper grocery bags stronger than plastic grocery bags?

Design a feeding dish or mechanism which will prevent a large dog from stealing food from a little dog.

Which dishwashing liquid produces the most suds?

What goes into the written report?

The school or teacher will probably have specifications for the written report. If not, your child should use the following format.

All parts of the science fair project should be explained in detail in a written report. The report should start with a title page containing the project's title; the date; and your child's name, grade, and teacher's name. Your child can also include a page of acknowledgments to thank the people who helped with the project. He should follow this with a table of contents and then the report.

THEY WROTE THE *BOOK* ON THE SUBJECT—A written report helps explain your child's project and what was learned.

The report can start with background information on the topic (from your child's research) and explain why your child chose the topic. Next, the report should state the question that your child set out to answer. A report on an experimental project should list the materials used and describe the experiment in enough detail that readers could reproduce the experiment.

Your child's report should include observations, as well as any charts, tables, or diagrams. The final section of the report should contain the conclusions your child made about the question being investigated. The last page should be a list of any references or sources used. And make sure your child *proofreads* the report!

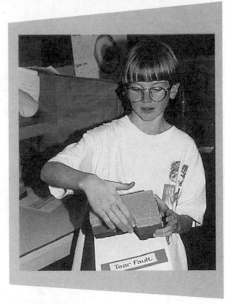

TELL IT TO THE JUDGE—During the science fair, your child has a chance to explain the project to judges and others.

What happens at the science fair?

HOW PROJECTS ARE JUDGED

Science fair projects are judged according to: originality, use of scientific process and procedure, individual effort, whether they follow the science fair rules, creativity, neatness, and accuracy.

First, a word about competition. Winning is fine, and your child should do the best he or she can to prepare for the science fair. But more than anything else, science fair projects are **learning experiences**. Whenever learning has occurred, we have a winner.

On the day of the science fair, your child will be assigned a spot to set up her display. She'll be expected to stand beside her project to answer any questions the judges or other observers may have.

If your child is shy, you can help in many ways. Remember that **preparation** is the key to a good presentation and to calming one's nerves. You can help your child practice answering questions ahead of time. Also, excitement about the project can go a long way toward reducing nervousness.

Sometime during the fair, make sure that you and your child get a chance to walk around and look at the other students' projects. Your child may see a project that sparks an idea for next year's fair.

GOOD LUCK!— We hope we've given you some useful ideas for helping your child. If your child needs more guidance or assistance, your child's teacher or a librarian are excellent resources. Remember—with preparation and a good plan, doing a science fair project can be a fun and rewarding experience for both your child and you!

To order a classroom set of 30 "Science Fair Projects—A Guide for Grown-ups" call ACS Education Products at 1-800-209-0423.

INDEX

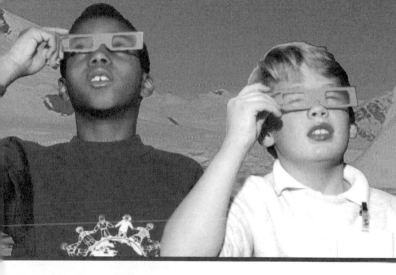